UP AGAINST THE
AMERICAN MYTH

UP AGAINST THE AMERICAN

MYTH

Written and edited by

TOM CHRISTOFFEL
DAVID FINKELHOR
DAN GILBARG

HOLT · RINEHART · WINSTON
New York Chicago San Francisco

PUBLISHED SIMULTANEOUSLY IN CANADA BY HOLT, RINEHART AND WINSTON OF CANADA, LIMITED.

LIBRARY OF CONGRESS CATALOG CARD NUMBER: 73–117290

FIRST EDITION

DESIGNER: CARL WEISS

SBN HARDBOUND: 03–085056–8
SBN PAPERBACK: 03–085378–8
PRINTED IN THE UNITED STATES OF AMERICA

CONTENTS

III. PROBLEMS OF U.S. CAPITALISM

IV. THE FAILURE OF LIBERAL SOLUTIONS

V. ALTERNATIVES AND STRATEGY

PREFACE

The materials in this book evolved out of a course at Harvard University—Social Relations 148-49—that was organized and presented by a group of radical students during the 1968–69 academic year (with the sponsorship of a sympathetic faculty member). Since that time many similar radical courses—both with and without academic credit—have been organized at other colleges and universities throughout the country.

The purpose of the Harvard course was to make available to students a radical analysis of the United States—to argue with them that meaningful social improvement is impossible in this country without the destruction of capitalism and, furthermore, that such a goal is achievable. This book continues that argument and—like the course—is aimed at a wide political spectrum, including liberals, radicals and especially people concerned with developing their political ideas. The common bond of this grouping is a shared commitment toward improving the world in which we live, a commitment accompanied by many political questions as to what the process of change will require.

Soc Rel 148-49 approached such questions through readings and discussions. The course had no formal lectures, consisting entirely of small groups of twelve to fifteen students, each including a discussion leader with some background in radical activity and radical thought. Readings served to provoke—and provide information for—discussion. As such, the readings played a secondary role, a fact with obvious implications for the present volume. For it is the hope of the editors that those reading this book will take the arguments it contains as ideas to be debated and discussed with others—to be tested and refined beyond the confines of the book itself.

We have tried to keep in mind some important lessons of Soc Rel 148-49, regarding the relationship between liberal and radical thinking. Many radicals, unfortunately, have a tendency not to take liberal ideas as a serious basis for discussion. They often treat liberals as though they were stooges. This is really an unnecessary kind of posturing. Liberal ideas, after all, have fairly deep ideological roots in this society, and are buttressed with a good deal of historical and analytical material interpreted in conformity with liberal conclusions. Thus, radicals should take seriously the fact that many liberals have solid ideas behind their liberal faith, not just blind conformity to accepted belief or blind fear of radical implications.

Soc Rel 148-49 taught us that radicals shouldn't assume that liberals just rationalize the status quo because they are privileged by it. A lot of liberals—particularly liberal students—share with radicals a sincere desire for a Good Society. They have certain disagreements with radicals about how much change is necessary and how it can be achieved, but these differences—as we will try to show—often rest on different interpretations of facts and weak or wrong arguments. We have found many of these liberals perfectly willing to change their ideas when presented with better ones, and we have learned much ourselves from such discussions with liberals.

We found that such liberal-radical discussions were not best generated by posing the issue point-blank: "Resolved: Capitalism does/does not stink." Instead, many more honest and informed ideas emerged from starting with a specific issue, e.g., "How are we going to solve the race problem?" or "Why did the civil rights movement fail?" Section leaders tried to be sensitive to and recognize liberal or radical assumptions underlying contentions about specific problems, and tried to bring them out in the open. It is one of our hopes that this book will delineate and speak to such underlying assumptions in a way that will provoke thought and discussion.

It is important to remember that discussions of this type take place far too rarely, and almost never in a college classroom. One of the most important aspects of liberal ideology is its contention that it is somehow objective and neutral. Such a claim protects the ideology from challenges to its particular way of looking at the world; it actually makes the capitalist system of economic organization a "given," to which contention would, by definition, be subjective and therefore not at all tolerable within neutral social science. Although events of the late 1960's have forcefully put the lie to this contention, it still serves as the guiding principle of university "education." Soc Rel 148-49 interested many nonradical students from the start by openly challenging this principle, by being open and frank in its own political bias, and by pointing out the obvious political bias in so-called objectively neutral courses. Our discussions, in fact, were intended to focus on the very difference between these two biases.

Such political discussions, involving contending liberal and radical ideas, can only be effective in relationship to involvement and experience with the real world. Ideas in the abstract can never be more than partially understood; if they have value and validity they must be the basis of action. In short, theory must be mixed with practice, analysis with action. Soc Rel 148-49 could play a real politicizing role only with the help of a radical movement on the Harvard campus. Through the movement activities on campus, classroom discussions on imperialism, racism, labor and other topics took on an immediacy that broke through the vacuous, academic tone of most course discussions Moreover, students could be brought to more than an abstract, academic understanding of radicalism only to the extent that they could involve themselves in ongoing political organizations and activities. Of course, the result of success in such an endeavor was a short-lived course . . . After a year of battling, it fell before the Administration axe.

The course experience provided us with some important lessons in radical education, which we have tried to make use of in putting together this book. The selections in the book are particularly well suited for provoking political discussion; and we have tried, through extensive introductory essays and blurbs, to tie each selection into the overall argument. Thus, if the book is used by a course or informal seminar, individual selections can be highlighted for particular attention according to the group's background and interest. At the same time, however, the book is organized so that it may be read from cover to cover as a coherent whole, for it does present a unified argument, rather than being a simple anthology of readings grouped together under a common theme.

This book contains only one tiny seed of what it takes to make a radical. It provides a beginning orientation and framework toward the goal of developing a radical analysis and critique of social change in America. There are several things that the book definitely is *not*:

1. It is not an adequate inventory of the injustices, irrationalities and problems of the society we live in. It merely begins to delineate the oppression, the waste, the horrible quality of life under capitalism—merely touches on the rotten values and the awful ways in which people treat one another. And it only mentions these to tie them into the basic analysis of capitalistic society, to relate them to the political economy. Much more detailed descriptions of these problems and their sources are desperately needed.

2. The book is not a discussion of the radical movement or of radical strategies. Most books about the Left in recent years have been more in that vein. Discussions of these sorts frequently fall completely flat when directed to people who do not already share certain radical perceptions about the society. It seems to us that it is relatively difficult for those outside the radical movement to gain access to the analysis radicals are making and to the radical critique of the prevailing liberal perspective. The book tries to fill some of this gap.

3. The book is by no means the final word on anything it contains. Individuals—including the present editors—can never be in complete agreement regarding political diagnoses and prognoses. Some of the analysis included herein would be hotly contested by other radicals. By and large, however, we have included those elements of the analysis on which we think radicals are in fairly wide agreement.

While a radical analysis of contemporary capitalism is continually developing, we think we have made as good a collection as could be made at this time. A limitation exists, however, since in most of the areas we have investigated, it is hard enough to find a clear and concise statement of a radical interpretation, let alone the depth of empirical and analytical work needed to convince the unconvinced of the correctness of these interpretations.

4. Finally, the book, in itself, is no substitute for an organized radical course or study group. The lone reader will have neither the experience of discussion or of political activity against which to relate and test ideas. Radicalization does not occur in an armchair; as Mao Tse-tung has written, correct ideas come from social practice, and from it alone. It is the hope of the editors,

however, that the materials included in this book will find themselves related to the readers' political functioning in such a way as to transcend this limitation of the written word alone.

One final word should be said about the relationship between this book and Soc Rel 148-49. We undertook work on this book because we hope it may contribute to radical change in the United States, the same reason, in fact, that Soc Rel 148-49 was first organized. That course involved the participation of literally hundreds of people, as organizers, discussion leaders, and students. All have helped in some way to bring this book into being and all deserve our heartfelt thanks.

The book is the culmination of the collective efforts of many of these people. The ideas contained in the book come out of a political movement that is growing by leaps and bounds in America today. We hope those who have lent a direct hand in the creation of the book and those who are testing and developing ideas in the practice of the radical movement will find this book useful and will see in it some of the results of their own work.

Tom Christoffel
David Finkelhor
Dan Gilbarg

—Spring 1970

UP AGAINST THE
AMERICAN MYTH

INTRODUCTION

Capitalism stinks! It is a highly destructive, wasteful, exploitative and irrational way to organize the resources of a society like ours. As a system, it stands in irreconcilable opposition to the fulfillment of the needs of the great majority of the people who live under its rule and to the creation of the Good Society. We can only solve our social problems and create that Good Society by doing away with capitalism and the institutions that support it. This is the point of the book, and we make it again and again. It is probably the most unsubtle book you will ever read.

In content, this book is about politics and economics in contemporary America. It is a radical critique of Corporate Capitalism, a term used almost exclusively by radicals to describe the system in which we live. The terminological difference is revealing. It is the general contention of liberal social thinkers that capitalism is not any longer the most basic characteristic of the system in which we live. Rather, our society should be termed "affluent," "post-industrial," "technetronic." We wish to diverge very sharply from this school of thought.

It is one general thesis of this collection that what happens in American politics and economics can be best explained by referring to America as a capitalist system. That is, the problems this system confronts—the wastage, the inequalities, the irrationalities and the oppressiveness—can be ascribed to the capitalist method of organizing society. More particularly, they can be traced to an economy where the productive apparatus is privately owned and where the major decisions about what will take place are made on the criteria of profit. Understanding the dynamics of a capitalist economy helps us to understand some very crucial things about our economic and political system. It helps us understand why great disparities of wealth and power exist. It helps us understand why billions are poured into military spending and little is allotted for schools and housing. And it helps us understand why basic needs go unattended, why people are alienated and manipulated, why black people and women are discriminated against, and a whole host of other problems. It helps us understand these things better than any other model offered by liberal social thinkers or others.

Besides showing how these problems are connected to capitalism, the book has a second theme: Such problems cannot be solved under capitalism. The present way in which our economic and political system is structured presents insurmountable obstacles to the solution of our major social problems. These problems require more drastic changes than the system will allow. Under capitalism vested interests oppose themselves to such changes; these changes strike at the fundamental privileges, priorities and operating principles of a capitalist society.

The book is also a critique of liberalism. Liberalism is the ideology of many people in America who are seeking social change and looking for a solution to our social problems. It is an ideology which argues that the necessary social changes required for a Good Society can take place within a capitalist framework and within the framework of already existing institutions. By implication, it says that a Good Society is in everybody's interest. No *irreconcilable* opposition exists.

Liberalism places great hopes in the role that reformed and liberalized government will play. It also places great stock in the future of technology and the opportunities created by affluence.

The book tries to point out the errors of such a view. It catalogues the nature and strength of the interests opposed to solving our social problems. It concludes that the government in America cannot be an agent for reforming the system. It shows how affluence and technology by themselves are not enough without a change in those who have the power to use it.

We hope the book can help to dispel certain conventional ideas people—especially liberals—have about radicalism. One frequently expressed view is that liberals and radicals have basically the same goals in mind—ending inequality, discrimination and so on—but that radicals are more impatient; they want these goals implemented right away.

This book should make clear that this is not an accurate presentation of the differences between liberal and radical. In the first place, radicals do not share the same goals as liberals. Radicals identify a whole set of problems to be solved—like work alienation, women's oppression—that liberals do not really take seriously as pressing problems. In addition, radicals are calling for a much broader and thorough transformation of the society—we are calling for socialism, that is, a fundamental revision of the economy, of the political decision-making mechanism, and of the cultural life of our society.

In the second place, radicals have a very different analysis of what stands in the way of having a Good Society. Radicals do not think, as do many liberals, that things are slowly getting better. In fact, they are getting worse. Radicals believe that corporate power under capitalism opposes even minimum improvements, and meanwhile, its antisocial priorities undermine whatever healthy aspects the society may already have.

Finally, liberals and radicals have very different strategies for improving society. The difference has little to do with patience, for, if anything, it is the liberals who are impatient, not the radicals. Liberals are proposing something of a "shortcut" to a Good Society via the route of electing reform politicians, legislating social welfare programs, using the power of the state to reform capitalist priorities from the top down.

Radicals do not think any of that will work. Corporate power effectively holds the state in check. Politicians, while paying lip service to people's interests, are easily co-opted and stymied by the mechanisms of corporate influence.

Radicals insist we must take the long hard road in changing society. That means building effective political power to oppose and eliminate capitalism from the bottom up. Such political power only follows from years of building and disseminating a critique of capitalist society, and from years of talking to people, changing ingrained attitudes and giving people a vision of a new society. It means not simply organizing the people but—given the forces that act to undercut and divert movements—organizing people for socialist revolution.

Where do these differences flow from? In part they flow from a different reading of history, as in the problem of whether the government can actually counter the capitalist priorities in our society. The book wants to take these differences up, as in the discussion of the New Deal and the Progressive Era.

In part, the differences flow from differences in analysis of the structure of present-day society. For example, radicals and liberals differ on the issues of how much power corporations have, how much progress has been made in solving problems like racism and poverty, and how dependent the system is on various of its components like the Military-Industrial Complex or the high level of unemployment. The book takes these up, too.

Other differences just stem from a commitment to different modes of social change. Liberals, because of their desire to be effective and realistic within the existing political system, tend to exclude demands that cannot be accommodated by that political process. Radicals, because they are prepared to accept the necessity of total transformation, are willing to be total in their critique. The book will try to elucidate the implications of the two strategies for social change and how they influence and grow out of two different critiques.

We have tried to take liberal ideas as seriously as possible. We think that many people who consider themselves liberals share many of the same ideals as radicals. They share a desire for the humanizing of our society, for the alleviation of oppression and suffering and inequality, and for the solution to specific pressing social problems. They generally have little sympathy for or attachment to those who presently run things. Radicals can talk sincerely with many liberals on the basis of these shared goals and, we think, convince them that the implementation of these shared goals requires more sweeping political changes than they had at first contemplated.

But liberals are often put off by radicals, and they may well be put off by many of the assumptions this book makes about liberals. We want to talk to some of these possible objections. First of all, although we make some sweeping generalizations about liberalism, we recognize that there are many shades and varieties of liberals. When we talk about liberal programs and liberal politicians, it is usually the liberalism of the Democratic party. When we talk about liberal ideology and liberal apologetics, it is usually the liberalism of academics and intellectuals—men like Arthur Schlesinger, Seymour Lipset and Daniel Moynihan. But most often when we say liberalism, we are referring to a political philosophy that says that significant social change can come about through already existing political institutions. This viewpoint encompasses all of the liberalisms mentioned above and also the liberalism of those like the McCarthy supporters.

Left-wing liberals, however, strenuously object to being lumped together with liberals like Schlesinger, Humphrey, Lindsay, Moynihan and, to our mind, Nelson Rockefeller—men we term "corporate liberals." But we do not think this is an unjustified classification for some purposes. In this case, we feel it is justified for our purpose of distinguishing clearly the radical viewpoint from the liberal one.

Moreover, liberals themselves make it very difficult to tell the difference among them. For one thing, they do not set out clear principles by which to distinguish one kind of liberal from another. Thus you find a John Lindsay proposing to break the garbage strike with National Guardsmen, an Arthur Goldberg arguing for the war in Vietnam, an Adlai Stevenson denying that the United States contributed to the Bay of Pigs invasion, and so forth. Second, left-liberals are always making common cause with corporate liberals. This is a central aspect to the liberal strategy of forming coalitions. The humanistic liberals are bound to enter these coalitions to preserve their claim of being able to exert some influence on those with power. But it makes it virtually impossible for outsiders to distinguish the so-called "good guys" from the ordinary politicians in the liberal league. Thus, if left-liberals wish to be distinguished from corporate liberals, they have to begin to draw more than *ad hoc* lines.

But most important for the purposes of this book, we think the particular aspects of liberalism we criticize most strenuously are shared in common by all strains of liberals. Among these shared aspects are a faith in gradualist reform, unwillingness to confront outright the dominant corporate elite, reliance on working *within* the present political system and belief in the reconcilability of the interest groups that compose our society. If such assumptions seem at first foreign to some of our liberal readers, we ask them only to hold back their indignation until they have familiarized themselves with the radical position and compared it to their own.

Finally, many liberals take offense at the reference to their political views as an "ideology." One of the tenets of liberalism has long been that it is not an ideology, that this is one of its improvements over radicalism and previous movements for social change. Rather, liberals think they are pragmatists. Solving problems is a matter of finding the facts and learning the techniques, not debating the advantages of one "system" over another.

We think this view liberals have of themselves is wrong. It is a defense through which they avoid taking seriously radical challenges; we hope to show why this is so as the book progresses. We think the liberal political beliefs can be formulated in terms of propositions about capitalism, about the nature of a Good Society, about what stands in the way of solving our problems, about the way in which social change can take place. We have already indicated what some of these propositions are. We think as such they constitute an ideology and can be openly debated in terms of how well they account for history and how well they describe reality.

We have enumerated some of the things we hope the book does. We also feel somewhat obliged to apologize for certain ways in which the book does not entirely meet our expectations.

For one thing, we wanted to put together a book that would be easy to read without requiring a degree in economics, political science or Marxian theory. As it stands, however, the writing frequently tends toward the academic. In many places, it is very dense and not at all lively. We believe there really is no excuse for bad writing. But, in so many instances, no other adequate statements of a radical view existed so we had to make do.

In many sections, too, the writing suffers from having been written for an exclusively radical audience. A certain jargon or the use of undefined terms may distract some readers in some of these selections.

In part, as well, the turgidness stems from our desire to cram the whole of a radical perspective into one volume, which is probably something that should not be done to any body of ideas that one has respect for. We have tried to make up for this by including some bibliographical suggestions, to which we hope people will turn, if confused or if looking for more extensive expositions of the radical point of view.

Many people are certain to ask why we have given such short shrift to the subject of American imperialism. Since liberalism has proved so unable to account for the war in Vietnam and the whole history of unprovoked aggressiveness of American foreign policy, it is here more than anywhere else these days that radical analysis is proving its merits over the liberal one. Many liberals have come to understand the nature of U.S. imperialism and its relation to our economic system. Through it they have often been brought to see the accuracy of other aspects of the radical analysis.

Our treatment of imperialism in the book is a token one, for two reasons: (1) It would have made the book much too long. We are hoping to be able to put together a companion volume on imperialism when our work on the present collection is completed. (2) More than any other area of radical analysis, good material here exists in commercially published form. We refer people to books by people like Oglesby, Magdoff, Baran, Barnett, Petras and Zeitlin, Horowitz, Williams, etc. (See Bibliography.) Much of what we might have included on imperialism in the short space we could have allotted it would have been from these generally available sources.

Finally, we would like to outline briefly how the book is organized and indicate what issues are dealt with in what sections. The anthology has five parts: Economic Consequences of Corporate Capitalism, Corporations and Government, Problems of U.S. Capitalism, The Failure of Liberal Solutions, and Alternatives and Strategy.

Keeping with the theme mentioned earlier, the first part tries to show that capitalism best describes the kind of political and economic system we have. It draws attention to the central role of the private corporation and the central role of profit. We lay out what the irrationalities of such a system are at its most general level: wastage, exploitation and insensitivity to real human needs.

The second part deals with the government under capitalism—we emphasize that the state is primarily an ally of the corporate interests, creating special opportunities for private gain and stabilizing the private economy as a whole. It is not an arbitrator over and above the corporations nor is it a servant of the people and the initiator of reform, as the liberal view would have it.

The third part examines the dynamics of a capitalist system from closer up, specifically with respect to the major unsolved social problems facing America. It tries to document the contention that these problems are products of the dynamics of capitalism. Its second thesis is that entrenched capitalist interests stand in the way of solution to these problems. Thus they will not be solved without a fundamental change in the nature of capitalism.

The fourth part illustrates this same point by examining liberal attempts to solve America's social problems. Liberal solutions have failed because they refused to confront the obstacles to these solutions inherent in a capitalist system. Some examples of liberal failures are given, and they are used as a vehicle for bringing to light some of the inherent contradictions of the liberal analysis.

The last part is intended to delineate some basic ideas about socialism. Some of the major improvements possible under socialism are indicated, and we try to offer some taste of what a Socialist society would be like by giving examples from socialism in developing societies. We conclude with a few observations on Revolution in America. We present reasons for optimism, some strategic outlines and some reasons for taking Socialist revolution seriously as a political goal to be achieved.

PART I

ECONOMIC CONSEQUENCES OF CORPORATE CAPITALISM

The major contention of this book is that the system of U.S. capitalism is in inevitable, fundamental conflict with the needs of the people who live under its rule. To satisfy those needs, capitalism must be destroyed.

This is a powerful contention, with rather profound implications for action. And it is a contention which would not be shared by most "prominent" intellectuals and social scientists. The prevailing ideology has concluded with much certainty that faith in the system is justified. The question "Is it possible for capitalism to produce a decent society" has rarely been asked, let alone answered.

The key concept in an attempt to answer such a question is that of power. Who has the power to make the decisions that determine the shape of our society? How do those who hold that power exercise it, and how will they exercise it in the future? The purpose of Part I is to show that a preponderant share of this power resides in the hands of the largest American corporations; that this power is used to make profits and to promote the self-interest of these corporations and the small class of people who own, direct and manage them—and finally, that unfettered use of this power is responsible for the persistent inequality in America, for the failure to meet most people's basic material needs, for the proliferation of waste in the form of military weaponry and useless consumer goods and for the insurmountable roadblocks placed in the way of serious social reform.

Many of the facts lying behind the radical argument are, surprisingly enough, fairly well accepted by many liberals. It is not only radicals who understand the tremendous inequality of income and wealth—Robert Lampman, a liberal, pioneered in studies of these questions. It is not only radicals who have discovered the existence of a ruling upper class—see the findings of Lloyd Warner, Digby Baltzell and others. It is not only radicals who are aware of the ties between the military and industry—just look at the hearings of the Senate Foreign Relations Committee, or at constant revelations in *The New York Times* or *Washington Post.* It is not only radicals who are aware of the tremendous concentration of the American economy and of the tendency to concentrate political power into the hands of these corporate giants—read what Bernard Nossiter has to say in selections in this book.

Nevertheless, these liberals and many others seem incapable of drawing the conclusions from these facts and piecing them into a global critique of the operation of our social and economic institutions. They fall back on the crutches of liberal ideology. This ideology in the past has served to satisfy both liberal ideologue and average American that things are fine—or at least getting better all the time.

What are the critical assumptions of the liberal ideology? In its most general form they are:

1. That the American economic apparatus is so fruitful and powerful as to be capable of creating through abundance a good life—in spite of waste and mismanagement. The fruits of such a productive system will eventually trickle down to everyone.

2. That the liberal idea is so inevitable that it will succeed in dislodging pockets of conservatism in the government and the economy and other obstacles—like race prejudice—that stand in the way of equality, democracy and peace.

3. That the growth of the liberal state should be heralded because it creates the potential to triumph public interests over self-interested, private ones, and to institute meaningful social reforms.

The political developments of the last decade—in particular, the deterioration of the cities and the overt militarization of foreign policy, all under "liberal" administrations—have cast grave doubts on these liberal assumptions. Another analysis has emerged, a radical analysis, which hotly challenges the liberal perspective.

1. The radical analysis questions whether things have been getting better, except in a superficial way. It poses a new criteria for judging our social progress: does it fulfill real human needs? The radical analysis attacks the idea that technology and affluence will solve problems. New money and new technology only go to enhance the power of the already powerful in the present order of things. The radical analysis suggests that the American economic system, rather than being fruitful and abundant, is irrational and oppressive, the source of many of our problems. Perhaps the solution to these problems requires not massive moondoggles, but social revolution and total reorganization of the society.

2. As to the obstacles to change, radicals point the finger at the basic institutions of the society, not the vanishing conservatives. These institutions are dominated by men whose interest is corporate empire building, not social problem-solving. Their institutions are responsible for many of the problems that plague our society. It is their stake in the status quo that prevents solution to social problems. Liberal victory means only new "enlightened" strategies for defending these institutions and the interests behind them.

3. Finally, the radical analysis has no illusions about the progressive char-

acter of the state. Given the present shape and power of private interests, the state will solve no problems. At best, the state will oil the gears to keep things running smoothly. At worst, the state will be the ruthless promoter of private interests and reactionary policies. The only hope for a good society can come from people taking power in their own hands.

This introduction tries to elaborate these contentions and extend the radical critique of the liberal mythology. It is divided into two sections:

1. The first argues that America is still a class society. Material inequality has remained great and the power to decide has grown more unequally distributed than ever before.

2. The second suggests that affluence as measured by GNP is not an adequate measure of our society's achievements. The system is simply not fulfilling people's real needs, but instead is manufacturing waste—particularly through defense production and in the consumer market—on a colossal scale.

The introduction to Part II of the book elaborates and extends these ideas. In particular, it speaks to certain kinds of objections commonly raised to the radical analysis. It discusses in depth the question of whether the government can be under capitalism the agency for social reform.

THE MIRAGE OF EQUALITY

The prophets of a Good Society under capitalism never stop harping on the idea that America is moving toward economic equality. Everyone is becoming middle-class. The income structure, which once looked dismally like a pyramid, now looks like a "fat man" with the bulge in the middle, they say.

A lot of monkey wrenches could be thrown into that self-satisfied vision of America. We could talk about the poverty that still besets nearly thirty million Americans. This is old hat to many people. We could talk about the painful reality faced by the average workingman. Much more of this revelation to middle-class social theorists we will leave until Part III. Here we will start with the income structure.

Distribution

The income structure in America has remained virtually static since 1910. This is the conclusion of Gabriel Kolko, whose study is included in Part I. While everyone may be getting more, the same *proportion* of income is going to the same income tenths then as now.

This finding has profound implications. It means that in spite of the deep economic and social changes of the last sixty years, those on top continue to appropriate the same lion's share of the pie. This testifies to the entrenched nature of the institutional forces maintaining this structure. It is good a priori evidence that those on top will in the future keep getting the disproportionate share they have gotten in the past. It also suggests that any changes in this allocation are going to require really massive changes in power relations.

Economic Concentration

But while the income structure has remained static, there is good reason to believe that, in back of this screen, those on top have been consolidating their power and resources. Real power in the economy lies not so much in individuals as in corporations. And the corporate economy is growing more concentrated year by year. In 1941 the top one thousand corporations controlled two thirds of all manufacturing assets. Today this same two thirds is controlled by a mere two hundred corporations. Real control is passing into fewer and fewer hands. The big corporations using their market leverage—as described by Nossiter here—are growing bigger. The conglomerate movement results in the marriages of a number of these giants to create bigger giants with more capital, more market power and more political leverage. Surely this increasing concentration of economic decisions cannot be passed off as a democratization of the society.

The most prominent trend in society is thus not the growth of the middle class, but the growth and consolidation of corporate power. But what about the new affluence?

Affluence

Although real income has increased substantially, doubling over the last twenty years, there are good grounds for questioning whether the lot of the average American has truly improved. Today the average American is buying products he could never before have purchased. But a substantial portion of his increased earnings is being gobbled up by superfluous and wasteful aspects of those products. He is paying for an enormous proliferation of frills, accessories, advertising needed to sell the product and engineering designed to make it outmoded.

For example, Baran and Sweezy in the selection below cite a study showing that the selling price of an adequate, modern automobile coming out of Detroit should be around $700–$800. The difference between that price and the conventional auto price of over $2000 is what the customer is presently paying out for advertising, and the unnecessary model changes that are made each year. Thus cars may be an advantage of affluence. But increases in income are rapidly eaten up without added satisfaction by these kinds of costs, not to mention the skyrocketing charges added on by insurance, gasoline, parking and the required new car every two and a quarter years.

The American consumer is never allowed to rest on his laurels. Having attained a certain level, immediately a higher style of living is projected to him as the new norm. He must now take on an extra job, go deeper and deeper into debt, send his wife off to work and worry twice as much in order to keep up. As even the U.S. Chamber of Commerce admitted, "only 54% of American families can afford what is now perceived by today's criteria as a low moderate life standard, and very few can afford the leisure-class life-styles popularized by the spread of education and promoted by the mass media. So paradoxically, personal insecurity grows as we become more affluent. The source of insecurity is the widening gap between the 'taught norm' of emerging life-styles and the economically supportable levels of living."

Let's take a look at what the Bureau of Labor Statistics calls a "modest" income for an average American urban family—$9076. Such a life is Spartan indeed by middle-class standards. In such an average four-person family, the husband can afford to buy a little over three pairs of pants every year, less than five pairs of underwear, one pair of shoes, a topcoat only every eight years, a sweater every five years and a pair of pajamas every three years. His wife can buy two dresses and two pairs of shoes every year, a coat every five years, a skirt every two years and pajamas every three years. They can spend $16.67 all year on books and $55.50 on education for both children. They can go to nine movies each year, consume 4.4 fifths of liquor and buy a television set every ten years. But it is even more impressive to realize that this family lives at an income level well above that of 50 percent of the population.

Talking about the average, however, leaves out of the picture those who remain at the bottom, plagued by poverty that doesn't go away on its own. Consumer statistics don't show houses without heat, six children to a room, rats, roaches and the works. Furthermore, poverty is also a relative concept. In many ways, the more advanced our society becomes the more expensive is a bare minimum existence. To purchase toothpaste, a poor man has to pay for the "extra-added-ingredients" and the costs of advertising all pegged for the man of "affluence." As jobs move to the suburbs, to take another example, a person can't have a decent job without a car to get there. Thus merely raising the bottom of the income ladder doesn't amount to "solving" the poverty problem. A good society requires economic equality, not just absence of poverty.

Meanwhile, the level of income may go up, but all aspects of living conditions over which an individual's income has no effect have been rapidly deteriorating. Cities are becoming unlivable. Pollution chases the average American wherever he goes. Public services rot (making the new car a necessity, not a luxury). Then the new car delivers him into the jaws of a gigantic traffic jam, morning and night. This is not exactly the promised land of affluence the prophets told us about.

A Class Society

What we have been describing is a "class" society. The major portion of the wealth and nearly all the power in the society are concentrated in the hands of a few giant institutions and the people that run them. Those who benefit from these institutions make up a cohesive group characterized by a myriad of social and institutional connections, relating the powerful and the wealthy, one to another. Access to this class, although possible, is highly restricted and requires a period of long apprenticeship in one of its guardian institutions.

On the other hand, the overwhelming majority of people in America live in a world dominated by the decisions of these institutions. As small businesses and marginal operations are squeezed out of existence, those Americans who don't have the fortune to belong to the ruling class are more and more obliged to work in or service one of these giant institutions. Such a world can only be termed a middle-class one in a very narrow sense.

All in all, Americans are beginning to question the myth of American affluence. If great inequalities of wealth continue to exist; if economic improvement brings more burdens than it relieves; if power is more and more centralized in the hands of the few, can we really be so confident that we are being led down the path to a Good Society?

PATTERN OF DEVELOPMENT: WASTE AND NEGLECT

Every year, America's national product gets larger. To look at the growth of the American economy over the years, it seems like a great success story. But we have to look underneath the statistics about more and more production to understand who has reaped the benefits of this increased production, and of what this production has actually consisted.

To begin with, we know that despite the growth in production, the American economy has failed miserably in the provision of collective goods and services. Mass transportation, medical care, education, housing, child care, recreation—all of these have been seriously neglected, much more than in other capitalist countries of Western Europe and far more than in the Socialist countries. Thus even increases in real income have not been able to satisfy those needs which require not simply consumer goods, but also collective facilities and action by public authorities.

Second, U.S. economic development has not taken place democratically. It has been directed by the corporate managers of America—out of control of the masses of people. Decisions about production priorities, or the use of technologies, or the balance between producing goods and increasing leisure, or the many other decisions that affect the day-to-day lives of ordinary people, have been kept out of popular hands. In fact, these decisions have remained jealously guarded managerial prerogatives; our society does not even in *theory* consider them to be the rightful property of the people.

This has meant that economic gain has been achieved at a serious human cost. Most people have continued to slave away on the job to keep the GNP rising. Work has remained largely meaningless, routine, alienating and in many cases brutal and dangerous. Existence for most people of the society consists of a constant rat race to make ends meet. There is the constant insecurity that losing a job or having an accident or getting sick or the coming of economic recession will wipe away all the hard-earned benefits gained by taking two jobs and going into debt. Interpersonal relations have remained isolated and competitive; materialism and the quest for success and status have infected people's ability to relate to one another and to make the best of their lives.

Third, as we have noted above, the major proportion of the benefits of economic development have accrued to those on top. These benefits have hardly trickled down to those on the bottom. One just has to look at the phenomenal increase in profit levels in the 1960's in comparison to the meager increase in wages to see this. (There has been an actual *decline* in real wages over the last five years.) Corporations have been raising prices on the whole much faster than productivity increases. That means people have had to work harder and faster (as the assembly line has speeded up, work load increased, etc.) just to keep up with prices. This pattern has been the case even in periods of the greatest increase of real income.

Finally—and this is the focus of the rest of this section—the *pattern* or *model* of development of the U.S. economy has been one founded on a high-level of military spending, on the one hand, and a huge amount of waste in the production of consumer goods, on the other. To put it another way—if we look at what our ever-increasing production has actually consisted of, we will see that billions represented military goods of all sorts that no one could use. In addition, we have paid in our purchases of consumer goods like automobiles not only for a product that could be used, but for the advertising and market research that went into selling it, for the research and style changes that went into making it look new and different, and for the repairs and the necessity to buy a new product when this one falls apart that comes from the systematic effort of producers to build obsolescence and a short life-span right into their product.

The consequences of this pattern of development—concentration on military spending and the proliferation of consumer waste—are felt not only in our pocketbooks. They have had clear effects on our culture and the prospects of human survival. Let's now try to see the roots of this pattern in the structure of our economy.

Militarism

Militarism looks easy to isolate: our society is presently spending $80 billion or close to 10 percent of the vaunted GNP on arms and related expenditures. This does not take into account that an estimated thirteen to sixteen million persons in 1962 out of a labor force of seventy-eight million were reliant for jobs on "national defense" efforts.[1] It does not include a picture of the sprawling defense bureaucracies or of the powerful giant corporations with stakes in the Military-Industrial Complex. It does not describe the vastness of the waste and profiteering that characterizes this sector. (See Reich-Finkelhor selection for all these.)

This incredible military complex constitutes the most advanced and rapidly developing sector of the economy. Electronics, aerodynamics and telecommunications are the pride and joy of American industry. The vast majority of the nation's research efforts plus the vast majority of the nation's newly trained scientists and engineers are poured into this sector at ever-increasing rates.

And with what result? A showy space program promising little for human betterment and wasting enormous resources for the sake basically of international propaganda. A growing arsenal of weapons many of which are never completed anyway. Aggressive military ventures all over the world. An empire we are obliged to protect, etc. How is this to be accounted for?

A certain portion of defense spending can be attributed to the problem of national defense. That, in less mystified lingo means protecting the world-wide American empire. Real threats to the people of this country are pretty few, except for nuclear annihilation—defense against which is clearly now *not* obtainable through increased armaments. But—as the wasteful way in which it is spent shows—there is an awful lot more behind defense spending than just defense.

Stagnation

Capitalism since its infancy has been plagued by the problem of stagnation. Demand tends to grow less rapidly than production. The market economy—unplanned and uncontrolled—heads into a tail spin—depression, unemployment and falling profits.

[1] From U.S. Arms Control and Disarmament Agency, *Economic Impacts of Disarmament,* Washington, D.C., 1962.

But in the wake of the last great economic crisis the system stumbled into a partial remedy. Massive state expenditures for rapidly disposable, expensive items like military weapons could maintain a fairly high level of demand over fairly long periods. What the New Deal was incapable of achieving in terms of bringing the capitalist economy back to life, World War II achieved. The result is the permanent war economy that continues to this very day.

A permanent military sector proved an ideal source of state-stimulated economic demand. (1) It provided virtually limitless projects which quickly became obsolete and required replacement. (2) It was bolstered by a tailor-made ideology—the Cold War. (3) State-financed defense, unlike, say, state-financed housing, in no way competed with the activities of private corporations who would oppose its expansion. These were advantages shared by no other type of possible government expenditure, like public housing or welfare spending. All in all, it spelled an immensely profitable opportunity for a vast array of corporations.

The military establishment is now a permanent feature of the capitalist landscape. It serves a crucial "safety valve" function to the boom-and-bust economy. And in addition, it is enormously profitable. So by now the most powerful corporations in the economy have tied their well-being and prosperity into it, by buying defense corporations and taking on government contract work.

America's international empire also has roots that trace to the heart of the economic system. In part, it too emerged as a response to the same problem of inadequate domestic demand. Corporations have found that markets abroad can be used to absorb goods unused by domestic demand. In addition, the international empire allows our corporations to dominate the world reservoirs of minerals and raw materials. This is the key to maintaining rates of profit far beyond that obtained in most domestic investment. Finally, sending plants overseas to cheap labor supplies can be a way of making big profits and of forcing wage levels down at home. Thus American corporate giants have staked out their claims all over the world. In order to protect this vast complex of economic interests, our political leaders must adopt a massive military arsenal and an aggressive posture toward popular and nationalist movements around the world.

Together, these two overlapping corporate interest groups—militarism and imperialism—are powerful forces behind the priority our system gives to a "garrison economy," as one writer put it. They lobby for it, they profit from it, they are prepared to defend it.

Exorcising this Leviathan is not like operating on a wart—some external excrescence. Since the vested interest in militarism has its roots in the heart of the economy, in the hundred or so largest corporations, eliminating the Military-Industrial Complex means fundamentally changing capitalism. In our view, these corporations cannot be satisfied by some nonmilitary spending substitute. The possibility for enormous profits there is too slim, the cost of changeover is too great. Those who think we can dismantle the MIC without a revolution have serious illusions about where power lies in America.

Consumerism

The model of development characterizing the nonmilitary part of the domestic economy is best described as consumerism. That means a commodity system based on the sale of products to a mass of private individuals for the purposes of individual consumption.

An economy based on consumption that seemed quite normal in a time of scarcity is coming to mean something quite irrational in an era of abundance. The market for consumer goods is now characterized by the sale of more and more useless items. Those items that are still necessary are more and more laden with useless accessories, fringes, decorations and anything that can be used to increase the price. Thousands of virtually identical products—produced with enormous waste in duplication—compete for consumers' attention in supermarkets and department stores under different brand names. To make the system work, billions are spent on advertising to assure a customer's preference for one identical product over another. To increase the general level of consumption, advertising is used to manipulate consumers to be aware of needs and desires they previously had never recognized. This is combined with intentional efforts to reduce the quality of goods, plan early obsolescence in order to obtain a quicker turn-over and repurchase of items. Vast quantities of technology and brain power go into the production of useless values and thinking up marketing schemes.

Here are the results: technological know-how that could be improving existence is wasted on uselessness. Productive capacity is squandered in duplication and needless variation. Human values are debased because people are goaded into placing market prices on everything, on consuming compulsively. Human relationships and aspirations all become associated with commodities, as people are told that buying a car or using a beauty product will make them loved, or give them an identity. The basis for cooperation and trust and openness in the society is undermined, as the most powerful economic institutions in the world manipulate people for profit, and this leaves them feeling exploited, bewildered and suspicious.

Profit

Such an organized system of misrepresentation and manipulation could only grow out of a production-for-profit economy. Companies plan obsolescence, manipulate consumers and market uselessness because it is enormously profitable to do so. It is cheaper than increasing the quality of their products, searching out new consumer needs to satisfy and helping consumers to rationally buy what they need. Under the constraints of competitive capitalism in the old days, companies had incentive to be constructive in these ways. But under monopoly conditions, with many basic commodity needs already satisfied and given the arsenal of manipulative techniques available, the real pathology of capitalism becomes apparent: production is not geared to satisfy needs, but to make money. The two do not coincide.

So a swamp of commercialism and a plethora of unneeded wasteful commodities have grown up around us. American development seems to be heading in the direction of an infinite expansion of this whole mode of production.

Collective Needs

We have isolated these two aspects of the capitalist system, because they represent leading developments. Militarism and consumerism are sectors of the society and the economy that will become more and more central as time progresses. But *over*development of these sectors—and the consequent waste of resources—goes hand in hand with the *under*development of others—most notably that of social services. Our society in its present development manifests a nearly total neglect of collective needs.

Any observer of our society cannot but be struck with the fact that the level of the provision of basic social facilities is truly inadequate—far below that of even other capitalist countries. The hospitals, schools, housing and public transportation are in miserable condition. Their improvement year by year is failing to keep track of the growth of our actual economic capacity to provide such facilities. As the market for individualized consumption spreads cancerously, the whole quality of collective existence atrophies. Besides the neglect of social services, the massive and manipulative institutions manage to deprive people of even simple social amenities—like rest and leisure, recreation, cleanliness, peace and quiet and privacy—all of which are becoming as extinct as the buffalo.

Color TV's are today within reach of the average American. But adequate medical treatment is available only for the rich. And good preventive medicine and public health aiming to prevent diseases before they occur and reduce the dangers in the environment aren't available to anyone. City transportation systems sink deeper and deeper into a morass. Smog and pollutants like DDT cannot be reduced. Well over 10 percent of thc population live in substandard housing—without hot water, or without plumbing facilities, or with holes in the walls that prevent heating, or with one bedroom to five children.

Collective Needs Unprofitable

What is it about these needs and the kinds of services ministering to them that allows them to be so neglected in our society? What it boils right down to is that these needs cannot be satisfied on a profitable basis. Corporations cannot produce these services and sell them to people for a profit. Public transportation, for example, has proved to be a deficit operation. Thus only public authorities can undertake to provide it. Housing, to take another example, is only profitable when built for rich people, not low- and middle-income levels. Hospitals, again, reveal the same story. The private sector, that is the corporations, just don't enthusiastically set up operations in these areas. They are left to public authorities, charitable institutions or no one at all.

A second aspect of these needs is that they can only be provided for on a collective basis. Many of them require a high degree of social planning and a large initial investment. Medical care requires bringing together a great variety of services and equipment. Transportation requires acquiring rights of way.

Collective services are not discrete products that an individual can use all for himself, but they are facilities that an individual must share with a larger number of other people. The private economy cannot organize the sale of such collective facilities in a highly profitable way.

Finally, some of these needs, like the need for privacy and cleanliness, require not services at all, but protections against certain trends developing in the society. The protection inevitably involves a collectivity taking action against the private industrial and commercial agencies which are polluting the environment and infringing on privacy. In a society where money means power, collectives just don't have what it takes to stop these private giants.

The central fact of our society is that profit-making pursuits take priority over socially needed pursuits. This occurs in large part because those who operate for profit—i.e., the corporations—determine to what activities the society will put its resources.

Private enterprise, however, goes beyond the sin of omission—i.e., ignoring the socially necessary—*here* to one of *commission.* For one thing, these private organizations are regularly engaged at present in the despoliation of the environment. They pollute waters and land capable of recreational use; they pollute air and create noise. They submit their workers to oppressive speedups and bad working conditions. And then they require the individual consumer to buy back at a high price and a profit to themselves the satisfaction of his needs for leisure and peace and health in the form of vacations and escapes to the suburbs.

On the level of collective institutions like state, city and Federal governments these same private interests lobby against the expansion of such services as could be publicly provided. They also fight against kinds of public regulation that would prohibit the continued despoliation of the environment. In the face of massive economic power, the public authorities have defaulted in the responsibility to provide even the most modest kind of control.

The ultimate lynch pin to a system of impoverished collective services is, of course, that citizens affected by the system are unable to even so much as formulate the existence of these needs. This happens not just because political leaders obviously will not call attention to problems they cannot conceivably solve even if they wanted to. More important, there are the media and the mandarins of public education who carefully damp any but the most circumscribed suggestions that the quality of life in America leaves something to be desired.

People are carefully groomed, on the other hand, to express their persistent feelings of inadequacy or unfulfillment—the result of inadequate collective services—through the market. Buy something new! Become something beautiful! People are so socially fragmented that the whole idea that they should band together for things like family planning services, better public transportation, recreation facilities, is regarded as suspect.

The Civilization of the Automobile

The best way to sum up this discussion of the model of development is with an example. We shall take that object which probably best characterizes America—the automobile. The automobile is the item of individual consumption par excellence. The average American is encouraged to express himself through the automobile. With it he can compensate for status anxieties; express his manliness; participate in America. Meanwhile, the automobile threatens to destroy our civilization. It makes cities unlivable; it pollutes the air; it spawns a network of congested highways tearing down everything in its path; it creates traffic jams that only intensify the anxiety and irritability acquired on the job; it causes thousands of deaths and millions of injuries per year; its economic costs include billions on highway building and billions on insurance policies.

Real questions are raised about whether it actually improves our quality of life. Congestion and parking mean that cars hardly make it any easier to get to work; a second car for many working-class families is an economic burden not a luxury—papa needs it to get a job, to which he drives the car everyday, only to leave it unused in the company parking lot. Meanwhile, families shell out an enormous amount on repairs, insurance, gas and the inevitable new car required by obsolescence.

No one questions that for an equivalent social expenditure we could build a fantastic system of rapid and low-cost public transportation within cities and between them. Many schemes of local car rentals or car pools have been devised, so that families could have cars for their use when public facilities did not suffice.

But the present system with all its waste is nonetheless enormously profitable, and the corporate interests that stand behind it sport a more enormous range of powers than capitalism has ever seen. What would the automobile companies do without *planned obsolescence* that enables them to furnish an average American with a new car every two and a quarter years? [2] Or the oil interests? Or the construction companies with their cornucopia of fat-filled road-building contracts furnished them by public authorities? Or the rubber and plate-glass interests? Or last but not least, the multibillion dollar insurance companies. It is not surprising that the American public cannot even formulate the idea of an alternative transportation system.

In conclusion, ours is a society that does not give priority to people and their needs, but to profit. There is little indication that this priority is being reversed, and substantial evidence that the irrational situation is being aggravated. Moreover, these priorities are not just arbitrary developments but rather stem from the deep-rooted underlying structure of our political economy.

[2] Cf. Vance Packard, *The Waste Makers* (New York: McKay, 1960), p. 76.

1 CORPORATE POWER IN THE ECONOMY*

by BERNARD D. NOSSITER

This chapter sets out some of the basic realities of the corporate economy. It details the concentration of economic power, the decline of the free-market constraints on corporate behavior and some of the new vistas of antisocial behavior now open to the giant corporations. Nossiter is a liberal (of the downy-cheeked if not the fuzzy-minded variety) who is upset by the ravages of selfish corporate power.

Social science has dealt only marginally with the implications of massive corporate power. Its comforting ideas about pluralism, "soulful" corporations and the "managerial revolution" are much too facile. Nossiter's evidence hardly creates much confidence that corporations are acting in anything but a selfish way. Moreover, Nossiter describes only a quite limited range of corporate activity—primarily the market behavior of large corporations. The type of immense power he points to applies its weight as well in the areas of politics and government, advertising, local economies, employment, and foreign policy, to name just a few. As we go along, we will try to draw attention to the impact of this corporate power in all these areas, and the way in which corporations impose their antisocial goals on all other spheres of activity in capitalist society.

Nossiter is particularly good in conveying one particular point that will be raised again in the Miliband selection. (See Part II.) He shows how the political goals of government, like anti-inflation policy, are directly dependent on corporate cooperation. This dependence is one of the crucial mechanisms through which corporations dominate government activity.

In economic affairs, the real and the spurious are often buried under layers of conventional belief and self-serving myth. Perhaps the most common distortion is embodied in the following contemporary fable:

"It is well to remind ourselves from time to time of the benefits we derive from the maintenance of a free market system. The system rests on freedom of consumer choice, the profit motive and vigorous competition for the buyer's dollar. By relying on these spontaneous economic forces, we secure these benefits."

The benefits are then described as the automatic production of the goods consumers want in the quantities they want them; automatic minimizing of waste in a world in which the most efficient producers triumph; encouragement of innovation and technological change through high rewards and competitive adaption.

"The free market is a decentralized regulator of our economic system. The free market is not only a more efficient decision maker than even the wisest central planning body, but even more important, the free market keeps economic power widely dispersed."

This is a contemporary restatement of Adam Smith's invisible hand. It was proclaimed by President Kennedy only a few months after he decried economic myths at Yale. The President's narrative had only marginal relevance to the modern world. Indeed, the Kennedy administration itself designed policies on a very different set of assumptions. In an atomistic, self-regulating economy there would be no point in trying techniques to restrain wage and price increases, devising tax programs to stimulate investment and worrying about the federal budget's impact on employment and output. In a world of pure and free competition, these problems solve themselves.

But the central fact about the American economy is that it is concentrated. In nearly every important manufacturing industry, a handful of firms produce a major share of the output, employ a significant portion of the work force and make the decisive investment decisions. The auto industry is dominated by a single firm with two lesser giants following behind it; in steel, three large companies control more than half of the total capacity while nine other firms own most of what is left; in electrical machinery, two great complexes stand out. While this concentration is especially visible in manufacturing, the most volatile sector of the economy, other areas like retailing and finance are shaped to some degree by a handful of leading concerns.

This overriding fact of concentration is taken for granted by the casual observer of the business scene. It is acknowledged but often ignored by economists. It is taken into account by government policy makers with reluctance and only when it intrudes on their vision with a prominence that can't be denied.

Instead of reckoning with large and concrete corporations, economists and government officials prefer to shape policy around large and impersonal abstractions. They think in terms of total demand, total employment; they manipulate broad-gauged tools like taxes, spending and the supply of money and credit. These concepts and tools were fitted together in the brilliant construction of John Maynard Keynes. His insights were apparently confirmed in World War II when the military economy's insatiable appetite for goods ended the great depression. As a result, attention has been diverted from the structure of the economy to more sweeping categories. Policy makers have examined the economy with a telescope, not a microscope. In the jargon of the professionals, the focus has been macroeconomic, not microeconomic. Only in the last few years has there been a growing, if limited, rediscovery of industry's shape. Preoccupation with the forest had hidden some important trees. Recent experience indicates that giant corporations, sometimes with the tacit support of large unions, can frustrate and upset broad-ranging policy designs.

The crucial fact of concentration has been snubbed for several reasons. This is, after all, a sensitive subject because it involves power. For a policy maker to cope with concentration can mean conflict with the strongest institutions in America.

Then, too, economists have invested considerable intellectual capital in exploring a model world of small, competing firms. If adequate account was taken of the fact that industries are generally organized by a few competitors, much of this capital stock would become obsolete.

Moreover, the existence of private power centers disturbs the soothing national belief in a pluralistic society. It is more agreeable to picture a world in which power is diffused, where one-man, one-vote expresses more than a formal political arrangement and reflects an underlying reality. Most of all, it is upsetting to acknowledge the existence of private power without public accountability. But the fact of concentration lends color to the unpleasant suggestion of Walter Adams and Horace M. Gray that America is moving towards "an Orwellian technocracy functioning under the aegis of socially irresponsible private power."

The features of the contemporary economic landscape can best be seen by comparing them with the economy of the less complicated texts, the classical world associated with Adam Smith, the simple world described by Kennedy in his account of the free market. In this setting, economic power is diffused. In every industry, no single firm is large enough to materially affect the price or supply of that industry's product. Each producer is confronted with an impersonal price, one he bears no share in making because it is determined by larger forces of supply and demand. Each producer tries to set his output so that the cost of turning out one more unit just matches this market price. In a world without price supports, this would be the situation of the wheat grower; his price would be set by forces over which he had no control.

In the classical economy of perfectly competitive industries, each producer tries to make the most profit possible. All are under continual pressure to search for cheaper methods of production and adopt the improved techniques of their peers. Happily for society, the self-interest of each producer in garnering the greatest profit insures an ideal arrangement for all. In this Smithian world, scarce resources of men, materials and investment are most efficiently distributed. Thanks to the carrot of demand and the stick of competition, resources are allocated in accord with the tastes of consumers and combined in the least wasteful fashion. The impersonal markets transmit the code for these ideal outputs through the signals of competitive prices. Thus, the invisible hand of competition rules economic activity and brings about the best of all possible material worlds.

In the everyday world, however, no such elegant mechanism is at work. Broad stretches of the economy are marked by much more personal markets in which giant firms have considerable discretion over their prices and a great deal more. General Motors is simply not in the same position as the wheat producer whose personal decision to raise or lower his price, increase or cut back his acreage, makes no difference to the price of wheat generally or the amount of wheat that will be sold.

On Capitol Hill, in the inspirational literature emitted by business and in the cruder textbooks, the small producer is hero. Indeed, if sheer numbers counted, he ought to be. Like the poor who must be blessed because there are so many of them, small firms make up the bulk of the business population. In 1962, there were about four and three-quarter million companies in the United States and the vast majority were small by any definition. However, their number is a poor index to the importance of small business in the economy. In a study covering data through 1958, Norman R. Collins and Lee E. Preston found that the 100 largest industrial corporations owned 30 percent of the assets of all manufacturing, mining and distribution companies. Even this aggregation of giants has its leaders. The 20 largest owned more than half of the group's assets and the four biggest, more than a fifth.

The Census Bureau periodically computes the degree of concentration for individual industries. The last survey also in 1958 disclosed that four[1] or fewer manufacturers account for more than half of their industry's sales in many sectors of the economy.

Here is the share taken by the top four in some leading industries, all with sales over $1 billion:

Motor vehicles and parts	75 percent
Steelworks and rolling mills	53
Aircraft	59
Aircraft engines	56
Organic chemicals	55
Tires and inner tubes	74
Cigarettes	79
Tin cans and other tinware	80
Synthetic fibers	78
Tractors	69

After an earlier 1954 survey appeared, Carl Kaysen and Donald F. Turner summarized these little noticed Census tables. In manufacturing, they listed 147 industries that sold their products across the country. Of these 147 industries, they distinguished 58 that were highly concentrated and another 46 that were simply concentrated.[2] In other words, two-thirds of the manufacturing industries with national markets are organized in a fashion that lies outside the world of classical economics. The typical manufacturing industry then is dominated by a handful of large competitors. They are not confronted by, but play a large role in determining, their prices.

Impressive as these figures may be, they only begin to reflect the extent to which the American economy rests on the giants. There are, after all, many industries; some, like rayon and cotton, compete with each other. So, to center on concentration in one industry might seem to exaggerate the lack of competition. However, another way of looking at the economy is to measure the portion of all industrial output produced by the large companies. Again, the figures don't fit the model of Adam Smith. For in 1958, the 50 largest corporations produced nearly one-quarter (23 percent) of all the value added in the manufacturing process. The biggest 100 firms claimed nearly a third (30 percent) and the top 200 almost two-fifths (38 percent).

Economists have been arguing for years over whether concentration is growing greater, smaller or holding steady. Are the big firms carving out an increasing portion of the economic domain? A look at individual industries

[1] The government does not break down its estimates and specify the shares of the biggest firm or top two or three in an industry. The calculations are limited to groupings of four on the somewhat dubious ground that a more refined count would give competitors information they now lack. Thus General Motor's 50 percent share of the auto market is supposedly a secret to be kept from Ford and Chrysler.

[2] A highly concentrated industry is one in which the eight largest firms account for half or more of the sales and the twenty largest, 75 percent or more. In a concentrated industry, the top eight account for at least a third of the sales and the top twenty, less than 75 percent.

is inconclusive. Since World War II, some like oil refining, aircraft engines, motors and generators and cigarettes have become less compact. The share of the four biggest companies in each has been slipping. Others, like motor vehicles and parts, bread and related products, paper and board products and ship building and repairing have become more concentrated. The big four have been gaining ground.

But a second look at the very biggest giants offers a strong hint that more and more of manufacturing is being drawn into fewer and fewer hands. Between 1947 and 1958, the top 50 firms enlarged their share of the industrial pie from 17 percent to 23 percent; the biggest 200 from 30 percent to 38 percent. In other words, the 200 greatest corporations increased their slice of a much bigger pie by more than one-quarter. The concentration of assets in the hands of the 100 industrial giants has also been growing slowly. Between 1948 and 1958, their share of all industrial assets rose from 26.7 percent to 29.8 percent. The top 20 firms were gaining on the second 80 at about the same pace.

If, however, concentration is shrinking in as many industries as it is growing, how did the largest corporations expand their sphere? The answer apparently is this: the big concerns have been breaking outside the bounds of their traditional industries and buying up firms in more or less unrelated fields. Since the end of World War II, the nation has been moving through the third great wave of corporate marriages in American economic history. Typically, these postwar mergers have united a big firm in one field with a smaller firm in another. These weddings are much more likely to escape the prohibitions of the antitrust laws than mergers between two clearly competing firms in the same industry.

The conglomerate merger, as these marriages across industry lines are called, is not a new phenomenon on the American scene. Partly as a result of mergers, General Motors has for years been a leading producer of diesel locomotives, refrigerators and trucks as well as autos. But the rapid spread of conglomerates is new and adds another dimension to the model of concentration in any one industry. Some of the corporate giants are not only powers in their native industry; they are figures of substance in several other industries as well. In the eleven years from 1950 through 1961, the 500 biggest industrial firms picked up 3404 other companies, an average of seven apiece. The top 200 acquired 1943 or an average of nearly ten each. Thus, Ford Motor Co. bought up Philco Corp., a major producer of radio and television sets. The General Dynamics Corp. embraced firms making missiles, radio and television equipment, building materials, welding apparatus and industrial gases. Textron, Inc., as its name implies, was once primarily a textiles producer; by 1961, textiles accounted for only 15 percent of its business and in 1963 it sold its last textile mill. Meanwhile Textron has taken under its wing makers of calendars, padding for auto seats, radar antennas, screw fasteners, brooms, storm doors, bathroom fixtures, plywood, watches, eyeglasses and shoes among others.

When these giants buy their way into highly competitive industries, the nature of competition within those industries changes from the classical model. The giant parent can use his greater resources to support price and output behavior by a subsidiary that the junior firm on its own could not afford. The Federal Trade Commission noted in 1948: "The giant conglomerate corporation may attain an almost impregnable economic position. Threatened with competition in any one of its various activities, it may sell below cost in that field, offsetting its losses through profits made in other lines—a practice which is frequently explained as one of meeting competition. The conglomerate corporation is thus in a position to strike out with great force against smaller business in a variety of different industries."

One further characteristic of the economic landscape should be noted: the landmarks are pretty stable. If life were perilous for the giants, if yesterday's pigmy became tomorrow's colossus, the economy would be much more competitive than concentration figures taken at one point in time suggest. But this does not happen. The behemoths generally maintain their dominance. Of the 50 largest manufacturers in 1958, some 34 were in this same sphere in 1947. The remaining 16 rose to their new eminence from the only slightly less exclusive top 200. In the postwar period, the industrial elite have not had to contend with many upstart new rich.

A relief map of the American economy, then, does not show a plateau of myriad indistinguishable, atomistic competitors. In region after region, distinct mountains emerge. Moreover, many of these mountains have foothills trailing off beyond their historic industrial boundaries. And towering above all the ranges are perhaps 200 corporate peaks whose features give the economy its essential contour.

The view of a market from a giant's executive suite is vastly different from the perspective of the Kansas wheat farmer. In the typical concentrated industry, the dominant corporations tend to abandon the law of the competitive jungle and substitute safety. Instead of survival of the fittest the prevailing mode is live and let live. To be sure, there are exceptions, breakaways from the pack, harassing attacks and defensive countermeasures. But in general, corporation executives yearn for stability. They don't seek the most profits possible, the spur of perfectly competitive markets. Instead, they seek satisfactory profits and institutional survival.

The typical manufacturing industry has a price leader and several important followers. So, in steel, no price increase can stick unless U.S. Steel goes along with it. In farm machinery, International Harvester is top dog. In electrical machinery, General Electric is the leader and Westinghouse the most important follower. In autos, General Motors is the kingpin. A Ford Motor Co. executive and a noted economist at that once insisted that Ford copied a GM price increase—not a decrease—"to meet competition." In this world, "meeting competition" means touching hands with a neighbor, not struggling with an enemy. Competition in the conventional sense becomes largely a matter of advertising and salesmanship, of attempting to establish a unique quality for similar or identical products. But competition in price, the key to the classical code, is vitiated or wiped out entirely.

The price leader is generally the largest single producer of a product. His followers respect the leadership as long as they believe they would gain nothing by revolt. As price-following companies have explained again and again to inquiring congressmen, there is no point in quoting a price below the leader's. The leader would simply come down to the lower price and all hands would be worse off.

If such leadership is to persist, there must be a tacit if not an explicit understanding that no firm will attempt to alter drastically its share of the market. If any firm does try to enlarge its share by quoting lower prices, the system falls apart and something resembling classical competition emerges. The recognition that stability and order are proper corporate goals is part of the language. The term "price cutter" is a pejorative in the talk of most businessmen.

The practice of price leadership does not require an illegal conspiracy, does not demand that representatives of the Big Three or Four gather secretly in a hotel room to set prices and carve up markets. At least it doesn't require an unlawful arrangement as long as all firms are selling similar products that are manufactured again and again. The corporate leaders are tempted to break the antitrust law only when they sell custom-built products for individual buyers. In the steel industry, Bethlehem and Republic are generally willing to let U.S. Steel select the price for such standardized products as cold rolled sheets. But in the steel forgings branch of the industry, each product is usually tailor-made. There can be no standard price because each sale is unique and there can't be a stable division of the market because the market is not continuous. Executives of the big steel companies have not been charged with conspiring to fix prices on most of their products; however, officials from U.S. Steel, Bethlehem and others in the steel forgings business were indicted in 1962 for illegal price fixing and pleaded their unwillingness to contest the charges.

Similarly, GE, Westinghouse and their rivals don't need to meet illegally to set prices and determine market shares in standard products with continuous production runs like toasters or electrical equipment sold off the shelf from stock. Here, price leadership and the live-and-let-live philosophy can guarantee order. But generators, custom-built for a single customer, are another matter. If this business is to enjoy price stability and undisturbed market shares, its executives must conspire. And so the electrical machinery makers did meet to set prices and slice up markets for years in the great price conspiracy uncovered in 1959. The purpose of the illegal gatherings, as officials repeatedly testified, was to bring order out of chaos, to stabilize prices and apportion the business.

The price leader in a concentrated industry does not have the wide-ranging power, the discretion of a monopolist. He has far more control over his price and his output than the lone farmer, but there are limits to his economic power. He must take into account the moves of his principal followers. This was dramatically illustrated in the 1962 steel crisis. Bethlehem, apparently frightened of retaliation by the Kennedy administration, broke away from U.S. Steel and the other major producers to cancel its price increase. Big Steel, in turn, was then forced to back down.[3]

Apart from the other members of the peer group, the price leader is restrained by several other forces. If he sets too high a price and earns too big a profit, he may attract new competing firms into the industry. This magnet may be more chimerical than real in some industries when the capital investment required to operate one plant is very great. Organizing an auto company

[3] Popular belief holds that the refusal of some smaller firms to go along with the increase—notably Inland Steel, Kaiser Steel and Armco Steel—was decisive in rolling it back. The evidence is far from conclusive, but it is not likely that these junior companies could have turned the tide. They lacked the steelmaking capacity to expand their output enough to make a consequential dent in the business of the larger firms. However, their stand undoubtedly embarrassed the giants who had raised prices and put added political pressure on Bethlehem.

from scratch takes enormous capital as even the wealthy Kaiser enterprises found out when their auto baby died in infancy after the second world war. But despite the great capital demands in most manufacturing industries, the danger of luring new firms is a limiting factor.

Another curb is the appetite of rival industries. Steel, for example, must keep a wary eye on plastics, cement, aluminum and other products which can be substituted for it if steel prices climb too far. The government may be a limiting force too. An excessive price or unusual profit gained through the exercise of economic power could invite political outcry, antitrust action, congressional investigation and other unpleasant consequences.

Finally, foreign producers constitute a limiting force. As trade barriers go down, imports from the revived European and Japanese industries shrink the market power of the concentrated industries. In time, steel, auto and other producers may attempt to achieve the live-and-let-live arrangements with foreign firms that have long marked the international oil business. But so far as is known, this degree of security has not yet been reached generally.

The price leader, then, is far from a free agent. But it is neither accurate nor practical to view him and his peers in the same light as the competitors of Adam Smith's world. Instead of being faced with an impersonally determined price, the industrial leader has a wide area of discretion. How this discretion is exercised, how prices are set in the modern world, has been explored by three scholars in a study for the Brookings Institution. One, Robert Lanzillotti, summarized the findings.

He reported that the typical industrial leader prices to achieve a target rate of return. The giant estimates its standard volume or "normal" output and sets prices to gain a predetermined rate of profit on this volume of sales. The profit goal is calculated as a percentage of the company's investment. If the economy is booming and the giant can sell more than its normal volume, it will take in higher profits than the target; if business slumps, the firm will probably not lower its price but simply pocket a smaller return. Over the course of any business cycle, however, the giant expects to turn out this standard volume and earn the target profit rate. Its expectations will be realized if it has selected realistic levels.

Lanzillotti has compared the target rate and actual performance for several price leaders over the 1947–1955 period. His findings are shown in the table below.

Apart from General Motors, which topped its target handsomely, the price leaders came very close to their goals. More efficient followers in each industry did better; less efficient followers, not as well.

The live-and-let-live characteristics of big industry also turn up in Lanzillotti's study. The giants told him that their price policies are designed to hold a particular share of the market, as well as a target rate of return. U.S. Steel executives said they wanted 30 percent of their market; Johns-Manville didn't want more than 20 percent of any market; International Harvester wanted "less than a dominant share" and General Electric, no more than 50 percent. This kind of self-imposed restraint is necessary if the system of peaceful price leadership is to survive and if the government is to keep its antitrust claws sheathed. An aggressive policy of price cutting to enlarge a slice of the market might wipe out weaker competitors but it would leave the leader exposed as a naked monopolist.

Price Leader	Target Rate After Taxes	Yearly Average of Actual Earnings After Taxes as a Percentage of Investment	Range
General Motors	20%	26%	19.9–37%
Du Pont	[a]	25.9%	19.6–34.1%
General Electric	20%	21.4%	18.4–26.6%
Union Carbide	18%	19.2%	13.5–24.3%
Standard Oil (N.J.)	[a]	16.0%	12.0–18.9%
Johns-Manville	15%	14.9%	10.7–19.6%
Alcoa	10%	13.8%	7.8–18.7%
International Harvester	10%	8.9%	4.9–11.9%
U.S. Steel	8%[b]	10.3%	7.6–14.8%

[a] Neither Du Pont nor Standard Oil (N.J.) would give Lanzillotti a specific target rate although they said they priced with a target in mind.

[b] U.S. Steel apparently raised its target in the middle 1950's and this was a major force behind its successive price increases.

Lanzillotti concluded: "Apparently the program of reaching no more than a given market share and of moving ahead against competition does not find expression in price reductions."

In less academic language, the system of target rates of return and target market shares lifts prices and profits above the level they would reach if the men in the executive suites were forced into the perfectly competitive world of classical economics.

In sum, modern corporate behavior resembles that of the atomistic, Smithian firm about as much as a coach and four does a jet airplane. But the consequences for the economy are not nearly so smooth and efficient as this image suggests. In the perfectly competitive mode, prices bear the force of changes in demand. When demand for a product declines or business generally slumps, prices drop. But in the modern world of concentration and target pricing, production and jobs bear the brunt of changes in demand. Prices in centralized industries are held more or less rigid or change slowly.

In the great depression of the 1930's, Gardiner Means found that prices in the concentrated industries were cut very little, but production and jobs were slashed drastically; in contrast, in competitive sectors like agriculture and textiles, prices fell sharply and employment and output were held up. The fact of concentration, then, tends to hold back the economy's potential output and to increase unemployment. A bizarre instance of this power over prices came in 1958 when U.S. Steel and its followers actually raised prices near the bottom of a business slump. If the industry had been forced to behave in classical fashion, prices would have been cut, more steel would have been produced and sold and more jobs would have been created.

On the upswing, when the economy's demand is climbing, the quest for stability also produces some peculiar effects. In the competitive world, increased demand will lift prices; in the world of concentration, however, a sharp rise in demand will produce a much smaller rise in prices. If the demand is strong enough, the concentrated firms will be selling everything they can produce; demand will be pressing against industry's capacity. Then, instead of letting higher prices ration goods among the clamorous, well-heeled buyers, the industrial giants will set up their own arbitrary system of allocation. It won't be foolproof, however, and some of their production will find its way into higher-priced "gray" markets. This is what happened in several concentrated industries after the end of World War II.

Concentration also tends to hold back innovation, the introduction of new machinery or technological change. At first glance, this seems surprising. Much business literature has insisted that the biggest firms are the most progressive, that advance comes from expensive research that only the giants can afford. This notion has become a part of conventional wisdom. But the logic of target pricing and the lure of security weaken the progressive strains of the giants. A big firm won't invest in a new process, a new machine or a new plant unless it promises to yield a return greater than the target.

For example, consider U.S. Polyglot and its target rate of 14 percent. A German firm develops a new and more efficient stamping machine that Polyglot might use. But if Polyglot figures that the machine will earn only 10 percent of its cost, Polyglot won't buy it. Not until a machine can earn 14 percent or more will it be worth Polyglot's while to invest. In other words, as long as target rates are above those that would exist in competitive markets, any innovation has a higher barrier to climb before it will be adopted by an industrial giant.

This is not merely a theoretical possibility. It is a commonplace of industrial life. The steel industry's belated introduction of the basic oxygen or LD furnace is a striking case in point. This technique for making steel was developed in Austria in the early 1950's. It produces steel $5 to $9 a ton cheaper than the open hearth furnace. Moreover, the initial investment cost has been estimated at $18 to $23 a ton less than an open hearth. A firm using a basic oxygen furnace is also well equipped to adopt another process called continuous casting that eliminates some costly steps in conventional steelmaking. American firms, however, ignored the basic oxygen furnace all during the years that they were pushing prices up at a rapid rate. U.S. Steel, for example, does not plan to install its first until some time in 1964.

Why the long delay? The controller of Bethlehem Steel, Frank Brugler, explained it to a writer for *Fortune*. Brugler said, "We don't want to invest in a facility unless it will return, on the average, 20 percent before taxes operating at 60 to 70 percent of capacity." Another Bethlehem official added, "We move only when improvements are so good we can no longer afford what we've got."

In other words, pricing to reach a target return on a "normal" volume of output placed a tall hurdle in front of the efficient, cost-reducing European technique. American steelmakers spurned the new furnace until their exacting profit standards could be met.

It is commonly claimed that invention itself comes chiefly from the giants. This however is dubious. Prof. John Jewkes of Oxford traced the origin of 60 major twentieth century inventions and found that only a minority were developed by large firms. More than half were the product of individual inventors working without institutional backing. Their contributions included the gyro-compass, the first successful system of catalytic cracking, the jet engine, safety razor and the zipper. Small firms came up with cellophane and

DDT among others. The high-powered and well-publicized research of the giants did bring such advances as nylon, tetraethyl lead, transistors and diesel electric motors. But in all, they accounted for a lesser share of the batch. Of course, the Jewkes list is a sample and does not measure the relative importance of each invention. But his study is suggestive. Taken together with the high profits barrier to innovation, it is likely that concentration and the existence of giant firms has impeded rather than advanced technological progress.

Another important consequence of concentration is the damage it does to the ideal distribution of rewards described in the harmonious world of textbook competition. In this elegant model, every actor in the economic drama is rewarded in accord with his contribution towards production. Each of the productive factors, the entrepreneur, the landowner, the laborer and the investor receives a profit, rent, wage or return that matches the value of his addition to the last commodity produced and sold in any industry. To be sure, this ideal never existed outside the pages of the texts. However, it embodies a powerful suggestion that impersonal justice tends to operate in the economic world.

In the real world of concentration, this logic is shattered and rewards can't be distributed in such a self-justifying fashion. One obvious example is the premium reward received by a stockholder of an industrial giant that has some power over its prices. In theory, stockholders are rewarded with dividends for supplying at some risk the capital of a corporation, the funds to pay for its investment in plants and machinery. Stockholders still fulfill this function for youthful, untested corporations. But the established industrial behemoth doesn't turn to its stockholders for financing. Instead, its investment is financed with what accountants call retained earnings. That is, U.S. Polyglot pays for its enlarged factories and new equipment largely out of its profits.

Polyglot, of course, gets these profits by selling its goods. Profits can be described simply as the difference between the cost of making a product and its price. So, it is Polyglot's customers who are actually supplying the capital with which Polyglot grows by paying the price that Polyglot charges. To be sure, the customers are supplying this capital involuntarily and not through any decision of their own. However, the yield or earnings from this increase in capital does not flow to Polyglot's customers. (Unless Polyglot is a regulated utility and a public commission insists that Polyglot give its customers a rebate of all profits above a competitive level.) Instead, some of the extra profits created by the new investment are distributed as dividends to Polyglot's stockholders. In effect, Polyglot is amassing from its customers what Representative Wright Patman of Texas has called "costless capital." Polyglot passes on the earnings of this capital to essentially passive stockholders who have risked no additional funds.[4]

One of the striking features of the 1962 steel price row was an argument, repeatedly advanced by Chairman Blough of U.S. Steel. He said that his company needed higher prices to pay for new, more modern equipment. In a

[4] Because income from dividends (and wages) is taxed more heavily than stock market profits, many corporations hang on to a large portion of their extra profits from new investment. The stock market then regards this accumulation as an increase in the value of the stock shares and the shares tend to rise in price. So, the stockholders are not only in line for an unearned piece of cake; they can consume more of it than if the same slice came to them as dividends or wages.

competitive world, he would be unable to finance his investment from increased prices paid by his customers. He would be forced to raise new capital in competition with other firms, either through borrowing funds or by issuing new shares of stock. This is what regulated utilities must do because they are prohibited from making customers pay for their investment. In unregulated and concentrated manufacturing industries, however, the bulk of the money for new investment is supplied by consumers.[5]

Costless capital is one reason why managers of large corporations vote themselves handsome stock options in their own companies. These options give them the right to purchase shares in their companies for extended periods of time at prices near current levels. As a company's capital expands, thanks to its power over prices, the price of the stock tends to rise. Indeed, the existence of stock options is a powerful incentive for corporation managers to keep pushing up the prices of their products. The faster their company's stock rises, the wealthier the managers become. And as a frosting on this cake, rewards from the exercise of these options have been protected from the impact of ordinary income taxes.

Just as incomes are not distributed in the fashion prescribed by the classical texts, so too are resources improperly allocated in the world of concentration. In the classical model, labor, material resources and capital move at the price signals flashed by competitive markets to firms and industries where they are in greatest demand. So, resources are combined most efficiently in accord with consumer tastes. In the real world of concentration, industrial giants interfere with this smooth-working, automatic arrangement.

When business generally is slack, firms in concentrated industries tend to hold prices above the level that competition would set. As a result, they sell and produce less than consumers would take in a classical world. When business is booming, the opposite takes place. Concentrated industries then hold prices down and sell more than they would in the textbook setting.

The giant's objective of a stable market share probably distorts investment in another way, too. Harald Malmgren and Benjamin Caplan have called attention to this phenomenon. Say that Western Widgets, a follower in the concentrated widgets industry, decides to enlarge its capacity by erecting a new plant. The industry's price leader, General Widgets, will probably follow suit—not because of any increased demand for widgets but in order to preserve its share of the market. One or both factories will be partly unused unless General violates the code and cuts prices. It is more likely that widget customers will be hit with a price increase to pay for the new and idle plants.

Something like this has been happening in the American economy. Between 1958 and 1962, manufacturers spent $13.3 billion dollars a year for new investment. But during this period, 18 percent of their productive capacity was idle. Of course, much of the investment was designed to reduce costs rather than enlarge capacity. But some of it very likely stemmed from copycat strategy to hold on to a potential share of a market. These outlays distorted the proper mix between investment and consumption spending. Moreover, the very exist-

[5] Since the end of World War II, corporations have financed from 70 percent to 83 percent of their investment out of their earnings. In 1962, for example, they raised $9.3 billion from the sale of stocks and bonds and $35.3 billion from profits and depreciation allowances. In other words, four of every five investment dollars came from the customers.

ence of excess idle capacity acts as a drag on the economy. When many plants are unused, corporations are less inclined to push ahead with new investment.

In contrast then with the watch-works world of classical economics, concentrated industries tend to push up prices, hold down production and employment, increase the barriers to technological progress, distort the flow of incomes and exert a distorting pull over the flow of resources.

The sluggish performance of the post-Korean War economy can be attributed in no small measure to the concentrated structure of business. To be sure, this sluggishness has occurred at a level high enough to enable many to live comfortably. There have been no deep depressions or massive unemployment like that of the 1930's or 1870's. The Keynesian lessons of World War II have not been entirely lost. Federal expenditures may not have been strong enough to create full employment but they have underwritten enough demand to prevent serious slumps and sustain some limited expansion. However, outlays for the Cold War have comprised an important part of the government's demand. Their abrupt removal could expose the economy to the full consequences of concentrated corporate policies. In the immediate future, there is considerable risk that the giants will undermine any more aggressive federal attack on the economy's ills. During the ten years following Korea, federal policy was often blunted by corporate pricing, investment and output decisions.

If concentration saps the economist's policies, it also raises some disturbing questions for political theorists. A democratic society assumes that power and responsibility are linked. The exercise of power in government is legitimate when officials are ultimately responsible for their actions to a sovereign people who can and do replace them. The problem of legitimacy does not arise in Adam Smith's world, for no producer in a competitive market has any power over price, output and investment. Each responds to the dictates of a sovereign market. But in a world of concentrated industries, the large corporations enjoy considerable discretion and they exercise an important share of economic sovereignty.

Indeed, their power extends directly to areas that are usually regarded as the exclusive preserve of the state. The large international corporations literally create a portion of American foreign policy. The investment, pricing and production decisions of Standard Oil Co. (N.J.) in Venezuela or Saudi Arabia are an integral element of national policy overseas. The operations of General Motors in France, United Fruit in Central America or Firestone in Liberia not only condition but are part of the stuff of relations with foreign nations.

"What all this seems to add up to," Edward Mason of Harvard concludes, "is the existence of important centers of private power in the hands of men whose authority is real but whose responsibilities are vague."

Where are the sanctions for the prices these giants set? What forces guide their investment and output decisions? Freed to a considerable if immeasurable extent of the restraints of competitive markets, to whom must they answer?

The standard reply in business literature is the stockholder. But even if this were true, why should it be so? The typical stockholder is no longer supplying capital out of his savings to competitive firms struggling in markets they can't dominate. For the large corporation, the stockholder is, as we have seen, a passive actor in the industrial drama. It is the customers who supply most of the capital.

In any case, stockholders are not likely to grumble over the actions of corporate managers unless the value of their shares is seriously threatened. Even then, the share holders are usually impotent. While the ownership of stocks is concentrated in a relatively narrow band of the population, ownership in any single large corporation is fragmented. Because of the diffusion of stock ownership in each major corporation, the managers become a largely self-perpetuating group. Indeed the managers' grip on the machinery that elects corporate directors is so firm that a fight for control of all but the sleepiest giants is unthinkable. As Professor Kaysen has said, "The power of corporate management is, in the political sense, irresponsible power, answerable ultimately only to itself."

Despite the worshipful hymns sung by and for the great corporations, there is nothing sacred or immutable about the business structure. It was not, after all, created in a burst of divine inspiration but is the product of a long evolution. The private corporation is merely one response to the modern world's technological demand for large aggregations of capital. The business structure, like any other institutional arrangement, is a means to an end.

The obvious purpose of an economic order is the provision of increasing material welfare, of a growing stock of widely distributed goods and services. Less apparent is the implicit demand that many make and this inquiry supports, that the economy should provide a setting which encourages the maximum play for the potential abilities of individual men. The concentrated American economy, however, tends to frustrate both ends.

2 PRIVATE PROFIT *versus* PUBLIC NEED*

by ANDRE GORZ

The Nossiter selection described the kind of power held by the giant monopolies. Gorz, in this selection shows how the capitalist power translates itself into irrational and antisocial priorities and puts itself into irreconcilable opposition to the fulfillment of human needs.

The selection is a little difficult to plough through, in part owing to the translation, and in part to Gorz's own abstract mode of reasoning. It is well worth the effort but we will touch on some of the major points he raises.

Capitalism does not fulfill people's real needs. The system is operated to do what is profitable for large corporations, not what is needed by people. Instead, the concern for profit results in enormous wastefulness and superfluous expenditure. This holds true not just in the consumer market, where advertising and obsolescence prevail, but in the system as a whole, where, for example, military spending takes priority over social spending.

A whole range of human needs is doomed to neglect because they cannot be expressed in market terms. Education, health, peace and quiet, etc., cannot be provided via profit-making schemes. Since the priority in the society goes to profit-making activities, these just do not get provided.

The irrationality has built up to such massive proportions, that we should doubt whether quality of life is really improving. New, but useless, products and advertising combine to provoke in people a bottomless yearning for products, which they feel so much the more inadequate without. Old ways of doing things are purposely obsoleted by the capitalist drive to create new needs, unnecessarily upsetting perfectly adequate styles of living. And the capitalist process bulldozes through the natural environment—creating new, but unfulfillable needs for privacy, cleanliness, quiet, etc. It is not at all certain that life is improving.

For example, the automobile, child of affluence, instead of improving existence, has turned on it and started to destroy it. While requiring ever-larger consumer expenditures to maintain in the form of repairs, insurance, gasoline and the inevitable new car every two and one-half years, the automobile strangles cities in massive traffic jams and suffocating air pollution. As public transportation rots, housing is torn down, communities bulldozed to make way for new highways. This is the society that profit built.

The profit motive is not content to hold sway over the private economy. The corporations reach out to impose their priorities of profit-making on politics, on culture and on people's personalities. Subservient to their power, the government gives them special privileges, it buys their products, it administers their foreign affairs, and it keeps stability and order for them at home. Meanwhile, they act to limit to a strict minimum any moves in the direction of providing public welfare.

In the area of culture, corporations try to create that individual who will be most susceptible to the appeals of the mass production market. In part, such an individual is created by the dehumanization, fragmentation, alienation and loneliness of work under conditions of capitalist production. In part, he is the product of the manipulation of the advertising and the corporation-dominated media.

Gorz, then, identifies what real human needs are and shows how they would be satisfied under socialism.

THE SUPERFLUOUS BEFORE THE NECESSARY

Does the man who eats red meat and white bread, moves with the help of a motor, and dresses in synthetic fibers, live better than the man who eats dark bread and white cheese, moves on a bicycle, and dresses in wool and cotton? The question is almost meaningless. It supposes that in a given society, the same individual has a choice between two different life styles. Practically speaking, this is not the case: only one way of life, more or less rigidly determined, is open to him, and this way of life is conditioned by the structure of production and by its techniques. The latter determine the environment by which needs are conditioned, the objects by which these needs can be satisfied, and the manner of consuming or using these objects.

But the basic question is this: what guarantees the adjustment of production to needs, both in general and for a specific product?[1] Liberal economists have long maintained that this adjustment is guaranteed by the mechanism of the market. But this thesis has very few defenders today. Doubtless, if we do not look at the overall picture in optimum human and economic terms, but only at each product taken separately, then we can still maintain that a product totally devoid of use value would not find a buyer. Nevertheless, it is impossible to conclude that the most widely distributed products of mass consumption are really those which at a given stage of technological evolution allow for the best and most rational satisfaction (at the least cost and the least expense of time and trouble) of a given need.

In fact, under capitalism the pursuit of optimum human and economic goals and the pursuit of maximum profit from invested capital coincide only by accident. The pursuit of maximum profit is the first exigency of capital, and the increase of use value is no more than a by-product of this pursuit.

For example, let us take the case of the spread of disposable packaging for milk products. From the viewpoint of use value, the superiority of milk in a cardboard carton or yoghurt in a plastic cup is nil (or negative). From the viewpoint of capitalist enterprise, on the other hand, this substitution is clearly advantageous. The glass bottle or glass jar represented immobilized capital which did not "circulate": empty bottles or jars were recovered and reused indefinitely, which entailed the cost of handling, collection, and sterilization.

[1] Structure of production; order of priorities between, for example, automobiles, housing, and public services. We shall return to this subject.

The disposable containers, on the other hand, allow a substantial economy in handling, and permit the profitable sale not only of the dairy product but also of its container. To increase their profits, the big dairy firms thus forced the consumer to purchase a new product at a higher price although its use value remained the same (or diminished).

In other cases, the alternative between maximum profit and maximum use value is even more striking. The Philips trust, for example, perfected fluorescent lighting in 1938. The life of these fluorescent tubes was then 10,000 hours. Production of these tubes would have covered existing needs cheaply and in a relatively short period of time; amortization, on the other hand, would have taken a long time. The invested capital would be recovered slowly, and the labor time necessary to cover existing need would have declined. The company therefore invested additional capital in order to develop fluorescent tubes which burned for only 1,000 hours, in order thus to accelerate the recovery of capital and to realize—at the price of considerable *superfluous* expenditure—a much higher rate of accumulation and of profit.

The same holds true for synthetic fibers, whose durability, for stockings especially, has decreased, and for motor vehicles, which are *deliberately* built with parts which will wear out rapidly (and cost as much as longer-lasting parts would have).[2]

Speaking generally, and regardless of the objective scientific and technical possibilities, technical development in terms of the criteria of maximum profit is often quite different from development in terms of criteria of maximum social and economic utility. Even when fundamental needs remain largely unsatisfied, monopoly capital objectively organizes scarcity, wastes natural resources and human labor, and orients production (and consumption) toward objects whose sale is most profitable, regardless of the need for such objects.[3]

In general, monopoly capitalism tends toward a model of "affluence" which levels consumption "upward": the products offered tend to become standardized by the incorporation of a maximum of "added value" which does not perceptibly increase their use value. At the limit (a limit attained by an impressive range of products), the usefulness of an object becomes the *pretext* for selling superfluous things that are built into the product and multiply its price; the products are sold above all for their packaging and brand names (that is to say, advertising), while their use value becomes a secondary part of the bargain. The packaging and the brand name, moreover, are expressly designed to deceive the buyer as to the quantity, quality, and the nature of the product: tooth paste is endowed with erotic virtues, detergents wih magic qualities, the automobile (in the U.S.) is extolled as a status symbol.

The apparent diversity of the products badly masks their true uniformity: the difference between brands is marginal. All American automobiles are iden-

[2] See Vance Packard, *The Waste Makers* (New York: McKay, 1960), which contains numerous examples of this type.

[3] In 1959 the Canadian government became worried by the fact that the cost of living had risen substantially in the space of a few years, while the price of agricultural and industrial products had remained stable. An investigating committee blamed the spread of supermarkets: after having eliminated independent grocery stores, the supermarkets (often linked to the monopolies of the food industry) established uniformly high prices. Above all, in order to extract the maximum profit per square foot of display area, they pushed the sale of expensive, luxuriously packaged products, to the detriment of products which have the same use value but are less costly.

tical with regard to the incorporation of a maximum of "packaging" and false luxury, to the point where an intense advertising campaign is necessary to "educate" the consumer, from school age on, to perceive the differences in detail and not to perceive the substantial similarities.[4] This dictatorship of the monopolies over needs and individual tastes was broken in the United States only from the outside, by the producers of European automobiles. "Upward" leveling, that is, leveling toward the incorporation of a maximum of superfluity, has been carried out in this instance to the detriment of the use value of the product, whose consumers were unable for years to reverse the tendency of an oligopoly to sell goods of a diminishing use value at a constantly increasing price.

The pursuit of maximum profit, to continue with this example of one of the pilot industries of the most developed country, was not even accompanied by scientific and technological fertility. The tendency to prefer the accessory to the essential, the improvement of the profit rate to the improvement of use value, has resulted in *absolute* wastage. None of the four major post-war technical innovations in automobile design: disc brakes, fuel injection, hydro-pneumatic suspension, rotating piston, originated in the American car industry—an industry which with every annual model change brings into conflict the two biggest manufacturing groups in the world. They compete mainly for maximum productivity, not for maximum use value. The notion that competition would be a factor in accelerating technical and scientific progress is thus, in large part, a myth. Competition does not contribute to technical progress unless such progress allows for the growth of profits. Technical progress, in other words, is essentially concentrated on productivity, and only incidentally on the pursuit of a human optimum in the manner of production and in the manner of consumption.

This is why, in all developed capitalist societies, gigantic waste coexists with largely unsatisfied fundamental needs (needs for housing, medical care, education, hygiene, etc.). This is also why the claim that capitalist profit (distributed or consumed) does not represent a great burden for the economy (about five percent of the French national revenue) is a gross myth.

Certainly the confiscation of the surplus value consumed by the capitalists would not result in a perceptible improvement of the condition of the people or the workers. But nobody claims any longer that in order to transform society the principal attack must be leveled against the profits pocketed by individual capitalists, against the incomes of the great families and the major employers. What must be attacked is not the personal incomes created by capitalist profits; it is rather the orientation which the system and the logic of profit, that is to say of capitalist accumulation, impress on the economy and the society as a whole; it is the capitalist control over the apparatus of production and the resulting inversion of real priorities in the model of consumption.

What must be constantly exposed and denounced is this organized waste of labor and resources on the one hand and this organized scarcity (scarcity of time, air, of collective services and cultural possibilities) on the other hand. On the level of the model of consumption, this combination of waste and scarcity is the major absurdity of the capitalist system. To attack the great families

[4] See David Riesman, *The Lonely Crowd* (Yale University Press, 1950). See also Ernest Mandel, *Traité d'Economie Marxist* (Julliard, 1962), Vol. II, Chapter XVII, pp. 354–359.

and the profits they make (in money terms) is always less effective than challenging the capitalist control and management over individual companies and the economy as a whole in the name of a different policy, that is to say in the name of an orientation of production to needs and not to greater profits. To show the possibility of this policy and the different results to which it would lead, to outline a *different* model of consumption, is of a much more real and revolutionary significance than all the abstract speeches about the billions pocketed by monopolies and about the need to nationalize them. Nationalization of the monopolies will not be a mobilizing goal unless linked to a concrete program which demonstrates why they must be nationalized, what presently unattainable results such nationalization will have, and what nationalization can and should change.

THE SOCIAL COST OF PRIVATE INITIATIVE

The effects of capitalist production on the environment and on society are a second source of waste and of distortion. In fact, what was said about the capitalist control over industry holds true *a fortiori* for the orientation of the economy in general. The most profitable production for each entrepreneur is not necessarily the most advantageous one for the consumers; the pursuit of maximum profit and the pursuit of optimum use value do not coincide when each product is considered separately. But if instead of considering the action of each entrepreneur (in fact of each oligopoly) separately, we consider the resulting total of all such actions and their repercussions on society, then we note an even sharper contradiction between this overall result and the social and economic optimum.

This contradiction results essentially from the limits which the criteria of profitability impose on capitalist initiative. According to the logic of this initiative, the most profitable activities are the most important ones, and activities whose product or result cannot be measured according to the criteria of profitability and return are neglected or abandoned to decay. These non-profitable activities, whose desirability cannot even be understood in capitalist terms, consist of all those investments which cannot result in production for the market under the given social and political circumstances, that is to say, which do not result in a commercial exchange comprising the profitable sale of goods and services. In fact this category includes all investments and services which answer to human needs that cannot be expressed in market terms as demands for salable commodities: the need for education, city planning, cultural and recreational facilities, works of art, research, public health, public transportation (and also economic planning, reforestation, elimination of water- and air-pollution, noise control, etc.)—in short, all economic activities which belong to the "public domain" and cannot arise or survive except as public services, regardless of their profitability.

The demand for the satisfaction of these needs, which cannot be expressed in market terms, necessarily takes on political and collective forms; and the satisfaction of these collective needs, precisely because it cannot be procured except by public services belonging to the collectivity, constitutes a permanent challenge to the laws and the spirit of the capitalist system. In other words, there is a whole sphere of fundamental, priority needs which constitute an objective challenge to capitalist logic. Only socialism can recognize the priority nature and assure the priority satisfaction of these needs. This does not mean that we must await the establishment of socialism or fight for socialism only by political campaigning. It means rather that the existence of this sphere of collective needs now offers the socialist forces the chance to demand and to achieve, in the name of these needs, the creation and the development of a sphere of services, a sphere which represents a popular victory and constitutes a permanent antagonism to the capitalist system and permanently restricts its functioning.

The acuteness of this antagonism—and the sharpness of the contradiction between capitalist initiative and collective needs—necessarily grows. It grows principally as a result of the fact that collective needs and the cost of their satisfaction are not in principle included in the cost of capitalist decisions and initiatives. There is a disjunction between the direct cost of the productive investment for the private investor, and the indirect, social cost which this investment creates to cover the resulting collective needs, such as housing, roads, the supply of energy and water; in short, the infrastructure. There is also a disjunction between the computation of direct production costs by the private investor and the social cost which his investment will bring with it: for example, expenses for education, housing, transportation, various services; in short, the entrepreneur's criteria of profitability, which measure the desirability of the investment, and the criteria of human and collective desirability, are not identical. As a consequence, the collective needs engendered by capitalist investment are covered haphazardly or not at all; the satisfaction of these needs is neglected or subordinated to more profitable "priorities" because these needs were not foreseen and included in advance in the total cost of the project.

Thus, when a capitalist group decides to invest in a given project and a given locality, it need not bother to ask itself what degree of priority its project has in the scale of needs, what social costs it will entail, what social needs it will engender, what long term public investments it will make necessary later on, or what alternatives its private decision will render impossible. The decision of the capitalist group will be guided rather by the existing market demand, the available facilities and equipment, and the proximity of the market and the sources of raw materials.

The first result of this situation is that the decision of a private trust to invest does not in most cases have any but an accidental relationship to the real but non-marketable needs of the local, regional, or national unit: the model of development which monopoly capitalism imposes on insufficiently developed regions is as a general rule a colonial model. The balanced development of Brittany or Southern Italy, for example, if it were to answer real needs would in the first place demand investments to revive agricultural productivity, to assure local processing of raw materials, and to occupy the underemployed population in industries having local outlets. Priority thus would have to be given to educational and cultural services, to food and agricultural industries, to light industry, chemical and pharmaceutical manufacturing, to communication and transportation. If these priorities were chosen, the local communities could develop toward a diversification of their activities, toward a relative economic, cultural, and social autonomy, toward a fuller development of social relations and exchanges, and thus toward a fuller development of human relations and abilities.

Capitalist initiative functions only in terms of the existing *market* demand. If there is no such demand in the underdeveloped regions for the products capable of bringing about balanced development, then capitalist initiative will consist of setting up export industries in these regions. The resulting type of development, besides being very limited, will reverse the real priorities: the underemployed local manpower will be drained toward assembly workshops (although not to the extent of providing full employment), toward satellite factories which are sub-contractors of distant trusts, and toward the production or extraction of raw materials or of individual components which will be transformed or assembled elsewhere.

The local community, instead of being raised toward a new, richer internal equilibrium, will thus be practically destroyed by having a new element of imbalance grafted onto its already out-of-date structures: agriculture, instead of being made healthier and richer, will be ruined by the exodus of manpower and the land will be abandoned; the local industries, instead of being diversified in terms of local needs, will undergo specialization and impoverishment; local or regional autonomy, instead of being reinforced, will be diminished even more, since the centers of decision making for the local activities are in Paris or Milan and the new local industries are the first to suffer the shock of economic fluctuations: the quality of the local community's social relations, instead of being improved, will be impoverished; local manpower will get the dirtiest and the most monotonous jobs; the ancient towns (*bourgs*) will become dormitory cities with new cafés and juke boxes in place of cultural facilities; the former civilization will be destroyed and replaced by nothing; those of the new workers who do not travel one, two, or even three hours daily by bus to go to and from their work will be penned up in concrete cages or in shanty towns: in the mother country as well as in the colonies there is a process of "slummification" ("*clochardisation*"). The colonies, at least, can free themselves of foreign colonialism; the underdeveloped regions in the mother country, however, are often irreversibly colonized and deprived of independent livelihood by monopoly capitalism, or even emptied of their population and turned into a wasteland.

The drift of industry toward the underdeveloped regions, in the conditions which have just been described, cannot really be compared to an industrialization of these areas. It tends rather to destroy all possibility of balance between the city and the countryside by the creation of new, giant agglomerations which empty the back country. The small peasants will not be able to rationalize their methods (that would require a policy of credit and equipment favoring cooperative or collective modes of farming); instead they will sell their holdings to the benefit of the agrarian capitalists. The former peasants will install themselves as shop keepers, café owners, or unskilled laborers in the new big city or in the capital. The drift of certain industries toward less developed regions is therefore not at all comparable to decentralization. On the contrary, it is only a marginal phenomenon of industry's tendency to concentrate geographically. Industry is attracted by industry, money by money. Both go by preference where markets and conditions of profitability already exist, not where these must first be created. Thus regional disparities tend to grow.

The principal cause of geographic concentration of industry has been the public pre-financing, during the past decades, of the social bases of industrial expansion in the highly dense zones: housing, transportation, trained manpower, infrastructure. Now, the savings realized by individual industries due to geographic concentration are an extra burden for the collectivity. After a certain point has been reached the operating costs of the large cities grow dizzily (long traveling time, air pollution, noise, lack of space, etc.). The overpopulation of the urban centers has as a counterpart the depopulation of non-developed areas below the threshold of economic and social viability, their economic and human impoverishment, and the obliteration of their potential; and the cost of the social reproduction of labor power is multiplied.

This double process of congestion and decline has one and the same root: the concentration of economic power in a small number of monopolistic groups which drain off a large part of the economic surplus realized in production and distribution and which reinvest that surplus where conditions of immediate profitability are already present. Therefore the resources available for a regional and social policy consonant with real needs are always insufficient, especially because monopoly competition engenders new consumer needs and new collective expenses which are incompatible with a government policy aimed at balanced development.

The costs of infrastructure (roads, transportation, city maintenance and planning, provision of energy and water) which monopoly expansion imposes on the collectivity as it spreads (namely in the congested zones), in practice make it impossible to provide such services in the areas where the need is greatest: the billions swallowed up by the great cities are in the last analysis diverted from economically and humanly more advantageous uses.

Furthermore, the cost of the infrastructure, which the orientation given by monopoly capitalism to consumption demands, represents an obstacle to the satisfaction of priority needs. The most striking example in this regard is that of the automobile industry. For the production of a means of evasion and escape, this industry has diverted productive resources, labor, and capital from priority tasks such as housing, education, public transportation, public health, city planning, and rural services. The priority given by monopoly capitalism to the automobile gets stronger and stronger: city planning must be subordinated to the requirements of the automobile, roads are built instead of houses (this is very clear in Italy, for example), and public transportation is sacrificed.

And finally the private automobile becomes a social necessity: urban space is organized in terms of private transportation; public transportation lags farther and farther behind the spread of the suburbs and the increasing distance required to travel to work; the pedestrian or the cyclist becomes a danger to others and himself; athletic and cultural facilities are removed from the city, beyond the reach of the non-motorized suburbanite and often even of the city dweller. The possession of an automobile becomes a basic necessity because the universe is organized in terms of private transportation. This process is halted only with difficulty in the advanced capitalist countries. To the extent that the indispensability of private automobiles has made life unbearable in the large, overpopulated cities where air, light, and space are lacking, motorized escape will continue to be an important—although decreasing—element in the reproduction of labor power, even when priority has returned to city planning, to collective services, and to public transportation.

COLLECTIVE NEEDS

Monopoly expansion thus not only creates new needs by throwing onto the market mass consumption products symbolizing an alleged comfort which becomes a need because it is available; it creates needs by modifying the conditions under which labor power can be reproduced. In point of fact, the development of needs in capitalist society often results less from the improvement and the enrichment of human faculties than from an increase in the harshness of the material environment, from a deterioration in living conditions, from the necessity for more complex and more costly instruments to satisfy fundamental needs, to reproduce labor power.

Between the natural origin of a need and its natural object, we note the interposition of instruments which not only are human products, but which are essentially social products. After the destruction of the natural environment and its replacement by a social environment, fundamental needs can only be satisfied in a social manner: they become immediately social needs; or, more exactly, fundamental needs mediated by society.

This is true, for example, of the need for air, which is immediately apprehended as the need for vacations, for public gardens, for city planning, for escape from the city; of the need for nightly rest, for physical and mental relaxation, which becomes the need for tasteful, comfortable housing protected against noise; of the need to eat, which in the large industrial cities becomes the need for food which can be consumed immediately after a day of work—that is, the need for cafeterias, restaurants, canned foods, and foods that require a minimum of preparation time; of the need for cleanliness, which in the absence of sunlight and natural beaches or rivers becomes the need for hygienic facilities, laundries, or washing machines, and so on.

In all these examples, the historical form which the fundamental need assumes cannot be confused with the historical need as such: the need in question is not a new and "rich" need which corresponds to an enrichment of man and a development of his faculties; it is merely an eternal biological need which now demands "rich" means of satisfaction because the natural environment has become impoverished, because there has been impoverishment of man's relation to nature, exhaustion or destruction of resources (air, water, light, silence, space) which until now were taken as natural.

Now the nature of capitalist society is to constrain the individual to buy back individually, as a consumer, the means of satisfaction of which the society has socially deprived him. The capitalist trust appropriates or uses up air, light, space, water, and (by producing dirt and noise) cleanliness and silence gratuitously or at a preferential price; contractors, speculators, and merchants then resell all of these resources to the highest bidder. The destruction of natural resources has been social; the reproduction of these vitally necessary resources is social in its turn. But even though the satisfaction of the most elementary needs now must pass through the mediation of social production, service, and exchange, no social initiative assures or foresees the replacement of what has been destroyed, the social reparation of the spoliation which individuals have suffered. On the contrary, once its social repercussions and its inverted priorities have aggravated the conditions in which social individuals exist, private enterprise then exploits at a profit the greater needs of these same social individuals. It is they as individual consumers who will have to pay for the growth of the social cost of the reproduction of their labor power, a cost which often surpasses their means.

The workers understand the scandal inherent in this situation in a direct and confused manner. The capitalist trust, after having exploited them and mutilated them *in* their work, comes to exploit them and mutilate them *outside* of their work. It imposes on them, for example, the cost, the fatigue, and the long hours lost on public transportation; it imposes on them the search for and the price of housing, made scarce by the trust's manpower needs and made more expensive by the speculations which increasing scarcity produces.

The same thing holds for air, light, cleanliness, and hygiene, whose price becomes prohibitive. For example, great industrial concentration forces women to go to work for pay, because one paycheck in the family is not enough to buy the means necessary for the reproduction of labor power[5] in the big city. In the absence of public services, the mechanization of housework becomes a necessity: washing machines, refrigerators, ready-to-eat foods, semi-automatic stoves, and restaurants come to be a necessity. But the satisfaction of this need, even though it has its origin in the condition of social production and of social life, is left to private enterprise, which profits from it. Individuals have to pay for this satisfaction, so that a very important part of a working woman's wages which once were (wrongly) considered as "supplemental" income, serves only to cover the supplementary expenses which women's work entails.

On the level of collective needs, and only on this level, the theory of impoverishment thus continues to be valid. The social cost of the reproduction of labor power (the simple reproduction, and as we shall show below, the wider reproduction) tends to rise as fast as or faster than individual purchasing power; the workers' social standard of living tends to stagnate, to worsen, even if their individual standard of living (expressed in terms of monetary purchasing power) rises. And it is extremely difficult, if not impossible, for urban workers to obtain a qualitative improvement in their living standard as a result of a raise in their direct wages within the framework of capitalist structures. It is this quasi-impossibility which gives demands in the name of collective needs a revolutionary significance.

The nature of collective needs, in effect, is that they often cannot be expressed in terms of monetary demands. They involve a set of collective resources, services, and facilities which escape the law of the market, capitalist initiative, and all criteria of profitability. These needs, inexpressible in economic terms, are at least virtually in permanent contradiction to capitalism and mark the limit of its effectiveness. These are the needs which capitalism tends to neglect or

[5] Labor power, according to Marx, is the quality of productive energy expended by a worker during the process of work. In order to keep on working day after day, he must constantly reproduce his labor power; that is, he must eat, rest, sleep, keep healthy, etc. Similarly, the working class as a whole must be constantly reproduced: workers must raise children to replace them when they are old, and skills must be passed on from generation to generation. The phrase, "simple reproduction of labor power" generally refers to all the means necessary to reproduce and maintain labor power as of now; while "wider reproduction" refers to the totality of vocational training programs, educational institutions, public information media, and cultural facilities necessary to maintain and reproduce over time the sort of educated working force and administrative personnel required by a complex society whose technology and knowledge evolve at an ever-quickening pace. See Karl Marx, *Capital,* Vol. 1, Ch. 4, Sec. 3. [Translator's note.]

to suppress, insofar as capitalism knows only the *homo œconomicus*—defined by the consumption of merchandise and its production—and not the human man, the consumer, producer, and user of goods which cannot be sold, bought, or reproduced.

Among these needs are:

—Housing and city planning, not only in quantitative but in qualitative terms as well. An urban esthetic and an urban landscape, an environment which furthers the development of human faculties instead of debasing them, must be re-created. Now it is obvious that it is not profitable to provide 200 square feet of green area per inhabitant, to plan parks, roads, and squares. The application of the law of the market leads, on the contrary, to reserve the best living conditions for the privileged, who need them least, and to deny them to the workers who, because they do the most difficult and the lowest-paid work, need them profoundly. The workings of this law also push the workers farther and farther from their place of work, and impose on them additional expense and fatigue.

—Collective services, such as public transportation, laundries and cleaners, child day care centers and nursery schools. These are non-profitable in essence: for in terms of profit, it is necessarily more advantageous to sell individual vehicles, washing machines, and magical soap powders. And since these services are most needed by those who have the lowest incomes, their expansion on a commercial basis presents no interest at all for capital. Only public services can fill the need.

—Collective cultural, athletic, and health facilities: schools, theaters, libraries, concert halls, swimming pools, stadiums, hospitals, in short, all the facilities necessary for the reestablishment of physical and intellectual balance for the development of human faculties. The non-profitability of these facilities is evident, as is their extreme scarcity (and usually great cost) in almost all of the capitalist countries.

—Balanced regional development in terms of optimum economic and human criteria, which we have already contrasted to neo-colonialist "slummification."

—Information, communication; active group leisure. Capitalism not only does not have any interest in these needs,[6] it tends even to suppress them. The commercial dictatorship of the monopolies cannot in fact function without a mass of passive consumers, separated by place and style of living, incapable of getting together and communicating directly, incapable of defining together their specific needs (relative to their work and life situation), their preoccupations, their outlook on society and the world—in short, their common project. Mass pseudo-culture, while producing passive and stupefying entertainments, amusements, and pastimes, does not and cannot satisfy the needs arising out of dispersion, solitude, and boredom. This pseudo-culture is less a consequence than a cause of the passivity and the impotence of the individual in a mass society. It is a device invented by monopoly capital to facilitate its dictatorship over a mystified, docile, debased humanity, whose impulses of real violence must be redirected into imaginary channels.

[6] All information media show a deficit; only advertising, that is to say the sale of commercial "information" which they are paid to sell, allows some of them to balance their budgets.

SQUALOR WITHIN AFFLUENCE

One can never emphasize sufficiently the fact that social, cultural, and regional underdevelopment on the one hand and the rapid development of "affluent" consumer goods industries on the other are two sides of the same reality. If collective facilities, social and public services (urban public transport, among other things), education, regional, and rural development are generally in a state of scandalous deficiency, while at the same time the oligopolies which produce articles for individual consumption enjoy a spectacular prosperity, the reason is not that the former are public and the latter private. On the contrary, it is because State-monopoly capitalism secures for the latter the driving role in economic development; because private accumulation diverts the greatest part of surplus value toward investments which yield a short-term profit; and because the portion of surplus value which can be utilized for social investment, for the satisfaction of priority necessities, therefore becomes insufficient.

In addition, the capitalist State subordinates its own investments, already insufficient in volume, to the interests of the monopolies: by pre-financing their expansion, by creating the infrastructure for them, by helping the monopolies (through its price, financial, fiscal, and military policies) to find a market for their anarchical productions. Always two steps behind, the State tries its best to finance out of public funds the social cost of private accumulation (urban congestion, transportation, professional education, infrastructure, public health, etc.) and, unable to catch up, cuts down those public investments (cultural, social, and industrial) which because they are relatively autonomous would be in a position to counteract the monopolist line of development.

The influence of the monopolies is felt, in effect, more or less openly in all spheres of civil life. And this is true not only because within certain limits the monopolist sector controls the prices of the products it sells as well as of the products and services it buys, and appropriates to itself an important part of the surplus value of other sectors (agriculture and industrial sub-contractors notably, as well as of the energy producing, mining, and transport sectors); but also because of the fact that the monopolist sector is in a position to impose a model of production and of consumption, and to orient the tastes of the "consumers" toward products which permit the highest profit rate, by the forced sale of services and goods. The results are the disparities and distortions common to all the State-monopoly capitalist economies: "public squalor within private affluence," to use Galbraith's phrase: megalopolis with gigantically expensive infrastructures and operations, and decline (going as far as the creation of wastelands) in so-called eccentric regions; slums with television and/or means of individual transport; illiteracy (real or figurative) and transistor radios; rural underdevelopment and superhighways; cities with neither hygiene, fresh air, nor sunlight, but with commercial cathedrals, etc.

The de facto dictatorship of the monopolies over all domains of economic and cultural activity is not, of course, exercised in a direct manner: it passes through a certain number of intermediate steps, it asserts itself essentially through the priorities it controls, by the subordination and conditioning of the range of human needs according to the inert exigencies of capital. Bourgeois ideologists sometimes attempt to deny this relationship of subordination by pointing to the sphere of autonomy (often real, incidentally) enjoyed by the State or by corporate bodies like universities. And it is true that to speak of a dictatorship of the monopolies over the State and over education, for example, is to oversimplify matters. The State plays the role of enlightened mediator between the direct interests of the monopolies and those of society; and this mediating role can include steps which seem to go contrary to the immediate interests of monopoly capital. In the short run, it is in the constant interest of monopoly capital to limit to a strict minimum all the activities of the public sector (education, health, hygiene, city planning, cultural and sports facilities, etc.) since the latter divert resources which have been deducted from individual income and buying power toward social uses from which no accumulation or profit can be realized. State-financed social consumption not only deflates or threatens to deflate the volume of surplus value, it also prevents a portion of individual buying power from flowing into the cash registers of private companies. It virtually creates a circuit of money not subject to the laws of the market and of capitalist profitability, a sector which is virtually antagonistic to the profit economy.

A permanent antagonism, therefore, opposes private capital to the State, even the capitalist State, as public entrepreneur active in unproductive, unprofitable sectors of general interest. But precisely what distinguishes neo-capitalism from traditional capitalism is that the former recognizes the necessity of the mediating role of the State; its efforts no longer aim at restraining public initiative, but at orienting it and even developing it for the benefit of monopoly accumulation. It is in the long-term interest of monopoly capital to insure that occasional redistributions of income render the capitalist system socially tolerable, that health and public hygiene slow the exhaustion of labor power, that public education cover future needs for trained manpower, that public city transportation, financed by the entire population, deliver manpower to the factories in good condition, that nationalization of energy sources and raw materials place onto the shoulders of the entire population the burden of supplying industrial needs at low cost. The expansion of public activity, in short, is welcome so long as it limits itself to publicly pre-financing the basis of monopoly expansion and accumulation; so long, that is, as it remains in a subordinate position to private capital and abandons to the latter the responsibility of determining the dominant orientations of the economy.

But that means precisely that the satisfaction of social and cultural needs is never considered as an end in itself, but only in a utilitarian manner; that the full development of human faculties (through education, research, information, and culture) including urban and rural development, is not pursued as a priority. These activities are developed only to the degree that they complement private initiative, or at least do not oppose its interests; or so long as they do not lead individuals to challenge the system. True enough, the University may be free, opposition and dissent may be voiced. Dissenters—mainly if they are celebrated writers or artists—are an essential ornament of neo-capitalist society. But an ornament only. Information is directed by the State or (in practice) by commercial interests; cultural facilities belong to the corporations or to the Church; publishing submits to the laws of the market and to pre- or self-censorship.

Economic, cultural, and social development are not oriented toward the development of human beings and the satisfaction of their social needs as a priority, but *first* toward the creation of those articles which can be sold with the maximum profit, regardless of their utility or lack of utility. Creative activity is limited by the criteria of financial profitability or of social stability,[7] while millions of hours of work are wasted in the framework of monopoly competition in order to incorporate modifications in consumer products, modifications which are often marginal but always costly,[8] and which aim at increasing neither the use value nor the esthetic value of the product.

Instead of putting production at the service of society, society is put at the service of capitalist production: the latter endeavors with all its ingenuity to offer to individuals ever-new means of evading this intolerable social reality; and the implementation on a grand scale of these individual means of escape (automobiles, private houses, camping, passive leisure) thereby re-creates a new anarchic social process, new miseries, inverted priorities, and new alienation.

Mature capitalist society, therefore, remains profoundly barbaric as a *society,* to the degree that it aims at no civilization of social existence and of social relationships, no culture of social individuals, but only a civilization of individual consumption. Simultaneously, the homogeneity and the stereotypes of individual consumption created by the oligopolies produce this particular social individual whose social nature appears to him as accidental and alien: the individual in a mass society.

One must not take this to mean—as sentimentalists of the age of artisans imply—that mass production itself induces the "massification" of social individuals. The latter is in no sense an inevitable consequence of assembly line production methods. It is, rather, the consequence of production which is social in its form but not in its ends. It is one thing to produce mass quantities of low priced agricultural equipment, mechanical pencils for the schools, work clothes, and lunch boxes—products which are designed to satisfy social needs as such, and which a social production is called upon to supply. It is another thing to work not for society but for a private company, producing objects which will satisfy no social need but will be offered to individual buyers as symbols of their liberation from social pressures.

For that is, in the last analysis, the mystique on which so-called affluent capitalism is based: production, which is social in form, scope, and consequence, never appears as such, it denies the social character of "demand," of work, and of needs which individuals have in common, which social production enriches and develops. What capitalism offers is consumer goods which are artificially and radically cut off from work and from the conditions of production which created them. And it does this for a reason: as a consumer, the individual is encouraged to escape his condition as a social producer, to reconstitute himself as a *private* microcosm which he can enjoy and over which he can reign as solitary sovereign.

The ideology implied by the model of "affluent" consumption is less that of comfort than that of the monad cooped up in its lonely, self-sufficient universe: the home with "all modern facilities" (a closed universe independent of exter-

[7] To a large extent, only the fear of being surpassed by the USSR has precipitated in the advanced capitalist countries the thrust toward automation, a development laden with explosive social problems for capitalism.

[8] The American automobile industry spends annually $500 million for marginal modifications of its models, while at the same time limiting their life, through "planned obsolescence" and without any saving of money, to about 40,000 miles. See Vance Packard's, *The Waste Makers.*

nal services) where one can look on the world as an outsider (thanks to television), which one leaves at the wheel of a private automobile to go enjoy "nature without people"—while venting anger against "the State" which does not build enough highways to make this escape easier; anger against the State, but not against the profit economy which makes this escape almost a necessity. The negation of the social origin and character of human needs, the negation of the necessarily social mode of their satisfaction, and the affirmation of the possibility of individual liberation through the acquisition of means of escape (whose social production is carefully masked) are the fundamental mystifications of the so-called affluent civilization.

The underlying reason for the "massification" of individuals is to be found in this refusal to take care of the social reality of individual life, a reality which is pushed back into the outer shadows, into the realm of the "accidental." This massification is the powerless and anarchic solitude of separated individuals, who suffer their social nature as if it were an external statistical reality, and who are manipulated in their individual behavior by the specialists of "hidden persuasion."

The passive and "massified" consumer required by capitalist production in order to subordinate consumption is not created by capitalism altogether by means of advertising, fashion, and "human relations," as is often asserted; on the contrary, capitalism *already* creates him within the relationships of production and the work situation by cutting off the producer from his product; and, what is more, by cutting the worker off from his work, by turning this work against him as a certain pre-determined and alien quantity of time and trouble which awaits the worker at his job and requires his active passivity.

It is because the worker is not "at home" in "his" work, because this work, negated as a creative activity, is a calamity, a pure *means* of satisfying needs, that the individual's active and creative needs are amputated, and he no longer finds his sphere of sovereignty except in non-work, that is to say in the satisfaction of passive needs, in consumption, and in domestic life.

3 CAPITALISM: THE ROOT OF THE PROBLEM*

by JOHN GURLEY

John Gurley, a Professor of Economics at Stanford, initially delivered this paper to a conference at MIT concerning the problem of "Economic Conversion." He sought to deal with the question, under what conditions could the resources of this country be used to solve the problems of environmental decay and poverty rather than to building up our military machine.

Gurley emphasizes the role of an expanding international capitalism in the perpetuation of militarism, and the primacy of profit-making in the continuation of poverty, pollution and unemployment. He also points out that the system that has spawned these problems and which blocks their solutions is now coming under attack, most powerfully from abroad in the form of national liberation movements, but also inside our own country as well. The solution to these problems is not reform of capitalism itself but the success of these anticapitalist movements.

I shall first describe, in thirty-three words, what I consider the problem to be. I'll then try to analyze its basic causes. Finally, I'll turn to some possible solutions. In between times, I'll hedge.

I. THE PROBLEM

What is the problem?

It is that many of our economic resources are apparently being used for wasteful and destructive purposes when, all around us, there is so much poverty, oppression, and maltreatment of people and nature.

I don't imagine that anyone here needs further description of *that*. However, I should note that economists have traditionally viewed economic activity in ways that question the very existence of such a problem. This view is through the competitive model, in which consumers demand various goods and services, either directly in marketplaces or indirectly through their government representatives, in accordance with their preferences and their incomes, while private businessmen, seeking profits, produce the goods demanded, and produce them efficiently at low costs and prices. Hence, the things that are wanted get produced, and what are not wanted are not produced. Under these conditions, there is no point at all in trying to convert anything!

While most economists recognize flaws in this picture, and so would want to modify the conclusion just drawn, it is still true that the influence of the

* Adapted from "Economic Conversion and Beyond" by John G. Gurley, published in *Industrial Management Review,* Volume 11, Number 3, Spring 1970.

competitive model has been so strong and so pervasive that it has all but eliminated economists as critics of the society in which they live. It is this model, applied domestically and internationally, which explains to a large degree why many economists have had to be told by their students and by others what the situation really is. This is an embarrassing fact, but it is a fact nevertheless.

II. CAUSES

What are the causes of the poverty, the environmental and urban decay, and the bloated military expenditures that we are all so concerned about?

Surely, some of the environmental and urban decay is caused by the very processes of industrialization itself, whether they occur in the Soviet Union or in the United States. And some of this decay has roots in large and growing numbers of people crowding into already densely populated areas. Some of our military expenditures are certainly necessary in view of the nuclear weapons now aimed at us. Poverty is relative—a reflection of the fact that in no society does everyone move up together at exactly the same pace. Much of what we observe and do not like can be seen most anywhere in the world.

But that is not the whole story. Much of the rest of it has to do with capitalism itself. One of the main roots of the problem is that there is a capital-owning class, which is largely supported by the State, and which has the primary drive of private profit-making within the context of a U.S.-dominated international capitalist system—which itself is under severe attack from anti-capitalist forces, both at home and abroad. These threats to global capitalism and the system's own driving forces and values largely determine how it uses the surplus economic resources at its disposal.

A. Military Expenditures

That requires explanation. So let's start with military expenditures. Why have these expenditures risen so rapidly in the postwar period? Certainly it is not because consumers have expressed growing demands, through any sort of marketplace or voting mechanism, for invasions by our military forces of one country after another, for the proliferation of nuclear and chemical and biological weapons, for hundreds of military bases around the world, for military aid to dictators, or for counterinsurgency in dozens of poverty-stricken countries. These expenditures are not meant to maximize the utility of consumers, by giving them what they have asked for.

No. Instead, much of these expenditures is intended to support the interests of a small class of people who own most of the business wealth in this country and who have business interests and ideological commitments to capitalism throughout a large part of the world. These expenditures are meant to defend, and, if possible, to extend, the area of the "Free World."

I don't think that anyone can really come to grips with this problem unless he realizes two things: first, that the "Free World" has relatively little to do with freedom and democracy and everything in the world to do with free enterprise, foreign investment, and capitalism; and, second, that the defense of the "Free World" is a very serious business, with not only the preservation of capitalist ideology at stake but also billions upon billions of dollars riding on every turn of the revolutionary wheel.

The "Free World" *does* exist. It is an international capitalist system, with hierarchical structures, composed of countries favorably disposed to private enterprise. The United States, sitting on top of this structure, dominates most of the countries just below it, which include the advanced capitalist countries of western Europe, Canada, Japan, Australia, New Zealand, and perhaps Israel and South Africa. The United States and many of these countries, in turn, control the economic and political destinies of quite a few low-income countries—in Latin America, Africa, and Asia—which are hospitable to free enterprise and especially to U.S. private investment, and which are at the bottom of the capitalist structure. Many of these lowly satellite countries are ruled by the rich and the powerful—by dictators, sultans, monarchs, feudal landowners, oligarchs of one sort or another. In most of them, the people are not free. The "Free World," as I have said, is not necessarily receptive to freedom, but it is always receptive to capitalism.

In this international capitalist system, individuals and corporations in the wealthy countries own large amounts of land, natural resources, and capital goods in the satellite countries, while the latter are often heavily in debt to the former. The wealthy countries have the industrial power that is fed by the oil, minerals, and raw materials of the satellites, and the latter in return receive industrial goods and some basic food items. Mostly by design, rather than by accident, there is much more trade between the wealthy and the poor countries than among the poor countries themselves. Finally, the international capitalist system is not really an alliance of "countries" or of "people." It is an alliance of the ruling classes in the underdeveloped countries with the capital-owning classes and their supporters in the industrialized nations.

So there *is* a "Free World"—and, what is most important for our purposes here, it is under attack. It is facing danger from almost every direction, both at home and abroad, from anti-capitalist forces. Some of the danger has been exaggerated, and some has been misrepresented. But most of it has been real enough to justify, in the name of the "Free World," not only billions of dollars of economic and military aid to the trouble spots, but also an extensive network of military bases, tens of thousands of troops in strategic locations, large-scale counterinsurgency operations, and numerous instances of military intervention.

It is true, as I have already observed, that some of our military expenditures can be explained, not in terms of the defense of the entire "Free World," but on the ground that nuclear weapons are in fact aimed right at us. And some military spending, as Galbraith has emphasized, has served the needs of a Technostructure, which has generated increasing demands for weapons systems quite independent of real dangers and threats. But most of this activity does not float on a cloud of Cold War Myth, as Galbraith supposes. It is instead firmly based on something very real, the defense of the international capitalist system, in the interests of a capital-owning class.

Vietnam, as the 41st military intervention by the United States since around the turn of the century, was no blunder. Every piece of the "Free World" is potentially of great importance for the viability of the whole system. Each part plays its role—economically, politically, and psychologically. A victory for communism in Vietnam would increase the danger to capitalism everywhere. It would, first of all, weaken the economic structure of capitalist countries and satellites in Southeast Asia; it would shake public confidence in leaders who have been propped up by a United States that may no longer be willing to meet its commitments; it would strengthen anti-capitalist forces, directly by economic and military aid from a Communist Vietnam to neighboring countries and friendly groups—and indirectly, by example to national liberation movements everywhere.

This view has recently been presented by a group of industrialists, bankers, militarists, and others, who call themselves the Citizens Committee for Peace with Freedom in Vietnam. As *The New York Times* reported:

> [Their] statement said that an abrupt withdrawal of United States forces would "represent an American sellout and encourage the victors to try for one, two or three more Vietnams. . . . America's word and leadership would be sharply devalued throughout the world. Every treaty that we have made, every agreement and commitment that we have entered into would be looked upon with suspicion by those countries who have counted on them. . . . The development of freedom and democracy would be reversed in Southeast Asia, and slowed in Africa and even in Latin America. Peaceful methods of social and economic change would be downgraded and violent methods encouraged. A huge part of the world would be increasingly vulnerable to Communist subversion and control. . . . And the lesson of the success of violent guerrilla tactics to bring about change would not be lost on those who seek to use violence to effect social change here at home.

If, in this statement, "freedom and democracy" are understood to mean "free enterprise," then the statement, in my judgment, reflects a fairly realistic picture of the dangers now confronting global capitalism. And so long as the dangers are there, and we insist on defending this international capitalist world, it will be terribly hard to hold back the growth of military spending—especially, if on top of this, we permit the military and their industrial contractors to play games with our scarce economic and natural resources.

B. Poverty and Environmental Decay

I previously suggested that the causes of environmental and urban decay and poverty are complex enough that no single determinant is likely to explain at all fully these social ills. Nevertheless, there is very little doubt that capitalism itself—its private profit-making drives and its values—must be held accountable for some of the inequities and deterioration that we observe and smell every day of our lives.

I can sum up what I have in mind in this way: if substantial private profits could be made in cleaning up our rivers and lakes, in restoring fresh, clean air to us once again, in eliminating hunger, malnutrition, substandard housing, and poor education, in doing something about congested and ugly urban areas and subhuman ghetto living—if, as I say, private capitalists could make a financial killing out of remedying these things, then, by God, they would be done faster than you could get a man to the moon.

In fact, however, not only is there very little private profit to be made in cleaning up the mess left in the wake of industrial capitalism, but—worse yet—it is the *creation* of much of the mess, not its elimination, that inflates the profits. Businesses make profits by keeping their costs as low as possible, and by charging higher prices for the products they turn out. The costs involved here are private costs, the costs incurred by the firms themselves in production. The social costs, those costs imposed on the rest of us by the firms' operations

—for example, river and air pollution, traffic congestion, blighted landscapes—do not have to be paid by the businesses and hence are no financial burden on them. In fact, the dumping of wastes into a river may be the cheapest way for firms to get rid of the stuff—if so, the drive for minimum costs and high profits would dictate that this be done. Industrialists, of course, are very reluctant to spend money to meet the social costs of their operations—simply because such costs lie beyond their private profit calculations.

This, indeed, is the way industrialists *should* behave, the way they are expected to behave, according to the rules of capitalism. Milton Friedman, as usual, has given the clearest statement of what capitalism expects of its capitalists:

> The view has been gaining widespread acceptance that corporate officials . . . have a "social responsibility" that goes beyond serving the interest of their stockholders . . . This view shows a fundamental misconception of the character and nature of a free economy. In such an economy, there is one and only one social responsibility of business—to use its resources and engage in activities designed to increase its profits so long as it stays within the rules of the game, which is to say, engages in open and free competition, without deception or fraud.

This doctrine of "open and free competition" has recently been invoked by Harrison Dunning, board chairman of the Scott Paper Company, when he argued, in effect, that so long as there is open and free competition among many firms in polluting a river, no one firm significantly lowers the quality of the water, and hence no one firm should be held responsible for its actions. This may seem a strange use of "open and free competition," but it is a reasonable one within capitalist rules.

At a recent conference in Washington, called by the Department of the Interior's Water Pollution Control Administration, and attended by 700 business executives, industry spokesmen made it clear that "they were all for the abatement of water pollution but that it should not be carried to the point of trying to make waterways too clean too soon or causing too great an impact on company profits." Brooks McCormick, president of the International Harvester Company, was reported to have said: "Any management today that does not understand its responsibility to society for degradation of the environment is derelict in its duty. But an even greater dereliction would be its failure to perceive and adopt a strategy of action that will provide the income for maintaining the profitability of the enterprise." Edgar B. Speer, president of the United States Steel Corporation, in discussing water pollution, said that "we oppose treatment for treatment's sake." There is something in that, but it does reflect less than complete enthusiasm for getting the job done.

And recently, *The New York Times,* in an editorial on the construction of a giant pipeline for carrying oil across Alaska, rebuked the oil companies on Alaska's North Slope, for "the greedy haste with which they are prepared to endanger a vast territory—the land, its people and its wildlife—for the sake of a quick and enormously profitable return on their investment."

But what do you expect? These are not evil men, and they are not necessarily cheating or engaging in fraud or deceit. The point is that private profit-making *demands* that they ignore the social costs of their operations. They should not be so castigated for doing what is required of them.

In saying this, I do not mean to deny the fact that some industrialists have made serious efforts and have spent large sums of money to clean up the mess they and others have made. But what they are doing is something that runs against the grain of capitalism, which is exactly why most of them acted only after heavy pressure was exerted on them by social-action groups of one type or another. The private profit-making drive is so strong and so much a part of our society that industrial capitalists must make heroic efforts to act in ways contrary to it.

The values of profit-making run even deeper than that, however. Private profit-making requires efficiency. To be efficient, a business firm builds on the best. This means that it does not hire the worst-trained workers, the disadvantaged, the poorly educated. Its strong inclination is to hire the best. Further, it locates where the most profits can be made—next to other factories that can give it low-cost access to supplies, or near markets where it can sell its products—even though a great social good might be served by locating in a depressed, poverty-ridden area. For the same reason, a banker extends loans to those who are already successful, or to those with the best prospects.

Such values permeate not only the business world, but the whole society. For example, primary and secondary education systems tend to devote their best teachers and best efforts to the superior students; universities offer admission to the ablest students, those who are best prepared; cultural centers are located in urban areas near the most cultured people; and even anti-poverty programs concentrate on those who have the best chance for success.

All of this ensures efficiency; it ensures the greatest returns for the cost, the best chance for making the operation profitable, whether it is business, education, culture, or whatnot. However, when such a high value is placed on efficiency, as it is throughout our entire society, the economic and social development that results is almost bound to be lopsided, uneven, inequitable —an economic development that builds on the best and in so doing bestows riches on some people while leaving many others in society's stagnant backwaters—an economic development that, by stressing efficiency, creates both wealth and poverty, fancy suburbs and miserable ghettos, development and underdevelopment.

Capitalism *is* highly efficient, marvelously innovative, technologically progressive. Being all of these things, it has created great material prosperity for many people. But, at the same time, it has created the opposite—poverty, maltreatment of many of its people and of much of its natural environment. Consequently, these social ills aren't just *problems* of capitalism; they are to some extent *creations* of capitalism. The wealthy industrialist and the poor tenant farmer are both products of the same system.

III. SOLUTION

What can be done to convert wasteful and destructive economic pursuits to ones more worthy of mankind?

If it is true that militarism, poverty, environmental decay, and other social ills are to a substantial extent products of U.S. capitalism, just as are TV sets, flashy cars, supermarkets, and all the rest, then there would appear to be only narrow limits within which economic conversion can be carried out, these limits being imposed by the existence of capitalism itself. Blueprints for economic conversion will turn out to be utopian—that is, rather useless—unless they reflect these limitations. And if they do reflect them, then they won't amount to much. These are the grounds for pessimism.

The prospects are not that bleak, however. For capitalism is not a static, unchanging creature, just daring someone to try to give it a once-and-for-all face-lifting. It is in fact a dynamic system, in constant change, continually in the process of economic conversion. The question, therefore, is not whether to have economic conversion, or even how to achieve it, but rather how to respond to, reshape, and take advantage of, the broad developments that are now taking place within the world economy.

Professor Kindleberger has recently pointed out that, three-quarters of a century ago, private corporations in this country broke out of local markets and developed into national corporations. In the past several decades, many corporations have burst their national bonds to acquire overseas operations. And out of these activities have come the proliferation of multinational corporations—those firms with allegiances to two or more countries—and the beginning developments of true international corporations—those with no strong loyalties to any one nation.

This international business expansion has radiated out from the United States to other advanced capitalist countries, raising and tending to equalize technological capabilities throughout the advanced capitalist sector, and so stimulating reciprocal movements of business expansion. At the same time, U.S. capitalism has expanded, almost explosively, into many Third World countries, drawing them more tightly into the exploitative capitalist structure. Capitalism has been and is a system in expansion.

So is communism. In the past half century, communism has grown to cover a third of the world's population and almost that percentage of the world's land surface. It has greatly reduced the area for capitalist expansion, and as a result the two giants have already collided with one another on several occasions.

These global economic trends have tended both to strengthen and to weaken the international capitalist system. It is being strengthened at the top by the growing economic cooperation and integration of the advanced capitalist countries. There are even indications that this affluent group will eventually draw into its economic orbit eastern Europe and the Soviet Union, and so further strengthen itself.

Simultaneously, however, U.S. capitalism, as it has spread to the Third World, has encountered increasing resistance which has come basically from expanding socialist forces and from growing nationalist movements. Both of these forces have tended to weaken global capitalism at the bottom of the structure, and have in fact defeated it on several occasions, Vietnam being potentially the most damaging defeat of all.

So capitalism is gaining some strength at the top, losing some at the bottom. The strength at the top helps to hold the system together at the bottom; it pits a strong combination of industrial countries, supported by the IMF and the World Bank, against weak, developing countries. But the decay at the bottom tends to spread to the top. There are now vigorous movements within the advanced capitalist countries, and especially within the United States, against capitalism. Capitalism in the advanced countries may be gaining technologically, but it is surely losing ideologically, as its Blacks, its youth, its minorities, and its poor turn against its values, and more and more associate themselves with anti-capitalist forces abroad.

I started out by suggesting that, if consumers always got what they wanted, as in the competitive model so dearly loved by academic economists, the correct position of this Conference would be: There is nothing that we should do.

I also noted that, if most of our economic and social ills are, in fact, created by an unchanging capitalism, the correct position would be: There is much that we should do, but nothing that we can do.

If, on the other hand, our economic and social ills are unrelated to capitalism and so are correctable within the capitalist system—as many young people with environmental concerns seem to think, and as Galbraith apparently views the military scene—then the Conference should adopt the position: There is much that we should and can do.

But if, as I have tried to argue, many of our difficulties come directly from capitalism itself—but from a capitalism that is in constant change, as its strengths fight its weaknesses in a dialectical war; from a capitalism that is still very strong but is presently on the defensive and so is vulnerable to forces for change—then there is room for some progress.

How much, is not certain. My own feeling is that, while there is much that we should do, there are relatively few things that we can do, within the existing system.

If this is so, there is a question as to whether we should devote our best efforts to trying to get a few more dollars eliminated from a huge military budget, a few more dollars devoted to alleviating hunger, a few more businessmen interested in the mess they create, and a few more city fathers concerned about ghettos—all the while trying to work within the present system. Or whether we should direct our energies forcefully to exposing the system itself. It can be argued that the former will achieve the latter. It may, if in the process of trying to improve things we increase our own awareness and the awareness of many others of the limits to our actions imposed by the system.

In that way, we can go beyond economic conversion to economic subversion.

4

WASTE UNDER CAPITALISM: THE SALES EFFORT*

by PAUL BARAN AND PAUL SWEEZY

The worshipers of the GNP have told us for a long time that the real improvement of life in America could be measured tangibly in the rising curve of national production. But when American "affluence" is dissected into the waste, duplication and irrationality that are its components, this kind of assertion seems a lot less tenable.

This selection from Monopoly Capital *maps out some of the bottomless pits of waste that are integral to the capitalist economic system. For one thing, there is advertising. The new style of competition among firms pours twenty billion a year into hawking virtually identical products. Then there's the obsolescence. The concern for rapid turnover of products leads to billions more squandered on engineering to reduce durability and on planning style changes. The system has such a hold over its captive market that it can now manufacture customers for its products rather than the other way around.*

How much is your new car really worth? If we took away the cost of the advertising, the cost of the model changes, the styling and excess, we could market a car for $700–$800. That's one third of what an average car now costs. If the income of the average American is being gobbled up by rising costs that give him so little in the way of use value in return, can we really conclude that increased affluence is really buying him a better life?"

This waste is really essential to capitalism. Advertising waste is crucial to the corporation that hopes to differentiate its product from the twenty identical ones already on the market. Advertising waste is also crucial to the system's stability as a whole. Without it people might save rather than spend money. They would tend to be much more discriminating about what they really needed to buy.

The same is true of planned obsolescence. Without the restyling and without the artificially shortened product lifetimes, customers would buy much less frequently. When consumer purchases decline, not only do companies make less money, but the whole economy heads into a tail spin. This compulsive addiction to waste is one of the major irrationalities of the corporate capitalist system.

But looked at another way, the waste, the advertising, etc., are not merely squandered resources that could have gone for something more constructive. Just as important, they are part of the downright antisocial nature of capitalism. The Sales Effort to do its job has to impose itself like a cancer on our culture, on our social values, on our personal identities, on all facets of human life.

For example, advertising really twists people's minds. It tries to make people feel inadequate—like "Are you sure you're a Real Man?" Of course, you're not until you buy their product. It also hawks truly destructive ideas and stereotypes. Women are told over and over that their only goal in life is to become a beautiful object. People in general are taught that they can only be loved, have a good time, have status, etc., if they possess the right objects or look the right way. All human relationships and feelings are reduced to a matter of materialism.

Of course, such notions are not confined to the medium of advertising. Those who use ads and create them dominate all the media—TV, films, newspapers, even to some extent schools. Their goal is to create masses of people as susceptible as possible to advertising appeals. The materialist mentality is at work subtly in all our communication to undermine our healthier values of who we are and what is important, and to turn us into docile and passive consumers.

The advertising business has grown astronomically, with its expansion and success being continually promoted by the growing monopolization of the economy and by the effectiveness of the media which have been pressed into its service—especially radio, and now above all television. Total spending on advertising media rose to $10.3 billion in 1957, and amounted to over $12 billion in 1962.[1] Together with outlays on market research, public relations, commercial design, and similar services carried out by advertising agencies and other specialized firms, the amount now probably exceeds $20 billion. And this does not include the costs of market research, advertising work, designing, etc., carried on within the producing corporations themselves.

This truly fantastic outpouring of resources does not reflect some frivolous irrationality in corporate managements or some peculiar predilection of the American people for singing commercials, garish billboards, and magazines and newspapers flooded with advertising copy. What has actually happened is that advertising has turned into an indispensable tool for a large sector of corporate business. Competitively employed, it has become an integral part of the corporations' profit maximization policy and serves at the same time as a formidable wall protecting monopolistic positions. Although advertising at first appeared to corporate managements as a deplorable cost to be held down as much as possible, before long it turned into what one advertising agency has rightly called "a must for survival" for many a corporate enterprise.[2]

[1] *Statistical Abstract of the United States: 1963,* Washington, p. 846.

[2] An extreme case of this "must for survival" principle is presented by a proprietary drug called Contac recently launched by one of the country's largest pharmaceutical firms. This drug's advertising budget is estimated at a "breathtaking $13 million, spent in probably one of the most elaborate drug product campaigns ever devised. Most of the budget is in television." For this outlay, the pharmaceutical firm "is said to be deriving about $16 million in drug store sales, expressed in wholesale prices." (*New York Times,* January 9, 1964.) Allowing for a handsome profit margin, which of course is added to selling as well as production cost, it seems clear that the cost of production can hardly be more than a minute proportion of even the wholesale price. And when the retailer's margin is added, the fraction of the price to the consumer must be virtually invisible.

The strategy of the advertiser is to hammer into the heads of people the unquestioned desirability, indeed the imperative necessity, of owning the newest product that comes on the market. For this strategy to work, however, producers have to pour on the market a steady stream of "new" products, with none daring to lag behind for fear his customers will turn to his rivals for their newness.

Genuinely new or different products, however, are not easy to come by, even in our age of rapid scientific and technological advance. Hence much of the newness with which the consumer is systematically bombarded is either fraudulent or related trivially and in many cases even negatively to the function and serviceability of the product. Good examples of fraudulent newness are admiringly described by Rosser Reeves, head of the Ted Bates advertising agency, one of the country's largest:

> Claude Hopkins, whose genius for writing copy made him one of the advertising immortals, tells the story of one of his great beer campaigns. In a tour through the brewery, he nodded politely at the wonders of malt and hops, but came alive when he saw that the empty bottles were being sterilized with live steam. His client protested that every brewery did the same. Hopkins patiently explained that it was not *what* they did, but what they *advertised* they did that mattered. He wrote a classic campaign which proclaimed "OUR BOTTLES ARE WASHED WITH LIVE STEAM!" George Washington Hill, the great tobacco manufacturer, once ran a cigarette campaign with the now-famous claim: "IT'S TOASTED!" So, indeed, is every other cigarette, but no other manufacturer has been shrewd enough to see the enormous possibilities of such a simple story. Hopkins, again, scored a great advertising coup when he wrote: "GETS RID OF FILM ON YOUR TEETH!" So, indeed, does every toothpaste.[3]

These examples could of course be endlessly multiplied. But from our present point of view the important thing to stress is not the ubiquity of this phenomenon but that it is confined entirely to the marketing sphere and does not reach back into the production process itself.

It is entirely different with the second kind of newness. Here we have to do with products which are indeed new in design and appearance but which serve essentially the same purposes as old products they are intended to replace. The extent of the difference can vary all the way from a simple change in packaging to the far-reaching and enormously expensive annual changes in automobile models. What all these product variations have in common is that they do reach back into the process of production: the sales effort which used to be a mere adjunct of production, helping the manufacturer to dispose profitably of goods designed to satisfy recognized consumer needs, increasingly invades factory and shop, dictating what is to be produced according to criteria laid down by the sales department and its consultants and advisers in the advertising industry. The situation is well summed up by the McGraw-Hill Department of Economics:

> Today, the orientation of manufacturing companies is increasingly toward the market and away from production. In fact, this change has gone so far in some cases that the General Electric Company, as one striking example, now conceives itself to be essentially a marketing rather than a production organization. This thinking flows back through the structure of the company,

[3] Rosser Reeves, *Reality in Advertising,* New York, 1961, pp. 55–56. This book is reputed to be the most sophisticated guide to successful advertising.

> to the point that marketing needs reach back and dictate the arrangement and grouping of production facilities.[4]

Vance Packard adds the information that "whenever engineers in the appliance industry assembled at conferences in the late fifties, they frequently voiced the lament that they had become little more than pushbuttons for the sales department," and he quotes Consumers Union to the effect that "a good deal of what is called product research today actually is a sales promotion expenditure undertaken to provide what the trade calls a profitable 'product mix.' "[5] And even this is not all. Researchers for *Fortune* magazine, that faithful chronicler of the mores and virtues of Big Business, looking into the Research and Development programs of large American corporations, found that this multi-billion-dollar effort is much more closely related to the production of salable goods than to its much touted mission of advancing science and technology.[6]

As far as the consumer is concerned, the effect of this shift in the center of gravity from production to sales is entirely negative. In the words of Dexter Masters, former director of Consumers Union, the largest and most experienced organization devoted to testing and evaluating consumers goods:

> When design is tied to sales rather than to product function, as it is increasingly, and when marketing strategy is based on frequent style changes, there are certain almost inevitable results: a tendency to the use of inferior materials; short cuts in the time necessary for sound product development; and a neglect of quality and adequate inspection. The effect of such built-in obsolescence is a disguised price increase to the consumer in the form of shorter product life, and, often, heavier repair bills.[7]

But for the economy as a whole, the effect is just as surely positive. In a society with a large stock of consumer durable goods like the United States, an important component of the total demand for goods and services rests on the need to replace a part of this stock as it wears out or is discarded. Built-in obsolescence increases the rate of wearing out, and frequent style changes increase the rate of discarding. (In practice, as Masters points out, the two are inextricably linked together.) The net result is a stepping up in the rate of replacement demand and a general boost to income and employment. In this respect, as in others, the sales effort turns out to be a powerful antidote to monopoly capitalism's tendency to sink into a state of chronic depression.

To answer the question as to how much of a product's cost is wastage we must compare the cost and quality of actual output with the cost and quality of hypothetical output. The problem is solved by Fisher, Grilliches, and Kaysen in their study of automobile model changes[8] by taking 1949 as their

[4] Dexter M. Keezer and associates, *New Forces in American Business,* p. 97.

[5] Vance Packard, *The Waste Makers,* p. 14.

[6] Eric Hodgins, "The Strange State of American Research," *Fortune,* April 1955. A similar conclusion is suggested by D. Hamberg, "Invention in the Industrial Research Laboratory," *Journal of Political Economy,* April 1963.

[7] Quoted by Vance Packard, *The Waste Makers,* p. 127.

[8] "The Costs of Automobile Model Changes Since 1949," *Journal of Political Economy,* October 1962. An abstract, omitting details of estimating procedures, was presented at the 1961 annual meeting of the American Economic Association and appears in the *American Economic Review,* May 1962, beginning at page 259. Our quotations are from the latter version.

point of departure and using the model of that year as the standard of quality and cost. The authors emphasize that the 1949 model was chosen as a standard not because of any particular merits but simply because that was the earliest year for which all necessary data were available. Conceptually, it would clearly have been possible to adopt as the standard a more rationally conceived and constructed model than that of 1949—safer, more durable, more efficient, more economical to operate. Perhaps such an automobile actually exists somewhere in the world, perhaps it would be necessary to have a team of experts blueprint one. From a methodological point of view, either could be substituted for the 1949 model, and such a substitution would undoubtedly result in much higher estimates of the costs of model changes. But even taking the imperfect product of 1949 as its yardstick, the investigation leads to an estimate of costs which the authors themselves consider to be "staggeringly high."

They "concentrate on the cost of the resources that would have been saved had cars with the 1949 model lengths, weights, horsepowers, transmissions, etc., been produced in every year. As there was technological change in the industry, [they] were thus assessing not the resource expenditure that would have been saved had the 1949 models themselves been continued but rather the resource expenditures that would have been saved had cars with 1949 specifications been continued but been built with the developing technology as estimated from actual car construction cost and performance data." These calculations showed that the cost of model changes "came to about $700 per car (more than 25 percent of purchase price) or about $3.9 billion per year over the 1956–1960 period."

And this is by no means the whole story, since "there are other costs of model changes which are not exhausted with the construction of the car but are expended over its life." Among these are costs resulting from accelerated obsolescence of repair parts, higher repair costs stemming from certain changes in car design and construction, and additional gasoline consumption. Confining themselves to estimating the last of these items, the authors found that

> whereas actual gasoline mileage fell from 16.4 miles per gallon in 1949 to 14.3 miles per gallon ten years later, then rising to about 15.3 in 1960 and 1961, the gasoline mileage of the average 1949 car would have *risen* to 18.0 miles per gallon in 1959 and 18.5 in 1961. This meant that the owner of the average 1956–1960 car was paying about $40 more per 10,000 miles of driving (about 20 percent of his total gasoline costs) than would have been the case had 1949 models been continued.

The additional gasoline consumption due to model changes was estimated to average about $968 million per year over the 1956–1960 period. And in addition, the authors estimated that "since such additional expenditure continues over the life of the car, . . . even if 1962 and all later model years were to see a return to 1949 specifications, the 1961 present value (in 1960 prices) of additional gasoline consumption by cars already built through 1961 discounted at 10 percent would be about $7.1 billion."

Summing up the costs of model changes proper and of additional gasoline costs caused by model changes, the authors concluded: "We thus estimated costs of model changes since 1949 to run about $5 billion per year over the 1956–1960 period with a present value of future gasoline costs of $7.1 billion. If anything, these figures are underestimates because of items not included."

All these calculations take for granted that the costs of automobiles include the enormous monopoly profits of the giant automobile manufacturing corporations (among the highest in the economy) and dealers' markups of from 30 to 40 percent of the final price to the purchaser. If these were omitted from costs, it appears that the real cost of production of a 1949 automobile built with the technology of 1956–1960 would have been less than $700. If we assume further that a rationally designed car could have been turned out at a cost of, say, $200 less than the 1949 model, and assume further the existence of an economical and efficient distributive system, we would have to conclude that the final price to consumers of an automobile would not need to exceed something like $700 or $800. The total saving of resources would then be well above $11 billion a year. On this calculation, automobile model changes in the late 1950's were costing the country about 2.5 percent of its Gross National Product!

It comes as a surprise that such a crucial component of the sales effort as advertising amounted to no more than $14 per car, about 2 percent of the cost of model changes. While automobiles are unquestionably an extreme case, this nevertheless may be taken as an indication of the scope and intensity of the interpenetration of sales and production activities, of the vast amount of selling costs that do not appear as such but are merged into the costs of production. In the case of the automobile industry, and doubtless there are many others that are similar in this respect, by far the greater part of the sales effort is carried out not by obviously unproductive workers such as salesmen and advertising copy writers but by seemingly productive workers: tool and die makers, draftsmen, mechanics, assembly line workers.

But what we would like to stress above all is that the Fisher-Grilliches-Kaysen study definitively establishes the feasibility in principle of a meaningful comparison between an actual and a hypothetical output, and between the costs incurred in producing the actual output and those that would be incurred in producing a more rational output. If carried out for the economy as a whole, such a comparison would provide us with an estimate of the amount of surplus which is now hidden by the interpenetration of the sales and production efforts.

This is not to suggest that a full-scale computation of this kind could be adequately carried out at the present time. No group of economists, no matter how imaginative, and no group of statisticians, however ingenious, could, or for that matter should, attempt to specify the structure of output that could be produced under a more rational economic order. It would certainly be very different from the structure with which we are familiar today; but, as so often, it is possible to see clearly what is irrational without necessarily being able to present the details of a more rational alternative. One need not have a specific idea of a reasonably constructed automobile, a well planned neighborhood, a beautiful musical composition, to recognize that the model changes that are incessantly imposed upon us, the slums that surround us, and the rock-and-roll that blares* at us exemplify a pattern of utilization of human and material

* Paul Sweezy and Paul Baran write a lot of great stuff, and we're very indebted to them for letting us reprint some of it. However, they do go a little far sometimes. Rock and roll inimical to human welfare!?!?! Egad! Hopefully what this reference means is that capitalism is always threatening to appropriate rock and roll, use it for its own ends, mold people's tastes, tell them what they "want" to hear and buy, and sell it to them.

resources which is inimical to human welfare. One need not have an elaborate plan for international cooperation and coexistence to perceive the horror and destructiveness of war. What is certain is the negative statement which, notwithstanding its negativity, constitutes one of the most important insights to be gained from political economy: an output the volume and composition of which are determined by the profit maximization policies of oligopolistic corporations neither corresponds to human needs nor costs the minimum possible amount of human toil and human suffering.[9] The concrete structure of a rational social output and the optimal conditions for its production can only be established in the fullness of time—by a process of groping, of trial and error—in a socialist society where economic activity is no longer dominated by profits and sales but instead is directed to the creation of the abundance which is indispensable to the welfare and all-round development of man.

After all, there is a fortune to be made in "youth culture." Somebody ought to write a good exposé of the rock and roll *industry*.

[9] That products designed according to the dictates of profit maximization can be in the most literal sense inimical to the elementary need for survival is illustrated by a report in the *New York Times* (March 3, 1964), according to which the American Automobile Association finds the automobile manufacturers guilty of grossly neglecting safety considerations for the sake of body glamor. Recommendations of competent engineers, said Robert S. Kretschmar, a national director of the AAA and head of its Massachusetts branch, "have been over-ridden by the body stylists and the merchandising people." And he continued: "The manufacturers look upon an automobile as 'glamor merchandise,' not as a mechanism that should be made as safe as possible." Among safety shortcomings were listed "a lack of fail-safe brakes, faulty tires, poor interior design, poor steering design, and weak and thin construction." And yet the automobile industry spends many millions of dollars every year on research and development!

5 INEQUALITY UNDER CAPITALISM*

by GABRIEL KOLKO

Throughout its history the capitalist economic system has produced startling extremes of riches and poverty. Since the means of production are held in private hands, certain individuals on the one end of the distribution receive wealth and income on a scale dwarfing that received by most other individuals in the society. On the other end, chronic unemployment, the system's need for low-paid wage labor, and other factors like discrimination doom many to a bare subsistence living.

This selection from Kolko's Wealth and Power in America *shows that the distribution of income has remained virtually constant for the last sixty years. Over all these years the rich have managed to keep appropriating the same lion's share of whatever new income was produced. It is strong evidence that there has been no decline in the power of the rich. This fact flies in the face of the widespread notion that the power of the wealthy has been in decline due to profound changes that have occurred in the economy and society.*

Kolko only refers to income. Even more powerful evidence exists that the wealthy have consolidated and magnified their power. In 1941, one thousand corporations controlled two thirds of the nation's manufacturing assets. Today that two thirds is controlled by two hundred; in 1968, the top ten corporations accounted for 22.5 percent of the profits of all U.S. industrial corporations. The tight grip of the corporate elite on the economy, far from letting up, is increasing all the time.

THE UNCHANGING PATTERN OF INEQUALITY

A radically unequal distribution of income has been characteristic of the American social structure since at least 1910, and despite minor year-to-year fluctuations in the shares of the income-tenths, no significant trend toward income equality has appeared. This, in brief, is the deduction that can be made from a study of Table I.

Throughout the 1950's the income of the top tenth was larger than the total for the bottom five income-tenths—about the same relationship as existed in 1910 and 1918. The income share of the richest tenth has dropped only slightly, if at all, since 1910. The average percentage of the national personal income before taxes, received by this group was about one-eighth less in 1950–59 than in 1910–41, omitting the exceptional years 1921 and 1929. This loss, however, disappears when the 1950–59 figures are corrected to allow for their

TABLE I. PERCENTAGE OF NATIONAL PERSONAL INCOME, BEFORE TAXES, RECEIVED BY EACH INCOME-TENTH[a]

	Highest Tenth	2nd	3rd	4th	5th	6th	7th	8th	9th	Lowest Tenth
1910	33.9	12.3	10.2	8.8	8.0	7.0	6.0	5.5	4.9	3.4
1918	34.5	12.9	9.6	8.7	7.7	7.2	6.9	5.7	4.4	2.4
1921	38.2	12.8	10.5	8.9	7.4	6.5	5.9	4.6	3.2	2.0
1929	39.0	12.3	9.8	9.0	7.9	6.5	5.5	4.6	3.6	1.8
1934	33.6	13.1	11.0	9.4	8.2	7.3	6.2	5.3	3.8	2.1
1937	34.4	14.1	11.7	10.1	8.5	7.2	6.0	4.4	2.6	1.0
1941	34.0	16.0	12.0	10.0	9.0	7.0	5.0	4.0	2.0	1.0
1945	29.0	16.0	13.0	11.0	9.0	7.0	6.0	5.0	3.0	1.0
1946	32.0	15.0	12.0	10.0	9.0	7.0	6.0	5.0	3.0	1.0
1947	33.5	14.8	11.7	9.9	8.5	7.1	5.8	4.4	3.1	1.2
1948	30.9	14.7	11.9	10.1	8.8	7.5	6.3	5.0	3.3	1.4
1949	29.8	15.5	12.5	10.6	9.1	7.7	6.2	4.7	3.1	0.8
1950	28.7	15.4	12.7	10.8	9.3	7.8	6.3	4.9	3.2	0.9
1951	30.9	15.0	12.3	10.6	8.9	7.6	6.3	4.7	2.9	0.8
1952	29.5	15.3	12.4	10.6	9.1	7.7	6.4	4.9	3.1	1.0
1953	31.4	14.8	11.9	10.3	8.9	7.6	6.2	4.7	3.0	1.2
1954	29.3	15.3	12.4	10.7	9.1	7.7	6.4	4.8	3.1	1.2
1955	29.7	15.7	12.7	10.8	9.1	7.7	6.1	4.5	2.7	1.0
1956	30.6	15.3	12.3	10.5	9.0	7.6	6.1	4.5	2.8	1.3
1957	29.4	15.5	12.7	10.8	9.2	7.7	6.1	4.5	2.9	1.3
1958	27.1	16.3	13.2	11.0	9.4	7.8	6.2	4.6	3.1	1.3
1959	28.9	15.8	12.7	10.7	9.2	7.8	6.3	4.6	2.9	1.1

[a] In terms of "recipients" for 1910–37 and "spending units" for 1941–59.

Source: Data for 1910–37 are from National Industrial Conference Board, *Studies in Enterprise and Social Progress* (New York: National Industrial Conference Board, 1939), p. 125. Data for 1941–59 were calculated by the Survey Research Center. Figures for 1941–46 are available in rounded form only. Previously unpublished data for 1947–58 are reproduced by permission of the Board of Governors of the Federal Reserve System, and data for 1959 by permission of the Survey Research Center.

exclusion of all forms of income-in-kind and the very substantial understatement of income by the wealthy, both of which are consequences of the post-1941 expansion in income taxation.

While the income share of the richest tenth has remained large and virtually constant over the past half century, the two lowest income-tenths have experienced a sharp decline. In 1910, the combined income shares of the two poorest income-tenths were about one-quarter that of the richest tenth; by 1959, their share had dropped to one-seventh. During this same period, the percentage of the next-lowest tenth also decreased, while the fourth and fifth from the lowest tenths (the sixth- and seventh-ranking) neither gained nor lost ground appreciably. Together these five groups, which constitute the poorer half of the U.S. population, received 27 percent of the national personal income in 1910, but only 23 percent in 1959. Thus, for the only segments of the population in which a gain could indicate progress toward economic democracy, there has been no increase in the percentage share of the national income.

The only significant rises in income distribution have occurred in the second- and third-richest income-tenths. Their combined shares increased more than one-quarter from 1910 to 1959, and by the end of that period their combined income share was almost equal to that of the richest tenth. It should be noted, however, that their gain was made almost entirely during the Depression years of the 1930's. Further, this group is largely made up of persons in occupations such as professionals, small businessmen, top clerical workers, and lesser managers, with rising salary or wage incomes and low unemployment, and by no means was in urgent need of a greater share of the national income.

Many recent explanations of rising real and dollar incomes in the lower-income groups since 1939 or 1941, which have been utilized to prove the occurrence of a radical and purportedly permanent income redistribution, ignore the fact that these increases reflect increased employment, not an alteration in the basic distribution structure.

Prior to World War II, it was commonly assumed that the different phases of the business cycle affected the distribution of income—that relative income inequality rose when unemployment rose. However, the relationship between employment trends and income is more important in the study of real income and dollar earnings than in the study of income distribution. During an upward trend in unemployment, the *dollar earnings* of the lowest-income classes decline much more rapidly than those of the other groups, and during an upswing in employment, both the dollar earnings and real income of the lowest-income classes rise much more rapidly than those of the higher-income groups. During full employment, the rate at which the dollar income of the poorer classes increases generally keeps pace with the rate of rise for the highest classes (although occasionally falling slightly behind—as from 1948 to the early 1950's).

However, even the pre-1941 data show that once common generalizations on the correlation between employment trends and income distribution did not always hold true. The income share of the highest tenth increased sharply in 1929, during a period of only moderately high employment. More important, even in the period of comparative full employment since 1941, the income shares of the poorer half of the nation have either declined or remained stable.

EXPENSE ACCOUNTS—INCOME-IN-KIND FOR CORPORATE EXECUTIVES

Material on money income must be supplemented by data on distribution of income-in-kind among income classes to arrive at more nearly accurate figures for total income and income inequality.

As income-in-kind declined in value for farm and low-income families, it gained new prominence in the highest income-tenth, and especially the top 5 percent of the spending units. Here it takes the form of the expense account and other executive benefits. A by-product of the steeper Federal personal and corporate tax rates instituted in 1941, the expense account is now an acknowledged form of executive remuneration. In 1959, a Harvard Business School study revealed that two-thirds of corporate executives regarded their expense accounts as tax-free compensation.

Legally, a corporation can deduct as expenses only bills incurred in the "ordinary and necessary" course of business, but the fact that a corporation in the top tax bracket is only 48 cents out of pocket for every dollar it deducts from its Federal tax bill has led to some broad interpretations of business costs. Especially at the extremes, in closely owned or very widely diffused corporations, extravagant use has been made of income-in-kind for management. The *Wall Street Journal* frequently mentions such items as $300-a-day hotel suites, $10,000-to-$25,000 parties, executive penthouses with marble walls and gold faucets. According to one *Wall Street Journal* report: "Hidden hunting lodges are one of the 'fringe benefits' awaiting officials who succeed in working their way up to the executive suite of a good many U.S. corporations. Other impressive prizes: sharing use of yachts, private planes and railroad cars, jaunts to exotic watering places and spectacular soirées—all paid for by the corporation. . . . Companies maintaining private retreats, planes and other facilities for fun or luxurious traveling generally report they are necessary to the conduct of their business. . . . This is the prime reason for some companies maintaining such facilities, though perhaps not for others. Even in the former case, executives generally manage to get considerable enjoyment from their firms' luxury properties. . . . In this way, a good many executives whose fortune-building efforts are impaired by today's high taxes still are enjoying the frills enjoyed by the Mellons, Morgans and Baruchs."

Company-provided luxuries are obvious indicators of a man's position in the hierarchy. For the top corporate elite, they generally include a company car, a gas credit card, vacations, excellent medical care, country-club memberships, dining and entertainment, and the cash difference between expense allowances and actual expenditures. Lesser corporate personnel receive lesser benefits, according to their rank.

In 1954, 37 percent of the Cadillacs registered in Manhattan and 20 percent of those registered in Philadelphia were in the names of businesses. Some 80 percent of the check totals of the most expensive restaurants and 30 to 40 percent of Broadway theater tickets are covered by expense accounts. Most of the items charged to Diners' Club, American Express, and other luxury credit-card clubs by members, who numbered well over a million in 1958, are paid for by businesses.

One-half of the executives in small companies and one-third of those in large companies are reimbursed for their expenses in social clubs and organizations. More than one-half of the executives in small firms and more than one-quarter of those in large companies are provided with private automobiles. One-fifth of the large corporations have their own country clubs and resorts for their executives.

Gifts received by executives—particularly those influential in purchasing—from personnel in other corporations are another type of income-in-kind. For Christmas, 1959, such giving accounted for $300 million—all tax deductible as business expenses.

Since nearly two-fifths of the top executives do not have to account to anyone for their expenses, and more than three-fifths are given no yardsticks to limit themselves, it is possible for executives to treat themselves to unusual indulgences, and from time to time some of these are revealed to the public—often in the form of advice on expense-account opportunities as suggested in the pages of business publications. One corporation president spent $17,000 of company funds on an African safari; another charged to business expenses

$65,000 in jewelry, $22,000 in liquor, $35,000 in night-club tabs, $25,000 in gifts, and $16,000 in boat outlays.

In scope and value, the income-in-kind of the rich presents a sharp contrast to the surplus flour, corn meal, rice, and butter provided as relief goods to the poor.

An unofficial Treasury Department estimate in August, 1957, placed the annual total for corporate expense-account outlays at more than $5 billion, and possibly as high as $10 billion. Certainly a portion of this total was in reality income-in-kind received by members of the top income-tenth. If only one-third of this amount is considered income-in-kind for the top tenth, it would add at least 1 percentage point to this group's share of the national income in 1956.

Although existing statistics do not allow us to calculate precisely the percentage of total expense-account outlays that represent personal income-in-kind, they are sufficient to indicate that income-in-kind was an item of major consequence to the share of the top income-tenth, especially to the style of living enjoyed by many of the richest members of the economic elite.

EVASIONS AND ERRORS: $30 BILLION-PLUS

The existing data on income distribution fail to account for a significant proportion of money income because of underreporting on tax returns and nonreporting to interviewers. Since automatic payroll deductions withhold the amount of money due for Federal income taxes, persons wholly dependent on wages or salary for their incomes—and this includes the vast majority of urban low- and middle-income earners—have little reason to underreport their incomes to data collectors. Whatever payroll earnings are underreported or nonreported are probably to be found in very small companies where executives or owners are in a position to alter their required earnings statements.

However, professionals, businessmen, and others receiving cash payments for their services are in an especially advantageous position to underreport their income on tax returns. Roughly one-half of unreported entrepreneurial income represented farm income, the better part of which probably went to low-income earners. The unreported half going to businessmen and professionals probably went to those already earning enough to underreport their incomes without arousing the suspicion of tax auditors. The result is ultimately indicative of an understatement of income by the upper tenths in tax and other statistics.

Refusal to report income data to interviewers also leads to an understating of income by the highest groups. Nonreporting is almost exclusively confined to the upper brackets. A 1941 Bureau of Labor Statistics study found that "the nonreporting rate tended to be higher in blocks with higher rent levels and with larger proportions of families at upper-income levels, ranging from about 1 percent at the under $1,000 level to 35 percent at the $10,000 and over level."

Nondeclaration of income to avoid taxes is illegal, but it is so widespread that no study of income distribution can ignore it. Between 1950 and 1953, the number of Federal income-tax returns reporting high incomes *declined,* a fact that the National Bureau of Economic Research, in view of "the almost certain increase in upper bracket salaries," found "puzzling" and meriting "close investigation."

In 1957, only 91 percent of the national personal money income was reported on individual income-tax returns, somewhat more than the 86 percent for 1944–46. The missing sum for 1957—$27.7 billion—comprised 3 percent ($7.1 billion) of wages and salaries paid, 14 percent ($1.6 billion) of distributed dividends, 58 percent ($5.5 billion) of interest, and 27 percent ($10.8 billion) of entrepreneurial income—the income of nonsalaried professionals, unincorporated businesses, and farmers. About the same amount of personal income is unreported in Census and Survey Research Center data. Obviously, the omission of income of this magnitude—especially if a large segment of it belongs in any single income-tenth—could produce a crucial distortion in the resulting income-distribution figures.

In 1952, spending units earning more than $10,000 owned more than 80 percent of the publicly held stock. So it is highly probable that spending units in the top tenth—in that year, those earning more than $7,090—received most of the unreported dividend income. The Bureau of Internal Revenue's sample audit of 1948 tax returns showed that those reporting $25,000-plus in income accounted for 7.2 percent of all returns with dividend errors and 38.4 percent of the dollar value of all errors, and that those reporting $7,000-plus in income accounted for 40.7 percent of all returns with dividend errors and 73.6 percent of the dollar value of all errors. Most interest-bearing savings, bonds, notes, etc., are owned by the top income-tenth, and thus a large segment of undeclared income in this category must be allocated to the economic elite. The 1948 tax audit found 52.6 percent of the dollar value of interest errors in the returns for the $7,000-plus bracket, the top income-tenth.

A good part of the existing income-distribution statistics fails to account for income earned in the corporate sector of the economy and—quite legally—not distributed to the owners of stock because of their desire to avoid high tax rates. But any nondistribution of corporate profits directly affects the income of the top income-tenth—especially of that small group within it that, as I will later show in detail, owns the vast bulk of stock. The relative importance of dividends grows with income, and above the $100,000 level, dividends are substantially larger than salary or wages. Since tax avoidance has become a primary concern of the highest income classes, especially since 1941, corporations increasingly retain dividends instead of distributing them. As Harvard economist William Crum has put it, "A group of wealthy directors owning stock in a closely held corporation may vote to retain earnings not so much because of the needs of the business as on account of the large surtaxes for which they would be personally liable were these earnings disbursed." In 1923–29, corporations withheld 27 percent of their net profits; in 1946–59 the figure was 51 percent. Had 1946–59 corporate profits been distributed at the 1923–29 rate, an average of $4.7 billion more in dividends would have been paid out annually to individuals, nearly all of them in the top income-tenth.

In this way, the economic elite can spread their dividend incomes evenly during fluctuations in the business cycle. Or they can increase the market value of their stock; then, if they sell it in the future, they will pay taxes on their profits at the much lower capital-gains rate. Corporations themselves have furthered this policy of personal tax avoidance since 1941 by sharply increased understatement and nonreporting of profits, accomplished by such devices as charging capital expenditures to current income. Thus the corporations represent vast income reserves for the economic elite.

If 1950 corporate profits had been distributed at the 1923–29 rate, the top income-tenth would have received 32 percent rather than 29 percent of the personal income. For 1952, they would have received 30 percent rather than 29 percent. In any postwar year, profits undistributed after allowing for a reasonable rate of corporate savings and self-financing would have added 1 to 4 percentage points to the share of the richest tenth. The value of corporate expense-account income-in-kind would have added at least 1 percentage point. Undeclared income, very conservatively assigning only one-third to one-half of it to the top tenth, would have added an additional 3 to 5 percentage points. Thus in 1952, for example, the top income-tenth actually accounted for at least 34 percent of all personal income rather than 29 percent.

THE DISTRIBUTION OF WEALTH: STOCK OWNERSHIP

The pattern of inequality that we have seen in the distribution of income also prevails in the larger picture—the distribution of stock, real estate, savings, and all other forms of wealth. Once again, we find the heavy concentration of holdings at the top, the thin scattering at the bottom.

The arresting fact is that, as of 1953, the 9 percent at the top of the income groupings owned more than 46 percent of the nation's net private assets. And, in that same year, the wealthiest 11 percent of spending units—those having a net worth of $25,000 and up—owned 60 percent of the private assets, according to the Survey Research Center.

Almost all the theorists who contend there has been a redistribution of wealth in America concentrate their attention on one form of assets—stock shares in corporations. In a characteristic statement, Ernest van den Haag writes: "Corporate ownership is no longer confined to the upper classes. An increasing proportion of industry, of the productive wealth of the country, is owned by the middle- and lower-income brackets. Their money is becoming indispensable for investment, because the rich no longer can save enough to provide for all the investment needs of the economy. This shift in the ownership of wealth may be described as a peaceful, but not slow, process of socialization of the means of production."

This idea of "people's capitalism"—the official and highly publicized concept of the New York Stock Exchange and the Advertising Council—is shared by too many social scientists who should know better. Popular economists, such as Adolf A. Berle, Jr., and Peter F. Drucker, have suggested that stock ownership has become very widely diffused and that there are no longer any sizable concentrations of stock held among individuals. In reality, stock ownership, like every other form of wealth and assets, is very highly concentrated. This conclusion is supported by every reliable study of stock distribution in the United States.

The fact is that the concentration of stock ownership has shown no appreciable change since 1929. In that year, 51,000 individuals received one-half the value of the cash dividends received by all individual shareowners; in 1933 and 1937, this number was 45,000 and 61,000, respectively. Also, in 1937, some 6.6 percent of the population owned stock; this figure dropped to 5.1 percent in 1956, and not until 1959 had it increased to 7.9 percent.

Within the already small minority of the population owning stock, a very small percentage has always controlled the bulk of the stock, no matter how large the total number of stockholders. The Temporary National Economic

Committee studied the distribution of shares among the 8.5 million individuals owning stock in 1,710 major companies in 1937–39. It found that 4.0 percent of the owners of common stock held 64.9 percent of it, and 4.5 percent of the owners of preferred stock held 54.8 percent of it.

The Brookings Institution, in a study of 1951 stock ownership in 2,991 major corporations, discovered that only 2.1 percent of the common-stock shareholdings owned 58 percent of the common stock and that 1.1 percent of the preferred stockholdings owned 46 percent of the preferred stock. Thirty-one percent of the common-stock shareholdings owned 32 percent of the shares, and two-thirds of the common-stock shareholdings accounted for a mere one-tenth of the shares. J. Keith Butters, in *Effects of Taxation—Investment by Individuals* (1953), estimates that in 1949, the spending units owning $100,000 or more in marketable stocks—who made up about one-fifth of 1 percent of the total national spending units and 2 percent of the stockholders—owned between 65 and 71 percent of all the marketable stock held by individuals.

These data unavoidably understate the concentration of stocks held by the wealthy few, for 36 percent of the total stock in 1937, and 33 percent in 1951, was owned by fiduciaries, foundations, etc., and these nonindividual shares are excluded from the stock distributions given above. However, even though these holdings are not listed by individuals, they remain largely controlled by top-bracket stockholders primarily interested in devising means for avoiding various taxes.

TABLE II. THE DISTRIBUTION OF COMMON STOCK IN PUBLICLY OWNED CORPORATIONS IN 1951

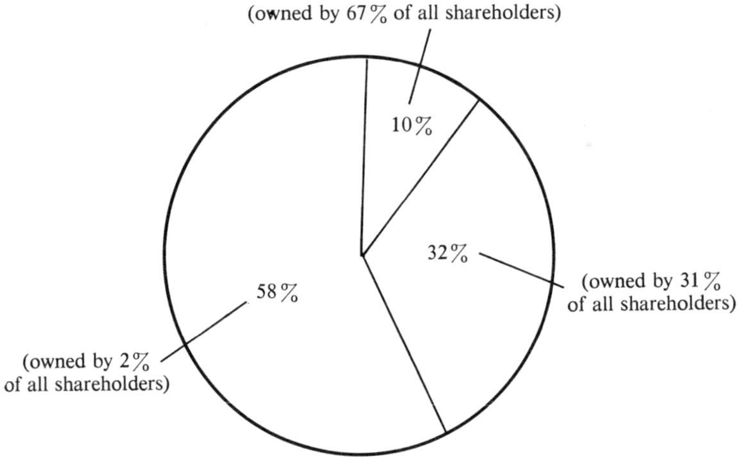

Source: Lewis H. Kimmel, *Share Ownership in the United States* (Washington, D.C.: Brookings Institution, 1952), pp. 43, 46.

As might be predicted, stock ownership is very inequitably distributed among the various income classes. In early 1959, only 14 percent of the nation's spending units owned stock; ownership ranged from 6 percent in the $5,000-or-less income class to 55 percent in the $15,000-or-more income class. The $10,000-plus income class accounted for more than half the stockholders and owned about 75 percent of the stock in 1949 and more than 80 percent in early 1952. In 1959, it accounted for nine-tenths of those with holdings of $25,000 and up.

Despite such conclusive data on stock-ownership concentration, the public has been subjected to a widespread advertising campaign alleging that the American corporation is owned democratically. They are told that the increase in the number of shareholders, from 6.5 million in 1952 to 12.5 million in 1959, is significant, even though there were 9 to 11 million stockholders in the smaller population of 1930. The annual stockholders' meeting is portrayed as a "town meeting," the epitome of democracy—despite the irony of a town meeting in which a few participants have most of the votes. Ignored is the fact that a growing number of these affairs are stage-managed by public-relations counselors, who are prepared for all contingencies. The conclusion is inevitable that there is little "people's" in "people's capitalism."

"People's capitalism" has drawn into the market persons ignorant of basic economics, many of whom have lost on their investments and have made the stock market more unstable during short-term political developments. Too many of these persons do little more than outright gambling in stocks. As a result, the Securities and Exchange Commission has been attempting since 1956 to curb the small but growing number of brokers seeking to sell nearly worthless securities to the public. Indeed, the only group consistently benefiting from the strong element of speculative mania in "people's capitalism" has been the brokers. In 1959, brokerage firms opened 203 new branch offices, compared to 73 the year before, and dozens of them moved into what the *Wall Street Journal* described as "bigger, plushier New York offices."

It is suggested that the supposedly growing ownership of stocks by worker pension funds and investment companies has made 50 million Americans indirect owners in the corporate structure, and that the proportionate returns of corporate profits to these Americans will rise as the holdings of pension and similar funds rapidly increase. "The corporate system," wrote Adolf A. Berle, Jr., in 1959, "is thus in effect operating to 'socialize' American industry but without intervention of the political state." Because pension funds and insurance companies supplied 10 to 15 percent of the industrial capital during the 1950's and are expected to supply even more throughout the 1960's, Berle foresaw the possibility of the managers of these funds achieving working control over the corporate structure.

However, this theory has a basic flaw. The trustees of these pension funds are not union officials, but, as Berle admits, primarily New York banks. These banks rarely vote their pension stockholdings, and they almost never oppose existing managerial control, since in most instances the employer has the right to transfer the pension account to another bank.

In nine out of ten instances, these funds buy no stock in their own corporation, and only occasionally have the total shares held by all pension funds amounted to more than 3 percent of the outstanding stock of any company. The pension funds are, in fact, a very long way from achieving control of the corporate system. At the end of 1959, the pension funds owned a mere 3.5 percent of all outstanding stock listed on the New York Stock Exchange. Robert Tilove, a pension-fund consultant, predicted in *Pension Funds and Economic Freedom* (1959) that by 1965, they would own no more than 6.5

percent. As more insured workers retire, the assets of the pension funds will decline, and their holdings will become even more inconsequential.

Investment companies, which owned 5.8 percent of the stock in 1959, are too limited by law to intimidate the corporations. Anyhow, they are hardly a force for democracy, since they are owned little more equitably than private stock.

We can only conclude that there has been an enormous exaggeration of the "socializing" effect of these institutions on the American corporation. Clearly, our only realistic yardstick for measuring the extent of democracy in corporate stockholding is the distribution of private ownership.

6 THE MILITARY INDUSTRIAL COMPLEX: NO WAY OUT*

by MICHAEL REICH
AND DAVID FINKELHOR[1]

What can be done about the Military Industrial Complex? Differences on this issue shed light on the nature of the disagreement between liberals and radicals. Examine these issues: "Is Waste endemic to capitalism?" Liberals see the MIC more or less as a blight on an economy that could otherwise easily be healthy and fruitful. The system could be restored to a productive operation if politicians would prune away the excessive military budget. Radicals say that capitalism has an endemic need for waste. Without a bottomless pit of military expenditures the system would collapse.

"Is the state really subservient to corporate power?" Here again, liberals feel that government has conspired in the creation of the MIC only in spite of itself. The majority of government officials are independent and enlightened but have been bamboozled and railroaded by a small group of military officials and their Congressional pimps, who used to their own ends their monopoly of information on our defense capabilities. Radicals emphasize the deliberateness with which the system was created. The most powerful corporate interests, rather than Machiavellian militarists, were the moving force behind the complex. They used their natural political power and the promise of economic benefits for one and all, not deceit, to build a massive interest group (including liberal politicians) behind the complex.

"Can capitalism reform itself and eliminate the MIC?" Liberals have been very sanguine. They point to the sincere desire of many liberal politicians to cut the heart out of the military budget. They point out the alternative possible outlets for government spending. Radicals think the MIC is in many ways synonymous with capitalism and cannot be eliminated so long as capitalism remains. The MIC is too fundamental to the system's stability, and too many powerful capitalist interests have a stake in it. This is the argument put forth by the following article.

Why does the United States spend $80 billion each year on military expenditures? Why are resources allocated so irrationally when basic social needs go unmet both within the United States and in the rest of the world? Much effort has gone into decrying this state of affairs, but not enough has gone into analyz-

* Used by permission of the authors.

[1] Our debts to Paul Sweezy and Paul Baran will be obvious to readers familiar with *Monopoly Capital,* New York, 1966. Much of the present article was precipitated in discussions among members of the Union for Radical Political Economics at Harvard.

ing its structural roots. Despite outward appearances presented by the media, the analyses of liberals and radicals are not very similar. Although liberals and radicals both agree that the resources commanded by the military are much too large, they disagree quite sharply on what is required to eliminate the war machine. This article explores these differences from a radical viewpoint.

Liberals concede that the problem of militarism is difficult, but argue that it is solvable. We can "convert" our national priorities from weapons to socially useful purposes without rearranging or too drastically upsetting the institutions basic to our economy and government.

Radicals, on the other hand, argue that the problem is not solvable; militarism is too intertwined with the basic structure of capitalist society. Only a social revolution and the establishment of a socialist society can eliminate militarist priorities.

Liberals see the problem of "conversion" as basically a political one. Politicians need to and can be convinced of the wastefulness of our militarized priorities. Corporations need to and can be convinced that alternative opportunities are available in other undertakings. Once the public is firmly persuaded and the necessary conversion studies have been made, the road to legislating away the military budget will have been cleared.

Radicals do not find this argument persuasive. It is based on a faulty analysis of how the military budget grew to its present size, and it minimizes the nature of the obstacles that exist to pulling it up from its roots. Far from being a political aberration, the development of the $80 billion military establishment is a phenomenon rooted in the nature of our economic system. Military spending is an integral feature of the development of domestic and international capitalism.

In this paper, we will sketch a critique of the liberal analysis of military spending. We shall focus primarily on the domestic aspects of militarism—its roots in the domestic economy and the obstacles to its "conversion." We begin with an outline of the liberal analysis and the radical challenge to that analysis. We then analyze in greater detail the impact of the military sector on the economy and consider some of its unique advantages for corporate capitalism. Finally, we discuss the obstacles to conversion inherent in the *domestic* economy.[2]

THE LIBERAL OPTIMISM

The liberal analysis can be outlined as follows:

1. Liberals like to lay the blame for the growth of the military budget on the doorstep of an unchecked troika. In their demonology, a scheming set of restless militarists in the Pentagon combined with a few large military contractors and enlisted the help of some "Neanderthal" Congressmen (mostly Southerners) to get the ball rolling. The Pentagon militarists used their privi-

[2] For purposes of exposition, we shall have to ignore the interrelations of militarism with other major social problems of America, such as inequality and poverty, the special subjugation of women and blacks, alienation, the destruction of community and of the environment, etc. See R. Edwards, A. MacEwan and others, "A Radical Approach to Economics," *American Economic Review*, May, 1970, for a discussion of the interrelations of these issues.

leged access to security to scare other Congressmen and the general public into support of massive defense expenditures. The contractors used the prospects of bringing the pork back to the home constituency to win over more legislators, while the Neanderthal Congressmen wheeled and dealt from their powerful positions of seniority in the important Congressional committees.

There are different versions of this analysis, some seeing conspiratorial political intrigue, others seeing only the confluence of mutual interests; some place more of the blame on politicians, others more on the corporate elite. But for our purposes, the difference among these views is not of central importance in understanding the outcome. All these liberal views emphasize the politics of bureaucracy and characterize militarism as essentially a political aberration.

The emphasis on the image of the Military-Industrial Complex as a subverter of the normal political process is crucial to the liberals' side of the story. What has been created politically can, by implication, be dismantled politically. Liberals feel confident that by strengthening the anti-military coalition in Congress and by achieving stricter supervision of the defense bureaucracy in the Executive branch, the basic combination that feeds and fuels the Military-Industrial Complex can be broken down.

2. The liberal conversion strategy is based on a second assumption that minimizes the dangers of the withdrawal of military spending from the economy. Keynesianism expounded by liberal economists says that any form of government spending is just as good as any other for the purposes of stimulating the economy, maintaining aggregate demand and keeping down the level of unemployment. Thus spending for needed social services could easily replace military spending without the economy's falling into depression. There are no economic obstacles to substituting for military expenditures; it is just a question of using the political process to change the particular mix of goods and services purchased by the government each year.

To bolster this claim, the liberals point out that the Federal government has in the past significantly reduced the scale of military expenditures, for example, after World War II and the Korean War. These cutbacks did not result in economic collapse. Furthermore, many other advanced capitalist economies, Sweden and Japan for example, spend relatively small amounts of their Gross National Product on military goods and services. Hence, there is a prima facie case that capitalist prosperity does not depend on a large military sector. The only economic obstacle to conversion is the problem of retraining workers with overly specialized skills.

3. Finally, what about the possibility of great corporate opposition to reductions in the military budget? The liberal analysis handles this problem, too. Although conversion is sure to hurt some important companies, these contractors constitute an economic enclave. There are a few large but isolated corporations who do most of the government work; they will have to suffer at first. They will, of course, kick and scream, but the other segments of the corporate community can be brought to see the wisdom of demilitarization and will provide more than adequate counterpressure. These are the three cornerstones of liberal optimism.

The radical analysis challenges the liberal approach at every step. In the first place, the militarism was not the creation of simple conspiracy nor subversion of the normal institutions. Military spending was the American system's only workable solution to the dangerous and profound crisis created by the Depression of the 1930's. No other solution is available which could adequately stem an inherent tendency towards economic crisis.

Although particular interests do benefit more than others, this military spending solution has had the tacit support of all the elements of the American ruling circles. The military sector is not an enclave. Its tentacles are implanted deep in the heart of the capitalist economy, and it is entirely fused with it. The vast majority of politicians, corporate executives and military officials have all contributed to its growth and each has benefited. Today they all stand to lose to some degree from the dismantling of the military-industrial establishment.

In the second place, the liberals' faith that equivalent forms of non-military spending can be found to substitute for military spending is a completely abstract one. An adequate substitute for the role military spending presently plays with respect to the economy would have to be equivalent in magnitude and expandability. But the social welfare spending alternatives proposed by many liberals are not an acceptable and expandable alternative. Such spending is neither economically feasible nor politically possible. It disrupts work incentives, profitability in the private sector and other key aspects of a capitalist economy. It also jeopardizes the existing structure of privilege, thus mobilizing the opposition of powerful vested interests.

In the remainder of this paper, we shall try to demonstrate the indispensability of militarism to the domestic economy. But this will, in effect, be only half of the radical argument. We also believe that the militarization of the economy is an integral part of American capitalism because of the natural importance of international operations to capitalism. While we have chosen not to examine this aspect of the argument in any detail here, a few words on the subject are necessary before passing on to the main body of the paper.

Liberals and radicals are both aware of the connection between the existence of the military-industrial establishment and America's international involvements. But once again they differ on whether militarization is essential to those involvements.

Liberals tend to see the Cold War as once justified, but now abating. The present overmilitarization stems from an over-extension of international military commitments, the legacy of a period of hysterical anticommunism. As United States leaders see the counterproductive nature of military intervention, the pressures for aggressively maintaining an overseas empire will slacken. When it does, militarization at home will also decline.

Radicals argue that the militarization of foreign policy and extensions of worldwide commitments are here to stay. The American role in the Cold War was not a response to Soviet aggression, but part of a strategy of capitalist encirclement of the Communist countries. American foreign policy is an outgrowth of the need to protect overseas economic expansion, to integrate the entire globe into the international capitalist system, and to maintain the dollar as the world's key currency. It also requires the containment of socialism and of national liberation movements. These goals imply a huge military machine. The United States could not fundamentally dismantle its international military operations without fatal harm to the process of capitalist development and growth.

THE IMPACT OF MILITARY SPENDING ON THE ECONOMY

Before World War II, military spending never exceeded 1 percent of the Gross National Product. Over $1 trillion have been spent on the military since 1951, consuming each year at least 9 percent of the GNP. In 1969, the United States spent about $80 billion on the military, about 10 percent of the total GNP. In 1967, 4.08 million civilian employees worked on defense-related jobs; add to this the 3.5 million soldiers in uniform and we have well over 10 percent of the entire labor force engaged in military-related employment.

The military sector of the economy is huge. Yet the image of the weapons industry often projected by liberals is of a small, albeit powerful, coterie of contractors, many of whom owe their existence solely to defense work. Producing exotic military hardware, these corporations form an economic *enclave* somehow separated from the remainder of the economy.[3]

According to the enclave view, most corporations in the country are not affected one way or another by the military budget (except, of course, insofar as aggregate incomes and demands are stimulated). There is some superficial evidence for this image. After all, only one hundred corporations receive over two thirds of all prime contract awards each year and fifty corporations receive 60 percent, and the list of the top one hundred contractors has exhibited very little turnover in the last twenty years.[4] Prime contract awards are concentrated among just four industries: aircraft (43%), electronics and telecommunications (19.3%), shipbuilding and repairing (10.3%) and ammunition (5%).[5] Moreover, subcontracts appear to be just as concentrated among the big firms.[6]

But this enclave image is highly misleading. First, a list of the top military contractors is virtually a list of all the largest and most powerful industrial corporations in America. (See Table I.) Nathanson estimates that, of the five hundred largest manufacturing corporations in 1964, *at least* 205 were significantly involved in military production, either because of the company's primary product, or its research and development contracts, or because of its diversification into the military market.[7] Among the top one hundred firms, sixty-five are significantly involved in the military market. As Table I shows, all but five of the largest twenty-five industrial corporations in 1968 were among the one hundred largest contractors for the Defense Department. Of these five, one—Union Carbide—is the largest Atomic Energy Commission contractor, two are oil companies indirectly involved in military sales, and one is a steel company also indirectly involved. It is difficult to think of these top corporations as constituting an "enclave."

[3] Emile Benoit, "The Economic Impact of Disarmament in the United States," in S. Melman, (ed.), *Disarmament: Its Politics and Economics* (Boston, 1962).

[4] W. Baldwin, *The Structure of the Defense Market, 1955–64* (Durham, 1967), p. 9.

[5] Research Analysis Corporation, "Economic Impact Analysis" in U.S. Congress, Joint Economic Committee, *Economic Effect of Vietnam Spending,* 1967, Vol. II, p. 827.

[6] M. Peck and F. Scherer, *The Weapons Acquisition Process,* (Boston, 1962), pp. 150–152, and M. Weidenbaum, *The Modern Public Sector* (New York, 1969), p. 40.

[7] C. Nathanson, "The Militarization of the American Economy," in D. Horowitz (ed.), *Corporations and the Cold War* (New York, 1969), p. 231.

TABLE I

The table below lists the top 25 contractors for the Pentagon, the Atomic Energy Commission and the National Aeronautics and Space Administration and the top 25 names on *Fortune* magazine's directory of the 500 largest industrial corporations. Note that only five of the 25 biggest corporations are not among the 100 largest contractors for the Defense Department, and one of the five, Union Carbide, is the largest A.E.C. contractor. Also noteworthy is the high coincidence of names on the Pentagon, A.E.C. and NASA lists. The table suggests that defense contracting is extremely attractive to big business.

Largest Defense Contractors			Largest Industrial Corporations[d]
Pentagon[a]	A.E.C.[b]	NASA[c]	
1 General Dynamics	1 Union Carbide	1 North American Rockwell	1 General Motors (10)[e]
2 Lockheed	2 Sandia Corp.	2 Grumman	2 Standard Oil (N.J.) (25)
3 General Electric	3 General Electric	3 Boeing	3 Ford (19)
4 United Aircraft	4 DuPont	4 McDonnell-Douglas	4 General Electric (3)
5 McDonnell-Douglas	5 Reynolds Electrical	5 General Electric	5 Chrysler (43)
6 A.T. & T.	6 Westinghouse	6 I.B.M.	6 Mobil (51)
7 Boeing	7 Bendix	7 Bendix	7 I.B.M. (30)
8 Ling Temco Vought	8 Holmes & Narver	8 Aerojet-General	8 Texaco (46)
9 North American Rockwell	9 Douglas United Nuclear	9 RCA	9 Gulf Oil (78)
10 General Motors	10 Dow Chemical	10 Chrysler	10 U.S. Steel (60)
11 Grumman	11 Goodyear Atomic	11 General Dynamics	11 A.T. & T. (6)
12 AVCO	12 Idaho Nuclear	12 TRW	12 Standard Oil (Calif.) (49)
13 Textron	13 Aerojet-General	13 General Motors	13 DuPont (38)
14 Litton	14 Atlantic Richfield	14 Ling Temco Vought	14 Shell Oil
15 Raytheon	15 E.G. & G.	15 Lockheed	15 RCA (26)
16 Sperry-Rand	16 Gulf General Atomic	16 Philco-Ford	16 McDonnell-Douglas (5)
17 Martin Marietta	17 Monsanto	17 Sperry Rand	17 Standard Oil (Ind.)
18 Kaiser Industries	18 Kerr-McGee	18 Martin Marietta	18 Westinghouse (27)
19 Ford	19 National Lead	19 T.W.A.	19 Boeing (7)
20 Honeywell	20 Mason & Hanger	20 Federal Electric	20 Swift
21 Olin Mathieson	21 North American Rockwell	21 Catalytic-Dow (joint venture)	21 I.T. & T. (29)
22 Northrop	22 Homestake-Sapin	22 United Aircraft	22 Goodyear Tire & Rubber (48)
23 Ryan Aeronautical	23 United Nuclear	23 Brown Engineering	23 General Telephone & Electronics (41)
24 Hughes	24 Pan American	24 Honeywell	24 Bethlehem Steel
25 Standard Oil (N.J.)	25 Phillips Petroleum	25 Control Data	25 Union Carbide

[a] 100 Companies & Their Subsidiary Corporations Listed According to Net Value of Military Prime Contract Awards (Fiscal Year 1968), Department of Defense.
[b] Annual Report for 1968, Atomic Energy Commission.
[c] Annual Procurement Report, NASA (Fiscal Year 1968).
[d] 500 Largest U.S. Industrial Corporations, Fortune Directory (1968).
[e] Number in parentheses indicates rank among 100 largest Defense Department contractors.
From Richard Kaufman, "We Must Guard Against Unwarranted Influence by the Military-Industrial Complex," *The New York Times Magazine*, June 22, 1969.

Second, there are no self-contained enclaves in the American economy. As the study of input-output economics has revealed, the structure of American industry is highly interdependent. Focusing only on the prime contractors is like looking at only the visible part of an iceberg. This is only the direct impact of the military budget; the indirect impact on subcontractors, on producers of intermediate goods and parts, and on suppliers of raw materials ties military spending into the heart of the economy. For evidence, look at Table II, which indicates the wide range of industries over which direct and indirect effects of military spending were distributed in 1967. With the exception of the aircraft

TABLE II. DISTRIBUTION OF PRIVATE EMPLOYMENT ATTRIBUTABLE TO MILITARY EXPENDITURES IN 1967

Sector	Percent of total military-related employment in sector
1. Agriculture, forestry and fisheries	2.5
2. Mining	1.3
3. Construction	2.3
4. Ordnance and accessories	6.2
5. Textile and apparel products	3.4
6. Chemicals and allied products	2.1
7. Petroleum and refining	0.5
8. Rubber and plastic products	1.1
9. Other nondurable goods manufacturing[a]	3.5
10. Primary metals	4.5
11. Fabricated metals	2.9
12. Machinery, not electrical	5.9
13. Electrical equipment and supplies	13.3
14. Aircraft and parts	16.0
15. Other transportation equipment	3.2
16. Instruments	1.9
17. Other durable goods manufacturing[b]	2.6
18. Miscellaneous manufacturing	0.3
19. Transportation and warehousing	6.9
20. Communications and public utilities	2.1
21. Wholesale and retail trade	5.6
22. Finance, insurance and real estate	2.1
23. Business services	4.3
24. Medical, educational services and nonprofit organizations	3.2
25. Other services	1.7
Total, manufacturing	68.0
Total, all private employment	100.0

[a] Food and kindred products, tobacco, paper and related products, printing and publishing, leather and leather products.

[b] Lumber and wood products, furntiure and fixtures, stone, clay and glass products.

From R. Oliver, "The Employment Effect of Defense Expenditures," *Monthly Labor Review*, Sept. 1967, Table I, pp. 10–11.

and electrical equipment industries, no one industry accounted for more than 7 percent of total private military-related employment. Aircraft and parts accounted for 16 percent, and electrical equipment and supplies accounted for 13 percent. This industrial profile shows that, despite the enclave image, a broad spectrum of the domestic corporate economy is involved in military production.

Third, corporations in the civilian market have been racing to get a piece of the military action. Between 1959 and 1962, years for which a study was done, "manufacturing firms outside the defense sector purchased 137 companies in the defense sector (i.e., aircraft and parts, ships and boats, ordnance, electrical machinery, scientific instruments and computers)." By 1966, 93 of the top 500 manufacturing firms had diversified into the defense sector from a traditional nondefense base.[8]

Military spending is very important for a large number of industries within manufacturing. As Table III shows, about 11.5 percent of all manufacturing

TABLE III. DIRECT AND INDIRECT DEPENDENCE OF INDUSTRIAL SECTORS ON MILITARY EXPENDITURES, 1958

Sector	Percent of total output attributable to military
1. Food and kindred products	1.6
2. Apparel and textile mill products	1.9
3. Leather products	3.1
4. Paper and allied products	7.0
5. Chemicals and allied products	5.3
6. Fuel and power	7.3
7. Rubber and rubber products	5.6
8. Lumber and wood products	3.9
9. Nonmetallic minerals and products	4.7
10. Primary metals	13.4
11. Fabricated metal products	8.0
12. Machinery, except electrical	5.2
13. Electrical equipment and supplies	20.8
14. Transportation equipment and ordnance	38.4
15. Instruments and allied products	20.0
16. Miscellaneous manufacturing industries	2.8
17. Transportation	5.9
18. Construction	2.1
Average, metalworking industries (Sectors 10–15)	19.9
Average, all manufacturing (Sectors 1–16)	11.5
Average, Sectors 1–18	9.6

Computed from W. Leontief and M. Hoffenberg, "The Economic Impact of Disarmament," *Scientific American*, April, 1961.

output in 1958 is attributable to military-related expenditures; the corresponding figure is 20 percent for the metalworking production sector, comprised of metals and metal products, nonelectrical machinery, electrical equipment and supplies, transportation equipment, ordnance, and instruments. The percentage of profits attributable to military spending are probably even higher, given that profit rates are higher on military contracts—as is shown below.

Within the key metalworking sector, a broad range of industries are dependent on miiltary sales, as Table IV shows.[9] The importance of the metal-

[8] *Ibid.*, pp. 215–216.

[9] Note that defense-related employment in 1967 in each industry is lower than defense-related production in 1958. This suggests that defense-related production is more capital intensive than civilian production, i.e., fewer jobs are generated by each dollar of government military spending than by each dollar of nonmilitary spending. The implications of this result are discussed below. The differences between the columns is *not* accounted for by the use of two points in time, nine years apart.

working sector in the domestic economy can be seen from the following statistics cited by Nathanson: in 1962, metalworking industries accounted for more than 47 percent of all manufacturing employment, 41 percent of total expenditures for plant and equipment, and 40 percent of the total value added in manufacturing.[10] And Table IV indicates that military-related demand

TABLE IV. DEPENDENCE OF SELECTED INDUSTRIES ON MILITARY EXPENDITURES

Industry	(1) Percent of Total Industry Sales Attributable to Federal Expenditures, 1958[a]	(2) Percent of Total Industry Employment Attributable to Defense Expenditures, 1967
Ordnance and accessories	86.7	64.8
Primary iron and steel manufacturing	12.5	8.8
Primary nonferrous metals	22.3	13.6
Stamping, screw machine products	18.2	10.2
Other fabricated metal products	11.9	6.4
Engines and turbines	19.7	11.5
Materials handling machinery and equipment	17.2	7.7
Metalworking machinery and equipment	20.6	11.2
General industrial machinery and equipment	15.3	7.7
Machine shop products	39.0	23.3
Electric industrial equipment and apparatus	17.0	11.3
Electric lighting and wiring equipment	14.5	8.0
Electronic components and accessories	38.9	26.1
Miscellaneous electrical machinery, equipment and supplies	15.1	8.3
Aircraft and parts	86.7	59.1
Other transportation equipment	10.1	22.5
Scientific and controlling instruments	30.2	14.2

[a] Military sales account for 85 percent of total government demand in these industries.
Sources:
1. U.S. Dept. of Labor, *Monthly Labor Review*, September 1967.
2. U.S. Dept. of Commerce, *Survey of Current Business*, November 1964.

accounted for at least 10 percent of 1958 sales for every detailed industry in the sector. A 1964 *Steel* magazine survey of 5,000 metalworking plants found that 40 percent were producing directly for the Pentagon; of these, 71 percent said that at least 31 percent of their output was for the military.[11]

[10] Nathanson, *op. cit.*, p. 223.
[11] *Ibid.*

HOW GREAT A STAKE IN THE MILITARY

Having seen that the Military-Industrial Complex comprises the very heart of Capitalist America, we can now ask what stake the economy has in the existence of this Leviathan.

First, we shall point out the stake of the most privileged and powerful segments of the economy. Military spending is in large part responsible for the increasing concentration of economic power in the hands of a small group. It plays a role in the perpetuation of substantial inequality among the population as a whole. And it is a key factor behind the profitability of many of America's largest corporations.

But we shall go further and argue that the entire capitalist economy has a stake in militarism. For military spending is responsible for most of the economic growth the country has experienced in the postwar period. Without militarism, the whole economy would return to the state of collapse from which it was rescued by the Second World War.

Military spending has been a key force behind the trend toward increasing concentration of economic power. We have already observed that prime contract awards are concentrated among a small number of corporations: fifty firms in an average year get 60 percent of the procurement contract dollar, about 94 percent of the research, development and testing contract dollar.[12] This makes the war industry much more concentrated than the economy as a whole, where the top one hundred firms usually account for only 35 percent of the manufacturing sales. The business of the war industry goes to the biggest firms and is used by them as a base from which to expand their area of control. So it is not surprising that between 1947 and 1963 the top two hundred industrial corporations boosted by defense business, increased their share of total value added in the economy from 30 percent to 41 percent.[13]

Let's look at the increasing concentration produced by military spending on an industry level. Almost all of military spending goes to the most concentrated industries in the economy. The standard measure of concentration in an industry is the percentage of sales accounted for by the top four firms. Four firms monopolized over 50 percent of the sales in about one third of all manufacturing industries in 1963.[14] But 90 percent of all military contracts went to these most concentrated industries. The most powerful elements in the economy have a large stake in the military production because of the opportunities it provides them to increase the concentration of their economic control.

Military spending has also created privileged interest groups within the occupational structure; it is an important factor tying many professionals, universities and labor union leaders to government policy. A large number of the most highly trained people in the economy owe their jobs to defense spending. For example, nearly half of all engineers and scientists employed in private industry are at work on military or space-related projects. Many of the scientists and engineers pursuing research in the universities receive money from the Pentagon.

[12] A. D. Little Co., "How Sick Is the Defense Industry" (1963).
[13] U.S. Census of Manufacturers, 1963, *Concentration Ratios in Manufacturing.*
[14] *Ibid.*

The military industries generally employ a highly skilled work force. A 1962 Department of Labor study of the electronics industry showed that at military-space-oriented plants 59.2 percent of employees were highly paid engineers, executives or skilled blue-collar craftsmen. In the consumer-oriented plants of the same electronics industry, in contrast, 70.2 percent of the employees were semiskilled and unskilled blue- and white-collar workers.[15] Professional and managerial workers comprise 22 percent of all private defense-related employment, but only 15 percent of all United States manufacturing employment.[16] Thus, a large proportion of the people in the most educated strata, many still university-based, are tied by military spending to a vested interest in existing national priorities. A large number of blue-collar workers are engaged in military-related work. The carrot the government can dangle in front of major union leaders has been a factor in their growing conservatism and endorsement of Cold War policies.

Military spending has a regressive impact on the distribution of income, i.e., benefits the rich and hurts the poor. This is suggested by the higher proportion of skilled workers in defense-related work. Computations by economist Wassily Leontief show that one dollar of military spending generates half as many jobs, but 20 percent more in salaries, then does one dollar of civilian spending.[17] This means that tax money extracted from the whole population is paid out in such a way as to benefit high earners much more than low earners. This is not just an accident. Military spending is one of the mechanisms by which higher income groups use the government to prevent redistribution of income from taking place.

Last, but not least, the military sector is a source of enormous profits for the corporate elite. It is an organized system of governmental subsidy for corporate coffers, or as C. Wright Mills called it, "Socialism for the rich." We can see how deeply wedded the corporate giants are to this arrangement by examining the opportunities the military sector presents to them.

ATTRACTIVENESS OF THE MILITARY MARKET

The attractiveness of the military market to big corporations—the opportunities for growth and fantastic profits—has been described by a number of journalists and muckrakers.[18] In recent years the hearings conducted by the Senate Subcommittee on Economy in Government (chaired by Senator William Proxmire) have provided further glimpses into the shadowy world of the military contractor. The mass media have reported horror stories from these hearings, and tales of corporate greediness and bureaucratic favoritism gleaned from the Proxmire investigations have been retold in excellent analyses by Henry Nieburg, Walter Adams, Richard Kaufman, and by the Proxmire Committee

[15] Bureau of Labor Statistics, *Bulletin*, 1963, October 1963, p. 37.

[16] *Monthly Labor Review*, May 1964, p. 514.

[17] From W. Leontief and M. Hoffenberg, "The Economic Impact of Disarmament," *Scientific American*, April 1961, p. 9, and Leontief et al., "The Economic Effect—Industrial and Regional—of an Arms Cut," *Review of Economics and Statistics*, August 1965.

[18] For example: F. Cook, *The Warfare State* (New York, 1961); V. Perlo, *Militarism and Industry* (New York, 1963); B. Nossiter, *The Mythmakers* (Boston, 1964), ch. 5.

itself (in its pamphlet, *The Economics of Military Procurement*).[19] The reader is strongly urged to examine one or more of these documentations of the waste and profiteering endemic to the military sector of the economy. These studies reveal that the excesses and horror stories presented in the mass media about the military contracting business are far from isolated or atypical examples. Where these studies fall short, however, is in failing to emphasize that the waste and profiteering have a systematic basis: the structure of the military market differs in several important respects from markets in the civilian economy.

Unlike other industries, military contract work is not determined in a "market" at all, in any usually understood sense of the word. Contracts are arrived at through negotiations between a company and Pentagon contracting officers. The arrangement is rife with opportunities for the companies. Government as purchaser is alleged to have the same interest as a private consumer in cutting costs and buying only what is needed. In fact, this is not the case. First of all, procurement officers—who represent the government in these affairs—have an interest as military men in expanding the arsenal of weapons and thus the power and prestige of their branch of service. And so long as there is slack in the economy, higher-ups don't pressure them to hold down costs. Secondly, if they are on the lookout for their future in the business world, and they are, they have the most appealing reasons for currying the favor of the corporations with whom they are supposed to "bargain." When they retire, many military men involved in procurement regulation go directly to jobs in one of the defense companies. In 1967, 2,072 retired regular military officers were employed by the ninety-five top contractors. The top ten contractors had an average of 106 former officers a piece on their payrolls.[20]

Contracting is supposed to take place competitively. In fact, it almost never does. Any one of a catalogue full of excuses can be reason for bypassing the competitive bidding procedure, e.g., if the item is critical, if delivery is urgent, if security considerations preclude it, etc.; 90 percent of the Pentagon's contract dollars are negotiated under such "exceptions." [21]

The exotic technologies involved in weapons provide a perfect opportunity for boondoggles. Only specialists understand what is a superfluous and what is a necessary expenditure. This allows for enormous padding and excessive costs, as a number of Senate investigations have charged. A contractor may sell the Pentagon a $2 billion missile when a $1 billion one would have worked equally well. Subcontracting creates the opportunity for pyramiding profits on multiple tiers of subcontracts. Moreover, once a contractor has done some work on a weapons system—whether in another contract or in a research and development study—he obtains a virtual monopoly over the area. Since he is the only one with relevant experts and the relevant experience, the government is stuck with giving him the business. It is practically impossible to oversee and account for the operations in these areas. Both the complex technology and security considerations bar most outsiders.

[19] H. Nieburg, *In the Name of Science* (Chicago, 1966); W. Adams, "The Military-Industrial Complex and the New Industrial State," *American Economic Review,* May 1968; R. Kaufman, "We Must Guard Against Unwarranted Influence by the Military-Industrial Complex," *The New York Times Magazine,* June 22, 1969; U.S. Congress, Joint Economic Committee print, *The Economics of Military Procurement* (May 1969).
[20] R. Kaufman, *op. cit.,* p. 70.
[21] *The Economics of Military Procurement,* p. 4.

So there is no bad blood created when costs of production far overrun those that were written into the contract. Final costs average 320 percent of original cost estimates.[22] That is, the average contractor ends up charging the government over three times the cost estimate he initially submitted to win the contract. His profits go up three times also.

Companies do not lose their privileged status if their weapons do not meet up to specifications or perform properly. A recent study of thirteen major aircraft and missile programs since 1955, which cost in total $40 billion, revealed that only four of these (costing $5 billion) performed at as much as 75 percent of the design specifications. Yet the companies with the poorest performance record reported the highest profits.[23]

What this all amounts to, of course, is that profits for defense work are higher than those in every industry except pharmaceuticals. This is obscured by the Defense Department which sometimes releases profits computed as a percentage of sales or costs. But, in the normal business world, profits are figured as a percentage of *investment*. Defense contractors invest very little of their own money because in most cases the government provides most of the investment and working capital needed by contractors to set up plants and machinery and to buy the necessary materials and parts. The profits when measured against investment are often huge.

A study by Murray Weidenbaum, formerly an economist for the Boeing Company and now an Assistant Secretary of the Treasury, of a sample of large defense contractors showed that between 1962 and 1965 they earned 17.5 percent on investment, compared to average civilian market earnings of 10.6 percent.[24] And this probably understates the case. Many military contractors also sell in the civilian market. The machinery provided free by the Pentagon, the allocation of all overhead costs to military contracts, and the technological edge gained in cost-plus military contracts can be of enormous importance in increasing profits on *civilian* sales for firms doing some business with the Pentagon. In one of the most outrageous cases that has come to light, a tax court showed in 1962 that North American Aviation Co. had realized profits of 612 percent and 802 percent on contracts in two successive years.[25]

Everyone—except the Pentagon, of course—agrees that laxity and profiteering are part and parcel of military procurement. Liberals take this to be indicative of the way in which the military complex has escaped the normal checks and balances of the political process. To radicals, this seems a gross understatement of reality. Politicians, bureaucrats and businessmen all know that these "excesses" exist. These "excesses" are not a subversion of normal government procedure—they are the normal government procedure. Waste is winked at because the entire economy has a stake in it.

Of course, military men dabble in corrupt practices. Of course, large corporations use strong-arm pressures to obtain favors. But waste of this magnitude is neither simple profiteering nor economic gangsterism. Massive, wasteful military spending is allowed to exist because it fulfills a need of the system as a

[22] Peck and Scherer, *op. cit.*
[23] *The Economics of Military Procurement,* p. 1.
[24] Weidenbaum, *op. cit.,* p. 56.
[25] R. Kaufman, *op. cit.*

whole. The waste is what helps military spending fulfill its function: providing a cushion to ward off stagnation and economic crisis.

MILITARY SPENDING AND STAGNATION

Among liberal optimists, one used to be able to find those who argued that government spending of any kind could be cut with no ill effects on long-run economic growth. The money freed from spending could be returned to taxpayers and corporations in the form of tax cuts. This would quickly be ploughed back into the economy in the form of increased consumption and increased investment—no slowdown necessary. There are few proponents of this view left.

Most everybody understands today that high levels of government spending are necessary for economic stability and growth. Economists such as John Maynard Keynes and Alvin Hansen, on the one hand, and Paul Baran and Paul Sweezy, on the other, have argued that monopoly capitalism has an inherent tendency to stagnate.[26] The Depression of the thirties illustrated the incredible levels of unemployment and business lethargy the system would generate if left alone.[27] Only World War II showed how to cope with the problem. Massive levels of government spending in defense were necessary to create demand and alleviate unemployment.[28]

In the post-war period too, military spending has been responsible for a large part of the economic growth that has taken place. The fluctuation of military spending has virtually determined the cyclical pattern of the economy. Declines in military spending have been followed by declines in overall economic growth. Those sectors of the economy that spurred economic growth when it did take place were generally sectors highly involved with the military. That includes the aerospace, the communications and the electronics industries. These have been among the fastest-growing industries in the economy in the post-war period. This is easy to understand, since the Pentagon has underwritten much of the technological development that has occurred in the economy: 75 percent of all research

[26] See P. Sylos-Labini, *Oligopoly and Technical Progress* (Cambridge, 1969) as well as P. Baran, *The Political Economy of Growth* (New York, 1957); Baran and Sweezy, *op. cit.;* Alvin Hansen, *The Post-War American Economy* (New York, 1961), and J. M. Keynes, *The General Theory of Employment, Interest and Money* (1936).

[27] An elaborate econometric study of the post-war period by the economist Bert Hickman concluded that, without the stimulus of government spending, the rate of economic growth in the United States would have been substantially lower. See B. Hickman, *Investment Demand and U.S. Economic Growth* (Brookings Institution, 1965).

[28] Not all advanced capitalist countries have leaned on military spending to the extent the United States has. In part this is because the United States, as the most industrialized country in the world, has the greatest problem of inadequate aggregate demand. But there is more to American militarism than this. After World War II, the United States emerged as by far the dominant leader of the worldwide capitalist system. It took on the task of defending the "Free World." This requires a large military establishment, and the United States, the only country with its industrial economy intact after World War II, was the only country capable of taking on this role. The resultant political-military leverage has helped U.S. exports and the key position of the dollar. Furthermore, the necessity of rebuilding in Western Europe and Japan postponed aggregate demand problems in these countries for almost two decades—the destruction of antiquated machinery also removed some of the fetters on production. Hence, the United States was far more in need of a stimulus for demand than other advanced capitalist countries. Finally, the tradition of etatism is much stronger in Western Europe, where most governmental functions are highly centralized. The decentralized and multi-level nature of government in the United States provides an additional fetter on civilian government spending.

and development activity in the country is paid for by the government, and of this 50 percent is disbursed directly by the Defense Department, and another 38 percent by the defense-related NASA and AEC.[29]

Liberals do not deny that arms spending has served the necessary function of averting stagnation. But they argue that other forms of public sector spending are equally feasible. Instead of weapons, the Federal government could sponsor vast projects to improve health, education, housing, transportation, etc., etc.—some even envisage a "domestic Marshall plan."

But in order to provide an equivalent aggregate economic stimulus, social welfare spending like that called for by liberals would have to be roughly the same magnitude as the present level of military spending. It would have to be just as expandable to keep pace with the growth of the economy. Can social welfare spending do this? The answer historically seems to be no.

Massive civilian government spending was tried as a stimulus in the 1930's, and failed. In the depths of the Depression, one of the impulses of the New Deal had been to increase social spending to stimulate the economy back to life. Between 1929 and 1939 government expenditures on nondefense purchases and transfer payments nearly doubled from $9.1 billion in 1929 to $17.9 billion in 1939.[30] (See Part IV, Chapter 29.) But this stimulus was not enough—the economy hardly budged. The GNP in the same period slumped from $104.4 billion to $91.1 billion and unemployment rose from 3.2 to 17.2 percent. Enough stimulus was just not generated by social spending. But government spending on arms, once the war mobilization had begun, was enough—exactly what the disease called for.[31]

NO POSSIBLE SOCIAL SPENDING SUBSTITUTE

Spending on arms succeeded where social services spending had failed, because only government spending on arms can be enormous and expandable without limit. Why is this so? For one, only military spending is so amenable to waste that can be made publicly and politically acceptable. Secondly, only military spending can expand so freely without damaging the basic framework of the economy. Massive social spending would compete with the private sector; it would damage the labor market; it would clash head on with hundreds of powerful vested interests at every level of the economy. Given such opposition, social spending could never expand adequately to fill the economic gap. Consider the factors that allow enormous size, rapid expandability and wastefulness of the military budget.

First, a convenient rationalization of the need for massive armaments expenditures exists. The ideology of anticommunism and the Cold War has been drummed into politicians and public alike for over twenty years. This is a power-

[29] S. Melman, *Our Depleted Society,* p. 76.

[30] Baran and Sweezy, *op. cit.*, p. 159.

[31] The decline in military spending after World War II from 40% to 5% of GNP with only a 1.7% increase in unemployment was accomplished only because of unique historical conditions. In particular, savings of $160 billion, accumulated during wartime, fueled a consumer goods boom, and 10 million servicemen went to school under the G.I. Bill. By contrast, the decline in military spending following the Korean War was accompanied by a sharp recession; the unemployment rate in the United States has never fallen below 4% during peacetime. See B. Nossiter, *The Mythmakers* (Beacon, 1964), pp. 171–173.

ful force behind defense spending as well as a general legitimizer of capitalism.

Second, armaments are rapidly consumed or become obsolete very quickly. Bombers get shot down over Vietnam, ammunition gets used up or captured, etc. More important, the technology of advanced weapons systems becomes obsolete as fast as defense experts can think of improvements over existing weapons systems (or as soon as Soviet experts do). Thus many weapons systems have proved obsolete even before production on them was completed. The demand for weaponry is a bottomless pit.

Third, the kind of machinery required for armament production is highly specific to particular armaments. So each time a new weapon is needed or a new process created, all existing production machinery must be scrapped. Extensive retooling at very great new outlays is required.

Fourth, there is no generally agreed-upon yardstick for measuring how much defense we have. How do we know when an adequate level of military security is achieved? National Security Managers can always claim that by some criteria what we have is not enough. Terms like nuclear parity and superiority are easily juggled. Military men always have access to new "secret intelligence reports" not available to the general public. Since few people are willing to gamble with national defense, the expertise of the Managers is readily accepted. Politicians and the general public have little way of adequately questioning their judgment.

These factors combine so that defense expenditures can be enormous and expandable probably without limit. But the same is not the case for social services spending. The above factors are all highly specific to the military sector.

No readily available rationalization yet exists behind massive social service spending. Of course, everyone has to admit health care, hospitals, and schools are good, but that does not mean they are prepared to see masses of federal tax dollars funneled into these areas. In fact, the dominant ideologies still oppose just such a development, particularly when they impinge on ingrained notions such as private medical care, local financing of schools, etc.

Investments in social facilities are usually durable—they do not become obsolete very quickly and are not rapidly consumed. Right now, of course, there are plenty of unmet needs in these areas. But once everyone is provided with a decent house, once there are new schools and health clinics stocked with materials, then what? They cannot be immediately torn down and built all over again.

The technology of social welfare facilities is not particularly exotic. Very conventional standards exist to tell us how much a house should cost and how much a hospital should cost. There is no possibility for enormous padding here to absorb funds.

Furthermore, there are generally accessible yardsticks to ascertain how well social needs have been met. The public knows when adequate and convenient public transportation is available. No one would want to extend it out to a suburb that did not exist.

In general, social spending beyond a certain point cannot be rapidly and wastefully expanded. The difference here is that investment in social services deals with people, not objects like weapons. People are much more resistant to allowing their lives to be dominated by the priorities of waste . . . even if it does help to keep the economy running.

For example, what would happen if a housing project were built in the same way as a new missile? If a missile doesn't work, the company is excused and the planners go back to their drawing boards, armed with another new contract. Since it already has the expertise, the same company is more than likely to get a new missile contract. Imagine the political repercussions of a lousy housing project? The tenants complain, a public scandal is declared, and all contracts are cancelled. The housing bill has a rough going the next time it comes up in the legislature.

So social spending can never provide the opportunities for waste that are provided by military spending. But this is not the most important reason why social spending is impossible. For massive social spending inevitably interferes with the basic operation of a capitalist system. How does this occur?

First, many kinds of social spending put the government into direct competition with the private sector. This is taboo in a capitalist economy. For example, if the government built low-cost housing in large amounts, it would cut heavily into profits of private builders and landlords who own the existing housing stock. It would add to the supply of housing and take land away from private developers who want to use it for commercial purposes. Similarly, building *effective* public transportation would compete with the automobile interests.

Second, social spending upsets the labor market, one of the essential institutions of a capitalist economy. Public expenditures on an adequate welfare program would make it difficult for employers to get workers. If the government provided adequate non-wage incomes without social stigma to the recipients, many workers would drop out of the labor force rather than take low-paying and unpleasant jobs. Those who stayed at jobs would be less likely to put up with demeaning working conditions. The whole basis of the capitalist labor market is that workers have no income source other than the sale of their labor power. Capitalist ideology has long made a cardinal rule that government must not interfere with the incentive to work. Powerful political forces thus operate to insure that direct income subsidization at adequate levels can never come into being.

Third, social service spending is opposed because it threatens the class structure. Education, for example, is a crucial stratification mechanism, determining who gets to the top and legitimizing their position there. Good universal education would put the whole system of inequality into question. Moreover, having the possibility to get an advanced education would undermine the labor market as well. Few workers would settle so willingly for the miserable, low-paying jobs they now do.

Finally, good social services—since they give people security, comfort and satisfaction, i.e., fulfill real needs—interfere with the market in consumer goods. Corporations can only sell people goods in an economy of abundance by playing on their unsatisfied needs and yearnings. In an era when most basic necessities have been provided, these new needs are mostly artificially created; the need for status, sex appeal, etc. They are based on fears and anxieties and dissatisfaction that people have and that are continually pandered to by the commercial world. But if people's needs were being fulfilled by the public sector, that is, if they had access to adequate housing, effective transportation, good schools and good health care, they would be much less prey to the appeals of the commercial hucksters. These forms of collective consumption would have interfered with the demand for consumer products in the private market.

In addition, massive social services spending runs up against the obstacles of the existing vested interests in the social services sector itself. The AMA opposes the extension of federal aid to medical education and is thereby able —in part with corporate assistance from the drug companies—to limit the supply of doctors produced each year. Entrenched civil service bureaucracies find grave threats in extensive federal intervention in local programs. The list could be prolonged indefinitely.

Any one of these interests taken by itself might not be sufficient to put insurmountable obstacles in the way of social spending. Most social service programs affect only one particular set of interests in the private economy. But there are so many forms of potential interference. Each of the vested interests understand this and they work to help one another out. They fuel a general ideology that says that too much social spending is dangerous. They refer to creeping socialism, the dangers of bureaucracy, the faith in individualism and self-help, and the unpleasant image of giving hand-outs to those who don't deserve it. Furthermore, the specter of interference haunts all those in the private sector. So they engage in the practice of "log-rolling." You oppose interference with me, and I'll oppose interference with you. Massive political opposition to rather minor increases in social spending is thus forged.[32]

The opposition of vested interests, the constraints of capitalist institutions and a much lower potential for expandability—these then are the most important factors distinguishing the social service sector from the military weapons sector. Defense spending is acceptable to everyone. It does not compete with already existing industries, it does not undermine the labor market, it does not challenge the class structure, and it does not compete with private markets. Social spending does all these things, and thus faces insurmountable obstacles for its own expansion. Liberals have not been able to overcome these obstacles to obtain even small increases in social services. How can they expect to overcome these obstacles on the massive scale that would be needed if the defense outlet were cut off?

The facile liberal response to this argument—one that views the problem in an abstract fashion—is that "anything can be made appealing" to corporations just by making the incentive sufficiently large. With enough promised profit, defense corporations can be lured away from defense to just about anything. Even assuming that a total giveaway to corporations could be somehow made politically palatable—a dubious assumption—this view lacks plausibility.

Corporations do not make large scale investment decisions just in terms of short-term profit from a particular project. Their minimum horizon is much greater, and a substantial element of inertia operates. First, what is to convince corporations that there are long-term growth opportunities in the social services sector? Corporate executives are well aware that social service spending has in the past been very capricious. Since the impetus behind a conversion program might well dry up after a few years, corporations are reluctant to make large long-term commitments for fear of becoming shipwrecked. The risk of navigating unchartered waters is large. No convincing proof will ever be offered that conversion is profitable like defense has been profitable.

There have been attempts by major defense contractors in the last twenty-five years to initiate large-scale conversion. But almost without exception, these have been failures. Murray Weidenbaum, an Assistant Secretary of the Treasury and former Boeing Co. economist, has reviewed the history of these efforts from the

[32] This point has been emphasized by Baran and Sweezy, *op. cit.,* ch. 6.

end of World War II to the late 1960's.[33] He concludes his survey of early diversification efforts as follows:

> Most of the diversification activities by the major, specialized defense contractors which were begun at the end of World War II were abandoned as unsuccessful or marginal or sold to firms traditionally oriented to industrial or consumer markets. The expansion of the military budget brought on by the Korean War soon turned the primary attention of these firms back to the military market. When faced with the alternative, few aircraft companies preferred to manufacture powered wheelbarrows or busses rather than bomber or fighter airplanes.

Efforts at diversification after the Korean War were equally unsuccessful:

> Most of these industrial diversification efforts outside of aerospace fields have since been abandoned. The surviving diversification programs continue generally at marginal levels—either actually losing money, barely breaking even, or at best showing profit results below typical military business returns.

The explanation of these failures is offered by Weidenbaum; many top corporate executives were convinced that military spending would continue to expand, perhaps a self-fulfilling prophecy:

> . . . the belief of the top managements (is) that there are adequate sales opportunities in government work and that the profit rates are, if anything, higher than on risky commercial ventures. *Interviews with chief executives of the defense industry repeatedly brought out their firm belief in the long-term nature and rising trend of the military market.* Also, their many prior unsuccessful diversification attempts have engendered a strong conviction that inadequate commercial opportunities exist for companies which have become oriented primarily to government work. (Italics added.)

The corporate elite is not going to sponsor a move away from military expenditures on its own. If they continue to oppose conversion, and we have every reason to believe they will, there is little reason to believe their opposition can be overcome within the existing political and economic framework. The conclusion which emerges: the military sector is just too crucial to capitalist stability and to capitalist profits.

We have tried to show in this article that the Military Industrial Complex is thoroughly integral to American capitalism. The only possibility for uprooting it, it would seem, is to challenge the legitimacy and structure of basic capitalist institutions and overthrow them. Furthermore, militarism is only one of many social problems resulting from capitalism. The problem with America has not been merely that too little money goes into social spending. Rather the problem is that the whole society has been dominated by capitalist priorities. The priority of production for profit and corporate aggrandizement takes precedence over the satisfaction of the real needs of the people in the society. These priorities would continue to predominate, even if corporations were making money by building schools instead of missiles. It is facile to believe that dollars alone are what is needed to build a decent society. For liberalism, the myth that we can dismantle the Military Industrial Complex is just one myth among many.

[33] See Weidenbaum, *op. cit.,* chapter 3. More recent expression of corporate sentiment on conversion can be found in a series of articles by Bernard Nossiter in the *Washington Post,* December 1968.

Others have cogently argued that achieving decent health care, a good and equal educational system, a fulfilling and creative work environment, a balanced ecological system, and the uprooting of sexism and racism each require the same thing: the destruction of capitalism. A socialist movement therefore has a strong base in the objective interests of most of the American people. The mobilized power of the people can overthrow capitalism and bring about a socialist revolution. Then a rational economy could be established that did not breed massive and murderous waste.

PART 2

CORPORATIONS AND GOVERNMENT

Part I sought to characterize the pattern of economic development that we have seen under American capitalism: tremendous inequality; the failure to meet basic needs, both in terms of the standard of living of individuals and the level of collective goods and services; the dependence of the U.S. economy on militarism and consumerism resulting in tremendous waste, perverted values and the danger of annihilation of the human species; the creation of unsolved economic and social problems through the normal functioning of the economy, like despoliation of the environment and pollution of water and air; and the cumulative toll that the rat race of American life takes on human sanity.

In the Introduction to Part II we delve more deeply into just why all these horrors result from the capitalist way of doing things, and we try to field some of the standard objections raised to this kind of radical analysis of modern capitalism. First, what are some of these objections?

In the first place, many liberal social theorists assert that the age of corporate rapacity is over. Corporations in particular and the economy in general have undergone a transformation and have become more socially responsible. We take this up first in a discussion of the "private" control of the economy and what that means.

Second, there are many who feel that forces *outside* the corporate economy have arisen that are capable of restraining corporate greed and irrationality and making it function in the public interest. Thus it is possible to restrict some bad aspects of corporate capitalism while maintaining its good aspects. This view particularly focuses on the state as an agency of reform and regulation. It asserts not only that government has promulgated social reform and restraint on corporate behavior in the past but that it will happen again in the future as social problems are spotted and understood.

THE MEANING OF A PRIVATE ECONOMY

Why in discussing capitalism is the idea of "private ownership" so important? "Private ownership" refers to the fact that decisions over crucial domains of social activity are left basically in the hands of people and institutions responsible only to themselves. Why do these decisions matter?

The first observation to be made about our capitalist—any capitalist—economy is that nearly all income-producing assets are controlled privately. That includes the factories that create goods and the organizations that provide services. The decisions affecting millions of employees of this private sector and the products they produce lie basically in the hands of these "private" institutions.

These "private" organizations make decisions of vast social consequences. They decide how much pay men will receive for their work. They decide who will work and who will not. With a single decision they can throw thousands of workers into unemployment and create economic wastelands of whole towns. By their investment decisions, they decide which regions will be highly developed and which not. They determine what products will be available to the society. They can devastate the environment with pollution. These and thousands of similar decisions are made in the private economy by small groups of corporate decision makers with no element of popular or public participation.

What is crucial about this decision-making is not merely its concentration and its lack of accountability. More important is the antisocial nature of these decisions. Basically the decisions are taken to enhance the self-interest of the corporate oligarchy making the decisions. They are made according to the criteria of profit.

As Gorz pointed out (see Part I), the decisions made via the criteria of profit only coincide by accident with the real needs of the society and people in the society. These corporations act according to what promotes their profit position. That may mean throwing many people out of work. It may mean tearing down forests and polluting streams. It may mean lobbying for useless weapons that will create a shower of lucrative contracts. It certainly does not mean determining what the top-priority needs of the people are—like health, job security, good information, etc.—and then proceeding to minister to them. Under a profit system the test of profit precedes the test of whether these actions benefit people and society as a whole.

Obviously there are some limitations. Individual corporations do not want to develop an "antisocial" image—one that would hurt their products or incense their customers. But, the basic dynamic to the decision-making on a system-wide level is to raise profitability to the ultimate criteria of determining what happens. Activities, products, ideas that are not profitable, never get started or get quickly sheared off. Human priorities that stand in the way of profitability are seen as necessary sacrifices and are trampled under foot.

The Ravages of Profit

In the Introduction to Part I we have described the irrationality of our society based as it is on military production and wasteful consumerism and oblivious to serious human needs. This set of priorities, we said, stemmed from this very fact of the profit criteria which decided what would be done.

The rest of the book, as well, is devoted to similar arguments. It shows how the profit motive and unfettered private selfishness have contributed to our social problems like racism, unemployment, the subjugation of women, the oppressiveness of work, etc. For the time being, we want to outline what are the most general ways in which the criteria of profit conflicts in the society with the needs of the people.

CORPORATE IRRESPONSIBILITY

Corporations are not responsible for the social impact of the decisions they make. Thus, profit-seeking may dictate the razing of a forest or the creation of a massive traffic jam, but corporations are not obliged legally or financially to clean up the social messes they indirectly create.

PROFIT AND WORK

The imperatives of profit-seeking put corporations into mortal struggle with their workers. In most instances the most profitable pathway is to squeeze out a maximum of work for a minimum of pay, with as little as possible expended on making the work pleasant or comfortable or safe.

Decisions about how work will be organized, how fast and under what conditions it will be done are all heavily determined by the concern of profit and cost-cutting. The needs of the worker—for exercise, cleanliness, safety, comradeship, autonomy, self-respect, education and psychological fulfillment—are subordinated entirely. It means insecurity for the worker, who never knows when the concern for profit and cost-cutting will deprive him of his job. It means boredom and meaninglessness. It means minimum pay for work nonetheless crucial to society. (See the Romano selection, Part III.)

PROFIT AND CONSUMERS

The demands of profit make the consumer an object of prey for the corporation. The goal of a profit-seeking producer is to get the customer to buy his product as often as possible at the highest price he will pay. Whether the customer really needs the product, whether he can afford the product, whether it is of any use to the society at large, are all questions irrelevant to the profit seeker.

We can see how this relation between profit and consumer leads directly to all the irrationalities of the consumer marketplace. The profit seekers are prepared to deceive the customer. Through advertising and media they will manipulate him to feel inadequate so that he will buy. Through loans and sales schemes they will make him think he can afford something he cannot. Through designing for obsolescence and waste they will insure that the customer has to buy frequently. All these strategies employed by the most powerful institutions in the world leave the powerless consumer confused about his own needs and desires, feeling an inadequacy he must deal with constantly through buying, frustrated by products that are not built for satisfactory use and suspicious of his every encounter with sales people. This gigantic maze is not built to help him rationally identify his needs and deal with them.

PROFIT AND POLITICS

Profit-seeking drives corporations to use their power to gain whatever advantages they can from the political process. The political process is full of opportunities for corporations. Through it they gain pork barrels—like military contracts—and special privileges—like tax exemptions. Through it they can administer and rationalize an economic system than can often get out of control. This impels them to control the political mechanisms.

How does this conflict with people's needs? It imposes corporate profit-seeking priorities on the activities of the state. Taxpayers' money is used for the pork barrels. Money that would go for nonprofit social services is blocked and redirected toward corporate profit. And, actions that would curb anti-social activities of the corporations themselves are nipped in the bud. The criteria of what is profitable for corporations thus comes to dominate and determine the actions of public officials.

PROFIT AND PLANNING

Profit-seeking creates anarchy for the system as a whole. Each of thousands of individual corporations makes decisions based on its own profit. The convergence of these uncoordinated decisions can frequently throw the whole system into turmoil. This is what happens when a depression occurs, when unemployment climbs, when inflation rampages. Whole sectors stagnate and decline; others take off and burgeon without any relation to what is really needed in the society, or what is really rational. Each industry clamors for its special privilege. Huge wasteful wars of take-over bids and product competition are fought. Whole regions are left to the mercy of powerful corporate giants. Planning is impossible because for the sake of profit-making each individual corporation must retain all rights to decide how to employ its assets. Between the competition and the anarchy, the system churns out its benefits to corporation owners and managers and leaves a wake of wastage and human suffering.

PROFIT AND VALUES

The imperatives of profit generate a system of completely inhuman values. These values encourage competitiveness and jealousy, selfishness, hatred and discrimination, suspicion, materialism, authoritarianism, etc.

To make larger profits, capitalists fuel insidious hatred among workers. Through granting selective concessions and playing groups off against one another, corporations have promoted racism, male chauvinism and ethnic rivalries. The sheer powerlessness and required obedience of so many jobs in the society build authoritarianism right into the social fabric.

Within the hierarchy of capitalist institutions personnel are goaded to compete; advancement, status, money, individualism, are offered as ultimate goals. In the market, profit creates a psychology based on deceit, watching out for one's own skin, imperviousness to suffering or exploitation of others.

Through such a system, people's real needs for love, friendship, feelings of adequacy, cooperation, mutuality, are completely destroyed. Profit makes these kinds of values nearly impossible.

Defenders of a system which results in this kind of perversion of human needs generally point to two limitations on the pathology we have described here. First, they say, the criteria of corporate decision-making has changed. The day of the avaricious, profit-greedy entrepreneur is over. Corporations are more "socially responsible." Second, they argue, the scope of such decision-making power has been reduced. Laws, regulatory agencies, private groups and the power of government now limit the domain in which corporate decision-making has free reign. We will take up these objections.

Corporate Self-Interest or "The Soulful Corporation"

We have said that the goal of corporations is to seek profits. Has this situation changed?

One line of apologist thinking in this matter has argued that the decline of the marketplace due to increased concentration has reduced the impulse of modern corporations to compulsively accumulate profits. Under the new ethic of an oligopolistic system, corporations seek only to maintain a stable market position. Stable and secure, the corporation is increasingly able to minister to the demands of labor, technology and the community at large. This new entity has been called the "soulful corporation."

Nossiter (see Part I) paints a picture quite at odds with this view. Decline of market constraints, he shows, only increases the potential for antisocial activity by the corporations. Today corporations can rake in larger and more secure windfalls than ever before. Their old impulse to respond constantly to consumers' demands and improve their products falls by the wayside. As to responsibility for its behavior, monopoly position, it has been shown, allows corporations to pass off nearly all taxes and government impositions on the backs of the consumer. Is this "soulful"?

Other economists, like James Earley, far from a radical, also express skepticism about the "soulful corporation." He concludes from his research that new techniques of corporation management, new forms of accounting and market analysis, all mean increased ability to predict and insure high profit levels. He concludes that high and rising profit levels are the key to all the large, "more sophisticated" goals corporations now see for themselves, including a strong competitive position, growth and high managerial salaries. The profit criteria still reigns supreme.

Another line of apologist defense argues that a "managerial revolution" has occurred, shifting control of corporations out of the hands of profit-maximizing entrepreneurs and into the hands of stability-oriented bureaucrats. This, too, is a line of reasoning not substantiated in reality. Even if managers, unlike the old entrepreneurs, had no direct financial interest in maximizing profits, this would still be their goal; all other corporate goals mentioned by the apologists—like stable market position and growth—require those high profits to maintain. But, in fact, managers do have important direct interest in the profit position of their corporations. The value of the stock options paid out to these new managers has a close relation to the level of a corporation's profits.

In short, it is impossible to imagine that corporations are engaging in anything but self-interested activity. As Sweezy points out in *Monopoly Capital,* modern corporations may avoid the old risk-taking, and they may take a new live-and-let-live attitude toward their competitors. But when human needs come into conflict with corporate gain it is still the same old story—profit over people.

DOES THE STATE RESTRAIN CORPORATIONS?

We now come to deal with the second line of liberal defense. Even if profit motive still runs free in the cabinets of corporate decision makers, they say, its ravages have been contained. An enormous force for social rationality and public interest has grown up in the guise of the Democratic State.

Since this argument is the cornerstone of those who place faith in the system and also is the basis on which people claim to choose our system over competing systems like socialism, we devote the rest of this introduction to it. In a capsule, we do not think the evidence shows that government acts to limit the priorities established by the private economy. Instead, we argue that government's primary role under capitalism is (1) the assistance of private interests and (2) the protection of the private sector.

We are not saying that the government is a simple tool—manipulated by the men who own the corporations. Clearly the national government has a capacity for independent initiative. But we are saying that the major thrust of government activity has the effect of benefiting and protecting the corporate sector. Ours is not a "public interest" government.

We are also saying that corporate influence over government means that there are a great many things our government is not capable of doing. One is imposing substantial controls on the activity of private corporations. Another is greatly expanding the range and extent of welfare services directly benefiting the public.

The activities of a government within our capitalist system are heavily determined by the interests of the capitalist class. This is not just because men in government share the same beliefs as the men in business. It is also because the power controlled by corporations in the form of money, control of markets and influence over the economy is a crucial "given" within the society which all governments and all politicians must reckon with. Cooperation with the corporate economy is a necessity for politicians who accept the capitalist system.

Has Corporate Power Declined?

The first observation that flies in the face of liberal assurances about the limitations on corporate power is the sheer magnitude and enormous concentration of that power. For example, General Motors in 1969 owned 3.3 percent of the assets, performed 5.6 percent of the sales and took in 7.2 percent of the income of the five hundred largest corporations together. The wealth and power controlled by the biggest is growing by leaps and bounds. In 1968 the top ten corporations in terms of sales accounted for 22.5 percent of the profits of all U.S. industrial corporations.

Pluralists often point out that corporations are not the only organized groups in society. We should not forget about labor unions, universities, conservationists, etc. But pluralists fail to see the limited scope of these groups. On the one hand, many—like universities and philanthropies—are dominated by business interests and basically service corporate America. Other organizations—like labor unions have accommodated themselves of necessity to the predominance of corporate power, and they can only force marginal adjustments. (See the Nossiter selection following.)

A second a priori observation is the contrast between the glittering, showcase private economy and the inadequate, impoverished nature of the public sector. The cupboards of education, health, housing and environment preservation seem bare in comparison. This too points toward the idea that the public authority in our system is subservient to the private sector rather than vice versa.

But what is underneath this comparison is quite revealing. The private sector is plush and the public sector starved not because the public authorities do nothing. They do a lot, but most of what they do is to enhance the plush private sector.

State as Promoter of Particular Private Interests

The instances of how government promotes specific private interests are well known. Uncle Sam commonly finances terrific pork barrels for some of the country's largest corporations—in particular through the military and space contracts and through road building. Thirty-seven billion in military contracts alone were let to private industry in 1969; 18.9 percent went to the five largest contractors.[1]

Government at all levels prefers to get things done via contracts to private corporations rather than mobilizing the resources of some government agency itself. Only completely unprofitable undertakings like mail delivery and certain urban transportation systems are taken on by public authorities.

Aid to private interests comes in all forms. Oil depletion allowances, for example, allow oil companies to pay an effective tax of 7.7 percent compared to a much higher rate for other corporations. A huge development contract for a supersonic transport promising billions in profits both in development and in service is let out to Boeing despite dire warnings from officials everywhere that the plane will create monstrous problems.

Foreign aid, which is usually thought of as benefiting other countries, is in reality a big gift to American companies. Eighty-five percent of the grants are spent right in the United States. And many of the "development projects" turn out like the road built in Guiana, useless to the automobile-less Guianans, which "happened" to connect the coastal port to Reynolds Aluminum's own bauxite mine.

Under the guise of defense contracts, billions are squandered to private corporations in cost-overruns, in government-owned equipment used for non-government production, in weaponry declared obsolete before it ever gets built (see the Reich-Finkelhor selection, Part I); these are just a few of the ways private corporations are given a helping hand. And, to mention just one other example, in the crucial area of financing technological progress, the Federal government picks up the tab for three fourths of the research and development spending that goes to keep the corporations now on top always on top. This only skims the top of the multitude of ways in which the government helps the corporations.

[1] *Business Week,* November 8, 1969, p. 130.

To understand this system of massive boondoggle, it is important to see that it is not just any old corporations that are the beneficiaries of the government glad hand. Rather, it is the most powerful corporations. It is the oil companies, among the most powerful international operations that ever existed, who get the depletion allowance. As for the rewards of the defense sector, twenty of the largest twenty-five corporations in America are among the largest one hundred defense contractors. This is no coincidence. These are the ranks of the powerful in America. The influence they wield traces through elective representatives, through government bureaucrats, through lobbies and through campaign contributions; it hangs like a pall over the activities of public agencies.

Protector of the System

Nobody really disputes that government spending has created some scandalous opportunities for the giant corporations. People also agree that these giants have set up and taken advantage of these pork barrels in large part because of the terrific power they wield. But the government does a lot more than just that. It makes economic policy, it makes foreign policy, it fights wars, it administers laws, it conducts political activities, and it cares for welfare, education and other services. These all appear to be the impartial activities of an agency that stands over and apart from the private economy. They seem to be the activities of an agency concerned with the public welfare.

Radicals think this is really an optical illusion. If you get down and examine closely these "impartial" activities of government, they are best understood not as implementing the "public welfare" but as protecting and defending the corporate economy. They are primarily aimed at preserving the profitability and oiling the gears of the system of corporate capitalism. What appears as "public welfare" is a very secondary function of government. Such welfare is primarily a device for buying off discontent or insuring against social and economic catastrophes.

Many of the "impartial" activities of government can be understood in terms of the need to protect the capitalist system from its own irrationality. On the one hand, the government is obliged to intervene in economic activities to keep the system profitable despite its tendencies to collapse. On the other hand, the government is obliged to intervene in social affairs to rescue the system from the discontent, rebellion and disaffection precipitated by the neglect of existing human needs.

Take the example of economic management. We have said that the profit motive leads to a highly anarchical economic system. For lots of familiar reasons the system has a tendency to instability—it falls into depression, it cannot dispose of all its production, etc. Under such conditions, profits drop precipitously and many firms are forced to close. Economic management and many related government activities are geared to help avoid this very problem.

How is this accomplished? On the one hand, the government just watches out for economic conditions. It has instruments like credit controls, taxation, budgeting, etc., to help steer the economy away from pitfalls. On the other hand, the government buoys up the economy by acting as a stimulator of massive economic activity. It buys huge quantities of production—largely through the Defense Department—at great profit to the corporate sector as we have already seen. (The Department of Defense alone purchases 15 percent of all finished manufactured products and more than 18 percent of all industrial durable goods.) It makes sure that a large demand for American products exists on the world market. This accounts for many governmental activities like foreign aid (11 percent of all exports are financed by foreign aid), tariff regulation and the defense of American business positions overseas from revolutions, nationalizations and foreign competition. Finally, the government stimulates economic activity at home by acting directly on the consumer market through tax cuts, Social Security payments and other things.

The fact that government activities are primarily oriented toward catering to the private economy can be illustrated in the case of public services, too. Take the case of the post office. The only reason the government operates the post office at all is that it could not be operated on a profitable basis by a private corporation, like the telephone system. Moreover, if you compare the rates for "junk mail," i.e., advertising, as opposed to those for personal correspondence, it is clear who benefits first from postal service. The taxpayers are paying a heavy subsidy on the real cost of carrying out advertising for private corporations.

A lot of other government activities that are usually thought of as "public welfare" activities can also be better understood in the same light—that is, in terms of servicing and defending the corporate economy. Education is a particularly good example. Many people think public education is primarily an opportunity for self-betterment provided by the government for the people. But looked at carefully, public education as it exists in America is better explained as a service to the corporate economy. Corporations need trained workers to maintain high levels of productivity and to perform more and more complicated jobs. If the corporations had to train workers themselves, the cost to them would be very high. Instead, the government supplies the trained manpower through the school system, with the taxpayer paying the costs. (See the Finkelhor and the Research Organizing Cooperative selections, Part III.)

That the schools work primarily as a service to the corporate economy becomes even more transparent if we think of just what schools do to kids. Recent research has shown that the main thing schools do is to teach kids to be obedient, to be passive and to do dull work for the sake of "extrinsic rewards"—that is, grades, and, of course, later on in life, money. Basically school molds them into good workers. This is a far cry from "bettering" people so they can enjoy fuller, more satisfying lives.

Welfare is another example. The way in which welfare is given out by government agencies—in a miserly, humiliating way—hardly leads one to think that welfare spending reflects the deep concern of a benevolent government for the well-being of all its citizens. Rather, it makes a lot more sense to see welfare as a kind of insurance against discontent, defending the system once again from its own irrationality. If the economy is always going to leave many people unemployed and impoverished, something has to be done to keep this outrage from providing fuel for revolt. Social tinderboxes cannot be allowed to smolder. So a welfare system exists. But what is important to note is that these welfare benefits are never provided in adequate quantities to really alleviate misery. Rather, they are grudging tokens to patch up the inhumanity of our system so that it does not spark revolt.

We think, in fact, that the government is incapable of coming forth with welfare programs that really do provide substantial benefits. This is because real welfare would require curbing corporate interests and diverting resources out of "profit"-making and into "people"-making. But the government can only sponsor reform efforts that have no detrimental effects on the corporate sector. That means only token programs to deal with emergencies like race riots that threaten to upset the whole apple cart.

So we all admit that powerful corporations feast at the trough of government spending. It also stands to reason that government management of the economy winds up helping to stabilize a system that is profitable to the same corporations. But don't corporations pay a price for that? Isn't that price the acceptance of a high degree of government regulation? Doesn't the government curb in this way the antisocial aspects of the private economy. We think the answer to this is a clear no.

Inviolability of Corporate Prerogatives

What evidence, first off, is there that the government cannot seriously counteract the private sector? One persuasive bit of evidence is that, as Kolko shows, there has been no substantial change in distribution of income since 1910, and this despite a gigantic increase in the state's role in the economy. (See the Kolko selection, Part I.) Another indicator of the impact of the state also provided by Kolko is that the income tax has no redistributive impact. If the government were actually curbing the greed of the rich, we would expect it to take some money from them in the form of taxes. Or, at least in the long run, it should reduce their cut in the pie. It does not. Still another indicator is offered by Baran and Sweezy in their book. They show how despite increases in the Federal tax rate on corporations, especially sharp during World War II, the level of profits made by the private sector has not fallen one iota; on the contrary, it has increased. That is, Federal taxes have not acted to curb corporations or reduce their profit rate. Nor is the government likely to nationalize any industry unless possibly that industry has ceased to be profitable and has become a burden to the private sector. In short, it is not capable of putting constraints on corporate activity that would significantly equalize wealth or stop the free, and by the same token antisocial, pursuit of profit.

How Much Reform Possible?

But, on the other side of the ledger, how do we account for all the apparent reform and even some seemingly anticapitalist activities of the state? Look at trust-busting, utility regulation, price regulation, etc.

Much of the image of the reformist bias of national government stems from the legacy of historical periods such as that of the Progressive Era and the New Deal. Many of the reforms instituted during these periods were made with a fanfare of anticapitalist ideology. However, a serious investigation of the character of these "reforms" indicates the real "conservative" role they played in the development of the political economy, the ways in which they served the private economy.

For example, in the Progressive Era certain reforms were instituted—from city-manager blue-ribbon government to trust-busting, to bank reform, to utility regulation—all smacking of democratic triumph. But underneath the surface rhetoric we find the efforts of newly ascendant commercial powers to provide a new rationality to the capitalist system. Urban reform was a strategy to break the back of ethnically controlled machines and institute control by the new corporate leaders over urban government. Bank reform was a self-imposed effort by banking interests to straighten out an anarchic and precariously balanced banking system. Regulatory agencies emerged as a by-product of the oligopolies' own desires to eliminate suicidal forms of intra-industry competition and so forth.[2]

Nor was the New Deal quite the orgy of democratic reform that is usually portrayed, either. The Brad Wiley selection included here shows how the measures instituted at that time represented the efforts of the more clairvoyant of the corporate class to put the old economy back on its feet, to avoid the pitfalls of the past, and to undercut the danger of revolution created by the worsened economic conditions—no anticapitalism here.

Although some real benefit did accrue to the people as a result of these measures, much of it has been destroyed since then, and much of it has simply failed to keep pace with the growth of other parts of the economy.

Trust-busting is one of the reform measures often cited as indicative of the government's anticorporate attitudes. It turns out often as not, however, that the illicit collusion among companies or the creation of enormous corporate empires is as threatening to other corporations as it is to the general public. It means they have to pay the higher prices for producer goods or suffer at the hands of a new competitive giant. They call on government intervention.

The trust-busting has, in other words, taken place mainly when it serves other corporations. It has had an impact on only a few industries, since the budget of the antitrust division of the Justice Department is just a thimbleful. Moreover, companies have found ways, when needed, of colluding just as effectively, as they used to in the crude combinations of old.

The myth that regulatory agencies really regulate corporate activity has been exposed for a long time. Agencies like the ICC and the FCC are known to be virtual tools of the industries they are supposed to control. These agencies were originally established to help rationalize away "destructive" competition in a legal way. Thus little real control in the interest of the public goes on. (See the Nossiter selection, Part II.)

Finally, we should take the example of civil rights. Several imposing-sounding laws have been put on the books in the name of equality. Of course, there is little evidence that the Federal government is prepared to infringe on corporate prerogatives to achieve real racial equality in this country. Housing codes and health codes have rarely, if ever, been enforced, and although government can withhold contracts from discriminating employers, this power has almost never been used to bring black employment up to parity. In general,

[2] Gabriel Kolko, *Triumph of Conservatism,* Chicago, 1963 and James Weinstein, *The Corporate Ideal in the Liberal State,* Boston, Beacon Press, 1968.

civil rights legislation and other laws that affect blacks have rarely been applied when it was a case of imposing them on powerful corporate interests.

It is true, however, that Federal legislation has created such power and this in itself is something of a threat to the private economy. What is important to note is that both government and corporate leaders are by now well agreed that black insurgency—positioned as it is in the hearts of American cities—could do inestimable damage to the private economy. This threat calls for some kind of collective sacrifice that corporations certainly would not ordinarily make. However, the main "sacrifice" that has been made so far has been the stockpiling of a great variety of new weapons and social-control devices, plus the beefing up of local police forces. With all the recommendations of the Kerner Commission Report, this is the only one that has been acted on in a resolute fashion.

These examples have shown that much of what passes for the government's taking action to curb corporations is nothing of the sort. Of course, businessmen complain, but this is all part of the complex ritual by which businessmen hold in line rambunctious politicians. (See the Domhoff selection, Part II.) In fact, these "reforms" have served crucial conservative functions for the private economy. We can analyze these functions as serving one of the following purposes.

Conservative Function of "Reform"

1. They are efforts to rationalize a situation becoming destructive for business itself. In such cases, the government enters in as a referee, as in the case of bank reform or regulatory agencies, usually under conditions of clear solicitation of help. Often the government can make use of the occasion with displays of antibusiness ideology. This is sometimes helpful in mobilizing people against any hold-out elements of the business community.

2. They act to shore up irrationalities created by the private economy. This includes cases of government-stimulated consumer demand, for example. In such cases, the government acts a bit more farsighted than any particular businessman would, so preoccupied is the latter with the maximization of his own gain. Government lets it be known that all must make sacrifices or take steps if general prosperity is to be preserved. This covers instances like the steel price showdown of the Kennedy years, where government had to take responsibility for saving all industry from the ravages of inflation.

3. They provide new services for industry. The business system has a need for services, the cost of which it would prefer not to pay. Such is the case with training and health care for the workers in the private sector. The government can be persuaded to provide education and a certain amount of public health, relieving the corporations of the costs.

4. They stave off insurgencies. In certain circumstances grievances explode, people are mobilized, great dissension threatens, as in the case of black rebellions. The government can sometimes provide the concessions needed to placate these groups and restore order. But, as illustrated in the case of civil rights, the concessions granted are as minimal as feasible under the given circumstances. They tend to lapse once the vigilance of popular forces begins to wane. The concessions are indicative of the power people can have, if militant. But constant remobilization, is their necessary price.

These are the kinds of conditions we see operating on the reform potential of the government. To our minds, these restraints mean that the government cannot create a good society in the face of private interests. The ravages of the private economy we have seen are very great. They are not leading us in the direction of a good society. Very pressing problems are at hand—that we outline in Part III—and these require enormous efforts to be solved. We maintain that real reforms will inevitably require (1) heavy restrictions on the private sector, private cupidity and its consequences, (2) redistribution of income and social benefits, (3) mobilization of masses of people to get and maintain real justice and social rationality. Serious reform will mean dismantling the institutionalized scandal of military spending and the profit that accompanies it. Any serious reform will restrict the scope of free reign presently enjoyed by corporate oligarchs. It will mean lower profits, less power, anticapitalist political movements. The state under capitalism is not capable of doing this. A stable set of structured relationships exists between the government and the private sector defining the limits of state activity. It cannot transcend these. To undersand why we will delve more deeply into the mechanisms by which the state is left subservient to corporation interests.

Mechanisms of Corporate Hegemony

Radicals are frequently caricatured as arguing that businessmen control everything, from what new military contracts will be given out to who will be the next President. This is obviously an exaggeration. There are many nonbusinessmen in politics and many politicians who believe that they are no man's pawn. But, the political system under capitalism is nonetheless closely wedded to corporate interests. Politicians accept the system as a given; they cooperate with and provide favors for corporate interests, and they buckle under when corporate opposition demands it. Why?

Accessibility

By its very nature, the corporate economy places vast amounts of wealth, power and, accompanying these, influence and prestige in the hands of the people who direct and benefit from the corporate empires. Such resources allow these men to finance campaigns, hire lobbyists, make their views known through media and even run for office themselves, if they are so inclined. All in all, this puts the political institutions in this country within easy reach of the men who make up the corporate elite.

For one thing, politicians come in disproportionate numbers from the upper classes. Their backgrounds are usually in law or business, and, through their careers or their families, they are usually quite wealthy. The very largest corporations and the very wealthiest families frequently have members in the highest positions of government—McNamara, Rockefeller, Kennedy, etc. (Franklin Roosevelt, to take what is probably the most blatant example of how narrow a class politicians come from, was related by birth or marriage to eleven other Presidents.)

Frequently as important for a specific corporation or industry is the fact that their representatives fill the government bureaucracy at all levels. As Nossiter indicates, the former corporate officials in regulatory agencies and in the Pentagon help make these agencies virtual tools of the corporations they are supposed to control and bargain with.

Second, corporations have the resources to maintain constant pressure on politicians at all levels of government. They hire "lobbyists" who make their home in the halls of Congress, and who play key roles in drawing up legislation and in advising Congressmen on appropriate positions to take. In 1949, according to one calculation, 825 out of a total of 1247 lobbies in the House of Representatives represented business. This is only the tip of the iceberg.

Third, the wealthy hold a tight grip over the political system, particularly by way of campaign contributions. Every politician needs money to run. In an era where Presidential campaigns run in the order of $20 million, this makes politicians quite beholden to men with money. The Democratic party, far from being the party of the "common man," is rather the party of the Lehmans, the Baruchs, the Kennedys, the Engelhards and the "Tex" Thorntons who provide the fuel on which it runs. Politicians who don't have the support of big money just cannot make it.

Finally, in order for people to pose a challenge to the Big Money, they need an understanding of what is happening. But information and ideas are controlled by the press, by the politicians and by the schools. These institutions promote certain ideas and not others, certain information and not other bits of information. The press, "free" as it may be, is entirely held in the hands of wealthy publishers. Certain large chains, like Hearst, control papers in home towns all across the country. Furthermore, for their information, the press is dependent on two big wire services and the government itself. Government officials "cooperate" with the media, to the extent that the media cooperates with them. In addition, newspapers are financially dependent on the big advertisers, i.e., other large corporate interests. These advertisers are unambiguous in their refusal to finance newspapers that are politically unorthodox. Thus, the ideas that are allowed currency in the public "forum" and that are free to have influence are the ideas of the owners of corporations and their allies.

Government Policy and Corporate Economic Power

Although the corporate elite influences politicians directly through personal contacts, lobbies, party finances and the press, this is not the only mechanism that keeps the government responsive to corporate interests. The structure of institutions under capitalism insures as well that the political leaders rely on business leaders. This is why even electing "uninfluenceable, idealistic, blue-ribbon" politicians cannot shake loose the government from its position of dependency.

The overriding reality for political leaders under capitalism is that their power coexists with enormous private power, concentrated in a few large corporations. Everything they wish to accomplish as politicians is contingent on that private power—whether it is a case of levying more taxes, of raising the general level of wages or of eliminating the pollution in the air and water.

Their political goals and their tenure in office can all be undermined by private centers of decision-making beyond their direct control.

The dependency is clearest in the case of local politicians. The representative who wants to bring prosperity to Podunk has to insure that there is in his district an environment congenial to business. High taxes, strict union or wage legislation and unfriendly political officials are plenty of incentive for a corporation not to settle there or to take its business and go elsewhere. The local politicians concern for business prosperity will also insure that he votes willingly for massive military expenditures, highway appropriations, tax loopholes and other boondoggles that benefit the corporations in his area.

On the national level, governments need the cooperation of corporations to achieve a healthy and growing economy, the key to all other political goals. Governments show this in their concern for the "business climate." If government goes too far in displeasing the private sector, its fate is sealed. Investment declines, unemployment rises, the stock market falls—all of which have deep and quick political impacts on the popularity of particular governments. Government equally needs business cooperation to stem inflation—another serious political pitfall.

If the corporate interests are really worried, as is the case when sweeping economic reforms like nationalizations are threatened, they have certain other retaliations to throw at the government. Capital flees the country as confidence declines. The government has difficulty financing its debt or floating bonds, most of which are controlled by capitalist institutions. Finally, corporations start to stir up and massively finance political opposition to the government and its policies. Such measures spell the death knell for governments that get really out of hand.

In summary, politicians under capitalism have much less leeway than it would appear from looking at the powers held in theory by government officials. The limitations on their power stem from the power and influence held over and above them by the privately controlled corporations. Politicians need the cooperation of these giants to accomplish any of the political tasks they may set out for themselves. They are conscious as well of the reprisals they may also incur. This structural situation of dependency has resulted in many years of long and happy alliance between political leaders and the corporate leaders who dominate the society. All in all, what this means is that the government is not an agent for social reform. The government cannot be seen as the instrument for countering the corporation-generated irrationalities and establishing a Good Society.

A Good Society would be one that gave priority to human needs. It would organize production to solve remaining social problems. It would use the human energies to make the institutions of the society responsive to the control of the people. It would allow men to organize to develop their own capacities and to gain satisfaction. Men would set their own priorities for institutions, rather than have them dominated by impersonal priorities such as those of profit.

Decisions responsive to people's needs can only be made when people have real power over the resources and institutions of a society. This means taking control from the hands of the few who dominate them and subjecting that power to democratic control. It also means bringing the resources together so that they can be used in a rational way, according to criteria that are democratically determined, not according to corporation criteria of profitability. This calls for socializing the resources and institutions, on the one hand, and radically democratizing control, on the other. That is socialism.

7 CORPORATE DOMINANCE AND THE MYTH OF PLURALISM*

by BERNARD D. NOSSITER

Anxieties about the growth of corporate power have in the past been assuaged by the idea of pluralism. Pluralism sees business as just one interest group among many. Citizens' groups, labor unions, consumers' groups, city machines, to name just a few, all interact to counter or moderate business influence. Most important, the national government has taken upon its shoulders the job of regulating business, keeping it in line and giving the proper weight to the ambitions of other organized groups.

This is really a pathetic apology. It ignores the tremendous power and resources at the disposal of the large corporations. It ignores the weakness of other groups and their dependence on the very same corporations they are supposed to counter. It ignores all the manifestations of the alliance between business and government—from oil depletion allowance, to military contracts, to regulatory agencies. Nossiter runs through the inventory, leaving the myth of countervailing powers where it belongs—in the trash can of history.

Given a world of large and impersonal economic institutions, there is some comfort in believing that the giants collide and neutralize each other. The theory of balancing or offsetting power helps sustain the democratic creed and nourishes economists who hunger for the equilibrium of the classical world. It lies behind the description of America as a pluralistic society; a vision embraced by many academics, journalists, politicians and those corporate officials who are uncomfortable about their power. Even apart from these uses, the concept of strong offsetting blocs has some tangency to the real world. Moreover, it does recognize that there are large and powerful organizations operating on the American scene.

But the confident assertion that these powerful institutions conflict and thereby cancel each other is more wish than fact. Indeed, the theory strains reality even further. It contends that the stalemate not only protects the public against an abuse of power but even yields many of the dividends promised in the classical world of diffused, atomistic power.

Whatever its shortcomings, the theory of countervailing power is undeniably a cornerstone of conventional wisdom. In its crudest form, it argues that Big Business is offset by Big Labor with Big Government watching both. One complication holds that Big Business is divided between Big Buyers and Big

Sellers, that Big Producers are confronted with Big Purchasers, and that their tug of war somehow redounds to the benefit of all. A representative version of the simple view is David Lilienthal's worshipful essay on the giant corporations. He writes:

"In short, as a result of the new comprehensive role of Government in economic affairs, the new power and influence of organized labor, the rise of the New Competition . . . a change in the power of large buyers . . . a change as to the social responsibility of Big Business . . . corporate control . . . is now divided and diffused . . . Against the danger of Bigness . . . we either already have adequate public safeguards, or know how to fashion new ones as required."

A more sophisticated elaboration is Professor Galbraith's witty and urbane treatise, *American Capitalism: The Concept of Countervailing Power*. Galbraith offers so many fruitful insights into the economic order that his book and his terminology have enjoyed a well-deserved vogue. Stripped of important qualifications and exceptions, Galbraith's central thesis is that the power of corporation managers, "though considerable, is deployed against others who are strong enough to resist any harmful exercise of such power." As a prescription for what should be, this notion may be unimpeachable. But as a description of what is, it is less than adequate.

One of Galbraith's most ingenious contributions is his conclusion that strong sellers beget strong buyers. This idea is so crucial to the theory that it deserves a closer look. At the retail level, Galbraith contends, these strong buyers exercise their countervailing power on behalf of consumers. Thus, in his view, the great chains like A & P, the great mail order houses like Sears, Roebuck and the great department stores like Macy's force concessions from the concentrated producers of goods and thereby give lower prices to consumers.

Galbraith's thesis begins to crumble at earlier stages in the productive process. Here, it is not likely that consumers derive much benefit from the big buyers. Think of American Telephone and Telegraph subsidiaries buying Anaconda's copper, of General Motor's purchases from U.S. Steel, of Consolidated Edison buying generators from General Electric.

There is no reason why these giant customers, partly or entirely free from competitive pressures, should force great concessions from their giant suppliers. At the production level, they operate in a live-and-let-live milieu. Why should they behave any differently when they are buyers? Even if the big buyers should extract concessions, what force compels them to be passed on to the dealers or consumers? In its quest for target returns, the corporate world wants stable prices and settles for higher prices as a second best. Price cutting is the last refuge to which corporation executives want to be driven. This fear of lower prices is reinforced by the prevailing corporate belief that demand is largely inelastic. That is, the typical corporation believes it won't gain enough extra sales from lower prices to compensate for the reduced revenue on each unit of sale. Given this frame of mind, corporations lack strong incentives to bargain down and pass on to consumers lower costs of supplies. Certainly the regulated telephone and electric utilities have little incentive to shop for lower costs. Their charges are set to yield a more or less fixed rate of return. The utilities are prevented in effect from pocketing any cost savings. And on the other side of that coin, increased copper or machinery costs can be translated into higher rates for consumers with the blessings of the regulatory commission.

In some industries, buyers and sellers are under the same corporate roof and obviously no genuine tug of war will take place. Crude oil production and refining afford a striking illustration of an industry in which some giants combine instead of countervail. In the Texas fields, the biggest buyers reporting their demand to the state regulatory agency in any month are subsidiaries of Standard Oil Co. (New Jersey), Standard Oil Co. (California), Standard Oil Co. (Indiana) and other giant producers.

In sum, whenever the big buyers are also big producers in a concentrated industry or whenever big buyers and big sellers are different arms of the same corporation, there are no grounds for believing that the ultimate consumer will enjoy any particular benefits from their dealings. If consumers are to gain from a struggle between buyers and sellers, the buyers who sell to consumers must be under strong competitive pressures.

Galbraith's selection of retailing to illustrate the theory of beneficent countervails is strategic. Despite the growth of chains linking many small stores or even large department stores, there is plenty of competition and relatively less concentration in this sector of the economy.

The trouble, as Professor George Stigler has observed, is that these large selling units buy most of their products from unconcentrated industries. Even if the chains are hard bargainers and share the fruits of their bargaining with consumers, they are buying from more or less weak sellers. The mail order chains and big department stores sell furniture and clothing chiefly; neither industry is dominated by a Big Four or Big Five. The A & P, Safeway and other grocery chains sell food; but farmers provide the textbook example of classical competitive markets. (Galbraith might retort with considerable justification that the Government has come to the aid of the farmers, giving them countervailing power in the form of price supports. While this may help shore up farm income, it is far from clear how it lowers prices to consumers.)

The other goods that consumers buy are generally distributed by weak sellers. These markets are characterized by a few giants on one side, the producing side, and a regiment of pigmies on the other, the retail side. The relative handful who manufacture autos, refine gasoline, make cigarettes, pour steel or manufacture building materials distribute through dealers or retailers who are rarely little more than dependent captives of the producers themselves. The local gas station, candy store or even Chevrolet dealer is not likely to impress Standard Oil Co. (New Jersey), The American Tobacco Co. or General Motors with his countervailing power.

If countervailing power in the corporate world is either nonexistent or malignant, can we hope for more from the confrontation of Big Labor with Big Business? The image of two equal and offsetting giants is particularly appealing to some celebrants of things as they are. Against corporate power, they cite strikes, large and wealthy unions and the prestigious positions of some union leaders. Thus the doctrine of pluralistic power is reaffirmed.

Whatever its value as a social and political check on the power of business, there is plenty of evidence that the confrontation between unions and managers often evolves into accommodation rather than conflict on the economic front. Again, Galbraith perceived this. When demand is strong, he said, "it is to the mutual advantage of union and employer to effect a coalition and to pass the costs of their agreement on in higher prices."

The coalition, of course, need not be overt, need not be collusive. Acting independently, countervails may coalesce and the consumer pays the price. The most striking example is the price-wage spiral that uncoiled in the steel industry from the end of World War II until the economy began to flatten out in 1958. The affair assumed a ritual nature. The United Steelworkers would press for a large wage increase. After some show of reluctance, the industry would grant a big packet and then use the bargain as an excuse to gain more than compensating price increases.[1]

A remarkable example can be found in the maritime industry—although admittedly shipping is a grotesque affair, a caricature of American industrial life. In this sector, the two leading unions tend to fight each other and to ally themselves with two separate sets of shipowners. Instead of offsetting the two types of carrier, the unions reinforce them.

One labor organization is the National Maritime Union or NMU. Its men sail for the most part on ships that receive building and operating subsidies from the federal government. The other union is the Seafarers International or SIU. Its membership is concentrated in lines that receive no such handouts.[2] The NMU works so closely with the major subsidized lines that they share the expenses of a Washington office for promoting bigger subsidies. The SIU has been looking for a formula that will weld it to its unsubsidized lines in a common effort to get a piece of this pie.

The strain between the two union-employer alliances led to a bizarre situation during the bargaining and strike of 1961. Then, the SIU found itself in the anomalous position of protesting the enormous wage increase that the subsidized lines were granting the NMU. The subsidized lines couldn't have cared less because the taxpayer would foot much of the added cost burden. The SIU's leaders knew they were undermining their position with their own members by asking for smaller gains than the NMU. But the SIU feared even more bankrupting some of its own nonsubsidized lines who would have to pay for the increase out of their own pockets. In the end, government mediators virtually compelled the SIU and its companies to accept the "bargain" struck by the NMU and its subsidized operators.

Scattered throughout the economy are similar union-industry alliances, typically in sectors that lack the price and market controlling influence of a few big firms. The International Ladies Garment Workers stabilizes the atomistic manufacturers of women's apparel. The United Hatters, Cap and Millinery Workers makes loans to keep alive weak (and possibly inefficient) hat companies. The United Mine Workers gives financial aid to large mines, helping to drive smaller, high cost and low paying companies to the wall. The Teamsters Union gives concessions in the terms of its contracts to large truckers and thereby promotes President James Hoffa's aim of eliminating the smaller firms.

[1] In the spiral's most virulent period during the 1950's, the union increased its members' pay and fringe benefits enough to lift steelmaking costs by 18 to 19 percent, according to Gardiner Means. But the companies raised prices by 36 percent.

[2] The inter-union rivalry is often ascribed to the thorny personalities of the two dominant leaders, Joe Curran and Paul Hall. Or it is blamed on their different CIO and AFL parentage. But neither factor is now so important as the differing economic interests of the shipowners with whom they bargain.

In some cities, building trades unions and contractors decide together who can bid on what jobs; at the national level, the construction unions and large employers collaborate to prevent industrial concerns from using their own workers on building tasks. On a much smaller scale, the secretary-treasurer of the New York newspaper reporters union in 1962 openly urged publishers during a strike to raise their circulation and advertising rates in order to pay bigger salaries. Whatever this was worth, two New York morning newspapers doubled their price after the strike was settled.

Apart from the various forms of combination, the popular notion of offsetting blocs is endangered on another front. The simple fact is that union power has been slowly ebbing away. Despite the noisy outcries over inconvenient strikes, Big Labor can't be equated with Big Business by capitalizing four words. The well-publicized union treasuries, the gleaming Washington headquarters and the infrequent, lengthy shutdowns give a misleading picture of union power. By the early 1960's, unions as a whole were losing about as many members as they were enrolling; their prospects of merely keeping pace with the growth of the labor force were dim. In the words of Sidney Lens, the typical union had become "an institution which carries out its accepted tasks in routine fashion, by rote, rather than . . . missionary force."

Behind this condition is the changing nature of the American economy and the comfortable, twilight repose of an entrenched leadership. The new economy is expanding in the very sectors where unions are weak or nonexistent and shrinking in the strongholds of unionism. In traditional union bastions like railroads and coal mining, jobs are vanishing under the impact of competing modes of transportation and fuel and a new technology that replaces men with machines.

The transformation of industrial sectors has been accompanied by a shift in occupations and the consequences for the unions are just as dismal. In the new automated, service-using economy, the nature of work is changing rapidly, and the unions are losing out. White collar clerks, technicians and professionals are growing; the blue collar semi-skilled worker, heart of the union, is falling back. For the first time in 1956, the number of white collar workers exceeded the number of blue collars.

Finally, an important postwar shift has taken place in industry's geographical location. The fastest growing regions of employment are the South and the West, historically indifferent or hostile to unions; jobs in the friendlier climate of the Northeast are also increasing but at a much slower rate.

These shifts within and between industries, in the nature of work and the location of industry have not reduced total union membership. But labor's rolls have generally remained static while the number of jobs slowly advances. The AFL-CIO estimated that labor had organized about 40 percent of its potential in 1953; by 1961, this had fallen to 38 percent. A union's power, like a corporation's, depends on its ability to impose its will. At the economic level, this power ultimately hinges on the union's ability to halt a productive process. In many sectors, unions still possess this strength; but in many of the rising sectors of the economy, this power is negligible or nonexistent.[3]

[3] One of the most common fallacies holds that "Jimmy Hoffa can stop the nation's wheels." Some arithmetic shows how little there is in this. Hoffa's membership includes at a generous estimate about 1.3 million truck drivers or enough to man perhaps 700,000 trucks. In 1961, there were 12.3 million trucks registered in the United States, or 17 for

If labor's economic power has been vastly overrated, its political strength has also been magnified out of all proportion. At the national level, labor's leaders have drifted into a satellite role within the Democratic Party. Union political endorsements are nearly as predictable as the movement of the planets. At the local levels, too, most union officials have become an integral part of a city or state machine, usually Democratic but occasionally Republican. The rewards for this loyalty have been largely honorific; prestige and place, positions on boards and commissions, an occasional ambassadorship, a few assistant secretaryships when the Democrats control the White House. The unions, in short, have fallen into what Mills called a nest of "status traps." But the price for this has been a marginal influence on programs and policies. A hard core of Representatives and even fewer Senators are wholly responsive to labor's organized views; they constitute a distinct minority.

The unions have become so much a part of existing political machinery that they can be and are taken for granted when policy and program decisions are made.

A striking example of just this occurred in the summer of 1962. The AFL-CIO was then as it had been for several years on record as favoring an immediate tax cut. But when the House Ways and Means Committee began hearings on a possible emergency reduction, Meany and other federation hierarchs were uncertain about their course. Some of Meany's staff strongly urged him not to endorse tax reduction because President Kennedy might not publicly favor it at that time. Others argued that Meany could not reject labor's own established position. Meany settled his dilemma by personally asking Kennedy what to do. The President told Meany that he should adhere to labor's line and so, with Kennedy's approval, Meany reaffirmed the AFL-CIO stand.

If labor's president has to ask the leader of the Democratic Party what position to take on a central issue of labor concern, and one on which the federation had already spoken, union legislative proposals are not likely to be regarded as imperatives by politicians of any stripe.

Labor's power is, even in an automating society, of great potential magnitude. Sometimes this power is displayed (and then some pluralizers think they detect excessive strength). But since the end of the second world war, this power has been confined to increasingly less important sectors of economic and political life. The erosion, however, has neither been startling enough nor rapid enough to shake most union leaders and their members from accustomed routines. But the steady decline in union power, coupled with the growing number of areas where unions and employers combine, unravels the concept of Big Labor as a countervailing force.

The artists of the political balancing act, however, have one more pole to swing. If Big Labor is a dubious offset, what about Big Government? Galbraith declared that "the support of countervailing power has become in modern

---

every one in Hoffa's domain. Hoffa's union embraces largely common carrier or for-hire trucks. But a large share of truck traffic moves on private fleets, outside the Teamsters' sway. Moreover, freight also moves on rails, barges, pipelines, ships and planes. In 1961 trucks accounted for less than one of every four freight ton-miles in intercity traffic. In other words, Hoffa at best "controls" a small fraction of trucking and trucks carry only a portion of all the freight. Hoffa could, if he dared, play hob with some particular city's food supply, but it is patent nonsense to talk of his halting the nation's transport.

times perhaps the major domestic peacetime function of the federal government." And Lilienthal, it will be recalled, assured his audience that "against the danger of Bigness . . . we either already have adequate public safeguards, or know how to fashion new ones as required."

If Big Government is indeed a countervail to Big Business, then an innocent observer might expect that the performance of the great federal regulatory agencies would support this view. These independent commissions, supposedly insulated from political manipulation, were created to rule over transportation, communications and the distribution of power, among other spheres. Their record, however, gives little comfort to the theorists of balance. Indeed, the overwhelming testimony is that the regulators in time become the captives of the regulated, that the commissions become the creatures of the industries they are supposed to police. This is not simply a question of venality; this is the record of nearly every agency since the establishment of the first in 1887.

As the agencies mature, after the flush of reforming zeal that called them into being has passed, here is what happens according to Professor Marver H. Bernstein of Princeton:

> The approach and point of view of the regulatory process begin to partake of those of business management . . . the commission becomes more concerned with the general health of the industry and tries to prevent changes which adversely affect it. Cut off from the mainstream of political life, the commissions standards of regulation are determined in the light of the desires of the industry affected. It is unlikely that the commission, in this period, will be able to extend regulation beyond the limits acceptable to the regulated groups . . . The close of the period of maturity is marked by the commission's surrender to the regulated . . . the commission finally becomes a captive of the regulated groups.

From inside the commissions, the same story is told. Here is Louis J. Hector, writing to President Eisenhower after resigning from the Civil Aeronautics Board.

> But no man can possibly work all day every day with the same people in the same industry . . . and then from time to time wipe out every bit of that out of his mind in order to become a judge . . . Commissioners circulate more or less freely in the industry they regulate . . . [Later] the same commissioner climbs on the bench and is supposed suddenly to become a judge . . . The system is actually so inviting to improper influence that it will inevitably occur from time to time.

Here is Howard Morgan, writing to President Kennedy as he resigns from the Federal Power Commission:

> Abandonment of the public interest can be caused by many things, of which timidity and a desire for personal security are the most insidious, the least detectable and, once established in a regulatory agency, the hardest to eradicate. Without the needed sense of public responsibility, a commissioner can find it very easy to consider whether his vote might arouse an industry campaign against his reconfirmation by the Senate, and even easier to convince himself that no such thought ever crossed his mind.

When commissioners lack character and courage, Morgan said, implying that his peers were deficient in both, "utility regulation ceases to be or never becomes a protection to the consuming public. Instead it can easily become a fraud upon the public and a protective shield behind which monopoly may operate to the public detriment."

The authorities could be cited without end, but perhaps one more should be invoked. In 1892, Attorney General Richard Olney, a prominent corporation lawyer, wrote a farsighted and soothing letter to a railroad president who thought that the recently created Interstate Commerce Commission should be destroyed.

> The Commission, as its functions have now been limited by the courts, is or can be made of great use to the railroads. It satisfies the popular clamor for a government supervision of railroads, at the same time that that supervision is almost entirely nominal. Further, the older such a Commission gets to be, the more inclined it will be found to take the business and railroad view of things. It thus becomes a sort of barrier between the railroad corporations and the people and a sort of protection against hasty and crude legislation hostile to railroad interests . . . The part of wisdom is not to destroy the Commission but to utilize it.

Olney's vision was realized beyond his fondest hopes. The ICC has become over the years so much of a tool of the railroads (except for the bureau regulating trucks which is a sturdy defender of trucking interests), that it is almost killing the lines with kindness. The ICC's habit of indiscriminately granting whatever rate increases the carriers seek has helped to drive freight and passengers to other modes of transportation.

The same story of subservience is found in most of the other regulatory agencies. The Federal Power Commission refused for years to enforce a Supreme Court decision requiring the agency to fix the prices charged by independent natural gas producers. In those sectors where the FPC has set prices, James M. Landis observed, the agency has displayed "disregard of the consumer interest." This disregard is so flagrant that state regulatory agencies have had to fight FPC's efforts to impose "monopolistic and excessive rates." That's the rare case of man bites dog. Normally, it is the state commissions who are most easily controlled by client industries and the federal government that offers consumers relatively stronger protection.

Similarly, the Civil Aeronautics Board has zealously protected the major airlines. The CAB shielded them from new competition by strangling with harassing regulations the nonscheduled airlines that flourished after the war and by refusing to certify any new scheduled airline despite the rapid growth in air travel. Again, the Federal Communication Commission's responsiveness to the television and radio networks has been so notorious that President Kennedy tried to give a new character to this servile and corrupted agency by staffing it with some of the most independent of the New Frontiersmen.

Students of the regulatory commissions often cite three reasons for the servility of the agencies: commission procedures do not allow a public representative or public counsel to press consumer views, so only an industry voice is heard; the commissioners tend to come from private industry and to leave government for the very industry they had been "regulating"; and, finally, the regulated industries can and do keep up a steady, one-sided pressure on their regulators. But there is nothing about these factors that is unique to the commissions. They are all present with varying degrees of intensity in the executive departments. When the Treasury, for example, plans to float a bond issue, it consults committees of bankers to find out what they want. The Agriculture Department tends to regard itself as the farmers' representative, not as a public interest body. Its subdivisions generally reflect the views of the commodity producers whom the bureaus are promoting as well as regulating.

Perhaps the process can be observed most nakedly in the Interior Department's Bureau of Mines and its treatment of petroleum. Oil production, unlike refining and transportation, is not concentrated but is divided among thousands of big and small concerns. In the name of conservation, the principal oil producing states set production quotas each month, limiting the amount that the wells may bring up. These state quotas, in turn, are based on forecasts made by the Bureau of Mines. The reports calculate the amount of oil that can be sold at existing prices. The system is reinforced by a prohibition against the interstate shipment of oil produced outside of a state quota and by curbs on the quantity of oil that can be imported. Here then is a complex federal-state system designed to keep oil prices above the production costs of relatively inefficient producers by tailoring supply to demand at going prices.

"Concern for the conservation of a scarce and essential raw material was made a justification for regulation, but the real stimulus to regulatory action was the desire of oil producers and allied interests to promote their own economic welfare."

This is the conclusion of a standard text, *Government and the American Economy* by Merle Fainsod, Lincoln Gordon and Joseph C. Palamountain. In other words, the state agencies and the Bureau of Mines become a legal substitute for a Big Three or for an illegal conspiracy to set prices.

In sum, the Big Government of the Cabinet departments suffers many of the defects of the regulatory agencies. The notion that either or both is an effective countervail to corporate power is dubious as long as the departments, bureaus and agencies are organized functionally, created to serve, regulate and promote separate producers and industries. The parochial nature of their task tends to turn officials of even the best will from broad-based public considerations to the establishment of a symbiotic partnership with the industry to which they are engaged. If a mechanism could be created so that government agencies and their client industries, as a matter of self-interest, thought in terms of the whole economy and the whole society, if representatives from other groups in the public were given a voice in their councils, a different result might take place. But in the present state of affairs, the government is much more likely to combine with than to offset business power.

The Cold War has added a new dimension to this problem. One of its principal consequences has been to blur the line between public and private functions. Under the impact of enormous military expenditures, government and private industry have become entangled at an astonishing number of points. The combination is most visible in the flow of top officials who shuttle between high military and government posts to corporate presidencies and directorships. Less apparent but just as important are the new ways in which the government conducts defense business.

The importance of the national security sector in the nation's economy cannot be exaggerated. For the accounting year ending on June 30, 1964, $56 billion was allotted to defense and space tasks, nearly three of every five dollars in the government's conventional budget and about 10 percent of the economy's total output.

Major industries have grown up almost entirely dependent on government military orders; others draw a substantial portion of their income from military buying. The companies in the aerospace industry receive from two-thirds to 99 percent of their total business from military purchases. The leading electrical machinery producers, General Electric and Westinghouse make nearly a third of their sales to defense buyers.

This breeds a dependency that works two ways. Government agencies become as bound to their military suppliers as the military suppliers to their federal customer. So, the Defense Department will deliberately award orders to a less efficient producer to maintain that producer's productive capacity. Officials in charge of the government's stockpile of strategic materials testified they had bought more than they needed to support the prices and profits of their industrial suppliers. A military service or its bureaus will develop as much of a vested interest in one company's weapon design as the company itself. The prestige and power of the service will depend on the appropriations it gets and this in turn may hinge on the approval of its chosen company's design. Just as some trade unions have fought against ending production of an obsolete weapon in order to preserve members' jobs, so too service officers struggle to hold what they have and to expand their domain.

The line between private and public becomes fuzziest, however, in the new administrative arrangements for parceling out defense business. The government does not as a rule award contracts for a rocket engine, a firing mechanism or the construction of a launching site. Instead, it hires a firm to produce a "weapons system" complete from soup to nuts, from blueprints to installation and possibly even operation. Indeed, the firm holding the prime or original contract for such a system will probably draw up the menu itself. The military agency may merely describe what characteristics a new weapon should have and let the prime contractor invent one to fit. The design and production of component parts and the erection of facilities like launching sites will be distributed by this prime contractor downward through successive tiers of subcontractors.

Since no one can reasonably estimate the cost of something that is yet to be invented, the military does not usually award these contracts by competitive bids to the lowest cost firm. Instead, the Defense Department typically negotiates with one firm, or a few selected firms, promising to cover all costs and add on a fixed fee for profit.

In this new twilight world, the government has turned over an endless variety of functions to private groups. Dean Don K. Price of the School of Public Administration at Harvard has noted "that private corporations have contracts to maintain the Air Force's bombers and its missile ranges, private institutions make strategic studies for the Joint Chiefs of Staff and foreign policy studies for the Senate Foreign Relations Committee, universities administer technical-assistance programs for the State Department all over the world, and telephone and radio companies are about to help the National Aeronautics and Space Administration carry our messages through outer space."

One study of the new defense contracting concludes: "While private firms have thus been freed from the restraints of the open market, they have acquired new public responsibilities. They are no longer merely suppliers to the government, but participants in the administration of public functions."

In this new world, arms length bargaining between independent parties disappears. Instead, as E. Perkins McGuire, former Assistant Secretary of Defense, said: "Some of these contractors by the very magnitude of the procurement we are involved in *are in reality agents of the government.*"

The two quotations underline the ambiguity of the new relationship. One suggests that the private firms have become public administrators; the other, that they are really government instruments. In either case, it is clear that they are not simply selling goods and services to a public customer.

The eggs have been so thoroughly scrambled that government officials are becoming worried about a silent abdication of responsibility. In a report to President Kennedy, some of his top advisers generally applauded the new partnership in contracting for research and development. However, the report, signed by Defense Secretary Robert S. McNamara among others, acknowledged "that in recent years there have been instances—particularly in the Department of Defense—where we have come dangerously close to permitting contract employees to exercise functions which belong with top government management officials."

Apart from the fusing of public and private roles, the great military expenditures undermine the theory of the government countervail in another and central way. The tens of billions of defense dollars contribute substantially to the centralization of American enterprise, to the dominance of the large corporations. This is because the lion's share of military contracts are placed with a relative handful of great firms. Concentration has marked defense outlays since the second world war. If anything, it is currently increasing rather than declining. During World War II, two-thirds of the military orders were awarded to the 100 largest defense contractors. During Korea, the share of the 100 largest dropped slightly to 64 percent. But in the accounting years from 1958 through 1962, it had risen to nearly three-quarters. The biggest 25 firms alone received more than half of the business during this latest period.

From the standpoint of economic dominance, the most important government dollars are those spent for research and development. These funds finance the search for new knowledge, and new applications of existing knowledge. Firms with the inside track to new technology have the best chance to command the markets of the future. The boxscore of research and development outlays in the United States shows three things. The government provides most of the money for scientific and technological advance. Within the government, the biggest source by far is the military-space-atomic-energy complex, the Cold War agencies. And like defense spending generally, government research and development expenditures are heavily concentrated among a few corporations.[4]

[4] In the year 1960–61, for example, the federal government supplied $9.2 billion of the $14 billion spent on research and development. Two years earlier, the federal share was $7.2 billion out of $11.1 billion. In . . . 1959, the government provided private industry with $5.6 billion for research and development or 59 percent of all industrial outlays. Of this sum, $4.2 billion went to the three defense-dominated sectors, aircraft and parts, electrical equipment and communications. Large firms, those with 5000 or more employees, received $5.1 billion or nine dollars out of every ten that the government gave industry for research and development.

The flow of federal military and research funds to the large corporations erodes the government's countervailing power in direct as well as indirect ways. The most obvious form of countervail is antitrust action, aimed at reducing the strength of large corporations. But under the stress of the Cold War, the Department of Justice will temper antitrust prosecutions at the request of the Defense Department.

The Justice Department, for example, brought an antitrust action against the American Telephone and Telegraph Co. in 1949. Among other things, the suit asked for the divorce of A T & T from Western Electric, its highly profitable equipment-producing subsidiary. But partly at the request of the Defense Department, Justice officials abandoned this decisive step and permitted A T & T and Western Electric to continue in wedded bliss.

This chapter's description of some of the relations between government and business does not imply acceptance of a crude Marxist formulation that the state is merely an agent of a ruling, capital-owning class. But it does raise serious questions about the equally crude notion that government is and can be an impartial umpire, above the battle, protecting the public interest against contending forces. Professor Earl Lathem wisely suggests that: " 'Government' is merely the device through which advantaged groups perpetuate their advantages, which disadvantaged groups would like to control, but cannot win." *

* Crass Marxists are certainly indebted to Mr. Nossiter. The government, it seems, is not an "agent" of the capitalist ruling class, but rather a "device" of that powerful and advantaged class. We must admit that, with our lack of sophistication, the subtlety originally escaped us.

8 THE STATE IN CAPITALIST SOCIETY*

by RALPH MILIBAND

What the pluralists are left with, once Nossiter is done, is a vague faith that at least our politicians, because they are elected by the people, must be immune from corporate domination. This idea also does not stand up for long. Corporations dominate the elective mechanism, too. They predominate in both political parties, and their financial support is crucial to winning campaigns. They own and operate the media, by which they influence popular attitudes—no politician can ignore that. They operate active, well-heeled lobbies which get in on the ground floor when legislation is being written or bills passed. They have easy access to politicians socially and professionally, since politicians and businessmen often come from the same class.

But to prove that the priorities of the private economic system dominate the activities of government, you don't have to rely on tracing the routes of easy access businessmen have to politicians. You just have to look at the relations of power. Corporations hold the economic system in their hand. A politician must take large account of that, because everything he might want to do depends on the economy, and thus depends on corporate power. If he wants to bring prosperity to his home state, then he has got to watch that he creates a good environment for attracting businesses there. If he wants to bring prosperity to the whole country, then he has to make sure the "business climate" is looking up, that investment is growing, that the stock market is going up, etc. When you are over the barrel like that, you are not busy plotting how you can take away corporate power.

The only politicians who can afford to oppose the will of the corporate sector are those who can afford to face the consequences of corporate backlash and who are willing to fight the corporate sector to its death. But only a popular movement can do that. Politicians under capitalism accept capitalism as a given, and once they have done that, then they have accepted cooperating with corporate power.

I

At first sight, the picture is one of endless diversity between succeeding governments, and indeed inside each of them; as also between governments of different countries. Presidents, prime ministers and their colleagues have worn many different political labels (often wildly misleading), and belonged to many different parties, or occasionally to none.

This diversity of views, attitudes, programmes and policies, on an infinite number of subjects, is certainly very striking and makes for live political debate and competition. And the impression of diversity and conflict is further enhanced by the insistence of party leaders, particularly at election time, on the wide and almost impassable, or actually impassable, gulf which separates them from their opponents and competitors.

The assertion of such profound differences is a matter of great importance for the functioning and legitimation of the political system, since it suggests that electors, by voting for one or other of the main competing parties, are making a choice between fundamental and incompatible alternatives, and that they are therefore, as voters, deciding nothing less than the future of their country.

In actual fact however, this picture is in some crucial ways highly superficial and mystifying. For one of the most important aspects of the political life of advanced capitalism is precisely that the disagreements *between those political leaders who have generally been able to gain high office* have very seldom been of the fundamental kind these leaders and other people so often suggest. What is really striking about *these* political leaders and political office-holders, in relation to each other, is not their many differences, but the extent of their agreement on truly fundamental issues—as they themselves, when occasion requires, have been wont to recognise, and as large numbers of people among the public at large, despite the political rhetoric to which they are subjected, recognise in the phrase "politicians are all the same." [1] This is an exaggeration, of course. But it is an exaggeration with a solid kernel of truth, at least in relation to the kind of men who tend to succeed each other in office in advanced capitalist countries. Marxists put the same point somewhat differently when they say that these men, whatever their political labels or party affiliations, are bourgeois politicians.

The basic sense in which this is true is that the political office-holders of advanced capitalism have, with very few exceptions, been agreed over what Lord Balfour, in a classical formulation, once called "the foundations of society," meaning above all the existing economic and social system of private ownership and private appropriation—Marx's "mode of production." Balfour was writing about Britain, and about the Whig and Tory administrations of the nineteenth century. But his point applies equally well to other capitalist countries, and to the twentieth century as well as to the nineteenth.

For it is no more than a matter of plain political history that the governments of these countries have mostly been composed of men who beyond all their political, social, religious, cultural and other differences and diversities, have at least had in common a basic and usually explicit belief in the validity and virtues of the capitalist system, though this was not what they would necessarily call it; and those among them who have not been particularly concerned with that system, or even aware that they were helping to run a specific economic system, much in the way that they were not aware of the air they breathed, have at least shared with their more ideologically-aware colleagues or competi-

[1] As witnessed, for instance, by the number of people in countries like Britain and the United States who, when asked whether they believe that there are important differences between the main competing parties, tend to answer in the negative.

tors a quite basic and unswerving hostility to any socialist alternative to that system.

There have, it is true, been occasions, whose significance will be considered presently, when men issued from working-class and formally socialist parties have occupied positions of governmental power, either alone or more commonly as members of coalitions, in many capitalist countries. But even though these men have quite often professed anti-capitalist convictions, they have never posed—and indeed have for the most part never wished to pose—a serious challenge to a capitalist system (or rather, as most of them would have it, a "mixed economy"), whose basic framework and essential features they have accepted much more readily than their pronouncements in opposition, and even sometimes in office, would have tended to suggest.

In this sense, the pattern of executive power has remained much more consistent than the alternation in office of governments bearing different labels and affecting different colorations has made it appear: capitalist regimes have mainly been governed by men who have either genuinely believed in the virtues of capitalism, or who, whatever their reservations as to this or that aspect of it, have accepted it as far superior to any possible alternative economic and social system, and who have therefore made it their prime business to defend it. Alternatively, these regimes have been governed by men who, even though they might call themselves socialists, have not found the commitment this might be thought to entail in the least incompatible with the ready, even the eager, acceptance of all the essential features of the system they came to administer.

However, even if we leave out for the present the particular role of formally socialist power-holders, it must be stressed again that this basic consensus between bourgeois politicians does not preclude genuine and important differences between them, not only on issues other than the actual management of the economic system, but on that issue as well.

Thus, it has always been possible to make an important distinction between parties and leaders, however committed they might be to the private enterprise system, who stood for a large measure of state intervention in economic and social life, and those who believed in a lesser degree of intervention; and the same distinction encompasses those parties and men who have believed that the state must assume a greater degree of responsibility for social and other kinds of reform; and those who have wished for less.

But the fact nevertheless remains that these differences and controversies, even at their most intense, have never been allowed by the politicians concerned to bring into question the validity of the "free enterprise" system itself; and even the most determined interventionists among them have always conceived their proposals and policies as a means, not of eroding—let alone supplanting—the capitalist system, but of ensuring its greater strength and stability. To a much larger extent than appearance and rhetoric have been made to suggest, the politics of advanced capitalism have been about different conceptions of how to run the *same* economic and social system, and not about radically different social systems. *This* debate has not so far come high on the political agenda.

Given their view of that system, it is easy to understand why governments should wish to help business in every possible way, yet do not at all feel that this entails any degree of bias towards particular classes, interests and groups. For if the national interest is in fact inextricably bound up with the fortunes of capitalist enterprise, apparent partiality towards it is not really partiality at all. On the contrary, in serving the interests of business and in helping capitalist enterprise to thrive, governments are really fulfilling their exalted role as guardians of the good of all. From this standpoint, the much-derided phrase "What is good for General Motors is good for America" is only defective in that it tends to identify the interests of one particular enterprise with the national interest. But if General Motors is taken to stand for the world of capitalist enterprise as a whole, the slogan is one to which governments in capitalist countries do subscribe, often explicitly. And they do so because they accept the notion that the economic rationality of the capitalist system is synonymous with rationality itself, and that it provides the best possible set of human arrangements in a necessarily imperfect world.

II

The first and most important consequence of the commitment which governments in advanced capitalist countries have to the private enterprise system and to its economic rationality is that it enormously limits their freedom of action in relation to a multitude of issues and problems. Raymond Aron has written that "it goes without saying that in a system based on private ownership of the means of production, measures taken by legislators and cabinet officials are not going to be in fundamental opposition to the interest of the property owners." This proposition, he comments, is too obvious to be instructive. It *should* perhaps be obvious. But it does not appear to be so to most Western political scientists who view the state as free from the inherent bias in favour of capitalist interests which Professor Aron's proposition implies.

That bias has immense policy implications. For the resolution, or at least the alleviation of a vast range of economic and social problems requires precisely that governments *should* be willing to act in "fundamental opposition" to these interests. Far from being a trivial matter, their extreme reluctance to do so is one of the largest of all facts in the life of these societies. Were it to be said about a government that though faced with a vast criminal organisation it could not be expected to act in fundamental opposition to it, the observation would not be thought uninstructive about its character and role. The same is true of the proposition which Professor Aron so casually puts forward and tosses aside.

On the other hand, that proposition tends to obscure a basic aspect of the state's role. For governments, acting in the name of the state, have in fact been compelled over the years to act against *some* property rights, to erode *some* managerial prerogatives, to help redress *somewhat* the balance between capital and labour, between property and those who are subject to it. This is an aspect of state intervention which conservative writers who lament the growth of "bureaucracy" and who deplore state "interference" in the affairs of society regularly overlook. Bureaucracy is indeed a problem and a danger, and the experience of countries like the Soviet Union has amply shown how greatly unrestrained bureaucratic power can help to obstruct the creation of a socialist society worthy of the name. But concentration upon the evils of bureaucracy in capitalist countries obscures (and is often intended to obscure) the fact that "bureaucratic" intervention has often been a means of alleviating the evils produced by unrestrained private economic power.

The state's "interference" with that power is not in "fundamental opposition" to the interests of property: it is indeed part of that "ransom" of which Joseph Chamberlain spoke in 1885 and which, he said, would have to be paid precisely for the purpose of *maintaining* the rights of property in general. In insisting that the "ransom" be paid, governments render property a major service, though the latter is seldom grateful for it. Even so, it would not do to ignore the fact that even very conservative governments in the regimes of advanced capitalism have often been forced, mainly as a result of popular pressure, to take action against *certain* property rights and capitalist prerogatives.

As against this, however, must be set the very positive support which governments have generally sought to give to dominant economic interests.

Capitalist enterprise *depends* to an ever greater extent on the bounties and direct support of the state, and can only preserve its "private" character on the basis of such public help. State intervention in economic life in fact largely *means* intervention for the purpose of helping capitalist enterprise. In no field has the notion of the "welfare state" had a more precise and apposite meaning than here: there are no more persistent and successful applicants for public assistance than the proud giants of the private enterprise system.

Nor need that assistance be of a direct kind to be of immense value to capitalist interests. Because of the imperative requirements of modern life, the state must, within the limits imposed upon it by the prevailing economic system, engage in bastard forms of socialisation and assume responsibility for many functions and services which are beyond the scope and capabilities of capitalist interests. As it does so, however, what Jean Meynaud calls "the bias of the system" ensures that these interests will automatically benefit from state intervention. Because of the private ownership and control of a predominant part of economic life, Professor Meynaud writes:

> . . . all the measures taken by the state to develop and improve the national economy always end up by being of the greatest benefit to those who control the levers of command of the production-distribution sector: when the state cuts tunnels, builds roads, opens up highways or reclaims swamps, it is first of all the owners of the neighbouring lands who reap the rewards . . . the concept of the "bias of the system" makes it also possible to understand that the measures taken to remedy the derelictions, shortcomings and abuses of capitalism result ultimately, where successful, in the consolidation of the regime. It matters little in this respect that these measures should have been undertaken by men sympathetic or hostile to capitalist interest: thus it is that laws designed to protect the workers and directed against their exploitation by employers will be found useful to the latter by inducing them to make a greater effort to rationalise or mechanise the productive process.

Governments may be solely concerned with the better running of "the economy." But the description of the system as "the economy" is part of the idiom of ideology, and obscures the real process. For what is being improved is a *capitalist* economy; and this ensures that whoever may or may not gain, capitalist interests are least likely to lose.

The "bias of the system" may be given a greater or lesser degree of emphasis. But the ideological dispositions of governments have generally been of a kind to make more acceptable to them the structural constraints imposed upon them by the system; and these dispositions have also made it easier for them to submit to the pressures to which they have been subjected by dominant interests.

Taxation offers a ready illustration of the point. The economic system itself generates extremely powerful tendencies towards the maintenance and enhancement of the vast inequalities of income and wealth which are typical of all advanced capitalist societies. Given that economic system, no government can achieve redistributive miracles. But the limits of its powers in this field are nevertheless not finally fixed—despite the system's tendencies to inequality and the fierce opposition of the forces of wealth to redistributive taxation. And the fact that taxation has not, over the years, affected more deeply than it has the disparities of income and wealth in these societies must to a major extent be attributed to the attitude of governments towards inequality, to the view they take of the conflicting claims of the rich and the poor, and to their acceptance of an economic orthodoxy which has, at any particular moment of time, declared additional burdens on the rich to be fatal to "business confidence," "individual initiative," the propensity to invest, etc.

The same considerations apply to government intervention in "industrial relations," the consecrated euphemism for the permanent conflict, now acute, now subdued, between capital and labour.

Whenever governments have felt it incumbent, as they have done more and more, to intervene directly in disputes between employers and wage-earners, the result of their intervention has tended to be disadvantageous to the latter, not the former. On innumerable occasions, and in all capitalist countries, governments have played a decisive role in defeating strikes, often by the invocation of the coercive power of the state and the use of naked violence; and the fact that they have done so in the name of the national interest, law and order, constitutional government, the protection of "the public," etc., rather than simply to support employers, has not made that intervention any the less useful to these employers.

Moreover, the state, as the largest of all employers, is now able to influence the pattern of "industrial relations" by the force of its own example and behaviour: that influence can hardly be said to have created new standards in the employer-employee relationship. Nor could it have been expected to do so, given the "business-like" spirit in which the public sector is managed.

Governments are deeply involved, on a permanent and institutionalised basis, in that "routinisation of conflict," which is an essential part of the politics of advanced capitalism. They enter that conflict in the guise of a neutral and independent party, concerned to achieve not the outright defeat of one side or the other but a "reasonable" settlement between them. But the state's intervention in negotiations occurs in the shadow of its known and declared propensity to invoke its powers of coercion, against one of the parties in the dispute rather than the other, if "conciliation" procedures fail. These procedures form, in fact, an additional element of restraint upon organised labour, and also serve the useful purpose of further dividing the trade union ranks. The state does interpose itself between the "two sides of industry"—not, however, as a neutral but as a partisan.

Nor is this nowadays only true when industrial disputes actually occur. One of the most notable features in the recent evolution of advanced capitalism is the degree to which governments have sought to place new and further inhibitions upon organised labour in order to prevent it from exercising what pressures it can on employers (and on the state as a major employer) in the matter of wage claims. What they tend to achieve, by such means as an "incomes policy," or by deflationary policies which reduce the demand for labour, is a *general* weakening of the bargaining position of wage-earners.[2] Here too, the policies adopted are proclaimed to be essential to the national interest, the health of the economy, the defense of the currency, the good of the workers, and so on. And there are always trade union leaders who can be found to endorse both the claims and the policies. But this does not change the fact that the main effect of these policies is to leave wage-earners in a weaker position *vis-à-vis* employers than would otherwise be the case. The *purpose,* in the eyes of political office-holders, may be all that it is said to be; but the *result,* with unfailing regularity, is to the detriment of the subordinate classes. This is why the latter, in this as in most other instances, have good reason to beware when the political leaders of advanced capitalist countries invoke the national interest in defence of their policies—more likely than not they, the subordinate classes, are about to be done in. Wage-earners have always had to reckon with a hostile state in their encounter with employers. But now more than ever they have to reckon with its antagonism, in practice, as a direct, pervasive, and constant fact of economic life. Their immediate and daily opponent remains the employer; but governments and the state are now much more closely involved in the encounter than in the past.

Quite naturally, this partiality of governments assumes an even more specific, precise and organised character in relation to all movements, groupings and parties dedicated to the transformation of capitalist societies into socialist ones. The manner in which governments have expressed this antagonism has greatly varied over time, and between countries, assuming here a milder form, there a harsher one; but the antagonism itself has been a permanent fact in the history of all capitalist countries. In no field has the underlying consensus between political office-holders of different political affiliations, and between the governments of different countries, been more substantial and notable—the leaders of all governmental parties, whether in office or in opposition, and including nominally "socialist" ones, have always been deeply hostile to the socialist and militant left, of whatever denomination, and governments themselves have in fact been the major protagonists against it, in their role of protectors and saviours of society from the perils of left-wing dissidence.

In this instance too, liberal-democratic and pluralist theorists, in their celebration of the political competition which prevails in their societies, and in their insistence on the political neutrality of the state, quite overlook the fact that the governments of advanced capitalist societies, far from taking a neutral view of *socialist* competition, do their level best to make it more difficult. In some countries, for instance Federal Germany, Communist and other left-wing parties and organisations are suppressed altogether, and membership made a crime punishable by law; in others, such as the United States, left-wing organi-

[2] See, e.g., Michael Kidron, *Western Capitalism Since the War,* London, Weidenfeld and Nicolson, 1968, pp. 190 ff; "Incomes Policy and the Trade Unions," in *International Socialist Journal,* 1964, vol. 1, no. 3; and "The Campaign Against the Right to Strike," in *ibid.,* 1964, vol. 1, no. 1.

sations, of which the Communist Party is only one, operate in conditions of such harassment as to narrow rather drastically, in their case, the notion of free political competition.

Nor is the state's hostility less marked in other countries, though it may assume different forms—for instance electoral manipulation as in France and Italy for the purpose of robbing their Communist parties of the parliamentary representation to which their electoral strength entitles them; the engineering of bias in the mass media, in so far as lies in the considerable and growing power of governments; and also episodic but quite brutal repression of left-wing dissenters.

The argument is not whether governments should or should not be neutral as between conservative and anti-conservative ideologies, movements, parties and groups. That question is not susceptible to resolution in terms of such imperatives. The argument is rather that the governments of advanced capitalist countries have never been thus neutral, and that they have for the most part used the state power on the conservative as against the anti-conservative side. And the further argument is that in so doing they have, whatever other purposes they might have wished to serve, afforded a most precious element of protection to those classes and interests whose power and privileges socialist dissent is primarily intended to undermine and destroy. Those who believe in the virtues of a social order which includes such power and privileges will applaud and support governmental partiality, and may even ask for more of it. Those who do not will not. The important point is to see what so much of political analysis obscures, often from itself, namely that this *is* what governments, in these countries, actually do.

The argument so far has centered on some of the main *internal* consequences which flow from the commitment of governments to the capitalist system. But the *external* consequences of that commitment are no less direct and important.

Here, perhaps even more than in other fields, the purposes which governments proclaim their wish to serve are often made to appear remote from specific economic concerns, let alone capitalist interests. It is the national interest, national security, national independence, honour, greatness, etc., that is their concern. But this naturally includes a sound, healthy, thriving economic system; and such a desirable state of affairs depends in turn on the prosperity of capitalist enterprise. Thus, by the same mechanism which operates in regard to home affairs, the governments of capitalist countries have generally found that their larger national purposes required the servicing of capitalist interests; and the crucial place which these interests occupy in the life of their country has always caused governments to make their defence against foreign capitalist interests, and against the foreign states which protect *them,* a prime consideration in their conduct of external affairs.[3]

The whole history of Western (and Japanese) imperialism is a clear case in point. It is certainly not true that these governments went into Africa or Asia

[3] As an American Secretary of State put it in May 1914 to the National Council of Foreign Trade, in words which have remained highly apposite: "I can say, not merely in courtesy—but as a fact—my Department is your department; the ambassadors, the ministers and the consuls are all yours. It is their business to look after your interests and to guard your rights." (Quoted in W. A. Williams, *The Tragedy of American Diplomacy,* 1959, p. 51).

simply to serve powerful economic interests. Nor did they embark upon imperialist expansion *simply* because they were "compelled" to do so by such interests. Vast historical movements of this kind cannot be reduced to these simplicities. But here too the many other purposes which governments have wished to serve in their quest for empire have involved, preeminently, the furtherance of private economic interests. They may *really* have been concerned with national security, the strengthening of the economic and social fabric, the shouldering of the white man's burden, the fulfilment of their national destiny, and so forth. But these purposes required, as they saw it, the securing by conquest of lands which were already or which could become zones of exploitation for their national capitalist interests, whose implantation and expansion were thus guaranteed by the power of the state. In this case too the fact that political office-holders were seeking to achieve many other purposes should not obscure the fact that, *in the service of these purposes,* they became the dedicated servants of their business and investing classes.

The same considerations apply to the attitude of capitalist governments towards the formally independent countries of the Third World in which their national capitalist interests have a stake, or might acquire one.

Thus, the attitude of the government of the United States towards, say, Central and Latin America is not exclusively determined by its concern to protect American investments in the area or to safeguard the opportunity of such investments in the future. When for instance the government of the United States decided in 1954 that the Arbenz government in Guatemala must be overthrown,[4] it did so not merely because that government had taken 225,000 acres of land from the American-owned United Fruit Company but because that action, in the eyes of the government of the United States, provided the best possible proof of "Communist" leanings, which made the Arbenz regime a threat to "American security."[5] But what this and many other similar episodes mean is that "American security" is so interpreted by those responsible for it as to require foreign governments to show proper respect for the rights and claims of American business. This may not be the only test of a government's "reliability"; but it is a primary one nevertheless. As a general rule, the American government's attitude to governments in the Third World, or for that matter in the whole non-socialist world, depends very largely on the degree to which these governments favour American free enterprise in their countries or are likely to favour it in the future. The governments of other advanced capitalist countries are moved by a similar concern. The difference between them and the government of the United States is not in basic approach but in the scale of their foreign investments and enterprises and in their capacity to act in defence of these interests.

In this perspective, the supreme evil is obviously the assumption of power by governments whose main purpose is precisely to abolish private ownership and private enterprise, home and foreign, in the most important sectors of their economic life or in all of them. Such governments are profoundly objectionable not only because their actions adversely affect foreign-owned interests and en-

[4] See, e.g. D. Wise and T. B. Ross, *The Invisible Government,* 1964, ch. 11.

[5] "In the era of the Cold War, keeping Soviet power and influence out of the hemisphere, and particularly out of the Panama Canal area, was far more important to Washington than old-fashioned style banana diplomacy. But certainly the seizure of United Fruit's holdings without adequate compensation forced Eisenhower to take action" (*ibid.,* p. 170).

terprises or because they render future capitalist implantation impossible; in some cases this may be of no great economic consequence. But the objection still remains because the withdrawal of any country from the world system of capitalist enterprise is seen as constituting a weakening of that system and as providing encouragement to further dissidence and withdrawal.

Here also lie the roots of the fierce hostility towards the Bolshevik Revolution which led the capitalist powers to try to crush it in blood—long before, incidentally, the notion of "Soviet aggression" had become the standard justification for their policies. And here too lies the main clue to the foreign policies of these powers since the end of the second world war, indeed during that war as well.[6] The purpose, always and above all else, has been to prevent the coming into being, anywhere, of regimes fundamentally opposed to capitalist enterprise and determined to do away with it.

Western office-holders have justified their attitude to socialist regimes and movements in terms of their love of freedom, their concern for democracy, their hatred of dictatorship, and their fear of aggression. In this instance, as in most others, it is not very useful to ask whether in these proclamations they were "sincere" or not. The important point is rather that they defined freedom in terms which made capitalist enterprise one of its main and sometimes its sole ingredient. On this basis, the defence of freedom does become the defence of free enterprise: provided *this* is safe, all else, however evil, can be condoned, overlooked and even supported.[7] Almost by definition, no regime which respects capitalist interests can be deemed hopelessly bad and must in any case be considered as inherently superior to any regime which does not. Given this attitude, it is not of major consequence that capitalist governments should have been concerned, in external relations, with more than the interests of their businessmen and investors. However that may be, *these* are the interests which their policies have most consistently served.

[6] See, e.g. J. Bagguly, "The World War and the Cold War," in D. Horowitz (ed.), *Containment and Revolution,* 1967.

[7] In October 1961, President Kennedy told Cheddi Jagan, then prime minister of British Guiana, that "we are not engaged in a crusade to force free enterprise on parts of the world where it is not relevant. If we are engaged in a crusade for anything, it is national independence. That is the primary purpose of our aid. The secondary purpose is to encourage individual freedom and political freedom. But we can't always get that; and we have often helped countries which have little personal freedom, if they maintain their national independence. This is the basic thing. So long as you do that, we don't care whether you are socialist, capitalist, pragmatist, or whatever. We regard ourselves as pragmatists" (A. M. Schlesinger, Jr., *A Thousand Days,* Boston, Houghton Mifflin, 1965, pp. 775–6). The trouble with such sentiments is not only that they are belied by American support across the world for regimes whose "national independence" consists in subservience to the United States, and about which the notion of "individual freedom and political freedom" is a grotesque if not an obscene joke. Equally important is the fact that the *real* test is always a regime's attitude to capitalist and notably American enterprise. Aid to Yugoslavia, or to any other dissident Communist country, comes within the sphere of Cold War politics, and scarcely affects the main point.

It is also worth noting that well before 1961 British Guiana was already the subject of attention by the C.I.A., which played a major role in the downfall of Jagan and in the assumption of power by a government wholly satisfactory to the United States government—and to American capitalist enterprise.

9 THE MYTH OF PROGRESSIVE TAXATION*

by GABRIEL KOLKO

One hard-dying liberal myth has been that the government has a redistributive impact on society. This goes part and parcel with the notion that the government acts to curb corporations or at least levy a heavy share of their profits for collective use. This Kolko selection argues against this idea.

Kolko shows that the tax system in itself is not progressive. Not only are the not-so-well-to-do taxed at rates nearly equivalent to those of the rich, but the costs of government fall heavily on the people through the personal income tax, and rather lightly on the corporations.

The impact of government is in all likelihood much more regressive than the simple incidence of taxation would reflect. If we take into account that the activities of government tend to benefit the rich and their corporations more than the rest, then the net impact of government is clearly a boon to them. Kolko gives some evidence to suggest that this is the case. For example, if we assumed even that all government welfare activities went to benefit the low-income groups, these groups still paid in more to the government coffers than they received. If we further consider that military spending, an enormous sector of the Federal budget, principally benefits the corporations via windfall profits and only indirectly helps the rest of the society, we see how government activity is redistributive in favor of the rich.

But the mere fact that corporations are taxed is often used to argue that the government curbs corporate power. Of course, levying a tax on the income of a monopoly corporation can hardly be equated with levying the same percent tax on a household. Corporations, as Nossiter shows, can easily pass off their tax burden on to the consumers. (Or in some cases, to their corporate customers, who in turn pass them on to consumers.) Baran and Sweezy, moreover, bring to light the remarkable fact that huge increases in theoretical tax rates at the beginning of World War II did not make even a little dent in corporate profit rates. This gives some indication of how immune corporations are from government taxation.

It is widely believed that, as Ernest van den Haag and Ralph Ross put it, "the effect of progressive income taxes in diminishing the income of the upper brackets is too plain to need rehearsing." But the impact of Federal income taxes on the actual distribution of wealth has been minimal, if not negligible. The desire to avoid the burden of high taxes has given rise to new factors in the distribution of wealth, which have so complicated the picture that a change in form has been mistaken by many for a basic change in content. A careful study of the topic will hardly sustain this illusion.

Contrary to common belief, heavy taxation of upper-income groups did not begin with the advent of the New Deal; it began only with the approach of United States involvement in World War II. Higher income taxation came as a response of the Roosevelt Administration to world events and not as a result of a conscious commitment to a social policy of reducing inequalities in the distribution of wealth.

As a matter of historical record, the New Deal was not seriously interested in taxation as a means of income equalization—despite its frequent assertions that it was. Roosevelt actively supported the Revenue Act of 1934, but his support for the somewhat stronger 1935 Act was equivocal and was finally obtained only because he feared the growing appeal of Huey Long's "Share-the-Wealth Clubs" and attacks by progressives in Congress. Even so, in a number of important areas, the provisions of the two Acts were hardly designed to redistribute wealth effectively or reduce the capital accumulations of the rich. The estate-tax rates, which the 1932 Act set at 2 percent for each bracket above $70,000, were raised to 3 percent on amounts above $70,000 and up to $4.5 million, after which the rate dropped to 2 percent. The corporate income tax was raised from 12 percent to 15 percent in 1936, to 19 percent in 1939; not until 1942 was it raised to 40 percent.

Before 1941, the New Deal practice on personal-income taxation was, despite its difference in verbiage, essentially a continuation of that of the Hoover Administration. In 1929 and 1940, when the national personal income was almost the same, Federal receipts from personal-income taxes were virtually identical—$1.323 billion in 1929 and $1.393 billion in 1940. But in 1941, the Federal personal income tax, increased because of the growing military budget, produced revenue one-half more than in 1940, although personal income increased only 14 percent. In 1944, personal income was twice the 1940 level, but the tax yield was twelve times as great. While much of this increased burden fell on the upper-income groups—enough to stimulate their search for new ways to avoid the highest tax brackets—the major weight fell on income groups that had never before been subjected to the income tax.

Thus, the ironic fact is that the extension of the income tax to middle- and low-income classes was the only original aspect of the New Deal tax policy.

TAXATION: THEORY AND PRACTICE

The feature of the income-tax structure that purportedly has had a major impact is the extremely steep tax rates (up to 91 percent) on the very largest incomes. Actually, the resulting varied and ingenious methods of tax avoidance have substantially lessened the importance of these theoretically high rates.

Since 1941, members of the economic elite have attempted to receive their income in nontaxable forms or to postpone receiving it until retirement, when they will be in lower income brackets. There has been a strong downward shift in income-bracket levels, with an increasing proportion in the $25,000–$100,000 bracket, and in some years there has been an absolute drop in the number of returns reporting more than $100,000. More important, however, has been the trend away from the forms of income subject to high tax rates (salaries, wages, and certain types of property income) and toward tax-free interest, capital gains, and many other forms of income taxed at much lower rates or not at all. The proportionate importance of these forms of income to total income rises sharply in every income category over $10,000 a year.

Under Roosevelt, up to 1941, the actual, as opposed to the theoretical, tax rates on very high incomes were not very different from those under Herbert Hoover. Theoretically, the statutory tax is levied on straight income, none of which is derived from capital gains or other sources taxed at lower rates, from which no deductions are made, and no evasion attempted. In 1932, the highest possible tax rate on incomes of $1 million and up was 54 percent, but only 47 per cent was actually collected. In 1938, the maximum theoretical tax rate had increased to 72 percent, but only 44 percent was collected. By 1957, the highest possible tax rate was 91 percent, but only 52 percent was collected. As J. Keith Butters, Harvard economist, has written in his major study of taxation and the rich, *Effects of Taxation—Investment by Individuals* (1953), "By far the most striking and significant feature . . . is the large excess of theoretical over actual tax rates on upper bracket individuals when these rates are computed for income inclusive of all net capital gains."

The income of the richest tenth is reduced less than 10 percent by Federal income taxes. And, of course, the other tenths also show a net reduction in earnings after income taxes. Thus, it should come as no surprise that the distribution of income by tenths after Federal income taxes, shown in Table I, is

TABLE I. PERCENTAGE OF NATIONAL PERSONAL INCOME RECEIVED BY EACH INCOME-TENTH AFTER FEDERAL INCOME TAXES

	Highest	2nd	3rd	4th	5th	6th	7th	8th	9th	Lowest
1947	31 (−2)[a]	15	12	10	9	8 (+1)	6	5 (+1)	3	1
1949	28 (−2)	15	13 (+1)	11	9	8	7 (+1)	5	3	1
1950	27 (−2)	15	13	11	10 (+1)	8	7 (+1)	5	3	1
1951	28 (−3)	15	13 (+1)	11 (+1)	9	8	7 (+1)	5	3	1
1952	27 (−3)	15	13 (+1)	11	10 (+1)	8	7 (+1)	5	3	1
1953	28 (−3)	15	12	11 (+1)	9	8	7 (+1)	5	4 (+1)	1
1954	27 (−2)	15	13	11	9	8	7 (+1)	5	4 (+1)	1
1955	27 (−2)	16	13	11	10 (+1)	8	6	5 (+1)	3	1

[a] Numbers in parentheses indicate change in percentage points from before-tax income.

Source: Bureau of the Census, *Statistical Abstract of the United States—1957* (Washington, D.C.: Government Printing Office, 1957), p. 309. These data, collected by the Survey Research Center, include capital gains but exclude income-in-kind.

practically the same as the distribution before taxes. The slight changes in income-shares effected by the income tax have benefited income-tenths in the upper half almost as frequently as income-tenths in the lower half. These fundamental facts have been ignored by those who interpret the tax system on the basis of their arbitrary preconceptions rather than on the basis of its actual effects.

THE REVOLUTION IN TAXATION

Now we see that progressive taxation of incomes has not been applied to the economic elite sufficiently to change the distribution of income-shares, and that although the economic elite has been subject to heavier Federal income taxation since 1941, the same factor that stimulated a higher tax rate on the rich also produced, for the first time in American history, permanent and significant income taxation of low- and middle-income earners.

In 1939, only 4.0 million families or persons were subject to Federal income taxation; in 1940, 7.5 million; in 1941, 17.6 million; in 1944, 42.4 million; and in 1957, 46.9 million. Similarly, the share of the national personal income subject to Federal income taxes was 10 percent in 1939, 24 percent in 1941, and 43 percent in 1957. The net effect, since there was a fairly stable distribution of income over that period, was to tax lower- and middle-income classes that had never been taxed before. This was done by reducing the minimum tax exemption and extending the tax scale. In 1957, 66 percent of all reported incomes were taxed at the base rate of 20 percent. For married couples, taxable income began at $3,500 in 1929, $2,500 in 1935 and 1936, $1,500 in 1941, $1,000 in 1944, and $1,200 from 1948 on. Inflation sharply increased this trend by reducing the value of both incomes and exemptions, and its influence continues. The percentage of Federal revenue yielded by personal-income taxes increased from a scant 9 percent in 1916 to 18 percent in 1941, 41 percent in 1946, and 53 percent in 1960. At the same time, the percentage of Federal revenue yielded by corporate-profits taxes grew from 8 percent in 1916 to 26 percent in 1941, and 30 percent in 1946, and fell to 28 percent in 1960.

In this process of incorporating more and more of the American population into the Federal income tax system, a moderate degree of progressive taxation has been maintained. The income tax is practically the only major tax that is not basically regressive. Nevertheless, the income tax paid by the average family in the lowest income-fifth—in 1957, amounting to 3.3 percent of their income—constitutes a greater hardship for those living on an emergency budget than does the tax burden of 13.7 percent paid in the same year by the average family in the richest income-fifth.

The basic tax rate on taxable income (i.e., income after all deductions for dependents, charitable donations, medical expenses, etc.) begins at 20 percent. A major proportion of legitimate expenses is unclaimed annually, and most of this can, we know, be attributed to low- and middle-income families. Fewer than 10 percent of those earning less than $2,000 take credit for deductible expenditures beyond their dependents and the flat 10 percent allowed on the short form. This failure is due in large part to the complexity of filling out a "long form" for deductions. Deductions, it should be pointed out, must be quite high before they will save a family anything. For example, a family that can claim no deductions for interest, state taxes, donations, casualty losses, or the like must have medical expenses amounting to at least 13 percent of its total income before it will save anything.

Joint-filing provisions for husbands and wives, intended to lower their tax burden, were of no benefit in 70 percent of the joint returns filed in 1957, which were from low- and middle-income groups. In the upper-income brackets, however, the joint return can be of enormous benefit. On an income of $35,000, it can realize a peak saving of 40 percent of the tax bill.

THE COMBINED IMPACT OF ALL TAXES

Most recent commentators who have credited the Federal income tax with redistributing income have ignored the fact that it is only one of a number of taxes—and the only one that is in some measure progressive. Therefore, any discussion of distribution of income after taxes must consider the consequences of all taxes.

In general, local and state taxes are regressive. More than half—59 percent in 1958—of all state tax revenues come from sales taxes. About one-half of the expenditures of an average spending unit earning a cash income of less than $1,000 a year are subject to general sales or excise taxes, but only one-third of the expenditures of those earning $10,000-plus are so taxed. In effect, corporations present the public with additional hidden taxes. The corporation income tax is, as the *Wall Street Journal* puts it, "treated by the corporations as merely another cost which they can pass on to their customers." It has been variously estimated that one-third to one-half of this tax is shifted to the consumers. Furthermore, at least two-thirds of American corporations add all payroll-tax costs to their prices.

The Tax Foundation has calculated actual taxes paid as a percentage of income for all income classes in 1958 (see Table II). Its figures show that

TABLE II. PERCENTAGE OF 1958 TOTAL INCOME PAID IN FEDERAL, STATE, AND LOCAL TAXES,[a] BY INCOME CLASS

Income Class (In dollars)	Share of Taxes (In per cent)		
	Federal	State and Local	Total[b]
0– 2,000	9.6	11.3	21.0
2,000– 4,000	11.0	9.4	20.4
4,000– 6,000	12.1	8.5	20.6
6,000– 8,000	13.9	7.7	21.6
8,000–10,000	13.4	7.2	20.6
10,000–15,000	15.1	6.5	21.6
15,000–plus	28.6	5.9	34.4
Average	16.1	7.5	23.7

[a] Social-insurance taxes are not included.
[b] Because of rounding, items do not always add up to totals.
Source: Tax Foundation, *Allocation of the Tax Burden by Income Class* (New York: Tax Foundation, 1960), p. 17.

state and local taxes are regressive, and that all Federal taxes combined, although tending to be progressive, fall much more substantially on the low-income classes than is generally realized. Included in its calculations are all local, state, and Federal personal-income taxes; inheritance, estate, and gift taxes; corporate-profit taxes (it assumes that one-half of this is shifted to the public); excise and sales taxes; customs and property taxes. Excluded are the highly regressive social-insurance taxes, which take 7.3 percent of the total income of those earning $2,000 or less but only 1.5 percent in the $15,000-plus class.

These Tax Foundation data indicate that the combined American tax system is scarcely "progressive" and hardly in accord with the image of it nourished by most social scientists and students of contemporary America. If, despite innumerable loopholes, the Federal income tax has introduced a moderately progressive but greatly misunderstood and over emphasized taxation, the Federal excise and customs—and most major local and state—taxes have seriously lessened its impact. The income tax paid by the lower-income classes is, for the most part, money that would otherwise go for essential personal and family needs; in this light, the tax burden is substantially heavier for the lower-income classes than for the higher-income classes.

WELFARE AND INCOME INEQUALITY

Theoretically, it would be possible for the revenues from regressive taxation to be directed to welfare expenditures for lower-income groups, and for the inequality of income distribution to be reduced thereby to a significant extent. This has actually been achieved, in the eyes of a number of proponents of the income-redistribution thesis. "Through a combination of patchwork revisions of the system—tax laws, minimum wage laws, subsidies and guarantees and regulations of various sorts, plus labor union pressures and new management attitudes—we had repealed the Iron Law of Wages," wrote Frederick Lewis Allen in *The Big Change*. "We had brought about a virtually automatic redistribution of income from the well-to-do to the less well-to-do." The plausibility of this thesis has only been strengthened by the attacks of conservatives on the alleged "welfare state" created by the Roosevelt Administration.

However, this viewpoint is not sustained by a careful examination of the motives for the revisions in the tax structure: The reason for high taxation, at least since 1933, has been not to redistribute income but to pay for extraordinary costs—primarily military from 1940 on—in the most expeditious way. We have not taxed the rich to give to the poor; we have taxed both the rich and the poor and, at least since 1940, contributed only a small fraction of the proceeds to the welfare of the poor.

Consider, for example, 1958. In that year, Federal revenue from personal-income, estate and gift, corporate-profit, and excise and customs taxes, excluding the self-financing social-insurance program, amounted to $69 billion. The families and unattached individuals in the $0–$2,000 class contributed $1.066 billion, those in the $2,000–$4,000 class contributed $4.971 billion. But the Federal government spent only $4.509 billion on what by the most generous definition may be called "welfare." Included were all expenditures for public assistance, public health, education, and "other welfare," and half of the outlay for farm parity prices and income, and public housing. In 1949, Federal expenditures for welfare were $2.037 billion; in 1954, they were $2.451 billion, and in 1955, $4.062 billion. In each of these years, however, the total Federal tax payments of the spending units earning less than $4,000 were greater than these welfare expenditures. If all Federal welfare expenditures went to the $0–$4,000 class—which was certainly not the case—this class more than paid for them.

In brief, welfare spending has not changed the nature of income inequality, nor raised the standard of living of the lowest-income classes above what it would have reached if they had not been subjected to Federal taxation. It might be claimed that these classes must assume some responsibility for the nation's "larger obligations," but this is not an argument advanced by those who assert that we have redistributed income through taxation and welfare measures.

MEANS OF TAX AVOIDANCE

The most effective way of avoiding taxes, of course, is by not declaring one's income. In 1957, 9 percent of the national personal income—$28 billion—never appeared in tax returns. Most of this $28 billion was received by the upper-income class.* This problem of undeclared income was negligible before 1941, but, as an Internal Revenue official suggested in 1959, "When the tax rates were low, there wasn't much to be gained." The strictly legal loopholes for tax avoidance are numerous. Still, as one tax accountant put it, "Taxpayers in the 50% bracket or higher start getting a feeling of anger . . . and they start looking for ways to lighten the load. First they take the legal steps of tax avoidance. But many find this doesn't give them enough relief." The wide extent of tax evasion makes it obvious that the risks involved are insufficient to discourage the practice.

Capital gains are the single most important means of avoiding the theoretically high tax on large incomes. The highest tax rate on capital gains—profits from sales of stock, property, etc., that have been held longer than six months—is only 25 percent. It is significant that in 1942, soon after the income-tax burden on the highest-income groups was increased, Congress reduced this holding period from two years to six months. The effect was to offset the increased tax burden on one form of wealth by reducing it on another. The act was based on the specious assumption that the flow of profits on stocks and sales was "long-term" windfall profit rather than income. In 1957, 20 percent of the total income of the $100,000-plus class was in capital gains, and this income was, at the most, taxed at a rate only slightly higher than the rate on the taxable income of the lowest-income classes. By way of contrast, only three-tenths of 1 percent of the total income of those in the $3,500–$4,000 class originated as capital gains that year.

As a result of the preferred tax status of capital gains, the wealthy have attempted to maximize the means for obtaining them, and the concept of executives' compensation in the corporation has been accordingly adjusted. "You can't compete for executive talent today without a gimmick," declared David Sarnoff, Chairman of the Radio Corporation of America, several years ago. These gimmicks take innumerable forms—deferred-compensation plans, profit-sharing trusts, stock options, and the like—but all have two common purposes: to maximize the amount of income going to executives as capital gains and to postpone disbursement of part of their income until retirement, when most will fall into lower-income categories. Before 1940, about 700 companies had such plans in operation; by 1946, 9,000 firms had them.

Under a deferred-compensation plan, the executive receives, after retirement, his own payments to the plan as tax-free income; he pays only a capital-gains tax on the company's contributions. These plans differ in detail but not in essential form. For top executives, special arrangements are often made. Harley J. Earl, a General Motors vice-president who retired in December, 1958, after having earned a peak salary of $130,000 a year, receives $50,000

* See Kolko selection, Part I.

a year until December, 1963, and $75,000 a year for the ten years thereafter. Although not always so generous, most companies, especially if they are closely owned, sponsor similar plans for top executives.

The stock option, a tax-avoidance factor of tremendous importance to corporate executives, was introduced in the 1950 Revenue Act, and it has become a major means of compensating members of the economic elite. By 1957, 77 percent of the largest manufacturing corporations had set up option plans. Under the terms of the Act, an option on a company's stock is offered to an executive at no less than 85 percent (in practice, it is generally 95 percent) of the current market value. The executive must wait at least eighteen months before he exercises the option—if he chooses to exercise it. If the market price rises, as it almost invariably does in an inflationary economy, the executive buys the stock at its original low price; then, if he waits six months to sell, he pays only the capital-gains tax on the profit. If the stock's price falls 20 percent or more below the option price, the option price can again be reduced to 95 percent of the average market price for the twelve months preceding the new change.

"In the past five years," *U.S. News & World Report* observed in 1955, "these options have produced a whole new crop of millionaires." One aircraft company gave thirteen executives an option on 30,000 shares in 1951; in 1955, they realized a 370 percent profit. A rubber company granted a vice-president an option on 10,000 shares worth $213,800 in 1951; in 1955, they were worth $574,000. In 1957, Frank Pace, Jr., and John J. Hopkins exercised their options to buy General Dynamics stock then valued at $1,125,000 and $1,220,000, respectively; their option price was about one-third the market value at the time of the stock sale. In January, 1956, Donald W. Douglas, Sr., of Douglas Aircraft, exercised an option for 15,000 shares at $16.50 each at a time when the market price had risen to $86—a profit of more than $1 million. During 1956, when executives at Pittsburgh Plate Glass purchased 40,000 company shares at an option price of $41, the market price ranged from $74 to $96. Beginning in 1951, U.S. Steel granted its executives stock options with a face value of $49 million; on August 8, 1957, the stocks were worth $133 million on the market.

Those in the high income-tax bracket find it profitable to receive part of their income in totally tax-exempt interest. In 1957, they received almost $600 million of income in this form. Kuznets, in his study of the top 5 percent, did not allocate any of this nontaxable income to this income group after 1940. However, we know that the economic elite have been rapidly increasing their tax-exempt holdings since 1929 and that they now own almost all available holdings of this type. We also know that the sales and yield of tax-free state and local securities have risen very sharply since 1939. Thus we can see the rising importance of tax-free income to the wealthy. These securities yield as high as 6 percent, although the 1959 average yield on high-grade municipal bonds was 4.0 percent. With a taxable income of $70,000 to $80,000 a tax-free return of 4.0 percent is equal to a taxable 21.0 percent return after taxes. In the $150,000–$200,000 bracket, a tax-free 4.0 percent return is equal to a taxable 40 percent after taxes, and a tax-free 5.25 percent is equal to a taxable 52.5 percent after taxes.

Contrary to common opinion, inherited wealth and large capital accumulations have not been seriously affected by the existing tax laws. Here the legal escape clauses are so numerous that the impact of the high estate tax—theoretically up to 77 percent on $10 million—is, in actuality, nominal. In 1951, the total net value of estates reported on taxable returns was taxed at only 14 percent.

A married man can divide his estate so that one-half is taxed at his death and one-half at his wife's death, thereby sharply lowering the tax bracket. In this way alone, the taxes on a $300,000 estate would be reduced from $62,700 to $17,900, and the taxes on a $10,060,000 estate from slightly more than $6 million to less than $2.5 million.

However, two major alternatives—gifts and trusts—allow persons with taxable estates of $100,000 and up to avoid the heaviest rates. Gifts made by wealthy individuals during their lifetime are taxed much less than the same gifts made as bequests after their death. The gift-tax rate on $1 million is 27.75 percent; the inheritance-tax rate is 31.4 percent. But even this rate is often avoided. A man may split up his estate by giving $6,000 a year to his wife and $3,000 a year—or $6,000, if his wife agrees—to as many other persons as he wishes. Only the donor is taxed on the gift at the gift-tax rate, which begins at 2.25 percent under $5,000. In addition, a $60,000 basic lifetime exemption is allowed every couple.

By 1951, about 45 percent of the value of estates worth more than $500,000 had been placed in trusts. The trust guarantees that estate taxes will be paid by a family on the amount set aside for at least two generations after the death of its founder. It divides the family fortune, for purposes of taxation, into smaller units and can result, under the 1952 tax laws, in tax savings as high as 70 percent on the income of property placed in trust. By September, 1959, all the states had enacted "custodian laws" to allow members of families to organize and manage trusts in the name of minors, permitting the eventual avoidance of estate taxes, division of income for current tax purposes, and elimination of cumbersome legal procedures for the organization of trusts.

Since the 1952 tax law, a rapidly growing number of special provisions have been created that apply to relatively small groups among the wealthy but add up to a cumulative trend toward legal tax avoidance. The fantastic complexity of the tax law has not succeeded in dimming the sheer genius of tax lawyers, who have aided the economic elite to circumscribe, in a perfectly legal manner, many of the more onerous tax provisions. Their ultimate success, however, can be attributed neither to their ingenuity nor to the intricacy of the tax law; it results from the failure of political administrations over the past four decades to enact tax legislation that seriously challenges the economic power of the wealthy. All recent Administration suggestions for closing these tax loopholes have been coupled with proposals to lower the tax rates on the richest income classes—thereby leaving the wealthy in substantially their present economic position.

Viewing this sharp contrast between the avowed equalitarian sentiments of most politicians and the legal and economic reality of the tax structure, Stanley S. Surrey, of the Harvard Law School, has rightly concluded that "the average congressman does not basically believe in the present rates of income tax in the upper brackets. When he sees them applied to individual cases, he thinks them too high and therefore unfair. . . . Since they are not, however, willing to reduce those rates directly, the natural outcome is indirect reduction through special provisions."

The complexity of the effect of taxation should not be allowed to obscure the basic trends—the growing tax burden on the low- and middle-income classes, and the huge disparity between theoretical and actual tax rates for the wealthy. The conclusion is inescapable: Taxation has not mitigated the fundamentally unequal distribution of income. If anything it has perpetuated inequality by heavily taxing the low- and middle-income groups—those least able to bear its burden.

10 WHY BUSINESSMEN COMPLAIN ABOUT GOVERNMENT*

by G. WILLIAM DOMHOFF

America has a Ruling Class. This is the not-so-very-surprising conclusion of Domhoff's book Who Rules America. *There exists in America a coherent Upper Social Class held together by marriage, social and educational institutions. This class also controls the vast majority of the country's wealth and is enormously overrepresented in the controlling chambers of America's major social institutions. Men from this class and representatives of the institutions they control—like businesses—hold positions of power in government, in the media, in the universities and elsewhere. Thus Domhoff concludes that the upper class is indeed a Ruling Class.*

In the selection of Domhoff's book reprinted here, he answers the question generally raised by people to the kind of analysis we have presented: "Why do businessmen seem to complain so much about the government, if they do indeed have so much power over it?"

The final, and most important, objection that is usually raised against a governing-class model concerns the apparent autonomy of the federal government. Critics point to the New Deal, the Democratic Party, anti-business legislation, and the intense hostility of business to government in support of the idea that the federal government is a relatively autonomous institution that adjudicates disputes among various interest groups. Talcott Parsons finds business opposition to government "impossible to understand" unless we assume "genuine, and in some sense effective" governmental control of business. Similarly, economist Edward S. Mason, an expert on corporations and a former president of the American Economic Association, was paraphrased as follows in *Business Week*: "Business' intense opposition to every proposed surrender of power to Washington is hardly consistent with the view that it itself dominates the U.S. government."

In answer to these objections, this study has shown who controlled the New Deal—liberal elements of the American upper class, including many ex-Republicans. We have stressed that the New Deal created a split within the power elite which has not yet healed. Many members of the upper class remain unreconciled to the New Deal, believing that aristocrat Franklin Roosevelt ("Rosenfelt") was a traitor to his class who was part of an international Communist-Jewish con-

* G. William Domhoff, *Who Rules America.* Copyright © 1967. Reprinted by permission of Prentice-Hall, Inc., Englewood Cliffs, New Jersey. (Footnotes have been eliminated from this version.)

spiracy. However, this does not mean that other members of the upper class did not control the New Deal. As Baltzell documents, the New Deal was actually the beginning of a more ethnically representative establishment within the governing class which pushed aside the Protestant Establishment made up of heavy industrialists, fiscal conservatives, and prejudiced personalities. On a larger time scale, 1932–1964, this study has answered the claim that the federal government is autonomous by showing that the now-dominant Executive branch is honeycombed to an overwhelming degree by members of the power elite. This same evidence, buttressed by studies of campaign financing, also disposes of the myth that the Democratic Party is not controlled by elements of the American upper class. As to the charge that the upper class is not omnipotent, and therefore not a governing class, the fact remains that a very wealthy upper class which makes concessions remains a wealthy upper class. It stoops to conquer, taking the advice of its English counterparts rather than the foolhardy path of the French landlords. Perhaps Joseph P. Kennedy put this point as well as anybody could in discussing his reaction to the Depression, a time of genuine panic and confusion for many members of the upper class:

> I am not ashamed to record that in those days I felt and said I would be willing to part with half of what I had if I could be sure of keeping, under law and order, the other half. Then it seemed that I should be able to hold nothing for the protection of my family.

There are several very good reasons why businessmen complain about the government, the first of which requires a slight detour into history. The original American political and economic system battled for many years against a centralized government in England. As Baltzell puts it, American institutions were "born in a revolt from the tyranny of a centralized government symbolized in the British monarchy and mercantilism. . . ." We would add that this long and bitter struggle created an anti-government ideology, especially against a strong central government, and that this hostility has remained one of the most prominent features of American thought, if not of American practice. In short, there are historical and ideological reasons why businessmen would verbalize hostility toward the federal government. This ideological hostility, we would argue, does not answer the question of whether or not members of the American upper class of rich businessmen control the government they criticize. A second "historical" reason for hostility to the federal government has been noted in the previous paragraph; that is, many businessmen do not accept the New Deal. They remember the good old days before the Depression, and they deny the claim by some of their colleagues that changes were necessary in order to forestall more serious socioeconomic and political difficulties. However, on this point it is necessary to emphasize that not all businessmen are hostile to a strong central government and the innovations of the New Deal. Some even find labor unions a useful stabilizing influence. We believe that these business liberals are coming to be the dominant influence within the upper class, as symbolized in the views of the Council on Foreign Relations, Foreign Policy Association, Committee for Economic Development, Business Advisory Council and National Advertising Council.

A third factor in understanding business hostility to the federal government is the fact that most businessmen are not part of the group that controls the government. The federal government is controlled by the corporate rich, and only a small percentage of American businesses are even incorporated, let alone large enough to sustain the owners as members of the national upper class. In short, it is necessary to specify *which* businessmen are complaining about the federal government. Small businessmen, for example, have good reason to complain. For them the government is largely an expensive nuisance which makes them keep annoying and costly records while doing very little for them. Needless to say, some of these small businessmen line up with the anti-New Deal members of the upper class to form the conservative wing of the Republican Party, which is very vocal in its hostility to a strong federal government. We suspect that this coalition would be the origin of most of the examples that Parsons and Mason could give in supporting their claim that businessmen are hostile to the federal government.

Other factors must be considered in explaining business hostility toward the federal government. First, much of this hostility is really hostility toward other businessmen, especially in the case of the regulatory agencies. For example, we have cited the case of the fight over an increase in natural gas prices, which was opposed by the other elements of the business community who would pay most of the increase in higher production costs. The FPC nonetheless took the brunt of the hostility. Along this same line, McConnell points out that "some industries, including the radio industry, the airlines, the railroad and trucking industries, and the oil companies, have actively sought regulation." Then too, many businessmen are temperamentally unsuited for the give-and-take of the political world. Nor are they comfortable with the hoopla of electioneering. They see government as a bureaucratic tangle opposed to the orderly, efficient atmosphere of the corporate world. Osborn Elliott goes so far as to call the corporate structure "authoritarian" in making this point. This would suggest that members of the upper class with temperaments and interests different from those of most businessmen would be more successful as political leaders. Neither President Roosevelt nor President Kennedy, for example, could get very enthusiastic about business careers.

As still another factor in considering business hostility to the federal government, it must be realized that even a government controlled by the corporate rich will often take measures which are distasteful to many corporations and corporate executives. Good examples from the mid-1960's would be the need to curtail overseas spending to halt the outflow of gold to other countries, and the need to curtail investment spending to discourage the inflationary tendencies which developed in an economy that was spending increasing sums on national defense. While both of these measures were in the interests of the system as a whole, they were not in the interests of the individual corporations, and many seemed to ignore the pleas of Secretary of Commerce John T. Connor, the former president of Merck and Company, and Secretary of Defense Robert McNamara, the former president of the Ford Motor Company.

Finally, there are good reasons why businessmen well aware of their power would pretend that they did not control the government. This is such a charged point, impugning as it does the motives of our corporate leaders, that we would not make it ourselves. Instead, we will let a respectable political scientist, Grant McConnell, and a highly regarded reporter, Bernard Nossiter, speak for themselves. After pointing to business antagonisms as the first element in explaining hostility to government, McConnell goes on as follows:

> Second, whether the issue is understood explicitly, intuitively, or not at all, the denunciations serve to establish and maintain the subservience of governmental units to the business constituencies to which they are actually held responsible. Attacks upon government in general place continuing pressure on governmental officers to accommodate their activities to the groups from which support is most reliable. Third, and probably most important, is that business attacks upon government are directed at any tendency toward the development of larger constituencies for the government units.

After noting that "some businessmen believe the myths cultivated by the image-makers of both major parties," and that pressure on President Kennedy brought the best results for business interests, Nossiter makes this important point:

> A second and related reason has to do with business sensitivity about its own power. To proclaim the triumph of business doctrine on the New Frontier might invite retaliation and counterpressure by organized labor, farmers, and other interest groups. Overt display of power in the corporate world is not only vulgar, it is unprofitable.

We believe the above arguments are an adequate explanation as to why many businessmen would express hostility toward the federal government. However, even if they were not, we would still argue that a decision about business domination of the government cannot be based upon the subjective feelings of the corporate executives, corporate lawyers, and aristocrats who provide the leadership of the State Department, Defense Department, and Treasury Department. We thus conclude from our empirical evidence that many social scientists are mistaken in their respective emphases on the New Deal, the Democratic Party, and business hostility as considerations which are contrary to the notion of a governing class.

11 THE MYTH OF NEW DEAL REFORM*

by BRAD WILEY

The New Deal is the key to the faith of many liberals that capitalism can be reformed. They believe that the State during the New Deal finally asserted itself to take responsibility for the public interest and for the well-being of the people. Democratic political power finally triumphed over and above the greed and irrationality of the private economy.

This view of American history just doesn't square with the facts. With the Depression of the 1930's, capitalism suffered an enormous setback from which many corporate leaders feared it would never recover. All energies of the political and corporate elite were directed toward a recovery of the healthy pre-Depression capitalism, and some highly unorthodox measures were taken. In particular, new administrative functions were taken on by the government to oversee the recovery of the economy. Strong measures were taken to alleviate the most acute suffering among the general population in order to avert social turmoil and development of anticapitalist movements. Care was taken to integrate and co-opt the development of the labor movement in its early years.

These measures were basically conservative in function. They were concerned with the preservation of the capitalist system. They did not question for one moment the need to preserve the system. Nor were basic structural reforms undertaken. A limited welfare budget was established, but clearly as insurance against social disruption. To assume that the New Deal was anticapitalist in its impact is to wreak a great distortion on history and ignore all the facts of the development of capitalism in the post-New Deal period.

THE NEW DEAL AND THE ROLE OF GOVERNMENT IN THE ECONOMY

The New Deal era represented the beginning of a decisive shift in both the extent and nature of government intervention in the market. Before 1929, participation in the economy had been in the form of subsidization and regulation. In the nineteenth century the economic activities of government at all levels—local, state, and national—had mainly consisted of measures to support the growth of industrial enterprise. National tariff policy was from the first calculated to protect infant American manufacturing. Later both state and national government used the basic source of early national wealth, land, to promote the development of the nation's first great industry, the railroads. Land grants to the rail corporations provided the capital basis for many of the key systems built between 1850 and 1890.

* Used by permission of the author.

Later, in the period of rapid industrialization between 1885 and 1925, government by subsidy was supplemented by a comprehensive system of regulation of private enterprise. This system of diverse legislative statutes and executive commissions reinforced a trend toward rationalization and stabilization in industry itself. It represented an attempt to bring some order to the virtually anarchistic growth of the great corporations and industries and the violent struggle for markets these new institutions of production found themselves engaged in.[1]

In this era there were created the Interstate Commerce Commission to attempt to bring order to the cutthroat competition in the rail transportation industry, the Federal Trade Commission to oversee manufacturing, and the Federal Reserve to solve the problems of the highly rigid financial and credit system. This was also the period of the Pure Food and Drug Act, the Hepburn and Mann-Elkins rail rate acts, the Sherman and Clayton acts, and other statutory attempts to regulate and standardize industrial competition and growth.

The 1929 crash and ensuing depression eventually forced both private enterprise and the government to recognize that rationalization of the corporations with the assistance of the government was not adequate. The expansion of private enterprise demanded subsidization of consumption capacity to sustain the growing productivity of the modern industrial corporation. Indeed, the history of the American economy between 1919 and the crash was a continuous attempt by capital to find markets domestically and abroad for the industrial capacity created by World War I. The crash and the ensuing decline of consumption subsequently cut production and the GNP in half by 1933.[2]

The economic programs of the New Deal introduced deficit spending as a permanent feature of public policy as a means of absorbing surplus production. The Roosevelt administration approached Keynesian spending warily after first attempting to rely mainly on the traditional regulatory means. Indeed the key tactic for recovery in the 1933–34 period, the NRA with its industrial codes, was nothing more than a plan to organize and regulate production, prices, and market shares in whole industries under the guidance of the government. Each NRA code simply provided the respective pre-existing trade associations with a set of more formal rules for conduct they were already practicing and then placed the associations under a centralized Federal Trade Commission-like supervisory agency. Some emphasis was put on deliberate government spending to generate purchasing power, through such programs as the Public Works Administration; but it was not until the 1937–38 period, the Roosevelt recession, that the New Deal accepted government spending as a prime instrument of recovery. And even then the scale of appropriations for the PWA, the WPA (Works' Progress Administration), and the National Youth Administration was scarcely of the scale necessary to promote real recovery and growth in the economy.

[1] For an analysis of the role of regulatory government in the economy between 1885 and 1914 see Gabriel Kolko, *Railroads and Regulation,* 1877–1916, Princeton, N.J., Princeton, 1965 and *The Triumph of Conservatism.* The problems of organizing legal administrative structures to control and administer the giant corporate manufacturers in the 1890–1929 period are carefully developed in Alfred D. Chandler, Jr., *Strategy and Structure,* Cambridge, MIT Press, 1962.

[2] See J. K. Galbraith, *The Great Crash,* for a good description of the structural weaknesses of the pre-1929 economy.

This brings us to the second important point about the New Deal and economic recovery: none of the New Deal recovery programs, including Keynesian spending techniques, really solved the basic problems of overproduction and underconsumption. In 1940, the last year of peace prior to U.S. entry into the war, unemployment was nearly as high as in 1933, and the Gross National Product was still lower than in 1929 despite the American role as "Arsenal of Democracy" to the Allies.

Essentially it was World War II rather than the New Deal which promoted both the recovery of the economy and the development of government policy and organization to play a permanent fiscal role in the economy. Only the scale of spending necessary to finance war objectives was great enough to overcome stagnation and stimulate permanent sustained growth in the economy.

Moreover, the types of controls imposed on domestic consumption—rationing, curtailing production of civilian durable goods in favor of military hardware, removal of 10–12 million soldiers from the civilian consumer market—were a consequence of the war economy, and they induced a kind of forced saving and redistribution of income which peacetime economic policy had not imposed.[3]

Finally, it was only during wartime and the postwar period that this type and scale of government intervention in the economy, permanent public spending to sustain consumption and economic growth, was institutionalized in the organization of the government. During the war it was the War Production Board that was instrumental in defining the level and quality of government spending for the war. In 1946, the Full Employment Act designated a President's Council of Economic Advisers to work in conjunction with congressional appropriations committees and the Bureau of the Budget to formulate the strategy of government to sustain economic growth. Twenty years later the federal budget directly sustained about 15 percent of the gainfully employed and an equal share of Gross National Product.

Thus if the New Deal neither promoted economic recovery nor established as permanent practice the new fiscal role of government in the economy, what was the significance of the Roosevelt programs mentioned earlier with respect to these occurrences? What the New Deal did accomplish was to establish the political precedent that legitimized the new economic function of government. More concretely it established the administrative machinery and pool of personnel and techniques necessary to run the new kind of government. Among other things this meant turning to the universities and professionals to staff the new agencies and bureaus. What the New Deal did then, rather than to promote recovery, was to provide the ideological and technical basis for government participation in the wartime and postwar recovery of the economy.

THE NEW DEAL AND AMERICAN POLITICAL LIFE

Most historians have recognized that the initial and basic assumption of New Deal economic programs was recovery rather than reform. They suggest that the importance of the Roosevelt era was political and social and that, as Burns

[3] Paul Baran and Paul Sweezy, *Monopoly Capital,* New York, 1966, traces the history of the modern economy and its growth pattern since 1900. This work also relates government spending to the problems of expansion and overproduction of corporate enterprise.

puts it, the state under Roosevelt became a "broker" redressing the political disadvantages of other groups against the power of corporate capitalism. Government policy as a counterbalance to vested interests was of course not new in the 1930s. What was innovative about the Rooseveltian politics, the historians indicate, was that it broadened popular participation in government by recognizing new interest groups in its legislative programs.

The New Deal's recognition of potentially antagonistic social groups served a conservative integrating purpose. If these groups could be led to cooperate with the dominant economic and political elite on the basis of the rules of corporate capitalism, any possibility that their demands for reform might begin to question fundamental property relations was eliminated. This arrangement, of course, meant that organizations demanding reforms had to accept the priority given to economic rationalization over social reform.

This process of co-optation, as we call it today, is illustrated by the growth of the labor movement during the Depression. Until 1935 the spontaneous strike action of the working class received little attention from the atrophied American Federation of Labor. By means of their militant tactics, workers were implicitly challenging the basis of the economic order. This kind of growing disruption could not be tolerated especially in a period of general economic chaos. Rather than repress the growing strike movement, an action which would have ensured greater disruption and, worse, the radicalization of the working class, most of the major corporations decided to cooperate with the newly formed Congress of Industrial Organizations. The CIO in turn channeled the generalized but inarticulate discontent of the workers into the "legitimate" confines of collective bargaining thereby limiting the concerns of the workers to wages and hours, a practice acceptable to their employers.

By means of the National Labor Relations Act, the Roosevelt administration legitimized this process by creating the machinery necessary to bring about collective bargaining. The result was that the workers were forced by their own organization to accept a minimal role in determining the conditions under which they worked. Their participation in the economic process was extended but only within limits determined by the profit system and only in order to keep them from demanding real participation in economic affairs. The "radicalism" of the CIO stemmed only from the workers' militant tactics and from the willingness of the leadership to integrate the previously ignored industrial workers into the modern capitalist order. The CIO furthered the process of rationalization of the economy by disciplining the working class through containing the militancy of the workers, eliminating the threat of strikes, and generally mediating between the boss and "his" workers.

The formal broadening of the base of politics, symbolized by the incorporation of the labor movement into the new order, has been offset, moreover, by other changes in American political life. The trend toward a corporate economy and urban society has created new social groups without giving them an organizational or programmatic basis for participation, à la the CIO, in the political system. All of these groups are unorganized, politically unrepresented, and basically powerless in the political system. They include the Negroes, the Puerto Ricans, the white urban and rural poor, and the new "middle class" of corporate and service employees.

Samuel Lubell's *The Future of American Politics* suggests that one of the politically most important aspects of the Roosevelt era was the rise to political importance of the urban areas in The Democratic coalition. The aspect of this phenomenon to which he attributes particular significance is the rise of ethnic groups to middle class status and their concomitant education in and concern for the political process. Though the program by program details are not clear, it is apparent that in the Depression this class group viewed the New Deal as a politically viable way of preserving its newly won status. But in the long run, this class, now one of the largest in the polity, has gained little from postwar political developments. The middle class has no representatives or lobby in Congress. It has no program to take to the political institutions of the country nor to the corporations for which the middle class serve as primary consumer clientele.

Another development of political life which has tended to isolate government further from popular authority was itself a consequence of the New Deal. That was the centralization of governmental functions in the hands of the executive branch. This trend began when Roosevelt decided that his administration would take the responsibility for solving the dilemma of the Depression and set up a "brain trust" to devise a legislative program to facilitate recovery. This policy was followed by the proliferation of permanent executive agencies and offices in the New Deal and thereafter; the growth of planned government spending during and after the war; the streamlining and integration of such policy planning agencies as Defense, State, Budget, and Resources in the postwar era; the subordination of Congress to a position where it could only approve or reject programs and policies worked out by the executive.

These trends, all based on the Roosevelt premise that government could be the decisive instrument in solving the problems of economic instability, have also severely limited the possibility for public participation in the machinery performing these functions. Government by permanent executive agency means that public policy is formulated by Presidential advisers and implemented by technicians none of whom are ever directly answerable to the commonwealth they ostensibly serve.[4]

SOCIAL IMPACT OF THE DEPRESSION AND THE NEW DEAL

Essentially little is known about the way the American people, various social groups, viewed the Depression—to what extent they saw it as a social crisis undermining the very viability of capitalism. On the one hand, the pronouncements of contemporary intellectuals upon this question no doubt reflected more the disaffection of their own class from the prevailing order; on the other hand, the present crop of historians, in their celebrations of the New Deal as a progressive movement, always pose the spectre of radicalism, fascist or communist, as the probable alternative to the failure of Rooseveltian policy.

Looking at the period from a broader perspective however, we may note two things. First, both of the interwar decades were years of political and social tur-

[4] C. Wright Mills, *The Power Elite,* New York, 1959, takes this view of political centralization one step further to the level of the political economy where he finds an integration of the leadership from the basic institutions (corporations, executive of the government, and military) in an informal interlocking directorate whose members can move at will from one of these basic sources of public power to another without recourse to the electoral process.

moil around the world. Beginning with the collapse of czarist Russia, most of the advanced nations of the West and East underwent some degree of internal unrest and dislocation. We need only mention the Civil War in China, the rise of Fascism in Germany, Italy, and Japan, the collapse of the British Empire and the ensuing economic crisis. Most of these trends began in the 1920s and reached crisis proportion during the Depression before culminating in World War II. Compared to what transpired elsewhere in the globe the economic and social crisis in the United States was of a relatively mild nature.

Second, it must be remembered that Depression time America merely represented an extreme of social and economic conditions which had prevailed in America since industrialization had begun. In the rural areas, for instance, farmers had been the victims of falling prices and rising costs for the whole post-Civil War period except for the years between 1900 and 1918. Indeed agrarian unrest manifested itself in such movements as prohibition, the Ku Klux Klan, and the LaFollette third party drive. These were signal departures from the Normalcy of the 1920s; they reflected the social as well as economic alienation of rural and small town life from the mainstream of urban, industrial America.

In the cities, too, many of the conditions of the Depression already prevailed in the 1920s. Unemployment, for instance, both seasonal and structural, was very high in many key industries where new technology was being introduced. Without listing them, it is important to remember in general that many of the features of the economic failure of the thirties were also part of the prosperity of the twenties.

Furthermore, it must be remembered that the period in question, 1920–40, was only an early phase of the mass consumption economy and that the vast majority of the population perceived the subsistence standard of living as a normal state of affairs. For these classes the Depression was merely another, albeit more severe, episode in the familiar business cycle which had always threatened the conditions of employment and subsistence.

What was the impact of the New Deal on American life during the Depression? We have discussed the more important ways Rooseveltian policies affected national economic political organizations. But how did the new scale of government intervention influence the way people viewed the political and economic institutions of capitalism?

The historians have for the most part portrayed the New Deal as a logical extension of the progressive-liberal political reform tradition of the 1885–1914 era. We remember to what pains Leuchtenburg goes to trace the precursors of the New Deal policies in the Theodore Roosevelt and Wilson programs. The eminent Schlesinger, Jr., court hagiographer of the Kennedy and other liberal "Renaissances" in American history, sees the emergence under Roosevelt of a government with expanded authority to intervene in the economy in order to promote the general welfare by assuring economic and social security. This is indeed the operating definition of the modern welfare state of the "mixed capitalist" system celebrated by the Schlesinger, Jrs., and Galbraiths, a political instrument whose negative functions are to mediate and regulate relations between institutions in the private sector of the economy and whose positive functions are to develop programs to enhance the economic and social well-being of its citizens.

The assumption here is that the political economy, this "mixed system" of enterprise, is a kind of peculiarly American derivation that lies somewhere between capitalism and socialism (Schlesinger, Jr., *The Age of Roosevelt,* III, 647–48). This review, on the other hand, emphasizes that while the New Deal represents a new *form* of government intervention in the economy, the role of the state continues to subordinate the problems of reform and reorganization of urban-industrial society to those of recovery and stabilization in the corporate-capitalist system of production. There is a distinction between recovery and reform, and the stabilization of the capitalist system as a political objective is in no way a necessary precondition for effective social reform. One means an attempt to reconstruct the *status quo ante,* the other means significant change in the economic and social basis of society.

We have already determined that prior to World War II the New Deal contributed little to economic recovery; we can now add that its contribution to reform was also nominal. Projecting ahead a few years, when we remember that a small percentage of government spending at all levels goes to education, health, personal security, or culture, we must recognize how small a welfare role the public sector of society presently plays in our lives. Thus the concept of the welfare state becomes an ideological tool in the baggage of modern capitalism.

FDR was not the first to coin a slogan of active government commitment to the general welfare. But since the New Deal the process of the political state has been successively termed Fair Deal, New Frontier, and Great Society. Indeed, in their own terms historians have recognized the importance of the ideology of the welfare state to the success of the New Deal. Henry S. Commager's article in the Heath series suggests that the New Deal implied "the responsibility of the state for the welfare of its citizens" and associates this with "the reassertion of faith in democracy." Leuchtenburg (*FDR and the New Deal,* 332–34) offers a similar evaluation of state commitment to individual security.

What the historians have identified is the Roosevelt strategy of engendering mass support for his administration, and indeed for the forms of political democracy and for capitalism itself, by promising that his programs could effectively redress the inequalities and injustices of the system. As we have indicated, however, the modern American government intervenes in the economy and society as a promoter, not of welfare and reform, but of capitalist stability and rationality. The contention that the welfare aspect of its activities is a decisive one does not stand up under scrutiny.

SUMMARY AND CONCLUSION

A historian such as Schlesinger, Jr. (*The Age of Roosevelt,* vol. I, ix), terms the 1930s the culmination of an era that began in the late nineteenth century, an era of reform and reorganization of society to deal with the problems of industrialization and urban society. This review, on the other hand, indicates that while the New Deal had its roots in the earlier period, 1885–1929, it was not merely a synthesis of the New Nationalism and New Freedom programs of the Theodore Roosevelt-Woodrow Wilson era. Rather the FDR administration became a transition period in which the Depression crisis demonstrated that the traditional role of state intervention in the economy was inadequate to deal with the weaknesses of capitalism as it developed after

World War I. Ultimately, however, it was the second war and the postwar era rather than the Depression that created the conditions for the recovery of the economy, enlargement and rationalization of the mechanics of the new form of state intervention, and the reorganization of government to facilitate implementation of its new role.

That the New Deal or some other political movement did not find a solution to the causes and manifestations of the Depression was symptomatic of the fact that the 1930s were not as severe a social crisis as historians have characterized it. Essentially no major social group or class, neither the owners and managers of the corporate system, nor the workers, farmers and middle classes felt themselves sufficiently threatened to commit themselves to more extreme forms of political and economic action. For unlike the situation in other countries, the growth of corporate capitalism in the United States in the 1900–45 period did not undermine the economic and social basis for the existence of any large or powerful class groups.

In conclusion, we will list the aspects of the New Deal which highlight the most important economic, political, and social developments of the era.

1. *Changing Role of State Intervention in the Economy.* A quantitatively larger and qualitatively different role for state intervention in the economy. The new role represents a shift from governmental concern with regulating the standards of corporate production and administration ("trustbusting" and the Federal Trade Commission) to concern with consumption and the aggregate national market.

Expanding demand as the key to economic stability and social well-being has been the basis for increasing the fiscal role of government in the economy. Keynesian deficit spending at both the national and international levels of the market has been the formal weapon.

Military spending initiated during World War II was the most important method of governmental disbursement and this means has continued on into the Cold War. Other means of creating markets for American production have included federal road construction projects, Area Redevelopment Agencies, Export-Import Bank and the foreign aid and loan programs. Altogether by 1967, the government budget had risen to include about 15 percent of the Gross National Product. About 60 percent of that amount is for military "defense" spending.

2. *Isolation of the Polity from the Arena of Political Decision-Making.* We found two aspects to this phenomenon, both to a degree immanent in the New Deal programs. First was the further subordination of political democracy to vested interest politics negotiated by the large-scale economic organizations. Those classes and groups not included in their membership were virtually excluded from access to the centers of effective political power. This trend had, of course, long predated the New Deal, but Rooseveltian policies greatly accelerated the process by concentrating political power in the executive branch and its appointed "non-political" agencies and bureaus.

3. *Government Intervention and the Ideology of the Welfare State.* The rise of government to a permanent and decisive position in the national economy was accompanied by an elaborate rationale, important to the success of the New Deal, of the reasons for its new role—a rationale emphasizing the relationship between the new scale of intervention and social justice and welfare. But this obscures as much as it illuminates the nature of the "welfare

state" in the modern capitalist system. This review has emphasized the difference between economic recovery and stability on the one hand, and social reform on the other. The equation between the two made by such ideologues of capitalism as Schlesinger, Jr., Burns, *et al.,* has little foundation in historic fact.

12 DEFENDING THE MYTHS: THE IDEOLOGY OF BOURGEOIS SOCIAL SCIENCE*

by ROBIN BLACKBURN

Capitalism stinks, but people with little stake in it still defend and have faith in it. Why?

Part of the answer lies in the question: who controls the ideas that predominate in our society?

The power and the wealth in the hands of the men who run and profit from American capitalism also give them easy access to people's minds. Corporate interests own and control the newspapers. They finance and operate the television networks and the wire services. They own publishing companies. Huge empires exist that interlock industrial corporations with the media and the media with one another. (RCA owns NBC and Random House; CBS owns Holt; Time-Life owns Little, Brown.)

The ideas they put in people's heads are ideas which justify the status quo. They are given as wide a currency as possible through the media, through the schools and through the pronouncements of politicians and intellectuals. They permeate much of the "social science" taught in high schools and colleges, where they are often foisted on students as "objective truth." Blackburn deals with such ideas in this selection.

Some of the ideas merely dress up reality in pretty colors. For example, the "soulful corporation" idea mentioned in the Introduction to Part II is used to explain why we shouldn't fear the steep growth of concentration in economic power. Other ideas merely deny that we can improve society any more than at present. Pluralism, for example, argues that the rotation of political elites like we now have is the closest a large society can ever get to democracy.

While one approach of status quo social science is to refute radicals and justify the present operation of capitalism, another approach merely treats such issues as unimportant. The social science disciplines have been shorn of any critical concepts or any modes of inquiry that might lead to a critical perspective. Blackburn takes each of these modes of social science to task, in the following selection, and shows how their ideas work to justify the status quo.

My intention here is to try to identify the prevailing ideology in the field of the social sciences as taught in British universities and colleges.* This ideology, I hope to show, consistently defends the existing social arrangements of the capitalist world. It endeavours to suppress the idea that any preferable alternative does, or could exist. Critical concepts are either excluded (e.g. "exploitation," "contradiction") or emasculated (e.g. "alienation," "class"). It is systematically pessimistic about the possibilities of attacking repression and inequality: on this basis it constructs theories of the family, of bureaucracy, of social revolution, of "pluralist" democracy all of which imply that existing social institutions cannot be transcended. Concepts are fashioned which encapsulate this determinism (e.g. "industrial society") and which imply that all attempts to challenge the *status quo* are fundamentally irrational (e.g. "charisma"). In short, bourgeois social science tries to mystify social consciousness by imbuing it with fatalism and by blunting any critical impulse. Those aspects of this social science which are not directly aimed at consecrating the social order are concerned with the techniques of running it. They are providing vocational training for future market researchers, personnel managers, investment planners, etc. And all this in the name of "value neutral" social science. The critique of these notions that follows is not intended to suggest that they are self-consistent or unified by any logic other than their common function within the society which produces them. As Joan Robinson has written: "The leading characteristic of the ideology which dominates our society today is its extreme confusion. To understand it means only to reveal its contradictions." [1] The source of the confusion must be sought in its apologetic function. The real achievements of bourgeois social theory for the most part lie behind it in that heroic epoch when the bourgeoisie was destroying an obsolete form of society and inventing a new one. Today it is incapable of understanding the major problems that confront mankind. The plight of the "underdeveloped" capitalist countries cannot be understood without questioning the viability of capitalism in those lands, and without a preparedness to expose the exploitation of the poor by the rich capitalist countries. The nature of the revolution in Asia, Africa or Latin America cannot be grasped in terms of the philosophy of counter-revolution. Moreover the systematic complacency of bourgeois social science about its own society and its instinctive pessimism about the possibility of creating a civilization which avoids its own misery and servitude blinds it to any understanding of the revolutionary stirrings within the advanced capitalist world itself.

THE ASSUMPTIONS OF CAPITALIST ECONOMICS

Let us begin where the capitalist system itself begins, with the exploitation of man by man. We shall see that capitalist economics refuses to consider even the possibility that exploitation lies at the root of inequality or poverty—one can acquire a first class degree in economics in Britain without ever having studied the causes of these phenomena. It is now a well established (though not so well known) fact that economic inequality within most capitalist countries has remained roughly constant for many decades. In Britain, for

* Not different from American universities and colleges.

[1] Joan Robinson, *Economic Philosophy,* UK, 1962, p. 28.

example, the share of national income going to wages and the share going as profits has remained more or less the same since the statistics were first collected towards the end of the nineteenth century: the richest 2 percent of British adults own 75 percent of all private wealth, while the income of the top one percent of incomes is in sum about the same as that shared out among the poorest third of the population. Marx and the classical economists tried to explore the causes of such phenomena in sharp distinction to their neglect by most modern bourgeois economics. The shift in emphasis is stated as follows by a recent historian of the subject:

> Marx inherited both the strengths and the weaknesses of his classical forerunners. In both theoretical systems, the central analytical categories were moulded to illuminate the causes and consequences of long term economic change and the relationship between economic growth and income distribution. The tools useful for these purposes were not, however, well adapted (nor were they intended to be) to a systematic inspection of other matters: e.g. the process through which market prices are formed and the implications of short term economic fluctuations.[2]

It is these latter questions which have for so long preoccupied the main bourgeois economists and all too often the conceptual tools developed in these inquiries are then used to tackle the larger issues with predictable lack of success. Thus in the age of attempted "incomes policies" economic theory is quite incapable of accounting for the share of national income represented by profits. In the most recent edition of a now standard text book we read:

> We conclude by raising the interesting question of the share of profits in the national income. We have no satisfactory theory of the share of national income going as profits and we can do little to explain past behaviour of this share, nor do we have a body of predictions about the effect on this share of occurrences like the rise of unions, wage freezes, profits taxes, price controls etc.[3]

In his conclusion on theories of income distribution as a whole Professor Lipsey confesses: "We must, at the moment, admit defeat; we must admit that we cannot at all deal with this important class of problems." His solution to the impasse is a little lame, faced with all this: "There is a great deal of basic research that needs to be done by students of this subject."

A re-examination of the tradition of Marx and the classical economists would have given these researchers the analytical categories they so evidently need. In fact the most promising work in this field is being done on precisely this basis but without acknowledgement from the mainstream of bourgeois economics.[4] For Marx, the tendency of capitalism to generate wealth at one pole and poverty at the other, whether on the national or international scale was a consequence of the exploitive social relations on which it was based. For bourgeois social science, the very concept of "exploitation" is anathema since it questions the assumed underlying harmony of interests within a capitalist society. But of course the rejection of this concept is carried out in the name

[2] W. J. Barber, *A History of Economic Thought,* Penguin, UK, 1967, p. 161.
[3] R. G. Lipsey, *An Introduction to Positive Economics,* UK, 1967, p. 481.
[4] The work of Piero Sraffa and his school.

of the advance of science not the defence of the *status quo*. For example, the whole question is disposed of in the following fashion by Samuelson in the other main economics text book: "Marx particularly stressed the labor theory of value that labor produces all value and if not exploited would get it all. . . . Careful critics of all political complexions generally think this is a sterile analysis . . ."[5] The tone of this remark is characteristic with its reference to the academic consensus which the student is invited to join. A more recent work on this subject makes greater concessions to the "sterile analysis" but preserves the essential taboo on the key concept: the author writes that we must "retain the germ of truth in Marx's observation of the wage bargain as one of class bargaining or conflict without the loaded formulation of the concept 'exploitation.'"[6] By excluding *a priori* such ways of analysing economic relationships, modern bourgeois economics ensures that discussion will never be able to question the capitalist property system. Thus Lipsey writes:

> Various reasons for nationalizing industries have been put forward and we can only give very brief mention to these. 1. *to confiscate for the general public's welfare instead of the capitalist's.* In so far as nationalized industries are profitable ones and in so far as they are not any less efficient under nationalization than in private hands this is a rational object. Quantitatively however it is insignificant besides such redistributive devices as the progressive income tax.[7]

Lipsey is to be congratulated for sparing a few lines to such thoughts in his eight hundred page tome—most bourgeois economists simply ignore the idea altogether. However, his argument is patently ideological. Firstly, his confidence in the redistributive effects of taxation is in striking contrast to his statements made a few pages earlier, and quoted above, that he cannot with current theory say anything useful about income distribution or the effects on it of taxation. More important is the implicit assumption that capitalists' profits are being confiscated but they are being compensated for the take-over of their property. Nationalization without compensation would have an immediate, massive and undeniable effect on distribution. Even when the bourgeois economist steels himself to consider the prospect of socialism being installed in an advanced capitalist country, he usually finds it impossible to imagine the complete elimination of property rights. In Professor J. E. Meade's *Equality, Efficiency and the Ownership of Property,* he constructs a model where we find that the fledgling "Socialist State" is burdened from the outset with a huge national debt. It seems that the mind of the bourgeois social scientist is quite impervious to any idea that "property is theft" or that the expropriators should be expropriated. Instead the only "rational" objectives for him are ones defined by the rationality of the system itself. A good example of this is provided by Samuelson's discussion of the problems raised by redundancy in a capitalist economy.

[5] P. A. Samuelson, *Economics,* Fifth Edition, USA, 1961, pp. 855–6. Samuelson's account of Marx's theory contains numerous factual errors: he attacks Marx's Iron Law of Wages, a concept of Lassalle's which Marx emphatically rejected; we are told that according to Marx the worker should receive in wages the full fruits of his labour, again a view which Marx explicitly rejected. cf. Karl Marx, *A Critique of the Gotha Program.*

[6] Murray Wolfson, *A Reappraisal of Marxian Economics,* USA, 1966, p. 117.

[7] R. G. Lipsey, *An Introduction to Positive Economics,* p. 532.

> Every individual naturally tends to look only at the immediate economic effects upon himself of an economic event. A worker thrown out of employment in the buggy industry cannot be expected to reflect that new jobs may have been created in the automobile industry! but we must be prepared to do so.[8]

The "we" here is all aspirant or practising economists. Nobody, it seems will be encouraged to reflect that workers should not individually bear the social costs of technological advance, that their standard of living should be maintained until alternative employment is made available to them where they live etc. For the bourgeois economist the necessities of the social system are unquestionable technological requirements. The passage quoted is dedicated to informing the student that: "the economist is interested in the workings of the economy *as a whole* rather than in the viewpoint of any one group." [9]

To make his point clear he adds:

> . . . an elementary course in economics does not pretend to teach one how to run a business or a bank, how to spend more wisely, or how to get rich quick from the stock market. But it is to be hoped that general economics will provide a useful background for many such activities.[10]

The one activity to which this brand of economics certainly does not provide a useful background is that of critical reflection on the economy "as a whole" and the social contradictions on which it is based.

Classical economics could analyse class relationships because it was a constitutive part of "political economy," the study of social relations in all their aspects. In contemporary social science the economic, political and sociological dimensions of society are split up and parcelled out among the different academic departments devoted to them. This process itself helps to discourage consideration of the nature of the economic system on other than its own terms. The whole design is lost in the absorption with details. It also allows inconsistencies to flourish within the ideology without causing too much intellectual embarrassment. For example, most economists studying the theory of the firm assume that the goal of businessmen is to maximize profits. Sociologists, on the other hand, assume that since the "managerial revolution," business decisions are not designed to maximize even long-term profits but are rather prompted by more positive-sounding considerations—public welfare, economic growth, etc. This apparent clash of assumptions reflects only the division of labour between the two disciplines. Economics, the more "practical" of the two, has to remain closer to the way things actually work in a capitalist economy while sociology provides a justificatory theory which does not interrupt "business as usual" in the real world. In its turn the economic assumption of profit maximization is validated by the theory that business decisions only reflect the needs ("utility curve" or "indifference curve") of the sovereign consumer. The naïveté of the utility theory is offensive to sociologists but then it is not necessary to them since they have opted for the (equally naïve) managerial revolution

[8] P. A. Samuelson, *op. cit.*, p. 10. The complex nature of capitalist rationality is admirably discussed in Maurice Godelier's *Rationalité et Irrationalité en Economie*, Paris, 1967.

[9] P. A. Samuelson, *ibid.*, p. 10.

[10] P. A. Samuelson, *ibid.*, p. 10.

thesis. However, on certain key concepts the same taboos operate in sociology that we have seen in economics. For example,

> In the now nearly forgotten language of political economy, "exploitation" refers to a relationship in which unearned income results from certain types of unequal exchange. . . . Doubtless "exploitation" is by now so heavily charged with misleading ideological resonance that the term itself can scarcely be salvaged for purely scientific purposes and will, quite properly, be resisted by most American sociologists. Perhaps a less emotionally freighted—if infelicitous —term such as "reciprocity imbalance" will suffice to direct attention once again to the crucial question of unequal exchanges.[11]

IMPERIALISM AND SOCIAL SCIENCE

The ideological character of a sociology which assumes on principle a harmonious economic system is particularly evident when the relations between advanced and backward countries are being examined. It is now widely acknowledged that the gap between them is growing and it should be equally evident that the relations between them involve the domination and exploitation of poor capitalist nations by rich ones. Between 1950 and 1965 the total flow of capital on investment account to the underdeveloped countries was $9 billion while $25.6 billion profit capital flowed out of them, giving a net inflow from the poor to the rich in this instance of $16.6 billion.[12] Yet we are informed by Professor Aron that "In the age of the industrial society there is no contradiction between the interests of the underdeveloped countries and those of advanced countries."[13] Talcott Parsons is also determined to ignore what he calls "irrational accusations of imperialism." He writes,

> My first policy recommendation, therefore, is that every effort be made to promulgate carefully considered statements of value commitments which may provide a basis for consensus among both have and have-not nations. This would require that such statements be disassociated from the specific ideological position of either of the polarized camps.[14]

Parsons's notorious obsession with values is patently ideological in such a context—especially since he goes on to assert that in creating this consensus atmosphere "the proper application of social science should prove useful." Nowhere in this essay on the "world social order" does Parsons discuss the role of the capitalist world market or the US Marine Corps as forces acting to maintain the *status quo*. Further, note the sheer fatuousness of Parsons's belief that anything would be changed by the promulgation of carefully considered statements, etc. Even Parsons's undoubted intellectual distinction is no protection against the feebleness imposed on its devotees by bourgeois ideology.

The radically distorted perspective encouraged by the Parsonian emphasis

[11] Alvin Gouldner, "The Norm of Reciprocity," in *Social Psychology*, edited by Edward E. Sampson, USA, 1964, pp. 83–4.

[12] Harry Magdoff, "Economic Aspects of U.S. Imperialism," *Monthly Review*, November 1966, p. 39. Of course, there are other aspects of imperialism than this. See, for example, *May Day Manifesto 1968*, edited by Raymond Williams, Penguin Books, pp. 66–85, and André Gunder Frank, *Capitalism and Underdevelopment*, USA, 1966.

[13] Raymond Aron, *The Industrial Society*, UK, 1957, p. 24.

[14] Talcott Parsons, *Sociological Theory and Modern Society*, UK, 1968, p. 475.

on the autonomous efficacy of values shows up very clearly in such studies as *Elites in Latin America* edited by Seymour Lipset and Aldo Solari. In a book supposedly devoted to elites there is no contribution on landowners who have traditionally been such an important element in the Latin American oligarchy. On the other hand there are seven contributions on aspects of the educational system including such topics as "Education and Development," "Opinions of Secondary School Teachers" and "Relations between Public and Private Universities." The general argument emerging from such works is that development of the underdeveloped regions will ensue if schoolteachers can be persuaded to instil healthy capitalist values in their pupils. The whole programme is offered as an alternative to social revolution:

> Although revolution may be the most dramatic and certainly the most drastic method to change values and institutions which appear to be inhibiting modernization, the available evidence would suggest that reforms in the educational system which can be initiated with a minimum of political resistance may have some positive consequences.[15]

Another striking instance of the excessive value emphasis encouraged by Parsonian theory is *The Politics of Developing Areas* by G. Almond and J. S. Coleman. This book, published in 1960, so persistently ignored Mao's dictum that "power grows out of the barrel of a gun" that the index contains no reference for "army," "armed forces," etc., and its discussions have been completely bypassed by the subsequent wave of military coups throughout the underdeveloped zone. The assumption usually made in such writings is that the "West" provides the model for the development of the underdeveloped world. The fact that the Western capitalist powers were plundering the rest of the world at the time of their industrialization, whereas the underdeveloped world is in the reverse position, is rarely considered. The profits of the slave trade, the sales of opium to China, the plantations of the Americas, etc. (not to speak of the expropriation of the common lands of the European peasantry and the grazing grounds of the American Indian), all contributed to the early capital accumulation of the Western Imperialist powers quite as much as their devotion to a "universalistic" value system. Curiously enough, bourgeois economists do not recommend underdeveloped countries to follow the Western model in this respect. In all the mountains of literature devoted to the strategy of economic development, writers who urge the poor countries to nationalize the investments of the rich are very rare. Martin Bronfenbrenner's excellent article on "The Appeal of Confiscation in Economic Development," first published in 1955, has evoked almost no response and most textbooks on development strategy ignore the question altogether.

Not surprisingly the best allies of foreign capital in the underdeveloped regions are the remaining traditional elites and the feeble local capitalist class. At one time it was hoped by Western strategists that the "middle sectors" could carry through the process of economic development in their respective countries. This ignored the fact that the context provided by the imperialist world market invariably poses an insuperable obstacle to the underdeveloped bourgeoisie of the poor capitalist countries. As a consequence they have usually sought en-

[15] S. M. Lipset, "Values, Education and Entrepreneurship," in *Elites in Latin America,* edited by S. Lipset and A. Solari, USA, 1967, p. 41.

richment through battening on a corrupt government or sponsoring a military coup rather than producing the hoped-for economic advance.[16] All this creates most unpleasant dilemmas for the bourgeois social scientist and accounts for the growing acceptance of development strategies based on an analysis such as the following:

> I am trying to show how a society can begin to move forward as it is, in spite of what it is. Such an enterprise will involve a systematic search along two closely related lines: first, how acknowledged, well entrenched obstacles to change can be neutralized, outflanked and left to be dealt with decisively at some later stage; secondly and perhaps more fundamentally, how many among the conditions and attitudes that are widely considered as inimical to change have a hidden positive dimension and can therefore unexpectedly come to serve and nurture progress.[17]

This fantasy enables the bourgeois social scientist to ignore the fact that the main obstacles to development are either directly provided by imperialist domination or buttressed by it.

The attraction of the Hirschman approach is increased as earlier illusions about "underdevelopment" are eroded. The economists, in particular, have often acted as if economic development can be induced as soon as a few well-meaning tax reforms are enforced. The fiasco of Nicolas Kaldor's policies in India, Ceylon, Ghana, Guyana, Mexico and Turkey illustrate this well:

> Since I invariably urged the adoption of reforms which put more of the burden of taxation on the privileged minority of the well-to-do, and not only on the broad masses of the population, it earned me (and the governments I advised) a lot of unpopularity, without, I fear, always succeeding in making the property-owning classes contribute substantial amounts to the public purse. The main reason for this . . . undoubtedly lay in the fact that the power, behind the scenes, of the wealthy property-owning classes and business interests proved to be very much greater than . . . suspected.[18]

On the whole, bourgeois economists only achieve such revelations in connexion with remote places whose local "privileged minority" appear to impede imperialist penetration. Even then they usually persist in believing that their technical nostrums can be made to work:

> In most underdeveloped countries, where extreme poverty coexists with great inequality in wealth and consumption, progressive taxation is, in the end, the only alternative to complete expropriation through violent revolution. . . . The progressive leaders of underdeveloped countries may seem ineffective if judged by immediate results; but they are the only alternatives to Lenin and Mao Tse Tung.[19]

The political exclusion of expropriation could scarcely be more unabashed.

[16] The writings of Frantz Fanon, Régis Debray, André Gunder Frank and José Nun explore different aspects of this process.

[17] Albert O. Hirschman, *Journeys Towards Progress,* USA, 1963, pp. 6–7.

[18] Nicolas Kaldor, *Essays on Economic Policy,* UK, 1964, Vol. 1, pp. xvii–xx.

[19] *ibid.*

The rejection of "entrepreneurial" values by the more militant representatives of the Third World is a problem for Western sociologists like Parsons. He attempts to explain it in terms of "the inferior status of the rising elements":

> Here, precisely because the core elements of the free world have already at least partially achieved the goals to which the developing nations aspire, there is a strong motivation to derogate these achievements. In ideological terms the aim of these nations is not to achieve parity but to supplant certain well-established elements of the "superior" society, for example, to substitute socialism for capitalism. . . . The direction of desirable change seems clear; ideological stresses must be minimized; those aspects of the situation which demonstrate an interest in order which transcends polarity must be underscored. One of the main themes here concerns those features which all industrial societies share in common. . . . An exposition of such features would necessarily focus on the standard of living of the masses—for obvious reasons a very sensitive area for the communists. . . . This discussion has been based on . . . the assumption that one side has achieved a position of relative superiority in relation to the important values.[20]

Parsons goes on to say that the reconciliation of the inferior elements and the core elements of the free world on the basis of the latter's superior values can be achieved partly by drawing on a "very important resource, namely the contribution of social science." This explicitly ideological orientation towards underdevelopment has already introduced us to a major theme of bourgeois ideology in the context of advanced countries—namely the category "industrial society." The time has come to consider its implications.

"INDUSTRIAL" SOCIETY AND TECHNOLOGICAL DETERMINISM

The category "industrial society" has now become the accepted definitional concept for modern capitalism. Raymond Aron, who has done much to promote it, makes clear its intention: it is, he writes, "a way of avoiding at the outset the opposition between socialism and capitalism and of considering them as two species of the same genus: industrial society."[21] This way of thinking in sociology owes much to Weber. It contains a large dose of technological determinism since it suggests that the industrial nature of technology dominates social organization as a whole. For pre-industrial societies values may act as an independent variable capable of re-shaping society itself in important ways. But

[20] Talcott Parsons, *Sociological Theory and Modern Society*, pp. 485–6.

[21] Raymond Aron, *Eighteen Lectures on Industrial Society*, UK, 1967, p. 42. The term "industrial society" can be used descriptively, without the intention here acknowledged by Aron, in which case its function need not be ideological. Recently some writers have been trying to popularize the term "post-industrial society" to describe the most advanced capitalist economy (the USA). Though the inner meaning of both concepts is technological determinism, the sponsors of the notion "post-industrial society" are right to fear that technological advance may make capitalist social institutions more fragile. As the material pre-conditions for liberation become undeniable in the advanced capitalist countries the defence of repressive institutions becomes more difficult. This is Daniel Bell's nightmare: ". . . to show that order has virtue becomes more difficult when the appeals to instinct and irrationality, bound up in the coil of pleasure, begin to weave their lure." Daniel Bell, *The Reforming of General Education*, USA, 1967, pp. 311–2.

once a society has industrialized the range of significant institutional alternatives available to it is very narrow. Thus the unavoidable concomitant of modern industry will be bureaucratic organization, the "nuclear" form of the family (i.e. the family system of the modern American middle class), etc. By deducing social organization from industrial technology bourgeois sociology can portray capitalist society as void of contradictions. In the "industrial society" there is no possibility of a clash between the forces of production and the institutions of the property system since they form a harmonious, non-antagonistic unity. Capitalist social relations cannot be rejected without abandoning modern technology. Nor with such a view can capitalist relations of production (private property, the sale of labour power as a commodity, etc.) act as a fetter on the development of the forces of production (technology, natural resources, etc.).

According to Talcott Parsons, Weber regarded "capitalism," including bureaucratic organization, both private and governmental, as essentially the "fate" of Western society

> clearly to him capitalism in some sense had to be accepted; but equally on a variety of grounds scientific and ethical, the prevailing interpretations were on the one hand inadequate to the phenomena itself, on the other out of accord with his feelings of rightness and appropriateness . . . with respect to my own country I have long felt that the designation of its social system as "capitalistic," even in Weber's highly sophisticated sense, was grossly inadequate.[22]

Parsons eschews the term capitalist, no doubt because its critical overtones are out of accord with his "feelings of rightness and appropriateness" as well as Weber's. But at the same time he manages to smuggle back the distinctive features of capitalist society in his theory of "evolutionary universals," that is the universal aspects of all societies as they evolve into modern industrial states. These evolutionary universals, according to Parsons, include "money and markets" and "bureaucracy." The sociological theory of bureaucracy deriving from Weber has marked fatalistic overtones, as Gouldner has noted.[23] Indeed the more alert defenders of bureaucratic domination, wherever it is found, draw on these ideas.

CHARISMA—A PSEUDO-CONCEPT

Weber identified social innovation and creativity with the irrational: they are subsumed under the category "charisma." The ascendancy of every popular leader who rebels against things as they are is "explained" in terms of his possession of charismatic qualities. In addition to absolving the social scientist from any real examination of the social forces and circumstances which produce popular movements it also enables him to lump together quite disparate types of leaders. For Weber, Napoleon and St Augustine were both charismatic figures: for the modern bourgeois sociologist a typical amalgam might be Hitler and Mao Tse Tung. Here is an example of how the concept is used:

[22] Talcott Parsons, *op. cit.*, pp. 99–101.

[23] Alvin Gouldner, "The Metaphysical Pathos of Bureaucracy" in *Complex Organizations,* edited by A. Etzioni, USA, 1964.

> Cuba did not prove that a Latin American nation could deliberately choose Communism; it proved, if proof were still needed that a charismatic leader can make a nation choose almost anything even in the act of denying he is choosing it for them. . . . Castro's charisma . . . cut across all classes; he established a mass relationship primarily with his person, not with his ideas.[24]

The term charisma is invariably used in this way, namely to imply that support for a popular leader is not to be explained by reference to his ideas, programme or actions, but rather, exclusively, by some quality of personal magnetism. As Marcuse has said: "It reveals the preconception that every successful ostensibly personal leadership is based on some religious inspiration." [25] The notion that "charisma" (initiative, innovation) could be diffused among all the members of an organization is quite alien to Weber. For him it is necessarily concentrated at the summit so that revolutionary movements are reduced to the personal qualities of their leaders. Moreover, he insisted that charisma could not sustain itself—it necessarily underwent a process of routinization, ending in some more or less effective form of traditional or bureaucratic domination.

THE MYTHS OF BOURGEOIS PLURALISM

Marx was fond of pointing out that if the appearance of things coincided with their essence then there would be no need for science. Bourgeois social theory assumes axiomatically that everything is exactly as it appears. It is wedded to fundamental conceptual empiricism. This becomes especially clear when we examine the analysis offered by bourgeois political science of power in the advanced capitalist part of the world, where social harmony is expected to prevail. Of course Marx always attacked bourgeois political economists for seeing power in a capitalist society as concentrated in the capitalist as an individual.[26] For Marx, the laws of capitalist accumulation imposed themselves "as an external co-ercive force" on the capitalist. The more *bien pensant* modern bourgeois economists are liable to get very worried when they discover that capitalist constraints still dominate the "masterful" modern manager.

The notion that he might be only the agent of the impersonal demands of the system itself is not considered. This approach would entail not just a superficial examination of managerial behaviour but also a critical study of the structural conditions of that behaviour. The bourgeois theory of "pluralism" exemplifies this failure in the field of political sociology. The concept of the "plural society" is another pleasing euphemism for capitalism. It seeks to suggest that power within contemporary capitalism is not concentrated in a single homogeneous "power elite" but rather distributed between a number of competing elite groups. Exhaustive studies are made of how given political decisions are made, analysing the different lobbies and interest groups which affected the outcome (see, for example, the work of Robert Dahl). What is neglected is what two American scholars have called the power of "non-decisions," the role of "institutionalized

[24] Theodor Draper, *Castroism,* USA, 1965, p. 127.

[25] Herbert Marcuse, "Max Weber," *New Left Review* 30.

[26] See Louis Althusser: *Lire le Capital,* Vol. II, p. 138. "Adam Smith's 'enormous oversight' was directly related to the exclusive consideration of the capitalist as individual, that is to say, as economic agent outside the whole, as the ultimate subject of the global process."

bias." [27] In capitalist society the property regime is installed at the heart of the productive apparatus of the society. Only political forces which are prepared to overthrow it can ignore its dictates. For others political decision making will not just be limited by the capitalist context; it will be dominated by it. The actions of the British Labour Government since 1964 are a clear example of this. From the beginning it sought to restore the failing fortunes of British capitalism, even though it probably discharged its function with great incompetence. This path was followed because of the structured exigencies of the situation, not because of the evil influence of Treasury officials, Zurich bankers, or City speculators. Short of overthrowing capitalism the only alternative is to make it work and this means accepting a very narrow range of choices. (It goes without saying that even the most super-revolutionary leadership could not overthrow even the most flagging capitalist society with a run-down electoral machine like the Labour Party, steeped as it is in the traditional subordination of the British Labour movement to ruling class hegemony.)

THE PLURALIST TRAVESTY OF POLITICS

I have so far dwelt on the unscientific character of bourgeois "pluralistic" theory without noting the ideological function to which this is related. Pluralism theory produces a quite new theory of democracy which seeks to justify the way contemporary bourgeois democracies actually operate. Naturally this involves a wholesale revision of classic liberal democratic theory to eliminate its dangerously populist tendencies and to accommodate the elitist features of contemporary capitalist society. The aim is a sort of apolitical politics. S. M. Lipset has summarized his position in the following terms:

> Essentially, I have urged the view that *realistically* the distinctive and most valuable element of democracy is, in complex societies, the formation of a political elite in the competitive struggle for the votes of a mainly passive electorate.[28]

The passivity of the electorate is most important: "It is necessary to look for factors which sustain the separation of the political system from the excesses inherent in the populist assumptions of democracy." [29]

For Parsons, the perils of "populist irresponsibility" are to be reduced by ensuring that "participation in the selection of leaders" is to be "structured." [30] What he might mean by this is indicated by Kornhauser:

> The present study has sought to show that directly accessible elites make ready targets for mass movements. Constitutional and other appropriate institutional devices are needed to regulate access to elites and to reduce pressure on them.[31]

[27] M. Bachrach and Baratz, "The Two Faces of Power," *American Political Science Review,* 1962.
[28] S. M. Lipset, *First New Nation,* p. 208. He is here summarizing views he set out in his earlier book, *Political Man.*
[29] *ibid.,* pp. 208–9.
[30] Talcott Parsons, *Sociological Theory and Modern Society,* pp. 517–8.
[31] Kornhauser, *Politics in the Mass Society,* p. 236.

Earlier in this book we have learnt that

> Mass politics in a democratic society . . . is anti-democratic, since it contravenes the established order. Mass politics occurs when large numbers of people engage in political activity outside of the procedures and rules instituted by a society to govern political action.[32]

It is not surprising that many "pluralist" theorists have been quick to denounce the student movement in the United States as a threat to their special brand of apolitical, elitist democracy. This approach to politics has recently led Ralf Dahrendorf to reflect that democracy in West Germany would be strengthened by strengthening the elite. This is how he puts it:

> The German power elite is not an established elite; it is for that reason incapable of that self-confidence which is a necessary condition of lively competition. . . . To create on the basis of equal chances of access, a political class homogeneous in the social biographies of its members, and, in that sense, established, is a task whose fulfilment might give democracy in Germany new and effective impulses.[33]

There is an unwritten premise of this argument. "Equality of access" to elite membership would not benefit one social class: otherwise their social biographies would not be "homogeneous." The wholesale revision of classical democratic theory undertaken by the theorists of the bourgeois "pluralism" naturally entails re-interpretation of the function of political apathy, ignorance and irrationality. These were vices for the founders of democratic theory but for the pluralists they can be virtues so long as they operate within the bourgeois framework:

> Just as the content and significance of voter ignorance and irrationality are often exaggerated, so are the content and significance of voter apathy. Apparently apathetic behaviour . . . may reflect widespread acceptance of the way disputes are resolved.[34]

The revaluation is based on the following reasoning:

> If the balance of power between the major social groups in society is unlikely to change rapidly or violently, if therefore, political dispute is limited to ways and means of improving the existing structure—and this seems a fair description of the situation in most advanced industrial nations—then there is little to get excited about.

This line of argument rapidly leads to the conclusion that mass involvement and participation in politics is a threat to democracy. The established elites are quite capable of producing the piecemeal reforms required and only passive acceptance is required of the masses. Occasional choice between competing sections of the elite provides them with all the political participation they require, or are competent to provide. The conclusion that there is really "nothing to get excited about" has a further consequence: "High electoral participation,

[32] *ibid.*, p. 227.
[33] Ralf Dahrendorf, *Society and Democracy in Germany*, UK, 1968, pp. 270 and 279.
[34] Peter Pulzer, *Political Representation and Elections in Britain*, UK, 1968, p. 129.

massive attendance at meetings, enthusiastic processions and heated discussions may, on the other hand, indicate fever not robust good health." [35]

This brings us back to Kornhauser's concern lest "mass politics" should destroy or disrupt the placid workings of bourgeois pluralism. Such writers are continually haunted by the fear that mass interest in politics can only portend an orgy of destruction and fanaticism. Better by far, they say, to become reconciled to the listless, apathetic irrationality of the electorate in a harmonious bourgeois democracy than risk the rampant generalized irrationality of mass politics. We must remember, "The extreme case of mass politics is the totalitarian movement, notably communism and fascism." [36]

In Kornhauser's use of the word "totalitarian" we see a very hackneyed theme of bourgeois ideology. We have already discussed the way the category "industrial society" is used to subsume the social institutions of all societies based on industrial production; this emphasizes that there exist no meaningful alternatives to society as it is. The concept "totalitarian" is used indiscriminately to refer to all modern societies which are not bourgeois democracies. In particular it seeks to imply that Fascism and Communism have a great deal in common. This involves ignoring the quite evidently "pluralist" (capitalist) features of Fascist societies.[37] It also involves a patently ideological attempt to identify Marxism and Leninism with the irrationality of Fascist ideology. The most notorious attempt to do this is Eysenck's attempt to prove that Communists and Fascists have a similarly "tough-minded" personality. He only succeeded in this by wholesale misrepresentation of evidence, errors of calculation and gross violations of his own evidence.[38]

"TOTALITARIANISM"

The scientific level of the main sociological writings on the category of "totalitarianism" can be judged from the fact that they invariably identified Nazi Germany with Stalin's Russia, and distilled from these the essence of their concept. In this manner purges, forced labour camps, cult of the leader and so forth are converted into the necessary features of all Communist regimes past, present or future.[39] The diverse contemporary evolution of China, Cuba, Romania and Yugoslavia have conclusively demonstrated that Stalin's Russia was an extreme, rather than a typical, instance of a Communist attempt to build a socialist society—no doubt the extreme historical conjuncture which produced the Stalin regime chiefly explains this fact. The error of the bourgeois theorists was again empiricism: that is, identifying the essence of a form of society (socialism) with its immediately given forms (Stalinism).

The drift of most bourgeois analysis of "totalitarianism" is to suggest that

[35] Peter Pulzer, *op. cit.*, p. 129. Other writers of this sort confess to being worried by apathy if it occurs on too large a scale since it means that the masses are beyond the reach of the control mechanism of pluralist politics. As always contemporary bourgeois society and its theorists want the masses to be energetic in performing the particular role allotted to them but passive with regard to society as a whole.

[36] Kornhauser, *op. cit.*, p. 236.

[37] cf. G. Roth, "The Isms in Totalitarianism," *American Journal of Political Science*, October 1964.

[38] cf. the critiques by Roszac, Christie *et al.* in *Psychological Bulletin*, 1955.

[39] See for example, "Totalitarianism," edited by C. Friedrick, USA, 1956.

the active transformation of their own society and polity by the mass of citizens must threaten a repetition of the horrors of Nazism. The need to portray in such black hues the consequences of any alternative to bourgeois society probably reflects an awareness that its intrinsic attractions are not sufficient to ensure loyalty. The recurring streak of pessimism in contemporary bourgeois thought is also evident here: "the idea of establishing a self-conscious mastery of all social processes is seen to be as impractical as it is depressing." [40]

Above all the concept "totalitarian" seeks to distract us from the fact that for a generation now it has been the so-called "pluralist" bourgeois democracies which have become the chief practitioners and supporters of wars of extermination, massacres, the use of torture, the bombing of civilian populations and the rest of the grisly catalogue of oppression employed by modern imperialism.

METHOD

The customary refuge of the bourgeois sociologist when it comes to verifying theory is the questionnaire. The results obtained in this way are thought to have unimpeachable scientific validity. Replies to interviews are invariably assumed to reveal a social consciousness which is homogeneous and consistent. A difficulty rarely considered is that interviewees are known to reply in a different sense to the same questions if these are put in different settings (the home, the factory canteen, the personnel manager's office, etc.). One of the best recent studies of class consciousness to be conducted in England illustrates the pitfalls involved. *The British Journal of Sociology* for September 1966 carried a report of a study of the Luton Vauxhall workers by John Goldthorpe. It concluded that

> in spite of the deprivation which their jobs on the line may entail, these men will be disposed to maintain their relationship with their firm, and to define this more as one of reciprocity and interdependence than, say, one of co-ercion and exploitation.[41]

Goldthorpe informs us that 77 percent of the workers had a "co-operative view of management" and that conditions in the plant were "no longer likely to give rise to discontent and resentment of a generalized kind." About a month after the publication of this report the Luton workers broke into open revolt. Two thousand workers tried to storm the management offices, "singing the Red Flag and calling 'string him up' whenever a director's name was mentioned." [42]

The possibility that the Luton workers might ever recognize the exploitation to which they were subject never occurred to Goldthorpe. Nor did he consider the probabilities that the workers there had at least two sets of "attitudes," as do many workers in a capitalist society. On one hand they are quite aware that the owners are profiting from their labour: on the other they know they cannot change the system so they are prepared to go along with it. In a study entitled *The Political Systems of Highland Burma,* E. R. Leach demonstrated that the Highland Burmese held two quite opposed world-views at the same

[40] H. B. Acton, *The Illusion of the Epoch,* UK, 1958, p. 189.

[41] John H. Goldthorpe, "Attitudes and Behaviour of Car Assembly Workers," *British Journal of Sociology,* September 1966.

[42] *The Times,* 19 October 1966. I discuss this episode at greater length in *The Incompatibles,* edited by R. Blackburn and A. Cockburn (Penguin Books), pp. 48–51.

time, bringing forth whichever was most appropriate to the situation. Sociologists rarely entertain the possibility that consciousness in an advanced capitalist country might have a similar ambivalence. Empiricist sociology insists that all attitudes should be neat and tidy. This approach can lead the bourgeois sociologist to refuse to admit as evidence anything which upsets his scheme. For example, a sample survey was conducted of all students at the London School of Economics during the sit-in of March 1967. The purpose of this survey was to discover the attitude of students (including those not taking a direct part) towards the sit-in. Professor Julius Gould has criticized this survey for the following reason: "It is hardly likely that a serious, scientific study could be carried out in the heated, near-violent atmosphere of the sit-in." [43]

As this study was precisely designed to investigate attitudes generated during the sit-in this is a most curious objection—to be explained no doubt by the fact that the survey indicated that the majority even of those students not taking a direct part in the sit-in tended to approve of it.

CONCLUSION

Through this essay I have stressed that contemporary bourgeois social science purges itself of any concepts which might suggest that capitalist society should be critically analysed. On the whole, bourgeois social scientists avoid altogether discussion of the ultimate prospects for their social system and unanimously shun any dialectical approach to the object of their investigations.

[43] Julius Gould, "Politics and the Academy," *Government and Opposition,* March 1968, p. 31.

PART 3

PROBLEMS OF U.S. CAPITALISM

We have so far focused on the political economy of American capitalism, analyzing who gets what and who governs. The capitalist form of economic organizations has been described as production for maximum profit, as contrasted to production according to collective human needs. From a social perspective capitalism is irrational and wasteful, offering economic inequality and exploitation instead of collective advancement. What capitalism does succeed at is perpetuating a class society which benefits the small minority of wealthy and powerful for and by whom it is run—at the expense of the great majority of the population. This corporate capitalist control—with a model of development which emphasizes militarism and consumerism—is maintained by the government in its roles as stabilizer and mopper-up. The capitalist contradiction between private profit and collective need makes significant improvement impossible as long as capitalism—in the form of an entrenched capitalist ruling class—continues to exist.

In Part III we focus on some of the specific consequences of capitalist rule, analyzing the implications of economic organization based on the profit and domination of a small group of people. We argue that profit comes from a very real source—the exploitation of workers—in a way that puts the majority of the society in antagonistic relationship with the economic system. To do this we discuss the nature of work under capitalism, explore some of the chief problems (or contradictions) faced by capitalism and analyze some of the controls the capitalists use to smooth over the effects of these problems. Against the view that these problems are transitory and will eventually be solved under capitalism, we argue that they are so intrinsically related to the needs and functioning of capitalism that only radical economic change can bring real social improvement.

WORK AND THE WORKING CLASS

In the early nineteenth century, 80 percent of the employed white population in the United States were self-employed, independent producers. By 1870, however, only 41 percent of the population were in this category and by 1967 the figure had reached 7 percent—i.e., 93 percent of the population were hired employees. The overwhelming majority of these hired employees—about 80 percent—could be classified as workers: of all employees 38.6 percent are manual workers, 15.1 percent clerical workers, 11.7 percent service workers, 7.5 percent sales workers, and 6.4 percent agricultural workers. The remainder are in professional, technical or managerial positions.[1] Incomes for these various occupations vary, but for the bulk of the population the range is relatively narrow. Fifty percent of the family units in the United States had incomes under $7973 in 1967, and roughly 25 percent of all families (and 65 percent of all individuals) had incomes under $5000.[2] Yet it was the laboring power of these men and women which produced $80.4 billion in corporate profits for the same year.

The fact is that as long as capitalism exists workers will have something taken from them by the capitalists. Under *any* economic system goods and services are created, transformed or performed by men and women employed to that end. In turn, the work they do creates something with a market value or price. In the capitalist system the consumer of the good or service pays that market price and the payment is apportioned out as wages or salary, overhead costs and profit. The size of the wage portion is largely determined by the workers' success in directing their organized strength against the capitalists. The profit, on the other hand, goes to the capitalists solely on the basis of their ownership and control of the productive system (rather than according to actual contribution to the process). Wealth produced by the collective labor of society is reaped by the class of capitalist owners, who thereby increase the realm of their power and make even more profit-making possible.

This arrangement, by its very nature, puts the capitalist and the worker in a relationship of permanent antagonism. The capitalist wants to get as much work as possible for as little pay as possible. Thus the whole work situation—and the very existence of particular jobs—depends upon the criteria of profitability. The Romano selection below shows how the antagonism between the demands of the job and the needs of the worker is a constant and preeminent factor in the life of workers.

Thus life for the American worker under capitalism is based on exploitation and alienation. The worker moves in a system wherein he has no control over his work situation and conditions, not to mention no control over the uses to which his productive activity will be put. Instead, he or she is faced with a dull routine of oppressive conditions, organized in a way which tends to isolate workers from the possibility of collective social functioning. One is

[1] Everett M. Kassalow, in A. Sturmthal, ed., *White-Collar Trade Unions,* Urbana, 1966.

[2] *Current Population Reports,* Bureau of Census, U.S. Department of Commerce: Series P-60, No. 64, October 6, 1969, "Supplementary Report on Income in 1967 of Families and Persons in the United States"; Series P-60, No. 60, June 30, 1969, "Income in 1967 of Persons in the United States."

locked into this system. The road upward—job mobility and advancement—is closed to all but a very, very few. Widespread unemployment and resultant job insecurity, however, keep the road downward a constant possibility and restraint. The worker's relationship to the capitalistic system is structurally antagonistic, and cannot be anything else given that his exploitation is the source of the capitalist's profit. He cannot, therefore, hope for significant amelioration of his position—in the sense of a humanized work situation—within the capitalist structure.

However, many liberals argue that this situation is changing—slowly but surely—for the better. Perhaps the leading myth in the capitalists' ideological bag of tricks is the idea that the United States is (or is rapidly becoming) almost entirely middle-class and, therefore, classless. For example, one of the nation's leading liberal political theorists—Louis Hartz—uses this myth as the key to his "refutation" of Marx. And Nixon is built up as representing a "new majority" of middle-class "silent Americans." A more sophisticated version of this myth is one of a society whose interests and values are becoming increasingly more middle-class—the working class ceasing to be a "proletariat" due to advancing technology and *embourgeoisment*. Such a picture is of course of great importance to those interested in radical social change, for its implication is that the major antagonism between capitalist and worker is disappearing into the mire of middle-class affluence, contentment and individualism, thus making fundamental change unnecessary and/or impossible. It is therefore most important to understand exactly why this liberal view of society is mythical, which means looking carefully at what it means to be a worker in the United States today.

We can first look at the statistical picture. As most people know, the distribution of income in the United States is grossly inequitable—with most of the wealth and income in the hands of a relatively small group. As Gabriel Kolko pointed out in his essay above (see Part I), throughout the 1950's the income of the top tenth of the population was larger than the total for the bottom five income-tenths. And one of the nation's leading experts on the topic—economist Robert J. Lampman—reports:

> In my own study, I found that the top 2 percent of wealth-holders held 29 percent of all wealth in 1949; this had risen to 30 percent by 1956. This trend was confirmed by the University of Michigan Survey of Consumer Finances which found that the top decile of wealth-holders had 58 percent of net worth in 1953, 61 percent in 1962. The lowest fifth of income receivers had 11 percent of net worth in 1953, 7 percent in 1962.[3]

Income figures are more meaningful in terms of what they can buy, and here the picture is quite striking. The U.S. Labor Department's Bureau of Labor Statistics publishes a City Worker's Family Budget by which an urban family of four could live at a "modest but adequate" level—*but* below what they consider "the American standard of living." A look at the detailed budget shows that it is calculated at rather rock-bottom levels. For 1967 this budget would

[3] Lampman, "Recent U.S. Economic Growth and the Gain in Human Welfare," in Walter Heller, *Perspectives on Economic Growth,* New York, Random House, 1968, p. 154.

cost $9076 before taxes.[4] Yet for 1967 the median income for all families was $7973.[5] According to the same government figures, 12.5 percent of U.S. *families* had income under $3000 in 1967; 25.3 percent income under $5000; 58.6 percent income under $9000. All in all, workers in the United States are not enjoying the unbounded affluence not infrequently heralded. As none other than the U.S. Chamber of Commerce puts it: "Only 54% of American families can afford what is now perceived, by today's criteria, as a 'low moderate' life standard, and very few can afford the leisure-class life styles popularized by the spread of education and promoted by the mass media." [6]

Moreover, this picture is at best static, at worst becoming even more widely inequitable. Because of tax cheating, payment in kind, changes in measurement technique, etc., it is difficult to compare income distributions over time. Most experts agree, however, that the distribution pattern has not improved at all since World War II and persuasive evidence exists to indicate that the pattern has shown no improvement since the early years of the century. Kolko, in fact, shows how income maldistribution in the 1950's bore the same relationship amongst income tenths as existed in 1910. (See Part I.)

For those who claim that U.S. workers are becoming middle-class the economic realities present a strong refutation. But there is still the argument that job conditions and attitudes toward work are changing for the better; more precisely, that the United States is becoming a nation of white-collar workers, making them middle-class in life-style if not in spending ability. The trouble with this argument is that it misconstrues the evidence. While it is true that advancing technology is replacing blue collars with white, it is also true that the workers in these white-collar jobs are exploited and dehumanized by the capitalists in the same way as are industrial workers. Benenson and Lessinger, in a selection below, review the evidence at hand and conclude that "the middle-class picture of the American workingclass . . . is largely irrelevant to the work experience of most blue-collar and white-collar workers."

It is true, of course, that there are far fewer sweatshops and fifteen-hour days today than there were fifty years ago. It is also true, however, that today's higher skill requirements are not well filled by workers who are dead on their feet. American capitalists have come to learn that it is in their self-interest to have workers alive enough to perform efficiently and consume prodigiously. This is capitalism's new *industrial revelation.* It is a revelation, however, that had to be forced on most capitalists by organized workers, and which still has little meaning for those people living in the most abject poverty.[7]

[4] See *Three Standards of Living for an Urban Family of Four Persons,* Spring 1967, Bureau of Labor Statistics, U.S. Department of Labor, p. 6.

[5] Bureau of Census, Series P-60, No. 64, *op. cit.* The 1967 individual median income was $3459; for all workers it was $5111, Series P-60, No. 60, *op. cit.*

[6] *Business Week,* December 6, 1969, p. 197. The Chamber's lower percentage figure apparently results from their using earlier, preliminary income figures for the comparison year.

[7] It is instructive to remember that after Henry Ford introduced his famous Five-Dollar Day in 1914 "he was denounced by other captains of industry as 'a Utopian,' 'a Socialist,' and 'a traitor to his class.' . . . By 1926, however, the leaders of industry had drastically overhauled their philosophy of wages. . . . Employers, apparently, had come to accept the mass-market purchasing-power theory. . . . 'To the new capitalism,' *Fortune* intoned, 'the wage-earner . . . is a purchaser, a partner, and the key to production. . . . His wages are dictated . . . by ambition for a market and a desire for willing coopera-

Thus, while the economy as a whole is advancing—absolute incomes rising, technology improving—the worker's relationship to the system has stayed the same. Work—for blue- and white-collar workers alike—remains oppressive and monotonous, with a pay scale quite low relative to what is justified by overall production, and with continuing job insecurity and unemployment. The primary antagonism within capitalism continues to be that between a capitalist ruling class, which owns and controls most of the wealth and productive capacity of the nation, and the working class, which provides the physical and mental labor needed to make things run. And while the organized strength of the working class has forced some material improvement, the major exploitation and alienation of work under capitalism remain. They are part and parcel of the capitalist system of economic organization, unreformable because of the profit and control dynamics inherent to that system.[8]

This perspective—a class analysis[9]—has profound implications in terms of analyzing the problems of the society, for it means that significant progressive change must alter this class structure. According to this analysis, those problems that are of such concern today—the war in Vietnam, poverty, racism, poor education, etc.—are inextricably related to the *needs* of the capitalist system of economic organization and—in many ways—actually help to continue that system. Thus the solution of these problems requires an end to the class structure on which capitalism is based. Stated most boldly, a society with adequate employment and decent education, and without war, racism and poverty, is impossible under capitalism. In the following pages we discuss these various problems—to identify the immediate human costs of capitalism and to show how these problems are caused by and help sustain the capitalist economic system. Specifically, we will discuss imperialism, unemployment, racism, male chauvinism, education, and law and order.

IMPERIALISM

The capitalist—as seen above and discussed more fully below—must continually extend and increase his return on exploitation—i.e., maximize his

---

tion.'" (Irving Bernstein, *The Lean Years,* Boston, 1960, p. 179.) When capitalism entered its next economic crisis, Ford found no difficulty in tightening the screws on his workers, cutting wages even more severely than other leading industrial giants.

[8] "In real life capitalism, it has taken the utmost efforts of the 90 percent of the population to prevent their share of the national product from falling, and so to enable their standard of life to rise with the rise of productivity . . . capitalism has in fact an innate tendency to extreme and ever-growing inequality. For how otherwise could all these cumulatively equalitarian measures which the popular forces have succeeded in enacting over the last hundred years have done little more than hold the position constant?" (J. Strachey, *Contemporary Capitalism,* New York, Random House, 1956, pp. 150–151.)

[9] This perspective may seem strange when viewed strictly contemporaneously but what we should be chiefly concerned with is a pattern over time. As E. P. Thompson has observed: "If we stop history at a given point, then there are no classes but simply a multitude of individuals with a multitude of experiences. But if we watch these men over an adequate period of social change, we observe patterns in their relationships, their ideas, and their institutions. Class is defined by men as they live their own history, and, in the end, this is its only definition." (Thompson, *The Making of the English Working Class,* New York, 1963, p. 11.) Some quite useful observations on this matter—especially in regard to the concept of a ruling class—can be found in T. B. Bottomore, *Elites and Society,* Baltimore, Penguin, 1966, especially in the first two chapters.

profits. One way of doing this is to prevent income redistribution at home (as with inflation). Another way is to seek increased profits through exploitation abroad.

The U.S. capitalist class has long felt keenly the need to extend its sphere of economic activity around the globe. American liberals, however, have preferred to view U.S. foreign involvement as part of an effort—admittedly not consistently successful or humanistic—to "make the world safe for democracy." Anti-communism has blinded them to the fact that Spain, Portugal, South Africa, South Korea, Formosa, etc., etc., are parts of a "Free World" that is free only in its openness to American capital. Thus the reality of Vietnam was a shock for liberalism, a shock the liberals sought to explain away as being exceptional—a mistake, the tragic final chapter of a bankrupt, Dulles brothers foreign policy.

But the roots of the modern American empire—to use William Appleman Williams' phrase—reach much deeper than the period of the Cold War. More important, they grow directly out of the nature and needs of capitalism itself. Thus American capitalism's first answer to domestic problems has always been to expand more and more into other countries, exporting their exploitation throughout the world.[10] As Dean Acheson told a Congressional committee on Postwar Economic Policy and Planning in November 1944, "my contention is that we cannot have full employment and prosperity in the United States without the foreign markets." [11]

Vietnam is actually a critical keystone in the network of U.S. imperialism that results from this economic need. The most important aspect of Vietnam is that it is the place where U.S. imperialism is being told most forcefully to get out—by the armed strength of the Vietnamese people. But Vietnam also has a special significance within the U.S. imperialist network. As Senator Gale McGee told the United States Senate: "That empire in Southeast Asia is the last major resource area outside the control of any one of the major powers on the globe. . . . I believe that the condition of the Vietnamese people, and the direction in which their future may be going, are at this stage secondary, not primary." [12] This realization as to the importance of Vietnam to U.S. world economic interests is made clear again and again by members of the capitalist class, in a way that provides verification of what their economic designs are for the world. Thus we find Henry Cabot Lodge commenting:

> He who holds or has influence in Vietnam can affect the future of the Philippines and Formosa to the east, Thailand and Burma with their huge rice surpluses to the west, and Malaysia and Indonesia with their rubber, ore and tin to the south. Vietnam thus does not exist in a geographical vacuum—from it large storehouses of wealth and population can be influenced and undermined.[13]

[10] On this point the reader should consult two most important books by William Appleman Williams: *The Tragedy of American Diplomacy,* New York, 1962; and *The Roots of the Modern American Empire,* New York, 1969. Williams has provided the theoretical groundwork for the study of the United States as an imperialist power. Also, for a detailed discussion of one period that explodes many fondly held liberal remembrances, see a book by one of Williams' students: Lloyd C. Gardner, *Economic Aspects of New Deal Diplomacy,* Madison, Wisc., 1964.

[11] Williams, *Tragedy, op. cit.,* pp. 235–236.

[12] See *Congressional Record* for February 17, 1965.

[13] *Boston Globe,* February 28, 1965.

And finally, we learn from Alfred Wentworth, vice-president of Chase Manhattan Bank in charge of Far Eastern operations:

> In the past, foreign investors have been somewhat wary of the over-all political prospect for the region. I must say, though, that the U.S. actions in Vietnam this year—which have demonstrated that the U.S. will continue to give effective protection to the free nations of the region—have considerably reassured both Asian and Western investors.[14]

Thus the war in Vietnam is not simply the result of mistaken or bad leadership, but is part of a conscious policy which backs up American capitalists' economic needs with American military strength. This economic penetration by force—U.S. imperialism—has required the placing of U.S. military and paramilitary forces, as well as money and materiel, around the globe. In September 1969 the United States had about 1.2 million military personnel stationed abroad, in more than thirty-three countries and foreign possessions. In addition there were 26,000 U.S. civilians, 350,000 dependents and 255,000 foreign nationals attached to U.S. overseas bases. All told, the United States maintained 2270 military installations overseas (not including Vietnam), of which the Pentagon designated 340 as major installations.[15] These figures do not include places—like Laos—where U.S. military personnel quite evidently are stationed despite government denials as to their presence.

Often United States involvement has been rather open and dramatic, as in Vietnam, the Dominican Republic, Greece, Lebanon, Thailand, Cuba, Guatemala, British Guiana, Iran and the Congo.[16] Most often, however, U.S. involvement is quite behind the scenes, as indicated—for example—by former Secretary of Defense Robert McNamara's statement to a Congressional committee as to how "the primary objective in Latin America is to aid, where necessary, in the continued development of indigenous military and paramilitary forces capable of providing, in conjunction with police and other security forces, the needed domestic security." [17]

The question most likely to be asked at this point is: Does this have to be? How deeply rooted, how necessary, is such economic and military imperialism? Cannot the path that led to Vietnam be reversed by better leadership and a more watchful public? The answer, of course, is that things are not so superficial and simple. Imperialism is a most important part of capitalism—the highest stage of capitalism, Lenin called it—and not merely the result of corrupted policies. It is, therefore, deeply rooted indeed. Harry Magdoff has shown[18] that in 1964 foreign sources of earning accounted for about 22 percent of domestic nonfinancial corporate profits. Furthermore, as Magdoff argues, if one looks at the largest and most powerful of U.S. corporations, foreign

[14] "Economic Considerations in Foreign Relations—An Interview with Alfred Wentworth," in *Political,* Vol. 1, No. 1, July 1965, pp. 45–46; as quoted in Harry Magdoff, *The Age of Imperialism,* New York, 1969, p. 176.

[15] *Congressional Quarterly Weekly Report,* October 24, 1969, p. 2075.

[16] For discussion of these cases, see Richard J. Barnet, *Intervention and Revolution,* New York, 1968.

[17] Testimony before Committee on Foreign Affairs, House of Representatives, *Hearings on the Foreign Assistance Act of 1967,* Washington, D.C., 1967, p. 117.

[18] *Op. cit.,* p. 182.

earnings become an even more important source of profits. Some of the biggest U.S. corporations get up to half their profits from foreign dealings.[19] The immensity of this situation is suggested by these comments of an investment banker writing in *Foreign Affairs*:

> The role of U.S. direct investment in the world economy is staggering. According to the U.S. Council of the International Chamber of Commerce, the gross value of production by American companies abroad is well in excess of $100 billion a year. That is to say, on the basis of the gross value of their output, U.S. enterprises abroad in the aggregate comprise the third largest country (if such a term can be used to designate these companies) in the world—with a gross product greater than that of any country except the United States and the Soviet Union.[20]

United States economic involvement abroad actually takes several forms; that is, there are several facets of foreign nations that are economically attractive to U.S. capitalists. First, there are the foreign markets, where goods made in U.S.-owned factories located in the United States, in the market country or in a third country can be sold. Second, there are the natural resources—oil, banana, chromium, etc.—which can be extracted for U.S. use. Third, there are sources of cheap foreign labor, to be used to produce goods for sale both abroad and for shipment back to the United States (thus, by the way, threatening the U.S. worker in his fight against the capitalists). And fourth, there are (especially in Europe) opportunities for direct investment, uniting the above three factors through involvement in overseas capitalist enterprises.

Because of their attractiveness for profit maximization, foreign markets, resources, labor and overall investment are becoming more and more important to U.S. capitalists. As the Gilbarg imperialism selection below shows, profits of U.S. corporations (excluding banks) earned off foreign operations grew from 10 percent of total profits in 1950 to 22 percent in 1964. As *Business Week* reported in 1963:

> Late in the 1940's—and with increasing speed all through the 1950's and up to the present . . . in industry after industry, U.S. companies found that their return on investment abroad was frequently much higher than in the U.S. As earnings began to rise, profit margins from domestic operations started to shrink; costs in the U.S. climbed faster than prices, competition stiffened as markets neared their saturation points.[21]

In recent years American investment emphasis has shifted from Europe and Canada, where the United States has already gained substantial control over major industry, to Latin America, Africa and Asia. Competition in Europe, Canada and Japan forced this shift, as is pointed out by John G. McLean, director of Continental Oil and Anderson, Clayton and Company:

> Manufacturers . . . have been forced to establish plants abroad to retain their business. . . . [U.S.] industries are finding their traditional export markets preempted by the growth of efficient, indigenous producers. The development of

[19] See *Business International* magazine, issues of August 4, 16, September 1, 29, October 13, 1967.

[20] Leo Model, "The Politics of Private Foreign Investment," *Foreign Affairs,* July 1967, pp. 640–641, as quoted in Magdoff, *op. cit.,* p. 59.

[21] *Business Week,* April 20, 1963, p. 70.

> local industries abroad has . . . made it impossible from a competitive and economical standpoint to continue shipments from this country.[22]

As Magdoff points out,[23] during the years 1950–65 the United States directly invested $9 billion in the poor countries (other than Europe and Canada) and brought back about $25.6 billion in profits. In the same period, U.S. business exported $14.9 billion to Europe and Canada in investments, but brought back a mere $11.4 billion in profits. The rate of profit is higher in the poor countries—and highest of all in Asia.

This network of U.S. imperialism constantly requires men and/or money to maintain and extend itself around the globe.[24] Its successes, moreover, serve to strengthen the dominance of the U.S. capitalist ruling class over the world capitalist system. Thus, while U.S. imperialism may avert economic stagnation and unemployment at home, it more than makes up for this in the way it directly hurts U.S. workers. Most obviously, it is largely working-class men who must fight wars to maintain the economic empire of U.S. business, and working-class people in general who are pressed economically by such wars. In addition, the actual and potential use of foreign labor is used as a threat to hold down wages at home (in much the same way as "runaway shops" to the Southern United States have served to hold down wages in the North). For example, *Business Week* of July 26, 1969 reports that "the only manufacturer of household sewing machines left in this country—the Singer Corp.—sells its domestic customers two machines produced in its overseas plants for every one made in the U.S. . . . Once, Singer had 10,000 workers at its Elizabethport, N.J. plant. Now Elizabethport employs 2,000 workers." And finally, the success of U.S. imperialism serves to strengthen the hand of the capitalists in exploitation and oppression of workers in this country.

All in all, as Harry Magdoff has written, "Imperialism is not a matter of choice for a capitalist society; it is the way of life of such a society." The struggle against U.S. involvement in Vietnam and elsewhere, the struggle against U.S. imperialism in general, and the struggle against U.S. capitalism are all part of the same struggle—and can only be won as one victory.

UNEMPLOYMENT

Imperialism is related in many ways to the second problem area of capitalism to be discussed, the area of employment and unemployment. The connection is seen most dramatically in the fact that in recent years it has been only during time of war that the nation's unemployment rate has dropped below 4 percent (a figure which itself is greatly understated).

One might think that a system which produces wealth out of the exploitation of workers would tend to exploit as many workers as possible on a full-time basis. But, in fact, capitalism does face problems in this regard. Full employment, it seems, produces a situation in which competition between

[22] McLean, "Financing Overseas Expansion," in John K. Ryans and James C. Baker, *World Marketing: A Multinational Approach,* New York, Wiley, 1967.

[23] *Op. cit.,* p. 198. He is using U.S. Department of Commerce figures.

[24] As President Calvin "The Business of America Is Business" Coolidge said several decades ago, "Our investments and trade relations are such that it is almost impossible to conceive of any conflict anywhere on earth which would not affect us injuriously." Williams, *Tragedy, op. cit.,* p. 123.

individual capitalists drives up wages and prices in such a way as to produce runaway inflation. Conversely, the existence of a pool or buffer of unemployed workers makes it easier to keep wages "competitively" low and to maintain inflation at a level satisfactory to prevent redistribution of income.[25] The result of this tension is that U.S. capitalism—aside from wartime—has continually faced a fairly high unemployment rate. As economist Robert Lampman has observed, "in a typical year [from 1947 through 1964] about 15 percent of the labor force experienced some involuntary unemployment." [26]

For all workers this situation is clearly bad. It results in great job insecurity and plays a big part in creating an overall situation in which the worker must run as hard as possible simply to avoid being pushed backward. But because unemployment tends to be concentrated in certain areas, its effects are particularly severe for certain groups of workers; namely, blacks, women and young people. These groups are last hired, first fired—generally in very poor-paying jobs. Their rates of unemployment are many times the overall average.

This situation is getting worse, not better. The job market is expanding at a rate slower than is the labor force. Over the past decade the various levels of government have provided the bulk of new jobs—primarily teaching—but not at a fast enough rate. Moreover, there would seem to be a limit to the number of unemployed to be absorbed by government hiring.

The liberal response to this situation has tended to be one of optimistic acceptance. Attention is focused on measures such as job training and income guarantees, the great unused potential of the U.S. economy is continually invoked, yet the simple fact remains that such measures do not get at the cause or magnitude of the job shortage. No realistic solution is brought forward because—within the framework of capitalism—no solution to the unemployment problem is possible. In fact, because of the way the system operates, capitalism's needs would be negatively served by full employment. Yet without a solution to the unemployment problem the other social problems of concern to liberals and radicals alike will not be abated.

The unemployment picture, however, does present the capitalists with a potentially volatile situation within the working class, a situation in which the poorly employed might possibly revolt against their plight. In fact, the factor that the Kerner Commission emphasized most strongly in reviewing the causes of ghetto rebellion was unemployment, especially among the young. Thus, viewed from the perspective of the capitalist, unemployment—like so many other aspects of capitalism—has both good and bad features. On the one hand, a pool of unemployed makes it easier to restrain wages and manipulate inflation. On the other hand, the lack of adequate employment raises the specter of revolt. In either event, unemployment stands as part and parcel of the operational structure of capitalism. To counter the radicalizing repercussions of unemployment the capitalists have been able to avail themselves of an age-old diversion, splits in the working class.

[25] The complexities of this situation are discussed in greater detail in the Christoffel selection, below.

[26] In Heller, *op. cit.*, p. 145.

RACISM

It is only when people begin to perceive that their problem is not a personal one but has its roots in the workings of the social and economic system that they are likely to fight back against that system. Racism serves to cloud such perception and realization, thereby protecting the system against revolt. Thus racism actually serves the needs of capitalism. By fostering the concentration of unemployment among black and brown people, racism eases somewhat the direct pressure of unemployment on white workers and, to a more important extent, serves as a psychological balm to white workers who see another group of workers even worse off than themselves. Moreover, by dividing white workers from black and brown workers, racism not only destroys the unity required if the working class is to effectively fight against capitalism, but goes beyond this to the point of getting workers to fight each other. Thus chronic unemployment, instead of being viewed as an intrinsic part of an economic system based on the overall exploitation of workers by capitalists, is viewed by workers as the threat presented by other workers of a different color. This dynamic of racism—which is the third problem of capitalism under discussion—is clearly not the cause or sole extent of racism itself. It is, however, very important in the continuation of racist attitudes and policies within the society.

Concerned Americans have been disturbed by various manifestations of racism for quite a long time; and the civil rights movement of the early sixties focused renewed concern on eliminating racist attitudes, injustices and inequity. But the basic approach of that movement—and of liberals today—viewed racism as primarily an attitudinal problem—of simply "white racism"—rather than one with economic content. (See, for example, the Kerner Report.) According to this view of the problem, racism will be uprooted through contact between the races and dissipation of racist attitudes. Thus, while the civil rights movement played an important role in the development of broader black and white radical movements, its own focus was insufficient in that it aimed at reforms—desegregated facilities, voter registration, etc.—which ignored the economic basis of racism. Desegregated restaurants are of little use to unemployed black workers.

The fact is that in order to change a pattern of activity you must first understand what keeps it going; specifically, who has a vested interest in its continuation. In order to effectively combat racism it is necessary to understand that the continuation of racism is economically profitable to capitalism—that racism is rooted in capitalism itself. Racism serves capitalism as a means of controlling a subgroup of the working class into which can be concentrated the various elements of exploitation. Such control is made possible because the subgroup is isolated, socially as well as physically, into ghetto areas. As a result, capitalism is better able to exploit all workers, while it is also able to exploit black and brown workers especially severely.

Additional ways in which racism benefits private interests under capitalism are outlined by Baran and Sweezy in their essay printed below. Because of racism, (1) owners of ghetto real estate are able to overcrowd and overcharge, (2) middle- and upper-income groups benefit from having at their disposal a large supply of cheap domestic labor, and (3) many small marginal businesses, especially in the service trades, can operate profitably only because of the extra-cheap labor available to them.

Beyond this are more institutional aspects of racism. For example, racism provides politicians with a sizable, yet generally powerless, group of voters—along with a not infrequently used emotional issue. And in a system where government services are financed, ultimately, out of profits, racism makes it easier to save billions on the schools, roads, welfare programs, houses, etc., that the black community does without. And finally, the myths and prejudices of racism have their own life—and a heritage that has given us various forms of segregation, racial violence, and—most destructively—the subtle racism that pervades us all.

One significant aspect of racism is the fact that people know it exists. Whether or not they share the belief that white people are superior to nonwhite people, they are aware that such a belief plays an important role in society. This means, first, that the nonwhite people can perceive the problem as being one faced by a *group,* thus making conscious and organized response possible and it means, second, that white people can develop a concern and response of their own. The situation is rather different, however, with the fourth problem of capitalism to be discussed: male chauvinism.

MALE CHAUVINISM

Women are not only discriminated against in all levels of society's functioning, but they are also taught to accept such a role. Their talents are not used, except in specifically limited areas of "women's work." The result is that women are seen by men primarily as sexual objects, as childbearers and raisers, and as the "old lady" tying them down to the old grind.

There are many parallels, both ideologically and structurally, between racism—the belief that white people are superior to nonwhite people—and male chauvinism—the belief that men are superior to women. Both beliefs are objectively baseless and wrong, yet deeply and pervasively held. Both are very effective in splitting the potential unity of the working class, making it impossible for working people to fully oppose their own exploitation under capitalism. As with racism, male chauvinism serves the needs of the capitalists by providing them with a pool of workers who can be poorly paid and inadequately employed without fear of well-organized response. In fact, this wage differential serves to split the unity of struggles for higher wages.

The parallel to racism should not be taken too far, however, for there are many special aspects of male chauvinism. Perhaps most obvious is the fact that women are not mistreated as a physically ghettoized *group;* rather, chauvinism is fostered within the family unit itself. Within the family the woman generally acts as a source of unpaid domestic labor and as the psychological scapegoat and escape for the man. Because of this one-to-one (rather than group) arrangement it is much harder for a consciousness of and response to chauvinism to develop. Unlike the case with racism, most people—both men and women—are unaware of the very existence and meaning of male chauvinism. Quite conveniently for those whose interests are served, the chauvinistic mistreatment of women is simply considered "natural." For example, a woman without a job is generally considered "not in the labor force" rather than unemployed, even though she might take—and need—a decent job if it were available. And when male chauvinism is recognized, it is most often—as with racism—considered to be simply an attitudinal social problem, growing out of backward prejudices and solvable by means of enlightened concern. But—again—as long as such "prejudice" is materially grounded in the profit self-interest of capitalists, the struggle against it is tied directly into the struggle against capitalism.

EDUCATION

The obvious, and quite important, question at this point is why these destructive policies and beliefs—imperialism, unemployment, racism, male chauvinism—are not more clearly perceived and opposed by those who are hurt by them? Or put another way, how are the capitalists able to perpetuate the system and the people needed to run it without being faced with revolt? One answer, which we will get to secondarily, is force. But while force can be used to contain active discontent, it cannot maintain and re-create the skilled and functioning labor force needed to operate the economy. For at least part of the answer we must look to a fifth problem area of capitalism, the educational system.

The standard, liberal analysis of the despicable state of education in the United States tends to point the finger of blame at the public's poor understanding of the importance of education, at a perverted set of social priorities, and at the shortsighted, pennypinching and selfish attitudes of (especially suburban conservative) voters and officials. Schools will remain mental deathtraps, it is argued, until the negative social cost of miseducation is fully and widely realized.

The fact that this analysis misses, however, is that schools actually do teach. The problem is that, rather than preparing the well-rounded-and-grounded, self-sufficient individual heralded by Horace Mann and John Dewey, the various levels of education concentrate instead on producing workers with—and only with—the necessary *skills* and *ideas* to make the capitalist economy operate efficiently. The function of education within capitalism is to provide a class-filtering process and to condition people to a repressive society.

The skills necessary to the operation of the capitalist economy include not only specific technological skills, like computer programming or carpentry, but also the basic skills needed to perform so-called unskilled jobs, e.g., the ability to read, do simple arithmetic, fill out written forms, etc. This type of skill instruction is organized by putting students into slots and limiting what is offered each slot according to what the future work demands of the slot will be. Sometimes this is done quite blatantly—the tracking system—while at other times the same end is accomplished by placing an entire school in a slot. Once an individual or group is put in a slot, they stay there.

Some skills needed by the economy, such as higher-level technological skills, require a rather high-level—but ideologically narrow—education. On the other hand, because of the unemployment dilemma discussed above, there are large supgroups of young people who are not needed in the labor force and who, therefore, get little in the way of skills. Thus, for most black and brown students elementary and high schools are ways of keeping them both off the streets and off the job market. In fact, for working-class children as a whole schools function more as people warehouses than anything else. The basic skills needed by most workers are quickly absorbed, and the teachers are left to spend quite literally the bulk of their time as disciplinarians and record keepers.

The people warehouse aspect of education does serve a useful function for the capitalists in that it accustoms the students to being in that role. Looked at in this way it seems no accident that high schools are one of the most oppressive institutions in capitalist society. For it is especially at the high school level that a certain type of ideological learning goes on that is helped by an oppressive atmosphere. Within the high school milieu many destructive prejudices—such as racism, male chauvinism, national chauvinism or super-patriotism—are fostered and heightened. Here also the ruling myths are presented most strongly and—perhaps most importantly—competing ideas are given the stamp of unacceptability.

Because of the demands of advanced technology, more and more young people are going on to college. This phenomenon is not, however, evidence of a more middle-class society. First of all, the bulk of the increase has been in state universities and junior colleges, rather than at the so-called elite schools. But whatever the type of school, college does not really provide escape from the working class. A fantastic percentage—close to half—drop out or are dropped out of college before graduation. And of those who do graduate, the great majority go on to work as technical workers, teachers, skilled workers, etc., rather than as managerial or professional personnel. Even at the traditionally elite schools the bulk of the graduates become teachers or social workers, not members of the capitalist class. Increased college enrollment, rather than indicating improving work situations, simply reflects capitalism's need for an ever more skilled and educated work force.

One result of this situation is that universities have become very big businesses. To borrow an example from Edward Greer's essay below, the University of California employs 40,000 people and budgets over $600 million annually. As Richard Greeman points out, below, "The activities of this super-industry include weapons development, real-estate wheeling-dealing, investment brokerage, publishing, counter-insurgency, lobbying for high drug prices, unsafe cars, and the bracero system, cigarette filters, rat poisons, poison gases, espionage, comic-books, and parlor games." At the same time the universities channel and indoctrinate—i.e., "teach"—in order to turn out individuals with the necessary skills and ideas. They produce competent engineers, respectable bureaucrats and sophisticated CIA agents. They also produce glib ideological defenders of the status quo, propounding the ruling ideas of the day, which—as Marx pointed out—are for any society the ideas of its ruling class.[27]

Universities, in their present form, may not be crucial to capitalism, but their present form is controlled by the needs of capitalism. What is crucial, however, is that a class-filtering process exists at some level, draining the super-talented working-class kids into a more useful and less troublesome middle-class milieu and rationalizing the class structure itself with the illusion that distinctions are based generally on some sort of merit standard. Criteria for improved education are incompatible with such functions. Good education would be nonrepressive and nontracked; it would make working-class students aware of their history and power as a class; and it would prepare students for working together, to

[27] Or, as Tom Watson remarked on one important area of ideas, "History has not been written by the laborer. It has usually been written by his enemy. Therefore we only catch glimpses of the truth from time to time."

change the world, rather than simply to fill a slot. Such a goal will not be achieved under a capitalistic system that must prepare people to take orders, work for extrinsic rewards and compete; under a system that cannot tolerate high aspirations among people destined for crummy jobs; or under a system in which a minority exercises ideological control over a majority. A revolution in education, therefore, will require a revolution for education.

FORCE—LAW AND ORDER

There are times, however, when passive acceptance is replaced with active discontent. There is, after all, a very important antagonistic tension within the very dynamic of capitalism. On the one hand, the capitalist must extend and increase his return on exploitation wherever possible—by avoiding increases in wages and avoiding income redistribution. But on the other hand, continuing exploitation increases, among the exploited, an awareness of their condition and a desire to resist and oppose it. In so doing they in fact challenge capitalism itself. Thus, despite all its protections—all the ideology that permeates and shores up the system—there are times of crisis when capitalism's ideological controls are not enough. Then the capitalists must call upon force—which is the sixth and last problem area of capitalism to be discussed in this section.

Large-scale domestic use of military and police power is a not uncommon part of U.S. history. The Stamp Act riots, Shays's Rebellion, John Brown's raid, Homestead, Pullman, steel organizing in the 1930's, Newark and Detroit in the 1960's—all were met with violent displays of official force. Today black people —the most exploited and most militant segment of the working class—are facing wide-scale use of official force (i.e., recent efforts to suppress the Black Panther Party by killing or framing its entire leadership).[28]

This type of violent response is resorted to when workers become so militant as to constitute an active threat to the continued functioning of capitalism. Capitalism, as a system of economic organization, has laid out political-legal guidelines as to what is permissible behavior and what is not—and clearly challenging the freedom of profit is not allowable. Historically, however, progress for the working class has come only when these guidelines—capitalism's law and order—have been challenged and overstepped. When the challenge has been strong—as with labor struggles in the 1930's—the capitalists were forced to loosen the guidelines or risk endangering their entire system. Progressive social change has come when those who would resist oppression used organized force to counter the force of day-to-day repressive society.

Yet capitalist law and order means more than simply forceful prohibition of revolutionary violence. Terry Cannon discusses, below, the various implications of the legal system as a weapon of the capitalist class. This includes not only direct control, but also harassment. For example, in the Spock and Chicago Demonstration trials the government was aware that—even under its own rules of the game—convictions would eventually have to be overturned. The effect of such prosecutions, however, was to harass and intimidate people opposing the

[28] The Kerner Report presents an interesting chronological history of the domestic use of Federal troops—see pp. 531–533 of the Bantam edition. In addition to being able to depend upon Federal and state troops and state and local police, capitalists have at times also directly employed their own private armies—often of Pinkerton agents—several hundred strong.

war in Vietnam. Or as in the case of Rap Brown, prosecution is brought under any flimsy statute—in Brown's case a statute already declared unconstitutional by the U.S. Supreme Court—so that travel restrictions can be attached to the bail requirements. Just as during a strike the police can be relied upon to attack the strikers, not the bosses, so can the courts be depended upon to rather consistently oppose efforts for social change. And by using injunctions, courts—working with companies and universities—can make up their laws as they need them.

However, the use of "legal" force is far from the most effective control available to the capitalist ruling class. Educational and ideological controls are to be preferred over the use of force, for the latter serves to strip away illusions about the nature of power in the society. As argued above, forcible controls face people with the realization that the only way they can improve their lot is by fighting against that force. For example, as Terry Cannon points out—and as workers learned long ago—"the only defense against the injunction is the force of numbers."

Thus, with force—as with the other problems of capitalism discussed—there exists an internal tension. Imperialism, unemployment, racism, male chauvinism, education, legal force—all work to serve the needs of the capitalist economic system. But at the same time all of them create problems within the society, problems which can potentially politicize the average man and woman in the society. The fact that these problems do form contradictions within capitalism can be nicely illustrated—in light of the arguments made above—by imagining a society in which such problems did not exist. A United States of America that did not exploit, oppress and attack peoples around the globe, which enjoyed virtually full employment at home, which was not weakened by racist and male chauvinist prejudices, and which maintained educational and legal systems based on equality, justice and full development of individual and social potentials, rather than on the maintenance of the class structure—such a society would be desirable indeed.

But—as was argued in the previous pages and is argued more fully in the essays that follow—such a society is incompatible with the needs of capitalism. United States capitalism *needs* to invest in the markets, resources and labor of foreign lands in order to maintain its control over the world capitalist system and in order to maintain its level of profits. Capitalism *needs* a significant level of unemployment in order to control wage levels and control inflation. Capitalism *needs* racism and male chauvinism in order to continue its especially profitable exploitation of black and women workers and in order to assure a disorganized working class. Capitalism *needs* a particular type of educational system in order to channel workers into properly controlled skill—and nonskill—areas, stabilize the social structure and inculcate acceptable values and beliefs. And capitalism *needs* a particular type of legal force system in order to guarantee continuation of the existing structure against challenges from below.

The conclusion suggested by all of this is that an equitable and just society, a society devoid of these very problems, can only be brought about through radical structural change—through the destruction of the capitalist system of economic organization. The specific nature of such a desirable society—and we assume it is desirable—is discussed later in this volume, as are ways in which it might be brought into being. The arguments made here suggest, however, that

(1) such a society would have to be socialist, not capitalist, and that (2) it is the tensions—or contradictions—within the problems just discussed which, especially during times of crisis, will clearly dramatize the need for such radical change. It is when people fully understand the real source of their problems, the ultimate cause of their unhappy condition, that they can begin to bring about fundamental change.

13 LIFE ON THE JOB*

by PAUL ROMANO

Over a century ago Karl Marx wrote in the Economic and Philosophic Manuscripts:

> In his work [the worker] does not affirm himself but denies himself, does not feel content but unhappy, does not develop freely his physical and mental energy but mortifies his body and ruins his mind. The worker therefore only feels himself outside his work, and in his work feels outside himself. He is at home when he is not working, and when he is working he is not at home. His labor is therefore not voluntary, but coerced; it is *forced labor.* It is therefore not the satisfaction of a need; it is merely a *means* to satisfy needs external to it.

Marx's words were true in 1844 and they are true today. Workers' labor under capitalism creates private profit for others, making the relationship itself economically exploitative. The labor is alienating because capitalism allows the workers little or no control over the conditions and speed of work, cuts them off from one another and cuts them off from the product of their labor (both because it is sold for the profit of others and because they have no say in whether it should be produced at all). This alienation from one's primary activity reflects itself (as Gorz argued, above) in a vain attempt—promoted by capitalism—to find fulfillment and self-expression in consumption.

The following selection by Paul Romano (the pseudonym of a Detroit factory worker) gives vivid firsthand content to these analytical observations on work. Although written in 1947, the essay remains valuable today because of the way in which Romano has related a sensitive portrayal of alienating day-to-day factory life to the actual causes of that alienation. No one reading it can have any doubt that factory work is hell.

At the same time, Romano shows how within the operation of capitalism there exists the basis and potential for workers overcoming this situation—for their running their own system more efficiently and more humanely. He shows how, even today, workers know more about their work than do the bosses; that they are constantly coming up with creative ideas to promote production despite an aversion to "helping the company." While most of this book concentrates on showing what the difference between capitalism and socialism means for the society as a whole, Romano shows quite clearly what that difference means for the workers in one factory.

INTRODUCTION

I am a young worker in my late twenties. The past several years have found me in the productive apparatus of the most highly industrialized country in the world. Most of my working years have been spent in mass production industries among hundreds and thousands of other workers. Their feelings, anxieties, exhilaration, boredom, exhaustion, anger, have all been mine to one extent or another. By "their feelings" I mean those which are the direct reactions to modern high-speed production. The present finds me still in a factory—one of the giant corporations in the country.

This pamphlet is directed to the rank and file worker and its intention is to express those innermost thoughts which the worker rarely talks about even to his fellow workers. In keeping a diary, so to speak, of the day-to-day reactions to factory life, I hoped to uncover the reasons for the worker's deep dissatisfaction which has reached its peak in recent years and has expressed itself in the latest strikes and spontaneous walkouts.

The rough draft of this pamphlet was given to workers across the country. Their reaction was as one. They were surprised and gratified to see in print the experiences and thoughts which they have rarely put into words. Workers arrive home from the factory too exhausted to read more than the daily comics. Yet most of the workers who read the pamphlet stayed up well into the night to finish the reading once they had started.

In direct contrast was the attitude of the intellectuals who are detached from the working class. To them it was a repetition of an oft-written story. They felt cheated. There was too much dirt and noise. They could not see the content for the words. The best expression of what they had to say was: "So what?" It was to be expected, for how could those so removed from the daily experiences of the laboring masses of the country expect to understand the life of the worker as only the worker can understand it.

I am not writing in order to gain the approval or sympathy of these intellectuals for the workers' actions. I want instead to illustrate to the workers themselves that sometimes when their conditions seem everlasting and hopeless, they are in actuality revealing by their every-day reactions and expressions that they are the road to a far-reaching change.

CHAPTER I. THE EFFECTS OF PRODUCTION

You've Got to Live

The worker has to work. There is no alternative but to produce in order to provide even the bare necessities of life. The greater part of his waking hours are spent in the factory. It is here that he, as a worker, must think and act. No matter what the conditions of life are in the factory, he has got to make a living. That is one of the strongest motivations governing the attitude of the worker in the modern productive system. He may not think of ever being anything but a worker, but that does not prevent the thousand and one pressures of factory life from leaving deep impressions upon him.

The worker is compelled on the job to perform a task which can only make him rebel: the monotony; the getting up every morning; the day by day drudgery which takes its toil. He labors under forced conditions. Not only that, but there is the fact that he compels himself to accept these conditions. Home, family, economics make him a slave to this routine. Theoretically, he is a free wage earner. Realistically, he cannot maintain such a policy and exist. In other words, he thinks he has the right not to accept his condition, but clearly realizes he must. These two pressures tend to foment a subterranean frustration within him.

The Shop's Hard on the Body

The factory worker lives and breathes dirt and oil. As machines are speeded up, the noise becomes greater, the strain greater, the labor greater, even though the process is simplified. Most steel cutting and grinding machines of today require a lubricant to facilitate machining the material. It is commonplace to put on a clean set of clothes in the morning and by noon to be soaked, literally, with oil. Most workers in my department have oil pimples, rashes and sores on their arms and legs. The shoes become soaked and the result is a steady case of athlete's foot. Blackheads fill the pores. It is an extremely aggravating set of effects. We speak often of sitting and soaking in a hot tub of water to loosen the dirt and ease the infectious blackheads.

In most factories the worker freezes in the winter, sweats in the summer and often does not have hot water to wash the day's grime from his body. How many thousands of workers have ridden the bus home with sweat and grime from the shop still covering their bodies. Even if the facilities are there, the desire to get home and away from the shop is so strong that workers often will not even bother to change out of their work clothes. On the other hand, some workers deliberately scrub themselves and take showers before leaving the factory. They attempt to leave every taint of the day's work on the inside of the plant gate. A new set of clothes and they are on the way home feeling a little relaxed from the day's grind.

X is a laborer. He pulls chips from the machines; fills the machines with cutting oil and helps stock up. Since a number of laborers were laid off, his job has increased in intensity. He has more machines to tend. As a result, he, like others, begins sweating profusely. The bad part is this. Upon filling the cart with chips, he pushes the cart outside of the plant. The constant change of temperature combined with the sweating gives many of these laborers colds and bone troubles (arthritis, etc.). However, they have discovered that if they wear a heavy sweatshirt, the perspiration will be absorbed. Of course, they are continually uncomfortable.

Factory lighting as I have known it has never approached daylight in being able to ease the strain on the eyes. Most often in the shops it is of a yellow hue. To illustrate the results of this, it is best to repeat what other workers have said on this score. A worker coming off the shift steps out into the sunlight. He blinks his eyes and says: "I feel as if I have just come out of the coal mines."

Sometimes workers who do not even know each other, greet each other in passing. One day a worker whom I did not at all know, walked by me and in a brief statement and a gesture of his hand towards the earth announced: "Down into the salt mines again."

Lunch time on the cafeteria veranda, an ex-GI says: "These goddamn factories are prisons. You are cooped up without a chance to get a decent breath of fresh air."

The plant is generally filled with a heavy smoke from the carburizing and heat treating departments. It fills the nose and throat. Some one wrote the following on the locker room bulletin board: "Why don't some one do something about this smoke hell-hole?" It remained there for a few days and then the following was written: "The union is no good, the smoke is still here."

In the various shops in which I worked, I used to notice that most old-timers chewed tobacco. Now there is a definite reason for this. To be exact:

1. It was one way to substitute for smoking on the job.
2. It seemed to absorb the fumes, dust and steel fragments that floated around.

I have noticed several young workers doing it now. I asked one why. He said that every night when he got home, his throat is coated and also his nostrils with the dust of the shop. He said it is a lung protection. Many of the workers have discolored teeth as a result. Snuff is also used.

I have made these observations of other jobs.

Foundry workers have the soles of their feet cooked on the job. It is a hot, filthy, smoky job and the feet ache from toasting. There is the ever-present danger of being burned by molten metal.

Crane operators inhale all fumes, dust, gas, heat, etc., which rise to the ceiling. In one shop, the crane men used to complain bitterly that they had to urinate in buckets because they were not allowed to leave the crane.

Production welding is also bad. The mask is over the head for long hours. It is a stifling job. The flash of a welding torch can blind a worker. Many such accidents happened during the war.

The factory routine often causes the worker physical discomfort and irritation of a very intimate kind. In the morning he faces the question: should he relieve himself by moving his bowels before he leaves the house, which will mean rushing in order to get to work on time; or should he be uncomfortable until he can relieve himself in the plant? On the other hand, in the plant he may not be able to leave his machine at the time he has the impulse to go to the men's room because of the production demands made on him. Sometimes in such a situation, he shuts down his machine in anger and says: "To hell with this. When you gotta go, you gotta go." No matter what course he follows, the result is that what should be a simple, personal routine, becomes a matter of pain, irritation and conflict.

There are times when a worker will cut himself badly. Although the company continually states that the hospital facilities are there for the use of the men, and that even the most minor cut or bruise should be reported to the hospital, the men do not report for treatment often. The reason for this is that they are afraid that they will receive a black mark on their record which might classify them as careless workers in this or any other factory where they might be working.

One day workers in one end of the shop are freezing from the cold. They get up a delegation and go into the front office. They say: "Either we get heat or we go home."

Monday morning on a dreary, cold, winter day: Workers are dressing and changing clothes. A worker comes in and in one word expresses the philosophical outlook and feelings of each worker present. In a frustrated, definitive, angry tone, he says, "Horse S . . ." Everybody understands and says to himself, "You can say that again for me, brother."

And Harder on the Mind

There are times when a worker suffers a nervous and mental breakdown as a result of attending machines for long hours over a period of months and years. It takes a period of sustained exposure to result in such a climax. In one shop where I was steward, I happened one day to look over at a machine where one of the workers was sitting. He had his head in his hands. It was immediately discernible that something was wrong. I went over to him. He told me if he didn't walk out that instant, he would break. I hurried him into the locker room and he left the building. A couple of days later he told me that was the closest he ever came to a physical and mental breakdown. In the same department I knew one worker who suffered a nervous breakdown after parts of his machine had showered him when the power was on and something went wrong. Home difficulties, combined with the machine often produce terribly nervous individuals.

On the job, as a result of constantly handling steel chips, the fingernails are torn away. Sometimes it is painful, but always irritating and annoying. Many accidents happen because of simple forgetfulness. The most usual is that of getting a cut by grabbing a chip coming off the machine. Many machines require a constant repetition of routine actions on the part of the worker. With the foot he steps on a lever while his hands are engaged in putting a piece of work in the machine and pushing other levers. The week in and week out repetition of these movements at certain times produces a sort of dullness or dizziness. The result is that one day the worker will put his hand in the machine instead of the piece of work. After such an accident, the operator asks himself, "Why did I do that?"

The militancy of the American worker is something of a sporadic nature. Now fierce, now subtle, now quiet. He may go for months without a violent outward expression. Even years. This does not belie the fact that continually within him is an ever-pressing force which drives towards eruption. Such an explosion at a particular time seizes any reason at hand as the basis for its manifestation.

A worker walks in and sits down in my aisle of lockers at the beginning of work. He is a veteran, was wounded overseas. He suddenly exclaims in a loud voice, "Let's go out on strike." I look at him and ask, "What brings this on?" He replies, "I can't stand it." "Stand what?" I ask. He answers: "The incessant pounding in my head. The goddamn bang-bang-bang of the machine is driving me nuts. It is driving me crazy. Back and forth, back and forth."

The machine he operates is a cold header. It chops off half-inch pieces of steel about one-half inch in diameter from a large roll of steel. It takes great pressure and is done without heat so that the result is a steady pounding noise, with the feeding arm going back and forth. I myself worked next to these machines for several weeks. When you leave work, there still remains the continued booming in your head.

I asked one worker how old he was. His reply was "30." I then said, "Well, you are as old as you feel in body and spirit." He replied, "Then here am I, an old man."

One young worker I know spoke of the fact that he was always under a strain because the boss was constantly yelling at him. As a result, whenever he sees the boss approach, he hides. In arguments with the boss, on the other hand, he suddenly becomes angry and threatens to quit.

There is the worker who arrives every morning in the locker room with, "Ours is not to reason why, ours is but to do and die."

The worker's attitude is: "All that the company is interested in is production and more production." This is his way of protesting against the complete disregard of the individual human element. This is also evidenced by such statements as: "What do they think we are, pieces of steel?"

CHAPTER II. A LIFE-TIME TRANSFORMED INTO WORKING-TIME

I Work All Week for Friday Night

The life of a worker is transformed into working-time. He does not know how to play. After working hours, in the company of other workers, the conversation invariably returns to the shop. It is like a drug that will not release his mind. The worker thinks of payday and the end of the week. His off hours are always conditioned by, "I can't stay up late as I have to go to work tomorrow." When Sunday night arrives, he thinks dejectedly of returning to work on Monday morning. The incessant process continually repeats itself. He looks longingly for weekends and they disappear before he has a real chance to absorb them. He says, "I work all week for Friday night."

There are times when the worker has several days off in a row. The knowledge of this almost immediately begins to loosen the psychological strain. After a few days, he begins to acquire rest and peace of mind. The work takes on a lighter aspect. He has the opportunity to look out of his limited sphere. The pressure of work temporarily leaves him. Oddly enough however, during fleeting moments of this period, a sense of unexplainable guilt for not being at work suddenly will come over him. The return to work is difficult. The first few hours back in the shop still finds the worker imbued with the spirit of his sojourn. Then comes the end of the day. The appearance and feeling of the worker are exactly what they were before the break occurred.

Effects of production are of a very insidious nature. Some of the cumulative effects reach heights of bursting power. There are days when some workers will go home early or not come in to work at all.

The worker often has to fool himself in order to keep working the whole week. On Tuesday he will promise himself a day off the following day. When Wednesday rolls around, he will say to himself: "I'll work today and take off on Thursday instead." He does this until Friday comes along and then he says: "I might as well finish the week. Another eight hours won't kill me."

One of the workers won $50 on a bet. When he learned of it in the plant, he worked 4 hours and then took off.

Now and then, the plant has a fire drill. The workers march out of the plant for five minutes. Everyone seizes the opportunity to smoke. Remarks of this kind can be heard: "I'd like to go right home," or "I wish we would stay out till quitting time."

Ten workers from my department are settled around the table at lunch time. As the half hour period ends, one worker states adamantly: "Let's stay here (cafeteria) and not go down to work. We work hard. What can they do to us if we stay?"

There is an old popular phrase used on payday, "Another day, another dollar."

When payday comes, the locker room buzzes as though a faucet was turned on. This one day of the week, there is whistling, chattering, and lively activity. The thing for which the workers have struggled all week has arrived, so it is natural that they should justify their suffering by the "good old pay check."

On the other hand, there is at certain times in the worker a psychological drive to remain in the plant. As we know, a worker spends most of his waking hours in the plant or at his labor. His life, therefore, revolves around this activity. His subconscious becomes overwhelmed with facts and thoughts concerning machine, workers, bosses, regularity of work hours, and incessant repetition. When out of the shop, he breathes a little more like a man. His home is more like the expression of his life. When the break occurs in the work and he has his week-end, for a fleeting moment he has loosened himself from the effects of the shop. Then crash! He must reorient himself back on Monday to the same old routine. The mental strain at many times is immense. This was much more so during the war when in many instances the work day was 12 hours, 6 and 7 days a week. As a result, having become acclimated to the shop, there were times he would rather remain than leave. The longer hours a worker puts in, the easier it is to drag him still further in the work day. There is a converse to this. As the work day shortens, and the work week correspondingly, the worker then begins to want a still shorter working period.

Once we were going back to a 40 hour week. I have heard many comments on this. The greater part of them are statements to the effect that these workers are very happy about it. They hate to lose the overtime pay (as they need it badly) but since the initiative was not theirs, they feel that they are not cutting their own throats. As I have heard it:

"I won't ask for overtime. If the company gives it to me, I will work, but I hope there is no overtime."

Speaking of overtime, workers sometimes resent other workers refusing overtime, because they are afraid that it will jeopardize their own overtime. They do not want overtime but are forced to take it by economic necessity.

Then I have heard rambling conversations. One worker says, "Let's work 6 hours a day, 5 days." Another says: "While you are wanting, how about 2 hours a day, 4 days a week?"

There Must Be a Better Way of Making a Living Than This

There exists today in the factory an attitude which was not apparent before the war. As stated by the workers, it goes, "There must be a better way of making a living than this." It is a distinct change. Several business suggestions have been bandied back and forth. Opening a tavern, ice cream parlor, launderette, etc. No one of the workers could finance it alone, so for a while they spoke about partnerships, but then gave that up. They feel the closeness of their economic position.

I have noticed the trend amongst the workers to speak more and more in terms of security. How it can be gotten, etc. There is a strong attitude prevalent to the effect that the worker gets pushed around too much on the job. They think in terms of a year or two at the present job. "When production really gets under way it will be a short time before the warehouses are flooded." In short, they expect bust. Every time a four day work week is scheduled, the workers speak as if the depression is already here. On the other hand, when they are sure of a full week's work, some workers will take a day off.

The married worker with a family feels that the single worker who supports himself only cannot be too responsible. He arrives at this conclusion this way. Factory life is drudgery. Anyone who is not forced by necessity to endure it is one who will at any moment up and leave or be irresponsible on the job. It is not uncommon to hear one worker say to another, "Why do you stay in the factory? If I was single, I would be out of here long ago."

One of the inspectors told me he is going into business. Day after day he gets up at the same time, goes through the same routine, and comes home. He says he refuses to take it any longer. This monotonous procedure is getting him down. He does not want to spend his life this way. He had best make a break before he gets old. He does not care if he loses all his savings, at least he will be free for a while. He was in the marines and did picket duty during the strike. I told him he was doomed to the factory and he became very upset. He took a month's leave of absence, failed, and then came back.

Workers often change jobs in the hope of finding conditions better in another situation. Often they will even take less pay if a certain job appears to offer peace of mind. It is apparent now though that conditions of work everywhere are the same. A change of jobs may bring a novelty, but it wears off in a week or so.

The Wife and Kids

The worker cannot express even to himself the real meaning of his suffering. When he arrives home, he finds that his wife, after a hard day's work in the home, often does not show any interest in his problems. His realization of this makes him at times resent the fact that he cannot even unburden himself to his wife. He often talks to his kids about his work though. Not so they will understand, but as a release for himself.

At other times, the wife is the only one to whom the worker can unburden himself. Many workers' wives know as much about the factory their husband is employed in as do workers in the shop. Over the supper table the many pressures which fell on the worker that day come out. Perhaps a fight with the foreman, some spoiled work, or trouble with the machine. If during the day the worker has made some creative work or found himself able to deal with some troublesome problem on the machine, he will report it to his wife in glowing terms.

Many times the worker awakens on a non-work day with the impression that it is a working day. Saturday or Sunday for instance. He wakes up with a start, not having set the alarm and frantically realizes he is late. The shop is ever in his subconscious.

About getting up in the morning, there is a technique which most workers use against being late. The clock is set and placed about 5 or 10 feet away. To shut it off, it is necessary to get out of bed and walk, stumble, and what have you, to the clock. This process insures the workers waking enough to realize it is time to get up. When the clock is placed next to the bedside, it is a common occurrence to reach out, stop the alarm, rest a few minutes and then wake up late for work. This provokes haste and nervous stomach, upset in the family, etc.

Often the wife must do the waking up at five or six in the morning. This adds to the trials of her day as she has to wake up a short time later for the kids. Many times home life is disrupted by this series of events. It results in early morning quarrels and arguments with the husband leaving for work without his lunch pail. Also a cause of this disruption in family life is the shift work. The third shift from 12:00 to 7:00 A.M. is the worst. Some call it the nightmare shift. The family can rarely get together and looks longingly for weekends. The worker gets home at the beginning of day and tries to sleep with the kids running around. He gets irritated at the kids and yells at his wife for not keeping them quiet. He works hard all night to come home to this.

Both second and third shifts prevent the husband and wife from sharing in a rational and human manner the normal intimacies of life.

Many young workers think of a new baby in the family in terms of support, or will they make enough to take care of it. If a slip occurs, the chain grows tighter. Many workers resort to having abortions for their wives. I know one such case in the shop where the woman became critically ill as a result and still suffers from the effects. This family already has two children. They like infants. The only apparent reason for the abortion was economic insecurity.

After supper, sitting in the living room, it is a matter of minutes before falling off in an exhausted sleep on the parlor chair. Here is the way it is told. "I put the radio on. I heard the announcer state the 'Lux radio for the evening,' and that is all. I woke up a few hours later. Stiff neck and backache and flopped into bed."

Here are some other aspects of home life. Many workers say, "I've already got my ice-box filled with beer. I generally drink a half a dozen bottles before going to bed." Or, "Relaxing with a bottle of beer."

Taking a ride on non-work days, a worker many times will deliberately avoid those streets which lead him to work. He comes to dislike all those buildings and landmarks which line the route to the factory. Or he will many times deliberately ride this circuit up to the plant and past, precisely because he is free to do so on this one day.

On the other hand, workers have often made it a point to bring their whole family down to the plant site on a Sunday. There they explain to the family what section of the plant is their working area.

The worker tries to bring a bit of his home into the factory, so he often shows to other workers the pictures which he carries in his wallet of his children. Sometimes it is the home in which he lives. It is not unusual for snapshots of all kinds to be on the inside cover of a worker's toolbox. One fellow had a snapshot of a filling station which he once owned, and another of his automobile.

In spite of the fact that workers continually go on strike, during periods when such is not the case, the attitude prevailing is one which would seemingly prevent a strike. Workers continually refer to the fact that they have a wife and kids and have responsibilities. They say, "I can't afford to be out of work or go on strike. If you were married, you would know and understand."

It is very difficult to reach workers at certain periods. To picture this point clearly we can say that the workers have drawn back into themselves to think things out. Events as they unfold are the lever which periodically brings forth these thoughts into actions. The average worker has too much responsibility to be persuaded by words alone.

CHAPTER III. SINCE THE WAR ENDED

The Speed-Up

At the time of the telephone strike, in the spring of 1947, we got an eleven and a half cents raise. Machines have been speeded up again to get it back. Most workers said when we got the raise that the company would take it out of our hide.

The worker used to be able to smoke more often. Now he has to spend all day watching, changing and cleaning tools. The interludes are briefer. The end of the day produces a more exhausted worker, mentally and physically. The moments of relaxation are continually diminishing.

On the other hand, the more the machine is speeded up, the more times the worker seeks to leave his machine even though this increases the chances of the machine's cracking up.

Workers in many departments now run 3 and 4 machines where previously a worker ran one. This keeps a worker jumping and on his toes. Invariably during every day someone will speak of his exhaustion.

A worker on a high speed automatic machine said: "I am geared up at a high speed pitch to run a fast machine. Kept busy piling up the work, loading and putting new tools in. If I was to be put on a slower machine, I couldn't stand the change of pace. At the same time it would be a vacation compared to the fast one I run."

I Dropped Dead

The shop has the incentive system. The company appears to cheat workers here and there out of parts of their bonus. Many ask "Why do they do this?" The computations of the bonus become complicated especially when time cards are given to workers. The company is often accused of ripping up time cards that were given to workers.

One worker went into a long, heated talk against the incentive system. Spoke of how a man has to exhaust himself to reach or go over the established norm. Also a normal day's work would relieve tension and is enough to expect from a worker. He stated vehemently that he would like to throttle the inventor of the bonus or incentive system.

When the operators fail to make bonus by the end of the day, they climax it with the expression, "I dropped dead." The essence is that the worker exhausted himself to no avail.

To Produce or Not to Produce

The machines are speeded up about 40%. The workers are caught in a contradiction. To continue to produce at that rate might soon put them out of work. The workers are divided on the subject. Some think that it matters little, and that when the big bust comes, it will hit them anyway. Others quietly begin to lower their production per day. The work, intensifying in pressure, also drives more workers to reduce their daily quota. To produce or not to produce under these conditions is the question. The cost of living soars upward, compelling the worker to produce in order to make extra money on incentive with which to meet his daily needs.

When time-study men are about, the worker will find a multitude of reasons for shutting the machine down. A resentment of large proportions grows as he sees the man from the office with the clock in his hand. It is then that he uses all the tricks he knows to slow down the machine and also his own action. The time-study man is unwanted in the shop. Everywhere he goes, resentment-filled eyes follow him. He is aware of this, and many times is almost apologetic, at other times surly.

The Company Checks Up

Relations between checker and worker have always been a strained affair. The worker always attempting to cheat, the checker always feels sure the worker is putting something over on him. Of course, the checker's personality becomes molded to his job and he becomes more or less of a "bastard" to the workers. He counts their work to see that they are not cheating, which they resent. However, the workers cheat at every opportunity by stealing work after collection or by deliberate miscount to the checker. Stealing pans of work from the company is an art which many practice. The worker in the morning will steal a pan of work. If in the afternoon, the checker accidentally should give him a miscount on a few pieces, he gets angry and demands the few pieces, even though they mean little.

On some machines, counters were placed to determine whether the worker was stealing work, and to determine the amount of cycles the machine made. A cycle is equivalent to one finished piece of work. It is clear that every means will be used to get the utmost out of the men.

The company is now checking the usage of electric power the last 15 minutes before quitting time. Many workers having reached their quota by then, shut down. It appears as though the company wants to determine the amount of labor they are not receiving.

The Worker Double Checks

The worker becomes a bookkeeper and carefully calculates his day's percentage, checking it against company receipts to see that he is not cheated. He does the same with his pay check every week. He is consumed with anger if the company has shorted him.

The plant took inventory this week. Many workers including laborers, machinists, heat-treat, grinders, etc., participated. For the past several months workers have been stealing pans of work to fill their bonus needs. Obviously, there will be a shortage of tens of thousands of pieces in inventory. The workers found the situation quite humorous.

We are on production in our department. One hundred percent is the norm you are told to achieve. It takes all day to reach that. It is generally in the last three quarters of an hour that you make your bonus. What has happened is this. The checker comes around to close the worker out just about then. Many lose their bonus because the checker comes too early. There have been some violent flare-ups on this score. Once a worker came around and told the others not to turn in their work until quitting time. However, there is a contradiction involved. The workers are told to shut down early but yet hate to lose their bonus. Here is how the workers get around this: After the checker has gone, they let the machines run for the next guy, so that when he comes in, lying in the pan will be the work he would normally lose at the end of the day. The next man does the same for him.

Some workers spend the last half hour making work for the next fellow. However, there are many workers who don't do so. Caught in the contradictions of company inefficiency, high piece-work rates and the desire to make bonus, the end of the day finds them too exhausted to change tools or to make extra work for the incoming worker. The desire to shut down the machine as soon as possible and to get away from it is always present.

Violations

In our shop there is a set of company rules. If any are broken, it means a violation. Three violations give the company the right to fire you. This can readily be used by the company when seeking to fire someone. One worker once told me, "They can fire you anytime. All they have to do is say your work is scrapped three times or catch you smoking, or coming in late." (However, this is dependent on the strength of the union.)

The company every once in a while sends a superintendent into the wash rooms to catch workers smoking or sitting down. Badge numbers are taken down and a black mark put against your record. The worker resents these sneaky tactics.

Workers have been restricted to machines till the bell rings. Formerly, they were able to go up five minutes or so earlier to the lunch room or at quitting time to the locker room. There is also to be no more eating of lunch at the machines. However, the men are already breaking it down. Violations are given out by the company. The plant superintendent complains that no sooner is the restriction announced than he catches a worker eating a sandwich. He says the worker has the gall to offer him a bite too. One worker was hauled in and threatened with a violation. His reply was, "I will eat three sandwiches and you can give me the three violations and try to fire me."

One worker I know has two violations. He is bitter over such treatment of workers. That is no way to treat your fellow men, he says. I asked him why he signed the violation when he should have fought it with the union. He says that while he was in the office, he was raging inwardly, but it could not be noticed outwardly. He signed it to show the company he was not afraid of them.

The company tries not to antagonize workers who are trouble-makers. Their attitude seems to be that if such a worker is irritated by the company, he will prove to be a greater source of aggravation for the company. Therefore, they attempt wherever possible to placate such workers.

The company has the right to fire workers who have been given violations. That is, for stealing work, making scrap, being caught smoking, etc. Although that is the law, so to speak, the company rarely invokes it. They could not in actuality enforce it. Instead they attempt to irritate the worker into obeying the law.

A worker once was caught stealing a pan of work to make up his bonus needs for the day. Upon being called into the office, he demanded that they should give him his final pay, and if they did not like his work, he would go elsewhere. The company declined to do this, but in order to penalize him, gave him a few days off.

Plant supervision has attempted several times to prevent men from using their half hour lunch to doze off in the locker room stretched out on benches. I used to do this in other plants. The idea is to eat your lunch surreptitiously before the bell and then escape into sleep for one-half hour. The awakening is only that much worse though.

The men often say: "If they were to fire us for all the violations that are committed, there would be no one working in the plant."

No Use Giving the Company Something for Nothing

The worker does not give freely of his fullest abilities. When he deems it necessary, he will cut his production. If he can't make out on the job, he will make sure he goes well under for the week. "No use giving the company something for nothing, as that is what they are looking for," he says. "You're here to work for yourself, not for the company."

There are days when a worker has become particularly irritated at the company. He vents his anger by putting out less work than usual. Other times, when the company speeds up the machines and increases the norm, a section of workers will tacitly agree to begin a slow down. Such a situation is occurring now in one department. In order to compel the company to reduce the rate, the workers are at present engaged in a daily reduction of their percentage. Since the company has refused by arbitration to reduce the rate, the men are relying on their own actions to compel a change.

The workers feel that strikes merely for wages do not get them anywhere. There is a direct, distinct and often openly voiced sentiment against another strike. However, it is easy to see from day to day, that as a result of the speed-up in the machinery and the increased exploitation, no excuse of wages will be needed for strike justification when the saturation point is reached.

CHAPTER IV. THE INEFFICIENCY OF THE COMPANY

The plant I work in is part of a giant corporation. The network is countrywide. It is a high degree of capitalist organization in industry. However, the bureaucratic supervision of work results in inefficiency on a tremendous scale in view of the effort involved. It appears that the company is sacrificing all for production. It is not so. More production could be gotten in a different manner. The intent is more at the subjugation and control of the laborer.

Wanton Use of Machinery

The machinery is speeded up to a high degree. As a result there are continuous breakdowns and a large crew of maintenance men is needed. The wanton use of the machinery is everywhere apparent.

A cam will be put in the machine to reduce cutting time. The tools as a result hit at high speed and both burn and break up. As a result of excessive speeds, bearings in the machines burn out, and some machines are always in repair. Such machine speeds induce the worker to say: "Some day these damn machines will take off and fly away."

The machines are geared to certain types of metal. Often the steel put at the machine is of a temper harder than that required. This once again causes burned up and broken tools.

For weeks on end, necessary repairs will not be made. A new hole needs to be tapped in a fixture to keep it secure. A slipping clutch or brake threatens the cracking up of the machine at any time with the added danger to the operator. Nothing is done.

The company is not interested in how many tools are burned up, or how often the men must change them. They are primarily interested in getting the machines to run at maximum speed and then it will be up to the operators to keep up with them.

"If I Had the Money Spent on This . . ."

The company continually attempts to cut down on the expense departments, that is, the non-productive departments. The production departments suffer by this and are constantly irritated by having to do incidental errands.

The grinding department has blueprints from which they calculate how to grind up the tools. The worker in his daily experience finds that the blueprint is no good and he asks the grinder to do it his way. The grinder says "okay," and for a while he cooperates with the machine operator. Management hears of this. A big argument takes place. The grinder is told that he is to take orders only from management and to follow the blueprint. He then says: "You're the boss," and does as instructed. What follows would be somewhat funny if it did not add to the troubles of the worker in the shop. The worker is then compelled to go to the crib, get the tool, find the foreman, tell him a change must be made in the tool, get a requisition from the foreman, go to the grinding room, and request the grinder to stop whatever he is doing to grind up the tool he needs. It should be remembered that from the moment the worker goes to the crib for the tool, it has already been ground up once.

A large conveyor belt has recently been installed throughout the plant. It goes from department to department. Hundreds of steel girders and steel baskets comprise its make-up. The cost ran into thousands of dollars. As far as the workers are concerned it is at this date a failure. The workers are constantly hurting themselves on it. It is in the middle of the machinery and serves as a hazard. The workers are becoming increasingly angry about it.

Whereas before the machine operator stacked up his work in pans and placed them on the floor for a laborer to pick up later, now the men are ordered to place the work on the conveyor. The laborer is now eliminated in this respect. The company had tried to institute this once before, but failed. Many of the workers rebelled at the new system, claiming it was out of their classification, etc. For some days there was a disturbance. Although the new system has proved in some ways more satisfactory, the fact that the men were not consulted and the company arbitrarily instituted it, brought on the revolt.

At this time, a layoff numbering into hundreds has been taking place. The workers contrast the cost of the conveyor and its waste of money and space to this layoff and say that the expense involved could easily have kept all these workers on the job. Many say, "If I had the money spent on this, I could retire for life." The layoffs have brought on increased labor on the part of those still remaining. The workers all understand and state openly and consistently that the company is trying to cut overhead and expense. These layoffs have affected all but the production departments, i.e., laborers, inspectors, toolroom, maintenance, and other non-production.

An incident happened in the shop one day. There was a shortage of laborers due to the layoff. Consequently when the checker came around, he asked the machine operators to load the work onto the conveyor. There was a rebellion expressed thus: "Give them an inch and they want a mile." As a result, a number of the operators refused to load. The laborers were put back on the job. It is obvious that the company is trying to get the machine operators to do the work of the chip-pullers and laborers as well.

A worker put in a suggestion, asking that the recently installed conveyor be used to carry tools to the machines. The company turned it down. The workers thought it was a good idea, but would fail because there never are enough tools anyway and most of them would be gone before half of the machines had been reached.

Management Complains

Management complains continually that the workers do not cooperate. They don't clean the machines or sweep the floor. There are seventy accidents in one month in one department.

Safety meetings are held once a month for one half hour following lunch. At the meetings, management attempts to superimpose the company's safety staff as a counter to the union apparatus. The workers are exhorted to bring their complaints to this safety committee. To stimulate workers' participation they appoint three shop workers as the first rung of the safety committee. Thereafter the committee consists of the company engineers and personnel.

The safety meetings are conducted by the company. A speech is generally given by the foreman for most of the allotted half hour. The last few minutes are left open for discussion by the ranks. If a worker or two speaks about something unimportant, they are patiently listened to. If, however, the men are in an uproar and begin jumping up to complain about this, that, or the other thing and the meeting runs away, it is immediately adjourned, and the company says: "Back to the machines, men, we have work to do."

These are some of the reactions of the workers to the safety committee meetings.

1. "Oh boy, another half hour to rest."
2. "What kind of safety meeting is this? All they did was yell at the porters."
3. Some doze off during meetings.
4. The foreman and superintendent always say: "The men are negligent and don't cooperate with the safety committee."
5. You are told to get enough sleep, not to drink, and to eat the right foods.
6. The men snicker sometimes.
7. The company maintains they are doing everything to help the men.

At one meeting the company stated: "We now have enough laborers to keep the plant clean, now do your part." Not long after, half the laborers were laid off. It seems to the workers that the company doesn't know its plans from one week to the next.

Why Such Inefficiency?

One grievance condition in the plant has existed for over a year. Heavy smoke from the heat-treating furnaces periodically covers the plant. This has been brought up in almost every committee meeting. The condition still exists. One worker says: "Someday, we are going to do something about this."

One day a worker is hauled into the office for making a pile of scrap work. They want to know why. His reply is this: "The lighting is poor. Those bulbs on the machine become coated with oil and I can't see. My eyes become strained looking into the machine and it was impossible to see what I was doing."

Inefficiency and red tape on the part of the company often drive the worker to the point of a combination of tears and anger. A shortage of tools at a critical moment, an improperly ground tool, a faulty machine left unrepaired and endangering the worker, help not around when needed, stock for the machines left not at the machine for which it is needed but ten machines down where it is not needed, passing the buck down the line when something goes wrong all contribute to the aggravating situation.

Workers often say:

"Why such inefficiency?"

"The company lost a day's work because of a lack of a piece of chain costing about 75 cents."

"Why are there no washers? Can't the company afford it?"

"It is getting so that supervision don't give a damn about anything."

Many workers become angry because of the fact that suggestions which they put in are ignored. These suggestions would add to efficiency and also increase production as well as save money.

There is a general tendency in all strata of the working class to work in as efficient a manner as possible. Also, workers feel pride when a plant is operated efficiently. The more complex and efficient the plant, the greater pride the worker experiences. The more conservative workers, i.e., the ones on higher paying and better jobs, those who have a perspective of going out on their own, or those who feel there is a chance for advancement, constantly seek and strive to make for more efficient operation. On the other hand, the majority of the workers face a frustrating contradiction. They feel their oppressed status and consciously and unconsciously struggle against it. They realize that any increase in efficiency is a further exploitation and oppression. As a result, they constantly have to struggle to maintain a balance between good and efficient workmanship and their class interests.

The company tries to increase production by every mechanical means. Management talks much about the human factor in production but it cannot conceive that the human factor lies in the collective capacities of the workers themselves.

The Violent Reaction of the Worker

The conditions of life in the factory often drive the worker into a fury. If windows supplying vital ventilation are closed, he will like as not pick up a piece of steel and break the window. That is the way I have seen it time and again.

In the toilets, water will deliberately be left running at full force when no one is using the sink. Fixtures are dismantled and doors broken.

I have seen workers methodically tear apart sections of machinery lying about and throw them away.

The conveyor has large steel baskets which hang from the chain belt. Periodically a dozen or so must be repaired. It seems that the workers twist the baskets as they go by, swing them back and forth, and in general mutilate them.

I have heard workers say that they wish that their machine would break up mechanically so that they would not have to run it.

There is the destructive fury manifested by the worker throwing a piece of work at the machine when it does not function properly. He bitterly curses the "goddamn machine."

Another worker slipped with his wrench and cut himself. He hurled the wrench on the floor in anger. This same worker during the same day had machine trouble. His anger reached new heights. He cursed the machine, the company, the foreman and kept shouting he was going to quit.

Going off the shift, a worker spits at his machine and curses the company and anybody in earshot.

A "Hammer Merchant" is a worker who uses a sledge hammer to adjust the fixtures on his machine. Instead of loosening the bolts keeping the fixture tight, he resorts to such activity as using the hammer in order to save him time on production. Over a period of time the machinery becomes mutilated. Many workers resent such a destruction of the machine and it causes arguments among them.

I once had trouble with a machine and said to the worker next to me, "If I owned this machine, I'd break it up." I was very irritated at the time. He replied, "Don't break your own machine but break this one, it belongs to the company."

The Dilemma of the Foreman

The position of the foreman is an extremely tenuous one. He is caught between two fires. He has to force the worker to produce as his job hinges on it. The pressure upon him from above is very heavy. An important slip on his part would mean his being broken. Those who are above him deliberately divorce themselves as much as possible from daily contact with the workers. This task they place upon the foreman and the first rank of supervisory help. Any difficulty the foreman has with workers is taken out on him. At the same time, there is the immense amount of red-tape and buck passing of responsibility which finally puts the whole burden of something not done upon the worker himself. In thc words of the worker, "Before you get something done around here you could drop dead."

All this, having its effect upon the foreman, produces a tense and strained individual. If he is at all sensitive, he is a mental wreck, always transmitting his unstable position to the worker.

I am acquainted at first hand with the situation concerning one foreman who had to take several weeks off as he was on the edge of a nervous breakdown.

Many foremen, in order to ease the pressure on themselves, will cultivate a shell of indifference. They vow to themselves that no matter what happens, it will not get the best of them. Then when trouble arises in the shop, the foreman will shrug his shoulders, and intimating there is nothing he can do about it, walk away, leaving those involved to figure it out for themselves.

Such situations sometimes develop into "hot potatoes." No one in the supervision will take responsibility. So from top management on down, the "buck" is passed. So confused does the issue get, that even the various layers of supervision wind up contradicting each other. No one will take the authority to give a decisive statement on the matter.

I once spent several months as a foreman over a few workers. I learned through this and experience as a worker in production that the supervisory help, i.e. the foremen, become irritated by the fact that they feel the workers are deliberately holding back on the job. The men are not producing as they could. They express it: "The men don't want to work, they are lazy." This feeling presses on the foreman and drives him to driving the worker.

On the other hand, many foremen are close to the workers. Some workers will even stop other workers from irritating a particular foreman. The men feel that these foremen are in a tough spot and are subject to discipline and firing as are other workers.

From a Detroit worker I learned that during the foremen's strike the workers felt a mixture of guilt at going back to work and not sticking with the foremen, and of satisfaction because of the chance to show how well they could work without supervision.

CHAPTER V. MANAGEMENT'S ORGANIZATION AND THE WORKERS' ORGANIZATION

The company for which I work is a gigantic industrial concern which employs hundreds of thousands of workers. From all accounts its assembly lines everywhere are vicious in their exploitation of the individual. Its technique is high speed production. On the other side we have the U.A.W., the most advanced union in the country. The class struggle has tripled in intensity and the workers speak in new terms and thoughts.

Management's Organization

It is clear to me that the reactions of the individual to production are of such a nature that they cannot be checked by the present-day utilization of the means of production. There is only one course open to the ruling class. It is to channelize, to corrupt, to disrupt, to coerce, to prevent any extreme expression from taking root or form with a view to change.

With this in mind, I shall proceed to discuss the manner in which this is done in the shop, the means used, and the divisions created.

THE PROBATION SYSTEM

The rebelliousness of the worker takes many forms. It is the conscious organization of this rebelliousness which the factory owners attempt to prevent. For example, the company in which I work insists on a six month probation period for a new worker. Exactly why? First let us get clear the fact that it takes but a month or two, more often a few weeks, to determine the ability and worth of the worker. Why then six months of probation? This six months period is the longest I have ever heard of in any union contract. Usually it is one month or two.

The six months period is a time in which new workers are provoked into revealing what their attitudes are. If such workers are stamped dangerous, out they go.

In certain departments, the company hires and fires en masse. Out of say, 40 laid off, a select few will be called back. By this means, during a trial period, the company can select more reliable elements. Then a mass layoff to avoid charges of discrimination. Then quietly, individuals are called back to work. The company is not bound to these temporary employees as there exists the six month probation period.

THE RUMOR SYSTEM

The company tries to keep the workers in a constant state of agitation and uncertainty by spreading rumors. Whenever a change is about to take place, a dozen rumors flood the shop. This is skillfully done. The workers never know what is coming next. First it is: we will work seven days a week, 12 hours a day. Then, three shifts at 8 hours. Then, two shifts at 9 hours. Then, no Saturday work or there will be Saturday work. There will be a big layoff in everybody's department, etc. The workers have a rapid grapevine over which flows information with an amazing speed. These rumors are spread by the company which then hits with a 5 day week, 8 hour day. That is the general idea. The conditions of employment are continually in flux. Finally the worker gets disgusted and says: "The hell with it, let them do what they want," or when angry, "What the hell are they up to now?"

THE KIND MASTER

The company tries to make the workers believe that it is looking out for their best interests. It sponsors all sorts of clubs. 25 year club, etc., bowling clubs, gun clubs, and fishing clubs. It goes in for paternalism, family circles. It likes to have members of the same family working in the shop. The company tries to imitate the workers' own tendency to organization.

Many times the company will deliberately issue sales of stock to employees in order to simulate part ownership. This however cannot counteract the miserable life of the worker in production.

The workers are not fooled any more by this sort of thing.

The company sponsors a nation-wide contest among all its employees. It is called "MJC," the "My Job Contest." The workers are exhorted to write letters as to why they like their jobs and especially why they like to work for this company. Over a hundred and fifty thousand dollars are being spent on the pushing of this contest. The factory walls are covered with signs advertising it. To induce the workers further, the prizes to be given away are brought to the plant. There are autos, refrigerators, washing machines, ovens, and the like. To date, 30% of my plant have made entries and on a nation-wide basis, about 100,000 have entered. The workers joke and laugh about the contest. Their remarks vary from: "The biggest liar will win," to "The winners are already picked out." Others say: "I like my job because I can feed my family," "I like my job because I want to win a new Cadillac," "I like my job because I want to keep my job," etc. Some workers at a loss for what to say ask their children. One worker's child said "because you buy me pretty clothes, Dad." When he asked his wife, she said: "Why don't they give you a steady day job?" The company is pressuring the workers to enter the contest. The foreman and plant superintendents have been going around trying to coerce workers into entering. One long employed worker was in the office about it. He noticed that the boss had a mark next to his name. He became furious and had an argument with him. He said that he would write a letter only if he himself decided. So far he had decided not to and no one was going to compel him.

The contest seems more to have stimulated workers to thinking about what they do not like about their jobs. Many are entering in spite of their hatred of the job. They feel that there are things which a worker likes. The company will accept letters in any language and will translate. They want the letters above all to be in the language of the worker and they stress this very much.

COMPANY MEN

There is a general feeling of insecurity throughout the plant. It is clear to me that the company is aggressively preparing for the next strike wave, or labor trouble, by building up a stratum of company men, or as it were, a labor aristocracy of a sort. These workers make it a practice to go out drinking and visiting other workers with a view to building up personal relations, and then to draw them into their circle.

Stool Pigeons Are Made, Not Born

When the bosses find a worker they want to corral, a certain type of treatment is employed. This treatment is of a most ingratiating nature. The worker is treated with kid gloves. In many instances the foreman will go out of his way for you. It places some workers under a tremendous mental strain to combat it.

In the past several months of my employment in this factory, I have been approached more than a dozen times by various workers who have attempted to bring me under the ideology of the company.

I have had discussions with various of these company men. It is necessary to lead these workers on in order to draw out the information. The point at which I was considered safe was the point at which a bolder approach could be used. So one quite bluntly tells me where the bosses drink on off days and then casually invites me to come down to the tavern and meet them over a few drinks.

Still another such worker recently quite frankly explained to me I was "busting my head against a stone wall. Why not play smart? Look out for yourself. A smart guy can go places if he looks out for himself." He went on to explain how the union is no good and is made up of bureaucrats approaching gangsters. This worker is a set-up man in the shop and the other workers know he is trying to get ahead.

The company stooge tries to draw out other workers by anti-company talk such as, "The damn company tries to get the best of you," etc. The unwise or unsuspecting worker finds himself out of a job in no time at all. The last shop I was in, I saw fifteen workers go by the board in four months because of one stool whom I immediately recognized after my experience in several other shops.

The Dilemma of the Company Stooge

The untenable economic situation pressing upon the working class brings certain sections to the point where they turn informer and betrayer of their fellow workmen. Combined with this is the drudgery and monotony of factory work as a whole from which these elements hope to escape by advancing themselves through their activity. As a result of their efforts in behalf of the company, many of these workers become foremen, set-up men, and in instances rise to even higher positions. At any rate, it is much easier for them to secure more financial benefits in their pay envelopes.

Another reason why such workers turn to such activity is the fact that they find the union incapable of satisfying their needs. At the same time the role of the union bureaucrat fills them with disgust. The anger at these fakers gives them some of their moral support.

There are many drives in back of a worker turned stooge. Home, wife, children provide his first impulse. At any rate that is his first conscious expression of what he is doing. In defense of these, he justifies all his actions and develops the attitude of: "The hell with everyone else. Every man for himself. Nobody does anything for you but yourself."

Some of these workers become fawning and servile, lose all self-respect. Others are decent men who are well-liked and who labor under a terrific mental strain as a result of the gulf which must be created between them and other workers. In general any self-respecting worker has a disdain and disgust, bordering at times on hatred, for the company stooges.

Self-seeking workers, e.g. company stooges, etc., will denounce each other to get ahead. They will inform on each other to higher-ups on being inefficient, etc.

The stooge in production today is more clever than most of his counterparts in years gone by. At all times he skillfully will try to cover his own tracks. He attempts to understand all the backward prejudices that workers have and use them against the worker. I have seen stooges brazenly condemn the existence of such workers as themselves to other workers.

These worker stooges are caught like other workers in the maelstrom of capitalist production. In seeking a way out, they choose to perform as they do, no other means appearing to them.

Infiltration into the Union

The company's network of stool pigeons and plants operates into the very heart of the union. Many times these agents employ a militant union exterior for their purpose, the betrayal of the workers for the sake of their own promotion.

In order to create anti-union sentiment, company stooges will infiltrate into union positions and then deliberately betray the workers. This infuriates the workers against the union inasmuch as they are unaware of what has happened.

At a recent union meeting, something of interest came to light. The chairman of the shop committee spoke of what transpired at union-management conferences. He stated that the company had no faith or trust in workers who would never join the union. In fact, their greatest satisfaction was to break away a fighting militant from the union and reward him with a good supervisory job. This type of worker the company felt it could trust. This same chairman had mentioned on several instances that the company had continually tried and still was trying to reach him.

In many instances, the company will attempt to demoralize a new committee-man or steward by ignoring him and not recognizing him. This was standard practice in other factories in which I have worked. This straightens out over a period of time depending in the main on the shop and the ability of the man involved.

In my plant it is well known that stewards and former militant union men get special treatment if they are amenable. Better jobs, more money, etc. At union meetings, it is not a rare thing for a rank and filer to take the floor and point-blank accuse various union representatives of being out and out company men. Such a rank and filer is immediately marked down as one to be approached by stooges. Recently one such rank and filer immediately got transferred from an unskilled job to one on a machine with an increase in pay.

It is interesting to note that this type of worker, in many instances, bands together with others in the shop in attempts to influence and maintain control of the union. This they do because they never fully trust the company and wish to have at hand the union as a counterweight should the company double-cross them. Of course, in achieving some sort of influence, they resort to bureaucratic tricks and scheming of all kinds to get their men in.

At a recent union meeting the local's president spoke of the company stooges and how they were trying to bust the union. He said that the plant was infiltrated with them and that the company was on the offensive. The union is invoking an old statute and will expel or exclude from membership any one who they discover is a company man. At the same time, it was announced that proceedings had been started against such an individual in one of the departments. The union chairman always warns that fifteen minutes after the meeting is over, the company will know exactly what took place during the meeting.

The company men constitute the minority of the workers in the shop, but during a period of quiet, they can give the impression that the company is strong and its eyes and ears are everywhere. Any worker who has had a few factory jobs throughout several years knows of the existence of these company men. In a new plant he learns to keep his mouth shut for a safe period of time. Many months pass before the gap is bridged between the new worker and his fellow workmen. He takes no sides. In answer to involving questions, he will answer with a nod or a knowing wink. What goes on about him does not escape him although to all appearances he has the aspect of disinterest. First impressions are almost always voided. Real trust is usually placed only in individuals with whom he has become more intimately acquainted through social intercourse outside the pressures of the factory.

This situation becomes completely altered during a critical period when the workers are in action. Then a new cohesion is established among the workers, and the company men seem to run for cover, while the workers speak their minds freely.

The Workers' Organization

I arrived in the plant two weeks after the "Big Strike" had ended. Things were tense for several weeks. Newcomers were eyed with suspicion by both workers and company so soon after the strike. My first day in the plant found me waiting in one of the departments for the foreman. A worker sauntered over to me. In a very brief discussion, he tried to determine my attitude towards unions. I shook him off and he walked away. His speech made it clear that he was anti-union. Union men made themselves conspicuous by their avoidance of newcomers.

THE AVERAGE UNION MAN

The average union man in my shop rarely talks about the union except to complain that it doesn't do enough for the workers. Nevertheless, he definitely feels he must have the union. The company would ride all over the workers without the union. In spite of his antagonism at the way the union is run, he still holds to this belief. He attributes the small attendance at meetings to several factors. One, the meeting hall is too far away from his home and the workers live all over. He says: "Why must they always hold it on a Sunday? A man likes to take his family and go for a ride or picnic on that day. A fellow works all week and should be with his family sometime." However, even when the meetings are called after work, the attendance is small. The workers reluctantly show up at a meeting. Most of the workers recognize this, but say: "Look how everyone turns out on a strike ballot, contract negotiation or election." They do not leave it to the leadership to decide crucial issues as they do not trust their decisions. The rest of the year, the ranks abstain almost completely from union activity, and angrily criticize the manner in which the leadership operates. They believe more could be done.

In spite of all this, the workers carefully watch developments in other unions throughout the country. When, in Pittsburgh, a union president was put in jail by the government, the ranks were in sympathy with the call of a general strike in that city to free him.

THE UNION LEADERSHIP

Many union representatives are sincere in their desires to lead, and to fight for, the workers, but most of the union leaders that I have seen, although they work on the machine or on the bench, do not react to most situations as the rank and file does. It is not rare for a committee man to attempt to persuade a worker not to put in a grievance.

The rank and file do not hesitate to demand departmental meetings when issues arise that directly affect them on the job. They do not trust these to the union leadership. They want to be there and to decide what action is to be taken. The workers go up and down the aisles saying: "We want a departmental meeting. If the committee man doesn't call one, we'll hold it ourselves."

The Taft-Hartley bill hung over the nation for some months. One day Congress made it into law. The next day I listened carefully for comment. One fellow says: "Those guys are really out to put chains on us." Another says: "Labor all over the country should walk out." A third says: "This will fix those union leaders."

As a member of the rank and file, I approach an official of the union, an executive-committee member. I demand that a plant-wide emergency meeting be immediately held in view of the situation. He refuses point-blank and says: "The usual monthly meeting will be held in two weeks." I talk to several workers. They say that they have heard rumors that the plant will walk out at twelve o'clock. The chairman of the shop committee then comes up to me. I demand an emergency meeting where the ranks can express themselves. He tells me: "You are going off half-cocked. Next week the C.I.O. is holding a National meeting in Washington on the subject and we must wait."

Several weeks after the initial crisis has passed, the leadership finally calls an after-work meeting on the anti-labor bill. A handful of workers shows up and the leadership rages on this point: "Such vicious attacks are being made on labor and when we call a meeting on this vital subject, the ranks don't show up."

The union leadership has a great deal of ridicule for the ranks. They constantly make fun of the fact that the ranks don't give a damn, and don't attend meetings. Their attitude is one of: "Here we are trying to do everything for them and they don't give a damn."

The union leadership is very much afraid of rank and file action. Recently a grievance of a serious nature came up. It was clear that to stop the company would require clear-cut action on the part of the workers. Just the presentation of a grievance on the matter was viewed with alarm by the bureaucracy. Their advice was: "Don't do anything rash." "Keep cool, and think it over," etc. The leadership is constantly on the defensive with the ranks.

Many times the leadership will agree to certain new proposals of the company which will have an effect on the rank and file. They do not notify the ranks of their agreement as they do not want trouble.

One day several workers are discussing the union contract with a union representative. The subject is the speed-up. The union official maintains that the workers must abide by the contract. He says, "Any change in the machinery which the company maintains is a change in method, gives them the right to raise the number of pieces per hour." At another time he reiterates that the union contract is binding. A rank and filer states: "It is binding just so long as we let it be."

The president walks about the plant with an aloofness almost comparable to that of the plant superintendent.

Even at a union dance there is this kind of separation. The union leaders have a central table at which they all sit with their friends. They have full bottles of liquor and other drinks. They engage in a cloistered bit of revelry. Some wear "Tux's" and most all wear white flowers in their lapels. They are somewhat boisterous at times. The atmosphere is not one of workers' comradeship. There appears to be a high degree of formality pervading the dance as a whole. A worker easily felt more at ease in the shop than he did at the dance.

The most disgusting sight is that of the company superintendent sitting at their table. They are all very friendly. There appears to be more friendliness than between the ranks and the union leaders.

What is the company superintendent doing at the workers' dance? He circulates around amongst those present, acting very friendly and trying to develop new friends in the ranks. Those workers who ignore him make it felt.

There are some 800 workers in the union but only about 150 attend the dance.

CHAPTER VI. ATTITUDES OF WORKERS

The Attitude of the Conservative Worker

There is in the factory today a stratum of workers which over a period of years has accumulated a high seniority. That is, these workers have spent several years in the same industrial plants. During this time they have observed and experienced various union regimes. More so than transitory workers, they have seen union leaderships develop into various patterns and effects. They are aware of the class collaborationist activities of the union bureaucrats. Bureaucratism has left a mark on them. This group of workers which represents a large section of the American labor movement is acutely aware of the rottenness of present day society. They harbor a deep and abiding hatred of the industrial ruling class. They are wise to its maneuvers, tricks and abuses of the workers. At the same time, not having a fundamental grasp of the economic laws governing society, many believe that the capitalist class is all powerful. They lean more to this conclusion as they see the trade union bureaucracies continually capitulate.

One old seniority worker said that the old workers were against the strike. Many claimed that the union leadership in the International had juggled the votes and called out the men when they should not have. One such worker claimed that "those who were for the strike were the new war workers who had never been in industry before. They did not know what our conditions of work were before the war. I was not against a strike as a strike, but against it being called when it was called. The company was being reconverted and was getting back tax refunds from the government. We were licked before we started. We used up all our savings in the strike and many of us had to go back into debt. It was tough enough getting out of debt from the pre-war years. I would not be against a strike now as the company needs production and is no longer getting tax refunds. No one broke the picket lines because the company itself after a while shut down the plants. Had they remained open, there would have been violence and workers would have attempted to bust the picket lines. As it was, very few workers from the plant manned the picket lines."

It should be stated here, that from the accounts of the strike ballots taken during the 1946 strike wave, the majority of workers overwhelmingly voted strike.

"IF I WORKED HERE AS LONG AS YOU HAVE . . ."

Throughout the years the process of production has steadily been working on these old workers and has produced an explosive latent force in them. More than all the other sections of the workers, they have been subjected to a steady and uninterrupted education and development by capitalist production. All the contradictions are there.

Their years of service in one factory have created in them a feeling or attitude of having a vested interest in the plant. This is expressed by other workers thus, "If I worked here as long as you have, I would want to own the factory." The manner in which these workers move about the factory indicates an attitude of ownership. The assuredness with which they move from department to department can be seen even in the way in which they walk.

The apparent inability of the union to solve their problems, the seemingly tremendous power of the boss, have contributed to making these workers cynical and conservative. Many sections of them become out and out company men. The company is forced to be lenient in one respect or another towards these workers because they know the ins and outs of the plant thoroughly. However, this does not prevent periodic explosions.

"FELLOWS LIKE ME KNOW PLENTY"

I would like to illustrate concretely the development of some of these long time seniority workers as I have seen and heard it. "Z" is a worker employed 20 years by the company. In the past few months he has come out with some revealing statements. It is clear that through the years he has given many worthwhile suggestions for production to the company, but has not been rewarded satisfactorily for them. One evening during the lunch period he tells a dozen or so workers from the department the following, "I have an idea now that would stop those machines from cracking up. But those sons of —— ain't going to get it for a measly fifty bucks. Either they give me a thousand bucks or they can go f— themselves."

At another time, the same worker angrily says, "While we are sweating our heads off, those bastard bosses are in Florida sunning themselves." He goes on to say, "The plant Super went out at seven and comes back at eleven all tanked up. Now if that son of a bitch said anything to me while I was taking a shower upstairs at eleven-thirty, I would let him have it."

From there we got into a discussion of our factory. I asked him about the efficiency in our factory and what he and the others with long years of experience about machinery could do if they had the opportunity to put their ideas into practice freely. He replied, "Fellows like me and workers 'X,' 'Y,' and 'Z,' know plenty. What do they (the company) know about production? They get more in our way than anything. Those engineers, who sit in the office, try to plan out things complicated so that they can keep their jobs. They've got to eat too, you know."

"SURE, ALL THAT STUFF IS TRUE"

The *Saturday Evening Post* of July 19, 1947, carried an article entitled: "The Union That Dared To Be Different." The article deals with a factory which was on the verge of bankruptcy. In order to forestall the layoff of hundreds of workers, the union and the company came to an agreement whereby the workers would have the full run of the shop to develop production to a point where the company would be able to remain in business. Not only did production increase, but absenteeism fell off almost entirely, and waste almost disappeared. I gave the magazine to one of the shop workers to read. He has been a worker for over fifteen years.

He was particularly struck by the manner in which the workers increased production when they were given a free hand. I present in the following an approximate account of his comments on this article.

"This guy has a lot of common sense. One shop I worked in I was set-up man. I used to stand at the machine and constantly try to devise new adaptations. I had hundreds of ideas. I have lots of them now, but what's the use of trying them out. The next guy would come in and change what I had done. I know ways of grinding tools now which I am positive would make the job easier and more efficient, but if I tried them out as things are everything would get more confused. What those workers have done is pretty good but I don't think we could do the same in our plant. Those engineers don't hold a candle to the guy on the machine. How can they know what we know when we spend hours right on the machine? There are things which it is impossible to learn unless you work at it every day over a period of years."

He ended up with an indication that the writer of the article might be a communist.

On January 1, 1947, immediately following the big post-war strike wave, *Collier's* weekly appeared with an article by Peter Drucker entitled, "What To Do About Strikes." I brought the issue into the shop and asked a worker who had been with the company over the past ten years to read it. He had been in the preceding strike and was in a position to understand what Drucker had to say.

He agreed that strikes were "essentially revolts." That the workers were psychologically unemployed in the midst of employment. He had gone through the depression years and remembered well.

"Sure. All that stuff is true," he told me. The deep penetrating unrest that upsets all workers he knew about.

The Women in the Shop

The outbreak of the war brought many women into the factory. I have seen many women operate machines which I have run. In one factory, they were employed as crane operators. The job required a great degree of sensitivity in the lifting of huge sections of steel throughout the factory. Women proved to be particularly able in this. I have seen them swing a heavy load of steel down the length of the factory and skillfully place it exactly where it was wanted. There were many women on grinding machines in this factory during the war. Today I know of but one or two.

The factory seems to have given a sort of assuredness to many of the women workers. The shop counteracts to some degree the unequal status between men and women in society generally. Although very few women attend union meetings, those who do show a surging desire to express themselves. Some think the union is the affair of the men and are afraid to interfere. Others think that the women don't stick together like the men. I had a talk with a woman worker in the shop one day. She was extremely scornful of the men in the factories of the Eastern states. She claimed: "they are all puny, no doubt from factory life, and do not compare with the healthy men of the Southwestern states and the wide open country. What's more, I'll equal and double anything any of you men do. I have held down three jobs at one time already." She was belligerent in trying to establish an equal status with the men.

The relations between the sexes are completely distorted by capitalism. Certain women in the shop are labeled as women who can be slept with. Whenever a woman goes down the aisle, whistles, cat-calls and phrases fly down after her.

At the time of the telephone strike, the workers were amazed at the militancy of the girls in that strike. Accounts of the picket line struggles were widely read by the workers. Their comments were: "Those girls sure have plenty of guts. Why they are fighting every one from the Company to the State and local governments. It sure is a surprise to me."

CHAPTER VII. THE CONTRADICTION IN THE FACTORY

Lowered Productivity of Labor

I had discussions with several workers on the lowered productivity of labor. Worker "R" agrees. Especially concerning the assembly lines. Says workers do not want to exist as slaves. Says production could be upped 20% or 30% if workers were given a free hand. Complains of the insuperable number of obstacles which a worker encounters during the day. Says if all red tape and annoying supervisory help were eliminated, and if workers ingenuity were allowed full play, production could be considerably upped. He says it is very difficult to know what the individual worker thinks as he isolates himself mentally in many respects from his fellow worker. He does not often say what he thinks. He says workers hold back on their production and never give their fullest.

JUST PUTTING IN TIME

I spoke with two other workers on the same subject. One worker says production could be doubled. The other is in doubt. Seems to think it means more work for the workers. I approached the subject on the basis of a 4 hour day, 5 day week and asked if that goal was possible. I tried to impress them with a plant-wide conception of cooperation. I explained what was in reality workers' control. One said that during the war in his section of the plant, the fellows used to knock out work fast deliberately and then spend a few hours in horse play. They enjoyed themselves and at the same time got the work out. He claims the mental attitude was entirely different then. Now the monotony is extremely evident. It is just a question of putting in time. He resents the pressure of the foreman when the production norm is completed and he is kidding around. The foreman, it seems, cannot stand workers being idle even though the norm has been filled. He spoke of the many skillful tricks applied by workers during the war.

A laborer one day confided in me the following: "You know, kid, being a laborer is really an art. The idea is not to be around when you are needed. There is a way to time all this, and the clever laborer need not exhaust himself."

I will add that this may have been much more true during the war. It appears that since some have been laid off, the laborers must work harder. But when the opportunity presents itself, the laborer will still seize it to lighten his load.

As the tempo of work increases and the oppression of the worker becomes greater, at a certain point in the process a change comes over the worker. At the moment the machine is inflicting its greatest damage on him, and when he is reaching the bottom depths of his despair, a sudden sense of defiance and then freedom envelopes him. This happens at rare moments but leads inevitably to lowering the productivity of labor as it exists under the present factory set-up.

On the other hand, I have seen workers almost wear themselves into the ground trying to put out an extra number of pieces purely from the desire to see how much they could do. In these instances, there was no extra money involved. In contradiction to this, workers will deliberately burn out tools in the machine at quitting time, by turning off the lubricant. Sometimes this is done to chastise the incoming worker for something ill-natured he has done.

THE DIVISION OF LABOR

The worker labors under contradictions. He may often wish to help another worker in some task, but because of the classifications and the fear of risking the resentment of his fellow workers, he refrains from doing so.

At the same time there is the ever present threat of the company using the worker's action against him in attempts to further the amount of work a man must do.

The wage scales and classifications in the shop are extremely numerous. It is a continual battle to reach a higher classification and more money, with one worker competing against another. Much anger is generated between workers and against the company over upgrading or promotions to new jobs. Every time a new job is open, a bitter wrangle takes place. It is not predominantly a question of the nickel raise involved, as it may seem on the surface, but a desire for recognition and a chance for exploitation of one's own capabilities.

In factories where different classifications of work are set up, workers confine themselves to their own classifications. For example, a machine operator runs the machine, the laborer sweeps and cleans, lifts, etc. This is usually the case. I have noticed, however, the distinct tendency on the part of workers to break these classifications by doing work not in their jurisdiction, so to speak. An operator does some laboring work, etc. This infraction of the rules is done on the workers' own initiative. That is, they take on the added tasks as long as they do it of their own accord. If the company orders them to do these things, immediately the men rebel and refuse. It is almost impossible to stop them when they decide of themselves.

Seniority regulations of the union very often prevent workers with real qualifications from getting ahead. For instance there are workers with a few years of experience who have outdistanced old time workers in ability and imagination. This is traced fundamentally to the type of technical and academic training they have received in the modern school system. I have heard even workers with seniority talk about how the seniority system is a brake on production. At the same time they would fight against the company's trying to override seniority. They are in a contradiction because they realize that workers need seniority as a defense and yet feel that such defensive measures do not allow the best productive talents of the workers to emerge. The workers say that if they had the opportunity in the ranks to decide who should be upgraded, they would be able to make better choices.

The last several months have shown signs of a swift development in the workers. They are stirred and moved by a deep unrest. They want a better life in the factory. Their desire to solve the frustrating contradiction of production can be seen everywhere. For example the worker who, sick to his stomach from the stench of his machine, shuts it down and shouts, "To hell with my classification. I can't stand it. I am going to clean out this goddamn machine."

The Creativity of the Workers

When a worker has the opportunity to sneak away, he investigates the other sections of the plant. Rarely does this happen. The longing to vision the whole of which he is a part is never satisfied. He does not get to know the routine and full mechanics of the next departments. When he can, the worker will stop at a machine which intrigues him, pick up a piece of work and comment on it. He will question the operator about it. An exceptional yearning can be seen in the watchful eyes of those whose job it is to perform some sort of laboring or unskilled manual task. It is not uncommon to hear one worker say to another, "Boy, that job's a good one to have."

However, when a worker is upgraded, the new job soon becomes routine and once again he feels the same dissatisfaction. Many workers express the hope to get into the tool room, but even in the tool room the work has been broken down into routine operations. One of the highest skilled men in my department is a set-up man. He does a variety of jobs in the course of the day, changing set-ups, devising fixtures, etc. Yet he is bored with his work. He says: "If you think this is such a good job you can have it. I'm fed up with it."

During the war, there arose a type of worker creativity known as a "Government Job." I don't think there is a worker who at some time or another has not made a "Government Job." It was always natural to observe a worker making something for himself during working hours. Hundreds of thousands have made rings, lockets, tools, and knick-knacks. If the foreman or boss would come over and ask "what are you doing?" the reply was "a Government Job." Many beautiful things were made and the workers used to show them to each other. This has carried over and it appears that it will remain. The term applies to anything the worker makes for himself on company time. But it also appears that the workers today don't have as much patience for this type of work and something more is needed.

The worker doesn't want to know how to do many things just for the sake of doing them. One worker will refer to another as a good all-round man. He would also like to be one but even that is not enough.

At lunch time, workers will often discuss how a job could be done more efficiently from beginning to end. They will talk about what stock to use, how to machine it, how to do certain operations on various machines with various set-ups. But they never get a chance to decide how and why things should be done. However, if they can't use all they know, they try to use some of it.

In order to make production, many workers devise ingenious adaptations. Some change gears when the foreman is not about. Some make special tools and fixtures for their machines to make it easier for themselves. They keep these improvements secret so the company doesn't benefit. At times they help each other and at other times they do not.

The other day, the worker on the next machine devised something of a skilled nature to better his machine performance. He insisted on showing it to me and explaining to me what he had done. He was pleased with his accomplishment but was frustrated that there were no others he could show it to.

Operators on steel-cutting machines have desires to speed up R.P.M.'s on them and then increase the feed to the maximum cut to see how far they can go. This is characteristic on lathes, boring mills, etc. I've done the same myself many times. Although destruction may result, the workers seek in this way completely to master the machine.

Since the workers are unable, in the shop, to express fully their creative instincts, outside the factory and in the home, they seek to give free rein to these instincts.

Many workers seek relief from tension of the shop on their off hours by working on their cars. Cleaning and polishing them. Tinkering with the motor and other parts. Workers continually paint and fix up their own homes.

But here too they feel that something is missing. They may interrupt such a project for weeks because they have lost interest and, unless they force themselves to finish, it remains undone. Many workers say to their friends in the shop: "When I finish a day's work here I have to go home and do the same thing there."

When a worker sees a new piece of machinery he eyes it with professional skill. "What a piece of machinery that is," he says. His appreciation is not based on a monetary calculation of the machine, but on its performance under his own command.

The Community of Labor

The miserable life in the factory is universal, so when some workers whine and continually complain to their fellow workers, it antagonizes them. Gripers are not liked and wherever possible avoided. The workers say to a griper: "Don't complain to me. Go tell it to the boss."

The average capable worker respects another good worker. It is his way of building up respect among his fellow workers in recognition of his capabilities. The community of labor brings this forth as part of an unstated code.

Workers have ways of testing each other. Sometimes a whole day will be spent plaguing a worker; for example, putting bluing on his machine, stopping his machine continually, upsetting his tool box, hiding his tools, etc. This is to determine if the worker will squeal to the boss and also to determine if he has a sense of humor and is a good guy.

Often a worker takes satisfaction out of coming to work on a very hazardous day. The initiative is his and he chooses to come as this is one day he is not expected to come to work. Those workers who do come that day find a certain enjoyment out of having arrived, especially if there are workers absent. There is then a certain camaraderie or light-heartedness apparent.

Workers in each department visit the toilet for a smoke and rest at certain periods during the day. No one has set the time, but in my department, we have set a custom of our own. The day is divided into sections. First smoke is at 10:00 A.M., second is at 2:00 P.M. At these specific times, some of the other workers will be there and there is company to talk with.

When a worker moves from one factory to another, a temporary feeling of being lost seizes him, an unsureness of whether he will be able to make good on the next job. One day in the new plant among the workers again, and his confidence in himself and his ability immediately returns.

When tragedy befalls a worker, death in the family, illness, or some such personal sorrow, the workers express deep sympathy. Often it is difficult to console such a worker in words, so in order to show his sympathy, the average worker will attempt some way in the day's work to aid the bereaved worker. When tragedy strikes a worker, he finds some relief back in the factory away from the sorrow at home.

AS THOUGH THEY WERE SOMEBODY

At lunch, one day, workers were discussing and lamenting the fact that there is so little real friendship amongst people. One was speaking in terms of what really amounted to comradeship. He remarked that it was tragic that relations between men were not harmonious.

All employees are numbered. Badge numbers are systematically replacing names of individual workers. Pay envelopes, work charts, etc., are all figured on the basis of number. Even workers begin to refer to each other as numbers. "No. 402 worked on my machine last night."

There are many workers in the shop who search for some expression of their importance as individuals. The company, knowing this, institutes a certain type of uniform. It is in the form of a smock or light work coat with the company insignia on it, usually worn by set-up men, inspectors, etc. I took care to notice the effects of this ruse on a few workers. For the first few days, they seemed to adopt a self-important air as though now they were somebody. After a few days, the coat was dirty, and added to this, from the very beginning the other workers ignored the new distinction which those who wore the coats seemed to think they had. The novelty soon wore off as no change was brought to their status and work continued in the same monotonous manner as before.

Workers now and then wear their names on their shirts. Many workers become identified by the distinct type and color of the clothing they wear.

I described above the conveyor system and the hostility of the workers to it.

There are some other aspects to this situation. Previously, the checkers came to the workers' machines and in a relationship exchanged receipts for the work which the operator created. Now the worker places his work on a conveyor from whence it travels to a central pay point. At various intervals during the week he receives his receipts. The old relationship no longer exists of contact between worker and checker. (This is very satisfactory to the checker.) The old system gave the worker a feeling of individual contact with the recipients of his work. The worker is angry at the new system and demands that the old relation be established. He insists that he be paid for his work at his machine. His reason is that otherwise he is cheated of some of his day's work. But this is no more the case than usual, the company goes to extremes to see no one is cheated. The new system as stated proves in many respects more satisfactory than before. But the worker, not understanding himself or his reason, is angry because he is becoming further divorced from, and automatized in, his work. He attempts to protect his individuality and resents the regimentation of his labor into a sterile path. So he protests not the fact that he is required to lift the work onto the conveyor, but the further divorce of himself from the end result and receivers of his efforts.

TEAMWORK

Production as it exists today in the shop seeks to divide the white from black, Jew from Gentile, worker from worker. But the shattering of the division can take place right at the point of production. As I have stated previously, workers have a basic respect of other good workers. The community of labor establishes a pride in this type of activity which is deeply rooted in the worker. No matter how much modern production distorts the worker, this instinct remains always there. This becomes a universal trait and cuts through barriers of race, creed, and religion. But there is no way for the worker to express this trait today in any productive manner. The result is that it appears in other ways.

At times, a wonderful camaraderie develops in the shop amongst the workers. Usually this is discernible in some sort of horseplay. Many times workers will sing songs together to lighten the day's work.

Or many will talk everlastingly of the baseball teams, their standings and who is playing. Specific detail is given to individual players and many know very exact information on some of the players and their health.

Workers will use any subject as a means of maintaining a bond of interest between them, e.g. baseball, betting, women.

A good worker always likes to keep his place of work clean. The conflict of classifications often prevents him from doing so.

One day the floor along the row of machines has become soaked with oil. Sawdust has been thrown down to absorb it. The result is a thick, heavy mess on the floor. Although this condition almost always exists, this one day the operators find a broom and clean about their machines. Then systematically the broom is passed on down the line. The company always exhorts the men to do this, but very rare are the times when they do, although they want very much to keep their places of work clean.

The workers are ready to act together to better their life in the factory.

CONCLUSION

The basic machine in production is the lathe. It was on the basis of the first crude lathe that the advanced machinery of modern production has developed. Almost all machinery is a modification of the lathe, e.g. the huge boring mills, or of the drill press, e.g. the thread-cutting machine, or of the lathe and the drill press. Most every worker who understands machinery knows this. The point which I wish to make is this: The mastery of any of these machines automatically prepares the worker to gain mastery easily over the others. I have seen this hundreds of times in the last 7 years. I as well as other workers have at some time or other been put on machines which we had never run. Most often it took about a half hour to be able to run them satisfactorily. This is a frequent occurrence in most factories. When work runs out on one machine, the worker is often put on another. I see it every day in the factory. In my present plant, during the first two months, I ran a drill press, air-chuck lathe, automatic-screw, foot press, etc. Two of these machines I had never run before.

I recall that during the war this was much more so. Another fact shown by the war was the ease with which newcomers to machinery could learn in a comparatively short space of time. This was proved to me by the fact that in the first three years of the war, I alone trained some twenty-odd workers, white and Negro, ranging in age from 17 to 50, in running engine and turret lathes.

It is clear, then, that the present-day organization of production itself develops certain strata of workers in a multiplicity of abilities. But this multiplicity of abilities the worker can never develop to its fullest in the factory as it is today.

The worker uses his five senses in the day-to-day labor in the factory. Every one of them is distorted and mutilated. The terrible frustration which is the product of years of exposure to an inhuman production apparatus drives relentlessly toward the overthrow of that apparatus and its replacement by a productive system which will enable the worker to give fullest expression to his senses.

In modern production, the worker is isolated on an island in the midst of men and machines. So divorced has the worker become from himself that he is divorced from his fellow worker. He cannot stand the chattering of men in the cafeteria, and can find ease better, alone at his machine. The anxiety of the worker is due to the fact that he is forever caught between the contradiction of wanting to let his instinct, to do a good job and be close to his fellow workers, have its way, and then having to reverse himself.

The deep undercurrent of protest which exists in the factory is slowly but surely beginning to concretize itself. The deepest hostility exists everywhere. It can be seen in the slumped shoulders of a worker trudging down the length of the factory; in the way in which a worker walks up to a drinking fountain and wearily bends over to meet the rising stream of water; and in the set lips and drawn features of the worker towards midnight on the second shift. What more profound expression of all this can be given than the words of worker X who, in speaking to his foreman, says, "I thought Lincoln freed the slaves." Later in the company of several shopmates, he mentioned something to the effect that it was time that someone came and freed us from the machines.

What the Worker Wants

Life, as he lives it in the factory and as it corrodes his home life, builds up this tremendous hatred in the workers. He struggles blindly to throw off the weight of a distorted factory system. His exasperation at the lack of efficiency is always apparent and is deeply rooted in him. It impedes him and tears at him internally. Day by day he attempts to circumvent the bureaucratic methods and orders from above. He takes note of all defects in the utilization of labor-power that result from the improper utilization of technical resources or from unsatisfactory administration. He attempts in vain to carry on a struggle against red tape, laxity and bureaucracy.

He wants every participant in production to understand the need for and expediency of the production tasks he is carrying out, and for every participant in production to take an intelligent part in remedying all technical and organizational defects in the sphere of production.

The worker expresses his hatred of the incentive system by saying he should write the union contract. This is no less than saying that the existing production relations must be overthrown. It is also much more. It means that he wants to arrange his life in the factory in such a way that it satisfies his instincts for doing a good job, knowing that it is worthwhile, and living in harmony with his fellow men. It is deeply rooted in the worker that work is the foundation of his life. To make his work a meaningful part of life, an expression of his over-all individuality, is what he would attempt to put into reality.

It is because I feel all this and see it around me in the factory that I am a revolutionary socialist. Socialism is not merely an ideal to be wished for. It must grow out of the daily lives and striving of the workers, and it must bring a new life to them in that which is closest to them and to society—their work.

It is not for today's leaders of society to solve this problem. They have shown inside the factory as outside it how helpless they are. It is from the workers that will come the men and women who will lead and guide the tremendous upheavals to come. Today they are being processed and prepared in the factory for a new reorganization based on the freed capacities of men in the labor process.

A powerful force is today preparing the socialist reality of tomorrow. I am a part of that, as a worker and as a revolutionary socialist. It is because of this that I have learned to see clarity in confusion. I see that in socialism the workers will gain the dignity which capitalism cannot give, and as a revolutionary socialist I have been able to clarify for myself and for other workers the coming revolution by which the workers will create a new world for themselves and for the rest of humanity.

14

ARE WORKERS BECOMING MIDDLE CLASS?*

by HAROLD BENENSON AND ERIC LESSINGER

A much heralded idea of the post-World War II period is that workers are becoming increasingly middle class; that growing affluence and expanded consumption is producing a middle-class America. The following selection casts doubt on this image.

If one takes the trouble to look at trends in real *wages, the growing-affluence argument loses most of its punch. Increases have been small. (In fact, over the last five years real wages have* declined.) *Despite absolute increases in pay levels, the average income in this country still falls short of that needed to finance the government's* own *"modest" model family budget (see page 173). Yet such statistics, dramatic and appalling as they may be, cannot convey the full meaning of what it means to earn that income . . . cannot convey the full meaning of work in the "affluent society."*

For the great majority of people work is, first of all, hateful. Most jobs are exhausting, demeaning, deadening, mindless, never-ending, almost completely lacking in mobility and filled with insecurity. Blue-collar work in particular is a draining dead end, and the workers know it.

Second, work is a full-scale rat race. Great numbers of workers—especially those in factory work—must put in all the work they can get in order to make enough to live on in an uncertain labor market. This means constant overtime (when possible), second—and sometimes even third—jobs, and employment for the entire family. The effects of all of this on family life are incalculable.

Finally, work in our society is psychologically destructive. Most work is degrading, and the worker's response is often to despise himself. Not infrequently this work attitude comes out, in a somewhat healthier way, through sabotage of product.

Paul Romano conveyed a feeling for this situation in his selection, above. Hal Benenson and Eric Lessinger add to Romano's firsthand observations with a summation of the systematic observations of others. They show that as long as bosses must get as much work as possible from their workers in as little time as possible the work situation will stay hateful and exhausting . . . and workers, despite their consumption patterns, will remain workers. They also show that most white-collar work meets the same negative work standards, that white-collar work is increasingly taking on more and more of the aspects of the assembly line. Except for professional and technical employees, a white collar is no longer a ticket to the middle class.

* Used by permission of the authors.

Two overall economic trends have transformed the character of the American working class in the twentieth century. The first is the increasing standard of living enjoyed by the blue-collar, industrial work force. The second is the fantastic growth in white-collar employment. Both trends have led social commentators to project an image of American society characterized by a "middle class," self-satisfied, even affluent social existence. Inconvenient facts, like widespread poverty at the bottom of the social pyramid and extreme concentration of wealth at the top, are for many of these writers the exceptions that prove the rule. The vast majority of Americans, they argue, who fall in between these extremes are able to spend an even greater part of their incomes on consumption items not directly related to subsistence needs. Their personal aspirations, styles of life, and social values reflect these new opportunities for acquiring material possessions. And the shift to white-collar employment has reinforced the tendency to status-conscious, individualistic attitudes which have always set white-collar employees apart from manual workers.

In this paper we will examine the ways in which this middle-class image distorts and obscures blue-collar and white-collar working-class realities, and in particular those aspects of working-class life which stem from the worker's immediate job situation. We will attempt to judge the impact of rising incomes on traditional blue-collar attitudes, and the effects of new trends in white-collar work on the traditional middle-class orientations of this group.

An analysis of the impact of rising incomes on the industrial working class, particularly for the workers in unionized mass-production industries, must begin with an assessment of the work experience of the industrial worker. It is this experience, and its place in the worker's social and personal existence, which together with the increasing possibilities for consumption, shape the attitudes of the industrial worker to long-term goals in life, collective action, and class conflict.

The work experience of industrial workers is not homogeneous. In the following discussion we will use that of auto workers as the primary example because of the large number of good studies about auto workers. Some aspects of work in auto plants are not representative of industrial mass-production work in general.[1] But it is possible to make some generalizations from the case of the auto industry.

Three characteristics of auto production and assembly work have a significant impact on the outlook of workers in the industry: the alienating mass-production characteristics of the work itself; the lack of job security in the industry; the lack of opportunities for advancement in the plants. The first and third characteristics are particularly marked in the auto industry, although they are found to a lesser degree elsewhere. Job insecurity is, on the other hand, more acute in other industries.

Jobs on the assembly line display the following "mass production" characteristics according to Walker and Guest in *The Man on the Assembly Line*: (1) mechanically controlled work pace, (2) repetitiveness, (3) minimum skill, (4) predetermination of tools and techniques, (5) minute subdivision of

[1] Robert Blauner, *Alienation and Freedom*, University of Chicago Press, Chicago, Illinois, 1960, p. 89.

product, (6) surface mental attention.[2] This means that the workers have almost no control over the quantity of goods they produce, and their effort is only minutely related to the quality of the final product. It means that 61% of the unskilled (mostly assembly-line) workers interviewed in 1947 found their jobs dull most or all of the time.[3] The human costs of assembly-line work are incalculable: as Walter, a fictional character in Swados' *On the Line,* puts it:

> The worst thing about the assembly line is what it does to your self-respect . . . It's hard to keep from feeling like a fool when you know that everybody looks down on what you're doing, even the men who are doing it themselves.[4]

A second part of auto work is job insecurity: "in 1953, 917,000 auto workers turned out 7.3 million cars, trucks and buses; in 1963, 723,000 workers produced 8.3 million vehicles."[5] The cutbacks in employment require layoffs, which often mean that workers will never work again. The shrinkage in production employment in manufacturing industries is not confined to the auto industry: from 1947 to 1959, jobs in production in textile mill products were cut back 30%; in lumber and wood products, 24%; in tobacco manufactures, 18%; in food and kindred products, and petroleum and coal products, 16%; in primary metal industries, 15%; in rubber products, and leather and leather products, 10%.[6] Among the unions hit hardest have been the Mine Workers, the UAW, the Steelworkers, the Packinghouse workers, the machinists, and others.[7] A young worker who gets a job in an auto plant can never be sure that he'll be able to work there in ten years, or fifteen years, much less until his retirement.

The lack of opportunities for advancement has been well documented by Chinoy in his *Automobile Workers and the American Dream.*[8] The openings for unskilled or semi-skilled workers in the ranks of skilled labor, the foremen or the white-collar staff are extremely limited. Most men give up hope of ever moving up inside the plant soon after they get there. In addition, the prospects for getting out of the factory, and going back to a farm or opening up a small business are also very remote. The typical worker can only hope to rise to one of the better semi-skilled jobs, paying at most a quarter an hour more than the job he started on, hopefully a "clean" job off the line, and also a job that is steady, although the prospects for layoffs are always uncertain.

These aspects of manual semi-skilled work in the auto industry are increasingly characteristic of mass-production industries in general as mechanization ties production workers to machines and conveyor belts; as employment de-

[2] Charles Walker and Robert Guest, *The Man on the Assembly Line,* Harvard University Press, Cambridge, Massachusetts, 1952, p. 19.

[3] Blauner, *op. cit.,* p. 207.

[4] Harvey Swados, *On the Line,* Little, Brown and Co., Boston, 1957, p. 65.

[5] Harvey Swados, "The UAW: Over the Top or Over the Hill?" in Howe, ed., *The Radical Papers,* Doubleday, Garden City, New York, 1965, p. 249. Quoted from *Newsweek,* April 1, 1963.

[6] Solomon Barkin, *The Decline of the Labor Movement,* Center for the Study of Democratic Institutions, Santa Barbara, California, 1963, p. 11.

[7] Ben Seligman, "Automation and the Unions," in Howe, ed., *The Radical Papers,* Doubleday, Garden City, N.Y., 1965, *passim.*

[8] Ely Chinoy, *The Automobile Workers and the American Dream,* Beacon Press, Boston, 1965. Chapters Four and Five.

creases for blue-collar workers in the manufacturing sector; as the growth of corporate bureaucracies and high educational standards for supervisory jobs makes rising from the ranks ever more difficult. Work alienation, job insecurity, lack of occupational mobility show no signs of diminishing with the advent of recent trends like the automation of some plants and processes.[9]

In addition, the labor movement has always been powerless in the face of these conditions. It has largely limited its demands to wages, grievance procedures covering arbitrary discipline and seniority rights in the shops, and fringe benefits which cushion the impact of some of these conditions (for instance, supplementary unemployment benefits for layoffs) without alleviating them.[10] Without a political party and a program to deal with control over work, loss of jobs, and education and employment in the entire economy, the trade unions will accomplish little in these areas in the future.[11]

It appears that these conditions are likely to continue to be everyday facts of life for the mass production industrial workers. How do these aspects of the work situation affect workers' attitudes and aspirations, their personal and social consciousness, in a period when these same workers are coming to enjoy a "middle-class" standard of consumption?

The higher levels of consumption permit an escape from the realities of the workplace. As workers adjust to never being able to do anything creative or meaningful on the job, they seek meaning in leisure activities: many purchase power tools, or do gardening, to have an opportunity to work creatively with their hands. But most watch TV and simply forget about the day at work: in fact, among the workers Berger studied, almost half said they watched for over 16 hours a week.[12] Daniel Bell distinguishes between play, which is merely a temporary release from work, and leisure or recreation which is creative as well.

Play (not leisure or relaxation) is a release from the tensions of work,

> an alternative use of muscle and mind. But a tension that is enervating or debilitating can only produce wildly aggressive play or passive, unresponsive viewing . . . If work is a daily turn round Ixon's wheel, can the intervening play be anything more than a restless moment before the next turn of the wheel? [13]

But the need for money to enjoy leisure activities and consumption items that are increasingly expensive is one of the main rationales for holding down a job. The alienating features of the work experience become somewhat bearable when the worker is able to look forward to spending his money at play.

Increased income, as Chinoy has shown, also permits an escape from the fact of failure on the job, in terms of failure to advance, to "get ahead." Buying a

[9] See William Faunce, "Automation and the Automobile Worker," in Galenson and Lipset, ed., *Labor and Trade Unionism,* John Wiley & Sons, New York, 1960.

[10] The unions are also concerned with job classifications and working conditions, but in these areas as well they have generally hesitated to challenge the right of management to determine the uses and impact of new technologies.

[11] C. Wright Mills, *The New Men of Power,* Harcourt, Brace and Co., New York, 1948. Chapter 14.

[12] Bennett Berger, *Workingclass Suburb: A Study of Autoworkers in Suburbia,* University of California Press, p. 119.

[13] Daniel Bell, "Work and its Discontents," in *The End of Ideology,* Free Press, New York, 1960, p. 259.

car or a house, or putting a few dollars in the bank, become talked about signs of success. As workers get older they view accumulating seniority, and saving money for retirement, as equivalent to having "made it." "If you're secure, then you're getting ahead," a thirty-nine-year-old oiler explained to Chinoy.[14] This concern with security is, however, extremely rational in the face of the temporary and permanent layoffs the auto industry has experienced in the past few years. But each worker seeks a personal way out of this danger beyond minimal seniority rights and pension plans won by the union. These latter gains will be of little help if a worker is laid off for good before his retirement and has to seek work elsewhere. The only answer is to accumulate a reserve of money, or to see that your kids get a good education so that they could support you temporarily if need be, or to own some property which could be sold at some future time.

The impact of a rising standard of living on the industrial working class is not easy to measure. First, it is clear that traditional problems associated with blue-collar work persist: the jobs, if they have changed, have usually changed for the worse. Speed-up and mechanization increase job dissatisfaction. Employment is insecure in a period of contracting demand for labor in the manufacturing sector. Advancement out of manual work is rare. And second, traditional working-class attitudes and cultural patterns remain strong: working-class self identification, working-class attitudes to social problems and politics, and working-class community living patterns continue to predominate among blue-collar workers studied by sociologists.

But on the level of personal aspirations, rising incomes have a significant impact. They have stimulated a "privatization" of goals, a search for fulfillment or simply pleasure in consumption and leisure after working hours. But these consumption patterns are often conditioned by the need to escape the insecurities and frustrations of life on the job. The inadequacies of the work situation continue to be felt strongly, and find an outlet in hostility to management, militant union activity, and identification with the union as a source of communal involvement for the individual.

But these tendencies do not appear to be as strong as the dominant type of union involvement: a narrowly economic "instrumental collectivism." The union, to many, has become an insurance policy, a service performed by paid professionals in return for dues payment and token loyalty. This attitude, which stands in sharp contrast with the sense of personal involvement, struggle and self-sacrifice which contributed greatly to the formation of the CIO in the 30's, corresponds to the worker's privatization of his own goals in life. It is this development, brought about by the rising incomes of industrial workers, which is the primary evidence for the thesis that industrial workers are acquiring a "middle class" outlook.

The other structural trend in the labor force in this century has been the great increase in white-collar workers. C. Wright Mills estimates that between 1870 and 1940, white-collar employment rose from 6% to 25% of the labor force, while the "old middle class" fell from 33% to 20%, and wage workers

[14] Chinoy, *op. cit.*, p. 125.

fell from 61% to 55%.[15] In the decade 1940–1950, white-collar employment showed a 41.9% increase, while manual work increased 36.9%. In the decade 1950–1960, white-collar employment increased 27.7% as against a 5.8% increase in manual work.[16]

The 26.6 million white-collar workers in 1960 made up 43.3% of the employed civilian work force. Of these, 7.2 million were professional, technical and kindred workers, 9.3 million were clerical and kindred workers, 4.6 million were sales workers, and 5.4 million were managerial workers, officials and non-farm proprietors. The professional and technical sectors were the fastest growing sector of the entire labor force, increasing 47.0% in the 1950–1960 decade.

The middle class has traditionally been associated with a certain social perspective and with working conditions which generally fostered the perspective. The social perspective has been most marked by individualism: "Those who have ability and initiative can overcome obstacles and create their own opportunities. Where a man ends up depends on what he makes of himself." [17] People who see themselves as middle class see the social structure as a highly subdivided hierarchy, and are very conscious of their own position in that continuum. The working conditions which have fostered their outlook are closeness to the management, which has made the ability to rise through the hierarchy an evident possibility, and has allowed workers to identify with the boss, and a certain amount of freedom in their work, which has allowed them to use their brains and be creative.

An examination of the work situation of white-collar workers reveals large areas for which the middle-class image is a very inaccurate description of reality.

In 1960, the six largest occupational groups in the professional and technical category were teachers, engineers, professional nurses (including student nurses), auditors and accountants, physicians and surgeons, and lawyers and judges, which altogether made up more than half the employment in that category.[18] For these groups, the middle-class model still has a fair degree of validity.

For many clerical and sales workers, however, the work situation has taken on alienating features formerly associated more exclusively with blue-collar work. These are the antithesis of closeness to management, ability to rise by individual effort, and freedom in the work environment which characterize "middle-class" jobs. They have their origins in structural economic changes: The increasing size of businesses, the bureaucratization and rationalization of managerial functions, the subdivision and mechanization of clerical tasks, and the standardization of qualification for white-collar employment.

The growing powerlessness of white-collar workers manifests itself in a lack of control over the conditions of employment and over the work process itself.

[15] C. Wright Mills, *White Collar,* Oxford University Press, New York, 1951.

[16] Everett M. Kassalow, "White-Collar Unionism in the United States," in Sturmthal, ed., *White-Collar Trade Unions,* University of Illinois Press, Urbana, Illinois, 1966, table p. 307.

[17] John Goldthorpe and David Lockwood, "Affluence and The British Class Structure," *The Sociological Review,* XI (2), July 1963, p. 141.

[18] Kassalow, *op. cit.,* p. 312.

White-collar workers have always enjoyed greater job security than manual workers. In some measure this has been due to the fact that in manufacturing, the white-collar force was relatively small and could be treated as fixed overhead costs.[19] However, recently white collar employment has increased as a proportion of employment in manufacturing. Moreover, the greatest increases in white-collar work are now coming in trade and service industries. Thus it will be increasingly difficult for the white-collar worker to remain immune to fluctuations in the business cycle. Nevertheless, taking into account other factors such as the high turnover among women workers, who account for well over half the white-collar force, it seems likely that white-collar workers will retain a somewhat greater measure of job security than blue-collar workers in the future.

Another aspect of the conditions of employment is working hours. While most white-collar workers continue to work nine to five, telephone operators are among several large groups which do not share this distinction:

> The hours, indeed, are likely to be less desirable than those in a factory, because the switchboards must be manned around the clock every day of the year, necessitating night-work, Sunday and holiday work, and split shifts.[20]

Powerlessness in the work process is a much more widespread phenomenon among white-collar workers than shift work, however. It is an unavoidable result of the economic processes mentioned above: increasing size, rationalization and so on. A girl who can type can no longer expect to become the boss's secretary in a big company; if she can type rapidly enough and passes other more or less objective tests she may be hired as a typist. As such, she does not operate various office machines, circulate and chat among the other secretaries in the office, take dictation from the boss, type his letters, and handle incoming and outgoing mail. She may be placed in a secretarial pool that receives material to be typed from all executive offices. She may transcribe tapes from nine to five, repeatedly using just her one machine, maintaining a rapid pace under steady pressure, unable to take a break or chat with her neighbors except at specified times, and unable to leave her machine and walk among her colleagues. Such a job incorporates all the powerlessness over pace, physical movement, and techniques as the most alienating factory work.[21]

Apart from the nature of the work, such jobs display other important characteristics which differentiate them from the middle-class model—they are not at all close to management, and, largely as a consequence, they do not permit the worker to rise as a result of his individual ambition:

> [C]oncentration into larger units and their specialization have made for many blind alleys, lessened the opportunity to learn about "other departments" or the business as a whole. The rationalization of white collar work means that as the number of replaceable positions expands more than the number of higher positions, the chances of climbing decrease. Also, as higher positions become more technical, they are often more likely to be filled by people from outside the

[19] *Ibid.*, p. 358.

[20] Seidman, *et al., The Worker Views His Union,* University of Chicago Press, Chicago, Illinois, 1958, p. 141.

[21] Robert Blauner has analyzed and categorized the aspects of alienation in factory work in his book *Alienation and Freedom.* He lists types of powerlessness over the work process as related to pace, pressure, physical movement, quantity, quality, and choice of techniques.

hierarchy. So the ideology of promotion—the expectation of a step-by-step ascent, no longer seems a sure thing.

A very important recent development which sharply accentuates these trends is the growth of office automation. While the potential for automation of the industrial production process is far lower than much of the fanfare might lead one to believe,[22] the automation of large clerical units is one of the few areas which is presently economically feasible, and which in fact has begun to occur at a significant rate.[23]

Ida Hoos has sketched the effects of the introduction of a computer into a large clerical operation:[24] with 500 "positions potential for computer application," the computer leaves in its wake 10–15 positions for programmers, and 50–100 positions for keypunch operators and others in actual operation of the system. Thus

> it remains evident that the number of programmers actively associated with computer installation is a relatively small proportion of the total office staff affected. . . . As for the change in classifications, key-punch and tabulating machine operators, for the present at least, replace bookkeeping and accounting clerks as well as routine clerical workers.

The work situation of the keypunch operator and tabulating machine operator is as alienating as any now found in the labor force, producing obvious tensions in the workers. It leads to no automatic promotions, is done in three shifts, permits no variations of technique or pace, no freedom of physical movement, and no conversation. The work is intrinsically meaningless. Work output measurement is "standard procedure" in both government and business, and the operator whose output lags is fired. The pace required is quite fast. All of this leads to a tremendous tension in each worker. One former keypuncher comments,

> If you just tap one of them on the shoulder when she is working, she'll fly through the ceiling.

Even if one attributes the brutal pace and output requirements to an initial over-zealousness to "make it pay," which will in time disappear, the inherent meaninglessness and alienating nature of the work remains. Thus, to whatever extent office automation turns out to be a significant trend, it will be to the further detriment of the work experience of the white-collar work force.

The idea of a "middle class" is naturally an ambiguous one; it can mean a variety of things to different people in different contexts, but whatever else it may connote in a given instance, it almost always carries with it the implication of being "in the middle" in terms of income strata. An examination of the incomes of white-collar groups shows that while their median incomes have been and continue to be somewhat above those of manual workers, thus placing them in middle-income strata, the income differentials between majority sectors of the two groups have shown a long-term narrowing.

[22] Georges Friedmann, *The Anatomy of Work,* Macmillan, New York, 1961, p. xiv.
[23] Ida R. Hoos, *Automation in the Office,* Public Affairs Press, Washington, D.C., 1961, pp. 23–25.
[24] *Ibid.,* p. 45.

Mills estimates that the average income of white-collar groups in 1890 was about double that of wage workers.[25] In the great period of unionization after the mid-30's, the incomes of manual workers rose much more rapidly than those of white-collar groups.[26] In the period 1950–1963, income for operatives still rose slightly faster than income for clerical workers, 76% against 71%, but income for laborers in the same period rose only 55% as against 88% for professional and technical workers. In 1963, the median annual income for these groupings were: professional and technical, $7182; clerical, $5318; operatives, $4830; and laborers, $2862. These figures can be misleading in two respects: first, the slower progress of manual workers reflects in part less steady employment, and therefore only in part a slower rate of wage increase, and second, which is probably much more important, these figures are calculated only for men, whereas women made up fully two-thirds of the clerical employment as of 1956,[27] and more than half of all white-collar employment (excluding managers) as of 1960, at which time they accounted for only 15% of the blue-collar force.[28] And men earn more, because, in addition to outright discrimination in pay rates,

> the disproportionately high number of women in white collar work made (and still makes) the promotion possibilities of the more "stable" male white collar workers much greater.[29]

Taking all these factors into account, we can say that white-collar incomes continue to be somewhat higher than those for manual workers, but also that the incomes of the mass of clerical workers are now only slightly if at all above those of the skilled and semi-skilled operatives, and that the closing of this income gap has been due largely to the strong unionization of blue-collar workers.

The thesis that American Society is becoming increasingly "middle class" has been discussed first in regard to the rising standard of living of the industrial work force, and second in terms of the increase in white-collar employment. We have examined, in addition, other trends: mechanization in blue-collar work, the contraction of employment in the manufacturing sector, the increasing size of modern businesses, the sealing off of avenues of advancement for both blue-collar and white-collar workers, and the rationalization and automation of white-collar work.

The net result of these social and economic developments has been ambiguous, although clearly white-collar workers are turning to trade unionism. In fact, the growth of white-collar unionism, along with the upsurge in militancy and rank and file revolts in the blue-collar unions, are the most significant new features of the labor movement in the middle sixties.[30] And among the industrial workers in mass-production industries, (1) working-class attitudes to poli-

[25] Mills, *White Collar,* p. 72.

[26] These and the following figures are from Kassalow, *op. cit.,* p. 361.

[27] Hoos, *op. cit.,* p. 23.

[28] Kassalow, *op. cit.,* p. 309.

[29] *Ibid.,* p. 356.

[30] Gus Tyler, "Fresh Breezes in the Labor Movement," *New Republic,* May 20, 1967, and Stanley Weir, *A New Era of Labor Revolt,* Berkeley, California, Independent Socialist Committee, 1967.

tics, social problems and class differences, (2) the need for collective action to deal with employers and (3) the persistence of the problems of work and employment security, have acted as barriers to the penetration of a thorough middle-class outlook. The middle-class norms of individual advancement through one's own efforts, of perceiving the social structure as a ladder to climb with no basic conflicts between those on the top and those further down, and of self-development and freedom in one's work are even more irrelevant to working-class realities today than they were fifty years ago. The only solutions a status-conscious, consumption orientated culture can offer to the real problems of blue-collar and white-collar life on the job are escapist and unreal.

The middle-class picture of the American working class is more a distortion of reality than a pure fabrication: it fails to account for the contradictory attitudes of many who accept collective action yet pursue individualistic goals. It misses the significant counter trends which limit the impact of rising living standards and white-collar employment, or which change the meaning of these phenomena for the workers involved. Above all, it is largely irrelevant to the work experiences of most blue-collar and white-collar workers.

15 THE WAR IN VIETNAM*

by DAN GILBARG
AND MILES RAPOPORT

Together with the growing black rebellion, the War on Vietnam was the most important event of the 1960's. As a result of the war, people in America have begun to consider the oppressive nature of the system in which we live. They have begun to wonder whether that oppressiveness is a result of the kind *of system we have.*

What have people learned about the American system as a result of the war? For one thing, they have learned that the American system is in mortal conflict with the great masses of people around the world. The United States has set itself resolutely on the side of the landlords, the military juntas, and the reactionary dictatorships of the world in its effort to crush popular revolutions. People have learned that American leaders are capable of perpetrating incredible crimes in the name of this policy.

From looking at Vietnam, people inside America have also begun to rethink a lot of traditional ideas about communism. If it was the Communists who gave land to the people, if it was the Communists who led the rebellion against the French, Japanese and Americans, if it was the Communists who built hospitals and schools in the liberated zones and organized people to resist attacks, could the Communists really be agents from Moscow (or Peking) conspiring to deprive these people of their freedom? In fact, beginning with Vietnam, a lot of people came to understand that communism has much more to offer the people of the third world than does the continued domination of U.S. Imperialism.

Finally, Americans have learned a lot about the nature of the American political and economic system and how it affects them. American political and military officials are willing to lie to the American people again and again about the war. They have manipulated the media, they have used scare tactics and they have been willing to beat, jail and smear many who sought to oppose them. Politicians have made promises over and over that they never intended to keep. And meanwhile, all the money, technology, armies and bombs that Americans are so good at making and using have failed to preserve the image of invincibility. In short, people learned that the system was organized to use them, too, for its purposes, and that the vaunted ideals of American democracy, benevolence and invincibility were nothing but a sham.

VIETNAM AND U.S. IMPERIALISM

We are told—by our government, our schools, our newspapers and TV—that our government is engaged in a worldwide conflict. On the one hand, there

* Used by permission of the authors.

is the "Free World," while on the other, there is totalitarian communism. Democracy or dictatorship; freedom or enslavement; our form of government or communism—these are the choices confronting the peoples of the world.

"To protect freedom and democracy and to limit the spread of communism," our government maintains a standing army of more than 3 million men, stationed in bases and countries all over the world. It spends over $80 billion a year on the military—more than all other items in the government budget combined. And, whenever communism threatens, we are asked to give up our money, our bodies, and sometimes our lives in order to meet that threat.

But as the war in Vietnam has dragged on, more and more Americans have been over there or have been forced to wonder about what is really going on in Vietnam. Growing numbers of us have begun to realize how we've been fed a bill of goods. They say we are fighting in Vietnam to protect freedom or democracy, but there seems to be none to protect. They say we are fighting in Vietnam to protect the little guy from Communist aggression, but it turns out that the little guy and the Communists are one and the same. They say we've been asked to come to Vietnam, but most of the people who want us to stay are some big landlords and generals.

THE WAR IN VIETNAM—FRENCH COLONIALISM

To understand the war and to judge the validity of what our government says about it, we have to understand the history of Vietnam. About one hundred years ago, the French took over Vietnam as a colony. They took land away from the people, set up rubber plantations that enslaved thousands of Vietnamese workers, conscripted peasants into the French army, and taxed the Vietnamese to support their colonial administration.

With all but a few rich landlords and generals opposed to French rule, it was only a matter of time before the Vietnamese organized a resistance movement aimed at kicking the French out of Vietnam. The invasion of Vietnam by the Japanese during World War II weakened the control of the French and provided an opportunity for the people—led by an organization called the Vietminh—to take control over their country. The Vietminh led the fight against both the Japanese and the French, and in 1946, the Vietnamese declared their independence (quoting word for word from our own Declaration of Independence) to set up the Republic of Vietnam under the Presidency of Ho Chi Minh.

The period 1946–1954 consisted of an effort of the French to win control of Vietnam back from the Vietminh. For our part, the U.S. was paying 80 percent of the French war costs by 1954. But popular support for the Vietminh and the isolation of the French were too great. Even the military power of the French couldn't defeat the Vietnamese Revolution, as was decisively demonstrated in the resounding defeat of the French at Dienbienphu in 1954.

THE GENEVA AGREEMENTS

At the Geneva Conference of 1954, the Vietminh and the French agreed to withdraw their armed forces to the North and the South respectively. Elections were to be held in 1956 to reunify Vietnam under a single government. President Eisenhower estimated in his Memoirs that ". . . had elections been held at the time of the fighting possibly 80% of the population would have voted for the Communist Ho Chi Minh."

An extremely anti-Communist columnist Joseph Alsop explained Ho's popularity after visiting Vietnam at the time:

> It was difficult for me . . . to conceive of a Communist government genuinely "serving the people." I could hardly imagine a Communist government that was also a popular government and almost a democratic government . . . The Vietminh could not possibly have carried on the resistance for one year, let alone nine years, without the people's strong united support. Relying almost entirely on their own resources, these Southern Vietnamese peasants had tremendous success.

Already, the United States had taken the wrong side—in supporting the French against the Vietminh. But now, our government became increasingly involved in the affairs of Vietnam. We handpicked a leader for the southern zone of Vietnam, a man named Ngo Dinh Diem, and rapidly went about building an independent South Vietnam under Diem's control. The French, who had been given responsibility in the South under the Geneva Agreements, withdrew from the picture. Even though Geneva clearly stated that elections would be held in 1956 to reunify the country, and that division between North and South was only to be temporary, the United States and Diem refused to hold elections—they knew they would lose. Fortunately for them, the Vietminh in the North chose to continue to build up North Vietnam rather than returning right then and there to continue the fight in the South.

THE DIEM GOVERNMENT

In the years between 1954 and 1960, the United States had a chance to show what it could do for the people of South Vietnam. The Diem government was largely its creation, and the U.S. government financed more than 80 percent of its budget. But rather than bringing liberty and economic justice and success to Vietnam, the United States and Diem brought misery and tyranny to all but a very few. The result was that by 1960, a large-scale rebellion had begun in the South and the National Liberation Front (NLF) had formed to coordinate that rebellion.

Diem's government was composed of generals and rich landlords—who had generally turned against their own people by supporting the French in their efforts to keep control over Vietnam. It reversed popular measures that the Vietminh had introduced while seeking to crush all opposition inside the South to the Diem government.

The Vietminh when it organized a village had followed the policy of "land to the tiller"—peasants who previously had to pay exorbitant rents to large landlords for the right to work the land now gained ownership of that land themselves. Smaller landlords who could be convinced to support the fight against the French were allowed to keep some or all of their land but were restricted in the amount of rent they could charge. In addition, the Vietminh reduced the amount of interest that could be charged on loans; abolished all past debt; and set up schools and health clinics in the villages.

The Diem government under U.S. guidance systematically reversed these policies. It reintroduced the power of the landlords in the countryside. First, it refused to allow village elections, instead appointing its own officials. These officials in turn administered a "land reform," which consisted of taking the land from the peasants and returning it to the landlords. Thus, peasants who had owned the land they worked for anywhere from one to eight years under the Vietminh were suddenly required to pay rent again, and sometimes back rent for the years that it hadn't been paid. Such actions led in many places to spontaneous demonstrations, riots, rebellions, and assassinations of Diem's officials.

Diem also tried to establish political control over the countryside. He did this not only by bringing back the old landlords but also by trying to destroy the militant and radical peasants. Anyone who had fought against the French—that is, any patriot—was liable to be arrested, tortured, interned in "political re-education" camps, or even murdered. Witch-hunts were held in many villages, under the watchful eye of Diem's army. Other times, Diem took even more extreme measures—bulldozing villages to the ground and moving the entire population at gunpoint to new areas where security could be more easily maintained. Little did it matter that the peasants felt attached to the land where their ancestors had lived and were buried, that the new villages often provided inadequate land, and that they were run by concentration camp rules and regulations (including the barbed wire fences that surrounded them).

THE NATIONAL LIBERATION FRONT

In response to these intolerably repressive policies of the Diem government, a full-scale revolt developed in South Vietnam. Sporadic rebellions began as early as 1957 and 1958, and by 1960, the National Liberation Front was formed. Increasing numbers of Vietnamese concluded that the only solution to their peoples' problems was armed revolution—and many of these who became Communists felt that the only solution following a successful revolution was socialism. The National Liberation Front was formed by Vietnamese from the South, many of whom were former Vietminh. The NLF sought like the Vietminh before it to mobilize the people of Vietnam to support the rebellion, to take power away from the landlord in favor of the peasant, and to get rid of foreign domination (the United States).

By 1963, just three years after its formation, the NLF had gained tremendous support from the people, especially in the countryside. The success of the NLF provoked a crisis in Saigon, leading to Diem's assassination by army officers. It also led President Kennedy to commit combat troops to Vietnam to supplement the numerous advisors already in Vietnam, thus beginning a process that only ended in 1968 with an occupation force of over 500,000 American troops in Vietnam.

WHY THE VIETNAMESE ARE WINNING

The only thing that has made the near defeat of the Saigon government and the United States possible has been overwhelming and enthusiastic support of the people for the NLF. The necessity of such popular support for successful guerrilla warfare is stressed in U.S. Special Forces doctrine. History also bears this out—one can see how popular support was essential for the NLF right from the beginning. It would have been a simple thing for some villager to let on to the authorities that an NLF organizer was being hidden in the village;

or that a secret meeting was being held at a certain time or place; or that certain people in the village were working closely with the Viet Cong; or that an attack on a particular fort was planned; or that there was a band of NLF guerrillas staying nearby. Indeed, Diem's secret police were trained precisely to find such information, and many Vietnamese suffered from their techniques of uncovering it. Yet, Saigon and the United States have been singularly unable to get accurate intelligence while the Viet Cong have always been well informed of the enemy's troop movements and plans.

The Tet Offensive

In the Tet offensive of spring, 1968, the NLF demonstrated once and for all that it could not be beaten. For weeks preceding the offensive, troops and arms were infiltrated into 140 cities throughout South Vietnam. NLF supporters in the cities fed and housed the troops, trained themselves to help them in combat, and moved supplies through the cities (one way was to hold a mock funeral, carrying guns in the coffin).

In February, 1968, NLF forces and supporters inside and outside the cities struck simultaneously, taking the United States and Saigon completely by surprise. No one had leaked the plans to the authorities. Tremendous damage was inflicted on aircraft, bases, barracks, troops, supply centers, communication centers, and police stations. While fighting took place inside the cities (at the U.S. Embassy, for example), NLF forces dug trenches and tunnels around the cities and bases to create strongholds for further attacks. ARVN and U.S. troops were rushed to the cities from the countryside, leaving the Viet Cong in undisputed possession of most of the country. Fighting over control of the cities continued for weeks—and cities from which the NLF could not be uprooted were bombed to the ground (like the city of Ben Tre and most of Hue, which were completely destroyed).

Tet demonstrated the depth of NLF support in the cities, struck the death blow to the United States and Saigon in the countryside, and set in motion a process by which elements that had previously supported Saigon—moderate Buddhists, shopkeepers, businessmen, conservative intellectuals, some government officials—went into opposition. The Alliance of National, Democratic, and Peace Forces was formed—and in 1969, this organization joined with the NLF to form the Provisional Revolutionary Government, which demands withdrawal of the United States from Vietnam. This government has been recognized by many of the countries around the world, and by the criterion of mass support, clearly represents the people of Vietnam. It maintains schools, health clinics, and a post office system in most of Vietnam.

ARVN and NLF troops

A comparison between ARVN and NLF troops gives further insight into the reasons for the success of the NLF. American officers and GI's alike return from Vietnam impressed with the morale, commitment, courage, skill, and discipline of Viet Cong soldiers. ARVN contrasts sharply: desertion rates have climbed to greater than 20 percent a year; ARVN is rarely willing to engage the NLF in battle, and frequently just sits by or gives up their arms while U.S. and NLF troops battle it out; ARVN boot camp is increasingly conducted behind barbed wire without leave to prevent new draftees from returning to their villages or joining the other side. The Viet Cong soldier is fighting for his land, for his country, and to avenge the crimes that Saigon and the United States have committed against his friends and family. His officers are from backgrounds similar to his own and are even more dedicated, committed, and skilled than he. The ARVN soldier is drafted to fight against his own people for a government of generals and landlords—most of whom were traitors against his own people in the war against the French. He is fighting for officers whose main concern is their own wealth and power, who find excuses to avoid combat, and who lord their privileges over their men.

GOVERNMENT LIES ABOUT VIETNAM

In order to make the war palatable to those of us who do the fighting and pay the bills for the war, our government has tried to make it look like we are in Vietnam to protect the South Vietnamese from the northern aggressors. But the rebellion developed in the South among southerners in response to the horrible conditions under Diem. The North did not even support the rebellion until 1960. After that time, it gave little concrete aid until after the bombing of the North was begun—1965. Senator Mansfield estimated that at the time of the bombing, the North had infiltrated only 400 troops into the South. The story for war materiel was similar—the Viet Cong captured most of its arms from ARVN and the United States. Even now, after the United States destroyed villages, bridges, hospitals, and many other structures in the North by heavy bombing, the NLF is still doing most of the fighting in the South. Furthermore, the whole issue of aggression from the North is a bogus one, since it was the United States and Saigon who prevented peaceful reunification of Vietnam in 1956 in the first place.

In addition, our government speaks of communism imposing itself on the people of Vietnam through terror. When it does so, it ignores the fact that most Vietnamese want *us* out. It also ignores the effects of saturation bombing of villages, and a policy that defines any moving body as the enemy. But in addition, to speak of terror contradicts what our government itself teaches its Special Forces about the necessity of trust and friendship as the basis of support in a guerrilla war. It is impossible to win durable political support through terror—especially in the beginning when you are weaker than the government you are trying to overthrow. NLF forces have used terror—but in a limited and specific manner. For example, assassinations of village chiefs were common in the early days of the Revolution. These were the officials responsible for the land reform by which people lost their land, and the witch-hunts by which they lost their friends, their families, and their freedoms. This is confirmed by Douglas Pike, ex-U.S. security attaché in Saigon and author of a book, *The Vietcong*. He points out that,

> . . . the killing of individuals was done with great specificity, as for example, pinning a note to the shirtfront of an assassinated government official, explaining the crimes he had committed. [In fact] the NLF theoreticians considered the terror to be the weapon of the weak, the desperate, or the ineffectual guerrilla leader.

Our government adds to all of this the myth that the NLF is cultivating the people now—only to sell them out once it gets power. This ignores who the

Communists in the NLF are—not power hungry despots from some other country, but people from South Vietnam who became Communists because they saw revolution and socialism as the only solutions for the problems of their people. It also ignores the achievements of North Vietnam—education, health, food production, equality, industry—which have significantly improved the lives of the people in North Vietnam and have laid the basis for further development.

Our government has consistently lied to us about the war in Vietnam. This is not the product of confusion or poor communications. The U.S. government has something to hide, and it knows it. At one press conference, Arthur Sylvester, chief information officer of the Pentagon, said to reporters: "If you think any American official is going to tell the truth, then you're stupid. Did you hear that? Stupid."

In fact—despite all the jive explanations for why we are in Vietnam—what the United States has done is to seek to crush—with nearly all the means at its disposal and at tremendous human cost—a popular movement for social justice and national independence whose policies and program have far more to offer the people of Vietnam than Saigon or the United States.

16 UNITED STATES IMPERIALISM*

by DAN GILBARG

Many people feel that Vietnam was somehow a mistake—leaving aside this war, they say, the basic pattern of U.S. relations with the world has been, if not benevolent, at least "concerned." People point to the existence of foreign aid, the Peace Corps, and particular examples of policy to prove this claim.

But to say that Vietnam was an accident is to ignore that Presidents Truman, Eisenhower, Kennedy, Johnson, Nixon, all devoted energies during their terms of office to crushing the Vietnamese Revolution. It is to say that a massive and costly war of genocide waged against a people fighting for their freedom against oppressive landlords and dictators is an act peripheral to our "real" foreign policy. This view ignores the fact that military and political interventions have been part and parcel of U.S. diplomacy for decades. Their real purpose has been to strengthen the hand of U.S. business around the world and to protect the property and trade of American corporations. Moreover, such a view ignores the actual content of the American "aid" program. Most aid has been military, propping up internal dictatorships and tying on "clients" to the American "Free-World" economic system. What economic aid exists has usually been a boondoggle for U.S. corporations functioning overseas. It has been used as a lever to make sure that foreign governments play the game the American way.

The American Empire may be different in many respects from the Roman Empire, or the British Empire—but it is the most powerful empire in the history of the world—and given the possibilities for revolutionary development in today's world, it is the greatest obstacle to human progress the world has ever seen.

Another conventional view holds that while American foreign policy may indeed be as reactionary as we suggest, all this is remediable by electing an enlightened, "anti-imperialist" brand of politician to high office. This view ignores the entrenched nature of imperialism and its necessity to the stability and health of the capitalist economy.

First off, the bedrock of the American Empire lies in the economic interests that invest, trade, extract raw materials and reap profits all over the world. Foreign sources of earnings account for over a fifth of nonfinancial corporate profits. Second, the interest groups that stand behind the government's enormous military expenditures—justified in large part thanks to the existence of an American empire—have a large stake in the empire, too. Finally, economic stability requires that America be able to dispose of a large part of her domestic production in foreign markets, many of which are created and kept open by America's world-wide military, political and economic presence.

In these ways, the American Empire is an integral feature to the kind of capitalism America has evolved. No mere policy changes are going to alter its

* Used by permission of the author.

nature. No mere politician is going to uproot it through his elective office. A solution, or rather dissolution, *to the American Empire will only come about from the combined forces of people around the world who mobilize to throw it out and the people within the United States who mobilize to uproot the capitalist system itself.*

We must try to explain why the United States government has been fighting in Vietnam for a number of years in an effort to preserve the rule of a corrupt clique of bureaucrats, generals, and landlords against the challenge of a popular and necessary social revolution. We have been told all our lives by our schools, media, and politicians that the purpose of U.S. foreign policy is the promotion of freedom and democracy. One might be inclined, then, to think that Vietnam is somehow an accident, an exception to the rule.

However, we also have more to go on than just Vietnam. We also know that the U.S. government's "free world" allies have included a number of *other* regimes no less reactionary than the Vietnamese dictatorship. Salazar's Portugal, Franco's Spain, Trujillo's Dominican Republic, Batista's Cuba, Chiang Kai-shek's China, Duvalier's Haiti, the military juntas of Brazil, Greece, Indonesia, South Korea, and Thailand, and the racist regimes of southern Africa —these are only the better known and the most vicious of such dictatorships. The U.S. position—considered in this context—is not quite so surprising.

What is it, then, about these rotten regimes that our government finds so attractive?

The answer to this question is that while such governments obviously have nothing to offer in the way of freedom and democracy in the manner that those terms are commonly understood, they do in fact provide one special kind of freedom, a freedom which our government cherishes greatly. This is the freedom they provide for businessmen, and especially United States businessmen, to make large profits. That is, while most of us would choose to judge a society according to the way in which it serves the people affected by it, the U.S. government chooses to judge societies according to the way they serve American business.

According to this view, the defining feature of the area known as the "free world" is hospitality to U.S. capital. A better name for the free world would be the American Empire: U.S. economic, political, and military power is dominant within the free world, as are American economic interests. The United States, through its government and international corporations, dominates the political economies within its empire for the purpose of extending the economic interests of American business. U.S. policy is most appropriately labeled *imperialism.*

What is the evidence for such a view?

We should begin by looking at the magnitude, and nature, of U.S. economic interests in the underdeveloped world.

U.S. business began to take a *serious* interest in the underdeveloped world in the 1890s. The depression of 1893 was the most severe in American history up to that time, and the third economic crisis in twenty years. Not only did such crises hurt profits, but they also threatened social stability. The '90s were the scene of bloody strikes, angry marches of the unemployed, and the growth of radical political challenges to the American system. Businessmen, looking for ways out of such crises, began to see the importance of foreign markets as a way to stimulate the economy. Some of the problems that producers were having in marketing their goods at home could thereby be solved. Interest focused on the markets of Latin America and China. The Monroe Doctrine for Latin America was restated—American interests would be dominant in the hemisphere. The Open Door Notes for China were issued—China would remain open to foreign trade and capital, and the United States (having newly arrived on the scene) should share equal rights of access with all other imperial powers. American determination to aggressively expand commercially was made absolutely clear from 1898 to 1903, in the wars to eliminate Spanish rule and to put down the revolutionary patriots in Cuba and the Philippines.

Since that time, U.S. interests have expanded tremendously. Preoccupation with foreign trade continued. As Franklin Roosevelt said in 1935 in the midst of the Great Depression, "Foreign markets must be regained if America's producers are to rebuild a full and enduring domestic economy for our people. There is no other way if we would avoid painful economic dislocations and unemployment." In addition, in the postwar years, U.S. foreign investments leaped ahead prodigiously. The *U.S. News and World Report* commented in 1964:

> Big U.S. firms find the pickings very good in their foreign operations. American executives are realizing, as never before, what the potentials in foreign lands are. Big growth in sales is to be abroad; not in the U.S. This is one of the most important business facts of the second half of the twentieth century.

Specifically: in 1950, 10 percent of the profits of U.S. corporations (excluding banks) were earned off foreign operations. In 1964, this proportion had risen to 22 percent. Over this period, while domestic profits for those corporations increased by 66 percent, profits off foreign operations increased 271 percent. Though somewhat *less* than half of all U.S. investments and trade is in the underdeveloped world (the rest are in the more industrialized capitalist countries—Europe, Canada, Japan), considerably *more* than half of U.S. profits is derived from interests in the underdeveloped world, because of the higher rate of profit there.

All of this begins to indicate the rapidly growing stake of American business in foreign operations and to explain the nature of its dependence on such operations. But global figures on profits give us only a first approximation. We should also note that the figures given on profits are an average over corporations that have a stake abroad and corporations that don't. If we look at the particular industries and companies that have foreign operations, we find that the dependence of these is far greater than that indicated by the average. Furthermore, we should also remember that even a company that depends on the underdeveloped world for only 2 to 3 percent of its profits will be interested in fighting to keep those profits.

Moreover profits don't tell the whole story. Some corporations have entered foreign markets which, if not tremendously profitable, still give the corporation a foothold for dominating markets that can be developed in the future or for outcompeting other local or international firms for existing markets. Other corporations in industries requiring particular raw materials for production (e.g., oil, copper) gain concessions to extract those materials in order to gain access to a long-term supply and to prevent competitors from having such access. The largest U.S. oil companies, for example, depend on a monopoly of two thirds of the world's crude oil reserves for their world preeminence in the refining and selling of oil. The importance of access to raw materials is brought home all the more sharply by considering that an increasing number of industries now depend on foreign supplies of raw materials and that many of these industries are key to the U.S. military establishment.

The companies with the largest foreign holdings are also the companies which dominate our economy here at home. The eight corporations that together gain 25 percent of all corporate profits in the United States (General Motors, Ford, AT&T, Standard Oil of New Jersey, Texaco, Gulf, Dupont, IBM) are all heavily committed overseas. This has important implications for the posture of the entire corporate community toward foreign expansion and the need for an aggressive foreign policy to protect economic interests. In particular, these giant corporations have allies throughout the U.S. economy—suppliers, customers, firms under the same ownership or top-level financial control. Furthermore, there is the overlapping set of interests that directly or indirectly are dependent on military contracts, which are responsible for 15 to 20 percent of our entire national product. The military contractors have a clear and obvious interest in an aggressive foreign policy. Taken together, these interests constitute a solid block of the very largest American corporations, deeply committed to preserving and extending the American Empire.

A leading businessman, Henry F. Grady, has said: "The capitalist system is essentially an international system. If it cannot function internationally, it will break down completely."

Whether or not the very survival of American capitalism does depend on its economic stake in the underdeveloped countries, there is no question but that a tremendously powerful group of corporate concerns have a great deal at stake in the American Empire. These corporations exercise decisive influence on the policies of the American government. They do so through a whole set of mechanisms that include their importance to the economy, massive campaign contributions sufficient to control both political parties, extensive lobbying, ties to commercially owned media, and direct representation in the Federal government. As President Woodrow Wilson pointed out in a moment of candor over fifty years ago:

> Suppose you go to Washington and try to get at your Government. You will always find that while you are politely listened to, the men really consulted are the men who have the big stake—the big bankers, the big manufacturers, and the big masters of commerce . . . The masters of the Government of the United States are the combined capitalists and manufacturers of the United States.

The fact of corporate influence in the government, together with the large corporate interest in an aggressive foreign policy to maintain and expand the American Empire (imperialism), leads to some clear conclusions. On the one hand, the U.S. government opposes socialist revolution all over the world, as it is an attempt to achieve independence from imperial domination. Such an attempt threatens present and future economic interests in the country in question. Furthermore, a successful socialist revolution would undermine the confidence of U.S. investors in other places, while encouraging revolutionaries and oppressed people around the world to fight for liberation against a colossus that has proven vulnerable. These are the bases for U.S. opposition to socialist revolution in Vietnam. While direct interests in Vietnam are limited (though growing), it offers some considerable opportunities for the future. More important, Vietnam is seen as critical to the remainder of the U.S. Empire, and particularly, to Southeast Asia. Henry Cabot Lodge, former Ambassador to South Vietnam and chief negotiator for the United States in Paris, puts it this way:

> He who holds or has influence in Vietnam can affect the future of the Philippines and Formosa to the east, Thailand and Burma with their huge rice surpluses to the west, and Malaysia and Indonesia with their rubber, ore and tin to the south. Vietnam thus does not exist in a geographical vacuum—from it large storehouses of wealth and population can be influenced and undermined.

The Vice-President of Chase Manhattan Bank in charge of Far Eastern operations chimes in with his concern:

> In the past, foreign investors have been somewhat wary of the over-all political prospect for the region. I must say, though, that the U.S. actions in Vietnam this year—which have demonstrated that the U.S. will continue to give effective protection to the free nations of the region—have considerably reassured both Asian and Western investors. In fact, I see some reason for hope that the same sort of economic growth may take place in the free economies of Asia that took place in Europe after the Truman Doctrine and after NATO provided a protective shield. The same thing also took place in Japan after the U.S. intervention in Korea removed investor doubts.

In addition to staunchly opposing social revolution around the world, the U.S. government serves American business on a day-by-day basis. The history of our relations with the underdeveloped countries is defined by a continual struggle on the part of the United States to extend and maintain the rights and privileges of American capital. Within the underdeveloped countries, wherever U.S. presence is at all significant, policy toward American interests is a major issue of public debate. The U.S. government uses its power to make sure that the issues are resolved in favor of U.S. companies.

Let's look, for example, at the case of Guatemala.

For a period of time in the late '40s and early '50s in that country, a liberal government was in power that took certain mild measures to improve welfare and to reform the economy. Inevitably, these policies came into conflict with the interests of U.S. companies and especially those of the giant United Fruit Company, banana producer and owner of a large railway subsidiary. The Guatemalan government encouraged the growth of trade unions, and it reversed earlier legislation outlawing strikes. In particular, a strong railway union developed. The legal minimum wage was raised from 26¢ a day to $1.08 a day, though enforcement of this measure was usually ineffective. Petroleum laws were amended to require refining of oil on Guatemalan soil (rather than the direct export of crude oil to be refined elsewhere) and 51 percent Guatemalan ownership of all oil companies. A tax was levied against profits, interest, and dividends of investors living outside of the country. To cap it off; a limited land reform measure was enacted in 1953. Under it, 234,000 acres of uncultivated land belonging to the United Fruit Company were expropriated, to be paid for in twenty-five-year bonds according to the value set on the property for tax purposes by United Fruit itself. This was considered unacceptable. The company wanted this land for further expansion, and to make sure that no competitor set up shop in the country. Further, as United Fruit saw it, underassessment of property for purposes of tax evasion didn't mean that the property should be undervalued for the purposes of compensation.

By the end of 1954, the reform regime in Guatemala was out on its heel, the victim of a military takeover organized by the CIA. Shrouded in secrecy at the time, the U.S. role in sponsoring an invasion force from Honduras, organizing the military junta to succeed in office, and bombing Guatemala City was later admitted by Eisenhower and others. The new government immediately revealed what the coup was about. Literacy was imposed as a condition for voting, thereby disfranchising 70 percent of the people. Strikes were outlawed, and the railway union broken. The only unions that were permitted to exist were those deemed acceptable by the dictatorship. An estimated 72,000 people were arrested without trial in the first four months of the new regime. All expropriated lands were returned, and the 100,000 peasants who had received land were thereby dispossessed. The minimum wage returned to 26¢. Restrictions on oil companies were removed, and numerous contracts with U.S. petroleum companies were signed. Profits were allowed to leave the country freely. And in 1955, as if in payment for services rendered, the man who engineered the coup for the CIA—General Walter Bedell Smith—became a Director of the United Fruit Company.

The case of Guatemala suggests by what methods differences between U.S. interests and the government of a client country may be resolved. However, the United States is usually able to repel attacks on American interests in ways other than overturning governments.

One of the chief ways in which the American government and corporations operate is through local allies. Strong efforts are made to develop local business, landowning, and military elites that can be organized to fight for U.S. economic interests. Local capital is often threatened by the same policies as is U.S. capital (e.g., tax reform, labor laws), and therefore can be mobilized to support U.S. interests. In addition—and very important—local capital is normally bound to American capital in a whole set of ways that leave it dependent on the American corporations. Investors in manufacturing, for example, often use American brand names, patents, parts, and technologies. In addition, they may share ownership with U.S. capital. Investors in raw materials usually sell to huge U.S. commercial concerns. In general, the largest business interests share much in common with American interests and are sufficiently dependent to support them in all cases. As for the military, its loyalty to the United States is cultivated by lucrative aid, training programs, and advisory help.

Also important as a means of everyday control, in addition to the loyalty of local elites, are the American economic aid programs. These programs are very revealing about the purposes of American foreign policy as well.

We are accustomed, in this country, to thinking of U.S. aid as a generous gift. If we are of a liberal persuasion, we have probably criticized our government for being stingy with aid. But in fact, aid serves American economic interests quite well. On the one hand, because client governments desperately need it, it provides a club by which to keep such governments in line. On the other hand, it provides an excellent means by which the interests of American corporations abroad can be extended.

Most governments in the underdeveloped world desperately need aid. Highly vulnerable to threats of insurgency from the masses of people who get nothing from the system but hunger and starvation, they need money for arms on the one hand and for government services on the other. In most underdeveloped countries, taxation mainly rests on the export and import of goods. But as raw material prices decline on the world market relative to the prices of manufactured goods, as they have for most products for the last fifteen years, the revenue from foreign trade for a country that mainly exports raw materials (most underdeveloped countries) does not keep pace with the needs of the government. This is one basis for the need for foreign aid. In addition, the decline of export earnings limits the capacity of the country to import goods. Foreign aid can also provide foreign exchange to permit further imports.

It may come as a shock to us that most aid is advanced in the form of loans, not grants. This means that the debtor government must pay the "aid" back, together with the interest on it. Thus, taking loans to support further government spending or to provide more foreign currency only serves to perpetuate the dependency. Soon, the client government must allocate part of its tight budget and foreign exchange requirements to paying back the loans in dollars. Some governments are in the position of having to allocate up to a third of their yearly budgets for the repayment of past loans. The result is simply to create the demand for still further loans.

Once in such a cycle of dependence, a client government is in a position of extreme subservience to U.S. interests. For the American government can exact many concessions in return for extending credit. As Eugene Black, former Chairman and President of the U.S. controlled World Bank has said:

> . . . our foreign aid programs constitute a distinct benefit to American business. The three major benefits are: (1) Foreign aid provides a substantial and immediate market for U.S. goods and services. (2) Foreign aid stimulates the development of new overseas markets for U.S. companies. (3) Foreign aid orients national economies toward a free enterprise system in which U.S. firms can prosper.

More than 85 percent of U.S. aid comes back to the United States for the purchase of U.S. goods. Most aid programs contain restrictions by which aid money must be used to "buy American." This is the case whether or not a particular item is more expensive in the United States than it is in some other country. In all, 11 percent of U.S. exports directly result from such foreign "aid."

Another condition of the extension of credit by the United States is the use of aid monies to *directly* benefit American foreign investors, many times at the expense of local competitors. For example, aid money is used to make investment surveys for United States firms; to provide foreign exchange to enable these companies to import parts and supplies from the United States; to provide loans to help them make investments in plant and machinery; and to build roads and ports that directly serve American commercial interests.

Further, extension of aid is used as a political bargaining point to resolve many of the issues of dispute between client governments and American interests. Many of these governments are brought to sponsor policies that favor U.S. interests as the price of getting continued aid. Concessions of mineral rights for U.S. companies; tax exemptions; anti-labor, anti-union, and anti-strike policies; freedom to repatriate profits to the United States without restriction; loans by the client government to U.S. firms; tariff policies that favor United States imports; import policies by which American companies get first claim on scarce foreign exchange to import goods—these are only some of the policies, favors, and subsidies that U.S. companies are usually capable of winning from client governments. Aid plays an important part in the process of influence.

Arnold Toynbee has said:

> America is today the leader of the worldwide anti-revolutionary movement in defense of vested interests. She now stands for what Rome stood for. Rome consistently supported the rich against the poor in all foreign communities that fell under her sway; and since the poor, so far, have always and everywhere been far more numerous than the rich, Rome's policy made for inequality, injustice, and the least happiness of the greatest number.

It is in supporting the rich against the poor, and in opposing socialist revolution by which the poor seek a place on the face of the earth, that U.S. imperialism has committed its greatest crime. The war in Vietnam should be opposed not only because the United States is fighting to destroy a *popular* movement, but also because it is fighting to destroy a movement that promises real solutions to the problems that the Vietnamese people have faced for the last century.

Under the present system in the underdeveloped world, a few large landowners control most of the land. The majority must work or rent someone else's land. Many starve; most suffer from nutritional disease; life expectancies are under 40 years in many places; death rates at birth reach greater than 50 percent. Food consumption, already ridiculously inadequate, has actually *declined* in many areas over the last three decades, according to UN statistics.

In the cities, the situation is almost as bad. Unemployment is tremendous and quickly growing in many countries. Masses of the unemployed live in rotting shanty towns, making their "living" (if they can) through scavenging, begging, prostitution, peddling, and occasional work. The postwar years have seen a phenomenal growth of these huge slums.

This is a picture that holds with some variation throughout the different parts of the underdeveloped world. It would be a mistake to think that these problems were unsolvable, inherent in the poverty of the country or in the steady increase of population. Rather, the failure of these countries to develop and to provide a decent living for all of their people have clear causes and clear solutions, as the success of socialist development has demonstrated.

The prime imperative of the underdeveloped country is land reform and social control over the resources of the society. The strangulation of the people by the large landlord and businessman must be ended. At present, these classes control the distribution of wealth for the majority of the people, and they keep most for themselves while letting those dependent on them live at starvation level. The large landowners decide whether land is to be used for the production of export crops, food crops, or nothing at all. The fact that food production is going down in many countries, and that the people desperately need land, does not prevent these landowners from holding large amounts of land fallow and from converting land from production of food to production of export crops according to what is profitable.

Furthermore, these landowners together with the big businessmen control the substantial portion of the wealth in the society. The priorities of human need and development of their countries would lead to using these resources to produce the goods that are most needed, to provide health, education, and housing, and to lay a basis for industrialization by building up heavy industry and by investing in the agricultural sector. Instead, those dominant classes that control the wealth in today's underdeveloped world choose to waste their wealth on lavish living, speculation in land, usurious loans to poor peasants, safe investments in New York and Swiss banks, and military spending. In the few countries where significant investment in industry has occurred, it has been for the purpose of providing luxury goods, it has depended on U.S. companies for know-how and parts, and it has been organized monopolistically so as to reduce the incentive for innovation and efficiency.

A socialist revolution is needed to take the power over society's wealth out of the hands of the dominant classes and to place it in the hands of the total community. The community can then decide how to distribute goods and what kinds of investments should be made. In general, it can take over the many important decisions now monopolized by the large landowners and businessmen. The practical results of socialist revolution have been remarkable, though variable, in most of today's socialist countries. The Soviet Union, the first socialist country, developed from a backward country in 1917 to become the world's second industrial power in the space of fifty years. However, it did this at the cost of great suffering (albeit abetted by the hostility of the West—intervention, invasion, economic quarantine) and in the process re-enacted certain class privileges. China and Cuba are better examples of socialist countries that have avoided the worst aspects of the Soviet experience. These countries saw early the need to avoid entrenched bureaucracy, to develop local institutions within which the people could participate and exercise power, to mobilize the entire people, and to emphasize the development and consciousness of their citizens. All of the socialist countries have spent large proportions of their resources on health and education. Increased food production through cooperative methods of farming and cultivation of new crops and land together with equal sharing of basic necessities has meant the end to starvation and nutritional disease.

Socialist revolution has come into direct conflict with the United States. The desire of the community to control its own resources on behalf of the entire people has meant kicking out U.S. economic interests. The desire of the country for independence has led to repudiation of debt and emphasis on self-reliance in the mobilization of resources rather than reliance on foreign "aid." The posture of the United States, in turn, toward socialist revolution has made it the most reactionary force in the world today.

As the above analysis has tried to suggest, the American government has chosen to play this role out of a desire to maintain and expand an economic empire that is extremely profitable to American business. The implications of such a view are clear: that to effectively oppose our foreign policy, both in its visible aspect as in Vietnam and its day-by-day aspect as in the functioning of its aid program, we must attack directly and powerfully the corporate interests and priorities that run our society. To do that, a majority movement of Americans must be built, embodying the goal of ending imperialism, and the understanding that such a goal can only be achieved via a socialist transformation of our own society. Our problems abroad lie at home.

17 IMPERIALISM AND UNDERDEVELOPMENT: THE CASE OF CUBA*

by EDWARD BOORSTEIN

What are the effects of the American system on the underdeveloped countries? Boorstein examines this question with respect to Cuba—a country which once had close political and economic ties to the United States. He documents the argument that liberation for the Cuban people and development of Cuban society required kicking out U.S. business and establishing socialism in Cuba.

The liberal myth asserts that U.S. policy toward the underdeveloped world is basically benevolent—with aberrations such as Vietnam. The United States will try to help out other countries—if only it has the chance. For example, U.S. companies can invest in these foreign countries, bringing their skills and capital and providing jobs and tax revenue for the host country.

But as Boorstein makes clear, such investment in Cuba, backed up by the U.S. government, brought only the strangulation of the Cuban economy.

Boorstein shows how the American economy in its contact with foreign societies breeds the same kinds of waste and oppression that it breeds at home—only on a larger scale. American corporations don't bother themselves with the needs of the people of the host country. Their job is to do business: that means paying labor as little as possible, extracting resources as cheaply as possible, paying as little taxes as possible, avoiding nationalization at any cost and then fleeing back home with a bundle of profits. No matter if this pattern strips a country of its resources, builds and sustains a reactionary parasite class of bureaucrats, dictators, profiteers and military men, in short, makes economic development impossible.

A second theme raised so far in the book which Boorstein illustrates is that American government serves as the handmaiden to these objectives of American corporations. In the underdeveloped country, this means giving foreign aid that benefits American corporate installations. It means using political power to win favors for U.S. business. It means using economic and military interventions to maintain or institute regimes favorable to U.S. business or to avoid nationalization of American enterprises. This complex of imperialist domination can only be thrown off by popular revolution.

The Cuban Revolution proved Boorstein's analysis to be a reality. Unemployment—20 to 25 percent before the Revolution—has been eliminated. Illiteracy—over 50 percent in many rural areas—was essentially obliterated in a mass literacy campaign in which educated people from all over the country were mobilized as teachers. Food consumption—declining per capita as it had been in many Latin American countries for a number of years—increased significantly with the application of new agricultural techniques, irrigation (there were no dams before the Revolution, now there are many) and the cultivation of lands previously held idle by the large companies. Medical care is now available to Cubans in every village, whereas doctors were available only in the larger cities before the Revolution and only if you could cough up the money.

A good description of what postrevolutionary Cuba is like is also found in the Goldfield selection. (See Part V.)

The central fact about the Cuban economy before the Revolution was neither its one-crop concentration on sugar, nor the monopoly of most of the agricultural land by huge *latifundia,* nor the weakness of the national industry, nor any other such specific characteristic. Until the Revolution, the central fact about the Cuban economy was its domination by American monopolies—by American imperialism. It was from imperialist domination that the specific characteristics flowed. Unless this is recognized, the Cuban Revolution cannot be understood.

Many of the specific characteristics of the Cuban economy are by now well known, so they can be summarized here in a few pages.

Sugar dominated the economy. Together with its by-products, alcohol and molasses, sugar made up about 80 percent of the exports and paid for the bulk of the imports. The sugar companies controlled 70 to 75 percent of the arable land; they owned two thirds of the railroad trackage; most of the ports and many of the roads were simply adjuncts of the sugar mills. The sugar industry employed about 25 percent of the labor force. The export of sugar and its by-products constituted 20 to 30 percent of the gross domestic product. But this last percentage does not give sugar its true importance: most of the rest of the gross product depended on sugar.

The sugar industry was seasonal, unstable, and stagnant, and it imparted these characteristics to the whole economy. It employed about four to five hundred thousand workers to cut, load, and transport the cane during the three to four months of the harvest season, and then left them to starve during the rest of the year. The price and demand for sugar rode up and down with war and peace and business cycles, taking the whole Cuban economy with them. Since export outlets for Cuban sugar were growing only slowly, the whole Cuban economy stagnated.

Even apart from sugar, there was great concentration in Cuban exports. When tobacco, minerals, and coffee are added, 94 to 98 percent of total exports is accounted for. Tobacco exports, next in importance after sugar, also stagnated; they were about as high in 1957–1958 as in 1920–1921. The earnings from minerals and coffee were small and uncertain.

With exports stagnating, the only way the Cuban economy could have advanced was by increasing production for domestic use. But here again there was little progress. Diversification and growth of agricultural output was blocked by the landholding system. National industry—industry not just physically located in Cuba but integrated into the Cuban economy—was stunted, squeezed in a restricted national market by deadly foreign competition. Some new manufacturing industries producing for the Cuban market were being established, but they were foreign enclaves, appendages of the American or some other foreign economy, and did not help solve Cuba's economic problems.

Most of the land in Cuba was monopolized by huge *latifundia*—sugar plantations and cattle ranches—that sprawled across the countryside. Both sugar grower and rancher practised extensive agriculture which wasted land, limited employment opportunities, and kept agricultural output down.

The sugar industry used for growing cane only about half the total area it controlled; it kept the rest in reserve, either idle or as low-yield natural pasture. To cover fluctuations in the demand for sugar, the industry kept much more acreage under cane than was harvested. Little money was invested in irrigation, little fertilizer was used, and no attempt was made to improve cane varieties. Cane yields per unit of land were among the lowest in the world.

On the large cattle ranches a few cowboys handled enormous herds which roamed over thousands of acres of land. Pastures were not fertilized. There were no silos for storing fodder. In the wet season much grass was wasted; in the dry season when the grass became brown and sparse, the cattle lost weight and milk yields dropped sharply. Outside the Havana basin, most cattle were not milked.

Most of Cuba's rural population and part of her city dwellers subsisted on a diet of rice, beans, and two or three tubers such as *malanga,* with practically no milk or dairy products, eggs, poultry, meat, fruit, or vegetables. To boot, Cuba had to spend large amounts of foreign exchange to import foodstuffs—lard and vegetable oils, rice, beans, potatoes—whose domestic production could have been increased.

The underutilization of labor-power and land in the countryside was enormous. But the idle labor could not get at the idle land because it was monopolized by the *latifundia.* The sugar companies had no interest in the full employment of the rural population. Their interest lay in unemployment. They needed a huge army of labor in reserve in the countryside for the cane-cutting season. One of the reasons they monopolized so much land was to keep the sugar workers from it. If the sugar workers had had access to land they would not have been available at miserable wages whenever the companies needed them.

National industry in Cuba was limited to a few types of goods. There were local slaughterhouses, bakeries, and factories producing milk and dairy products, soft drinks, and candy. Local factories, shops, and cottage industries turned out shoes, clothing, furniture, brick and tile, and a few other clay products such as water jugs and flowerpots. A few factories were large and used modern machinery. But most characteristic were the hundreds of little shops and cottage industries.

How could Cuban national industry grow? The poverty which blanketed the countryside limited the effective demand: over a third of the population did not buy anything other than a few staple foodstuffs and articles of clothing. And into the truncated market that did exist, a flood of goods was poured by the giant corporations of the North.

Cuba's internal market was dominated by imports. Not only did the imports greatly exceed the domestic manufactures in value, but they were infinitely greater in variety. Every conceivable type of goods was imported—from cornflakes to tomato paste; from nails and tacks to tractors, trucks, and automobiles; from thread to all types of clothing; from goods for Sears and other department stores to accessories for the home, fertilizers and insecticides for agriculture, and materials and equipment for industry and construction.

The sugar mills, mines, and almost all the large manufacturing plants in

Cuba were foreign enclaves. They pre-empted Cuba's best land, her mineral resources, her raw materials; they dominated the internal market for many products. But they could not give steady employment to a large number of people, and they prevented rather than promoted the creation of a national market.

These enterprises were foreign enclaves even though some of them were owned by Cubans. Whether foreign-owned or Cuban-owned, they were meshed with the American or some other foreign economy; they were dependent on foreign equipment, materials, or markets, and most of their profits were transferred abroad.

The sugar industry—counting the whole complex—employed a total of about half a million people, but it provided year-round work for fewer than 25,000. The nickel plant at Nicaro provided about 1,850 jobs and the copper mine at Matahambre, 1,250;[1] the other mines had fewer employees. For a few thousand jobs and some tax payments, all Cuba's mineral resources were taken over.

The foreign plants turning out cement, tires, paint, soap, detergents, toiletries, bottles, tin cans, paper, and oil and gasoline were typical of most U.S. investment in "manufacturing" in Latin America, and thus especially interesting. I have been through about 25 such plants in Cuba. In their economics, almost all were essentially the same.

They were mechanized or automated, turning out a large output with a small labor force. One plant, employing 30 people mostly engaged in watching instrument panels or sweeping and cleaning, turned out half the detergents consumed in Cuba, with a sales value of several million dollars. Three or four tire plants, each employing about 250 people, monopolized the Cuban tire market. The plants operated with foreign equipment and raw materials which were usually imported in a fabricated state. The tin can plant used imported tinplate; the soap and detergent plants imported fats, alkalis, and silica rock; the tire plants imported rubber, carbon black, etc. The profits were, of course, remitted abroad. And the products went to the upper 15 percent or so of the Cuban population; most Cubans did not have cars on which to put tires or paint, and could not afford canned tomatoes or a 40-cent package of detergent.

These plants were established in Cuba for a variety of reasons: to escape customs duties on finished goods, to get a more secure grip on the internal market, to be able to continue to use machinery that had already been written off as obsolete in the United States. They were technically impressive, even when the machinery was obsolete by American standards. They blew up the local production statistics. But they provided jobs for less than 3 percent of the Cuban labor force. Their economic effect was not much different from that of the packaging which a sales representative performs locally on goods brought in from abroad. These plants were little more than disguised American export operations.

The most striking examples of foreign enclaves in the Cuban economy were the three large oil refineries owned by Standard Oil, Texaco, and Shell. With their large control rooms full of instrument panels; their mazes of pipes, towers, tanks, and furnaces all operating automatically; their tankers, internal railroad

[1] *Investment in Cuba, Basic Information for U.S. Businessmen,* Washington, D.C., U.S. Government Printing Office, 1956, p. 73.

systems, and trucks; their cleanliness and order, they were little communities unto themselves—marvels of technology. The value added by these refineries to the imported crude oil and other materials with which they worked was over $50 million a year, and this amount went into the statistics as Cuban output. Many an economic report has discussed the growth of "the Cuban economy" on the basis of these statistics. But in what sense was the output of these refineries Cuban? They employed fewer than 3,000 people, and most of those in the higher positions were foreigners.

The composition of Cuba's imports also reflected the basic split in the Cuban economy between foreign and national Less than 20 percent of Cuban imports consisted of items serving the needs of the mass of the people, such as rice, lard, beans, codfish, cloth, and medicines. Little foreign exchange went for economic development. Eighty percent of Cuban imports went to the upper classes and the large corporations, whose products either went abroad or also to the upper classes. Tens of millions of dollars went for goods which, in a country as poor as Cuba, can only be classified as luxuries: passenger cars, air conditioners, record players, fancy foodstuffs. In 1957 when total imports were $770 million, $30 million were spent on passenger cars alone. Over $60 million went for petroleum to refine into gasoline to run the cars, and into fuel oil to produce electricity to run the air conditioners and other appliances.

The whole way of life of the Cuban well-to-do depended on American goods, and the market they formed was also an enclave. Most Cubans, and almost all rural Cubans, lived in a different world. A survey taken by the Catholic University in 1956 showed that average per capita income in the countryside, including homegrown food supplies, was less than $100 per year.

It is evident even from the telling that these characteristics of the Cuban economy were not accidents; they were interrelated. The sugar plantations, the sugar mills, the sugar railroads and ports, and the sugar boats were all links in a chain; so also were the large import houses, the foreign plants pumping goods into the Cuban market, the mines, the tourist industry, the banking business. And at the other end of the chain stood the giant foreign corporations—American imperialism.

It was the monopolies that geared the Cuban economy to sugar, dominated its resources, suffocated its industry with the goods they pumped in, and drained out its foreign exchange for luxuries.

The monopolies did not deliberately plot to strangle Cuba. They simply acted naturally. They made sure of the land and labor they needed, took control of mineral resources the way monopolies do everywhere, secured easy access into Cuba for their exports. They took control of resources and markets not only for their own use but to deny them to others. And just by being themselves, by taking normal advantage of their size and strength to promote their interests, the monopolies could not help but strangle the Cuban economy.

What could possibly be the result of competition for resources and markets between the giant corporations of the United States and the small economic units of Cuba? What sort of competition could Cuban workshops offer Westinghouse or General Motors? Just by selling goods in Cuba, the American giants were stunting the growth of Cuban industry.

It was inevitable that the monopolies would turn the Cuban economy into an appendage of the American economy. Their Cuban operations were only part of their total operations and their aim was profits—maximum profits on their operations as a whole. They were not interested in how their operations fitted into the Cuban economy, or how to develop that economy. They had to fit their Cuban operations into their total operations in the way that would make the most money.

What could the sugar companies be expected to do in Cuba other than what they did? Should they have produced a diversity of agricultural products for the Cuban market? They were in Cuba for a different purpose. They had positions of great value in the American sugar market, and to realize the most out of these positions, they needed control of a supply of sugar. The production of diversified products for the Cuban market was irrelevant to this need.

The corporations exporting to Cuba were also acting in accordance with business principles. Their job was to sell Cadillacs or whiskey, not to worry whether the importing country could put its foreign exchange to better uses than providing luxuries to a privileged foreign-oriented minority.

Decisions about investment in Cuba were also governed by the interests of the foreign corporations. Why put a plant in Cuba at all if the Cuban market could just as easily be supplied from the United States? And when a plant did get established in Cuba it was bound to be part of a broader complex. There were no good business reasons for setting up integrated, self-sufficient operations in Cuba. On the contrary, the plant which depended on foreign raw materials and spare parts was a safer risk against nationalization.

The very size and strength of the foreign corporations meant the loss for Cuba not only of her economic independence, but also of her political independence. Can there be any true independence for a poor country—especially a small one like Cuba—which has guests like United Fruit and Standard Oil?

Like the giant corporations, the U.S. government also acted naturally in Cuba. It pushed through reciprocal trade agreements so that American goods would have no difficulty entering Cuba. It promoted a monetary policy that permitted profits to be taken out with no trouble. It prevented Cuba from maintaining diplomatic relations with the socialist countries and pressured her into keeping trade with them at a minimum.

Throughout the years, the U.S. government promoted and defended American investment in Cuba, keeping a watchful eye on anything that might threaten that investment—attempts to limit the rights of foreign business, to increase tariffs or taxes, to lower electric power and telephone rates, to regulate the discharge of workers. The United States government used its influence to defeat Cuban legislation that was unfavorable to American business—or saw to it that if such legislation did happen to pass, it was not enforced. And it made sure of Cuban governments that were friendly to American business. What the United States government did in Cuba was no different from what it does in all countries to the extent that its strength permits.

Until 1934 the Platt Amendment, which had been forced into the Cuban constitution in 1901 by the United States, gave the United States the right to "intervene" in Cuba for "the maintenance of a government adequate for the protection of life, property, and individual liberty." There were many gross interventions. The United States landed troops in Cuba in 1906, 1912, and 1917.

In 1933, when the Cuban people began to move toward open revolt against

Machado, "the Butcher," the United States sent Sumner Welles as a special ambassador to try to save his regime. Welles tried; he felt at first that the removal of Machado would mean "chaos"—the destruction of American property. But when he saw that Machado could not be saved, Welles employed a maneuver often used by the United States when it finds that a dictator it has supported has outlived his usefulness; he organized a palace revolt, a movement among army leaders and conservative politicians to replace Machado with someone else satisfactory to Washington. The maneuver worked for a while. Machado was removed by an army *coup d'état* which placed a conservative approved by Welles in the Cuban Presidency. But within a few weeks the new regime was overthrown. A "radical" government headed by Grau San Martín came to power and began to institute reforms. Washington found this government unsatisfactory and denied it recognition while Welles and his successor worked to replace it. A number of American warships were sent into Cuban waters and units of the Marines were mobilized. Again American officials connived with the Cuban Army and within a few months Batista was installed in power.

But United States intervention in Cuba did not really depend on the Platt Amendment. The United States has engaged in countless armed interventions—in Santo Domingo, Mexico, Nicaragua, and throughout the world—without Platt Amendments. Also, there is more to intervention than shows up when it becomes necessary to resort to armed force. There is the ordinary day-to-day action of the U.S. government and its embassies abroad—the exertion of influence and pressure in a thousand ways on local newspapers, businessmen, legislatures, government officials, and army officers. The United States was constantly intervening in Cuba.

The U.S. government was unconcerned about what it meant for the Cuban people to live under a dictatorship. What the U.S. government wanted in Cuba was the "order," "tranquility," and "favorable investment climate" required by American business. Whenever these conditions could best be attained by dictatorship the United States supported dictatorship. In Cuba this meant supporting dictatorship most of the time. The U.S. government only turned against a dictator when it was necessary to do so because he could no longer hold on.

Many liberal writers have commented on the intimacy with Batista of United States Ambassadors Arthur Gardner and Earl E. T. Smith, as though this were an idiosyncrasy of these individual ambassadors. These writers seem unaware that there were communications, a steady flow of instructions and reports, between Washington and Havana. Washington's repudiation of dictators after they have fallen means nothing. Its real attitude comes out in a publication like *Investment in Cuba,* written for businessmen without much demagogy. During the 1940's, complains this volume, "the whole machinery of government was geared to favor labor. . . . The situation improved materially during the period 1953–1955. A more balanced emphasis in government policy brought the interests of labor, capital, and the public into better focus." [2] The "balanced emphasis" came when Batista took over for the second time in 1953; the fact that he came to power through a *coup d'état* and was a dictator was not considered relevant.

But Cuba's problems—its underdevelopment and poverty, its lack of inde-

[2] *Ibid.,* p. 21.

pendence—did not result from any policy or failure of policy. They resulted from the simple presence of the U.S. monopolies and the monopoly-dominated U.S. government engaged in their normal business. They resulted from imperialism. Imperialism is not a policy; it is a system.

To what extent could the ills of the Cuban economy have been cured through reforms? How far could a Cuban government go in curing the Cuban economy without coming into conflict with American imperialism?

What reforms? Would a wage increase for the sugar workers who were unemployed six to nine months a year have solved any basic problems? With such heavy unemployment, could a meaningful system of social insurance have been set up? Suppose it had been possible to carry out a tax reform. What would it have meant?

Take economic development. How far could Cuba have gone with the standard recipes? It already had an excellent "investment climate." "The main manufacturing opportunities," said *Investment in Cuba,* "await the development of new and improved applications for sugar-cane products. . . ." [3] But a few factories making paper or wax from cane would not constitute significant industrialization. Cuba's need for economic development could not be met by creating the type of development bank sponsored by the United States—a bank which can lend money only for nonindustrial projects, for projects outside the domain belonging to private enterprise.

Cuba needed land reform. But a true land reform is not a technical measure that can be accomplished to the satisfaction of everybody. A true land reform means taking the land away from the large estates and making it available to the people. A true land reform hurts; it changes the balance of political power; it begins a process of broader change. A true land reform is not a *reform;* it is a *revolutionary* measure.

Cuba could not afford artificial restrictions on its foreign market. Population was growing steadily. Unless the foreign market expanded, the Cuban economy would go backward. Cuba had to break the U.S. monopoly of its foreign trade.

Cuba needed full independence and sovereignty—not simply as a matter of justice and freedom, but also for practical economic reasons. The task of economic development is complicated enough for free countries; it cannot be accomplished by a country that is hamstrung by foreign domination.

Could the large foreign corporations in Cuba have been reformed? Could they have been prevented from acting according to business principles? Could they have been subjected to anything more than minor controls which would not have touched the heart of Cuba's problems?

What could a Cuban government have done to solve Cuba's problems without touching some American interest? It could not have regulated public utility rates, touched the land, broadened foreign trade, imposed foreign exchange controls, increased taxes, raised tariffs, subsidized new industry. It could not have changed the charter and policies of the National Bank and tried to use it to promote development; nor could it have greatly increased public expenditures for education or medical care—such actions would have endangered the kind of monetary stability required by the foreign corporations. It could not have promulgated and enforced laws against racial discrimination because this

[3] *Ibid.,* p. 8.

would have interfered with the tourist business. American interests were so omnipresent in Cuba that if a Cuban government were to try to make any significant reforms, it was bound to collide with one or another of these interests. And given the nature of the United States government, what could be expected from it in the event of a collision?

No matter where you start probing the Cuban economy, if you cut at all deep you will hit the core of the malignancy—American imperialism. Cuba had many problems. But its chief problem was the United States. The precondition for being able to make a serious attack on Cuba's specific problems was the elimination of imperialism. A true revolution in Cuba had to be a revolution against American imperialism.

18 THE PERMANENT JOB SHORTAGE*

by TOM CHRISTOFFEL

Can United States capitalism reduce its high level of unemployment? In the following selection Tom Christoffel argues not only that it cannot, but states that unemployment rates are much higher than ordinarily realized. There is, in fact, a massive permanent job shortage which capitalism cannot alleviate; from which, in fact, capitalism actually benefits, since it is primarily by means of such high unemployment that wages are kept down.

A basic tenet of modern-day liberalism holds that our most pressing social problems can be—and will best be—solved under the present system; or, in popular phraseology, reform rather than revolution. Racism, poverty, inequality and injustice can, slowly but surely, be eliminated. The road is long and hard, but it holds out great promise. Thus the Kerner Commission was following in the best tradition of liberalism when it told the nation:

> Only a commitment to national action on an unprecedented scale can shape a future compatible with the historic ideals of American society.
>
> The great productivity of our economy, and a federal revenue system which is highly responsive to economic growth, can provide the resources.
>
> The major need is to generate new will—the will to tax ourselves to the extent necessary to meet the vital needs of the nation.

This statement makes an important assumption—a very important one. It assumes that, given the will to attack social ills, our economy can provide the necessary resources. Yet, at best, this is a questionable assumption. As the Kerner Commission itself emphasized, the main source of social ill in the United States—from which so many other problems flow—is the lack of full or adequate employment. If full employment could be attained, with no inflation and with adequate economic growth, then it would be possible to solve other problems—at least to the point of muffling discontent. Clearly the commission and other liberals are right in seeing job improvement as the number-one item on the liberal agenda. The question is whether they are right in thinking that U.S. capitalism can provide sufficient jobs. This chapter will argue that they are not—that U.S. capitalism cannot solve its unemployment dilemma.

* Used by permission of the author.
Particular thanks are owed to Gal Alperovitz and Bill Tabb for their help on this essay.

I

Since 1929 the overall unemployment rate in the United States has dropped below 4 percent only during time of war, except for the years 1946–48 when it stood at 3.8–3.9 percent. During the nonwar years of the past two decades the unemployment rate varied from a low of 4.1 percent to a high of 6.8 percent. Yet these figures represent only a part of the picture. They are calculated from the number of persons estimated to be out of work at the time of the week or month when the Federal government takes its sample. Because the rate is not a continuous measure of unemployment and because it uses a quite narrow definition of unemployment, it underestimates severely. A much more meaningful rate would measure the percentage of workers forced into nonearning idleness for some significant part of each year. Thus economist Robert J. Lampman finds that "in a typical year [during the period from 1947 through 1964] about 15 percent of the labor force experienced some involuntary unemployment." [1]

How does one arrive at such a figure? The government, of course, does not provide adequate information on the employment crisis. Various factors must be pieced together, with the Census Bureau figure as a poor starting point. But as journalist Hobart Rowen explains:

> The problem is more pervasive. There are different groups of persons employed and unemployed at different times—and some of the jobless have two or three periods of unemployment during the year. According to the Department of Labor, in recent years nearly one in every five persons in the labor force has been out of work for some significant period of time during the calendar year. The actual figure for 1962, for example, was 15,256,000 persons, or 18.2 percent of the labor force.
>
> The breakdown for 1962 was as follows:

Total working or looking for work	83,944,000
Total with unemployment	15,256,000
Did not work, but looked for work	1,887,000
Year-round workers with 1 to 2 weeks' unemployment	1,129,000
Part-time workers with some unemployment	12,240,000
—1 to 4 weeks	2,993,000
—5 to 10 weeks	2,759,000
—11 to 14 weeks	1,700,000
—15 to 26 weeks	2,768,000
—27 weeks or more	2,020,000
Total with two spells or more of unemployment	5,219,000
—2 spells	2,524,000
—3 spells or more	2,695,000

> What becomes clear from this table is that the well-publicized monthly reports on unemployment represent *different* groups of people who are out of work. Thus, in contrast to the 1 to 1.5 million generally listed by the Labor

[1] Lampman, "Recent U.S. Economic Growth and the Gain in Human Welfare," in Walter W. Heller, ed., *Perspectives on Economic Growth,* New York, Random House, 1968, p. 145.

> Department as the "long-term unemployed"—those who have been idle for 15 weeks or longer—the true hard core is much bigger.[2]

The reason that the standard overall unemployment figure is so poor a benchmark is rather complex. First, as Rowen clarifies, unemployment is not static. For example, the University of Michigan's Survey Research Center reported that in June 1961, 14.5 percent of the families in a nation-wide survey had some member of the family unemployed for a period of time during the preceding year. Of the families that experienced some unemployment, 28 percent of the household *heads* had been unemployed two or more times during the year. Also, of the unemployed, 54 percent experienced more than 15 weeks of unemployment.[3]

Second, the inability to find a job often results in the unemployed person dropping out of the labor force completely—or, with teenagers, not entering it in the first place—so that many unemployed are not counted. (The Federal government presently counts as unemployed only those persons who had "engaged in some specific job seeking activity within the past 4 weeks"—i.e., prior to the survey week.) Moreover, an individual desirous of full-time work but able only to find a part-time job does not show up in the statistics. Using *only* this aspect of undercounting the United States Senate's Subcommittee on Employment and Manpower, using data compiled by Charles Killingsworth, reported in 1964 estimates of a "real" unemployment rate of between 7 and 9 percent of the potential labor force. The so-called "nonparticipation" rate is increasing over time as more and more people are forced to give up trying to find employment. Ben Seligman reports:

> The proportion of nonparticipants in the labor force—those who have given up looking for work—*among men in their prime years* increased from 4.7 percent in 1953 to 5.2 percent in 1963. For Negroes the nonparticipation rate leaped from 5.3 percent to 8.2 percent over the same period. Indeed, if adjustments were made for nonparticipation, requiring some shift in statistical definitions, the unemployment rates would be a good deal higher than the Federal figures show. When California officials made such adjustments for both part-time employment and nonparticipation in the work force, they came up with an unemployment rate for the state more than twice the figure issued by Washington.[4]

Along with the nonparticipation rate it must also be remembered that for the decades of the Cold War from 3.5 to 4.5 percent of the potential labor force has been removed from job competition by the military draft.

Any realistic picture of the unemployment situation would also have to include part-time workers unsuccessfully seeking full-time work as well as those persons who are employed in dead-end, low paying jobs—for in terms of income and identification such individuals are virtually unemployed. Such a calculation cannot be made with any real precision, but according to the Kerner Commission, "Today there are . . . about ten million underemployed,

[2] Rowen, *The Free Enterprisers,* New York, Putnam, 1964, pp. 268–269.

[3] Mueller and Schmiedeskamp, *Persistent Unemployment, 1957–1961,* Kalamazoo, 1962, p. 6; as cited in William Haber, *et al., The Impact of Technological Change,* Kalamazoo, 1963, pp. 10–11.

[4] Ben B. Seligman, *Most Notorious Victory,* New York, Free Press, 1966, p. 214.

6.5 million of whom work full time and earn less than the annual poverty wage."[5] This ten-million figure, which does not include the unemployed, makes up almost 13 percent of the nation's labor force.

Perhaps the most persuasive testimony as to the inadequacy of standard unemployment statistics comes from the U.S. Department of Labor itself:

> Over 11 million American workers were jobless and looking for work at some time during the prosperous year 1966. This was almost four times the average number (2.9 million) unemployed in any one week of the year. The total number out of work during 1967 was probably somewhat higher. . . . About four times as many workers had 5 or more weeks without work during 1966 as is suggested by the monthly data. For the number out of work 15 to 26 weeks, the corresponding ratio was almost 5½ to 1. Any complacency as to the limited impact of extended unemployment among men in the central age groups, who are generally the most employable and have the heaviest family responsibilities, should be ended by these data. Close to 1.3 million men aged 25 to 44 had 5 or more weeks of unemployment during 1966, almost six times the number (226,000) shown by the monthly surveys. . . . Clearly, the number of men of prime working age who are severely affected by joblessness is much higher than is indicated by the monthly unemployment data. And, to a lesser degree, the same is true for women.[6]

II

The simple facts of history indicate that, barring war, capitalism does not provide for full employment. Even with all the fiscal and monetary tools available—deficit spending, adjustment of the tax rate, credit adjustment via the rediscount rate, etc.—the level of unemployment cannot be significantly lowered without resulting in an unacceptable rate of inflation. The direct correlation between employment and inflation is such that we find Nixon's economic advisers urging a higher—6 percent—unemployment rate on him in order to slow down inflation. The uniformity and directness of the unemployment-inflation trade-off is quite dramatic. If one were to graph this relationship, with changes in the price level plotted on the vertical axis and the unemployment rate increasing horizontally along the bottom axis and with dots representing the intersection of those two rates for each of the last thirty years (for any capitalist country), the points would produce a smooth, outwardly concave curve, holding very close to both axes.[7]

To better understand the unemployment-inflation relationship one can visualize the capitalist economy as a giant steam kettle, constantly in danger of blowing up from too much pressure of inflation. One way to alleviate this danger is to expand the size of the kettle by increasing aggregate demand. Another way is to condense and drain off some of the steam in the form of increased unemployment.

[5] New York, Bantam, p. 414.

[6] *Manpower Report of the President, including Report on Manpower Requirements, Resources, Utilization and Training by the U.S. Department of Labor,* 1968, p. 18.

[7] The reader should consult, for example, Paul Samuelson, *Economics,* 7th ed., New York, McGraw-Hill, 1967, pp. 333–334, Cambell R. McConnell, *Economics,* 4th ed., New York, McGraw-Hill, 1969, pp. 392–393, for an actual representation of the *Phillips Curve.*

As more men and women are thrown out of work the economy as a whole is "cooled" down. The cause-effect relationship is of course complex, but most important are two facts. First, with increased employment, firms begin competing for skilled workers, driving wages up. Conversely, as the rate of unemployment increases, it becomes more difficult for the workers to win livable wages. Thus, *as a trend,* increasing employment is troublesome for the capitalist. Second, at times of increasing unemployment, total wages paid out increase slowly or not at all, so that consumption begins to slow down. This in turn leads to reduced production and even less employment and slowly reverses the inflationary situation. Thus, *as a mechanism,* reduced employment can help the capitalist control inflation.

One seemingly obvious solution to this problem would be to increase output —i.e., speed up the economic growth rate and expand the productive capacity. Increasing the output of goods and services would normally be expected to produce inflation, but many liberal economists claim that this would not be the case if savings were diverted to a greater extent into long-term investment, i.e., if spending and demand is deferred. This result, it is argued, will come about because increased growth will be manifested in efforts to increase the capacity and efficiency of the productive economy—in efforts such as research and development, job training and education. In the long run this would increase the economy's ability to produce, thus giving the desired result of increased employment without inflation.

Aside from the fact that there is no guarantee that oligopolistic control would not be used to restrict the results of increased capacity and thereby produce price increases anyway, an even larger objection to the growth theory exists in simple economic history. The economic growth rate has rarely approached the levels needed to have the desired effect. Most economists agree that a yearly growth rate of 4 or 5 percent would be needed to even begin making a dent in the unemployment problem. Such a rate has been achieved during wartime—as during the early Cold War-Korean War period, 1947–53, and after troop escalation began in Vietnam—but otherwise, the rate has averaged below 3 percent. Overall, the annual gain in gross national product between 1909 and 1960 averaged 2.9 percent.[8]

Attempts to boost this rate through government spending also result in unbearably high degrees of inflation. Even as respectfully liberal an economist as John Kenneth Galbraith has admitted that "I once considered it possible that by adequate compensation, a volume of unemployment consistent with stable prices could be made socially and politically tolerable. Cf. *The Affluent Society,* pp. 298–307. This I now doubt." [9]

A second flaw in this growth vision is the fact that Federal expenditures needed to bolster aggregate demand cannot be of the WPA variety—i.e., schools, housing, the poor, etc. Rather, as Galbraith himself has written, "Substitute spending would need to have somewhat of the same relation to technology as the military spending it replaces." [10] This point is very important, for the number-one dream of American liberals has long been substitute spending (i.e., "Once the Vietnam—or Cold War is over we can transfer billions

[8] Bernard Nossiter, *The Mythmakers,* Boston, Beacon, 1964, pp. 158–159.
[9] *The New Industrial State,* Boston, Houghton Mifflin, 1967, p. 259.
[10] *Ibid.,* p. 231.

from military to social spending!" or "We shouldn't spend any more tax dollars on conquering space until we have first conquered poverty!"). The reason that such thinking is chimerical is somewhat complex, although in practice the results are quite apparent.

Basically, as Galbraith says, government expenditures for goods and services must have somewhat of the same relation to technology as military—and space spending. These latter types of expenditures are made on inflated cost-plus bases and are justified by the almost mystical expertise required by the "new technology." The economics of building a house or a school, on the other hand, are quite straightforward; construction costs are fairly standardized, competitive and generally familiar. Thus, in short, General Dynamics, General Electric, AT&T, etc., can't start building houses because (1) the Federal government could not justify paying them for such activity at rates well above going construction costs and therefore (2) these companies would be unable to sustain their present profit levels in such endeavors. Given these facts, and given the power of these—the nation's largest—corporations, government spending will *not* be transferred to technologically different—and smaller—areas of the nation's economy.[11]

Seymour Harris, one of the leading economic admirers and advisors of the Kennedy Administration, writes:

> But in the last twenty years or so, recourse to increased public spending as a means of stabilizing the economy and increasing the rate of growth has become less fashionable. For example, in the 1964 Budget of President Kennedy, the stress is not on increasing non-military spending but on reducing taxes as a means of stimulating the economy. In fact the rise in the 1964 Budget can be explained by the increased expenditures for military and space programs. When one considers that annual average increase in wages is about 3 per cent; in population, 2 per cent; and in prices, 1.5 per cent; it might be expected on the average that the total budget would rise by about 4 per cent in the year without any new programs or extensions of old programs. Therefore, when the President announces that he has increased the budget by roughly the amount of spending on space and defense, he has in fact reduced his real expenditures on welfare and other non-military purposes.[12]

Thus during the Kennedy Administration—a liberal administration—the response to a stagnant economy was "reactionary Keynesianism"—a tax cut unaccompanied by expenditure increases (Medicare standing as the *only* new government responsibility undertaken during the Kennedy era).

Such a situation is, of course, not the fault of Kennedy or of the conservatives in his Congress, but rather a basic contradiction of the capitalist system of organization. Thus the economic history of this country has not been one of slow but steady improvement of the employment and income situation—as liberals like to think—but simply the swinging back and forth of the unemployment-inflation pendulum. And throughout the Cold War this has hap-

[11] This logic does not apply to the "administration" of welfare programs, a boondoggle area that—because of their administrative and systems expertise—many of the large military contractors are moving into. Of course, just as at present, very little of the welfare monies involved manage to trickle down to the poor.

[12] Harris, "U.S. Welfare Programs and Policies," in Edgar O. Edwards, *The Nation's Economic Objectives,* Chicago, University of Chicago Press, 1964, p. 131.

pened, with 3.5–4.5 percent of the potential labor force kept off the unemployment rolls by the simple expedient of being "employed" in the military. Were it not for the Cold War, in all its facets, American capitalism would be unable to avoid unemployment of tremendous proportions.[13]

III

A situation with close to 15 percent of the labor force unemployed during the year and almost an equal percentage of families affected by inadequate employment is of course a highly volatile situation. For if people perceive that their problem is not a personal one but has its roots in the workings of the social and economic system, they are likely to fight back against that system. The prospect of rebellion by unemployed and poorly employed workers is not a happy one for the capitalists. Nor is it a safe one. Somehow the ruling class must get the bulk of the working class to accept such a situation. They do this in many ways, using anti-communism, racism, anti-intellectualism, anti-scientism, liberalism, national chauvinism and male chauvinism. Especially important within this ideological arsenal is racism.

Racism serves capitalism in many ways. Although, overall, many more whites than nonwhites are unemployed, by especially concentrating unemployment among black and brown people it eases somewhat the direct pressure of unemployment on white workers and, to a more important extent, serves as a psychological balm to white workers who see another group of workers even worse off than themselves. Moreover, by dividing white workers from black and brown workers, racism not only destroys the unity required if the working class is to effectively fight against capitalism, but goes beyond this to the point of getting workers to fight each other. Thus chronic unemployment, instead of being viewed as an intrinsic part of an economic system based on the overall exploitation of workers by capitalists, is viewed by workers as the threat presented by other workers of a different color.

The effect of racism on unemployment is easily seen in the heavy concentration of unemployment—and poor employment—among nonwhite workers. Today, as Rashi Fein has pointed out, the black American faces an unemployment rate unknown to the white American except during the depth of the Great Depression. LBJ's own Kerner Commission found that at least a third of all ghetto residents in big cities either are unemployed or work only part time, seasonally or in grossly underpaid jobs. And they found, for example, that urban black teenagers collectively faced a 26.5 percent unemployment rate

[13] Eleanor G. Gilpatrick's *Structural Unemployment and Aggregate Demand,* Baltimore, 1966, is notable in that the author tries to find a new way out of capitalism's unemployment dilemma. "The demand theorists," she explains, "have been identified with the position that unemployment can be reduced to about 4 percent through aggregate fiscal means without affecting over-all prices. At the other pole the structuralists have been associated with the claim that inflationary pressure would appear before 4 percent is reached. A third position is presented here, namely that simultaneous treatment of structural and demand problems could make possible an unemployment rate as low as 2.9 percent (achieved in 1953) without inflation." (p. 203) The argument Gilpatrick presents, however, is not particularly convincing, especially when she reveals: "Thus the best means of reducing unemployment might be wage increases, not decreases." (p. 210) A nice suggestion, but somewhat at odds with the basic principles of capitalism and not likely to be followed by those controlling the nation's wealth and power.

(compared with 10.6 percent for white teenagers), with the rate at times over 50 percent in some ghetto areas.

Since World War II the black unemployment rate has—according to official figures—maintained a two-to-one ratio with the overall unemployment rate. And for urban ghetto areas the rate is about 10 percent, or approximately three times the average for the rest of the country.[14] Moreover, the duration of unemployment is longer for black workers. In 1964, for example, nonwhites represented 11 percent of the labor force but they accounted for 23 percent of those unemployed for over half a year.[15]

When one looks beyond the "officially" unemployed, the situation is equally bad for black and brown people. The Department of Labor estimated in late 1966 that the "subemployment rate" (i.e., unemployed workers, part-time workers looking for full-time work, full-time workers earning less than $3000 per year or dropouts from the labor force) in ten ghetto areas surveyed averaged 33.9 percent.[16] And, presumedly, the situation for black and brown people in rural areas is even worse.

"Even more important perhaps than unemployment," reports the Kerner Commission, "is the related problem of the undesirable nature of many jobs open to Negroes. . . . In the riot cities which we surveyed, Negroes were three times as likely as whites to hold unskilled jobs, which are often part time, seasonal, low-paying, and 'dead-end'—a fact that creates a problem for Negroes as significant as unemployment." The commission explained that "Negro workers are concentrated in the lowest-skilled and lowest-paying occupations. These jobs often involve substandard wages, great instability and uncertainty of tenure, extremely low status in the eyes of both employer and employee, little or no chance for meaningful advancement, and unpleasant or exhausting duties." [17]

Finally, as with unemployment and underemployment in general, automation has hit the black and brown man and woman with much greater severity than it has hit white men and women. In a paper on "Technology and the Negro" prepared for the National Commission on Technology, Automation, and Economic Progress, M. T. Puryear of the National Urban League explains:

> At this time we don't have adequate statistical data concerning the impact of automation on the employment structure generally, nor on the Negro labor force in particular. However, we do know that automation and related technological change tend to create the greatest displacements in these occupational classifications where the bulk of the Negro labor force is concentrated. Furthermore, when we place automation in its proper context within the total employment structure and examine the status of the Negro worker within that structure, the information is ample to make a crystal clear picture—and dismal it is. Job opportunities for the Negro worker have traditionally been, and are

[14] U.S. Department of Labor, "A Sharper Look at Unemployment in U.S. Cities and Slums—Summary Report," 1967; Charles Killingsworth argues that the overall black-white ratio is really three-to-one. See his paper presented to the Princeton Manpower Symposium, printed in William Bowen and Frederick Harbison, *Unemployment in a Prosperous Economy,* Princeton, Princeton University Press, 1965, p. 89.

[15] Rashi Fein, "An Economic and Social Profile of the Negro American," in Parsons and Clark, *The Negro American,* Boston, Beacon, 1966, pp. 827–828.

[16] U.S. Department of Labor, *op. cit.*

[17] *Op. cit.,* pp. 253–255.

> now, severely restricted. Predictions for the immediate and long-range future indicate that the plight of the Negro worker is very likely to get worse instead of better unless drastic countermeasures are instituted now to offset current trends. This is no wild-eyed alarm stemming from irresponsible visionaries. It is plain, honest, though unpleasant fact, supported by nationwide figures from the U.S. Employment Service and by regional estimates from local Urban League affiliates.[18]

With inflation, speed-up and other methods of further exploiting working people, the plight of the average worker cannot be said to be getting ever better and better.[19] While hurting all workers, this situation particularly hurts black and brown workers, because of their position in the job hierarchy. The Kerner Commission reported that "although it is growing, Negro family income is not keeping pace with white family income growth. In constant 1965 dollars, median nonwhite income in 1947 was $2174 lower than median white income. By 1966, the gap had grown to $3036." [20] Herman P. Miller, of the Bureau of the Census, comes to the same conclusion in his book *Rich Man, Poor Man.* "The income gap between whites and nonwhites did narrow during World War II," says Dr. Miller. "During the last decade, however, it shows some evidence of having widened again. The census statistics demonstrate this dismaying fact." [21] And Rashi Fein reports that "in spite of the considerable out-migration during the 1950's of Negroes from the South to higher income regions . . . the ratio of Negro to white income for males fell during the period of 1949 to 1959 in every region of the country." [22] Finally, Smooth Society director Sargent Shriver dramatizes the situation by pointing out that "while the Negro was earning $1 in 1949, his white counterpart earned $1.90; in 1959 every time the Negro earned $1.75 the white man earned $3.20." [23]

IV

And what about the near future? The National Commission on Technology, Automation, and Economic Progress concluded that over the next decade

> The number of unskilled jobs will not decline, though unskilled jobs will continue to as a proportion of all jobs. Growth patterns in both the economy and the labor force provide an important warning: Unless Negroes and, to a lesser degree, youth, are able to penetrate growing occupations and industries at a

[18] From Federal Role in Urban Affairs hearings, Exhibit 46, pp. 528–531.

[19] The April 1964 *Survey of Current Business* reported that the poorest one fifth of the population received 4.9 percent of the total income in 1944, compared with 4.6 percent in 1963. And Robert J. Lampman reports in Heller, *op. cit.,* p. 154, that "In my own study, I found that the top 2 percent of wealth-holders held 29 percent of all wealth in 1949; this had risen to 30 percent by 1956. This trend was confirmed by the University of Michigan Survey of Consumer Finances which found that the top decile of wealth-holders had 58 percent of net worth in 1953, 61 percent in 1962. The lowest fifth of income receivers had 11 percent of net worth in 1953, 7 percent in 1962."

[20] *Op. cit.,* p. 251.

[21] New York, Signet, p. 41.

[22] *Op. cit.,* p. 835.

[23] See Robert Will and Harold Vatter, *Poverty in Affluence,* New York, Harcourt, Brace & World, p. 157.

> more rapid rate than in the past, their high unemployment rate will continue or even rise.[24]

Why should this government commission, or more notably, the Kerner Commission, be so concerned with the plight of "Negroes and, to a lesser extent, youth"? After all, the Federal government serves as the faithful arm of the capitalist ruling class, and if concentrating unemployment among black and brown people helps the capitalists keep the lid on, should not government commissions be expected to excuse away, rather than crusade against, this phenomena? The answer is seen in a complication growing out of the use of racism to handle unemployment difficulties: black and brown people are rebelling.

By the early 1960's the United States had reached the point where over 46 percent of the nearly five million workers who were unemployed for a minimum period of fifteen weeks were black.[25] And liberal solutions have become more and more clearly illusory. For example, the theory that small spurts in overall aggregate demand will positively affect the hard-core unemployment problem proved hollow when the 1963 tax reform resulted in a widened, rather than narrowed, black-white unemployment differential.[26] The reaction to this situation has not been passive. It is to be expected that those people who are most exploited will be the first to fight back against that exploitation. And in doing so they become a big danger to the capitalist. It is not so much the economic cost of the rebellion-caused damage—although that is a not insignificant factor—but rather the fact that ghetto rebellions produce a new clarity in the class consciousness of black working people and, as a result of such consciousness, a growing tendency toward political organization. Such a situation is, of course, completely unacceptable to the capitalist class. To have within the society a large mass of people organized politically to fight actively against their own exploitation cannot long be tolerated. Nor can it be so simply repressed. It is a tremendous problem for the capitalists—and it is a problem that can only intensify. For the job market, as shall be shown, is expanding at a much, much slower rate than is the labor force, and thus the basic contradiction—men without jobs and capitalism unable to provide them—is accentuated.

The situation, almost ironically, stems in large part from increases in productivity. The National Commission on Technology. Automation, and Economic Progress found that from 1909 to 1947 the annual growth rate of output per man-hour in the private economy was 2 percent per year; from 1947 to 1965 it was 3.2 percent per year.[27] The result, as reported by William Appleman Williams, is that

> American capitalism is simply not creating enough jobs. . . . Nothing really dramatized the extent to which American capitalism relies and depends upon the taxpayer as effectively as the fact that *government created more than half the new jobs that appeared between 1960 and 1963*. Private enterprise provided 76 percent of the job growth between 1947 and 1957, but since then the government has supplied 64 percent of new employment.

[24] *Technology and the American Economy,* Report of the National Commission on Technology, Automation, and Economic Progress, February 1966.

[25] Rowen, *op. cit.,* p. 269.

[26] See Killingsworth, in Bowen and Harbison, *op. cit.*

[27] *Op. cit.,* p. 53.

> There has been a 20 percent drop in unskilled jobs between 1950 and 1960. Unemployment among such men and women, which had dropped from 30 percent in 1940 to 12 percent in 1950, had by 1961 begun moving back (passing 20 percent) toward the depression figures. The same cycle appeared in the semi-skilled sectors of the labor market. In 1940, for example, 13 percent of the semi-skilled workers were unemployed, whereas only 6 percent were out of work in 1950; but the total was back to 12 percent in 1961. The statistics for unemployed skilled workers were 15, 6, and 10 percent for the same years.[28]

The problem Williams outlines results from a system's inability to deal with its technological input; specifically, with capitalism's inability to make rational use of more efficient—rather than more intensive—human labor power. As Williams points out, "between 1952 and 1961, when production went up jobs went down by 5.8 percent." [29] Unemployment among clerical workers rose from 2.8 percent in January 1957 to 4.6 percent in January 1962.[30] The Bureau of Labor Statistics' data revealed that clerical employment increased by only 0.6 percent in 1962–63, as compared with a 2 percent increase the year before and almost 4 percent the year before that.[31] Unskilled labor, which accounted for 20 percent of all jobs in the 1930's, now accounts for only 5 percent.[32] From 1957 to 1961 there was a net loss of 1.1 million production jobs in manufacturing, while output increased by 8 percent and output per man-hour by 18 percent.[33] By the end of 1962 the Buick plant in Flint, Michigan, was employing only half the number of workers to produce the same number of cars as it had manufactured approximately five years earlier.[34] Fourteen people controlling fourteen machines can produce 90 percent of all the light bulbs used in the United States.[35] Seymour L. Wolfbein, speaking as director of the Labor Department Manpower Office before the Senate Select Committee on Small Business in 1963, estimated that between 1960 and 1970, 22 million jobs would be "affected" by automation and technological change.[36] And the Council of Economic Advisors estimated in 1963 that automation destroys 28,000 jobs *a week*.[37] The old belief that automation would produce more jobs than it destroyed—carriage maker to automobile worker—has proven to be a myth.

Businessmen themselves no longer seriously sing employment praise of automation. When asked in a 1965 Manpower Research Council survey whether they believed automation would increase the nation's supply of jobs during the next five years, over half the business respondents replied negatively. And only 29 percent of the respondents foresaw automation increasing jobs in their own branches of industry—only 22 percent for their own companies' production areas.[38]

[28] *The Great Evasion,* Chicago, Quadrangle, 1964, pp. 84–85. (Emphasis added.)
[29] *Ibid.,* p. 95.
[30] *Ibid.,* p. 93.
[31] Seligman, *op. cit.,* p. 192.
[32] Rowen, *op. cit.,* p. 270.
[33] Seligman, *op. cit.,* p. 209.
[34] Williams, *op. cit.,* p. 96.
[35] *Ibid.,* p. 96.
[36] Rowen, *op. cit.,* p. 264.
[37] Seligman, *op. cit.,* p. 356.
[38] *Automation: Research Report No. 2,* as cited in Seligman, *op. cit.,* pp. 385–386.

During the decade of the 1960's it has been necessary to create about 3.3 million new jobs each year merely to hold the jobless at their present level.[39] So far the demands of the Vietnam War have saved capitalism from being swamped by this tidal wave of job demand. The National Commission on Technology, Automation, and Economic Progress found that "the output of the economy, and the aggregate demand to buy it, must grow in excess of 4 percent a year just to prevent the unemployment rate from rising, and even faster if the unemployment rate is to fall further, as we believe it should. Yet our economy has seldom, if ever, grown at a rate faster than 3.5 percent for any extended length of time." [40] Or as Leonard Lecht has calculated, "If GNP were to grow, as in the 1950's at about 3 percent a year, unemployment by 1975 would be expected to reach 10 percent of the labor force or more." [41] Ben Seligman states that "By 1970 the labor force is expected to reach some eighty-five million workers; yet the rate of increase in jobs promises to leave nine or ten million of them without work—an unemployment rate of 11 or 12 percent—unless the war effort can absorb them." [42] And *Business Week* (July 26, 1969) reports that

> manufacturing employment rose by only 3.5-million jobs between 1961 and 1968—2.5-million of them since 1965—despite accelerating production for the Vietnam War and widespread prosperity. Many unionists suspect the Vietnam War is masking an actual loss of jobs in non-defense industries, in part from growing imports. They fear unemployment problems when peace removes the mask.

And after the war, most signs point to a continuation of the "upward drift" of unemployment—the fact that each recovery from the last three recessions has left an even higher unemployment level.

The job burden, as indicated earlier, has fallen almost entirely on the public sector of the economy, with state and local governments providing most of the new jobs of recent years, largely in the school systems. Ben Seligman reports:

> Most of the new jobs prior to the Asian affair were supplied by government—federal, state, and local—and for the 1953–1963 decade, it is more than likely that *private profit-making industries contributed to unemployment rather than to employment.* During these ten years the civilian labor force increased by 8.9 million; employment by 6.6 million [of which 3.2 million were part-time]; unemployment by 2.3 million.[43]

V

More people to be employed, not enough jobs to employ them in, and rebellion by those formerly used to absorb this problem. How can the capitalist ruling class alleviate this situation before it endangers them even further? Let us consider several possibilities.

[39] Nossiter, *op. cit.,* p. 159.
[40] *Op. cit.,* p. 15.
[41] Lecht, *Goals, Priorities, and Dollars,* New York, Free Press, 1966, p. 309.
[42] Seligman, *op. cit.,* p. 212.
[43] *Op. cit.,* p. 210.

Full-Scale Repression of Black and Brown People

Repressive techniques are only employed as a last resort, since they have many counterproductive aspects. When the oppression of capitalism becomes blatantly open, even if for only one segment of the working class, it becomes harder for the ruling class to maintain myths and false consciousness among the working class as a whole. Since ideological controls are more efficient and less disruptive than open repression, they are to be preferred. (See the Blackburn selection, Part II.) In a sense, open repression is a point of no return; it destroys all illusions, making physical rather than mental controls primary, and necessitates the actual smashing of the repressed group by the repressor. American capitalism is always ready to use repression if need be, but to do so on a large scale is at best dangerous and at worst an act of desperation.

Job Training and Education

The structuralist explanation for unemployment—that the unemployed simply lack the skills needed by an advancing technology—should be obviously unsatisfactory. Certainly there are some job vacancies unfilled because of the lack of properly trained personnel. This irrational use of manpower is, in fact, a situation the capitalists are quite interested in eliminating. Ergo the array of much publicized job training programs. But *in terms of overall numbers* of unemployed, these "pockets" of unemployment do not provide the key to the permanent job shortage.

From the capitalists' perspective it is more rational for the pool of unemployed workers to be unskilled men and women (as, in the main, they are), since this allows for greater flexibility in hiring and firing. It is therefore sensible to fill in "pockets" of *skilled* job vacancies and lump unemployment at the bottom of the labor hierarchy. But such efforts to rationalize this aspect of the work force will not significantly affect the overall unemployment rates. Nor, in fact, have these efforts been as extensive as the hoopla surrounding them has made them seem. According to Alfred Friendly, in a *Washington Post* study of the Office of Economic Opportunity in 1966, the Job Corps and individual projects in the Community Action Program "will touch only from 3 to 10 percent of their particular 'universe of need.' " [44] In mid-1967, fewer than 300,000 persons were being trained or employed under the various Federally supported manpower programs.[45] Job placement by such programs was also very poor, at times with only half the trainees successfully placed.[46] When job training is undertaken, its real purpose is often more than that which first meets the eye, as with a Federally funded 1968 program to train black women from Boston's Roxbury section as telephone operators—begun in the face of a threatened telephone strike. Most of the women, being on welfare, found it hard to refuse either training or scab jobs.

[44] *Washington Post,* February 12, 1966, p. A17.

[45] Sar Levitan, *Alternative Approaches to Manpower Policy,* U.S. Chamber of Commerce, p. 2.

[46] See Steve Kurzman report to the Senate Subcommittee on Employment, Manpower, and Poverty, 1967, pp. 156, 176.

All in all, job training and education as a solution to the job shortage—i.e., as a solution which would significantly affect the overall employment rate—seems spurious.

Increasing the Rate of Economic Growth

As has been seen above, expanding the size of the economy is the only real answer to the inflation-unemployment dilemma; but, also, American capitalism has shown—over the last sixty years—that it is incapable of growing at anywhere near the rate necessary to provide for lower unemployment.

Subsidizing a Permanent Pool of Unemployed Workers

To a certain extent this is what is happening at present, but clearly there is a limit to the number—or percentage—of the potential work force that can be so subsidized. As the ultimate source of all surplus, the working class itself must provide such subsidies. This is actually handled directly through the tax mechanism. (See the Kolko selection, Part II.) Thus the percentage of its own numbers that the working class can subsidize in unemployment—while this very unemployment helps to keep wages down—is self-limiting. Moreover, the subsidies provided are a bare minimum for the continuation of life and, therefore, no means by which the ruling class can ultimately buy off discontent. As Brian Glick has shown (see selection on the guaranteed annual income, Part IV), even with the current levels of unemployment it would be impossible for capitalism to provide all persons within the economy with a modest, but adequate income.

Spread Unemployment More Evenly Among All Sections of the Working Class

Since the immediate problem for the capitalists is the active rebellion of the highly unemployed black and brown sections of the working class, a more even distribution of unemployment may seem to be the best bet. Actually this is not the case, for different reasons in the short run and in the long run. In the short run, such a solution is made impossible by the very racist mechanisms that capitalism has so long been relying on. This is seen most clearly in the trade unions, where the leadership so congenial to capitalism in general uses its "protect your own," nonclass approach to keep black and brown people out of the labor market. "By the time of the AFL-CIO merger," writes Sumner Rosen, "the CIO had largely abandoned any vigorous commitment to an improvement in the position of Negroes through direct union action, either in collective bargaining or by internal reform." [47]

Three unions (the Packinghouse Workers, the United Mine Workers and the United Auto Workers) have maintained something of a nondiscrimination record. But the same cannot be said of any other major union. Herbert Hill reports that U.S. Census Bureau data indicate that in the construction industry—which is an expanding industry—there were exactly 2190 black apprentices in

[47] Rosen, "The CIO Era, 1935–1955," in Julius Jacobson, ed., *The Negro and the American Labor Movement,* Garden City, N.Y., Anchor, 1968, p. 190.

1950 and 2191 in 1960. A gain of one in ten years.[48] Elsewhere, Hill has thoroughly documented organized labor leadership's efforts to exclude black and brown workers from available jobs, including the particularly gruesome record of the liberal ILGWU, which has succeeded in forcing the closing of OEO job training programs aimed at preparing black and brown jobless for work in the garment industry.[49]

Liberals have sought to attack this aspect of "structural" unemployment by writing antidiscriminatory labor clauses into civil rights legislation and into Federal contracts. But as Hill has revealed, "The history of federal power in relation to enforcing the legal prohibitions against racial discrimination in employment is a tragic example of the politics of nullification. Today a Negro worker seeking employment may be protected by as many as six anti-discrimination laws and Executive Orders, none of which is effectively enforced."

The situation, of course, is one in which the various mechanisms and agencies developed by the ruling class to handle its problems are not susceptible to immediate change. Thus while more sophisticated capitalists, as represented by the Kerner Commission, may realize that more jobs for black and brown people may be a tactical necessity for capitalism at present, the politicians, sell-out trade unionists, and general racist attitudes fostered by capitalism suddenly come home to roost. Such things are not like a spigot that can be continually turned on and off at will.

Of course in the long run capitalism could bend these agents and attitudes to their ends, but they are actually not interested in such a *long-run* goal. Black rebellion is an immediate problem for them; in the long run, eliminating this immediate problem would leave them with the very problem sought to be avoided in the first place—a general uprising by the entire working class. To ease the concentration of unemployment among black and brown workers can only be carried out if it can then be reconcentrated in some other subgrouping of the working class—rather than evenly spread around.

Male Chauvinism

An obvious direction for the capitalists to move from this seeming dilemma is to rely more and more heavily on *male chauvinism—using women as the buffer component in the labor force*. In general, women are more highly exploited than men under capitalism in three distinct ways: First, they are paid less than men for equivalent work as well as being concentrated into the worst jobs. Second, they are a source of unpaid domestic labor as housewives, so that the capitalist does not have to pay his male employees anything to cover such living costs. Third, they form a very flexible component of the labor force which can easily be forced into unemployment, with unrest being contained by the male chauvinist attitudes of both men and women. (These points are expanded upon in the Kaufer and Christoffel selection below.)

For each individual capitalist enterprise the first of these factors is perhaps the most important, for it means that women cannot only be employed at lower wages than men, but also that this wage differential splits the unity of the workers in any struggle for higher wages. But in the long run some of this

[48] *Commonweal,* March 15, 1968, p. 711.

[49] See Hill, "The Racial Practices of Organized Labor," in Jacobson, *op. cit.,* p. 334.

advantage may have to be sacrificed to the third factor: using women workers as the area in which to concentrate unemployment by using male chauvinism in the way racism is used now. This is of course very much the situation at present, since the great majority of women—unlike men—are not employed. In 1967, 72 percent of all men over 14 were in the labor force—at a median income of $6610—compared to 38 percent of women—at a median income of $3157. The 1967 median income of all men over 14—employed or not—was $6020, compared to $2351 for women.[50] This low participation rate for women in the labor market is generally treated as "natural." Just as during World War II women were suddenly "taught" that their presence in the factory rather than the home was better for them *and* their children (as well as the war effort), women —and men—can be "taught" that it is unnatural and unfeminine for women to be employed. High unemployment would still exist—single women, women heading households and women whose husbands earn less than $5000 a year currently make up two thirds of the female labor force—but much of this unemployment would be disguised. And women fighting back against such a situation would be frowned upon—if not actively opposed—by male workers.

Thus just as racism—the idea that black and brown people are inferior to white people—is effectively used by the ruling class to split and pacify the working class, so is male chauvinism—the idea that women are inferior to men —used in this way. But just as racism need not be a permanent means of maintaining capitalist hegemony, neither should male chauvinism.

Export the Problem

One final method by which the capitalists can seek to alleviate the problems growing out of the permanent job shortage is to send certain side-effect problems abroad—especially inflation. That is, inflation can be made somewhat acceptable by using United States economic power to force other countries to adjust to U.S. inflation by upvaluing their currencies, thereby eliminating the "competitive" disadvantage of inflation. United States efforts to institute a world dollar standard, Special Drawing Rights, a "crawling peg" plan for world currency values, etc., are aimed at this end. These aspects of economic imperialism could not, of course, alleviate all the discontinuities of unemployment, but they would be of tremendous help to the capitalists in keeping the lid on. Their success, however, is circumscribed by the working-class struggles United States capitalism is now facing around the globe.[51]

VI

The primary effect of the permanent job shortage is that working-class militancy is contained. Poorly paid, unskilled workers can easily be replaced, know it, and are kept constantly in flux and disorganized. More highly skilled workers, on the other hand, are made very aware of the fact that they could

[50] "Income in 1967 of Persons in the United States," U.S. Department of Commerce, Bureau of Census Current Population Reports, Series P-60, No. 60, June 30, 1969, p. 35. The median earnings for black and brown people was: men, $3669; women, $1635.

[51] For an interesting discussion of U.S. efforts to export inflation, see David Deitch's financial column in the Boston *Globe,* September 4, 1969, p. 33.

be worse off, are fed a line about professionalism and superiority and encouraged to protect their edge in a dog-eat-dog world. Racism and male chauvinism stand out as particular variations of the way in which those workers lumped at the bottom of the labor pool—largely blacks and women—are used to ease the direct pressure of unemployment on the majority of (white, male) workers, to provide a psychological balm to this majority of workers and, most important, to divide workers from one another such that they lack the unity to fight for their collective interests.

If full employment did exist, workers would not feel as threatened by other workers, and racism and male chauvinism would become much less effective tools of the capitalists. Women and black people would become full-fledged members of the labor force. Full employment, therefore, would force up wages not only because of increased competition between employers for workers but because of new unity within the working class. For capitalists to end the job shortage would be for them to mark the beginning of their own end. Therefore all that capitalism *can* do is to attempt various ways of avoiding the disruptive consequences of a permanent job shortage. It is the working class that suffers from unemployment and it is the working class that might actively rebel against conditions of unemployment. It is such working-class discontent, and not unemployment itself, that capitalism seeks to avoid.

19 RACISM AND CAPITALISM

Hundreds of years of racism—of enslavement and near-enslavement of black people—has finally caught up with America with a Bang. Over the last fifteen years, a militant and increasingly revolutionary black liberation movement has developed in this country, demanding what rightfully belongs to it. Our cities are in a state of crisis. Major rebellions have taken place in over two hundred of them. The "race problem" is on everybody's mind, and few people really believe that it has any easy solution.

When the black movement started, it was demanding integration: the right to live a life in America just like that of white Americans. But over the last five years blacks have moved beyond integration. They have recognized that integration has always been a one-way street—integration on the terms of capitalist society. They have also recognized that equality with whites means very little when whites have so little themselves. Black people are not demanding the right to a lousy job or a lousy education, but the right to a fulfilling life, class liberation.

The black movement also learned that it could not expect any gifts. Its original demand for integration—a seemingly innocuous goal—met up with terrific resistance, not only in the South but in the North, as well. At one time, perhaps, many blacks had illusions that the government was sincerely committed to ending racism. But the experience of the civil rights movement conclusively showed that this was not the case. Political leaders failed time and again to speak to the demands of blacks in the Northern ghettos, except with more guns, more police and other techniques of military control, just placing more fuel on the fire. More and more, black people have come to speak of revolution. Groups like the Black Panthers have formed and grown around a program of socialist revolution.

Liberal leaders think this goes too far. They have a blind faith that somehow, someway, blacks will be given their share in America. But little has happened to indicate this goal can be realized. Many of the oppressions blacks suffer are endemic to capitalism. For example, they are massively unemployed. But capitalism cannot provide full employment; it propels the system into dizzying inflation. Or on another front, blacks are subject to racist, dehumanizing education. But education under capitalism cannot be geared to fulfilling men's needs. Its main task is to make men docile and obedient enough to fit into the dull and subservient slots in the capitalist labor force. Liberal solutions to the black problem constantly run up against insurmountable obstacles.

In addition, many powerful interests within capitalism seem to have a direct stake in the special oppression of blacks. Baran and Sweezy in the following article lay some of these out. Ghetto merchants and realtors profit from the limited geographical areas into which blacks can move. Low-wage employers benefit from the availability of black, marginal workers. All employers benefit from the racial division of the labor force, which justifies lower wages and undercuts working-class solidarity.

These particular obstacles, when combined with the priorities of a capitalist system which responds to profit rather than to crying human and social needs, mean that an assault on racism is far off. One, two, many National Commissions may demand action, but the kind of massive social spending programs even they know is required has never been contemplated under capitalism.

The following selections give two facets of the reality for black people. Baran and Sweezy show how racism had its origins in the needs of the capitalist economy; and they show how capitalism continues to have a stake in racism today. They say the strategy of tokenism and co-optation is doomed to failure, as the lot of the great masses of blacks fails to improve.

"Black Oppression in Newark" shows some of the conditions of life in the black ghetto that lie behind the rebellions. It is significant that this was an article written for GI's at Fort Dix who were being trained for riot control work.

MONOPOLY CAPITALISM AND RACE RELATIONS*

by PAUL BARAN AND PAUL SWEEZY

Race prejudice as it exists in the world today is almost exclusively an attitude of whites and had its origins in the need of European conquerors from the sixteenth century on to rationalize and justify the robbery, enslavement, and continued exploitation of their colored victims all over the globe.[1] When the slave system was introduced into the American South, race prejudice naturally came with it, and the ideological justification of the system was perhaps elaborated with greater diligence and subtlety there than anywhere else in the world. From colonial times, Americans both North and South have been systematically and continuously subjected to a barrage of propaganda fostering the ideas of white superiority and Negro inferiority.

It was, of course, always easy to adduce evidence purporting to "prove" the white-superiority/Negro-inferiority thesis. Having been enslaved and deprived of all opportunity to share in the benefits of civilized living, Negroes were visibly and undeniably inferior in all respects by which civilized societies judge superiority and inferiority. The argument that this *de facto* inferiority

[1] For excellent treatments of this subject, see Eric Williams, *Capitalism and Slavery*, Chapel Hill, 1944, Chapter 1; and Oliver C. Cox, *Caste, Class, and Race*, New York, 1948, Chapter 16.

was due to inborn racial characteristics was convincing to those who wanted to believe it. And it was not only whites who accepted it; many Negroes were successfully brainwashed into believing in the reality of their own inherent inferiority, and this self-depreciation acted as one of the most important bulwarks of the racial system.[2] It should be noted that the slave system, while assiduously fostering the idea of Negro inferiority, does not necessarily imply hatred by whites of Negroes as such. As long as the Negro knew and kept his "place," he was tolerated and even liked by whites. What whites hated was the Negro who believed in and acted on the principle that all men are created equal.

The Civil War was not fought by the Northern ruling class to free the slaves, as many mistakenly believe. It was fought to check the ambitions of the Southern slave-owning oligarchy which wanted to escape from what was essentially a colonial relation to Northern capital. The abolition of slavery was a by-product of the struggle, not its purpose, and Northern capitalism had no intention, despite the interlude of Reconstruction, of liberating the Negro in any meaningful sense. Having subdued the Southern planters, it was glad to have them resume their role of exploiters of black labor whom it could in turn exploit. The notorious compromise of the 1870's was a tacit recognition that the renewed colonial status of the South had been accepted by both sides, with the Southern oligarchy exploiting the Negro and in turn paying tribute to Northern capital for the privilege of doing so.

Under these circumstances, new methods of control over Negro labor were needed to replace slavery, and they were found in various forms of wage labor, sharecropping, and peonage. When Negroes tried to take advantage of their legal freedom to organize along with poor whites in the Populist movement, the planters answered with violence and the Jim Crow system of legalized segregation. By the turn of the century, the oppression and exploitation of Negroes was probably as bad as it had ever been under slavery, and racist propaganda was at least as virulent—and even more successful in the North because racism no longer had to bear the moral stigma of out-and-out slavery.[3]

It was of course inevitable that Negroes should enter the urban economy at the very bottom. They were the poorest, most illiterate, least skilled on arrival. They were doubly burdened by historic race prejudice and discrimination and by the prejudice and discrimination that have greeted every group of impoverished newcomers. The questions we have to ask are: How have they made out since moving to the cities? Have they been able to follow in the footsteps of earlier immigrant groups, climbing the economic ladder and escaping from their original ghettos?

In answering these questions, we must be careful not to mix up the effects

[2] This subject is illuminatingly treated by Harold R. Isaacs who convincingly shows that "the systematic debasement and self-debasement of the Negro . . . has begun with or been underpinned by the image the Negro child has gotten of the naked, uncivilized African." *The New World of Negro Americans,* New York, 1963, p. 161. This goes far to explain the enormous psychological significance to American Negroes of the emergence of independent African nations and leaders, and their full acceptance into the comity of nations.

[3] See Rayford W. Logan, *The Negro in American Life and Thought, the Nadir, 1877–1901,* New York, 1954. These last two decades of the nineteenth century were, in Harold Isaacs's words, "the peak years of Western white supremacy all over the world." *The New World of Negro Americans,* p. 119.

of moving from country to city, a process which has been continuous for more than half a century, with what has happened after arrival in the city. The move from countryside to city has on the average unquestionably meant a higher standard of living for Negroes: if it had not, the migration would have ceased long ago. In other words, the bottom of the urban-industrial ladder is higher than the bottom of the Southern agricultural ladder, and when Negroes stepped from the one to the other it was a step up. This is not what primarily interests us, however. It was similarly a step up for impoverished European peasants to leave their homelands and move to the United States: again the proof is that the flow continued until it was cut off by war and legislation. The point is that after they got here, they soon started to climb the new ladder, and fresh immigrant groups took their place at the bottom. What we want to know is whether Negroes have followed the same course, climbing the new ladder after moving to the cities.

A few have, of course, and we shall discuss the role and significance of this minority when we come to the subject of tokenism. But for the great mass of Negroes the answer is, emphatically and unambiguously, no. The widespread opinion to the contrary, to the extent that it has any factual basis, rests on confusing the step from one ladder to the other with a step up the new ladder. This important point was explained to the Clark Committee by Herman P. Miller, Special Assistant to the Director of the Bureau of the Census and one of the country's leading authorities on income distribution:

> We heard this morning from Professor Ginzberg that the Negro made a breakthrough in the 1950's. Senator Javits, in his excellent book, *Discrimination, U.S.A.*, also speaks about the improvement of the economic status of the Negro. Even the Department of Labor refers to the occupational gains that have been made by the Negro in the past 20 years. This is all very true, but I think it can be shown, on the basis of census statistics, that most of the improvement in occupational status that the Negro has made since 1940 has been through his movement out of sharecropping and agricultural labor in the South and into your Northern industrial areas.
>
> When we look at the figures for the Northern and Central states we find that the occupational status of the Negro relative to the white has not improved appreciably since 1940.

Negroes have thus not improved their occupational status relative to whites since 1940, nor their income status since the end of the war. Moreover, in certain other key respects their position has been clearly deteriorating.

After exhaustive investigation, the Commission on Race and Housing reported: "Segregation barriers in most cities were tighter in 1950 than ten years earlier. . . . The evidence indicates, on the whole, an increasing separation of racial groups as nonwhites accumulate in the central city areas abandoned by whites and the latter continually move to new suburban subdivisions from which minorities are barred." [4] And a statistical study based on the Censuses of 1940, 1950, and 1960 by Karl E. and Alma F. Taeuber showed, in the words of a *New York Times* report, that "with some notable exceptions, racial segregation, far from disappearing, is on the increase in the United States." [5]

[4] *Where Shall We Live?* Report of the Commission on Race and Housing, Berkeley, 1958, p. 3.

[5] M. S. Handler, "Segregation Rise in U.S. Reported," *New York Times*, November 26, 1964.

On the basis of the data presented, which could of course be made much more comprehensive and detailed, the conclusion seems inescapable that since moving to the cities, Negroes have been prevented from improving their socio-economic position: they have not been able to follow earlier immigrant groups up the occupational ladder and out of the ghetto.

As always happens in social science, answering one question leads to another. What social forces and institutional mechanisms have forced Negroes to play the part of permanent immigrants, entering the urban economy at the bottom and remaining there decade after decade? [6]

There are, it seems to us, three major sets of factors involved in the answer to this crucially important question. First, a formidable array of private interests benefit, in the most direct and immediate sense, from the continued existence of a segregated subproletariat. Second, the socio-psychological pressures generated by monopoly capitalist society intensify rather than alleviate existing racial prejudices, hence also discrimination and segregation. And third, as monopoly capitalism develops, the demand for unskilled and semi-skilled labor declines both relatively and absolutely, a trend which affects Negroes more than any other group and accentuates their economic and social inferiority. All of these factors mutually interact, tending to push Negroes ever further down in the social structure and locking them into the ghetto.

Consider first the private interests which benefit from the existence of a Negro subproletariat. (a) Employers benefit from divisions in the labor force which enable them to play one group off against another, thus weakening all. Historically, for example, no small amount of Negro migration was in direct response to the recruiting of strikebreakers. (b) Owners of ghetto real estate are able to overcrowd and overcharge. (c) Middle and upper-income groups benefit from having at their disposal a large supply of cheap domestic labor. (d) Many small marginal businesses, especially in the service trades, can operate profitably only if cheap labor is available to them. (e) White workers benefit by being protected from Negro competition for the more desirable and higher paying jobs. Hence the customary distinction, especially in the South, between "white" and "Negro" jobs, the exclusion of Negroes from apprentice programs, the refusal of many unions to admit Negroes, and so on.[7] In all these groups—and taken together they constitute a vast majority of the white population—what Marx called "the most violent, mean, and malignant passions of the human breast, the Furies of private interest," are summoned into action to keep the Negro "in his place."

With regard to race prejudice, it has already been pointed out that this characteristic white attitude was deliberately created and cultivated as a rationalization and justification for the enslavement and exploitation of colored labor.[8]

[6] "The Negro population," says the Commission on Race and Housing, "in spite of its centuries of residence in America, has at present some of the characteristics of an incompletely assimilated immigrant group." *Where Shall We Live?* pp. 8–9.

[7] "There has grown up a system of Negro jobs and white jobs. And this is the toughest problem facing the Negro southerner in employment." Leslie W. Dunbar, Executive Director of the Southern Regional Council, in testimony before the Clark Committee. *Equal Employment Opportunity,* p. 457.

[8] Among colored peoples, race prejudice, to the extent that it exists at all, is a defensive reaction to white aggression and therefore has an entirely different significance. It may serve to unify and spur on colored peoples in their struggles for freedom and equality,

But in time, race prejudice and the discriminatory behavior patterns which go with it came to serve other purposes as well. As capitalism developed, particularly in its monopoly phase, the social structure became more complex and differentiated. Within the basic class framework, which remained in essentials unchanged, there took place a proliferation of social strata and status groups, largely determined by occupation and income. These groupings, as the terms "stratum" and "status" imply, relate to each other as higher or lower, with the whole constituting an irregular and unstable hierarchy. In such a social structure, individuals tend to see and define themselves in terms of the "status hierarchy" and to be motivated by ambitions to move up and fears of moving down.[9] These ambitions and fears are of course exaggerated, intensified, played upon by the corporate sales apparatus which finds in them the principal means of manipulating the "utility functions" of the consuming public.

The net result of all this is that each status group has a deep-rooted psychological need to compensate for feelings of inferiority and envy toward those above by feelings of superiority and contempt for those below. It thus happens that a special pariah group at the bottom acts as a kind of lightning rod for the frustrations and hostilities of all the higher groups, the more so the nearer they are to the bottom. It may even be said that the very existence of the pariah group is a kind of harmonizer and stabilizer of the social structure—so long as the pariahs play their role passively and resignedly. Such a society becomes in time so thoroughly saturated with race prejudice that it sinks below the level of consciousness and becomes a part of the "human nature" of its members.[10] The gratification which whites derive from their socio-economic superiority to Negroes has its counterpart in alarm, anger, and even panic at the prospect of Negroes' attaining equality. Status being a relative matter, whites inevitably interpret upward movement by Negroes as downward movement for themselves. This complex of attitudes, product of stratification and status consciousness

---

but once these goals have been achieved it rapidly loses its *raison d'être.* As Oliver Cox has pointed out: "Today communication is so far advanced that no people of color, however ingenious, could hope to put a cultural distance between them and whites comparable to that which the Europeans of the commercial and industrial revolution attained in practical isolation over the colored peoples of the world. And such a relationship is crucial for the development of that complex belief in biological superiority and consequent color prejudice which Europeans have been able to attain. Therefore, we must conclude that race prejudice is not only a cultural trait developed among Europeans, but also that no other race could hope to duplicate the phenomenon. Like the discovery of the world, it seems evident that this racial achievement could occur only once." *Caste, Class, and Race,* pp. 348–349. The other side of this coin is, since the colored races obviously can and will attain cultural and technological equality with whites, that the race prejudice of modern whites is not only a unique but also a transitory historical phenomenon. It needs to be added, however, that completely eliminating it from the consciousness of whites, even in a predominantly non-exploitative (that is, socialist) world, may take decades rather than months or years.

[9] The crucial importance of the status hierarchy in the shaping of the individual's consciousness goes far to explain the illusion, so widespread in the United States, that there are no classes in this country, or, as the same idea is often expressed, that everyone is a member of the middle class.

[10] At this level of development, race prejudice is far from being reachable by public opinion polls and similar devices of "sociometrics" which remain close to the surface of individual and social phenomena. Incidentally, we have here another reason for believing that the eradication of race prejudice from whites will be, even in a rational society, a difficult and protracted process.

in monopoly capitalist society, provides an important part of the explanation why whites not only refuse to help Negroes to rise but bitterly resist their efforts to do so. (When we speak of whites and their prejudices and attitudes in this unqualified way, we naturally do not mean all whites. Ever since John Brown, and indeed long before John Brown, there have been whites who have freed themselves of the disease of racial prejudice, have fought along with Negro militants for an end to the rotten system of exploitation and inequality, and have looked forward to the creation of a society in which relations of solidarity and brotherhood will take the place of relations of superiority and inferiority. Moreover, we are confident that the number of such whites will steadily increase in the years ahead. But their number is not great today, and in a survey which aims only at depicting the broadest contours of the current social scene it would be wholly misleading to assign them a decisive role.)

The third set of factors adversely affecting the relative position of Negroes is connected with technological trends and their impact on the demand for different kinds and grades of labor. Appearing before a Congressional committee in 1955, the then Secretary of Labor, James P. Mitchell, testified that unskilled workers as a proportion of the labor force had declined from 36 percent in 1910 to 20 percent in 1950.[11] A later Secretary of Labor, Willard Wirtz, told the Clark Committee in 1963 that the percentage of unskilled was down to 5 percent by 1962.[12] Translated into absolute figures, this means that the number of unskilled workers declined slightly, from somewhat over to somewhat under 13 million between 1910 and 1950, and then plummeted to fewer than 4 million only twelve years later. These figures throw a sharp light on the rapid deterioration of the Negro employment situation since the Second World War. What happened is that until roughly a decade and a half ago, with the number of unskilled jobs remaining stable, Negroes were able to hold their own in the total employment picture by replacing white workers who were moving up the occupational ladder. This explains why the Negro unemployment rate was only a little higher than the white rate at the end of the Great Depression. Since 1950, on the other hand, with unskilled jobs disappearing at a fantastic rate, Negroes not qualified for other kinds of work found themselves increasingly excluded from employment altogether. Hence the rise of the Negro unemployment rate to more than double the white rate by the early 1960's. Negroes, in other words, being the least qualified workers are disproportionately hard hit as unskilled jobs (and, to an increasing extent, semi-skilled jobs) are eliminated by mechanization, automation, and cybernation. Since this technological revolution has not yet run its course—indeed many authorities think that it is still in its early stages—the job situation of Negroes is likely to go on deteriorating. To be sure, technological trends are not, as many believe, the *cause* of unemployment: that role is played by the specific mechanisms of monopoly capitalism.[13] But within the framework of this society technological trends,

[11] *Automation and Technological Change,* Hearings Before the Subcommittee on Economic Stabilization of the Joint Committee on the Economic Report, 84th Cong., 1st Sess., pursuant to Sec. 5(a) of P. L. 304, 79th Cong., Oct. 14, 15, 17, 18, 24, 25, 26, 27, and 28, 1955, p. 264.

[12] *Nation's Manpower Revolution,* Part 1, May 20, 21, 22, and 25, 1963, p. 57.

[13] Under socialism there is no reason why technological progress, no matter how rapid or of what kind, should be associated with unemployment. In a socialist society technological progress may make possible a continuous reduction in the number of

because of their differential impact on job opportunities, can rightly be considered a cause, and undoubtedly the most important cause, of the relative growth of Negro unemployment.

All the forces we have been discussing—vested economic interests, socio-psychological needs, technological trends—are deeply rooted in monopoly capitalism and together are strong enough to account for the fact that Negroes have been unable to rise out of the lower depths of American society. Indeed so pervasive and powerful are these forces that the wonder is only that the position of Negroes has not drastically worsened. That it has not, that in absolute terms their real income and consuming power have risen more or less in step with the rest of the population's, can only be explained by the existence of counteracting forces.

One of these counteracting forces we have already commented upon: the shift out of Southern agriculture and into the urban economy. Some schooling was better than none; even a rat-infested tenement provided more shelter than a broken-down shack on Tobacco Road; being on the relief rolls of a big city meant more income, both money and real, than subsistence farming. And as the nation's per capita income rose, so also did that of the lowest income group, even that of unemployables on permanent relief. As we have seen, it has been this shift from countryside to city which has caused so many observers to believe in the reality of a large-scale Negro breakthrough in the last two decades. Actually, it was an aspect of a structural change in the economy rather than a change in the position of Negroes within the economy.

But in one particular area, that of government employment, Negroes have indeed scored a breakthrough, and this has unquestionably been the decisive factor in preventing a catastrophic decline in their relative position in the economy as a whole. Table 1 gives the essential data (all levels of government are included).

TABLE I. NON-WHITE EMPLOYMENT IN GOVERNMENT, 1940–1962
(FIGURES ARE FOR APRIL, IN THOUSANDS)

	1940	1956	1960	1961	1962
Government employees, total	3,845	6,919	8,014	8,150	8,647
Non-white government employees	214	670	855	932	1,046
Non-white as percent of total	5.6	9.7	10.7	11.4	12.1

Source: United States Department of Labor, *The Economic Situation of Negroes in the United States*, Bulletin S-3, Revised 1962, p. 8.

Between 1940 and 1962, total government employment somewhat more than doubled, while non-white (as already noted, more than 90 percent Negro) employment in government expanded nearly five times. As a result non-white

years, weeks, and hours worked, but it is inconceivable that this reduction should take the completely irrational form of capitalist unemployment.

employment grew from 5.6 percent of the total to 12.1 percent. Since non-whites constituted 11.5 percent of the labor force at mid-1961, it is a safe inference that Negroes are now more than proportionately represented in government employment.[14]

Two closely interrelated forces have been responsible for this relative improvement of the position of Negroes in government employment. The first, and beyond doubt the most important, has been the increasing scope and militancy of the Negro liberation movement itself. The second has been the need of the American oligarchy, bent on consolidating a global empire including people of all colors, to avoid as much as possible the stigma of racism. If American Negroes had passively accepted the continuation of their degraded position, history teaches us that the oligarchy would have made no concessions. But once seriously challenged by militant Negro struggle, it was forced by the logic of its domestic and international situation to make concessions, with the twin objectives of pacifying Negroes at home and projecting abroad an image of the United States as a liberal society seeking to overcome an evil inheritance from the past.

The oligarchy, acting through the federal government and in the North and West through state and local governments, has also made other concessions to the Negro struggle. The armed forces have been desegregated, and a large body of civil rights legislation forbidding discrimination in public accommodations, housing, education, and employment, has been enacted. Apart from the desegregation of the armed forces, however, these concessions have had little effect. Critics often attribute this failure to bad faith: there was never any intention, it is said, to concede to Negroes any of the real substance of their demand for equality. This is a serious misreading of the situation. No doubt there are many white legislators and administrators to whom such strictures apply with full force, but this is not true of the top economic and political leadership of the oligarchy—the managers of the giant corporations and their partners at the highest governmental levels. These men are governed in their political attitudes and behavior not by personal prejudices but by their conception of class interests. And while they may at times be confused by their own ideology or mistake short-run for long-run interests, it seems clear that with respect to the race problem in the United States they have come, perhaps belatedly but none the less surely, to understand that the very existence of their system is at stake. Either a solution will be found which insures the loyalty, or at least the neutrality, of the Negro people, or else the world revolution will sooner or later acquire a ready-made and potentially powerful Trojan horse within the ramparts of monopoly capitalism's mightiest fortress. When men like Kennedy and Johnson and Warren champion such measures as the Civil Rights Act of 1964, it is clearly superficial to accuse them of perpetrating a cheap political maneuver. They know that they are in trouble, and they are looking for a way out.

Why then such meager results? The answer is simply that the oligarchy does

[14] If the data were available to compare income received from government employment by whites and non-whites, the picture would of course be much less favorable for Negroes since they are heavily concentrated in the lower-paying categories. But here too there has been improvement. A study made by the Civil Service Commission showed that between June 1962 and June 1963 Negro employment in the federal government increased by 3 percent and that "the major percentage gains had been in the better-paying jobs." *New York Times,* March 4, 1964.

not have the power to shape and control race relations any more than it has the power to plan the development of the economy. In matters which are within the administrative jurisdiction of government, policies can be effectively implemented. Thus it was possible to desegregate the armed forces and greatly to increase the number of Negroes in government employment. But when it comes to housing, education, and private employment, all the deeply rooted economic and socio-psychological forces analyzed above come into play. It was capitalism, with its enthronement of greed and privilege, which created the race problem and made of it the ugly thing it is today. It is the very same system which resists and thwarts every effort at a solution.

The fact that despite all political efforts, the relative economic and social position of Negroes has changed but little in recent years, and in some respects has deteriorated, makes it a matter of great urgency for the oligarchy to devise strategies which will divide and weaken the Negro protest movement and thus prevent it from developing its full revolutionary potential. These strategies can all be appropriately grouped under the heading of "tokenism."

If we are to understand the real nature of tokenism, it is necessary to keep in mind certain developments within the Negro community since the great migration from the Southern countryside got under way. As Negroes moved out of a largely subsistence economy into a money economy and as their average levels of income and education rose, their expenditures for goods and services naturally increased correspondingly. Goods were for the most part supplied by established white business; but segregation, *de jure* in the South and *de facto* in the North, gave rise to a rapidly expanding demand for certain kinds of services which whites would not or could not provide or which Negroes could provide better. Chief among these were the services of teachers, ministers, doctors, dentists, lawyers, barbers and beauty parlors, undertakers, certain kinds of insurance, and a press catering to the special needs of the segregated Negro community. Professionals and owners of enterprises supplying these services form the core of what Franklin Frazier called the black bourgeoisie.[15] Their ranks have been augmented by the growth of Negro employment in the middle and higher levels of the civil service and by the rapid expansion of the number of Negroes in the sports and entertainment worlds. The growth of the black bourgeoisie has been particularly marked since the Second World War. Between 1950 and 1960 the proportion of non-white families with incomes over $10,000 (1959 dollars) increased from 1 percent to 4.7 percent, a rate of growth close to three times that among whites. During the same years, the total distribution of income among Negro families became more unequal, while the change among white families was in the opposite direction.[16]

[15] E. Franklin Frazier, *Black Bourgeoisie: The Rise of a New Middle Class in the United States,* Glencoe, Illinois, 1957.

[16] All data from Herman P. Miller, *Trends in the Income of Families and Persons in the United States: 1947 to 1960,* Bureau of the Census Technical Paper No. 8, Washington, 1963, Table 9, pp. 168–189. The measure of inequality used by Miller is the so-called Gini coefficient which increased for non-white families from .402 in 1950 to .414 in 1960, while for white families it was declining from .372 to .357.

Apart from the direction of change, the greater degree of income inequality for non-whites which these figures indicate should not be interpreted to mean that there is really a greater degree of equality of material circumstances among whites than among

The theory behind tokenism, not often expressed but clearly deducible from the practice, is that the black bourgeoisie is the decisive element in the Negro community. It contains the intellectual and political elite, the people with education and leadership ability and experience. It already has a material stake in the existing social order, but its loyalty is doubtful because of the special disabilities imposed upon it solely because of its color. If this loyalty can be made secure, the potential revolutionizing of the Negro protest movement can be forestalled and the world can be given palpable evidence—through the placing of loyal Negroes in prominent positions—that the United States does not pursue a South African-type policy of *apartheid* but on the contrary fights against it and strives for equal opportunity for its Negro citizens. The problem is thus how to secure the loyalty of the black bourgeoisie.

To this end the political drive to assure legal equality for Negroes must be continued. We know that legal equality does not guarantee real equality: the right to patronize the best hotels and restaurants, for example, means little to the Negro masses. But it is of great importance to the well-to-do Negro, and the continuation of any kind of disability based solely on color is hateful to all Negroes. The loyalty of the black bourgeoisie can never be guaranteed as long as vestiges of the Jim Crow system persist. For this reason we can confidently predict that, however long and bloody the struggle may be, the South will eventually be made over in the image of the North.

Second, the black bourgeoisie must be provided with greater access to the dominant institutions of the society: corporations, the policy-making levels of government, the universities, the suburbs. Here the oligarchy is showing itself to be alert and adaptable. A *New York Times* survey found that:

> Business and industry here, in the fact of the civil rights revolution, have been reassessing their employment policies and hiring Negroes for office and other salaried posts that they rarely held before.
>
> Many national concerns with headquarters in New York City have announced new nondiscrimination policies or reaffirmed old ones. Personnel officers are taking a new look at their recruiting methods and seeking advice from Negro leaders on how to find and attract the best qualified Negroes.
>
> On a nationwide basis, about 80 of the country's largest companies enrolled under Plans for Progress of the President's Committee on Equal Opportunity have reported substantial increases in the hiring of Negroes for salaried positions. . . .
>
> The latest figures for the 80 companies that filed reports in the last year . . . showed that nonwhites got 2,241 of the 31,698 salaried jobs that opened up. This represented an increase of 8.9 percent in the number of jobs held by nonwhites in those companies.[17]

The same thing has been happening in government, as already noted; and in addition to being hired in larger numbers in the better-paying grades, Negroes are increasingly being placed in executive jobs at or near the cabinet level, in federal judgeships, and the like. And as Negroes are brought into the economic and political power structure, they also become more acceptable in

---

Negroes. In the upper reaches of the social structure, income is less significant than property; and while we know of no data on Negro property ownership, it seems beyond doubt that the disparity between Negroes and whites in this regard is immeasurably greater than in incomes.

[17] *New York Times,* November 12, 1963.

the middle- and upper-class suburbs—provided of course that their incomes and standard of living are comparable to their neighbors'.

Not many Negroes are affected by these easings of the barriers separating the races at the upper economic and social levels—in fact, it is of the essence of tokenism that not many should be. But this does not deprive the phenomenon of its importance. The mere existence of the possibility of moving up and out can have a profound psychological impact.

Third, the strategy of tokenism requires not only that Negro leadership should come from the black bourgeoisie but that it should be kept dependent on favors and financial support from the white oligarchy. The established civil rights organizations—the National Association for the Advancement of Colored People, the Urban League, and the Congress of Racial Equality—were all founded on a bi-racial basis and get most of their funds from white sources; they therefore present no potential threat. But it is always necessary to pay attention to the emergence of new and potentially independent leaders. Where this occurs, there are two standard tactics for dealing with the newcomers. The first is to co-opt them into the service of the oligarchy by flattery, jobs, or other material favors.

If co-optation fails, the standard tactic is to attempt to destroy the potentially independent leader by branding him a Communist, a subversive, a troublemaker, and by subjecting him to economic and legal harassments.

Finally, there is a fourth aspect of tokenism: to open up greater opportunities for Negro youths of all classes who because of luck, hard work, or special aptitudes are able to overcome the handicap of their background and start moving up the educational ladder. For a "qualified" Negro in the United States today, there is seemingly no limit to what he may aspire to. A report in the *New York Times* states:

> Dr. Robert F. Goheen, president of Princeton University, said yesterday that the competition among colleges and universities for able Negro students was "much more intense" than the traditional competition for football players. . . . Dr. Goheen said: "It certainly is very clear that the number of able colored who have also had adequate educational opportunities is very small. And we find we are all extending our hands to the same relatively few young men and women." [18]

Here we can see as under a magnifying glass the mechanics of tokenism. With the country's leading institutions of higher learning falling over themselves to recruit qualified Negro students—and with giant corporations and the federal government both eager to snap them up after graduation—the prospects opened up to the lucky ones are indeed dazzling. But as President Goheen stresses, their number is very small, and it can only remain very small as long as the vast majority of Negroes stay anchored at the bottom of the economic ladder.

The fact that the great mass of Negroes derive no benefits from tokenism does not mean that they are unaffected by it. One of its purposes, and to the extent that it succeeds one of its consequences, is to detach the ablest young men and women from their own people and thus to deprive the liberation movement of its best leadership material. And even those who have no stake in the system and no hope of ever acquiring one may become reconciled to it

[18] *New York Times,* October 21, 1963.

if they come to believe there is a chance that their children, or perhaps even their children's children, may be able to rise out of their own degraded condition.

It would be a great mistake to underestimate the skill and tenacity of the United States oligarchy when faced with what it regards—and in the case of race relations, rightly regards—as a threat to its existence. And it would be just as serious a mistake to underestimate the effectiveness, actual and potential, of the strategy of tokenism. Yet we believe that in the long run the real condition of the Negro masses will be the decisive factor. If some improvement, however modest and slow, can be registered in the years ahead, a well conceived policy of tokenism may be enough to keep Negroes from developing into monopoly capitalism's "enemy within the gates." But if the trends of the recent past continue, if advances are canceled out by setbacks, if the paradox of widespread poverty and degradation in the midst of potential abundance becomes ever more glaring, then it will be only a matter of time until American Negroes, propelled by the needs of their own humanity and inspired by the struggles and achievements of their brothers in the underdeveloped countries, will generate their own revolutionary self-consciousness.

If this assessment of the situation is correct, it becomes a matter of great importance to know whether the kinds of reforms which are possible within the framework of the existing system—the kinds advocated by the established civil rights organizations and their white supporters—are likely to yield any real benefits to the Negro masses.

It seems clear to us that the answer is negative; that the chief beneficiaries of reforms of this type are the black bourgeoisie; and that, regardless of the intentions of their sponsors, their objective effect is merely to supplement the policy of tokenism.

This might be thought not to be the case with prohibitions against discrimination in the hiring of labor, which unquestionably helped open up many new jobs to Negroes during the war. In a period of heavy and growing unemployment, however, no such effect can be expected. Even if color is not the reason, Negroes will be discriminated against because of their inferior qualifications. Only those with special talents or training will benefit, and they are already set apart from the ghettoized masses.

Nor can the ghetto dwellers hope to gain from anti-discrimination measures in the field of housing. The only kind of housing that would benefit them would result from construction on a large scale of low-rent units for those who most need it where they need it. Under existing conditions, there is no chance that such housing could be integrated. Attempts to build low-rent housing in marginal neighborhoods and to keep it occupied on a bi-racial basis necessitate the enforcement of so-called "benevolent quotas"—in other words require that Negro occupancy be kept low and hence that few Negroes benefit. As to the prevention of discrimination in the sale of private housing, either by law or by judicial nullification of restrictive covenants, this certainly helps well-to-do Negroes to move into previously all-white neighborhoods. As far as low-income Negroes are concerned, however, the most that can be said is that it facilitates expansion of the ghetto itself through what has been called the "invasion-succession sequence." In this strictly limited sense, anti-discrimination measures do help low-income Negroes: after all, they have to live somewhere. But it does nothing to raise their status or to promote racial integration in the lower reaches of the social structure.

With appropriate modifications, the story is not different in the case of school integration. Where neighborhoods are racially mixed, school integration follows naturally and is unquestionably good for all concerned. But this affects few Negroes, mostly of the higher-income group. The real problem is the ghetto schools. Some upgrading of schools attended by ghetto dwellers may be achieved by placing them on the margins of the ghetto and drawing school districts so as to include both black and white areas. But this does not touch the problem of the ghetto schools themselves, and here all the forces of tradition, inertia, prejudice, and privilege come into play to block or abort attempts at reform. Programs of driving a certain number of Negro children by bus from ghetto areas to white schools elsewhere merely evade the problem, and there is considerable evidence that they increase the insecurity and self-distrust of the children involved.[19]

There is really no mystery about why reforms which remain within the confines of the system hold out no prospect of meaningful improvement to the Negro masses. The system has two poles: wealth, privilege, power at one; poverty, deprivation, powerlessness at the other. It has always been that way, but in earlier times whole groups could rise because expansion made room above and there were others ready to take their place at the bottom. Today, Negroes are at the bottom, and there is neither room above nor anyone ready to take their place. Thus only individuals can move up, not the group as such: reforms help the few, not the many. For the many nothing short of a complete change in the system—the abolition of both poles and the substitution of a society in which wealth and power are shared by all—can transform their condition.

Some will say that even if this is true, it does not mean that the Negro masses will necessarily become aware of the causes of their degradation, still less that they will achieve a revolutionary self-consciousness. May they not be blinded by the mystifications of bourgeois ideology and paralyzed by a leadership drawn from the tokenized elite? After all, there have always been oppressed classes and races, but the achievement of revolutionary self-consciousness is a rare historical event. Why should we expect American Negroes to do what so few have done before them?

There are, we believe, two reasons, equally compelling.

First, American Negroes live in a society which has mastered technology and advanced the productivity of labor beyond anything dreamed of even a few years ago. True, this has been done in search of profits and more perfect means of destruction, but the potential for human abundance and freedom is there and cannot be hidden. Poverty and oppression are no longer necessary, and a system which perpetuates them cannot but appear to its victims ever more clearly as a barbarous anachronism.

Second, the tide of world revolution against imperialist exploitation, which in our time is simply the international face of monopoly capitalism, is flowing strong, much too strong to be turned back or halted. Already, the rise of inde-

[19] See A. James Gregor, "Black Nationalism: A Preliminary Analysis of Negro Radicalism," *Science & Society,* Fall 1963, pp. 427–431. Gregor also presents valuable evidence on the negligible importance to the Negro masses of anti-discrimination programs in housing.

pendent African nations has helped to transform the American Negro's image of himself. As Africans—and Asians and Latin Americans—carry their revolutions forward from national independence to socialist egalitarianism, the American Negro's consciousness will be transformed again and again—by his own knowledge and experience and by the example of those all over the world who are struggling against, and increasingly winning victories over, the same inhuman system of capitalist-imperialist oppression.

The Negro masses cannot hope for integration into American society as it is now constituted. But they can hope to be one of the historical agents which will overthrow it and put in its place another society in which they will share, not civil rights which is at best a narrow bourgeois concept, but full human rights.

BLACK OPPRESSION IN NEWARK*

ANONYMOUS

TROOPS IN THE GHETTO

Two weeks ago New Jersey State Police received riot-control training at Fort Dix. They were housed in the 759th MP barracks and were given their training by military personnel. The training consisted of the techniques of crowd dispersion, i.e. proper use of the billy club; uses of tear gas, mace, and CS; implementing mass arrests; and the employment of confinement vehicles. It has been learned that other State Police units will also receive riot training at Dix within the next month.

The events of the last few weeks and our knowledge of past summer occurrences make it important for us to understand what riot training is really aimed at, since we all will be subjected to mandatory training and in some cases will be called to "pacify" areas here at home. Vietnam, Berkeley, Newark, and Columbia are all recent examples of the armed power of the state in action against the people. In the past, the army has been used against workers fighting for economic rights and union recognition, most infamously during the Pullman Strike of 1894, during the Haymarket Square Affair of 1886, and during the Flint Strike of 1936. And today as the student and anti-war movement grows, police and National Guard troops are used increasingly to suppress it.

The most vicious use of armed power by the state has been against people of color—at first to annihilate the Indians and take their land, later to preserve and protect the slave system, and today to control the ghettos of our country.

* Used by permission of the editors of *Shakedown*.

The Newark ghetto is really like every black northern ghetto in America. It contains all the conditions which have fueled the anger that has flared into the explosions and rebellions that have rocked the ghettos. Many white people don't understand why black people revolt, and since it doesn't seem right to them, they put it down.

The facts of Newark are pretty ugly, and they speak for themselves. It has the highest percentage of slum housing in the nation, the highest rate of VD, maternal mortality, and new cases of TB, and it rates seventh in absolute number of drug addicts. Newark has the second highest birth rate in the nation and also the second highest rate of infant mortality. The unemployment rate in the black community is consistently more than 15%.

In the summer the ghetto is hot to baking in the "homes," and crowded and sweating in the streets. Even the parks are not within walking distance of the ghetto. In the winter landlords don't provide enough heat, and people have to light their ovens and pay huge gas bills. Rents in the black community are higher than in the more spacious tree-lined area that is white populated. One man paid $140 for a small four-room cold-water flat with cracked paint, broken plumbing, and the usual company of rats and roaches that share everything but the rent. The residents of the ghetto are always on the move, looking for a decent place to live, but they never find one. Many landlords in Newark won't rent to black people, others won't rent to people with children, but nobody will rent to black people with black children.

Families are crowded into apartments with their relatives who come up from the South looking for "freedom" in the North, only to discover that they cannot find jobs and places to live. Usually there are two or three beds in every room, two or three or more children in a single bed. People are stacked on top of each other like animals, in tenement houses and huge high-rise projects.

Newark's black population is the MAJORITY population in the city, which is at least 55% black. But blacks have no voice in the affairs of their city. There are a few blacks in token government positions, but the real control is by whites. The black people in Newark have nothing to say about THEIR city. Almost all of them are squeezed into two wards, which means simply that they get to elect only two of the nine men that make up the city council. In other words, the black people of Newark haven't really even had the "power of the vote." (Whether that "power" really means anything is a matter for another discussion.) The essential fact of being black in Newark—or of being black anywhere in America—is powerlessness.

Not only don't blacks control their city, they are also not allowed to control their own neighborhoods. The economy of their community is owned and controlled by basically the same white structure that controls the city.

And the money leaves the community at 5:00, when the whites leave the city for the comfort of their suburban homes. In other "ethnic" neighborhoods, the corner grocery store or tavern is owned by someone of the same ethnic group. In the black community however, black people owned practically nothing—not the stores, not the bars, not the houses—until the rebellion two years ago. The reason blacks didn't own anything (still don't CONTROL anything) was not because they didn't want to make money like everybody else. It is because they HAVEN'T BEEN ALLOWED TO! Black people who owned their own homes were constantly harassed by local officials about the condition of their homes or the sidewalks in front, while the white slumlords who owned blocks of houses that violated every section of the city's housing code were never bothered—they paid off and the City shut up.

Blacks (and all poor people) have to pay MORE for LESS than the middle class or rich. All food prices are higher—and they go up on the 1st of each month when welfare checks arrive. All food quality is lower; any meat dealer will tell you (if you're white and suburban-looking) that only the lowest grade—often BELOW commercial grade—is packaged and delivered to ghetto stores. This is even true of supermarkets that are part of a chain. It is impossible for most people to get outside of the area to more suburban markets; many people don't have cars, a family's groceries cannot be carried on the bus, and by the time they lay out for a cab, they have spent what they were going to save. And it doesn't matter how smart or thrifty you are—if you've got to have furniture and you don't have cash, you've got to get it from the man who will give you credit. There is only one man like that. He is the "loan shark" who charges four times in interest what the merchandise is worth!

If you're on welfare and you go get a job, as much money as you earn is deducted from your welfare payments. So it doesn't make sense to work—the hard, bad-paying, humiliating jobs that most women are able to get don't pay any more, so why not be at home with your kids? It's important to note, too, that black people didn't create welfare—the state did.

What people on "the outside" don't understand is that the ghetto is a trap. Black people don't like to be poor, wear raggedy clothes, or eat neckbones all the time and steak never. In Newark, significant sections of the community had organized for change. People had gotten together peacefully in all kinds of ways over a period of several years. They had protested bad conditions and unfair practices. They had signed petitions to the City Hall, made phone calls, written letters, gone on rent strikes, demonstrated for better garbage removal, construction of traffic lights and recreation centers, an end to split-sessions in the schools, an end to the worst practices of the Welfare Department, an end to police mistreatment of the people and creation of a civilian review board, etc., etc. THEY HAD TO DO IT THAT WAY BECAUSE THEY HAD ALREADY FOUND OUT THERE WASN'T ANY SUCH THING AS DOING IT ALONE—by pulling your own butt up by your own bootstraps. So they did it together. And the City responded. It responded by framing rent-strikers on phony charges or having them evicted; it responded by jailing peaceful pickets; it responded by calling local leaders communists. The police in the local precinct arrested and beat teenage kids who were associated with protest activities. Neighborhood action offices had their windows busted out. Welfare mothers were left without their food money for a month.

At first the people were afraid because they knew all this shit would come down on their heads if they got together. But then people started getting LESS SCARED and more ANGRY. It seemed there was no way to make things better. The more "reasonable" you were, the less you got any place at all. The officials handed down a lot of bullshit—and did nothing. Often the City didn't even pretend to listen.

What people learned was that demonstrating got them next to nowhere too. People aren't fools. When they try to do something and get slapped down over and over again, most people have the good sense NOT to get up and try it the same way again. They figure out how to deliver their own punch.

THE COMMUNITY HAD TO BE HEARD

Finally in July of '67 the last straw fell. The ghetto erupted to the sound of a black cab driver being beaten by white cops. Everybody got everything—a whole lot of things they needed and didn't have. The cops got theirs too—"looting" like everybody else. People replaced their broken-down chairs with new ones. They stocked up on food for months. Kids brought home clothes not only for themselves but for all the other kids in their family. People took things and gave them to other people. People risked their lives for such things as rubber-thonged sandals and hair rollers. And a lot of people died. Most of them were not doing anything that was in any way "illegal"; most of them were minding their own business, like Mrs. Spellman, the mother of 11 children, who was shot to death in her own living room. People were murdered sadistically, like 19-year-old Jimmy Rutledge, who was shot point blank at least 39 times—whose body would have been unidentifiable had not some of his friends witnessed the killing. What was Jimmy Rutledge's crime? Being in a boarded-up tavern and coming out with his hands up.

It's important to realize WHO HAD THE GUNS in Newark. The City Police, the State Troopers, and the National Guard (Jersey Blues) had the guns. That's how come 26 black people were killed and only two whites (who died from related causes). They acted as though they believed that every black person was armed and mobilized to kill them. So they got crazy—ran around terrified and trigger-happy in the streets—and spent from Friday to Monday shooting at EACH OTHER, instead of at snipers. Supposedly the Guard was there just to quiet things down, but in fact their presence made people more furious than ever. They totally occupied the town; they helped the local police who had always acted like brutes to the people of the neighborhood; they helped the State Troopers who—during the period of curfew when the residents had to be in their homes—went through town busting out windows and destroying the merchandise in the few stores owned by blacks. In other words, the Guard was called into Newark to defend the interests of the people who had always controlled the city and exploited and colonized the black community.

Even now, almost two years after the rebellion, blacks are still angry at the way the white government of Newark opposes all efforts of the black community to defend itself from the landlords, merchants, and police. The "poverty program" in Newark has not helped the people at all. For every dollar that was supposed to go to black people, three more went to local businesses. There has been such misuse of funds in a city known for corruption, with the poverty program controlled by the Democratic Party machine. Investigations of the program reveal that officials appointed to the program by the Mayor have taken big slices out of poverty money. Then these same politicians have turned around and complained to white people living in Newark that black people were getting too much.

Unemployment is still high in the black neighborhood, and it's not because people don't want jobs. Just this past week, Newark businessmen said that they did not have summer jobs for even half of the people who want them.

Housing is getting harder and harder to find. Newark-Rutgers University, Newark College of Engineering, and Essex County College have evicted thousands of black people from their homes in order to expand. To suit the needs of suburban commuters, the city is building two six-lane highways right through the black neighborhood. Already 7,000 have been evicted. Where are they to go?

Consequently, people have been forced to pay higher and higher rent because housing is harder and harder to find. If they can't afford the rent, and few can, black people have no choice but to apply for public housing in the "projects."

It is clear that powerful whites in Newark have begun an economic war on the black community to force it out of Newark.

If the Army is called into Newark, it will not be there to free the black neighborhood, but to protect the shops and property of landlords and merchants. The Army will not fight poverty, hunger, sickness, or the merchants; it will perpetuate them at a high cost of human life. Black people have learned something about the need for self-defense from the incidents of the last few years. More and more black people are fighting back, not just in Newark, but in every American city.

CONCLUSIONS

Most institutions in the society are a reflection of society as a WHOLE. As people strike out against the oppressive institutions in their lives, they see certain similarities in the ways that the institutions try to prevent people from getting what is rightfully theirs. The Vietnamese fighting to liberate his country is basically fighting the SAME fight as the black community which is trying to liberate itself. Like workers, students, and blacks, GIs are beginning to engage in struggles for liberation. The real heroes of the people are not the John Wayne-type "Green Beanies" or lifers, but men like those at Fort Hood who refused to be used against the people in Chicago. Why should American GIs or NGs go armed into an American city to put down people who are fighting for decent lives—people who are defending themselves in the only way they have left? Why should American GIs fight to keep corrupt politicians in office or to protect businesses which, after all, are interested in profit and not people's lives?

We must break down the false barriers which are constructed to keep the people separated from each other. The same way we must smash the Army's attempts to separate company from company here at Dix; we must join with those whose interests are in giving power to people rather than those who would use us for cannon fodder in order to hold on to privileged positions. People should control their communities, workers their factories, nationalities their countries; and we must not let ourselves be used to keep that control in the hands of a few. The NGs who refused to bayonet, gas, or shoot their brothers and sisters in Berkeley saw how they were being used, and they spontaneously said "NO!" It came home to those NGs as it's coming home to GIs. It's a common struggle to defend ourselves. We must be prepared and organized to deal with the armed power of the state, especially when the state actually uses us indiscriminately to pursue its aims. This is true be it Nam, Berkeley, or Newark.

If we are to be successful, we must not only begin to say NO when ordered to commit crimes against the people, but we must think about how to refuse together. It's easy to pick off one guy acting alone, but there's almost nothing can be done against a whole company or battalion—and when all GIs act together as one, GIs can join with the people and stop letting themselves be used as pawns against their fellow human beings. We must talk with the guys in our own platoons and companies. SPREAD THE WORD AND ORGANIZE! We MUST support those who begin to move first, just as we need their support when we move. Support must come from all over the base, whenever our brothers begin to defend those beliefs which we know are right. Riot duty is WRONG, Vietnam is WRONG! We MUST refuse that which is wrong and against the people. We are beginning to learn; now we must begin to ACT!

20 CAPITALISM IN ACTION: THE OPPRESSION OF WOMEN*

by BEVERLY JONES

Many men refuse to believe that women are oppressed in our society. If they are unsophisticated in their argument, they say that women prefer to perform the domestic and maternal functions they usually perform; "ask them," they say, "they'll tell you they like it." Many women say they do. If the men are somewhat more sophisticated, they don't rely on the argument that these functions are "natural." They merely argue that men's roles in life are no bed of roses, either, so how can you say that there is any qualitative difference in their oppression.

Of course, men are also oppressed in our society. But the form and content of women's oppression are of a different order of magnitude. The argument about women preferring other functions resembles the racist attitude that blacks don't mind having the "left-over" jobs, because they get their real satisfaction out of "lazin' around, shuckin' and jivin' and sex." What is important to see about the roles women are allowed to play in the society is that women have many fewer roles they are allowed to play and that the content of the roles they are allotted is just plainly less satisfying, less engaging than the roles men are allowed by the very standards we establish ourselves to judge what is satisfying and engaging.

1. Men are told by the society that they will find their identity in a job or a profession. Their potential roles are as varied as the kinds of work available. Women, however, are told that their identities are fixed by the men they marry and the functions of motherhood and homemaker they are destined to play. Although women are told that their identities can be as varied as the different kinds of husbands they can marry, this is a crude deception. Living vicariously through another individual is as much a variety of identities as watching a dozen different movies is a variety of activities.

2. The content of women's roles is really limiting, too. First, women play the role of accessory and dependent. The fulfillment in these roles is always highly contingent upon the judgment of the person or people on whom they are dependent. They must please their husbands and win the love of their children. In a society where stable emotional relationships are the exception, not the rule, this leaves women especially vulnerable. When they are rejected by husband, lover or children, they have no internally generated identity to which to turn.

Being an accessory means being not quite a person. The problem of catching a man—the key one in a woman's life—is a downright dehumanizing experience. Women must constantly mold themselves to the presumed expectations men have of them. They must treat themselves as objects. They are taught that actually cultivating their own inclinations—intelligence, curiosity, and talents of various sorts—is risky because it jeopardizes the ease with which they will please men.

Second, women's roles are just plain menial. Keeping house is basically drudgery. For purposes of commercialism, women are conned by advertisements into trying to "express" themselves through buying homemaking products. But basically the hours are lengthy, the fruits do not last long, and the work is unexpressive. Society recognizes these facts in the generally low regard it has for housework. Being a mother is also a menial service job in most ways. It has its rewards, but the feeding and the cleaning and the caring are rarely the labor of love they are pictured to be.

Women are treated as inferior creatures. They are treated as being less intelligent, less capable of rational action, less dependable, etc. A great many people in the society actually believe these are immutable characteristics attached to women in some biological way.

This is only to begin the inventory of the ways in which subordinate status is imposed on women. The Beverly Jones article communicates forcefully how the roles women play and the stereotypes they are forced into deprive them of freedom. It illustrates the vulnerability of dependency roles. It shows how little self-respect women can eke out of their roles, because they are so self-contradictory and because they deny such basic human ambitions and ideals.

Many people think at first that the complaints Jones registers are trivial. They are the quirks of a specific relationship, they say, not the description of a general condition of women. The experience of a vast number of women says this is not true. The injustice of deeply ingrained and traditional roles is not experienced at first as massive existential doubts about meaningfulness. It is experienced in day-to-day frustration. No matter how hard she tries, the role does not fit. Out of the seeds of this frustration can come a mighty gut awareness of the facts of oppression, and from there, a dynamic force for a movement for social change.

There is an almost exact parallel between the role of women and the role of black people in this society. Together they constitute the great maintenance force sustaining the white American male. They wipe his ass and breast feed him when he is little, they school him in his youthful years, do his clerical work and raise his and their replacements later, and all through his life in the factories, on the migrant farms, in the restaurants, hospitals, offices, and homes, they sew for him, stoop for him, cook for him, clean for him, sweep, run errands, haul away his garbage, and nurse him when his frail body falters.

Together they send him out into his own society, shining and healthy, his mind freed from all concern with the grimy details of living. And there in that unreal world of light and leisure he becomes bemused and confused with ideas of glory and omnipotence. He spends his time saving the world from dragons, or fighting evil knights, proscribing and enforcing laws and social systems, or just playing with the erector sets of manhood—building better bridges, computers, and bombs.

Win or lose on that playground, he likes the games and wants to continue playing—unimpeded. That means that the rest of the population, the blacks and females, who maintain this elite playboy force, must be kept at their job.

Oh, occasionally it occurs to one or another of the most self-conscious, self-confident, and generous white men that the system could be changed. That it might be based on something other than race or sex. But what? Who would decide? Might not the change affect the rules of the game or even the games themselves? And where would his place be in it all? It becomes too frightening to think about. It is less threatening and certainly less distracting, simply to close ranks, hold fast, and keep things the way they are.

This is done by various techniques, some of which are: sprinkling the barest pinch of blacks and women over the playground to obscure the fact that it is an all-white male facility; making a sacred cow out of home and family; supporting a racist and antifeminist church to befuddle the minds of the support force and to divert what little excess energy is available to it; and most importantly developing among white men a consensus with regard to blacks and females and a loyalty to each other which supersedes that to either of the other groups or to individual members of them, thus turning each white man into an incorruptible guard of the common white male domain.

The gist of that consensus which is relevant to the point at issue here is:

1) Women and blacks are of inherently inferior and alien mentality. Their minds are vague, almost inchoate, and bound by their personal experiences (scatterbrained, or just dumb). They are incapable of truly abstract, incisive, logical, or tactical thinking.

2) Despite or perhaps because of this inferior mentality women and blacks are happy people. All they ask out of life is a little attention, somebody to screw them regularly, second-hand Cadillacs, new hats, dresses, refrigerators, and other baubles.

3) They do not join mixed groups for the stated purposes of the groups but to be with whites or to find a man.

WOMEN STUDENTS

FOR AT LEAST TWO REASONS RADICAL WOMEN DO NOT REALLY UNDERSTAND THE DESPERATE CONDITION OF WOMEN IN GENERAL. A. In the first place, as students, they occupy some sexy, sexless, limbo territory where they are treated by the administration and by males in general with less discrimination than they will ever again face.

It may seem strange but one of the main advantages of a female student, married or unmarried, with or without children, is that she is still public. She has in her classes, in her contacts on campus, the opportunity to express her ideas publicly to males and females of all ranks. Indeed, she is expected to do so—at least in good schools, or in good seminars. Anyway, she has this opportunity on an equal basis with men.

Moreover, her competition with men, at least scholastically, is condoned—built into the system. This creates in the girl an illusion of equality and harmony between the sexes very much as a good integrated school (where students visit each others' homes even for weekends and are always polite) creates in the black the illusion of change and the faith in continued good relations upon graduation.

These female illusions are further nurtured by the social life of students. Since many live in dorms or other places where they cannot entertain members of the opposite sex, most social intercourse of necessity takes place in public. I mean that people congregate in coffee houses, pubs, movies, or at parties of the privileged few with off-campus apartments or houses. And since most students are unmarried, unsure of themselves, and lonely, they are constantly on the make. Thus they dance with each other and talk with each other. The conversation between the sexes is not necessarily serious or profound but it takes place and, as we have said, takes place, in the great main, publicly. Each tries to find out more about the other, attempts to discover what future relations might be possible between them, tries to impress the other in some way.

So that the female student feels like a citizen, like an individual among others in the body politic, in the civil society, in the world of the intellect. What she doesn't understand is that upon graduation she is stripped of her public life and relegated to the level of private property. Enslavement is her farewell present. As things stand now she is doomed to become someone's secretary, or someone's nurse, or someone's wife, or someone's mistress. From now on if she has some contribution to make to society she is expected to make it privately through the man who owns some part of her.

If as a secretary she has a criticism of the firm she works for and a money-making idea of improvement for the company, she certainly doesn't express her view publicly at the board meeting of the firm, though she may be there taking minutes. Nor does she speak to her boss about it at an office party or in any other public place. She is expected rather to broach him in private, in a self-effacing manner, indicating that she probably doesn't really know what she is talking about but it seems to her . . .

He then proposes the idea to the board and receives both the credit and the raise or promotion. And the peculiar twist is that this holds equally true even if in passing he mentions that the idea was brought to him by his secretary. For in the eyes of the board, as in the eyes of all male society, the female employee has no independent identity. She belongs to the boss as a slave belongs to his master. If slaves are exceptionally productive, the slave holder is given credit for knowing how to pick them and how to work them. Slaves aren't promoted to free men and female secretaries aren't promoted to executive positions.

But slavery is an intricate business. As an institution it cannot be maintained by force alone. Somehow or other slaves must be made to conceive of themselves as inferior beings and slave holders must not be permitted to falter in the confidence of their superiority. That is why female secretaries are not permitted to offer public criticism. How long, after all, could the system survive if in open *public* exchange some women, even in their present downtrodden position, turned out to be smarter than the men who employ them?

What is feared most is that women, looking out at their natural surroundings, will suffer a reversal of perspective like that one experiences looking at optically balanced drawings where background suddenly becomes subject. That one day looking at men and women in full blown stereotype a woman will suddenly perceive individuals of varying ability, honesty, warmth, and understanding. When that day comes her master stands before her stripped of his historical prerogative, just another individual with individual attributes. That has ponderous implications for their relationship, for all of society.

In the world of the graduated and married this situation is forestalled in perhaps the most expeditious way. Men simply refuse to talk to women publicly about anything but the most trivial affairs: home, cooking, the weather, her job, perhaps a local school board election, etc. In these areas they are bound to be able to compete and if they fail—well, men aren't supposed to know anything about those things anyway. They're really just trying to give the girls a little play.

But even that routine has its dangers. Women are liable to change the topic, to get to something of substance. So generally to be absolutely safe men just don't talk to women at all. At parties they congregate on one side of the room, standing up as befits their condition and position (desk workers in the main) and exhausted women (servants and mothers) are left propped up by girdles, pancake make-up, and hair spray, on the couch and surrounding chairs. If the place is big and informal enough the men may actually go into another room, generally under the pretext of being closer to the liquor.

Of course, most women don't understand this game for what it is. The newcomer to it often thinks it is the women who withdraw and may seek out what she imagines to be the most stimulating company of the men. When she does, she is quickly disillusioned. As she approaches each group of men the conversation they were so engrossed in usually dies. The individual members begin to drift off—to get a refill, to talk with someone they have just noticed across the room etc. If she manages to ensnare a residual member of the group in conversation, he very soon develops a nervous and distressed look on his face as though he had to go to the bathroom; and he leaves as soon as possible, perhaps to make that trip.

There is another phenomenon not to be confused here. Namely, men being stimulated to show off in the presence of an attractive female, to display in verbal exchange what they imagine to be their monstrous cleverness. But the rules of this game require the women to stand by semi-mute, just gasping and giggling, awed and somewhat sexually aroused. The verbal exchange is strictly between the men. Any attempt on the woman's part to become a participant instead of a prize breaks up the game and the group.

This kind of desperate attempt by men to defend their power by refusing to participate in open public discussion with women would be amusing if it were not so effective. And one sees the beginnings of it even now, while still students, in SDS meetings. You are allowed to participate and to speak, only the men stop listening when you do. How many times have you seen a woman enter the discussion only to have it resume at the exact point from which she made her departure, as though she had never said anything at all? How many times have you seen men get up and actually walk out of a room while a woman speaks, or begin to whisper to each other as she starts?

In that kind of a hostile, unresponsive atmosphere, it is difficult for anyone to speak in an organized, stringent manner. Being insulted she becomes angry, in order to say what she wanted to say and not launch an attack upon the manners of her "audience," she musters the energy to control her temper, and finally she wonders why she is bothering at all since no one is listening. Under the pressure of all this extraneous stimulation she speaks haltingly, and if she gets to the point at all hits it obliquely.

And thus the male purpose is accomplished. Someone may comment, "Well, that is kind of interesting but it is sort of beside the main point here." Or, whoever is in charge may just look at her blankly as if, "What was that all about?" The conversation resumes and perhaps the woman feels angry but she also feels stupid. In this manner the slave relationship is learned and reinforced.

Even if the exceptional case is involved—the woman who does sometimes get up front—the argument holds. I know whom you are thinking about. You are thinking about the girl who has thirty IQ points over almost anyone in the group and therefore can't be altogether put down. She is much too intelligent, much too valuable. So she is sometimes asked by the male leadership to explain a plan or chair a meeting and since it is obvious that she is exercising *male*-delegated authority and because she is so bright people will sometimes listen to her. But have you ever known the top dog in an SDS group to be a woman, or have you ever known a woman to be second in command? Have you ever seen one argue substance or tactics with one of the top males *in front* of the full group? She may forget her place and do so, but if she does she receives the same treatment as all other females. The rules may and sometimes have to be stretched for the exceptional but never at the price of male authority and male control.

Almost all men are involved in the male mystique. No matter how unnecessary it may be, particularly for the bright and most able among them, each rests his ego in some measure on the basic common denominator, being a man. In the same way white people, consciously or unconsciously, derive ego support from being white and Americans from being American.

Allowing females to participate in some group on the basis of full equality presents a direct threat to each man in that group. And though an individual male leader may be able to rise above this personal threat he cannot deviate from the rules of the game without jeopardizing his own leadership and the group itself. If he permits the public disclosure in an irrefutable manner of the basic superiority of half of the women to half the men, of some of the women to some of the men, he breaks the covenant and the men will not follow him. Since they are not obliged to, they will not suffer this emasculation and the group will fall apart.

To think that women by asserting themselves individually in SDS, can democratize it, can remove the factor of sex, is equally silly. In the first place the men will not permit it and in the second place, as things stand now, the women are simply incapable of that kind of aggressive individual assertion. The socialization process has gone too far, they are already scrambled. Meeting after meeting their silence bears witness to their feelings of inferiority. Who knows what they get out of it? Are they listening, do they understand what is being said, do they accept it, do they have reservations? Would urging them to speak out have any effect other than to cut down their numbers at the next meeting?

The Limbo

Though female students objectively have more freedom than most older married women their life is already a nightmare. Totally unaware they long ago accepted the miserable role male society assigned to them: help-mate and maintenance worker. Upon coming to college they eagerly and "voluntarily" flood the great service schools: the college of education, the college of nursing, the departments of social work, physical therapy, counseling, and clinical psychology. In some places they even major in home economics.

Denied most of them forever is the great discovery, the power and beauty of logic and mathematics, the sweeping syntheses, the perspective of history. The academic education in these service schools varies from thin to sick, two-semester courses in history of western civilization, watered down one-quarter courses on statistics for nurses, and the mumbo-jumbo courses on psychoanalysis.

It is no wonder that women who may have come to college with perfect confidence in themselves begin to feel stupid. They are being systematically stupefied. Trying to think without knowledge is just a cut above trying to think without language. The wheels go around but nothing much happens.

The position of these women in college is very much like the position of black kids in the black public schools. They start out with the same IQ and achievement scores as their white counterparts but after the third year they begin to lag further and further behind in both measurements. Those blacks still around to graduate from high school usually measure at least two years below graduating whites. Of course, black kids blame the discrepancy on the schools, on the environment, on all kinds of legitimate things. But always there is the gnawing doubt. It is hard to believe the schools could be so different; white women, being at the same school and from the same families understand that they are simply, though individually, inferior.

But that is not the only reason female students are scrambled. They are also in a panic, an absolute frenzy, to fulfill their destiny: to find a man and get married. It is not that they have all been brainwashed by the media to want a husband, split-level house, three children, a dog, a cat, and a station wagon. Many just want out from under their parents. They just can't take the slow slaughter anymore but they don't have the courage to break away. They fear the wrath of the explosion but even more they fear the ensuing loneliness and isolation.

Generally a single girl's best friend is still her family. They are the only people she can rely upon for conversation, for attention, for concern with her welfare, no matter how misdirected. And everyone needs some personal attention or they begin to experience a lack of identity. Thus the big push to find the prince charming who will replace the chains with a golden ring.

But that is not as simple as it may seem. It is not proper for women to ask men out. They are never permitted the direct approach to anything. So women must set traps and, depending upon their looks and brains, that can be terribly time consuming, nerve-racking, and disappointing. Thus the great rash of nose jobs, the desperate dieting, the hours consumed in pursuit of the proper attire. There is skin care, putting up one's hair each night, visits to the hairdressers, keeping up with, buying, applying, and taking off make-up, etc. The average American woman spends two hours a day in personal grooming, not including shopping or sewing. That is one-twelfth of her whole life and one-eighth of the time she spends awake. If she lives to be eighty, a woman will have spent ten whole years of her time awake in this one facet of the complex business of making herself attractive to men. It is staggering to think what that figure would be if one were to include the endless hours spent looking through fashion magazines, shopping and window shopping, discussing and worrying about clothes, hair style, diet, and make-up. Surely one-fourth of a woman's waking time would be a conservative estimate here. Twenty years of wakeful life!

So, one-fourth of a female student's day goes down the drain in this manner, another one-fourth to one-half is spent getting brainwashed in school and studying for the same end. What does she do with the rest of the time? Often she must work to support herself and she must eat, clean, wash clothes, date, etc. That leaves her just enough time to worry about her behavior on her last date and her behavior on her next one. Did she say and do the right thing, should she change her approach? Does he love her or does he not? To screw or not to screw is often a serious question. It is taken for granted amongst the more sophisticated that it helps to nail a man if one sleeps with him. Still, it is no guarantee and there are only so many men with whom a woman can cohabit in the same circle and still expect a proposal. Movement men seem prone to marry the "purer" non-movement types. And at that age and stage, when girls are worried about being used, about pregnancy and privacy, still ignorant of the potentials of their bodies, and hung-up by the old male sexual code which classifies so much as perversion and then demands it, sex usually offers only minimal gratification anyway. Given the girls' hang-ups and the insecurity and ineptness of young men, even that gratification is more often psychological than sexual.

Sex becomes the vehicle for momentary exchanges of human warmth and affection. It provides periods in which anxiety is temporarily allayed and girls feel wanted and appreciated, periods in which they develop some identity as individuals. It is ironic indeed that a woman attains this sense of identity and individuality through performing an act common to all mankind and all mammals. It bespeaks her understanding that society as it is presently organized will not permit her to function at all except through some male. The church used to say that "husband and wife are as one, and that one is the husband," or "the husband and wife are as one body and the husband is the head." As though fulfilling a prophecy unmarried women go about like chickens with their heads cut off.

In this terrible delirium between adolescence and marriage the friendship of female to female all but disappears. Girls, because they are growing duller, become less interesting to each other. As they slip into the role of submissiveness to male initiative, male intelligence, they also become increasingly uneasy with one another. To be the benefactor of female intelligence and to respond with warmth and affection brings with it anxieties of "homosexual tendencies." To initiate, direct, or dominate brings with it the same apprehensions. To insure a female for every male (if he wants one), to insure his freedom and his power through the enslavement of our sex, males have made of homosexuality *the* abomination. Everyone knows what happens to them; they go crazy and get buried at some intersection. It is too terrible to think about; it can only be feared.

And that fear, initiated by men, is reinforced by both men and women. Perform a simple spontaneous act like lighting another woman's cigarette with the same match with which you've just lit your own and there is panic on all sides. Women have to learn to inhibit these natural, asexual gestures. And any close and prolonged friendship between women is always suspect.

So women use each other as best they can under the circumstances, to keep out the cold. And the blood-pacts of childhood where one swore not to reveal a secret on penalty of death turn into bargains about not leaving each other until both are lined up for marriage. Only these later pacts are never believed or fulfilled. No woman trusts another because she understands the desperation. The older a woman becomes the more oppressive the syndrome. As one by one her contemporaries marry she begins to feel the way old people must when one by one their friends and relatives die. Though an individual in the latter condition is not necessarily burdened with a sense of failure and shame.

So there you have the typical coed, ignorant, suffering from a sense of inferiority, barely perceiving other women except as mindless, lonely, and terrified. Hardly in any condition to aggressively and individually fight for her rights in SDS. It seems, in a way, the least of her problems. To solve them all she is fixated on marriage. Which brings us to the second arm of this discussion, the point we raised earlier.

MARRIED WOMEN

FOR TWO REASONS, RADICAL WOMEN DO NOT REALLY UNDERSTAND THE DESPERATE CONDITION OF WOMEN IN GENERAL. B. Because so few are married, or if married have no children.

No one would think to judge a marriage by its first hundred days. To be sure there are cases of sexual trauma, of sudden and violent misunderstandings, but in general all is happiness; the girl has finally made it; the past is but a bad dream. All good things are about to come to her. And then reality sets in. It can be held off a little as long as they are both students and particularly if they have money but sooner or later it becomes entrenched. The man moves to insure his position of power and dominance.

There are several more or less standard pieces of armament used in this assault upon wives but the biggest gun is generally the threat of divorce or abandonment. With a plucky woman a man may actually feel it necessary to openly and repeatedly toy with this weapon, but usually it is sufficient simply to keep it in the house undercover somewhere. We all know the bit, we have heard it and all the others I am about to mention on television marital comedies and in night club jokes; it is supposed to be funny.

The husband says to the wife who is about to go somewhere that doesn't meet with his approval, "If you do, you need never come back." Or later, when the process is more complete and she is reduced to frequent outbreaks of begging, he slams his way out of the house claiming that she is trying to destroy him, that he can no longer take these endless, senseless scenes; that "this isn't a marriage, it's a meat grinder." Or he may simply lay down the law that God damn it, her first responsibility is to her family and he will not permit or tolerate something or other. Or if she wants to maintain the marriage she is simply going to have to accommodate herself.

There are thousands of variations on this theme and it is really very clever the way male society creates for women this pre-marital hell so that some man can save her from it and control her ever after by the threat of throwing her back. Degrading her further, the final crisis is usually averted or postponed by a tearful reconciliation in which the wife apologizes for her shortcomings, namely the sparks of initiative still left to her.

The other crude and often open weapon that a man uses to control his wife is the threat of force or force itself. Though this weapon is not necessarily used in conjunction with the one described above, it presupposes that a woman is more frightened of returning to an unmarried state than she is of being beaten about one way or another. How can one elaborate on such a threat? At a minimum it begins by a man's paling or flushing, clenching his fists at his sides or gritting his teeth, perhaps making lurching but controlled motions or wild threatening ones while he states his case. In this circumstance it is difficult for a woman to pursue the argument which is bringing about the reaction, usually an argument for more freedom, respect, or equality in the marital situation. And of course, the conciliation of this scene, even if he has beaten her, may require his apology, but also hers, for provoking him. After a while the conditioning becomes so strong that a slight change of color on his part, or a slight stiffening of stance, nothing observable to an outsider, suffices to quiet her or keep her in line. She turns off or detours mechanically, like a robot, not even herself aware of the change, or only momentarily and almost subliminally.

To understand the desperate situation of married women you have to remember that women before marriage have on the whole only superficial, competitive, and selfish relationships with each other. Should one of them have a genuine relationship it is more likely with a male than a female. After marriage a woman stops courting her old unmarried or married female sidekicks. They have served their purpose, to tide her over. And there is the fear, often well founded, that these females will view her marriage less as a sacrament than a challenge, that they will stalk her husband as fair game, that they will outshine her, or in some other way lead to the disruption of her marriage.

Her husband will not tolerate the hanging around of any past male friends, and that leaves the woman isolated. When, as so often happens, after a few years husband and wife move because he has graduated, entered service, or changed jobs, her isolation is complete. Now all ties are broken. Her husband is her only contact with the outside world, aside, of course, from those more or less perfunctory contacts she has at work, if she works.

So she is desperate to talk with her husband because she must talk with *someone* and he is all she has. To tell the truth a woman doesn't really understand the almost biologic substructure to her desperation. She sees it in psychological terms. She thinks that if her husband doesn't talk to her he doesn't love her or doesn't respect her. She may even feel that this disrespect on his part is causing her to lose her own self-respect (a fair assumption since he is her only referent). She may also feel cheated and trapped because she understood that in return for all she did for him in marriage she was to be allowed to live vicariously, and she cannot do that if he will not share his life.

What she does not understand is that she cannot go on thinking coherently without expressing those thoughts and having them accepted, rejected, or qualified in some manner. This kind of feedback is essential to the healthy functioning of the human mind. That is why solitary confinement is so devastating. It is society's third-rung "legal deterrent," ranking just below capital punishment and forced wakefulness, or other forms of torture that lead to death.

This kind of verbal isolation, this refusal to hear a woman, causes her thought process to turn in upon itself, to deteriorate, degenerate, to become disassociated from reality. Never intellectually or emotionally secure in the first place she feels herself slipping beyond the pale. She keeps pounding at the door.

And what is her husband's response? He understands in some crude way what is happening to her, what he is doing to her, but he is so power-oriented he cannot stop. Above all, men must remain in control; it's either him or her. The worse she becomes the more convinced he is the coin must not be turned. And from thence springs anew his fear of women, like his fear of blacks.

Sooner or later, if she can, the wife has children. Assuming the husband has agreed to the event, the wife's pregnancy does abate or deflect the drift of their marriage, for a while anyway. The pregnancy presents to the world visible proof of the husband's masculinity, potency. This visible proof shores up the basic substructure of his ego, the floor beyond which he cannot now fall. Pathetically his stock goes up in society, in his own eyes. He is a man. He is grateful to his wife and treats her, at least during the first pregnancy, with increased tenderness and respect. He pats her tummy and makes noises about mystic occurrences. And since pregnancy is not a male thing and he is a man, since this is cooperation, not competition, he can even make out that he feels her role is pretty special.

The wife is grateful. Her husband loves her. She is suffused with happiness and pride. There is at last something on her side of the division of labor which her husband views with respect, and delight of delights, with perhaps a twinge of jealousy.

Of course, it can't last. After nine months the child is bound to be born. And there we are back at the starting gate. Generally speaking, giving birth must be like a bad trip with the added feature of prolonged physical exhaustion.

Sometimes it takes a year to regain one's full strength after a messy caesarean. Sometimes women develop post-partum psychosis in the hospital. More commonly, after they have been home awhile they develop a transient but recurring state called the "Tired Mother Syndrome." In its severe form it is, or resembles, a psychosis. Women with this syndrome complain of being utterly exhausted, irritable, unable to concentrate. They may wander about somewhat aimlessly, they may have physical pains. They are depressed, anxious, sometimes paranoid, and they cry a lot.

Sound familiar? Despite the name one doesn't have to be a mother to experience the ailment. Many young wives without children do experience it, particularly those who, without an education themselves, are working their husband's way through college. That is to say, wives who hold down a dull eight or nine hour a day job, then come home, straighten, cook, clean, run down to the laundry, dash to the grocery store, iron their own clothes plus their husband's shirts and jeans, sew for themselves, put up their hair, and more often than not type their husband's papers, correct his spelling and grammar, pay the bills, screw on command, and write the in-laws. I've even known wives who on top of this load do term papers or laboratory work for their husbands. Of course, it's insanity. What else could such self-denial be called? Love?

Is it any wonder that a woman in this circumstance is tired? Is it any wonder that she responds with irritability when she returns home at night to find her student husband, after a day or half-day at home, drinking beer and shooting the bull with his cronies, the ring still in the bathtub, his dishes undone, his clothes where he dropped them the night before, even his specific little chores like taking out the garbage unaccomplished?

Is it any wonder that she is tempted to scream when at the very moment she has gotten rid of the company, plowed through some of the mess, and is standing in a tiny kitchen over a hot stove her husband begins to make sexual advances? He naively expects that these advances will fill her with passion, melting all anger, and result not only in her forgetting and forgiving but in gratitude and renewed love. Ever hear the expression, "A woman loves the man who satisfies her"? Some men find that delusion comforting. A couple of screws and the slate is wiped clean. Who needs to pay for servants or buy his wife a washing machine when he has a cock?

And even the most self-deluded woman begins to feel depressed, anxious, and used, when she finds that her husband is embarrassed by her in the company of his educated, intellectual, or movement friends. When he openly shuts her up saying she doesn't know what she is talking about or emphasizes a point by saying it is so clear or so simple even his wife can understand it.

He begins to confuse knowledge with a personal attribute like height or a personal virtue like honesty. He becomes disdainful of and impatient with ignorance, equating it with stupidity, obstinacy, laziness, and in some strange way, immorality. He forgets that his cultivation took place at his wife's expense. He will not admit that in stealing from his wife her time, energy, leisure, and money he also steals the possibility of her intellectual development, her present, and her future.

But the working wife sending her husband through school has no monopoly on this plight. It also comes to those who only stand and wait—in the home, having kiddy after kiddy while their husbands, if they are able, learn something, grow somewhere.

Women who are not mothers can also suffer from the "Tired Mother Syndrome." Once a mother, however, it takes on a new dimension. There is a difference of opinion in the medical and sociological literature with regard to the genesis of this ailment. Betty Friedan, in the sociological vein, argues that these symptoms are the natural outgrowth of restricting the mind and body of these women to the narrow confines of the home. She discusses the destructive role of monotonous, repetitive work which never issues in any lasting, let alone important achievement. Dishes which are done only to be dirtied the same day; beds which are made only to be unmade the same day. Her theory also lays great emphasis on the isolation of these women from the larger problems of society and even from contact with those concerned with things not domestic, other than their husbands. In other words, the mind no more than the body can function in a straight jacket and the effort to keep it going under these circumstances is indeed tiring and depressing.

Dr. Spock somewhat sides with that theory. The main-line medical approach is better represented by Dr. Lovshin who says that mothers develop the "Tired Mother Syndrome" because they are tired. They work a 16-hour day, 7 days a week. Automation and unions have led to a continuously shortened day for men but the workday of housewives with children has remained constant. The literature bears him out. Oh, it is undoubtedly true that women have today many time-saving devices their mothers did not have. This advantage is offset, however, by the fact that fewer members of the family help with housework and the task of child care, as it is organized in our society, is continuous. My mother used to boil her wash in the basement and the children made out down there as best they could sometimes getting burned. Now a woman puts the wash in a machine and spends her time reading to the children, breaking up their fights, taking them to the playground, or otherwise looking after them. If, as is often said, women are being automated out of the home, it is only to be shoved into the car chauffeuring children to innumerable lessons and activities, and that dubious advantage holds only for middle and upper class women who generally can afford not only gadgets but full or part time help.

THE RETURN FROM NEVER-NEVER LAND

Women who would avoid or extricate themselves from the common plight I've described, and would begin new lives, new movements, and new worlds, must first learn to acknowledge the reality of their present condition. They have got to reject the blind and faulty categories of thought foisted on them by a male order for its own benefit. They must stop thinking in terms of "the grand affair," of the love which overcomes, or substitutes for, everything else, of the perfect moment, the perfect relationship, the perfect marriage. In other words, they must reject romanticism. Romance, like the rabbit at the dog track, is the illusive, fake, and never-attained reward which for the benefit and amusement of our masters keeps us running and thinking in safe circles.

A relationship between a man and a woman is no more or less personal a relationship than is the relationship between a woman and her maid, a master and his slave, a teacher and his student. Of course, there are personal, individual qualities to a particular relationship in any of these categories but they are so overshadowed by the class nature of the relationship, by the volume of class response as to be almost insignificant.

There is something horribly repugnant in the picture of women performing the same menial chore all day, having almost interchangeable conversations with their children, engaging in standard television arguments with their husbands, and then in the late hours of the night, each agonizing over what is considered her personal lot, her personal relationship, her personal problem. If women lack self-confidence there seems no limit to their egotism. And unmarried women cannot in all honesty say their lives are in much greater measure distinct from each other's. We are a class, we are oppressed as a class, and we each respond within the limits allowed us as members of that oppressed class. Purposely divided from each other, each of us is ruled by one or more men for the benefit of all men. There is no personal escape, no personal salvation, no personal solution.*

* This should be contrasted with the discussion in the Christoffel and Kaufer selection below.

The first step then is to accept our plight as a common plight, to see other women as reflections of ourselves, without obscuring, of course, the very real differences intelligence, temperament, age, education, and background create. I'm not saying let's now create new castes or classes among our own. I just don't want women to feel that the movement requires them to identify totally with and moreover love every other woman. For the general relationship, understanding and compassion should suffice.

We who have been raised on pap must develop a passion for honest appraisal. The real differences between women and between men and women are the guideposts within and around which we must dream and work.

Having accepted our common identity the next thing we must do is get in touch with each other. I mean that absolutely literally. Women see each other all the time, open their mouths and make noises but communicate on only the most superficial level. We don't talk to each other about what we consider our real problems because we are afraid to look insecure, because we don't trust or respect each other, and because we are afraid to look or be disloyal to our husbands or benefactors.

Each married woman carries around in her a strange and almost identical little bundle of secrets. To take, as an example, perhaps the most insignificant, she may be tired of and feel insulted by her husband's belching or farting at the table. Can you imagine her husband's fury if it got back to him that she told someone he farted at the table? Because women don't tell these things to each other the events are considered personal, the women may fantasize remarriage to mythical men who don't fart, the man feels he has a personal but minor idiosyncrasy, and maledom comes out clean.

And that, my dear, is what this bit of loyalty is all about. If a man made that kind of comment about his wife he might be considered crude or indiscreet; she's considered disloyal—because she's subject, he's king, women are dominated and men are the instruments of their domination. The true objective nature of men must never become common knowledge lest it undermine in the minds of some males but most particularly in ours the male right-to-rule. And so we daily participate in the process of our own domination. For God's sake, let's stop!

I cannot make it too clear that I am not talking about group therapy or individual catharsis. (We aren't sick, we are oppressed.) I'm talking about movement. Let's get together to decide in groups of women how to get out of this bind, to discover and fight the techniques of domination in and out of the home. To change our physical and social surroundings, to free our time, our energy, and our minds—to start to build for ourselves, for all mankind, a world without horrors.

21 THE POLITICAL ECONOMY OF MALE CHAUVINISM*

by TOM CHRISTOFFEL

AND KATHERINE KAUFER

Women are specially oppressed under capitalism, as the Jones selection has outlined. Male chauvinism, the notion that women are inferior to men, is part of the ideological baggage of capitalism that surrounds and supports this oppression. But it has its basis in the economic structure of capitalism, for the latter profits in many ways from male chauvinism.

In the following selection, Tom Christoffel and Katherine Kaufer identify the ways in which male chauvinism serves capitalism. Women in our society are paid less for equivalent work, channeled into more undesirable jobs, or simply excluded from the labor force. As a result they form a gigantic reserve labor pool for the convenience of employers and employment trends, are forced into dependent relationships with men and are condemned to unpaid household drudgery.

Because of capitalism's stake in male chauvinism, the struggle for female equality must be part of the anticapitalist struggle, and vice versa. Capitalism and male chauvinism can only be eliminated together.

"Women!—give 'em an inch and they'll take a mile!"

—GRUMPY, IN WALT DISNEY'S
Snow White and the Seven Dwarfs

A system of exploitation can only survive if those who are exploited fail to rebel against their situation. The crudest and most direct barrier to such rebellion is force; less direct but more efficient means are the granting of concessions and the manipulation of ideology. Capitalism, while ready to use force whenever it is deemed necessary and willing to offer concessions within the limits of exigency and practicality, prefers to win voluntary acceptance through a broad complex of ideas and values which divide and weaken the working class by distorting its understanding of reality. Anticommunism, racism, nationalism, sectionalism, anti-intellectualism, antiscientism, religion, liberalism and male chauvinism are among the ideologies that serve capitalism in this way, and to understand how capitalism maintains itself, it is necessary to understand how these various ideologies work.

* Used by permission of the authors.

This essay deals with one such ideology, male chauvinism, which in its simplest sense involves the belief that men are innately superior to women in many ways. It is a belief widely held by both men and women, and is used to justify inferior treatment of women, including their economic exploitation under capitalism.

Chauvinism justifies treating men and women differently on the basis that "natural" differences between the sexes inevitably determine the roles that are appropriate to each. In this view, women are "naturally" intended to complement men, who are "naturally" intended to work, provide and command. Thus women "belong" in the home, and it is their biologically determined nature to be full-time mothers, housekeepers and helpmates. Cleaning, cooking, shopping, sewing and childrearing are "inherently" women's work, and "real" women find these tasks far more self-fulfilling than work outside the home, which is "inherently" a man's domain.

Perhaps the most compelling "natural" role of women, according to the chauvinist man, is that of the sex mate—who fulfills her husband's sexual needs as seductively—but unaggressively—as she possibly can.

This male chauvinist view of the proper relationship between men and women is pervasive and powerful. It molds our views of ourselves and others, dictates our tastes and buying habits, shapes our attitudes and, to a large degree, determines our social and work patterns and controls the sex and nature of our labor force. The majority of women don't work outside the home unless there is an economic need. And when they do they most often gravitate to "women's jobs"—housekeepers, clerks, secretaries, social workers, nurses, teachers—rather than working as mechanics, riveters, truck drivers, doctors, administrators or college professors, all of which are considered male jobs. And while some men may sew, cook or clean professionally, most consider it demeaning to do so in their own homes.

So pervasive are the influences of chauvinist thinking that, even when some aspects are recognized as wrong and harmful, others continue to be accepted, despite the fact that such thinking condemns one half of the population to a more restricted, less respected, less interesting, less independent way of life and robs society as a whole of the skills, talents and creativity that half of the population might otherwise contribute. What accounts for the tenacity of chauvinism in the face of ever-mounting evidence that it is costly to most men and women and is based on a lie?

There is, of course, a real difference between the sexes: women bear children; men do not. During earlier stages of social organization this difference provided a rational basis for various divisions of labor. In pre-industrial society it made sense for childbearing women who were needed to nurse their babies to work in or near home and for men to venture away from home to hunt or fight.[1] But in an industrial society such a division of labor has become senseless because the "maternal" role—insofar as it is biological and not otherwise parental—has become very much less time-demanding. "In the 1890's in England a mother spent 15 years in a state of pregnancy and lactation; in

[1] The differences in musculature between men and women quite possibly evolved sometime early in primate evolution, in part as adaptation to this quite reasonable division of labor.

the 1960's she spends an average of four years." [2] And the secondary physical differences between men and women—size, strength, musculature, cyclicity—have at most marginal effects on workers' participation in the larger economy. The United States Public Health Service reports that employed men aged 17 years and over lost an average of 5.3 days from work due to illness during the period from July 1966 to June 1967, while employed women lost 5.4 days.[3]

If the homebound and economically dependent woman is anachronistic and irrational in modern society, why does the practice survive? A partial but insufficient answer is that it is part of our heritage. Sex role divisions have existed for millennia and have had a profound effect on our history. But the same may be said of witchcraft, cannibalism and many other ancient beliefs and practices; yet these have died out as science and technology have left them behind. To understand why chauvinism remains socially and economically powerful, we must look at the role it plays in modern capitalist society. Viewed from this perspective it becomes clear that the role of women in our society and the ideology that supports it play an important part in capitalist exploitation of the working class.

First, as long as society continues to accept the notion that a woman's primary place is in the home, women will constitute a large available source of unpaid domestic labor, economically dependent on the men who support them. Second, the assumption that women are inherently less capable than men at tasks outside the home makes it possible to keep those women who are in the work force at the more menial jobs and to pay them less for doing the same work men do. Third, since women are considered peripheral members of the work force, they provide capitalism with a flexible supply of labor which can be drawn upon as needed. And finally, the socio-economic division between men and women encouraged by the chauvinist ideology makes it much more difficult for the working class to unify in opposition to capitalist exploitation.

Let us review these four points in order. The unpaid work of women in the home is considered far less important than their husband's paid labors. It can be made a secondary function during periods of labor shortage, but becomes the woman's main role when jobs become scarce. In addition, the fact that housewives are not expected to be paid for their labors in the home makes it possible to keep the wages of their husbands far lower than they would have to be otherwise.

The fact that women are not paid directly for their work at home makes them dependent on their husbands for any improvement in their working conditions. To lighten their housekeeping load they must convince their husbands to reapportion the limited family income toward that end, or to make increased funds for housekeeping an issue in wage bargaining. But male chauvinism makes it hard for working men to demand a wage increase for housekeeping expenses, with the result that housekeeping costs and conditions more often become family issues than the wage issues that they really are. Thus women are uncompensated domestic workers often pitted against their

[2] See Juliet Mitchell, "Women: The Longest Revolution," *New Left Review,* December 1966, p. 28.

[3] See Caroline Bird, *Born Female,* New York, 1968, p. 259.

husbands, an example of how male chauvinism benefits capitalists by dividing the working class.

Furthermore, the capitalist profit level is supported in an important way by reliance on "unpaid" women who provide the household chorework for the society; i.e., keeping these jobs off the market. The value of such unpaid domestic labor has been estimated at one fifth to one third of the total Gross National Product, or approximately $150–$250 billion.[4] Finally, the work of women in the home actually builds male chauvinism by making women seem less essential to the economy of the family. It does this by keeping women in "supportive" roles and by restricting the vistas and experience of housewives—making them often in fact quite limited. In a society that prizes earning ability and versatility, "women's work" has attached to it a whole aura of worthlessness and failure.

That women who work outside the home are paid less for their labors is an acknowledged fact. In 1967 the median income for men in this country was $6020 as compared to $2351 for women. This discrepancy particularly reflects the higher proportion of women who do not have jobs, but even if only year-round full-time workers are counted, the median income figures are widely separated at $7182 and $4150.[5] What is even more important, this differential in median income ratio has been steadily growing over the past several decades.[6]

Today over one third of the total work force is composed of women, most of them concentrated in traditionally "women's jobs."[7] The President's Commission on the Status of Women reports that, "The largest concentration [of women workers]—7 million—is in the clerical field. Three other main groupings—service workers (waitresses, beauticians, hospital attendants), factory operatives, and professional and technical employees (teachers, nurses, accountants, librarians)—number between 3 and 3¾ million each."[8]

"By and large," as one recent study of employment points out, "women are found in jobs that men don't want—jobs with low wages and poor prospects for advancement."[9] And most often they receive lower pay for doing the same work as men. This situation is often justified on the grounds that women are only working to supplement their husbands' incomes and therefore do not need to earn as much as men. But this is clearly more myth than truth. One of every eight urban families is headed by a woman. And two thirds of all women employed in 1965, for example, were either single, widowed, divorced, separated or married to husbands earning under $5000 a year.[10] Of

[4] For the lower estimate, see Bird, *ibid.*, p. 227; and for the higher, David Deitch's financial column in the Boston *Globe*, September 17, 1969.

[5] *Income in 1967 of Persons in the United States*, U.S. Department of Commerce, Bureau of the Census Current Population Reports, Series P-60, No. 60, June 30, 1969, p. 39.

[6] See Joan Jordan, "The Place of American Women: Exploitation of Women," *Revolutionary Age*, vol. 1, no. 3, Seattle, 1968; reprinted by New England Free Press, pp. 6–7.

[7] One third are clerical workers. See A. J. Jaffe and Joseph Froomkin, *Technology and Jobs*, New York, 1968, pp. 98–105.

[8] See *American Women*, The Report of the President's Commission on the Status of Women and other publications of the Commission, New York, Charles Scribner's Sons, 1965, p. 45.

[9] Jaffe and Froomkin, *op. cit.*, p. 105.

[10] *Underutilization of Women Workers*, U.S. Department of Labor, Women's Bureau, 1967.

the remaining 34 percent one would expect that a significant proportion were in families where the husband's income was insufficient to maintain a decent standard of living (given that the U.S. Department of Labor has suggested somewhat over $9000 as the income necessary for a "modest but adequate" 1966 budget for an urban family of four).

Overall, then, women earn less and have less appealing jobs for no reason other than their sex. The result of this situation is greater profit for the capitalist:

> Using 1950 Census reports, and figures from the Federal Reserve Board and also from the Securities and Exchange Commission, Grace Hutchins calculates that manufacturing companies realized a profit of $5.4 billion in 1950 by paying women less per year than the wages paid to men for similar work. The extra profits from employing women at lower rates than men formed 23% of all manufacturing company profits.[11]

It is hardly surprising, then, that the number of women in the work force has been rising steadily—mainly in nonunionized, poorly paying service jobs. Thirty-one percent of all women in the country were employed in 1947; 34 percent in 1957; and 39 percent in 1967. Women make up nearly half the nation's white-collar force: three out of every four clerical workers are female.[12]

"Equal opportunity" [for women], writes Caroline Bird, author of *Born Female,* "could raise our labor costs, make it harder for us to adjust supply to demand, and reduce the flexibility of our economy . . . equal opportunity would have the same effect as raising the minimum wage." [13] The advantage to capitalism of an inequality between the sexes is clear: it delivers one fourth of manufacturing profits. Capitalism would have great difficulty surviving "equal opportunity for women."

The third enormous benefit of male chauvinism to those who control the capitalist economy is that women constitute a vast reserve of labor power which can be mobilized when needed, but is not considered unemployed when jobs disappear.

As Table I indicates, the majority of women, unlike the majority of men, are *not* gainfully employed; and the current popular ideal is that of the happy housewife busy with home and children. When the labor market is glutted, the ideal gets a great deal of publicity; but in times of labor shortages, the ideal that is publicized is that of the working woman.[14]

During World War II, when the nation was desperately short of labor, women were assured that their menstrual periods did not have to immobilize them for several days a month, that bottle feeding was preferable to breast feeding and that it was better for them and for their children if they got out of the home and into a job. Thousands of day care centers were set up to make it possible for women to contribute to the war effort. But as soon as the war ended, 300,000 women workers were fired.[15]

[11] Jordan, *op. cit.*, p. 16.
[12] Manpower Report of the President, 1968, p. 232.
[13] Bird, *op. cit.*, pp. 231, 237.
[14] Fran Ansley, "Function of the Theory and Practice of Male Chauvinism," *Female Liberation Newsletter*, Vol. 1, No. 1, 1969, pp. 3–6; and Jordan, *op. cit.*
[15] Bird, *op. cit.*, p. 42.

TABLE I. EMPLOYMENT OF PERSONS 14 YEARS AND OVER AS OF MARCH 1968

	MEN		WOMEN	
	Numbers in Thousands	Median Income	Numbers in Thousands	Median Income
Total	66,519	5,571	73,584	1,819
Employed	47,622	6,610	27,887	3,157
Unemployed	1,680	3,017	1,332	1,382
Armed Forces or not in labor force	17,217	1,634	44,365	913

Source: Based on U.S. Department of Commerce, Bureau of the Census, *Current Population Reports*, Series P-60 No. 60, June 30, 1969, p. 35.

"Immediately following World War II," writes Joan Jordan, "when the returning veterans needed jobs, women at work created juvenile delinquents at home, were competing with men, and surveys showed eight out of ten infants who died of stomach ailments within the first year of birth were bottle-fed." [16]

World War II demonstrated how easily women could be moved in and out of the labor force—and also how profitable it could be for business to employ women. As soon as the postwar recovery permitted, the employment of women sky-rocketed. The 1950's was the first decade in American history in which more women than men entered the labor force.[17] The number of working mothers also increased dramatically. In 1940, one out of ten mothers of children under 18 were working; by 1967, the figure had risen to four out of ten, or 38 percent of all women in the labor force.[18]

So persistent are the chauvinist assumptions, however, that many wives and mothers feel guilty about the fact that they work. Nine out of ten working wives in a 1956 Detroit area study, for example, felt that their job made personal relations in the home more difficult, hurt their husbands' pride or simply disrupted the home.[19] Thus, there is little danger of organized rebellion when women are forced out of their jobs by a tightened labor market.

The flexibility in the size of the labor force provided by male chauvinism is especially important because of the inability of capitalism to provide full employment—at least without runaway inflation. Thus, the lesson of this century has been that capitalism can have full employment and full-scale war, or full employment and intolerable price levels, or—the option generally followed—a relatively high level of unemployment. But if the real unemployment level were widely recognized as being at about 15 percent (see the Christoffel selection above), the capitalists would run a high risk of a working-class rebellion. This true level is camouflaged, however, because unemployment does

[16] Jordan, *op. cit.*, p. 15.

[17] See Jaffe and Froomkin, *op. cit.*, pp. 98–105.

[18] *Who are the Working Mothers?* U.S. Department of Labor, Wage and Labor Standards Administration, Women's Bureau, Leaflet 37, 1968.

[19] Harold Wilensky, "Women's Work," *Industrial Relations,* May 1968, p. 235; as reported in Marilyn Goldberg, "New Light on the Exploitation of Women," *Liberation,* October 1969, p. 23.

not strike the working class across the board, but is concentrated within certain subgroups. Very old and very young workers, unskilled workers, black workers, women workers, have unemployment rates far above the national average—and workers who suffer less severely are convinced that their own situations would worsen if conditions were appreciably improved for other, worse-off subgroups. This antagonism between parts of the working class is fostered by such ideologies as racism and male chauvinism, with the result that the true unemployment picture remains an unchallenged obscurity.

Dependable statistics on unemployment are generally hard to find; with respect to female unemployment they are virtually nonexistent. This is because standard tallies count as unemployed only those who are actively looking for work. But there is no way to measure how many of the forty-five million women over 14 not in the labor force would want to work if they could find jobs and if society sanctioned their working. It has been estimated that as many as ten million women might be added to the labor force under such circumstances,[20] and even this may be a conservative estimate.

The fact that a large number of women are employed in part-time jobs helps ensure the female-based flexibility in the size of the working force. In 1960, for example, 13 percent of all employed men held part-time jobs; it was true of 32 percent of all employed women.[21] In other words, although women constitute only 37 percent of the total work force, they hold over half of all part-time jobs.

Part-time work is convenient for some women, but its greatest value is to the capitalists. It is a great deal easier to fire and replace part-time than full-time workers. Job security is generally viewed by full-time workers and their unions as a privilege of full-time employment; and in most instances part-time workers are looked upon by their employers and their full-time co-workers as temporary employees, without the protection of seniority. In addition, many hard-won fringe benefits, such as sick leave, vacations with pay, medical insurance, retirement pensions, and so on, are often denied to part-time employees; and where this is so, huge savings in labor costs may result from breaking up full-time jobs into two or more part-time positions. Finally, extensive use of part-time workers makes it much more difficult for all the workers on a job to unite in organized struggles for better wages, working conditions, benefits and the like. It is interesting to note that in clerical work, a major area of female employment, temporary jobs have been institutionalized in the form of temporary worker agencies—Kelly Girls, American Girl Service, Girl Power, Inc., etc.—which provide part-time labor and ensure all these advantages to the employer.

Because so many women hold part-time jobs and women workers provide flexibility for the labor market, many people still believe that female workers are marginal to the economy (e.g., Juliet Mitchell, Margaret Benston). But while it is true that the major increase in female employment over the past 15 years has been in those industries where—because of little technological

[20] Alva Myrdal and Viola Klein, *Women's Two Roles,* London, 1956, cited in Bird, *op. cit.,* p. 231.

[21] Report of the Committee on Private Employment to the President's Commission on the Status of Women, Washington, D.C., Government Printing Office, 1963, p. 42.

advance—productivity has increased *least,* it is also true that more than one out of every three employed persons in America today is a woman. Approximately one out of every four factory workers is a woman, and two of every five such women work in "heavy" industry.[22] Clearly, a high percentage of the total GNP and of all profits can be attributed to women workers. Far from being marginal, women constitute a crucial part of the productive capacity of the economy.

Nevertheless, working men most often fail to recognize working women as equals, a fact which weakens and divides the working class in struggles against their bosses. The capitalists, of course, recognize this situation and try to perpetuate it. For example, one fifth to one third of all companies have different pay scales for men and women doing the same kind of work.[23] In other companies, work which could be done equally well by men or women is defined by the employer as "men's jobs" or "women's jobs," closing off employment opportunities for one group or the other. And in a tactic often used by employers during strikes, letters are sent to strikers' wives, calling upon them to urge their husbands to return to work.

By failing to fight for equal wages and job security for women, trade unions have weakened *all* workers struggles. For as long as men must fear replacement by lower-paid women, they are weakened in their fight for better wages and working conditions; and as long as women are not fighting alongside men, all workers are weakened. Yet working men have been conditioned to believe that their own exploited situation is relatively "good" because it is slightly better than that of women, and have been misled into believing they have a vested interest in keeping women down.

Women workers, as a result, often resent the men who work alongside them, and the two groups who should be working together are kept—profitably for their bosses—at odds with one another.

The same harmful division is often carried into the home, where wives must often bear the brunt of their husbands' anger and dissatisfactions on the job. Frustrated by the economic treadmill they must run on, working men all too often come to view their families as burdens and blame them, rather than the exploitation of capitalism, for their discontent. Thus male chauvinism divides the working class and turns its discontents back upon itself.

It is important to be clear, however, that male chauvinism not only hurts women, but hurts men as well—and quite directly. For as long as women are kept economically and psychologically dependent, men are charged—psychologically, if not always in fact—with the sole and complete burden of providing for their families. (And this is true even if their marriages should be dissolved by divorce.) To be sure, men are reputed to enjoy many advantages in their "superior" role. But the so-called advantages tend to crumble under examination.

The light and lively companion who is so flatteringly unchallenging to the male ego is seldom a friend to share experiences, doubts, and problems with; and the wife who is sheltered—and isolated—by the confines of her home and

[22] Manpower Report of the President, 1968, p. 232; Elizabeth Baker, *Technology and Women's Work,* New York, 1964, p. 206.

[23] Report of the Committee on Private Employment, *op. cit.,* p. 48.

family all too often becomes a bore and a nag that her husband yearns to escape from. Keeping women "in their place" may help some men avoid housework. But a good marriage calls for more than being kept by a housekeeper and a marriage based on shared burdens and desires is a good deal more satisfying than one based on a well-darned sock. The satisfaction of feeling superior compares poorly with mutual respect, and command and subservience compares poorly with cooperation.

Despite the fact that male chauvinism hurts both men and women, it persists. For the attitudes that support it are pervasive and deep. Boys and girls are taught practically from birth that men are expected to run the world and women are expected to stay sweet, sexy and at home. While most young men are raised to prepare for a job in order to support their family (their role being that of provider and authority first and only secondarily that of husband and father), the goal for women, first and foremost, is that of wife and mother, and they learn early that they are expected to venture beyond those roles only as required to help husband and children get along. The implications of such conditioning are profound and all-pervasive, and they serve capitalism well.

Because it helps them, capitalists foster male chauvinism. The media they control are well-run schools for indoctrination in male chauvinism. Sex-oriented marketing practices serve the dual function of increasing markets (two razors) and maintaining male chauvinist ideas (Be a *real* man; win a *real* woman; wear, use, *buy*) that increase profits through a sex-divided labor force. The survival of male chauvinism in advanced capitalist societies rests firmly on its economic basis. And unless that basis is clearly understood, the persistence of chauvinist myths and prejudices will be quite confusing.

The importance of that understanding is strategic: because male chauvinism is so integral a part of capitalism, it can only really be eliminated when capitalism is destroyed. And the effort to replace capitalism with socialism can succeed only as male chauvinism—and the other divisive ideological underpinnings of capitalism—are defeated. For unity of men and women is essential to real socialism, a form of social organization based on and built by people sharing equally their wealth and responsibility.

Because the underpinnings of capitalism and chauvinism go very deep, the defeat of male chauvinism and the advent of socialism will take an unforeseeably long time. Even after a socialist revolution, it will be a very long time before all of the effects of these ideologies on our thoughts and actions become fully apparent. And the struggle against them goes on and on.

Of all the divisive ideologies, male chauvinism goes perhaps the deepest. Its added strength and tenacity is due to the childbearing capacity of women, which no longer provides a real material basis for male chauvinist sex roles, but which is a functional difference between the sexes that can be pointed to to justify male chauvinism. The other ideological underpinnings of capitalism have never had functional bases.

In the absence of a demonstrable functional basis—however unimportant—an ideology can be expected to grow weak in the face of evidence to contradict it and to show its harmfulness. Similar weakening is not impossible—but is much slower—for the ideology of male chauvinism. Furthermore, male chauvinism goes deeper simply because it involves sex, which intimately and ritualistically and often neurotically pervades our social and personal lives, and even our language.

What this all adds up to is that the struggle against male chauvinism will be at least as prolonged as it is essential, at least as difficult as it is promising. So long as we keep that in mind, it is a struggle that can be won—and during which we will all become stronger and freer.

22 EDUCATION UNDER CAPITALISM*

by DAVID FINKELHOR

The following article was originally intended as an introduction to the selections on education. It grew to such proportions, however, that it is herewith presented on its own.

Liberals have long felt that public education was a bright spot in the social landscape. Not that public education was good. But the existence of universal, public education demonstrated that the system was indeed responsive to the aspirations of the people. Through education everyone had the possibility for self-improvement, and universal education would ultimately result in a humanizing and liberalizing of the society.

And even if education was bad, they said, in the long-run it was sure to improve. After all, good education is in everybody's interest, even those who run the economy. Better-educated people make better workers and better citizens. But given this alleged general interest in better education, what has always puzzled liberals is why education should be so bad, and why so little money flowed into it.

Radicals, on the other hand, have applied a class analysis to the school system, and with it have gained many insights into why schools are as bad as they are. They have seen the present organization of the school system as a crucial stabilizing mechanism in our modern capitalist society. Specifically, the schools serve the following functions: (1) they create and maintain a social class hierarchy; (2) they legitimate the existence of inequality and class privileges; (3) they socialize the great mass of people to prepare them for and make them accept oppressive jobs; and (4) they indoctrinate people into the political and social ideas that help strengthen the system. "Improving" the schools a la liberal rhetoric often jeopardizes one or more of these central functions. That's why there's no reform.

MAINTAINING THE CLASS SYSTEM

Those who benefit from the class privileges of the society hope naturally to pass these privileges on to their children. To serve this interest, the public education system provides a series of institutions that are biased toward advancing the children of the well-to-do into important positions, but which is meanwhile financed mainly from the pockets of the poor-to-do. In addition, the capitalist economy needs a work force neatly stratified to provide workers who will fit in comfortably to their destined job slots. For employers, the system de-

* Used by permission of the author.

livers up stratified classes of people who are clearly intended for factory work, for clerical work, for white-collar work, etc. This means employers don't have to spend time evaluating people's abilities to figure out where they should go. It also means that workers will see their job situation as their "destiny" and will not have ambitions terribly out of line with their situation—a conflict that could easily lead to discontent and inefficiency. The Research Organizing Cooperative selection (see below) documents how this system works in a highly premeditated way in the California school system—supposedly one of the most "progressive" in the country.

LEGITIMIZING PRIVILEGES

Besides giving advantage to the children of the upper classes and stratifying the labor force, schools operate to give the impression that it is perfectly just and right that they should do this. Children are conventionally taught that those who succeed in school are those who are "intelligent," those who work hard and those who live up to the expectations of their teachers and other authorities. These are virtues supposedly accessible to everyone. Moreover, it is drilled into our heads that society needs such people in high position, and therefore their privileges are well deserved. What is covered over is that these qualities—like intelligence and good behavior—as they are measured by the schools, are nearly synonymous with coming from a privileged background.

The results of such a system of legitimizing privilege are, on the one hand, that the advantaged kids feel justified in their privileges and believe they are now sanctioned to occupy the positions in the society where they will command and oppress all the rest. Those who fail in the system think they have only themselves to blame. They lost out in fair and square competition. Moreover, they believe that those who did succeed and now oppress them have the right to do so because they had the laudable qualities of intelligence and diligence.

MAKING GOOD WORKERS

A third need for the capitalist system is to assure itself of a supply of trained and obedient workers. The key thing about work under capitalism is that the vast majority of jobs are oppressive, dehumanizing, unsatisfying and require ideally (for the boss) a high degree of obedience to supervisors. Schools work to provide workers who are suitable for this kind of work.

Most people think that the main training kids get in school is reading, writing and arithmetic. A quick trip through a school for anyone illustrates how few of these "cognitive" skills—history, math, etc.—get learned, particularly by those who are going to take up the lower ranks of the work force. We all know that most jobs in our society don't require those skills anyway.

What skills do they require? They require men and women who will do repetitive and meaningless work, day after day, year after year. They require men and women who will willingly take orders from superiors and implement them efficiently. They require men and women who will compete with one another to get ahead by obediently carrying out their assigned tasks. They require men and women who will suffer this meaninglessness willingly, even enthusiastically, for the sake of a reward like money. They require men and women who will not grumble or band together and fight back.

The schools train kids in all these personality characteristics. They are a prototype of the work experience. Kids do repetitive and meaningless tasks. They are taught to take orders and compete. And they are made to respond to some sort of external reward for this meaninglessness, i.e., grades. In a word, they are repressed. The main message of the school is authority. Kids are subjected to a never-ending series of rules: dress codes, haircuts, talk periods, lines, sitting still, bubble-gum chewing. They are brought to conform. And authority is ever present in the form of suspensions, beatings, grading and make-up work. These all seem extraneous to what liberals see as "learning." But they are not at all extraneous to what schools in our society want their future workers to learn.

IDEOLOGY

Finally, it is relatively important that people under capitalism learn to accept it, and see it as the best of all possible worlds. Most of the few ideas the schools do communicate to kids are about what a great society we live in and about how people should have faith and trust in the system. Kids are taught that American history has been a democratic pageant. The great "soap opera" of government is run by and for the people. They are taught a hatred of communism or socialism and the superiority of the American system. They are taught that those who hold power do so because they have special talent, and that we should trust in their ability to handle things for us. All suggestions that America leaves something to be desired are carefully avoided. Kids are molded into citizens who will be passive and who will not question the justice of the system.

REFORM?

Progressive school reformers usually say they will change all this. But if we understand how the schools serve to stabilize capitalism, then we can see how reform or improvement of the schools threatens to upset the system. For example, what would happen if a college education were available to everyone. For one thing, it would be much more difficult for the children of the rich to monopolize positions of importance. Their claim to do it on the basis of more education would have been undermined. Second, those who would have to go perform the menial functions in society would do so a lot less willingly. Since their aspirations had been raised, they would feel much more acutely the oppressiveness of their fate. They would probably rebel against the degradation and meaninglessness of their work.

What if schools were made less authoritarian, as liberals often propose, and more time was given to learning than discipline? For one thing, kids would not adopt the discipline and the necessary personality characteristics to tolerate the work they will later have to do. They would think their jobs ought to be creative. They would get the idea that maybe they had the capability to do something else. In fact, a rebellion based on an awareness of this sort is presently underway in many schools around the country.

So a lot of what liberals think is "bad" about schools is just precisely what the schools are supposed to be doing. Reforming the schools threatens to eliminate the crucial functions the schools perform for the capitalist system. Reform also costs money. Corporate managers and their political allies do not particularly think the schools fail in providing the kind of manpower they need. So they are not so keen on spending on school reform billions that could go into more profit-making kinds of undertakings. Spending on education runs up against the same kinds of corporate obstacles as other welfare spending.

A real change in the nature of education cannot occur until there is a change in the nature of work and an abolition of the class structure. Since capitalism breeds work that is inherently alienating and oppressive, education under capitalism will have to prepare people to do that work. Since it spawns a class system, education will have to stratify people and justify doing so. Good education for everyone aimed at ministering to the needs of kids as people, not to the needs of the system, can only occur once capitalism has been eliminated.

23

THE FAILURE OF GHETTO EDUCATION*

by ERIC MANN

Many studies have been done and they all show the same thing—black students fail in school. They do worse than whites at all levels, and the gap becomes greater and greater the higher you go.

Mann's article addresses itself to the question of why this is. Many people have the interpretation that black children are "deprived" by their environment—that the solution is to enrich their environment or to make up for the deprivation at school itself. Others, of course, interpret this as evidence enough of either black stupidity or black laziness. But neither the liberal interpretation nor the blatantly racist interpretation speaks to what is really going on.

The virtue of Mann's article is to point out that school is an arbitrary and oppressive game. No one would naturally want to learn what schools have to offer. Students play along because it is the ticket for getting ahead. It may be that the kids with the most brains and the most spirit do the worst in school because they can't hack the boredom and the lies. This is part of the explanation for the "failure" of black students. For a whole set of reasons, they have little incentive for playing. They are less eager than whites from the start to dig into Dick and Jane.

Blacks just don't get ahead going to school the way whites do. Economists show that black income increases very little with additional years of schooling. It may even be economically rational for black kids not to go to school; to drop out and start making money right away.

The racism in the schools makes it a hard pull to get through. Blacks get less attention, more punishment and discipline; teachers expect them to fail from the start and they get channeled into the lowest tracks and the worst schools. Why should they want to hack this?

Finally, schools are middle-class institutions bent on preparing middle-class people. Black kids' homes don't prepare them for middle-class institutions. That doesn't mean they're deprived; it means that they get prepared for survival in a world of "leftovers"—probably a much more essential preparation for a ghetto kid. Black kids just don't relate to the middle-class material, and they naturally won't respond to the demands for behavior that violate their tested code for survival.

EDUCATION IN THE GHETTO

The problems in ghetto education manifest themselves in two major areas: academic performance and classroom behavior. In the three elementary schools in our area the average reading score in the sixth grade on the Stanford October Reading Test was 1.8 years below the national average. The average score on the Stanford Mathematics test—given in the seventh grade—was 2.0 years below the national average. Recently, 150 students at the junior high school in our area were suspended in one day by a principal who declared, "Something has to be done to shock these students into proper behavior."

Like many public-school educators we, too, are deeply concerned about the academic and behavior problems of ghetto youth. Unlike many public-school educators, however, we believe that the public-school system is primarily responsible for these problems.

Public education—for the middle-class child as well as the ghetto child—is largely irrelevant to the child's interests and contrary to his creative capacities. The middle-class child, however, has more incentive to adapt himself to an unstimulating school situation. Although school itself is not particularly satisfying, the middle-class child learns at an early age to postpone immediate gratification to earn future rewards. He enters school with well-developed prereading skills and usually achieves reading competence with relative ease. Thus, the initial school experience reinforces postponing gratification: the student didn't particularly care what Dick said to Jane but by learning how to read he won the approval of his teacher and parents.

IMMEDIATE GRATIFICATION

The ghetto child does not enter school with the same skills as the middle-class child. The exigencies of a large family and the small number of material rewards from his parents have made the pursuit of immediate gratification a logical life style. His initial experience with nonstimulating curriculum does not produce the same success that the middle-class child experiences. The work is harder for him and he is less willing to attack a difficult and boring lesson for the promise of future rewards. Some ghetto students refuse to accept the challenge and "turn off" at a surprisingly early age. Others accept the challenge and fail: they also didn't care what Dick said to Jane but despite making some effort to learn they do not get the rewards and reinforcements of reading success. A third group manages to get through the obstacle course of immediate gratification and difficult work and is on its way to developing middle-class skills.

As the middle-class child grows older the unpleasantness of the school situation often becomes a stronger force than the rewards stemming from academic competence. At this point a more fundamental reward system comes into play. By fourth or fifth grade the middle-class child is conscious of some kind of relationship between academic success and his middle-class environment. Although this relationship is often explained by his parents in crude economic terms, it is doubtful that the child studies hard because he is afraid of jeopardizing his long-range financial situation. He is, however, capable of perceiving his parents in more generalized material terms: they are successful; they tell him that school is the key to his success. His desire to please his parents and his general feeling that his parents are able effectively to deal with the world give their arguments considerable force. Learning becomes even more removed from an intrinsically rewarding activity. It gets tied up in a complex set of expectations which the middle-class teacher and parent convey to the student, and which eventually becomes internalized in the "well-adjusted" student.

MODELS OF FAILURE

As the ghetto child grows older he discovers that the arguments about the material benefits of a good education are, at best, quite tenuous. He has seen most of his friends, relatives and neighbors with varying degrees of education living in similar conditions. The Negro college graduate rarely moves back into the ghetto and, therefore, does not provide a role-model for the student who is struggling in the public school. The Negro high-school graduate, more often than not, still lives in a rundown building, still experiences police abuse and brutality, and still is unable to get a good job. The ghetto family often is lacking a father, and even in families where a father is present the success models projected by the schools and television make the child increasingly aware of his parents' "failure." Thus, the ghetto students who hardly tried at all and the students who tried and failed become further demoralized as they get older. As the sequential presentation of irrelevant material continues these students become hardened into a disloyal opposition. This large body of alienated students obviously affects the performance of all the others. Even the ghetto students who were more successful in the early stages find their numbers dwindling.

The teacher in the middle-class school starts out at a great advantage. His students have already developed many basic skills before coming to his class and are reinforced by strong pressures from home. A process of mutual reinforcement takes place. The teacher, while adhering to the basic curriculum, employs a few new twists in presenting the material. The students respond by enthusiastically participating in the lesson and learning the material presented. The teacher feels successful, becomes more confident and more open, and rewards the students for their success. These rewards, in the form of verbal praise and good grades, encourage the students to continue to participate in the learning process. A whole success syndrome is created.

In spite of the large numbers of teachers who are racially and culturally prejudiced, a large minority of teachers in ghetto schools start out with a genuine concern for the students and the ability to communicate with them in a non-school atmosphere. These teachers in the ghetto schools have a terribly difficult task. They, too, try to make small innovations in teaching methods and curriculum, expecting the same enthusiasm that such improvements would receive in a middle-class school. Since they accept the basic conceptions of learning theory, curriculum and classroom discipline, however, they soon discover that their students are unresponsive and unappreciative. Their attempt to sell the status quo in the face of this student rejection produces a warfare situation between the teacher and his class. The students have little interest in the material presented, little reason to believe they will be successful someday, little reason to believe their new teacher will be different from the oppressors of previous years and little incentive to be cooperative members of a classroom group. Since the school has become associated with embarrassment and failure the only real pleasure remaining for the student is to take out his aggressions on the teacher.

"THE KIDS ARE ANIMALS"

If the teacher is extremely competent at repressive discipline practices, he may be able to defeat the students in this war and force them to hide their aggressions behind a mask of compliance. It is the teacher who tries to avoid such repressive measures—while still trying to push the basic educational program of the school—that finds himself most victimized by the students. He is the "easy mark." As the students express their hostility to the school by verbally—and sometimes physically—attacking him, the well-meaning teacher often finds himself losing much of the sensitivity and concern he came in with. Rather than evaluating the situation and deciding the students' hostility is justified—perhaps the irrelevance and inhumanity of ghetto education creates "blackboard jungles" —the teacher usually decides that his original conceptions about the kids were romantic. Somewhat reluctantly, he finds himself feeling a certain amount of empathy with the teachers who complained all along that "the kids are animals."

This inability to accept the validity of the students' rebellion is not surprising. Many teachers are overwhelmed by the massive powers that stand in the way of educational reform—principals, school boards, city administrations—and feel threatened by arguments that link educational reform with challenging those in power. Also, despite the fact that the school administrators are most responsible for the educational policies in the ghetto, it is the teacher who experiences the hostility that these policies produce. After becoming involved in a warfare situation with his class it is difficult for him to extricate himself from his emotional framework and develop a new analysis of what went wrong. Perhaps most importantly, the systematic discouragement and weeding out of innovators among the new faculty and the absence of experimental private schools in the ghetto provide the ambivalent teacher with no visible models to support his initial faith in his students.

24

EDUCATION AND THE MAINTENANCE OF SOCIAL CLASSES*

by THE RESEARCH ORGANIZING COOPERATIVE

Schools service the corporate economy in crucial ways. One of these ways is to select out ahead of time those who will staff positions of authority in society and those who will man the machines. In other words, schools create a hierarchy; they determine who will get ahead and who won't. One way this is accomplished within the schools is through tracking. It is also accomplished through college admissions and through grades.

Tracking only works if it manages to limit the number of people who advance so that they match the number of positions of responsibility there are to be filled. If too many get ahead, those who have to suffer menial jobs anyway are much more likely to grumble. Corporate leaders really worry about controlling things like that. This article by the Research Organizing Cooperative shows how the hierarchy produced by the system of California schools was a deliberate creation of political and corporate leaders in the state.

The article is part of a pamphlet that came out of the strike at San Francisco State. For four months during the winter and spring of 1968–69 there was a strike led by black and Third World students (Chinese, Mexican American, Japanese). They were demanding an end to the systematic exclusion to black and Third World students and the establishment of a Department of Black and Third World studies. This pamphlet explained how the exclusion of blacks and Third World students was part of the deliberate discrimination established by the tracking system in the California schools.

"To get a good job, get a good education."

America is the "land of opportunity" because everyone has a chance to get a good education. That's why we have free public schools from kindergarten to high school. And here in California, that's why we have "mass" higher education. Right?

Wrong.

Many people put up with the way their lives are run—hard work, low take-home pay, prices and rents going up all the time—because they believe that their children, at least, have a chance to make a decent life for themselves. If your kid studies hard and if he's got something on the ball, maybe he can make it.

This is a myth.

The reality? A factory worker's son has a smaller chance of getting a four-year college diploma today than he had ten years ago. For Third World children—those of African, Asian, Latin American and American Indian descent—the situation is even worse. At San Francisco State College in 1960, for example, 12 percent of the students were black. By 1968 this had dropped to 3 percent.

How did this happen? For the answer, we have to go back to the late 1950s.

Thanks to the post-war "baby boom," the number of children in school was expected to double between 1960 and 1970. The bonus crop of babies who were born after World War II was growing up, and there had been a steady migration of families to California. Just to keep up with this increase—not to mention improving education—the state would have to build as many schools in one decade as it had built in the previous forty or fifty years.

Books, teachers, school buses—all would have to be doubled. And college facilities would have to be expanded too. Where was the money to come from?

As usual it would come from California's working people, the people the state squeezes most of its income from. These are the families who make less than $10,000 a year—and they pay the lion's share of the retail sales, cigarette, alcoholic beverage, motor vehicle and gasoline taxes. Together these taxes bring in 55 percent of the state's revenue. And these same people pay a generous share of the state's personal income tax, as well.

What about the corporations? Last year, bank and corporate taxes brought in less than 12 percent of California's tax revenues. Could they afford any more?

The huge war industries of California are bloated with dollars. Lockheed Aircraft made a profit of $54 million in 1967; North American Rockwell made $68 million; Standard Oil of California, $421 million—and this is only what these companies report.

Any one of these corporations could cough up another $10 million in taxes without straining. But they don't have to because they control the governor's office and the state legislature. (By making big contributions to both political parties, the corporation bosses come out on top no matter who wins the election.)

In short, there was no way to pay for mass higher education. The workers had already been taxed to the gills. And the corporations refused to pay. Obviously something had to go.

What "went" was the notion that higher education was for everybody. In 1959 the state legislature authorized the Regents to figure out ways to cut the costs of education and make the school system more "efficient." In February 1960 the Regents came out with their report, the "Master Plan for Higher Education" in California. Two months later the report was enacted into law, killing any hope for equal opportunity in education. And it all had the approval of Democratic Governor Edmund "Pat" Brown.

The Master Plan had two major effects. It established the tracking system throughout the state. And it cut down on the number of working-class students who attend college and reduced spending on those who do attend.

What is the "tracking system"? Since the Master Plan there have been two standard "tracks" in the elementary and high schools of California. One is for children who are considered "college material," the other for those who are "not academically inclined." If your child is placed on the "college" track, he will be in a classroom with other children who are headed for college. What he is taught will prepare him for college.

If your child is placed on the "vocational" track, he will be taught different materials, by teachers who know that he is not likely to go to college. And they are right. Once he is put on this track he hasn't much chance of getting off.

Why is there a tracking system? In America today, the number of good jobs is limited, and there are many jobs that are poorly paid. If everyone got a good education, it would be hard to find people to fill the poorer jobs. Also, the extra education would be "wasted"—there would be no way for the bosses to make money out of it.

Even more important, the people who have good jobs now are not satisfied just to have good jobs. They want to make sure their children have them too. But in a fair competition for the good jobs, many privileged kids of average ability would be edged out by brighter working-class kids.

The tracking system solves this "problem." It eliminates most working-class children from the competition for good jobs, by preventing them from getting the education they need to compete. Yet it seems normal to many working people. Why is this?

Very early in their school careers—usually by the third grade—children are placed on either the college track or the other track, on the basis of seemingly "objective" reading and "IQ" tests. But in fact these tests are far from objective.

They measure "intelligence" by comparing a child's test scores to those of an average group of white, privileged city children of the same age. But the "IQ" test is based in part on things that a child living in a higher-income city neighborhood is more likely to know about. So if you are a factory worker and you live in a neighborhood of other workers, or if you live on a farm, your child will be handicapped in the test. And the cultural bias of IQ tests makes it extra hard on black and brown children.

It is not a matter of the privileged children having a "better background" or being "better prepared." Some of the questions on the Stanford-Binet IQ test for young children, for example, involve the use of wooden building blocks. Nearly all middle-class parents buy blocks like these for their children. A great many poorer children, on the other hand, have never seen a set of building blocks before the day of the IQ test. Clearly, the children who have played with them for many hours at home will do a better job with them than the children who have never seen them before. Does this make the practiced, middle-class child brighter? According to the IQ test it does.

When it comes right down to it, IQ tests measure income, not intelligence. It may be news to some parents that the IQ tests discriminate in this way. But teachers, professors and testers have known it all along.

In theory it is possible for a child to get onto the college track even if he starts on the lower track. But it is very difficult. Often, racial or class discrimination is at work. Teachers and guidance counselors cannot believe that a child from "that kind of background" could be "college material."

Often it is simply that once a teacher learns a child's "IQ," she "knows" how much to expect of the child—and children quickly understand when they are not expected to do well.

An experiment that took place in the New York City schools proved this. Some teachers were told that an objective test had identified some "late bloomers" in their classes. They were told that certain children who had been doing only average work would soon show a dramatic improvement in their classroom performance.

Actually the children were just average children, selected at random. But once the teachers believed that these children were about to do better, the children DID do better. The teachers "knew" they were not ordinary children and treated them more patiently and respectfully—and the children responded.

For ethical reasons, the people who ran this experiment did not try telling the teachers that any of the children had "no potential." They did perform that experiment on rats. The people who put rats through mazes were told that some of the rats were more intelligent and that other rats were dumber. Sure enough, the "intelligent" rats (actually they were all the same) did better in the mazes!

In effect the school system is doing the same thing to your children that the experimenters did to the rats. They tell the teachers that some children are not as bright as other children. And then these children do not do as well because they are not expected to.

The lesson is clear. Once a so-called "objective" system of testing like this takes hold, it will actually hold back the children from Third World and white working-class backgrounds.

The tracking system isn't the only problem Third World and white working-class children have to face in the schools of San Francisco. Just as important are the problems of blatant inequality in faculty, staff, facilities, supplies and curriculum. The highest paid teachers (the best and most experienced) are concentrated in the predominantly white schools, teaching students from the higher-income neighborhoods. And the least experienced and poorest trained teach the poorest students—in schools that are overwhelmingly black and Spanish-speaking.

More money is spent on each pupil at the "whiter," richer schools. This is because the channeling of funds favors the college-trackers over the vocational-trackers. And the biased tests push the wealthier white students into the pre-college program.

The Third World communities suffer most. The greatest overcrowding in San Francisco schools occurs in the black ghettoes of the Fillmore and Bayview-Hunters Point. And many of these schools are in older, deteriorating buildings, with bad plumbing, bad lighting, no playground equipment, inadequate fire escapes, etc.

Children from Third World communities rarely have teachers from a background similar to their own. Six out of ten public school students in San Francisco are nonwhite, but only one teacher in ten is nonwhite. Programs in ethnic studies developed by teachers at Polytechnic High, Mission High and Wilson High have not been seriously considered by the Board of Education.

The school system has been callous toward Third World children speaking foreign languages. There is no bilingual instruction in San Francisco, even in the primary grades where children from non-English speaking homes need help in making a transition. Yet one-third of the students come from homes where a language other than English is spoken.

What is the effect of all this? Let's just give one example: the results of a third grade reading test given at two elementary schools. At the wealthier, 70-percent-white Alamo Elementary School, the children were found to be reading a year *ahead* of their grade level. At poverty-ridden, nearly-all-black Golden Gate School, the children were more than a year *behind* their grade level, and two years behind the Alamo children.

That test spells bright careers and high salaries for most of the Alamo School class. It dooms the Golden Gate third-graders to lives of poverty and under-employment.

By the time they get out of high school, more than three-quarters of all graduates from the working-class schools either look for a job right away, take vocational training, or go into the Army. But what about those working-class and Third World students who still want to go to college? To understand their fate it is necessary to go back to the Master Plan for Higher Education.

The Master Plan, which became law in 1960, outlined the official policy of class discrimination that determines who gets into college.

> The State College and University admission requirements "should be exacting," the Plan stated, "because the junior colleges relieve them of the burden of doing remedial work."

Translation: Those Third World and white working-class children who have been crippled by the "educational" system can be kept out of the better colleges by using so-called "objective" entrance tests. They won't complain because they can always go to junior college.

> "Special admissions" should not exceed 2 percent of the regular enrollment.

Translation: If protests force the admission of students outside of the regular, discriminatory standards, at least they will be only a token group. The great mass of Third World and white working-class youth will be kept out. (This remains true despite the recent concession, which may raise the "special admissions" quota to a maximum of 10 percent at S. F. State—if the Legislature approves.)

> "A study of the transfer procedures (from the junior colleges to the four-year schools)" should be undertaken "with the view of tightening them."

Translation: The main purpose of junior colleges is to turn out skilled workers, not four-year college graduates. Make it more difficult for junior college students to get into a four-year program, or else they will get more education than they need to do their jobs.

> "Retention standards" at the junior colleges should be "rigid enough to guarantee that taxpayers' money is not wasted on individuals who lack the capacity or the will to succeed in their studies."

Translation: Instead of helping those students who were badly prepared by their high schools, flunk out as many as possible to keep costs down. That way you can preserve the myth that higher education is available to everyone, when in reality higher education is only intended for some.

> "Vigorous use of probation and the threat of dismissal may help some 'late bloomers' to flower sooner."

Translation: Train the workers to know who's boss. Get them used to being afraid. That will be useful to them on the job or in the Army.

Finally, the Master Plan conceded: "The selection and retention devices . . . will not guarantee that all able young Californians will go to college."

It was the understatement of the year.

All of these measures have worked out precisely as expected. Before the Master Plan was adopted, anyone in the top 33 percent of his high school class was supposed to be able to get into the University of California. And anyone in the top 70 percent could get into State College.

Today, only students in the top 12½ percent are supposed to be able to get into the University, and only the top 33 percent can get into State College. But good grades are not enough to get you into college any more. Since the Master Plan, you also have to do well on the College Board examinations.

Like the IQ tests for tracking students in school, the College Boards have a racial and class bias. Again, membership in the privileged classes gives you a better score.[1]

Adding the discriminatory College Board examination to the requirements for admission wiped out any chance that most Third World and white working-class high school graduates had of going on to college.

San Francisco's Mission High School, the lowest income school in the city, is a good example. In June 1966, only 2 percent of the graduating class went to either the University of California or San Francisco State College. In all, 5 percent of Mission's seniors went to some four-year college, as against 50 percent for Lowell, one of the highest income schools in the city. This is how the San Francisco school system serves its working-class and Third World majority.

A recent interview (March 1969) with the Dean of Admissions of San Francisco State College, Charles Stone, tells a lot about who gets to go to our "local" four-year college. Dean Stone admitted that 60 percent of San Francisco State freshmen come from outside the city. He also admitted that "almost half of the San Francisco people we admit come from private schools"—despite the fact that three-quarters of the high school students in the city go to public

[1] The Scholastic Aptitude Test, the main part of the College Board exams, is only a variation of a test invented by Edward Thorndike, the "father" of intelligence testing —who believed that nonwhite people were genetically of lower intelligence than whites. This man, who has had a tremendous influence in American education, not only wanted to exclude people of color from the colleges, he wanted to exclude them from the human race. He wrote in 1940: "One sure service, about the only one, which the inferior and vicious [his term for nonwhite people] can perform is to prevent their genes from survival." Although he was most hostile to people of color, Thorndike wanted to deny all working people the right to an equal education. He opposed "extending culture to the masses," favoring instead "giving special education to the gifted (privileged) child."

schools. This means that a boy or girl in private school has a three times better chance of getting into our publicly financed State College than a boy or girl from public school. Last year only 4 percent of San Francisco public school graduates enrolled at San Francisco State.

But Dean Stone's preferential treatment does not apply to just any private school. Take the Sacred Heart High School in the Western Addition, for example. Half of the student body of this low-tuition school is nonwhite. But San Francisco State accepted only five boys from Sacred Heart last year.

No, the Dean is talking about high-tuition, mostly white private schools like Stuart Hall for Boys in Pacific Heights, or St. Ignatius High School in the Richmond district. Last year Dean Stone admitted more students from the distant (and expensive) Bellarmine Preparatory School in San Jose than he did from Mission and Wilson High Schools combined.

The Dean was asked why this was so, when so many youths here in San Francisco want a college education. "You understand," he replied, "the boys at Bellarmine are mostly San Jose boys, so naturally they want to get away from home." To Dean Stone it means more that these rich boys should be able to go to school away from home than that poor boys and girls from our own city should go to college at all. The result is that the family income of the average State College student is $10,000 a year. (At the University of California, the average is even higher: $12,000.)

The main excuse the educators give is that everyone can go to a junior college. But even the two-year junior colleges—supposedly "open to everybody with a high school diploma"—are more exclusive than they pretend to be. Once admitted, many students are promptly flunked out—and no wonder, since most of them come from impossibly bad high schools. Most of those who enter City College of San Francisco, for example, do not complete two years there, and only 15 percent go on to higher education.

Given the systematic exclusion of black and Spanish-speaking people from State College and U. C., you would think they would show an extra high enrollment at junior colleges. But this is not the case. Black and brown people make up 22 percent of San Francisco's population—but only 16 percent of the students at City College of San Francisco.

Two-thirds of the students at the junior colleges come from families earning less than $10,000 a year. These are the families, Third World and white working people, who actually pay most of California's taxes. Yet the junior colleges their children go to get only 10 cents out of every dollar the state spends on education. While their own kids get a second class education, working people subsidize quality education for the rich.

For the junior colleges are really nothing but glorified vocational high schools. Their job is to make workers out of the children of workers, just as the University's job is to make managers and professionals out of the children of managers and professionals. The corporations, which benefit, have found that this "educational division of labor" is more efficient for them.

Junior college facilities, libraries, teacher salaries and working conditions are all below standard. Their massive counseling and testing programs combine to discourage most students from going ahead to a four-year college. Instead, students are encouraged to become hairdressers, technicians or secretaries.

It doesn't "just happen" that so few junior college students go ahead to a four-year education—that's the way it is meant to be. At the College of San Mateo, for example, only 5 percent of the students normally go ahead to a four-year institution. However, when a "College Readiness Program" for Third World students there encouraged them to continue their education—and 90 percent of the Third World students in the program did so!—the director of the program was told that not enough of his students were going into vocational training. "I didn't know I had a quota," he told the administrators. "You don't," they replied, "but you still should have put more students into vocational training." Precisely because the College Readiness Program was succeeding, it had to be crippled.

Whenever you run into a strange situation like this—educators discouraging students from getting more education, "economy" at the expense of those who can least afford it—the question you have to ask is: Who benefits?

In California and the rest of America, it is the corporations. When Governor Reagan and Superintendent Rafferty get together to talk about how to create a real educational system that meets people's needs—they talk about the "manpower requirements" of private industry and the state. (Even the San Francisco State catalogue talks about serving "the technical and professional manpower requirements of the state.")

The fact is that higher education in California is controlled by big business. The Regents who control the University of California, the Trustees of the State Colleges, and the trustees who supervise every other public and private college in the state, are almost always members of the white business class. They range from officials of the biggest corporations and banks, to the presidents of important local businesses. They are almost all white, Protestant, male and over 50.

And they have made sure that the school system in the state of California contributes its share to the production of their most important product: Profits.

APPENDIX—CLASS EDUCATION IN A NUTSHELL: WHO GOES TO COLLEGE AND WHO PAYS FOR IT

	Family Income Under $10,000	Family Income Over $10,000
Percent of California families	71.9%	28.1%
Percent of San Francisco families	75.8%	24.2%
Percent of California Third World families	Over 90%	Under 10%
Percent of state non-corporate taxes paid	62%	38%

Colleges Attended			Relative Amount Spent per Student
(Full-time student enrollment in California, 1967)			Out of every $100 of taxpayers' money spent by the State of California to educate students in public colleges . . .
Junior Colleges (217,000)	2/3 of students	1/3 of students	—an average of $10 is spent for each Junior College student.[a]
State Colleges (122,000)	1/2 of students	1/2 of students	—an average of $30 is spent for each State College student.
University of California (91,000)	1/3 of students	2/3 of students	—an average of $60 is spent for each University of California student.
Private colleges and universities (78,000)	1/4 of students	3/4 of students	

[a] While Junior Colleges are mainly financed by local rather than state taxes, local taxes are mainly property taxes which hit poor and working people hardest. The brunt falls on tenants (due to a shift from landlord to tenant) and on small homeowners.

WHAT THIS MEANS . . .

1. Seven out of 10 of the 270,000 who graduate from California public and parochial high schools come from families with total income under $10,000—the income group that pays most of the state's taxes.

BUT . . .

2. Fewer than 10 percent of the under-$10,000 high school graduates enroll at the University of California or State Colleges upon graduation. (Two percent go to private colleges; 41 percent enter Junior Colleges; and 47 percent of them go to no college at all.)

AND . . .

3. Nearly 35 percent of the over-$10,000 high school graduates enroll at the University of California or State Colleges. (Almost all go to college somewhere.)

THEREFORE . . .

4. Four-year college is mainly for the minority of higher-income families. But the lower-income families, most of whose children can't get in, pay most of the bill.

25 THE CORPORATE INTEREST UNIVERSITY

Capitalism needs and uses its schools to maintain the kind of society it finds most conducive to its own ends. While the selection on tracking concentrated on the school system as a means of controlling and molding the students involved, the following two selections broaden the focus to consider other ways in which universities serve capitalism.

Under capitalism universities perform four major functions: first, they train students, providing the mental workers the system needs; second, they do research, to service, among other things, corporate expansion and government policy; third, they promulgate ideas, polishing the system's image and its self-justification; and fourth, they perform the ordinary functions of any corporation —owning stock and property, employing workers, and so on.

Moreover, the training includes ROTC, as well as CIA and police institutes; the research often focuses on Defense Department hardware and counterinsurgency scheming; the ideas promulgated are heavily racist, anti-working class, individualistic and cynical as to change; and the business functioning includes low wages, racist hiring practices, slumlordship and destruction of generally low-income housing to make room for all these functions. Rather than standing as a neutral *ivory tower, the university is "an ivory tower atop a castle which is part of a kingdom which, in turn, directs a far reaching empire."*

In the following two selections Edward Greer and Richard Greeman make some beginning observations on the corporate interest university (Greeman in the form of a book review). More such analysis (such as Who Rules Columbia? *and* How Harvard Rules) *is being produced as students rapidly learn—through that best of all teachers, experience—that universities are forcefully committed to their capitalist functions. They are learning, in short, that the universities are an important part of an enemy and that they must be fought. This, rather than a generation gap, explains the present turmoil on campus.*

THE PUBLIC INTEREST UNIVERSITY*

by EDWARD GREER

"Intellect has also become an instrument of national purpose, a component part of the 'military-industrial complex.'"

—Clark Kerr, *The Uses of the University*

To understand the function of the contemporary American university, it is necessary to reconstruct certain key features of our political economy of which the university is a part. By showing how the national economy needs the universities to perform certain specialized functions, and how the universities duplicate in microcosm the dominant organizational patterns of the political economy, a new explanatory theory of university behavior emerges: the theory of the "public interest" university. If this theory is correct, operations like chemical and biological warfare (CBW) research, which have been viewed as alien to the university, may be better understood as *integral* to its nature. And this recognition, in turn, suggests that it is not reform of the university itself which will abolish such operations, but the reconstitution of our nation's economic and political institutions.

CORPORATE HEGEMONY

The one hundred largest corporations in America own 55% of the total net capital assets; the men who control these oligopolies also largely control the United States government—a government which defines the "public interest" as a situation where stability is maintained for a social order which maximizes corporate profits. In such a system the common man cannot hope to control the events which shape his life; he is subject to impersonal social forces before which he is powerless. The "public interest" is rarely in his interest.

The critical fact to bear in mind when reviewing the strange symbiosis between public and private which characterizes our political economy, is the continually growing weight of the government in the administration of the economy within the limits of the logic imposed upon it by the hegemony of private corporate power. The historic decline of competition and its free market price mechanism due to the rise of oligopoly power required a shift to a different mechanism for determining prices; and it was this historical transformation which opened the path to direct government administration of the economy.

How does this administration work today? First, government socializes the risk for oligopolistic industries by directly undertaking, subsidizing, or insuring the "risk capital" in the new frontiers of the economy such as computers, atomic energy, electronics, and aerospace. Thus public tax coffers absorb the risks our mythology more glamourously assigns to the private entrepreneur. As a corollary, the government rescues by tax benefits and nationalization failing industries. Socialism for the rich, at the poor man's expense: it is the American version of Marx.

Second, the government's foreign policy of economic imperialism guarantees the profits of many corporations directly through defense contracts, and indirectly by guaranteeing favorable trade terms and protecting foreign investments (45 firms claim 57% of total U.S. business investments abroad). For most oligopolies in the capital goods industries these markets in combination provide 20%–50% of their sales, and probably more than half of their net annual profits.

Third, the government constantly intervenes in the economy in a massive fashion through its fiscal and monetary adjustments. Government payrolls have increasingly been called upon to assume the burden of warding off mass unemployment.

Fourth, the government has been called upon by the most politically powerful faction in industry after industry to end the uncertainties and risks attendant to free competition by suppressing it and administering prices. This task has been accomplished by the creation and rise to power of the independent regulatory commission—the legal form through which oligopolistic control, and positive federal aid and protection, can be guaranteed. Historically, the railroad executives pioneered this system through the creation of the Interstate Commerce Commission. With modification this instrument has proven adaptable to a multiplicity of cases from forest use through communications satellites.

In each case, legislation is enacted ostensibly to control private power. In reality, vast new powers which are virtually unreviewable by legislature or the courts are granted to the private interests who inevitably capture the commission.

Fifth, the government continues to undertake, as it has throughout our history, the role of providing the infrastructure necessary to permit private interests to profit. Land grants, the financing of canals and other public works, and the turning over of vast mineral resources to private developers is an often told tale; and the despoliation of our natural heritage is evident everywhere. What is somewhat less evident is that public provision of the social services which has earned our society the title of a "welfare state" can also be viewed as infrastructure for the profits of the corporations.

THE SOCIAL INFRASTRUCTURE

In fact, for the interests of large corporations to be properly served, the government must assure continuous accretions in public welfare. This is because modern capitalism, which is constantly revolutionizing the productive process, requires an ever more skilled and educated work force. It is no accident that the percentage of high school graduates has risen from 6.4% in 1900 to over 70% today. Corporations need computer repairmen, not day laborers, and the public treasury pays the bill.

In more theoretical terms, the creation of such a labor force requires an ever higher cultural and economic standard of living for the population. Our system rests not on the "iron law of wages," but on its ability to produce an ever higher real standard of living for the working class. This need holds not only for production, but for consumption as well, for a growing market is essential to the flood of goods industry pours forth.

However, there is a counter-tendency to restrict the provision of social services such as medical care and education, and reduce payments like Social Security to the smallest possible extent compatible with the needs of the economy and the overall standard of living. This counter-pressure cannot be explained by an ideological reluctance of corporate executives to rely on government services, nor by their fiscal conservatism. It arises from a sensible fear that the proliferation of such services threatens the system because it suggests to the people that it is possible for their human needs to be met on a basis outside of the market which puts a price on everything, even beauty, truth, and health.

THE POWER BASE

The result of corporate hegemony over our economy is that despite fifty years of progressive taxation, mass unionization, Social Security, trust-busting, etc., no significant redistribution of income or wealth seems to have occurred. The social power of capital is as great as it was at the time of the robber barons; expanded social welfare benefits have served to rationalize the system, not change it; liberal reforms generally have sought to adopt ill-served men to the political economy rather than to adjust the economy to serve the common man. And one can reasonably conclude that the continued preeminence of corporate economic power, despite government regulation of such power in the "public interest," results from its control of the bases of national political power. And inasmuch as the regulatory powers of a "public interest" government function as *alternatives* to socializing the decisive portion of the productive plant, the corporate leaders of America have assured the continuation of a society based upon a small administrative minority planning and executing the decisions which affect everyone's life.

The methods of this domination are little understood, but they include a variety of mechanisms encompassing legal procedures, an ideology afraid of social change and committed to technological control systems, and an ability to manipulate the psychic forces of the individual so that an equilibrium is reached under which people come to accept their powerlessness as a tolerable, and indeed inevitable, phenomenon. It is this last factor which is perhaps most pernicious and which most fully reveals the inability of our society to create decent conditions of life for its people. Alienation from one's work intensifies as tasks become more subdivided and complex, but in contemporary America anger and despair are subsumed in an endless search for *ersatz* gratification through mass consumption. Thus, one works harder to earn more leisure and consumer goods; the work itself is pallid, but one acquiesces in the general system because it alone appears to guarantee material rewards, and because its reform, like its present control, appears out of reach. This social order denies fulfillment of the instinctual and cultural aspiration of men to be free to determine the circumstances of their own lives.

THE "PUBLIC INTEREST" UNIVERSITY

The university exists in the image of the corporation; the college classroom is administered analogously to the assembly line. In both cases production is for purposes extrinsic to the free development of the participants, but appropriate to the logic of private profit and national political power.

As a handful of oligopolies dominate industrial production, so, too, do a handful of universities dominate higher education. For example, in contrast to a liberal arts college with 1,500 students and an annual budget of some $3 million, stands the University of California with 40,000 employees, an operating budget of almost $500 million, a student body of 100,000, and annual construction expenditures of almost $100 million.[1]

While a few corporations receive the bulk of federal largesse, so, too, do the favored universities. Federal funds for scientific research are concentrated so that the top ten schools receive 35% of the total; the top fifty institutions obtain 75%. In absolute terms, in 1964 the top twenty-five recipients of federal funds for research and science education obtained $880 million out of a total of $1.5 billion.[2]

These are the "public interest" universities and their fate is of consequence. Their trustees are men who sit in the seats of power in the great corporations and are prominent in public affairs: they are men who do shape national and international events. The preeminence of the "public interest" university with its access to both governmental and corporate wealth has cast smaller colleges into the shadows of permanent mediocrity. Unable to obtain adequate funds, limited by the general tendency of our political economy to hold public expenditures to a minimum, the other institutions cannot provide adequate staff or facilities. Hence the majority of students do not have access to really adequate higher education. This is especially true for schools in the South, Negro colleges, women's schools, and the institutions catering to students from the lower rungs of the economic ladder.

Two modifications of this system are worth noting. One is that different types of schools tend to educate students from different economic classes. SDS Secretary Carl Davidson has observed that "the traditional Ivy League schools shape the sons and daughters of the ruling class and old middle class into the new ruling and managerial elites. The state colleges and universities develop the sons and daughters of the working class and petty bourgeoisie into the highly skilled sectors of the new working class, the middle sector white collar workers, and the traditional middle class professionals. Finally, the new community and junior colleges serve the increasing educational needs of, for the most part, the sons and daughters of the working class."[3] The second modification is the tendency of schools to differentiate among their student bodies by "social types." By having colleges which will cater to bohemians and radicals—Reed, Antioch, Bard, etc.—most students are kept largely insulated from these potential influ-

[1] Clark Kerr, *The Uses of the University* (Harper and Row, New York: 1966), pp. 7–8.

[2] U.S. Congress, House Committee on Government Operations, *Conflicts between the Federal Research Programs and the National Goals for Higher Education* (Report No. 1158, 89th Congress, 1st Sess., 1965), pp. 30, 60.

[3] Carl Davidson, *The Multiversity: Crucible of the New Working Class* (SDS pamphlet, n.p., n.d.), p. 7.

ences. It is interesting to note that at Brooklyn College, the University of Wisconsin, and Michigan in 1967, local and even state police forces were called in to prevent student behavior taken for granted at "prestige" colleges. Students from some families are more equal than students from others.

Like the large corporations they emulate, the "public interest" universities have over time become increasingly dependent on federal financing. At present, some 15% of the higher education budget comes from federal funds, but for the "public interest" universities the proportion may reach toward the 80% mark when research centers are included.[4] These schools must maintain their government research projects or face bankruptcy.

The Secretary of Health, Education, and Welfare, John W. Gardner, once suggested that retrenchment of government subsidies would come to prove almost impossible politically as the liaison with the universities grows tighter.[5] In reality, the "public interest" university is already an integral part of the military-industrial complex: an end to the cold war would prove as disastrous to it as to an aircraft company. Specifically, the "public interest" university performs three vital services for the system. It carries out government subsidized research and development; it performs specialized cold war political tasks; and it trains the personnel required by the corporations and government.

About $24 billion is spent annually for research and development in the United States, $16 billion by the federal government. This "risk capital" is concentrated in the military sector (through disbursements by the Defense Department, NASA, and the AEC); and it is carried out by corporations, $10 billion, the federal government itself, $2.9 billion, and the "public interest" universities, $1.8 billion. Of this $1.8 billion, $1.1 billion is apportioned directly to universities and $700 million to research centers and laboratories, such as the Columbia Radiation Laboratory and the Cambridge Electron Accelerator, which the universities operate.[6]

Through interlocking personnel, foreign affairs centers, etc., a variety of specific cold war projects enmesh professors and administrators in a network of dual loyalties and secret commitments. It gives one pause, for example, to observe the liberal former Dean of the Yale Law School testifying before Congress as Under Secretary of State for Political Affairs on the desirability of subsidized arms for underdeveloped nations. Such public servants are endemic to the "public interest" university, for they are a key link in the chain of command which coordinates the needs of business, government, and education.

Finally, the university serves to train the experts who man the economy and the polity. Hence, *professionalism* becomes the dominant personality trait at the "public interest" university, and underachievement becomes the most abhorred student deviation. The administration attempts to minimize those conflicts within the institution which might interfere with the production of students with marketable skills. This emphasis is doubtless best for the economy as presently organized, but it surely does not promote the maximum well-being of the students.

[4] Kerr, p. 55.

[5] John W. Gardner, "Government and the Universities," *Politics, Economics, and the General Welfare*, ed. Michael D. Reagan (Scott, Foresman and Co., Chicago: 1965), p. 112.

[6] House Committee on Government Operations, pp. 2, 17.

To carry out these services, power within the university must remain focused in the hands of those amenable to this type of university. It is no accident that there has been a transfer of power from the faculty and students to the foundations, business community, and government agencies—though one would perhaps hesitate to accept Clark Kerr's liberal pluralistic conclusion that this result is historically "inevitable." [7]

The faculty, much like Congress, has been reduced to the "middle levels" of power: delaying, modifying, and commenting upon administrative initiatives and decisions.[8] The students, of course, are outside the system of power completely; they are like a "mass public," subject to manipulation from men above them who hold different priorities and values. Not the inhabitants of its dormitories, but the state and its corporate partners define the "public interest" served so faithfully by the American university.

If one undertakes the utopian exercise of imagining a community of scholars where one learns out of sheer curiosity and not for grades, where one teaches what is exciting and not what is useful for making money, then it becomes clear just how perverse our universities have become. For the present, nevertheless, it is not utopian to urge that each time a struggle is waged on a campus for some reform, an opportunity be seized to demonstrate how the problem derives from the larger irrationality of America's political economy. After all, it is not so difficult a lesson, that a system which literally prepares germs of death in its institutes of learning is unfit to long endure.

[7] Kerr, pp. 26–27, 122.

[8] *Ibid.*, p. 100. Cf. C. Wright Mills, *The Power Elite,* for an explication of this concept.

A REVIEW OF THE CLOSED CORPORATION: AMERICAN UNIVERSITIES IN CRISIS BY JAMES RIDGEWAY*

by RICHARD GREEMAN

This book should be required reading for all college teachers, especially those who still retain illusions about the American academy being some kind of "oasis" in an increasingly materialistic, manipulative, and anti-human society. Mr. Ridgeway's thesis is simple, and he states it on the very first page: "In all likelihood most Americans believe . . . that universities are places where professors teach students. They are wrong. In fact, the university looks more like a center for industrial activity than a community of scholars." He then goes on to investigate "the different sorts of relationships universities and professors have with the rest of society," and the evidence he comes up with is impressive.

In page after page of anecdote, case-history, interview, and statistic, he documents the phenomenal growth of a "university industry" consisting of 2200 institutions with an annual revenue of $10 billion, a growth rate of 10 percent, a half-million instructors, and 6.7 million students. The activities of this super-industry include weapons development, real estate wheeling-dealing, investment brokerage, publishing, counter-insurgency, lobbying for high drug prices, unsafe cars, and the bracero system, cigarette filters, rat poisons, poison gases, espionage, comic books, and parlor games. Somewhere along the way the ostensible humanistic goal ("educating the whole man" was the phrase used when I was a Freshman) gets lost. What does emerge is the impression of a "kind of data-processing center: part bank, to provide the money for the activities of the different subsidiaries; part brokerage, for arranging deals among quarreling faculty members or between a faculty group and the government."

What disturbs Mr. Ridgeway about this state of affairs is that this industry is largely paid for, directly or indirectly, out of our tax dollars. To begin with, over half of the university's revenues (all for state-supported institutions) come from the government. In addition, all of their holdings and lucrative activities are tax-free. However, the profits which accrue when all this publicly financed research and development is put to practical use are reaped by the professors (who often set up "spin-off" corporations on the margins of the campus), big business (especially those with representatives on the university's board of trustees), and the institutions themselves (through the exploitation of patents or cost-plus sub-contracts). "Education" enters the picture largely as a necessary pretext to get the taxpayer to shell out the cash.

The following pattern emerges: the public pays its government to finance tax-free enclaves where greedy technicians are paid to develop products and systems for profit to themselves, for big business, or for the Defense Department, CIA, and State Department which protect the investments of big business abroad. Meanwhile, on the basis of this pattern, the institutions themselves and the "action-intellectuals" who run them are busy carving themselves out places of power and influence in government and the military-industrial complex. So happy is this intermarriage between big government, big business, the multiversity, and the high-powered jet-age "scholars" who exploit it, that there is no time for the kiddies. Another casualty of this happy marriage is the truth or at least any truth detrimental to the powerful interests represented on campus. No university sponsors research on why insurance premiums or drug prices are rising despite record profits. Cornell research on automobile fatalities due to manufacture is released only to the companies, never to the public at large or even the victims themselves.

After reading Mr. Ridgeway, the American university system begins to look like an enormous Teapot Dome scandal. You wonder why the public has not heard of it before. Mr. Ridgeway has a ready answer, as his title indicates. This conspiracy, like all good conspiracies, is secret: "It is difficult to gain any clear understanding of the university because it remains as one of the few large secret organizations within the nation. One can find out more about the activities of a public corporation than about a university. The trustees of private universities are invariably self-perpetuating bodies of businessmen who meet in private and do not publish accounts of their activities." People who were indignant about the invasion of President Grayson Kirk's "private" files by rebellious Columbia students last spring might well ask themselves how else they were to find out about the secret weapons research and land-grabbing he was sponsoring out of their parents' tuition fees and tax dollars. These students, of course, didn't need to read Mr. Ridgeway's carefully documented book (he even footnotes SDS!); they knew already because they knew somehow they had been had. But most of the professors, especially those who actually do teach students, never even knew the name of a trustee until the explosion last spring. Mr. Ridgeway so delicately puts it: "The professors at Columbia don't know who runs their factory, or how it is run. They don't especially care. What they care about in the end is preserving their jobs."

But Mr. Ridgeway's most serious journalistic defect is the absence of a theoretical framework, for which his admirable sense of outrage is no substitute. He paints the university as a secret conspiracy of greedy, manipulative intellectuals with tentacles on Washington, the Army, and big business, who make their living fleecing the public out of their hard-earned tax-dollars under the guise of "philanthropy" and "education." If we only had to deal with our old friend, the international Jewish-intellectual-homosexual-Communist-Fascist-banker-conspiracy, the world would be a lot easier to deal with. Unfortunately, things are much simpler and much more complicated, and moral indignation is no substitute for political-economic analysis.

Mr. Ridgeway sees the multiversity as some kind of dream, a deviation from an ideal norm. Since he is unable to comprehend this phenomenon historically, his own point of view is basically contradictory. On the one hand, as a reporter, the evidence of his eyes forces him to conclude (p. 215) that "The idea that the university is a community of scholars is a myth." Yet, four pages later, when he attempts to formulate a solution, he can only retreat into a restatement of the pious myths of the liberal academy: "One may hope that the country will pursue the idea that the university is a place where great teachers and students are brought together." Moreover, the means by which this liberal ideal is to be resuscitated is that of purification. The academy is to be cleansed of the dirty admixtures of business and politics and returned to education: "Professors are paid by the university to teach students, not lobby. If they want to work for the CIA or some soap company, then they should quit and do so."

Part of Mr. Ridgeway's confusion stems from his false dichotomy between "teaching" and other activities, in which he sees teaching neglected for the production of systems and hardware. In fact, the universities do teach: they teach young people to become good CIA-agents, good IBM managers, and good advertising executives. Mr. Ridgeway thinks that students are merely tolerated as a pretext, providing the rationale for financing the university. In fact, as Mario Savio put it four years ago, they are the "raw materials" from which the university-industry works up another product, equally as important as the new computers and non-lethal gases: technicians and managers to perpetuate the system.

Far from being held passively "in holding pens, off the labor market" (page 15) the students are carefully channeled, processed, manipulated, tested, inspected, indoctrinated, programmed and eventually packaged (the diploma) as products for a waiting market in laboratories and bureaucracies of government and business. Moreover, it is precisely the increasing demand for such standard human products (even more than the demand for university produced hardware and systems) that accounts for the increasing investment by government and industry in the university factory. Further, like any other investors, government and industry must maintain control over the process of production and its products, which they do through the absolute power of Regents and Trustees.

To hope, as Mr. Ridgeway does, that control of the university industry will somehow be turned over to students and faculty is like hoping that the directors of General Motors will turn the auto industry over to the auto workers. Both of these transformations may some day take place, but they will only occur as part of a process of total social revolution. But to ask that one such industry—the university—be "democratized" in the context of capitalist society is a Utopian pipe-dream. At most, one would end up with the kind of bogus "participation" which in the long run only reinforces the system by creating an illusion of democracy where none exists. The radical students of SDS clearly understood this when they refused to get involved in a phoney "dialogue" with university officials who are only the pawns of the Trustees, and instead put forward the slogan of "a free university in a free society." A frustrated Columbia professor, who had wasted his summer on one of the myriad committees that have sprung up at Columbia since last spring's rebellion, came to the same conclusion when he asked: "How do you reason with a Trustee?"

What both SDS and that professor had understood—and what Mr. Ridgeway evidently has not—is that the university is a class institution which quite naturally reflects the interests and priorities of the ruling class. Mr. Ridgeway's ideal of the liberal university, shared by thousands of naive academicians, is merely the historical form of that class institution in the past century. It was "liberal" only because it educated a tiny elite and existed on the basis of a relatively simple technology. Today's multiversity reflects the post-war technological and bureaucratic revolutions and the relatively broader social basis of today's ruling class. No "conspiracy" is necessary to maintain this relationship because it is organic. The professors who are part-time CIA-employees or management consultants are neither betrayers nor anomalies. They merely reflect a social division of labor which makes it increasingly more efficient for government and industry to pool their intellectual resources in large banks (universities) rather than trying to maintain separate armies of "experts" directly on their respective payrolls.

In the context of monopoly state-capitalism based on an advanced technology, the call for a revival of the independent liberal university is about as historically relevant as Bill Buckley's or Ayn Rand's demands for a return to "free enterprise" and "rugged individualism." The answer is not to attempt to sterilize the university or turn it back into a monastery, as if that were ever possible. Nor is it to passively accept it in its current form as the reflection of a manipulative, exploitative, technologically sophisticated, and ultimately destructive and anti-human society. It is rather to struggle against it, from without and within, as part of an on-going process of social revolution which includes the struggles of blacks in the ghettos, of rank-and-file workers wild-catting against management and the labor bureaucracy in industry, and youth rebelling in the schools. Only in the context of a totally new society based on new human relations can the university actually be democratized or humanized. Meanwhile, in the process of this struggle (which has already begun) the university will produce not just new systems, hardware, managers, and technicians to replace the existing ones as they grow obsolete; it will also produce its own grave-diggers—that significant layer of rebellious students whose actions this spring at Columbia, as well as in Paris and Prague, point the way toward a new society.

In conclusion: *The Closed Corporation* is a useful expose, full of juicy scandals and outrageous incidents, of the near-total subjection of the university to the exigencies of the CIA, the Defense Department, the federal bureaucracy, and the chemical, electronics, computers and other industries. A muck-raking work, a la Vance Packard and Fred Cook, it aims at "arousing public indignation" by presenting the workings of a new and vital capitalist industry as if it were a sex-scandal. At best, its charts and indexes might be used by SDS militants as a guide to where to sit in next. I think, however, they already know.

26 LAW AND ORDER IN AMERICA*

by TERRY CANNON

"Don't I think a poor man has a chanst in court?" snorted Mr. Dooley. "Iv coorse he has. He has the same chanst there that he has outside. He has a splendid poor man's chanst." In the following selection Terry Cannon describes the way in which courts act as class institutions. It should be remembered, however, that he is basically describing the tip of the iceberg. For supporting the arbitrary "justice" of local-level courts is a whole system of class-oriented law.

American constitutional law explicitly defines corporations as persons (deserving of Lockean liberties) and implicitly considers them Very Important Persons. It is not just that judges come from the capitalist class (or aspire to it), that money buys legal talent and connections, or that, in fact, it was judges and legislators with a particular bias that evolved the laws in the first place; the fact that is so particularly crucial about the class character of the legal system is that it is structured to continue the existing distribution of wealth and power. Any challenge to that distribution is viewed with prejudice, not just by the judges but by the rules of the game themselves.

The number one rule of the game is time. If a challenge to the status quo can be delayed long enough, it will eventually be moot. Arrest them on the picket line and allow them a meaningless victory in court after the strike is over. Or get an outrageous temporary restraining order, where—quite revealingly—violation of the order is punishable even if the order is eventually removed as unjustified and illegal. Or—as is particularly the case in labor law—do what you want (if you're a company), send your lawyers to court to argue with the NLRB, and two years later be told you should not have done what you did . . . without penalty. Many working-class movements have been forced to spend so much time running through judicial corridors that their organizing efforts have fallen apart. One company lawyer can file an awful lot of papers.

If you didn't know anything about how the law works in America, if all you did was read the papers, you would know that American courts and American law are the enemies of the people. If you're too poor to pay the rent, who puts you out on the street? The law. If workers go out on a wildcat strike, who lays an injunction down on them? The law. When people rebel against tyranny, what does the President call for? Law—law and order.

Law is the tool that politicians and businessmen use to keep down the people they oppress.

Did you ever hear of a cop busting in the head of a supermarket owner

* Used by permission of Terence M. Cannon.

because he charged too much for food? Was Lyndon Johnson ever arrested for the murder of Vietnamese? No. Law is the billyclub of the oppressor. He isn't about to use it on himself.

FREEDOM TAX

Let's take "a typical case of American blind justice," as Arlo Guthrie says. A man gets arrested. The heavy odds are he's a working man, a poor man, or black or brown. The gyp artists, price fixers, money lenders, war profiteers, capitalists—they don't get arrested. So first of all the defendant comes from certain classes of society.

To get out of jail you have to pay money. We got rid of the poll tax a few years ago; you don't have to pay to vote. But you still have to pay to get out of jail. Freedom under the legal system is a commodity you have to buy—if you got enough money. If you can't bribe your way out you stay in until you come to trial. Most felony cases do not come to trial for a year or more from the time of arrest. This time does not count toward your sentence! If you get 5 in the pen, that means 6½ in jail, counting the time you spent waiting trial.

So you make it to trial. You have to buy a lawyer. A lawyer gets paid per case: the more cases he has the more money he makes.

A lawyer, like any other businessman, makes money on a high turnover. He gets $100 just for filing a piece of paper that takes him an hour to write. A three-week trial cuts him out from handling a lot of flat-fee deals that are pure profit. The economic system pressures him to avoid trials. He doesn't want you to go to trial—he'll lose money.

Trials cost the city, county, state, or country big money to put on. The government and the judges don't want trials. If you can't afford a lawyer, you are assigned a Public Defender. Since there are so many people who can't afford lawyers, the Public Defender is loaded down with cases. He gets paid a salary so the more cases he gets the more work, but no more money. He wants to get cases out of the way fast. He doesn't want a trial.

NOBODY IN THE LEGAL SYSTEM WANTS A TRIAL BY JURY—EXCEPT THE DEFENDANT.

Trial by jury—the right given us in the Bill of Rights—is the exception, not the rule. Only a tiny fraction of legal cases ever come before a jury. Trial by jury is a shuck promise—the name of the legal game is "How'd you like to cop a plea?"

"Copping a plea" runs like this. The District Attorney meets with the lawyer and offers to drop four of the five charges against you if you will agree to plead guilty to the fifth charge. The reason you had five charges against you in the first place is that the cop who busted you knows that a deal will be made so he adds on a lot of extra charges to make sure that you are found guilty of one of them.

The lawyer, the District Attorney and the judge gang up on the defendant. They put it simply: cop a plea and the judge will go light. Insist on a trial by jury and you'll get the maximum. Some judges will tell a defendant point blank: plead guilty and you get 6 months; go for a jury trial and you get a year. Few defendants have the resources or the knowledge of the law to withstand the pressure.

(They say that ignorance of the law is no excuse—but who the hell keeps us ignorant of the law? Who writes legal verdicts in hocus-pocus language full of Whereases and Parties of the First Part? Who set up the legal system in terms of back-room and countryclub deals where the average person can't even get in the door? Not us, brothers and sisters, not us.)

TRIAL BY JURY

If you make it past this part—and most don't—you get a trial by jury. The "law" says that a man has a right to a jury of his peers, which means people like himself. Jury members don't get paid (maybe they get $5 a day). Working people can't afford to serve on juries; they can't take a pay cut down to $5 a day for two or three weeks. Black and Third World people are excluded from juries by District Attorneys because they have a tendency to go easy on people like them, knowing the reasons why their brothers and sisters are forced to commit crimes. Juries are also selected from the voting rolls of the county. Non-whites tend not to register to vote because they know that voting doesn't mean shit. Young people are also kicked off juries for the same reasons.

That leaves the middle class and the rich, who fill most juries. They are the classes of order and they sit in judgment on the classes of rebellion.

You face a jury of people who share none of your experiences, know nothing of your motivations, and who are threatened by the desires and angers of your people. When you plead your case you are not allowed to use motivation to defend yourself.

Were you poor, hungry, sick and tired? Were you unemployed? Did you have to break the law just to survive? Were you mad, or too proud? American class justice does not recognize these as defenses. All we want to know, buster, says the court, is did you rip off that liquor store, or get drunk, or call a rally without a permit?

After the jury finds you guilty, the judge lays down the sentence on you. The judge owes his job to the people who run the state; he serves the rulers. In California several months ago, a Congressman called a meeting of Superior Court judges. He laid it on the line. He told them that if he caught any of them giving light sentences to student demonstrators, they would face "well-financed opposition" to their re-election as judges.

The election of judges is a farce anyway. A retiring judge usually agrees to resign in the middle of his term. The State Governor appoints his successor—from a lower court. This gives the Governor another spot to fill and makes sure that the lower court judges kiss up to him in order to get higher court appointments. Once appointed, a judge runs in election unopposed (unless he goes against the wishes of the ruling class and they put up a "well-financed" campaign against him).

People take trial by jury, freedom from illegal search and seizure and free speech for granted. The Constitution as written says nothing about the rights of the people. The original Constitution is an aristocratic, racist document. The first ten amendments, the Bill of Rights, were only added to the Constitution after the left-wing of the revolutionary aristocracy under Thomas Jefferson forced its acceptance.

In practice, the aristocratic, racist intention of the Constitution is carried over in the application of our so-called legal rights. The Bill of Rights has never set well with those who profit from the business of racism, war-making, and industry.

Last year a group of Congressmen confronted a member of the Justice Department, demanding to know why Stokely Carmichael hadn't been busted. The Justice Department man was a little embarrassed.

"He hasn't committed any crimes we can get him on," he said.

"What about all that stuff he says?" said a Congressman.

"He's protected by the First Amendment," said the Justice Department man.

"Well, then what are we going to do about that goddamn First Amendment?" the Congressman shouted.

An injunction is an order by a judge to make somebody stop doing something. It began as a way of putting down labor struggles.

When labor first began fighting for its liberation, businessmen got the cops to arrest workers on all kinds of phony charges, of which the most effective was conspiracy. Groups of workers trying to organize a union were arrested for "combining, confederating, and conspiring in restraint of trade." The first charge was brought in 1803 against cordwainers in Philadelphia who wanted to organize a union. They were sent to jail.

In the 1880's this changed. Juries of the time were made up of small businessmen and small landowners. They were being squeezed out of business by the monopoly capitalists, the robber barons and big bankers. They recognized that monopoly capitalism, the enemy of the working man, was also their enemy, and they set free the labor organizers brought before them for conspiracy.

The businessmen weren't about to let themselves be beaten in the courts. They stopped demanding conspiracy indictments, and sought a way of getting around the jury trial. They turned to their most reliable class allies, the judges, and introduced the injunction against strikers.

The only defense against the injunction is the strength of numbers. Standard Oil got an injunction against the oil workers in Richmond, California, earlier this year. The strikers called for student support, pulled out hundreds of supporters to walk the picket line, defied the injunction, and won. The injunction was not enforced.

The city government of Berkeley got an injunction against the Stop the Draft Week Committee in 1967, forbidding it from holding meetings on the Berkeley campus. Two thousand people showed up for a series of illegal rallies on the campus. The pigs didn't come near.

PART 4

THE FAILURE OF LIBERAL SOLUTIONS

The 1960's will go down in history as the decade of the frustration of liberal politics. During this period, the hopes of the liberals came to a head with the election of two liberal Presidents and the election of an unprecedented liberal majority in Congress. In spite of these opportunities, however, the decade ended with little measurable progress on the fronts of eliminating discrimination and poverty, legislating improvements in the situation of the workingman or substantially bolstering the pathetically impoverished areas of education and health care.

Instead, liberals saw the military establishment gobble up increasing amounts of government spending at the expense of domestic programs. They witnessed the progressive alienation of black people, working people and young people from the political system and the emergence of an active left. They found themselves making bedfellows more and more openly with conservatives and businessmen, in order to deal with social reform and social unrest. All these represented the dashing of hopes for liberals in America.

A quick index of the fate of liberalism can be seen from the amount of money in the Federal budget going to nondefense spending. In 1960 the figure was a little more than 5 percent of the GNP. In 1969, at the end of the liberal reign, the figure was still between 5 and 6 percent. The percent of the GNP going to welfare spending has remained virtually constant since the 1930's. The notion of the rise of the welfare state is a myth; increases in the Federal budget have gone almost entirely into defense, roadbuilding and irrigating the immense Federal bureaucracy.

As the decade draws to a close, the problems the liberals set out to solve are festering close to the surface, ready to erupt any minute. Liberal faith has been shaken to the point that eternal optimist Arthur Schlesinger, who entered the Cold War with the publication of the *Politics of Hope,* has now written of *The Crisis of Confidence.*

The end of the sixties found the lot of black people barely changed. True, the threat of black rebellion and a strategy of tokenism had touched off the rapid promotion of middle-class blacks to higher positions in the government and corporate hierarchies. But the mass of blacks stay locked into a position of inferiority with respect to whites. In 1967, black median income stood at $3448, a bare 59 percent of the white median income of $5862. Although this is five percentage points higher than in 1960, the improvement is only part of a cyclical pattern explained by the war boom that does not bode any permanent improvement. In 1946, and then again in 1951, black income reached as high as 61 percent of white income before falling back down to 50 percent, in the midst of the next economic slowdown. By contrast, on another crucial indicator—unemployment—black joblessness has stayed fixed, in 1967 standing at 2.22 times the rate of joblessness for whites, virtually no improvement at all over the 2.23 figure for 1960.

Meanwhile, ghettoization increased. School desegregation proceeds at a snail's pace. Blacks are still almost totally excluded from craft unions—like carpenters, electricians, etc. Only the quality of the riot control weaponing in the nation's police arsenals has improved.

The War on Poverty, for its part, is faring not much better than the War on Vietnam. According to economist Ben Seligman's calculations, there are still thirty million poor people in America. This shame has easily survived the $18 billion per year poured into poor aid in a hodgepodge of public housing, food stamp programs, manpower training and old age insurance programs—much of it financed by the poor themselves. Testimony to the liberal Poverty Program's ineffectiveness was made by OEO's own former deputy director, who estimated that the War on Poverty did not reach more than 6 percent of the poor, or about 1.8 million persons.[1]

Even the plight of the ordinary workingman took a nosedive. By the end of 1969, in the face of inflation, real income had been in steady decline for almost five whole years. Weekly wages in 1957–59 dollars for the wage earner of a family of four stood at $77.62 in April 1969, compared to a figure of $78.53 for 1965. This decline in real wages occurred amazingly enough in the midst of the longest economic boom in the postwar period. With economic managers trying frantically to apply the brakes, the future for the wage earner held only increasing unemployment and decreasing wage levels.

In the area of health care (not to mention education and housing) things are reaching crisis proportions. The ratio of doctors per thousand population, long in decline, is due to fall below the World Health Organization's "crisis" level by 1972.

Grim realities. But die-hard liberals have taken refuge in the claim that their aspirations were frustrated by the untimely war in Vietnam. Once the war is over, they add confidently, liberals may once again take the helm to promulgate the sweeping series of reforms that have long been their historical mission.

This view of what has frustrated liberal reform and what is its future is quite superficial, however. A more convincing explanation of the failure of

[1] Ben Seligman, "The OEO," *Commentary,* Vol. 48, No. 4, October 1969.

liberalism lies in an analysis of liberalism itself. What is to blame is liberalism's own inadequate prescriptions for change, and liberalism's naive view of what lies in the way of effective solutions.

Liberalism as we will refer to it is a doctrine of gradualist, reform politics. For the last thirty years, it has claimed leadership in identifying and calling attention to the problems that remained to be solved in America. These problems —tainting an otherwise fairly impressive record of social progress—are (1) the persistence of economic inequality, (2) race prejudice and its consequences, and (3) inadequate legal protections and inadequate individual rights. This is not an exhaustive inventory of the problems liberals see, but they argue that solution to these will lay a basis for solutions to others.

Liberalism has assembled a political program to implement these goals. The main pillars of this program are guarantees of equal rights to blacks, labor legislation to increase union strength and the well-being of workers, income maintenance programs like minimum wage laws and negative income taxes, increased welfare responsibility by the state, such as for medical care, education and child support. There are also some secondary reforms liberalism pushes, such as pollution control, consumer protection, liberalized sex laws and others. A society with some such combination of liberal solutions would be a Good Society.

Liberalism sees such reforms as all possible within the structure of American capitalism. In part, this is because it believes in the long run the antisocial features of capitalism are on the decline. In addition, it thinks that many enlightened elements among the ranks of the powerful will ultimately come to support such reforms, since they are reforms that benefit almost everybody.

But why then have these programs been blocked in the past? Liberalism tends to view the real culprits here as being the conservative Republican and Southern legislators, who oppose welfare spending (1) because they hold to an atavistic ideology of "individualism"—abhorring the handout—and (2) because they represent rural constituencies, which stand to lose out since welfare spending gets directed primarily at urban problems. These influences are on the decline, they argue, as "individualism" wears thin as a coherent ideology and as redistricting and urbanization of the South give urban areas the political weight they deserve.

This book thus far has tried to suggest a very different interpretation of the evidence. We have argued that the problems continuing to face us are products of our own economic system. Solution to these problems will have to involve an entire reordering of that system. Powerful interests—primarily corporate interests—have a stake in the system as it stands and even in the mechanisms that create these problems. They oppose with their considerable power attempts to solve these problems. Liberalism, we argue, because it does not realistically come to grips with the task of destroying the power of corporate interests cannot implement programs that will effectively solve problems.

In this introduction we try to sketch a short critique of liberal program and liberal strategy. We focus, first, on the inadequacy of the liberal vision. Second, we comment on liberalism's unrealistic assessment of the obstacles to reform; and third, we take up the shortcomings of the liberal strategy for coming to power.

WHO ARE THE LIBERALS?

Liberals come in all shades and sizes. The liberal program is diverse enough, and vague enough, that nearly all politicians give lip service to it in one form or another. But a crucial distinction should be made.

We must differentiate between corporate liberals on the one side and humanist liberals on the other. Both of course want change to take place within the existing system; both oppose a radical reorganization of our society. The humanist liberals, for their part, however, give a high priority to the solution of our social problems and the creation of a humane society. They think that if you have to change quite a few things around to give equality to black people, then this should be done.

In the case of corporate liberals, on the other hand, their first and fundamental commitment is to the corporate economy. They want to keep it profitable, and they are fairly content in the status quo. Liberalism for them is a strategy to keep the boat from rocking. It is an enlightened way to avoid social unrest and ward off economic and social problems that might someday erupt. Politicians of the corporate liberal variety also use their liberalism to attract votes, particularly from labor, minority groups and middle-class professionals.

For such men, liberalism is not seen as a commitment to a Good Society and a ruthless attack on everything that stands in its way. It is rather a call urging corporations and politicians to quell the complaints of black people before they erupt and jeopardize the system. It is a call to make sure that American foreign policy doesn't irreparably alienate the youth of the society from the two-party alternative presently offered. By its very definition, corporate liberalism puts strict limits on the kind of reform measures it is willing to entertain. It is often more interested in the show of reform and the rhetoric than in any results. It refuses to consider any reform measures that seriously infringe on corporate privileges. When social reform and corporate interests run into collision, it is the first that gets tossed out not the second.

For the distinguishing feature of corporate liberalism is that it is the politics of those with power and is used to maintain and justify that power. Thus, while the great army of humanist liberals toil in the political vineyard, it is the corporate liberals who generally call the shots. This explains much of the erratic kind of success liberalism has had in mounting a sustained attack on social problems.

Humanist liberals have sometimes seen the dead end of corporate liberalism. Sometimes they have moved toward more radical ways of achieving their goals. But more often, they have deluded themselves about the prospects for liberalism. They have thought they could make common cause with corporate liberals. They have mistaken corporate liberal rhetoric to mean that support for thoroughgoing reform was more widespread than it was. But again and again, they have been left in the lurch when problems called for massive solutions, usually involving sacrifices on the part of the corporate class.

Thus many of the fundamental failures of liberalism stem from the fact that it is at base a conservating ideology. Because it refuses to tamper with basic social arrangements, it provides a refuge for many who want only to preserve the status quo.

INADEQUACY OF LIBERAL VISION

Because it is basically committed to reform under capitalism, liberalism does not make a penetrating critique. Laying out all the problems of our society at their roots is dangerous because it raises too sharply the possibility that what we need, in reality, is a new society. So it makes a modified critique.

Liberalism puts its finger on a certain number of the inequities and injustices that plague American society—like discrimination, poverty, inadequate welfare services. But their program falls woefully short of constituting a program for a truly Good Society.

Problems Ignored

In the first place, liberalism doesn't come to grips with a whole range of problems that confront present-day America. What are some examples? Take the problem of work alienation. For the vast majority of people in this country, work is something terrifically unpleasant, not simply because "work is always unpleasant," but because capitalism is particularly insensitive to workers' needs. (See Part III.) Clearly we must end the alienating aspect of work if we are to ever achieve a Good Society—a society where people are fulfilled and improved by the social activity in which they invest most of their time. We could. The technology exists to move in that direction. But the liberal vision is silent on this point.

Another issue liberals conventionally overlook is the problem of the family and the oppression of women. A Good Society will have to eliminate the gross economic and social discriminations perpetrated on women and totally weed out the complex of stereotypes and roles that relegate women to a permanent inferior status. Nothing less than a cultural revolution and a complete attack on the institutions that have a vested interest in this discrimination will be able to bring this about. Certain liberal women's rights organizations have come into existence. For the most part, however, they call for limited solutions much akin to the "assimilation" strategy called for by early white civil rights proponents. The argument that liberalism does not search for a thorough critique of the problems of capitalism still holds.

Still another issue is the U.S. role in world affairs. Although sickened by the War in Vietnam, liberalism has hardly acknowledged the systematically oppressive nature of America's world role. It has failed to see the underlying role the American International Capitalist Economy plays in wreaking exploitation on less powerful nations and creating an empire that necessitates world policing operations like that in Vietnam to protect it. No "Good" American society could come into existence that continued to prosper at the expense of the rest of the world's inhabitants.

Other issues left almost completely out of the liberal picture (and discussed in previous sections) include: the wastefulness and irrationality of the economic system and specifically advertising, commercialism, etc.; the totally inadequate nature of public and community facilities; the extent and depth of psychological alienation and the pathology of interpersonal relations.

No Critique of Process

Second, liberals mainly seek to change social outcomes—poverty and discrimination, but they do not seek to reform social processes—the reasons why these outcomes are so awful. For example, liberals hardly speak to the problem of the concentration of political power and the need for radical democratization.

In fact, they usually find themselves proposing more centralization. They don't recognize the need to mobilize the community, to put effective power in the hands of local groups, to create control by workers, to give people control over the decisions that affect them.

Moreover, liberals don't have much concern about the ravages of a private-enterprise economy. They don't meaningfully criticize the effects of a system of decision-making based on the criteria of profit. Although they sometimes attack concentration of corporate power, they don't call for change in the process of capitalist control that leads not just to the concentration, but to waste, customer manipulation, despoliation of the environment, antisocial collusion and dangers to health and safety. It is difficult to imagine a Good Society that retained these aspects of our present system.

Outmoded Ideals

Third, liberalism fails to take account of the constantly expanding capabilities of the society. It does not revise its critique of society in terms of the new potentials offered by the presently higher levels of technology. The Freedom Budget, for example, would channel ever-increasing amounts of Federal money into welfare. But the uses the Freedom Budget sees for this increased spending are fairly traditional liberal welfare goals. It does not consider qualitatively new possibilities of social organization made possible by vastly expanded resources. It is stuck with a secondhand idealism. An image of a Good Society that took into account the new potential our society has attained would go far beyond just calling for the elimination of poverty and discrimination. It would call for the implementation of new technologies to change the nature of work, to create new social institutions like communes, to achieve new levels of direct democracy and control, to sponsor massive assaults on the world problems of disease and hunger, etc. Liberalism is not this kind of radical idealism. It sticks with its "realistic" program, conceived in the era of the New Deal, precisely because it has never had much success in achieving its original goals. Instead of revising strategy in the face of frustration, liberalism tries to explain away defeat.

INADEQUACY OF PROGRAMS

Sometimes, however, liberalism has hit the mark. It has fueled great concern recently over the persistence of problems like racism and poverty. But even when it correctly identifies a problem, what it proposes is rarely adequate to the task. Take some examples.

Income inequality is a problem. But, as Glick shows in his essay below, the liberal income subsidy programs are hardly up to providing a decent life for everybody. Really dealing with inequality requires trampling on the toes of those with wealth and power.

With poverty, liberal programs also proved completely inadequate. Since poverty has its roots in racism, unemployment, a measly billion-dollar increase in welfare programs couldn't do much more than was already being done. Once again, a coordinated all-out attack on poverty means sacrificing some of the privileges of those who presently are powerful.

In the case of race, blacks themselves have quickly been disenchanted with the skimpy solutions liberals have proposed. Liberals have called for equal rights, for school integration. But where racism really hurts—in the unemployment, the low-paying jobs, in the political powerlessness—liberalism could only give lip service, for as we have seen, capitalism just cannot provide the needed jobs.

This insufficiency masks two facts about liberalism: First, liberalism is unwilling and unable to challenge vested interests, when they stand in the way of solving a problem. Adequate solutions imply reforms that adversely affect powerful interests. E.g., military spending must be cut back; discriminatory hiring policies must be curbed. But liberals are committed to staying within the capitalist framework and to not provoking powerful opponents.

Second, liberalism lacks the political strength to compel adequate programs. Can it ever provide the power it needs for adequate solutions with the strategy it offers? To deal with this question we will proceed in two steps. We will first ask what are the real obstacles to liberal solutions. Our answer: corporate power.

If this is so, we must then ask, how does liberalism pretend to cope with the obstacle of corporate power? Answer one: It offers corporations incentives to play along. Can that work? Answer two: It tries broadening its base of popular political support. Can this work?

OBSTACLES TO CHANGE

Liberalism thinks that over the long run solving social problems is in almost everybody's interest, but this ignores the powerful corporate interests in our society. Because it deludes itself about this fact, liberalism thinks it can change things without really making a fight, without changing the nature of the society.

In Part III, we described the connection between our persistent social problems like racism, poverty, women's oppression, unemployment and our capitalist form of economy.

In each case, the persistence of a problem stemmed from something more than a case of political "neglect." Problems resulted from the nature of the corporate economy and powerful interests were responsible. To reiterate an example, we said, unemployment is a kind of safety valve to the economy, consciously relied upon to keep the economy from overheating. To eliminate unemployment means to seriously jeopardize the private economy, because it drives up the price of labor and creates manpower bottlenecks. Powerful interests fight to keep unemployment at fairly high levels.

Solving other social problems runs into similar contradictions. Of course, precisely how a solution to each of these problems would threaten vested interests varies from problem to problem, but we can summarize some of the major factors involved.

Class Interests

Certain of our problems stem from the unequal way in which wealth and other social benefits are distributed in our society. The answer is to distribute benefits more fairly. Redistribution, however, implies that one class must sacrifice to the benefit of another. The rich, of course, are best able to afford it, but they have the instant political power to block such schemes.

Interference with Market Mechanisms

Other reform efforts clash with corporate interests, because they hinder the free and profitable operation of the market economy. For example, corporations depend heavily on a free labor market to provide relatively cheap labor, when and where they want it, for jobs that are unpleasant and that would not be done without the coercion of poverty staring workers in the face. Programs like a guaranteed annual income, public works, elimination of the pool of unemployed, elimination of discrimination against blacks and women, all have the effect of interfering with the free labor market. They make workers difficult to get, or else they drive up the price corporations have to pay to get them.

Certain other reforms, such as universal and good public education, would have similar effects. They would eliminate the present stratification of the labor force, created by a limited supply of schooling. This stratification leaves the great majority of people without real salable skills and they must seek the menial jobs. If everyone had lots of education, workers would be overtrained for the kinds of jobs presently provided by the economy and they would have too high aspirations to docilely submit to the work that needs to be done.

Competition with the Private Sector

Another series of obstacles to liberal programs arises from the opposition of those in the private sector who fear that social spending programs will put the government into economic competition with private corporations. Public works is one obvious such case; under public works a government agency builds buildings that would otherwise ultimately have to be built by private builders. Public housing deprives private contractors of opportunities, too, with the additional feature that it puts the government into the competition for the scarce urban real estate.

Diversion from Profitable Government Spending

One crucial, unpleasant facet of welfare spending is that it does not provide a direct source of profits for corporations, as in the case of military contracts or road building. (For elaboration on this point, see the Finkelhor-Reich selection, Part I.) Thus, when new tax monies are available, corporations tend to oppose spending on welfare, since it subtracts from the money that could go into profitable military contracts. The corporate opposition wants particularly to prevent any long-run increase in the government's welfare commitments, which would automatically freeze up substantial amounts of future government spending. This opposition to a general commitment to welfare goals translates itself into a general ideological opposition to welfare spending.

Alliances

Some of the proposed reforms threaten vested interests other than the corporations. School spending, for example, is very threatening to local Board of Education bureaucrats. Black ghetto capitalism is threatening to local, small, white businessmen. Although these voices alone would not amount to much, they have the opportunity to ally often with bigger corporate interests. They trade opposition support on one kind of welfare measure for opposition support on another. These coalitions—a practice known as "logrolling"—can carry great political clout. (All these issues and particularly the last one are well treated by Baran and Sweezy in this section of the book.)

POLITICAL POWER

What does this opposition from private interests mean for liberal programs? On the one hand, it means that effective liberal programs generally arouse the opposition of business lobbies and face nearly impossible legislative battles. But more basically, corporate opposition means that programs really implementing the liberal goals never get proposed.

The corporate liberal-type politicians are plenty sensitive to the needs and desires of the private sector, and they act to muzzle programs that could be potentially threatening. They know how to pull the teeth out of a program by loading it down with limiting provisions. They know how to stifle it by putting it under hostile bureaucratic jurisdiction so that it is hardly implemented or enforced. Often it is even handy for ineffective programs to make it through—it provides an illusion of liberal success.

A reading of the *Congressional Record,* even in the liberal heyday, reveals that programs adequate to liberal specifications were never even proposed. Even when corporate liberals have tried to promote programs to quell the most obvious social tinderboxes, they have often been stymied by less enlightened colleagues. Administration after liberal administration has admittedly toned down requests for social spending, as they came to understand that even modest programs just weren't politically feasible in the face of corporate opposition.

Liberalism has sometimes been able to disguise its effective lack of political power by sneaking through the political obstacle course a few hard-fought victories—like the War on Poverty of 1965. But such victories were more propaganda than anything else, since to win them, liberals were obliged to pretend that a fundamentally inadequate program was an important step toward social change. However this approach usually backfires.

For example, liberals in high offices during the Johnson administration believed they could legislate some welfare spending to deal with the poverty problem. But to make it fit the proportions of what was politically feasible, they had to define a solution modest enough to pass, but significant enough to look like a solution.

The logic of the antipoverty effort devised under these constraints was that people were poor, not primarily because they were unemployed or underpaid, but because they lacked training. Training programs were politically feasible, and the poverty program centered around them.

Of course, the constraints of the situation barred the poverty warriors from treating the problem for what it was. Ending unemployment or effectively raising wages required measures that would have run into serious corporate opposition: measures like public works projects, guaranteed income levels, etc. So naturally, the war on poverty, with its modest solution, made hardly a dent. Retrained poor had no more success in finding jobs that did not exist than they had before. The result in many cities of raised expectations, but no opportunities, was the inevitable: rebellion.

REFORM FOR CORPORATE PROFIT

On the whole, the most "successful" liberal answer to their predicament has been to try to win corporations over to reform by offering them rewards and incentives for playing along. Sometimes it happens the other way around: corporations, through corporate liberals, dress up profit-making opportunities in the cloak of liberal reform in order to get liberal support. In both cases, however, experience shows it is the reform part of the deal that suffers while the profit part prospers greatly.

A clear-cut example of this approach was the Great Urban Renewal drive of the 1950's. Urban renewal was initially conceived as a way of solving the housing needs of the poor. In actuality, the urban renewal programs ended up serving real estate and commercial interests, universities and middle- and upper-income home owners, while actually decreasing the net supply of low-income housing.

This is how it worked. Government authorities obtained the slum land, moved the poor out, and then turned it over to private developers. The developers built what was most profitable, in other words, shopping centers, office buildings and housing for the rich. Public housing doesn't pay. It is easy to see how the private interests cashed in on all the goodies and how benefits for the poor came to zero. (The Wilhelm selection below documents the specifics of urban renewal programs in great detail.)

Recently we all have heard of the much touted plan for giving corporations incentives to set up plants in ghetto areas to train and employ black workers. This is the same kind of "reform for profit" scheme. There are good grounds to think that this scheme, too, will not go very far toward solving the real problem.

Although the "gilded ghetto" strategy may marginally reduce black unemployment, as we have seen, corporations are not likely to want to go too far toward eliminating unemployment. The penalties of creating a tight labor market very easily outweigh the short-run profits some corporations might make by feeding off this government pork barrel.

Moreover, many business experts have predicted that few corporations are going to commit themselves to this quagmire, even if it looks enticing at first glance. The uncertainties—including fickleness in the government's commitment to support this kind of boondoggle over the long term—are just too great. The business of social reform can never match the welter of lucrative opportunities afforded by military contracts and the opportunities of the consumer market. (See the Finkelhor-Reich selection for elaboration.)

This then is the plight of liberal reform. It either must settle for a program so modest that it cannot possibly make a dent in the problem. Or it must directly subsidize those responsible in large measure for the problem, with little hope for positive results. Meanwhile, each new liberal failure only fuels conservative opposition and undermines liberalism's own base of support.

BUILDING POLITICAL SUPPORT

Of course, liberals are not fully unaware, as may seem to be suggested here, of the bind they are in. Some liberal thinkers acknowledge, for example, that it is corporate power that holds liberal reform at bay. They argue that this is a surmountable obstacle. Corporate power can be defeated through *electoral mobilization,* they say.

The liberal prescription for building political power is straightforward: elect more liberals. Committed liberal legislators and executives once in power will act as a counterforce to entrenched corporate interests. Once there are enough of them, liberal programs will be possible.

As we have argued, however, corporate power is built right into the political system. Through campaign financing and through their control of the economy, corporate interests have enormous leverage even over unsympathetic politicians. But let us ignore this reality for a moment and merely examine the liberal strategy for building a popular base.

The strategy for electing more liberals has several components. One is the politics of charisma. It calls for throwing financial and popular support to a handful of young politicians who will popularize the liberal ideals. A second is the politics of the "lesser of two evils." It believes that wherever possible liberals should reinforce the more liberal candidate of any group of candidates running in an election—virtually no election is to be ignored.

The base of the liberal electoral support will come from a coalition of blacks, labor and white progressives. Liberalism sees a long-term trend in its favor. The impulse toward widespread redistricting provided by recent Supreme Court rulings should more and more give a valid weight to the urban groups who make up the liberal coalition. Liberalism thus attaches great importance to redistricting and fights for it tooth and nail in courts and state legislatures.

So far liberalism has not had its optimism rewarded. Conservatives are making a comeback, and liberal politicians, not to mention liberal programs, are stymied. Why?

For one thing, the country doesn't get more liberal just by itself. For example, on the redistricting issue, liberal optimism proved way off the mark. Redistricting has ended up benefiting the burgeoning suburban areas—a bastion of middle-class conservatism—not the cities.

Second, the old liberal coalition is rapidly falling apart. Labor has defected rapidly. White workers are balking at the prospect of "liberal" programs like the "gilded ghetto," which redistribute money from white workers to the black poor. Rank-and-file discontent makes it difficult for the union bureaucracy to "deliver" on call any more for liberal candidates.

For their part, liberal whites are disaffected too. They are turning tail because of the war. The equivocal position of old liberal war horses like Humphrey and Johnson has completely alienated them.

Finally, the blacks especially are dropping out of the coalition. They are coming to understand through the idea of black power that their automatic support of liberal candidates has made them for all intents powerless. Black power—a more rational strategy—calls for organizing their own political force and playing extremely coy to liberal appeals.

This disaffection on all sides of the liberal coalition is not irrational as often pictured by liberal ideologues. It reflects the fact that years of coalition have not brought anything but frustration to the goals of the groups involved. Groups break off to look for new roads to political influence. The result is the fatal inability of the liberals to mobilize a base, elect candidates and even agree any more on a commonly acceptable program.

ELECTORAL WEAKNESSES

But even when the coalition still held together, the liberal approach contained grave weaknesses in its electoral strategy, which now in its decline only seal its fate. For one thing, the "lesser of two evils" electoral method has not brought an increase to the liberal camp. Left-center politicians elected in this way by liberal support do not give much but lip service to liberal causes. They know they can count on the liberals, who have no other place to go, and they want to stay close to the center to keep the crucial swing votes for times when the chips are down. Such men only succeed in weakening support for liberalism back home. To rank-and-file supporters, such meager returns don't seem to be worth all that electioneering effort.

For another thing, liberalism is trying to fight fire with fire—the politics of media and manipulation with more of the same. In an oversimplified capsule, American politics works like this: politicians gain support by manipulating a fairly narrow set of ideas—"arousal ideas"—by putting them into juxtaposition with various programs or practices. Thus, money for schools will be advocated to "keep America first" or opposed because it will "raise taxes" or open the door to "creeping socialism." This and a few more constitute the political vocabulary. Since people react favorably to issues, presented in formula ways, what determines whether people are pro or con usually is who has the resources to present the issues that way to the public. These resources lie with politicians who have lots of money to spend.

Liberals can't win by competing on this same level. They cannot possibly muster the resources of their powerful opponents and their corporate allies. So many liberals chart another course. They play a straight game, they make the claims of all the other candidates; they leave themselves ideologically indistinguishable from the other candidates, except for a small bit of excitement, youth or some other stylistic feature. Compromises on their principles, they argue, are justified, because once elected, the candidate will be free to act on the basis of his underlying liberal convictions.

But such compromises never build a clear-cut or long-lasting base for the candidate. He never actually changes people's attitudes. He never really prepares a solid base for long-lasting political support of himself and his programs. He may gain a temporary lead because of his marginal attractiveness. But soon his real politics rouse the ire of those with the resources to effectively oppose him. Next election he finds his marginal attractiveness swamped under a mass of "arousal formula" generated by his conservative opponents. This is what happened to liberals like Senator Clark from Pennsylvania and Senator Douglas from Illinois.

Without a committed and active base, it is ludicrous for liberals to think of confronting corporate power with elected liberal power. The slightest retaliation from the corporate interests, either through financing political opposition or through economic blackmail, uncovers the tenuous nature of the liberal support and the nakedness of their threat. Given the weakness inherent in the kind of politics and strategy they pursue, it is not much wonder that they stop far short of challenging corporate interests.

The alternative to the politics of media and manipulation is the politics of organization and political education. Organizing means that grass-roots organizations are set up, geared to the participation and control of the people in the community or in the shop. Discussions on a one-to-one basis and personal contacts must serve as substitutes for money and media. Organizations have to function all the time, not just during elections. They must involve people, provide services that play a real function in people's lives, raise issues and do new organizing.

Political education must be open and honest. The full implications of the views held by the organization must be brought out. Differences should not be hidden, but made explicit and discussed. Organizers cannot shy away from presenting radical or other unpopular ideas on socialism, foreign policy, power or other issues.

Real political education means presenting clear positions on national and broad ideological issues as well as on local grievances. Organizers try to tie these together wherever possible. Protests and direct actions show the class nature of society and demonstrate that people acting together are not powerless. Such actions help to overcome the general alienation from politics created by electoral campaigns, where everyone feels manipulated and passive. Ultimately, popular power is created as a counterforce to corporate interests.

Communities organized in such a way can, if they see value in it, run their own candidates. But rather than hoping to influence national politics by way of a victory, the politics of organizing sees campaigns as a good situation for reaching people and changing their ideas. Elections become organizing tools.

Of course, liberal politics has great difficulty incorporating this kind of strategy into its own. Such politics builds a mass movement. This raises the specter of a radical insurgency, which is precisely the eventuality many of the elements of the liberal coalition see themselves as actively combating. Such a movement would not be patient with the continual frustration of liberal solutions at the hands of corporate interests. It would be radicalized. It would start calling for the drastic and effective measures that are really needed.

Thus liberals choose the road of relying on conventional politics. They remain incapable of marshaling political power to institute even moderate reforms, and are stymied in the face of corporate power. It is in the face of this impasse that radical politics begins to take root.

In conclusion, liberalism isn't on the wane because the "Neanderthals"—as one liberal put it—are staging a comeback. Liberalism is collapsing from the force of its own failures. Liberalism raised up great expectations in its behalf, as it purported to offer a roadmap to the Good Society. But it was a cruel deception. On the one hand, liberalism was a cynical tool for those who only sought to reinforce the status quo of privilege and inequality. On the other hand, liberalism was the illusion of those who thought that American social problems could be solved without fundamentally changing the nature of the American economy. Both groups foundered on the rock of corporate power—which one didn't dare and the other didn't want to confront.

What results is a set of stunted solutions, a series of political defeats and an electoral strategy doomed to impotence. The solutions hardly get to the source of the American pathology and never provide adequately for the diseases they seek to cure. The political programs are watered-down and ill-conceived and only produce an embarrassment. The electoral strategy fails to create a base for liberal ideas in the nation at large.

Only a realistic political conception can take its place. That conception must acknowledge the obstacles to change and organize to eliminate them. That means a movement to change the basis for power and privilege in America, to uproot the corporations and overpower the basic decision-making mechanism—profit. Short of this, the liberal idea will continue to beat its head against a wall.

27 THE FAILURE OF CORPORATE LIBERALISM: THE TRAGEDY OF RICHARD LEE*

by JOHN WILHELM

Liberals have maintained that everyone has an interest in the solution of our urban problems. All we need is enlightened liberal politicians and the help of modern expert assistance. It can be done with the help and cooperation of the large corporations and the local corporate elite.

This was the strategy of liberal mayor par excellence Richard Lee of New Haven. John Wilhelm shows why he failed. Forced to choose—which would you prefer in New Haven?—liberal reform or the status quo?

Summer 1967 was too much for liberals in America. When Watts exploded in 1965, they blamed it on the 400-year oppression of American Negroes. The more widespread uprisings of 1966 produced doubts, but liberal America still maintained that the basic causes were sociological, not criminal.

But 1967's nationwide violence has produced a new schizophrenia in the liberal mind.

Whatever illusions the American people once had about a swift end to the war in Vietnam have disappeared. A new band of black revolutionaries has appeared at home, and every day brings new suspicions that the black masses are following their advice. Revolution abroad and insurrection at home: these two crises together pose too serious a threat to American stability.

Liberal rhetoric continues, more hesitantly, to assign much of the blame to the poverty in which one-third of America lives. But the suspicion grows that the black people have taken advantage of their deprivation to wreak unnecessary and wanton havoc. Many well-intentioned and capable people are working hard to eradicate ghettoes; "riots" simply set the cause back, liberals believe.

In New Haven the schizophrenic response to black rebellion has become sharply defined. Liberalism has been in power for 14 years, and the city has become nationally famous for its efforts to solve the urban crisis. Nevertheless, the city's ghettoes blew up in mid-August.

The immediate spark for the disturbance was typical: a white snack bar owner on Congress Avenue, in the Hill section, shot a young Puerto Rican late one Saturday afternoon. Puerto Ricans and blacks in the Hill erupted that night.

Sunday afternoon both local and state police, equipped with rifles, shotguns, tear gas, and MACE (a new aerosol-spray nerve gas), deployed in large numbers in the city's ghettoes. That night violence spread throughout the city. By the time it stopped Wednesday night, millions of dollars of damage had been done, countless stores looted, and 500 people arrested.

Black militants were bitter. They could have stopped the violence, they said, if Mayor Richard Lee had kept a series of agreements made and immediately broken Sunday. City Hall says the militants did not have enough influence among their own people to stop it.

The city's basic policy was to seal off the black and Puerto Rican areas and arrest anyone who moved. Ghetto leaders say the people felt they were being counter-attacked by police, and that this provocation made the violence much more serious than it might have been.

In late September Community Progress, Inc., the Mayor's anti-poverty program, released its annual report. It was prefaced by a statement called "Violence and CPI."

Many of the "disadvantaged," the report said, have taken heart from New Haven's public dedication to progress. Too many, however, "look out on a world where their people still live in the worst parts of town, hold the poorest-paying jobs, suffer most from disease, are looked down on and shunned." CPI declared renewed war on the "privation and frustration and anguish whose continuance can mean recurrent violence and threats of violence in this and every other city."

These sections of the CPI analysis are in the best liberal tradition of recognizing basic social problems. There is a quite different side to the report, however; it reads almost as if two different people wrote it.

Most of the rioters, it says, were "teenage hooligans" with "a thirst for revelry"; they were a tiny minority of the ghetto population. "Few if any of the incidents of the four days bespoke any widespread discontent. There is no basis for reading into the four-day flareup (as a few have done) an Inner City-wide indictment of the physical and human-renewal efforts of 14 years."

Furthermore, "the fact is that City Hall and CPI are the chief militants in the Inner City crisis. The most strident critics . . . rarely address themselves to the most difficult, vexing task of meeting urgent day-to-day needs."

This despite the fact that the most publicized "strident critic" is Fred Harris, whose Hill Parents Association ran four CPI-funded programs this summer. CPI workers in the Hill readily admit the programs were a huge success, in particular because they were planned, administered, and staffed almost entirely by the blacks and Puerto Ricans of the Hill.

This is the liberal response to New Haven's rebellion. The basic sources are still recognized; but the Lee administration is unwilling to admit that anything more than demagoguery and teenage hoodlumism really caused it.

The Mayor fully intends to lend reality to that analysis by eliminating the "demagogues." Since the August uprising the liberal Lee administration has been working with that most conservative of governmental institutions, the FBI. Early this month a Federal grand jury subpoenaed Fred Harris and other black militants. Local police leaked to the press that the object is to put them in jail.

Mayor Lee is making his choice. Daniel Patrick Moynihan, a leading Kennedy liberal, succinctly defined that choice in a speech to the Americans for Democratic Action. Liberals, he said, must "see more clearly that their essential interest is in the stability of the social order, and that . . . it is necessary to seek out and make much more effective alliance with political conservatives who share that concern . . ."

What Moynihan suggests nationally the country's most liberal Mayor is carrying out locally: the "essential interest" is not justice but stability. Why has Mayor Lee made that tragic choice? Why does he cooperate in the effort to jail the man whose organization did more with $45,000 in one summer to involve the hard-core poor in constructive self-help programs than CPI does in a year with over $6 million?

The answer lies in an examination of the forces the Mayor has brought together to keep liberalism in power.

Richard C. Lee was in the 1950's an extraordinary mayor. Liberal America had to sit out the quiescent Eisenhower years, its radical cutting edge sapped by McCarthyism, its new blood shut off by the silent generation. Liberals roused themselves just often enough to cheer Adlai Stevenson on to defeat; the years between were lean.

One of the few bright spots on the national horizon was New Haven, a middle-sized industrial city then noted mostly as the site of Yale University. When Dick Lee became mayor in 1953, on his third try for the job, he did for a city of 160,000 what Stevensonians had failed to do for the country: he brought liberalism to power.

Lee has never been a Stevenson-style egghead. He is, on the contrary, a political genius who also happens to sincerely believe that American cities must be rebuilt.

Lee came out of a working-class Irish neighborhood in New Haven, worked his way up through the local Democratic Party, and received his polish and finesse as director of the Yale News Bureau. In his 14 years as mayor—and he will win an eighth term this fall—Lee has completely reshaped local politics and adapted it to his drive to rebuild the city.

When Lee started in 1953, Washington was not, as it became during the New Frontier, a playground for bright, sharp young liberals. Lee was able to bring a talented group of high-powered, sometimes visionary, young men to New Haven—the kind who worked for John Kennedy, flocked to the swollen staff of Robert Kennedy, or found a spot in the liberal refuges in Johnson's Washington.

This group—Lee gleefully called the building they worked in the "Kremlin"—was headed until 1961 by Edward Logue.

Lee and his young hot-shots got in early on the Federal urban money grab-bag. William F. Buckley pointed out that if every American city got the amount of per-capita Federal money New Haven brought back from Washington, the national budget for urban programs alone would be something like $146 billion.

New Haven's out-of-proportion success at landing Federal money is no accident; by the time other cities were waking up to the New Frontier and the Great Society, Lee and his Kremlin were veterans at the politics and the red tape of extracting money from Washington.

Lee's planners have not only had more money than any other city to work with; they have also had greater political freedom. By using redevelopment and later the war on poverty as his tools, Lee has completely reshaped the power bases of the New Haven Democratic Party.

When Lee assumed office in 1953, power within the party was split between

John Golden, the aging Irish boss who is now Democratic National Committeeman from Connecticut, and Arthur Barbieri, the new Town Chairman who brought dissident Italians into the Democratic fold.

Lee has let those men keep the traditional party organization and traditional patronage sources like the Public Works Department.

His strategy has been to bring new muscle into the Party—muscle which ultimately is much more important than the old-line ward organization which Barbieri still runs.

Unlike old-style reformers, Lee made no attempt to capture the traditional city structure; he doesn't even control the Board of Aldermen, although all of its 33 members are Democrats.

Lee has his people in these institutions, but the basic strategy of control is much simpler; he just created another city government parallel to and eventually above the old one. It's not in the City Charter, but Lee's private government is what is shaping the city.

This new government is the Redevelopment Agency and the complex of organizations around it, plus since 1962, Community Progress, Inc., the local anti-poverty program. At the head is the Development Administrator, who in fact is the deputy mayor.

Logue occupied this post until 1961; L. Thomas Appleby, who had the job for four years, and Melvin J. Adams, who has it now, both started under Logue in the Kremlin. The actual boss of this whole complex is, of course, the Mayor.

This highly paid, well-staffed, sophisticated bureaucracy has assumed control of New Haven. It makes all important decisions about the shape of the city: which stores occupy the downtown, which industries get new plants, what highways go where and who gets new houses. It has a monopoly of information and expertise, so that whoever challenges it can neither disprove what it says nor criticize its future plans.

Traditional government agencies cannot compete: many of the non-salaried aldermen, who lack even secretarial help, did not even read the 1967 city budget before they passed it. While the city has done well in school construction, which falls under the Redevelopment Agency, the educational program itself—which is under the Board of Education—has made little significant progress.

Allan Talbot, in his book *The Mayor's Game* (published early in 1967), provides an excellent account of Lee's techniques in transferring power from the traditional city government to his private bureaucracy.

What is important, however, is not the politics by which this was done—although it was a brilliant piece of work—but the implications of this power transfer.

Lee's private government has provided him with a vast patronage pool, financed not by local taxes but by Federal and foundation money. The Board of Aldermen has been rendered impotent so that the people cannot make their views felt at the polls short of throwing out their apparently impregnable Mayor.

Lee has tied his nationally known liberal image to his renewal programs; and the agencies that run those programs act as one of the biggest and most efficient public relations organizations any politician ever had.

The most important fact about this new power, however, is that it has *integrated the city government with the real powers in New Haven life: the banks, big business, and Yale*. It is these groups who give Mayor Lee decisive backing both in the city and within the Democratic Party.

Corporate power has traditionally left municipal politics to its own devices, because local government has rarely interfered with business. With the advent of an administration that proposed to rebuild New Haven, that relationship had to change.

Yale was the first corporate power in the city to recognize the potential of the Lee program. The Mayor had become friends with top Yale people during his 10-year tenure at the University's News Bureau.

A. Whitney Griswold, the late President of Yale, was vital in rallying University support for Lee, from the Corporation on down. One of Lee's unparalleled feats at the News Bureau was getting Griswold on the covers of both *Time* and *Newsweek* the same week.

His Yale connections are very important to Lee, personally as well as politically. His dress and mannerisms reflect his Ivy League tutelage. The Mayor regularly gets his afternoon rubdown at the Payne-Whitney gym, and Mory's is a frequent luncheon spot, as well as a regular location for political confabs.

The relationship is not emphasized to the working people of New Haven—anti-Yale sentiment is rife in town—but when he speaks to Yale groups, Lee likes to use phrases like "When I was at Yale . . ."

Most of Lee's numerous enthusiastic supporters—those in print range from Yale Divinity School Prof. William Lee Miller's embarrassingly panegyric *The Fifteenth Ward and the Great Society* to Talbot's more analytic *The Mayor's Game*—like to emphasize that Yale's support for Lee stems from his liberal social philosophy.

Talbot quotes former Law School Dean Eugene V. Rostow as finding in the Mayor "a simple, yet intense moral purpose . . . He was attacking fundamental ills of our time, the moral, economic, and social injustice of the slums."

The relationship has its more concrete, mutually advantageous aspects. Yale likes to be surrounded by a clean, bright, modern downtown area. A Yale education rests on an upper-class style of life and on the consideration of intellectual problems in isolation from the outside world. Yale's very architecture—forbidding stone walls, moats, heavy locked gates, and opulent, comfortable, self-contained interiors—embodies this approach to education.

Beginning in the early 1950's the Oak Street and Dixwell slums pushed tighter and tighter against the University; and Yale considered neither the slums nor the shabby downtown area proper neighbors.

Mayor Lee's first redevelopment project dealt with part of this problem. When Oak Street, the city's worst slum, was torn down in the middle 1950's and replaced with the turnpike connector, a series of new office buildings and stores, and two of the most nondescript luxury apartment buildings anywhere—Madison and University Towers—Yale thus had its most discomfiting neighbor excised.

The downtown renewal project finished that part of the job by installing Malley's, Macy's, a new bank, Paul Rudolph's parking lot, and finally, after several years as a giant hole in the ground, the new Chapel Square shopping mall.

Two more projects now on the drawing boards, one Yale's and the other the city's, will complete the encirclement of the University by an environment acceptable to it.

The Mellon Art Gallery will take care of a pesky block of small stores and apartments along Chapel. The projected inner loop road will effectively isolate

Yale from Dixwell and the rapidly expanding black population in the Dwight neighborhood across Howe Street. It will also save the Medical School from the blacks and Puerto Ricans in the Hill.

This loop, part expressway and part boulevard, will start from the I-91 Trumbull Street exit, an engineering disaster, circle behind the Grove Street Cemetery and Payne-Whitney and go down Howe and Dwight to the turnpike connector, which is being extended, and then circle beyond the medical school-hospital complex and join State Street, by then a six-lane road.

To please Yale, which does not want Vassar's proposed Prospect Street site and the science complex to be cut off from the rest of the University, Lee has made a tentative agreement with Brewster to bury the Trumbull Street section of the loop underground.

Another of the many instances of mutually beneficial cooperation between Yale and the Mayor is Yale's $3 million purchase of the old Hillhouse and Boardman Commercial high schools, now the site of Morse and Stiles, in 1955 for a price much higher than market value. Lee got money needed for working capital; the large profit margin, and the city's free use of the schools until 1958, helped overcome political opposition to the sale.

Another piece of cooperation is in the offing if Vassar comes to New Haven and locates, as projected, on Prospect Street. Upper Winchester Avenue and Newhall Street, below Prospect Hill, are rapidly becoming serious slum areas, and Vassar will not tolerate a ghetto next to it. An employee of the Redevelopment Agency says that the area will be "cleaned out."

Yale gains from its cooperation with the Mayor, then, by insuring the kind of clean, undisturbed surroundings it requires for its methods of training the nation's leaders.

The Lee administration has also given many Yale people the chance to dabble in local politics—examples are Law School Dean Louis Pollack on the Board of Education and University Secretary Reuben Holden as president of the board of CPI.

Yale has generously repaid the Mayor for his help. The University's local political and economic power are enormous, and both are solidly behind the Lee administration. Yale has consistently bestowed upon Lee official praise and recognition.

Yale faculty has been an important resource for the Mayor for expertise, free advice, and image-building publicity. A lot of valuable publicity has also been generated for New Haven by Yale's practice of hiring famous architects to design its new buildings.

In marked contrast to Yale, the banks and big businesses were slow in recognizing Lee's value. Many influential businessmen viewed him for several years as a threat; all have now accepted him as a phenomenon here to stay, and most are enthusiastic supporters of his programs.

To overcome business animosity, Lee first had to demonstrate to the retailers that a downtown location was ultimately more profitable than fleeing to the suburbs. The middle and upper classes, Lee argued, would shop downtown and eventually live there when his redevelopment program had done its job. The convincing wasn't easy, but Lee did it. For instance, when the Mayor decided to announce plans for the Church Street South project (the vacant land in front of the railroad station), he did it in a speech to the Chamber of Commerce.

The 800-plus housing units there, he said, would be at least 90 percent middle-income and luxury housing; this would constitute a "captive market" for the new downtown shopping area.

But it took the big businesses some time to come around. The man who helped Lee win the argument was Roger L. Stevens, who in addition to making an immense amount of money from real estate, also produces Broadway plays and contributes heavily to the national Democratic Party. He was President Johnson's adviser on the arts, and chairman of all sorts of national councils on the arts. The most legendary of Stevens' grandiose financial moves was in 1951, when he bought and sold the Empire State Building.

Lee and Logue got Stevens to become the financier for the original four-block downtown commercial redevelopment. The obstacles were numerous.

The small businessmen there were overwhelmed without too much difficulty, but the big problem was getting the big businesses in.

Malley's, an old New Haven family firm, was convinced to buy into the new project. The real turning point, however, was when Macy's agreed to come to town; and once again Yale helped out.

In 1962 the University lent Stevens $4.5 million for short-term financing. J. Richardson Dilworth, financial adviser to the Rockefellers, was on the Yale Corporation when the loan was approved. He was also on the board of Macy's, and a chain of events that began with a Dilworth-Lee meeting at Mory's culminated when Macy's agreed to build a $5 million store in downtown New Haven. Macy's arrival broke the back of local big business opposition to Lee's programs.

Charles Abrams, in his book *The City Is the Frontier,* explains in some detail how urban renewal enabling legislation—which with a little gerrymandering the downtown project became eligible for—guarantees large profits for big construction companies and lending institutions.

Retailers, money-lending banks and insurance companies, and construction and real-estate interests all began to understand their opportunity. A whole new field for investment opened up to them—or would if they became Democratic Party backers.

Fusco-Amatruda, for instance, a huge construction company based in New Haven, became the developer for the Chapel Square shopping mall; and Arthur Barbieri, the Democratic Town Chairman, landed the Chapel Square rental agents job for his real estate company.

It is since 1961, when he came the closest to losing an election, that Mayor Lee has demonstrated to the corporations that he is right: there is big money to be made in his urban renewal program.

It is also since 1961 that the Democratic Party has demolished the Republicans in New Haven. In 1965 Lee pulled down the largest victory margin ever for a New Haven Mayor. And the Republicans couldn't seem to raise any money for the mayoralty election.

With Yale and the big business support, the Democratic Party now runs New Haven—but it is not the same Democratic Party that captured the mayoralty for Dick Lee in 1953.

The Mayor is fond of saying that when he and his Kremlin started, they didn't know where they were going or how they were going to get there—just that they wanted to rebuild their city.

It is clear that Lee had no idea what his Democratic Party would look like after 14 years of his administration. It is not true that he set out on his renewal program simply to solidify his political power; power, of course, is important to him, but equally important is his belief that he is rebuilding New Haven.

This drive for the "new New Haven" began with the redevelopment program in 1953.

After nine years of what the city calls "physical renewal," Lee decided that only half the job was being done. The result was $2.5 million from the Ford Foundation in 1962 to start Community Progress, Inc., the city's anti-poverty program. Once again, New Haven pioneered; when the Federal government opened the Office of Economic Opportunity in 1964, many of its initial programs were modeled on CPI's experience. Today the Federal government provides over 80 percent of CPI's $6 million-plus annual budget. CPI, Lee says, does the job physical renewal neglects: "human renewal."

In both of these programs, "coalition" is the key word. Lee's approach is the most comprehensive attempt in the United States to implement the basic liberal theory of change: that those in power will use their power to significantly improve the lot of the disadvantaged, once they are made aware that it is in their self-interest to do so.

At bottom is the assumption that the entire community, rich or poor, black or white, shares a common interest.

The ensuing years of redevelopment have yet to prove that this is true. The face of New Haven is being dramatically changed, but the corporations have changed it by building the things business finds profitable or necessary: big stores, expressways and parking lots that service these stores, office buildings, a hotel, and middle-income and luxury housing.

All of these projects are money-makers. Only one kind of construction is seriously needed in the city that is not profitable: low-income housing.

The poor people have simply been moved from place to place. When Lee and his Kremlin tore down the Oak Street slum, most of its white residents headed for Fair Haven or Wooster Square and the blacks went to Dixwell.

Redevelopment followed them to Wooster Square and Dixwell, and it is on its way to the Hill, Fair Haven, and Newhallville. The extension of the turnpike connector is taking care of the Legion Ave. area, perhaps the worst slum pocket in the city.

Because discrimination in housing is still widespread and blatant, the problems for blacks and Puerto Ricans have intensified. The non-white population nearly doubled between 1960 and 1967, from about 20 percent to an estimated 35 percent this year.

Redevelopment Agency figures say that the city has relocated 6776 households, 4785 of them in the same period. This figure does not include families who don't wait for the Relocation Agency, but move out when they hear the bulldozers are on their way.

Of those families relocated between 1960 and 1967, 2076 have been white and 1794 black; this means that, by the Redevelopment Agency's own admission, less than five percent of the city's white people but almost 30 percent of the blacks have been moved. A Yale planning student's study, based on 1965 figures, calculated that 40 percent of the total Negro population had been relocated.

What was built for these people? In mid-1965 redevelopment had erected

1676 housing units; 700 were luxury apartments and 976 were middle-income. More in those categories have been opened since 1965. A low-income public housing project with about 25 units is about to open in Fair Haven, and about 100 other poor families have received rent supplements.

Beyond that, nothing has been done since the big public housing projects were built in the late 1940's and early '50's except some housing for the elderly; only token numbers of low-cost units are even on the drawing boards.

The attempt to relocate tenants from the path of Route 34, the turnpike connector extension, points up the seriousness of the housing crisis for low-income families particularly blacks. The Legion Avenue area is being torn down for this road, which will be one of the widest roads in the world, with six lanes of traffic, an immense grassy median strip, and a wide bank on either side—even though it runs through the middle of the city.

This neighborhood has the biggest concentration in New Haven of large families on welfare. The State Highway Department, which is building the road, had hoped that relocation could be finished by this fall so construction could start, but over one-half of the families are still there even though the state now owns all the properties.

The buildings are falling to pieces; the first week of October saw two major fires in these apartments. Relocation officials admit in private that there is just no place to put these families. A top official of the State Welfare Department said in Hartford that some large welfare families have already had to move out of New Haven because there is no place for them to live.

It is clear that the interests of the poor have not been properly represented in the redevelopment program. CPI, some people hoped before they saw it in action, would overcome this problem by organizing the people to make their needs known.

Allan Talbot claims in *The Mayor's Game* that a new political force—"direct citizen action"—is at work in the city. CPI, Talbot says, has "played key behind-the-scenes roles in most of the recent stir and action." In its first four years, according to this analysis, CPI invested $1,639,574 in "neighborhood organization."

The bulk of this "neighborhood organization" money in fact went for the CPI neighborhood offices, which in no sense organize neighborhoods. CPI is a very tightly administered, top-down organization, with every major decision made by the executive staff and the Mayor. The neighborhood offices simply carry out the directives from downtown. What little community organization CPI indulges in has been designed to create pressure for goals selected in advance by the CPI staff.

CPI, like the development program, is a coalition of those in the community who already have power. These power groups do not believe that those who dominate society are responsible for the depressed condition of the poor and the blacks; implicit in their programs is the assumption that the poor are where they are because something is wrong with them, whether it be lack of education, poor motivation, or something else.

The CPI approach denies that powerlessness is an important factor in the ghettoes; and it denies, by its top-down control and its predominantly white middle-class policy makers, that the poor ought to have an important voice in programs designed to help them.

Some individuals have been able to begin the climb out of poverty with CPI help, but the organization will never significantly affect large groups so long as it tries to pull individuals out and up rather than mobilizing the masses of the poor in their own behalf.

Maurice Sykes, a black CPI neighborhood worker, put the problem succinctly: CPI, he said, has "done a helluva job, but they overlooked the grass roots."

All of Mayor Lee's vaunted programs overlook the fact that the economic structure of the United States has always rested on an underclass. Previous immigrant groups have been able to rise in the society only because they were replaced by another group of immigrants.

In this way the Italians replaced the Irish as the lower class in urban industrial centers, and as the blacks and Puerto Ricans moved to the cities they replaced the Italians.

Because there are no more new immigrant groups, and because this country is racist, the blacks and Puerto Ricans have remained on the bottom, along with some whites who didn't make it. There is no replacement group in sight.

The implication, clearly, is that those who are poor now will remain that way unless the structure of the society is changed in some basic way. It is foolish to expect that programs run by those who have gained power in the present structure will do anything but perpetuate that structure.

Large corporations are making a lot of money these days, and there is no reason to expect them to disturb the status quo when they profit so much from it.

If those who make decisions now continue to have that power, the poor will remain where they are: on the bottom. If the poor are going to have some voice in the decisions that affect their lives, they are going to have to *take* power. No one is going to give it to them.

This is the fatal shortcoming of the Lee programs for change. They are based on the liberal assumption that a community of interest exists between the poor and the powerful. That is demonstrably untrue, for in New Haven the lot of the poor has not improved despite the millions of dollars spent on renewal programs.

The tragic fact about all this is that Mayor Lee does not understand what is wrong with his programs. He is fond of saying in public that "if New Haven is a model city, then God help urban America"; but he is at bottom convinced that he has done well.

Talbot quotes him as replying, when asked if he regretted passing up the 1958 Senatorial nomination which eventually went to Thomas Dodd, "Sure, every once in a while I have my regrets, but . . . I've already done something that few men will ever do—I've rebuilt a city, not just any city, mind you, but a city I love."

There is clearly something amiss in that city. The "riots" pointed up the problem, but Dick Lee does not understand what the problem is. When the Mayor swept into office, a bright star in a dismal decade for liberals, he stirred hope in the hearts of the poor as well as middle-class men of good will. The goal was, he said, nothing less than a "slumless city." It is significant that Melvin Adams, Lee's Development Administrator, said that the "slumless city" wasn't, after all, possible: "controlled slums" is actually the goal.

Why the current uneasiness? The war in Vietnam has cut down funds for liberal domestic programs, and it has also alienated many blacks because they bear such a disproportionate burden in the fighting. New Haven's programs are no longer unique in the country, as they were when Lee started in the 1950's, and it is becoming difficult for the city to get such an out-of-proportion share of Federal money.

Many of Lee's sharpest administrators have moved on, part of a new group of floating anti-poverty and renewal professionals who shift from city to city not because the work is done in one place but because their personal ambitions dictate that they keep climbing in the "human resources business," as Mitchell Sviridoff, the first executive director of CPI, calls it.

Sviridoff has excelled in this game of personal advancement through fighting poverty: he left his job at CPI to head New York's new Human Resources Administration—at a substantial salary raise—and after a little over a year there, he resigned to take a $50,000 job as a Ford Foundation vice president.

There are many other examples; New Haven is a training ground for renewal administrators all over the country. Logue resigned as chief of the Boston Redevelopment Authority to run for mayor of that city; L. Thomas Appleby, who followed Logue as Development Administrator, now runs renewal in Washington, D.C.; the list is practically endless.

These factors have all contributed to New Haven's unrest. Basically, however, the problem is very simple: the years of rhetoric by the Lee administration have simply never been fulfilled. CPI's training programs are a stopgap which help only a small percentage of the poor.

Redevelopment may be rebuilding the city, but its major effect on all but the well-off is to tighten the housing market. The poor have not been effectively organized to make their needs felt in the city; they have depended on the good will of the Lee administration.

They have been forced to depend on good will because they have nothing to say about what happens. Lee's government is a tightly run operation, with every major decision cleared over his desk. Information about the city's plans is kept secret until final decisions are made. Consensus is the goal and too often the reality; plans are made not by discussion and disagreement but by administrative fiat.

The director of a major service project in New Haven says that he constantly gets calls from the Mayor's office, saying "You guys take it easy over there. We're running this town." In that kind of administration the only disagreement tolerated is from those who already have significant power. The voices of the protesting poor are shunted aside as quickly as possible.

When the city holds Federally required "public hearings" for some of its programs, Lee's officials can never understand why people protest. They usually return from these meetings shaking their heads and wondering "why those people don't understand . . . why they're so unreasonable." Then whatever plan was being aired goes ahead, on the assumption that the Mayor's people know best.

It is ironic, in fact, that people at Yale make so much of the fact that they at last have a chance to participate constructively in city politics. It is, after all, their University and their class of people for whom the city is being rebuilt.

According to Allan Talbot, "New Haven's message to other cities is written in optimism . . . It has demonstrated that the work of restoring our cities can be challenging, fruitful, and even fun. . . . New Haven shows that there can be nobility in action, that it is far better to participate than to watch."

That would make ironic reading for the poor who are pleading with the Lee administration to let them run their own programs and rebuild their own neighborhoods before it is too late.

Dick Lee is hardly campaigning at all this fall [1967], although he is running for his eighth term as Mayor of New Haven. This is, he says, a time of crisis, "no time for ordinary politics." He can afford not to campaign this year because his Democratic Party is supported by virtually every group in the city with any political power. The Republican Party has been reduced to a joke. There are two new sources of potential opposition in the city, but neither has yet organized a sufficient political base to be a threat at the polls.

The first of these new additions to the city's political scene is the American Independent Movement, which ran Yale sociology professor Robert Cook for Congress in 1966 as an independent. Cook polled a little over 4000 votes within New Haven. AIM is basically a white middle-class group, drawing its hard core from young professionals and intellectuals who have banded together because of a common anger with the condition of the country.

AIM makes no bones about its radical opposition to America's policies, both foreign and domestic. Bob Cook, writing about the "riots" in New Haven, bluntly said "that the forces which control the community are in fact *illegitimate,* that their law and order are in fact *illegal,* and that at bottom their position rests upon force and violence."

AIM presents an often incisive intellectual analysis to back up this radical stance; but so far it has not done any real organizing, and it has failed to acquaint the community at large with its analysis and its program.

For that reason AIM is powerless, and poses a political threat to no one.

The other new force in New Haven politics is, of course, the angry black people. They have not yet organized themselves into a force which can contend for power at the polls, but they have certainly made themselves felt politically. The message they carry—the message of Fred Harris, the quiet little man who is their most impressive leader, and of the nameless angry men on the street-corners—is that if the white people can't solve the problems they had better just get out of the way and let the black people try.

Harris' Hill Parents Association and its allies are a real challenge to those in power, and that is why they are being threatened with Federal prosecution. The militant blacks have made it too clear that they understand that basic changes are necessary.

The Lee administration has demonstrated that a determined liberal can do everything possible to rebuild urban America, so long as he does not challenge the right of those in power to make the crucial decisions on priorities.

The real powers—the corporations—can, Lee has demonstrated, even grow to appreciate a liberal program. The Mayor has built a political coalition that rests on those who have money and resources—and this coalition therefore does not include the blacks and the other poor people in New Haven.

The tragedy of all this is that Richard C. Lee does not understand why his city is racked with unrest. Lee is not evil; he is a sincere man who wants to make New Haven a better place for its people.

The Mayor has used his political genius to wring everything possible out of those who hold power; but to step outside the existing structure simply does not occur to him.

Lee has built his political career on the assumption that America as he knows it can solve its urban problems. The nation as a whole has certainly not demonstrated that this proposition is true; and neither has the Lee administration.

Friends of the Mayor say he calls people over to him at cocktail parties now, and insists on telling them about all these upstart critics. He has been fighting for a better New Haven for 14 years, the Mayor will say—and where have these critics been all that time? They just don't understand, he says.

28 THE LIMITS OF LIBERAL SOLUTIONS: THE CASE OF INCOME GUARANTEES*

by BRIAN GLICK

Liberals often view the creation of some kind of negative income tax as the final solution to the problems of poverty and income inequality in America. But like many liberal solutions, they are inadequate as programs for a Good Society and a hoax in terms of their prospects for realization.

Glick in this article illustrates why. Real welfare can't be provided by the NIT. To give everyone an adequate income ($8000 according to Glick), it would require a massive redistribution of money from the wealthy to the poor. Second, it would totally undermine the willingness of men to work for the meaningless and low-paying jobs offered by the capitalist economy.

Since no serious program will be instituted, what will be instituted will be a cover for conservative intentions. When conservatives get hold of it, as they always do, they will turn it to their own purposes, in this case, to simply streamline away the administrative costs of welfare without materially affecting benefit levels. Liberals often get the form of their programs instituted (a la Poverty Program or a la School Desegregation), but rarely do they have the power to solve the problem and usually they are only used to serve a stabilizing and status quo function.

Glick's estimate of what an adequate income would be raises the question whether redistribution is even adequate itself to create a Good Society. Capitalism impoverishes society most basically by limiting the kinds of goods and services to those that serve profit-making. Income levels can be raised from here to Kingdom Come, but if the society still works to manipulate and exploit people, if people have no control, if all they can buy with increased income is waste and longing and false security, but not services and goods that minister to their needs, then this is not a Good Society by any stretch of the imagination.

Guaranteed Annual Income has been admitted into the litany of liberal ideology, but not in a form which offers hope to the poor. The plans which corporate and political leaders are now considering will neither pay a living wage nor safeguard civil liberties, though they may well promote social and economic stability while diverting attention from the basic issues of wealth and power.

Once the esoteric vision of eccentric economists and the Ad Hoc Committee on the Triple Revolution, Guaranteed Annual Income has recently been endorsed by four presidential commissions (riots, crime, automation and income maintenance). Eugene McCarthy has publicly endorsed it along with Daniel P. Moynihan, the ADA, National Association of Social Workers, the Conference of Mayors, over 1000 economists, and many corporate heads including Henry Ford II. The Office of Economic Opportunity recently funded a three-year pilot project and several congressmen have introduced modest legislative proposals.

Endorsement does not, of course, entail adoption. An undefined GAI serves many of its supporters as no more than a convenient political slogan. For the moment, and probably for the next several years, liberal leaders can advocate GAI without fear of favorable action by congressional reactionaries. By pretending to consider it seriously they can excuse inaction on immediate reforms or divert attention from unpopular decisions, as when LBJ announced the new income maintenance commission along with his acceptance of regressive welfare legislation.

It is not at all clear, however, that corporate and political leaders would have much to lose from adoption of the kind of GAI they support, or that the poor would have much to gain. GAI is merely a general label for any plan to guarantee every person some specified minimum income. The plans can take a variety of forms. Some would protect privacy by giving every person the same flat grant; they would make no special inquiry into financial circumstances and would rely on progressive income tax to redistribute the burden of poverty among the nonpoor. Robert Theobald and the Triple Revolution committee would use GAI to cut the traditional link between jobs and income and free recipients from the need to work in order to live decently. (Theobald, however, proposes two levels of guaranteed income, one for the poor and a higher one for middle class workers displaced by cybernetics.)

Universal flat grants and allowances sufficient to cut the job-income link are not necessary features of GAI, however, and the new supporters of income maintenance do not discuss them. Their intellectual leader is not Theobald, but Yale's James Tobin, a former member of Kennedy's Council of Economic Advisors. The model for their GAI is based on conservative economist Milton Friedman's Negative Income Tax (NIT).

FROM POSITIVE TO NEGATIVE INCOME TAX

NIT would not distribute money automatically. Every tax unit, either an individual or a family, would have to compute its total income and file a return. A unit whose income exceeded a level specified in the NIT plan would, as now, pay tax to the government, but any unit whose reported earnings fell below the specified level would pay no tax and instead would receive a "negative tax" or NIT allowance. The Internal Revenue Service could advance periodic allowances to poor units who filed a declaration of estimated income, just as it now collects advance payments from wealthy tax units.

In theory, NIT could simply rebate to every poor unit the entire difference between its reported and guaranteed income, deducting all earnings from the amount of the government's payment. Tobin and his followers reject this "100 percent tax on earnings" for fear it would discourage people from working for wages not substantially in excess of the guaranteed income. They prefer to have only a part of a unit's earnings (generally 33 to 50 percent) deducted from the unit's guaranteed minimum income to determine the size of its NIT allowance. Their mathematically complex proposals are carefully designed to reinforce the job-income link which Theobald would cut, to integrate the poor into the work force.

Economists consider NIT more adaptable than current welfare programs to sophisticated systems of work incentives. If they are right, NIT could be used to significantly strengthen social cohesion. Effective work incentives would increase poor people's stake in American corporate economic success. Given a stake in the system and tired from working all day, poor people would have neither the will nor the time and energy for rebellion or politics. At the same time NIT would free welfare caseworkers for more effective social reclamation programs. Corporate leaders, who undoubtedly value these functions, also see NIT as an inexpensive tool for expanding ghetto markets and stabilizing the economy.

Liberals stress that NIT, unlike welfare, would cover all needy persons and distribute aid as a matter of right with full respect for freedom and privacy. In large part, however, NIT exhibits these characteristics only because its proponents choose to define it that way. Congress could enact an NIT which excludes certain needy people: those judged immoral, lazy, or simply "employable" (as some NIT advocates recommend). It could also require detailed investigation of all returns which indicate financial need. Federal investigators, assigned the powers and duties of local welfare workers, would not necessarily interfere less in a recipient's private life. Indeed, NIT proponents endorse infringements on privacy and freedom similar to those complained of in current programs. Tobin, among others, would reduce grants to large families to encourage birth control and would retain the type of man-in-the house rule which includes in a family's income the earnings of an unmarried woman's sex partner whether or not those earnings are in fact available to the family.

On the other hand, the liberal's admirable objectives can be fully achieved without NIT. Congress does not need NIT to require, as a condition of federal subsidy, that each state extend its traditional welfare programs to all its needy. Congress and the Department of Health, Education and Welfare (HEW) can protect welfare clients' civil liberties under the current structure; HEW has to some extent already done so rhetorically. In 1962, HEW's Advisory Committee on Public Welfare recommended reforming the existing welfare system to aid all the needy, set a national standard of need, and determine eligibility by affidavit and spot check. NIT merely wraps these old proposals in a new package.

HOW MUCH IS "GUARANTEED"?

Few current NIT plans could fully implement even the HEW Advisory Committee's recommendations. Most proposals guarantee a minimum income far below the generally accepted "poverty line" and many assure a family of four as little as $1500 a year. With only a portion of their minimum financial needs met by NIT, poor families would require supplementary assistance from existing welfare programs which the NIT would neither replace nor reform.

NIT proponents treat as secondary and merely technical the crucial question of how much to guarantee. Their most generous proposals set the minimum income at the official poverty line (around $3000 for a family of four). But this index vastly underestimates the money a family needs to maintain its health and live decently. It allows no more than the better northern welfare budgets, which everyone recognizes as grossly inadequate. (Similarly, $3000 is the standard deduction for personal exemptions allowed four-member families under current income tax laws. Whatever its merit when first established, this allowance no longer reflects family needs.)

OEO's $3130 line (over $3300 at current prices), developed by Mollie Orshansky of the Social Security Administration, is hardly more rational.[1] On the assumption that families generally spend an average of one third of their income on food, Miss Orshansky estimates total needs by tripling the cost of the U.S. Department of Agriculture's (USDA) lowest-cost "economy" diet (currently priced at about $1100). But her multiplier of three, based on 1955 USDA studies, is too small according to 1961 Labor Department data showing an average income-food expenditures ratio of more than four to one. Moreover, the diet she uses is only a guide for "temporary or emergency use when funds are low." USDA developed the economy plan because welfare agencies refused to grant a food allowance sufficient to purchase its more expensive "low-cost" diet. Even the low-cost plan indicates only the lowest price at which it is theoretically possible to obtain a proper diet, assuming no deviation from the prescribed diet, skillful no-waste food preparation, maximum shopping efficiency, and no eating out. The Labor Department regards USDA's "moderate-cost" plan (priced at about $2000 assuming some meals out) as necessary since only 23 percent of those who spend no more than the low-cost amount actually have nutritionally adequate diets.

Retaining Miss Orshansky's procedure of multiplying the minimum food expenditure by the ratio of income to food expenditures, but using the more accurate figures, one finds that a family of four needs over $8000 a year ($\$2000 \times 4.2 = \$8400$). Roughly the same estimate results from independent calculations by the Labor Department's Bureau of Labor Statistics (BLS). BLS determines periodically the cost of the goods and services which an urban family of four needs for "modest but adequate" living, more than mere physical survival but less than the "American standard of living." As of Autumn 1966 this City Worker's Family Budget required $7825 after taxes and other payroll deductions; later figures are certain to indicate a substantially higher minimum.[2]

BLS's is not an advocate's budget. It was not developed to prove a point or promote reform. Most of the figures it uses are rock-bottom. Under this budget, as well as under a properly computed version of Miss Orshansky's poverty line, today's family of four seems to need at least $8000 a year, or more than double the minimum income guaranteed by the most generous of current NIT plans.

THE EFFECTS OF GUARANTEED ADEQUATE INCOME

Despite our apparent affluence, the U.S. government cannot guarantee this large a minimum income without both giving up effective work incentives and radically redistributing income. An NIT which guarantees $8000 to a family of four and deducts from 33 to 50 percent of earnings would cost nearly $200

[1] My critique of this poverty line is based largely on Alan Haber's excellent article "Poverty Budgets: How Much Is Enough?" *Poverty and Human Resources Abstracts*, May–June 1966.

[2] The BLS requirement increases rapidly not only to adjust for price rises, but also because of changing standards of minimum needs and increasing urbanization (as of 1966 metropolitan families of four needed $1000 more per year than those living outside metropolitan areas).

billion a year. The National Income (personal plus corporate income) would not be sufficient to support the federal government as well as this NIT plan. Although it is financially possible, an NIT program which deducted a far higher proportion of earnings would still drastically redistribute income and also threaten social cohesion and productivity.

Economists agree that a man would have incentive to work under NIT only if no more than 50 percent of what he earned was counted toward reducing the government's payment. Tobin argues that incentives can be effective only if no more than 33 percent is counted.

If every family of four were guaranteed $8000 a year and only 50 percent of its earnings were deducted to determine its allowance, the family could take in up to $16,000 ($4000 per person) before losing its eligibility for an allowance and having to pay tax to the government. This is computed as follows:

Earnings	$0000	$6000	$9000	$12,000	$16,000
50% of Earnings	$0000	$3000	$4500	$6000	$8000
Govt. NIT Payment	$8000	$5000	$3500	$2000	$0000

If the same family had only one third of its income counted, it could earn up to $24,000 ($6000 per person) before moving from negative to positive tax brackets.

Because fewer than 10 percent of the nation's families now earn over $16,000 a year (let alone $24,000), an NIT which guarantees $8000 for a family of four and counts only half or a third of a family's earnings would have to pay some allowance to over 90 percent of the people in the country. This would be economically impossible. The full cost of these allowances plus all other government expenses would have to be borne exclusively by the remaining 10 percent, and the corporations—the combined income of which was $230 billion in 1966 (the last available figure). The federal budget in the same year was $100 billion, which left $130 billion for an NIT. However, an NIT which guarantees $8000 per family of four and deducts only 50 percent of income would cost $170 billion, which leaves a $40 billion deficit. To balance, an NIT plan would have to deduct at least three quarters to four fifths of every unit's earnings.

Most workers, guaranteed a decent income without working and only marginal benefits with work, would probably quit, losing the economic stake crucial to social cohesion. As an example, consider a family whose income is $6000. Four fifths of that is $4800. Subtracting $4800 from the GAI, $8000, the government allowance then becomes $3200. Adding the NIT payment to the family's income, we get $6000 + $3200 = $9200. The family would take in a total of $9200 if the husband worked all year to earn $6000 independently, whereas it would have received $8000, very little less, if no one worked at all. In our society, relying as it does on economic motivation for work, the only financially feasible form of an $8000 minimum GAI would dangerously reduce the work force and, consequently, total productivity.

Even if economic collapse could be averted, perhaps through rapid automation, such an NIT would substantially redistribute income. Guaranteeing $8000 to a family of four provides an income of $2000 per person. If no person in the nation received less than $2000, the limited amount of money available for distribution as income would permit no more than half the population to receive as much as $3000 per person. This can be seen easily by looking at the size of the national "personal income" (wages, etc. after taxes): $500 billion. If everyone received no more than $2000 per year, $2000 × 200 million persons = $400 billion, showing that we could afford to let part of the population have a higher income. Say only half the population earned $2000 per person; $2000 per person × 100 million persons = $200 billion. If the other half of the population earned $3000 per person, $3000 per person × 100 million persons = $300 billion. The total of these two income figures equals the present national "personal income"; thus if no one is to receive less than $2000, neither can anyone receive more than $3000 if an adequate workforce is to be sustained. Because no one's after-tax income would be much more than his minimum needs, accumulation of wealth would become very difficult, and non-economic incentives would have to be devised to induce the requisite number of people to work.

By stressing the method of distribution and not the amount distributed, GAI and NIT proponents obscure the fact that it will be necessary to nearly equalize income in order to end poverty in the United States. While this is hardly their intent, a simple projection of their program (such as we have made here) raises the obvious question of whether a capitalist economy *can* guarantee everyone sufficient income to live decently. Guaranteed-income proponents evade their own evidence, but the answer seems clearly no.

GAI proponents also ignore the key issue of power. During the past two years, welfare rights organizations, composed mainly of black "Aid to Dependent Children" mothers, have begun to build local political power which is bound to be substantially enhanced when black political leaders, already sensitive to client demands, take control of municipal governments across the country. At that point clients would be able to influence local welfare agencies and perhaps gain the power to elect local welfare boards.

Federalization of welfare would make this impossible. It would shift legislative and administrative authority to white officials geographically and politically removed from welfare clients. Client groups, unable to win extra money for their members or focus anger against identifiable local officials, would lose most of their already limited organizational strength. Like welfare clients before the formation of welfare rights groups, the beneficiaries of NIT would be powerless to block the restrictive amendments and harsh administration from which NIT would be no more exempt.

NIT reinforces the fiction that income can be guaranteed "as of right" by congressional declaration and administrative arrangement without a transfer of power. Both the legalistic and humanitarian language of NIT proposals mask its basic function of preserving social stability while maintaining the present distribution of national wealth and political power in the United States.

29

CORPORATE OBSTACLES TO SOCIAL SPENDING*

by PAUL BARAN AND PAUL SWEEZY

Liberals have argued that the main obstacles to the solution of social problems are political. Conservative legislators beat back liberal social spending. But with a liberal congressional majority the way would be clear for a massive assault on social problems.

One part to this line of logic is that under liberal hegemony large reductions would be possible in the size of the military budget. The Reich-Finkelhor selection (Part I) earlier explained why massive institutional interests will prevent such a cutback. The following chapter from Baran and Sweezy also shows why the massive military expenditures provide the only solution American capitalism has ever found (and ever will find) to its basic tendency to stagnate. An alternative was tried during the 1930's and it didn't work. Obviously the obstacles to reducing the Military-Industrial Complex lie not with conservative politicians. They lie at the heart of the system's economic stability, with entrenched economic interests.

Leaving aside the MIC, for a moment, it is also true that it is not conservative politicians who are primarily responsible for the tight lid kept on the level of the government's welfare spending. Welfare spending, independent from military reductions, is opposed by powerful corporate interests. They do so for a number of reasons: It threatens to put the government into competitive position with private interests (as in the TVA). It threatens to undermine the low-wage labor market. It threatens redistribution and the dismantling of class privileges. Baran and Sweezy here illustrate how this opposition operates in the cases of river valley development and public housing.

Such realities spell failure for liberals. Their strategy for a short cut to the welfare state runs again and again into the stone wall of corporate opposition. Electing more liberal politicians won't work. The only way to get the system to serve the needs of the people is to mobilize the masses of people against the domination of the corporations.

Baran and Sweezy make reference in this selection to the problem of "surplus absorption" which they outline in earlier parts of their book (and which is outlined briefly in the Reich-Finkelhor selection). It is, in capsule, that under monopoly conditions, corporations cannot find enough outlets for their investment, and thus surplus accumulates in corporate coffers. With inadequate investment, the economic system slows down and rumbles into depression and unemployment. The only workable solution, i.e., possibility for absorbing the surplus, has been for government to stimulate the economy through massive expenditures, which in turn creates outlets for corporate investment, which in turn keeps the economy ploughing ahead.

The main facts about the changing composition of government spending in the period of its most rapid growth (since 1929) are well known. Table I,

TABLE I. GOVERNMENT SPENDING, 1929–1957 (PERCENT OF GNP)

	1929	1957
Non-defense purchases	7.5	9.2
Transfer payments	1.6	5.9
Defense purchases	0.7	10.3
Total	9.8	25.4

Source: F. M. Bator, *The Question of Government Spending*, 1960, Tables 1 and 2.

comparing 1929 with 1957, shows government spending, broken down into three major components, as percentages of GNP. "Non-defense purchases" includes all purchases of goods and services for civilian purposes by federal, state, and local governments. "Transfer payments" includes unemployment benefits, old age pensions, veterans' allowances, etc.; interest on government debt; and subsidies less surpluses of government enterprises. "Defense purchases" includes all purchases (almost exclusively by the federal government) of goods and services for military purposes less sales of military items.

During the interval 1929–1957, total government spending increased from roughly one tenth to one quarter of GNP. Of this proportionate increase in the ratio of government spending to GNP, almost nine tenths was transfer payments and defense purchases, little more than one tenth non-defense purchases. How are we to interpret these figures?

In the first place, government's direct contribution to the functioning and welfare of society is almost entirely subsumed under non-defense purchases. Here we have public education, roads and highways, health and sanitation, conservation and recreation, commerce and housing, police and fire protection, courts and prisons, legislatures and executives. And here, despite an enormous increase in outlays on highways, associated with a more than doubling of the number of automobiles in use since 1929, there has been very little expansion relative to the size of the economy as a whole. Increased non-defense purchases of goods and services have thus made almost no contribution to the solution of the surplus absorption problem.

Transfer payments, on the other hand, have grown significantly, expanding from less than 2 percent to nearly 6 percent of GNP. While an appreciable fraction of this increase (12 percent) represents expanded interest payments (which go largely to banks, corporations, and upper-income individuals), by far the larger part is accounted for by various forms of social security payments (unemployment, old age and survivors, veterans) which certainly do enhance the welfare of large groups of needy citizens. This is the only substantial element of truth in the common assertion that since 1929 this country has become a "welfare state." In other respects expenditures affecting the welfare of the people have grown only about as fast as the economy as a whole. As to surplus absorption, the growth of transfer payments has undoubtedly made a significant contribution.

It is of course in the area of defense purchases that most of the expansion has taken place—from less than 1 percent of GNP to more than 10 percent, accounting for about two thirds of the total expansion of government spending relative to GNP since the 1920's. This massive absorption of surplus in military preparations has been the key fact of postwar American economic history. Some six or seven million workers, more than 9 percent of the labor force, are now dependent for jobs on the arms budget. If military spending were reduced once again to pre-Second World War proportions, the nation's economy would return to a state of profound depression, characterized by unemployment rates of 15 percent and up, such as prevailed during the 1930's.

This is of course widely denied, the dissenters falling into two main categories. First, there are those who claim that if taxes were cut simultaneously with a reduction in arms spending, private spending would increase to a compensating extent. Much of this book [*Monopoly Capital*] up to this point has been devoted to showing why the system does not and cannot work this way, and there is no need to repeat the argument here. The second group recognizes that arms spending is now acting as a prop to the economy (though generally tending to underestimate its importance) and that its removal would have serious consequences. These consequences, they argue, can be avoided by substituting other kinds of government spending for arms spending. In place of the warfare state, they say, we can and eventually should build a genuine welfare state.[1] And they have no difficulty in enumerating useful and needed projects which would require government outlays as large as, or even larger than, the present arms budget.[2]

The argument that non-defense spending is as effective in sustaining the economy as defense spending, and that "we" therefore should substitute the one for the other is no doubt valid enough as a statement of what is desirable. Whether it is also valid as a statement of what is possible, within the framework of monopoly capitalist society, is a different question, one which advocates of the change-over too often ignore. Yet this is clearly the crux of the matter for anyone who is interested in understanding how the system really works.

To answer this question, it is necessary to take into account the modalities

[1] For a succinct statement of this position, see J. K. Galbraith, "We Can Prosper Without Arms Orders," *The New York Times Magazine,* June 22, 1952.

[2] For example, Reginald Isaacs, chairman of the Department of City and Regional Planning at Harvard University, after extensive research for the American Council to Improve Our Neighborhoods (ACTION), concluded (in 1958) that required outlays for urban renewal would total just under two trillion dollars by 1970 and that the "necessary federal participation expenditures alone will rival those for national security." Reginald R. Isaacs, in Committee for Economic Development, *Problems of United States Economic Development,* New York, 1958, Volume 1, p. 339.

of political power in a monopoly capitalist society, and more specifically in its particular American version. Since this is a large subject which cannot be dealt with at length in the present study, we shall have to confine ourselves to a few observations and suggestions.

Except in times of crisis, the normal political system of capitalism, whether competitive or monopolistic, is bourgeois democracy. Votes are the nominal source of political power, and money is the real source: the system, in other words, is democratic in form and plutocratic in content. This is by now so well recognized that it hardly seems necessary to argue the case. Suffice it to say that all the political activities and functions which may be said to constitute the essential characteristics of the system—indoctrinating and propagandizing the voting public, organizing and maintaining political parties, running electoral campaigns—can be carried out only by means of money, lots of money. And since in monopoly capitalism the big corporations are the source of big money, they are also the main sources of political power.

It is true that there is a latent contradiction in this system. The non-property-owning voters, who constitute the overwhelming majority, may form their own mass organizations (trade unions, political parties), raise necessary funds through dues, and thereby become an effective political force. If they succeed in winning formal political power and then attempt to use it in a way which threatens the economic power and privileges of the moneyed oligarchy, the system is confronted by a crisis which can be resolved according to its own rules only if the oligarchy is prepared to give up without a fight. Since to the best of our knowledge there is no case in history of a privileged oligarchy's behaving this way, we can safely dismiss the possibility. What happens instead is that the oligarchy, which controls either directly or through trusted agents all the instrumentalities of coercion (armed forces, police, courts, etc.), abandons the democratic forms and resorts to some form of direct authoritarian rule. Such a breakdown of bourgeois democracy and resort to authoritarian rule may also occur for other reasons—such as, for example, a prolonged inability to form a stable parliamentary majority, or successful resistance by certain vested interests to reforms necessary for the proper functioning of the economy. The history of recent decades is particularly rich in examples of the substitution of authoritarian for democratic government in capitalist countries: Italy in the early 1920's, Germany in 1933, Spain in the later 1930's, France in 1958, and many more.

In general, however, moneyed oligarchies prefer democratic to authoritarian government. The stability of the system is enhanced by periodic popular ratifications of oligarchic rule—this is what parliamentary and presidential elections normally amount to—and certain very real dangers to the oligarchy itself of personal or military dictatorship are avoided. Hence in developed capitalist countries, especially those with a long history of democratic government, oligarchies are reluctant to resort to authoritarian methods of dealing with opposition movements or solving difficult problems, and instead devise more indirect and subtle means for accomplishing their ends. Concessions are made to pull the teeth of trade-union and labor political movements professing radical aims. Their leaders are bought off—with money, flattery, and honors. As a result, when they acquire power they stay within the confines of the system, merely trying to win a few more concessions here and there to keep the rank and file satisfied, yet never challenging the real bastions of oligarchic power in the economy and in the coercive branches of the state apparatus. Similarly, the oligarchy alters the machinery of government to the extent necessary to prevent any stalemates and deadlocks which might involve the breakdown of democratic procedures (for example, the number of political parties is deliberately limited to prevent the emergence of government by unstable parliamentary coalitions). By these methods, and many others, democracy is made to serve the interests of the oligarchy far more effectively and durably than authoritarian rule. The possibility of authoritarian rule is never renounced—indeed, most democratic constitutions make specific provision for it in times of emergency—but it is decidedly not the preferred form of government for normally functioning capitalist societies.

The United States system of government is of course one of bourgeois democracy in the sense just discussed. In constitutional theory, the people exercise sovereign power; in actual practice, a relatively small moneyed oligarchy rules supreme. But democratic institutions are not merely a smoke screen behind which sit a handful of industrialists and bankers making policies and issuing orders. Reality is more complicated than that.

The nation's Founding Fathers were acutely aware of the latent contradiction in the democratic form of government, as indeed were most political thinkers in the late eighteenth and early nineteenth centuries. They recognized the possibility that the propertyless majority might, once it had the vote, attempt to turn its nominal sovereignty into real power and thereby jeopardize the security of property, which they regarded as the very foundation of civilized society. They therefore devised the famous system of checks and balances, the purpose of which was to make it as difficult as possible for the existing system of property relations to be subverted. American capitalism later developed in a context of numerous and often bitter struggles among various groups and segments of the moneyed classes—which had never been united, as in Europe, by a common struggle against feudal power. For these and other reasons, the governmental institutions which have taken shape in the United States have been heavily weighted on the side of protecting the rights and privileges of minorities: the property-owning minority as a whole against the people, and various groups of property-owners against each other. We cannot detail the story here—how the separation of powers was written into the Constitution, how states' rights and local autonomy became fortresses for vested interests, how political parties evolved into vote-gathering and patronage-dispensing machines without program or discipline. What interests us is the outcome, which was already shaped before the end of the nineteenth century. The United States became a sort of utopia for the private sovereignties of property and business. The very structure of government prevented effective action in many areas of the economy or social life (city planning, for example, to cite a need which has become increasingly acute in recent years). And even where this was not so, the system of political representation, together with the absence of responsible political parties, gave an effective veto power to temporary or permanent coalitions of vested interests. The positive role of government has tended to be narrowly confined to a few functions which could command the approval of substantially all elements of the moneyed classes: extending the national territory and protecting the interests of American businessmen and investors abroad, activities which throughout the nation's history have been the first concern of the federal government;[3] perfecting and protecting property rights at home; carving up the public domain among the most powerful and insistent claimants; providing a minimum infrastructure for the profitable operation of private business; passing out favors and subsidies in accordance with the well-known principles of the log-roll and the pork barrel. Until the New Deal period of the 1930's, there was not even any pretense that promoting the welfare of the lower classes was a responsibility of government: the dominant ideology held that any reliance on government for income or services was demoralizing to the individual, contrary to the laws of nature, and ruinous to the system of private enterprise.

This was the situation which prevailed at the time of the collapse of the boom of the 1920's. But with the coming of the Great Depression, the need for government to play a larger role suddenly became acute. How was this need met in the liberal New Deal period? In order to answer this question we have constructed Table II, which is the same as Table I except that it compares 1929 with 1939 instead of with 1957:

TABLE II. GOVERNMENT SPENDING, 1929–1939 (PERCENT OF GNP)

	1929	1939
Non-defense purchases	7.5	13.3
Transfer payments	1.6	4.6
Defense purchases	0.7	1.4
Total	9.8	19.3

The changes which took place between 1929 and 1939 are in sharp contrast to those which took place between 1929 and 1957. Even though the Second World War had already begun before the end of 1939 and American involvement was clearly a possibility, defense purchases were still of quite minor importance. On the other hand, both categories of civilian spending—non-defense purchases and transfers—increased sharply relative to GNP. Of the total increase in government spending relative to GNP during the decade of the 1930's, more than 60 percent was in non-defense purchases and more than 30 percent in transfers, less than 10 percent in defense purchases.

Here, it might seem, is evidence that the problem of inadequate surplus absorption can be solved, as some liberals claim, by increased government spending for welfare purposes. In actual fact, it is no such thing. Not that we wish to call in question the welfare goals which the New Deal increases in government spending were intended to serve. True, a large part of these out-

[3] Failure to understand this is one of the greatest weaknesses of most American historical writing. There are exceptions, however. See, for example, R. W. Van Alstyne, *The Rising American Empire,* New York, 1960, where the decisive character of foreign relations in shaping the nation's development from earliest times is correctly appreciated.

lays were in the nature of salvage operations for depression-threatened property owners of various sizes and descriptions,[4] but also much of genuine value for the non-owning classes was accomplished or at least initiated. But this is essentially beside the point. What was wrong with the government spending of the 1930's was not its direction but its magnitude: there was just not enough of it to come anywhere near offsetting the powerful depressive forces at work in the private sector of the economy. Measured in current dollars, government spending increased from $10.2 billion in 1929 to $17.5 billion in 1939, more than 70 percent. At the same time, however, GNP itself declined from $104.4 billion to $91.1 billion (a fall of 12.7 percent) and unemployment as a percentage of the labor force rose from 3.2 percent to 17.2 percent.[5]

Regarded as a salvage operation for the United States economy as a whole, the New Deal was thus a clear failure. Even Galbraith, the prophet of prosperity without war orders, has recognized that the goal was not even approached during the 1930's. "The Great Depression of the thirties," in his words, "never came to an end. It merely disappeared in the great mobilization of the forties." [6]

War spending accomplished what welfare spending had failed to accomplish. From 17.2 percent of the labor force, unemployment declined to a minimum of 1.2 percent in 1944. The other side of the coin was an increase of government spending from $17.5 billion in 1939 to a maximum of $103.1 billion in 1944. This is not to suggest that in peacetime an increase in spending of this magnitude would have been required to produce the virtual disappearance of unemployment. If it had not been for the fact that during the war civilian spending had to be restrained in various ways, near-full employment would have been reached at a considerably lower level of government spending. But a very large increase over the 1939 level—probably of the order of a doubling or tripling—would surely have been necessary. Why was such an increase not forthcoming during the whole depressed decade? Why did the New Deal fail to attain what the war proved to be within easy reach?

The answer to these questions is that, *given the power structure of United States monopoly capitalism,* the increase of civilian spending had about reached its outer limits by 1939. The forces opposing further expansion were too strong to be overcome.

In analyzing these forces and the limits they place on the expansion of civilian spending, it is relevant to point out first of all that spending originating at the state and local levels is much less flexible than spending originating at the federal level. Property taxes play the dominant role in state and local finance. They are harder to shift or evade than the taxes which provide the bulk of federal revenues (corporate and personal income taxes, payroll taxes, excise taxes, customs duties), and indeed to the extent that they fall on the personal property of individuals they cannot be shifted at all.

With this background, it is hardly surprising that there has been little change in the relative importance of state and local outlays during the last three dec-

[4] This often neglected aspect of the New Deal is ably dealt with by A. H. Hansen in his *Fiscal Policy and Business Cycles,* New York, 1941, Chapter 4.

[5] Even measured in constant (1957) dollars, GNP grew only from $193.5 billion in 1929 to $201.4 billion in 1939, which was not enough to keep real per capita GNP from slightly declining.

[6] J. K. Galbraith, *American Capitalism,* London, 1957, p. 69.

ades when the role of government spending as a whole has undergone such a radical transformation. State and local expenditures constituted 7.4 percent of GNP in 1929, and 8.7 percent in 1957. It is true that the proportion rose to nearly 13 percent at the bottom of the Great Depression, and fell to less than 4 percent during the war. The explanation in both cases, however, is clear: it was impossible to curtail the functions of state and local governments in line with the precipitous drop in GNP which marked the Great Depression; and during the war, controls prevented state and local spending from rising in step with GNP. What is important is that, with the return to "normalcy" after the war, the percentage reverted to approximately the level of the 1920's.

Given the structure of United States government and politics, then, any further variations in the role of government in the functioning of the economy will in all likelihood be initiated at the federal level. What follows must therefore be understood as applying largely to the forces which determine the amount of federal spending.

Here, as we have seen, the size of the tax bill, though not without influence, is far from being a decisive factor in determining the amount of government spending. With productive resources idle—the normal situation for monopoly capitalism—more spending means higher incomes out of which increased taxes can be paid. Some people will get hurt, but few of them are likely to belong to the moneyed oligarchy which holds political power. The oligarchy as a whole stands to gain and hence has a strong incentive to keep pushing up the level of government spending.

If taxes are not the decisive factor, what does determine the limits on the expansion of civilian spending? The answer is the particular interests of the individuals and groups which comprise the oligarchy and the way these interests are affected by the various types of spending.

We can postulate that for every item in the budget there is some minimum amount which has general approval and which evokes no appreciable opposition. As this amount is exceeded, approval for further increments gradually declines and opposition builds up until an equilibrium is reached and further expansion stops. Starting from this schema, we might attempt to determine the equilibrium points for the major budget items, hoping in this way to discover the individual spending limits and, by aggregation, the overall limit. This procedure, however, would be wrong. It ignores the existence of what may be called an "interdependence effect," which rules out simple aggregation of individual limits.

The point can be elucidated by considering two budget items simultaneously, say housing and health. Very few people nowadays are opposed to a modest public housing program, and of course everyone is in favor of at least enough spending on health to control epidemic diseases. But beyond a certain point, opposition begins to build up in each case, at first from real estate interests to housing and from the medical profession to public programs of medical care. But real estate interests presumably have no special reasons to oppose medical care, and doctors no special reasons to oppose housing. Still, once they have each gone into opposition to further increases in their own spheres, they may soon find it to their joint interest to combine forces in opposing both more housing and more public health. The opposition to each individual item thus builds up faster when two items are under consideration, and fastest of all for across-the-board increases in the whole budget. We might say figuratively that if one item is being considered, opposition grows in proportion to the amount of the increase; while if all items are being considered, opposition grows in proportion to the square of the increase.[7]

In practice, of course, no such simple quantitative relationships can be postulated, still less demonstrated. We need only keep in mind that resistance from the moneyed oligarchy as a whole to each item in a proposed general increase of civilian government spending will be much more intense than if the same items were being considered in isolation.[8] This is of great importance for our problem, because what we are concerned with is situations where the need is for a large expansion of total government spending, something which could hardly be achieved unless many budget items were increased at the same time.

In the case of almost every major item in the civilian budget, powerful vested interests are soon aroused to opposition as expansion proceeds beyond the necessary minimum. This occurs whenever a significant element of competition with private enterprise is involved, but it is also true of other items where competition with private enterprise is largely or even wholly absent.

There are many urgent social needs which government can satisfy only by entering into some form of competition with private interests. River valley development, for example, an area in which private enterprise could never hope to operate effectively, is essential for flood control, water conservation, rebuilding eroded soils, etc. But it also produces electric power which competes with private power and thus provides a yardstick by which the performance of the private power monopolies can be measured. For this reason, river valley development is bitterly opposed not only by the utilities themselves but also by the entire Big Business community. The history of the Tennessee Valley Authority affords eloquent testimony to the effectiveness of this opposition. TVA had its origin in the government's need for nitrates during the First World War. A dam, hydro-electric generating facilities, and a nitrate plant were built at Muscle Shoals, Alabama, to satisfy strictly military requirements. During the 1920's, a campaign to turn Muscle Shoals into a broad river valley development scheme was led by Senator Norris of Nebraska; but, in this period of capitalist prosperity, nothing came of it, and even the original investment was allowed to deteriorate in idleness. It was only during the "Hundred Days" after Roosevelt's inauguration in 1933—a period of near-panic for the moneyed oligarchy—that Norris's determined efforts were crowned with success. And the oligarchs have been regretting their moment of weakness ever since. From their point of view, the trouble with TVA was that it was a tremendous success. It gave the American people their first glimpse of what can be achieved by intelligent planning under a governmental authority equipped with the powers necessary to carry out a rational program. To cite only one of its achievements, by the later 1950's a typical household in the TVA area was paying only half as much for its electricity and consuming twice as much as the national

[7] The following observation from a letter to *The New York Times* (August 5, 1962) by James MacGregor Burns, professor of political science at Williams College, is apropos: "The gap between President and Congress today is too wide to be bridged by the usual techniques of pressure and bargain. The opposing elements are so strong and interlocked that he cannot push one policy as much as might seem feasible to the outsider without activating the whole machinery of opposition."

[8] This rule does not apply to increases in military spending.

average. And on a world-wide scale, TVA had become a symbol of the New Deal, a light showing others the way to democratic progress. Under these circumstances, the oligarchy did not dare destroy TVA outright. Instead, it organized a long-range campaign of unremitting criticism and harassment destined to hedge TVA in, curtail its functions, force it to conform to the norms of capitalist enterprise. And this campaign has achieved considerable successes: TVA has never been allowed to realize anything like its full potential. Nevertheless, its popularity with the people of the seven-state area in which it operates has protected it from being gutted and perverted from its original aims. The greatest triumph of the anti-TVA campaign, therefore, has been its total success in keeping the principle of the multi-purpose river valley authority from being applied to any of the other numerous river valleys of the United States where it could so richly further the people's welfare. The need for more TVA's is easily demonstrable to any rational person; during the 1930's and later, expanded government outlays on river valley development would frequently have made excellent sense as a partial solution to the problem of inadequate surplus absorption. But what Marx called the Furies of private interest, having been thoroughly aroused, easily repelled any further encroachment on their sacred domain.

Public housing, potentially a vast field for welfare spending, is another activity which encroaches upon the realm of private enterprise. A really effective low-cost housing program would necessarily call for extensive building in open spaces, which abound in most cities in the United States. But this is precisely what the powerful urban real estate interests are against. On the rock of this opposition, all attempts to launch a serious attack on the twin problems of insufficient and inadequate housing have foundered. Instead we have had fine-sounding "slum clearance" or "urban renewal" programs, which, while liberally rewarding the owners of run-down property, typically throw more people on the streets than they house. Moreover, the mausoleum-like "project" which is the usual embodiment of public housing is no kind of environment in which a viable community could take root and grow. "Slum clearance" is thus in reality slum creation, both off-site and on-site; and "urban renewal" is a system of outdoor relief for landlords in the decaying "gray belts" which are inexorably creeping out from the centers of our big cities. So grim indeed has been the American experience with public housing since it first became a political issue during the 1930's that today it no longer commands even a modicum of popular support. "Back in the 30's," writes Daniel Seligman, an editor of *Fortune* magazine, "proponents of public housing were possessed of a missionary fervor. New housing, they believed, would by itself exorcise crime and vice and disease. But public housing didn't do what its proponents expected. Today, public-housing people are searching for a new rationale and their fervor is gone; the movement today is so weak that most real estate groups hardly bother to attack it any more." [9] A deliberate plot to sabotage public housing could hardly have succeeded more brilliantly: the private interests don't have to oppose any more—the public does it for them.

River valley development and public housing are but two examples of government activities which trespass upon the territory of private interests. In all such cases, since private interests wield political power, the limits of

[9] William H. Whyte, Jr., and others, *The Exploding Metropolis,* New York, 1958, p. 93.

government spending are narrowly set and have nothing to do with social needs—no matter how shamefully obvious. But it is not only where there is competition with commercial enterprise that such limits are imposed: the same thing happens in areas like education and health where direct competition is either non-existent or of relatively minor importance. Here too the opposition of private interests to increased government spending is soon aroused; and here too the amounts actually spent bear no relation to demonstrable social need.

It would be possible to run through the gamut of civilian spending objects and show how in case after case the private interests of the oligarchy stand in stark opposition to the satisfaction of social needs. Real competition with private enterprise cannot be tolerated, no matter how incompetent and inadequate its performance may be; undermining of class privileges or of the stability of the class structure must be resisted at any cost. And almost all types of civilian spending involve one or both of these threats. There is just one major exception to this generalization in the United States today, and it is very much the type of exception which proves the rule: government spending on highways.

There is no need here to detail the importance of the automobile to the American economy. We need only say that the main business of several of the largest and most profitable corporations is the production of motor vehicles; the petroleum industry, with some ten corporations having assets of more than a billion dollars, makes most of its profits from the sale of gasoline for use in motor vehicles; several other major monopolistic industries (rubber, steel, glass) are crucially dependent on sales to automobile makers or users; more than a quarter of a million persons are employed in the repair and servicing of automobiles; and countless other businesses and jobs (trucking, motels, resorts, etc.) owe their existence, directly or indirectly, to the motor vehicle. This complex of private interests clustering around one product has no equal elsewhere in the economy—or in the world. And the whole complex, of course, is completely dependent on the public provision of roads and highways. It is thus only natural that there should be tremendous pressure for continuous expansion of government spending on highways. Counter-pressures from private interests do exist—notably from the railroads, hard hit by the growth of highway transportation, but the railroads have been no match for the automobile complex. Government spending on highways has soared; limitations posed by state and local finances have been overcome by increasingly liberal federal grants-in-aid. And today highways are second only to education as an object of civilian government spending.[10]

This fact does not in itself prove that spending on highways has gone beyond any rational conception of social need. What does prove it—dramatically and overwhelmingly—is the frightful havoc which has been wreaked on American society by the cancerous growth of the automobile complex, a growth which would have been impossible if government spending for the required highways had been limited and curtailed as the oligarchy has limited and curtailed spending for other civilian purposes. Cities have been transformed into nightmares of congestion; their atmosphere is fouled by disease-bearing pollutants;

[10] In 1957, total government purchases of goods and services for civilian purposes came to $40.4 billion. Of this, $13.6 or 33.7 percent went for education and $7.2 billion or 17.8 percent for highways—the two items together accounting for more than half of civilian government spending.

vast areas of good urban and rural land are turned into concrete strips and asphalt fields; peaceful communities and neighborhoods are desecrated by the roar and stench of cars and trucks hurtling past; railroads, which can move goods and passengers efficiently and unobtrusively, lose traffic and correspondingly raise rates in a vicious circle which threatens the very existence of commuter service for our biggest cities; urban rapid transit systems are at once starved and choked, so that getting around the downtown area of New York, Chicago, and dozens of other metropolises becomes an ordeal to which only the necessitous or the foolhardy will submit. And the usual remedy for this increasingly frightful and frightening state of affairs? More highways, more streets, more garages, more parking areas—more of the same poison that is already threatening the very life of an increasingly urbanized civilization. And all this is made possible by lavish grants of public funds, eagerly sought and approved by an oligarchy of wealth which fights tooth and nail against every extension of those public services which would benefit the great body of their fellow citizens. Nowhere is the madness of American monopoly capitalism more manifest, or more hopelessly incurable.

The New Deal managed to push government spending up by more than 70 percent, but this was nowhere near enough to bring the economy to a level at which human and material resources were fully employed. Resistance of the oligarchy to further expansion in civilian spending hardened and held with unemployment still well above 15 percent of the labor force. By 1939 it was becoming increasingly clear that liberal reform had sadly failed to rescue United States monopoly capitalism from its own self-destructive tendencies. As Roosevelt's second term approached its end, a profound sense of frustration and uneasiness crept over the country.

Then came the war, and with it salvation. Government spending soared and unemployment plummeted. At the end of the war, to be sure, arms spending was cut back sharply; but owing to the backlog of civilian demand built up during the war (compounded of supply shortages and a massive accumulation of liquid savings), the downturn associated with this cutback was relatively mild and brief and soon gave way to an inflationary reconversion boom. And the boom was still going strong when the Cold War began in earnest. Military spending reached its postwar low in 1947, turned up in 1948, received a tremendous boost from the Korean War (1950–1953), declined moderately during the next two years, and then in 1956 began the slow climb which continued, with a slight interruption in 1960, into the 1960's. As a percentage of GNP, the variations of military spending have followed a similar pattern, except that there was very little change from 1955 to 1961.[11]

There is more to say about the performance of the economy in the postwar period. Here we need only note that the difference between the deep stagnation of the 1930's and the relative prosperity of the 1950's is fully accounted for by

[11] Here are the percentages of GNP, 1946–1961:

1946–8.9	1950– 5.0	1954–11.0	1958–10.1
1947–4.9	1951–10.3	1955– 9.8	1959– 9.6
1948–4.5	1952–13.4	1956– 9.9	1960– 9.0
1949–5.2	1953–11.0	1957–10.0	1961– 9.4

Source: *Economic Report of the President,* January 1962, p. 207. The figures are slightly different from those cited earlier from Bator for 1957 and earlier years.

the vast military outlays of the 50's. In 1939, for example, 17.2 percent of the labor force was unemployed and about 1.4 percent of the remainder may be presumed to have been employed producing goods and services for the military. A good 18 percent of the labor force, in other words, was either unemployed or dependent for jobs on military spending. In 1961 (like 1939, a year of recovery from a cyclical recession), the comparable figures were 6.7 percent unemployed and 9.4 percent dependent on military spending, a total of some 16 percent. It would be possible to elaborate and refine these calculations; but there is no reason to think that doing so would affect the general conclusion: the percentage of the labor force either unemployed or dependent on military spending was much the same in 1961 as in 1939. From which it follows that if the military budget were reduced to 1939 proportions, unemployment would also revert to 1939 proportions.[12]

Why has the oligarchy, which keeps such a tight rein on civilian spending, become in the last two decades so openhanded with the military?

[12] Obviously this conclusion does not follow in the prevailing liberal logic of today. One group of liberals, having apparently forgotten all about Keynes and never having understood the relation of monopoly to the functioning of the economy, asserts that if there were less military spending there would be more private investment and consumption. They do not explain why it failed to work out that way during the 30's, when there was in fact less military spending, nor do they explain why unemployment has crept up during the 50's and 60's, when military spending as a proportion of GNP has remained generally stable. Until they can offer a rational explanation of these phenomena—which we believe can be done only along the lines sketched out in this book—their pronouncements on the probable effects of military cutbacks are not entitled to be taken seriously. Another group of liberals, who at least have not altogether forgotten the Great Depression, postulate with equal fluency a substitution of welfare spending for military spending. But they neglect to reveal their magic formula for converting the oligarchy to their way of thinking. We must say of such liberals what Marx said of the bourgeois reformers of his day: "They all want the impossible, namely, the conditions of bourgeois existence without the necessary consequences of those conditions." Karl Marx and Friedrich Engels, *Selected Correspondence,* New York, 1935, p. 15.

30

A NOTE ON THE RELATION OF RADICALISM TO LIBERALISM*

by JEREMY BRECHER

The last several selections have shown the hollowness of liberal approaches to social problems. They have been examples of how the government (even under a liberal President and liberal Congress—as in 1965–66) will venture into the social welfare field only if violent disruption of the status quo is threatened or if a private interest stands to make most of the money involved.

Does our critique of liberalism imply that radicals should attack liberals at every turn and consider them tools of the status quo? Or should radicals make common cause with them on certain issues? These questions have perplexed the left for many years. The history of the Communist Party, for example, is riddled with confusion on this issue. Jeremy Brecher lays out in the following short selection some points that in general reflect the discoveries the New Left has made about the best way to deal with liberal ideas and liberal movements.

The broad political movement in our society known as liberalism, bridging a spectrum from the "radical liberalism" of Arnold Kaufman to the corporate liberalism of Hubert Humphrey, must be understood as part of the great historical tradition of capitalist democracy, stretching back to the English Chartists, the French Jacobins, and the American Jeffersonians. But while this movement died out in Europe after 1848, it experienced repeated rebirths in the United States, in the Civil War, the Progressive Movement, the New Deal, and most recently in the McCarthy movement. It is based on a vague notion of the middle-class "people" developing their political power against a minority of plutocrats, monopolies, imperialists, or whatever. Its strength lies in its ability to appeal to the people as a whole; its weakness in its inability to challenge—or even to understand—the contemporary structure of society, based not on the free competition of individuals and ideas in the market-place, but rather on hierarchical organization and direct social domination. Its persistence in the U.S. is a reflection of the society's failure to assimilate intellectually its total transformation from a nation of small proprietors to a nation of employees, paralleling the similar persistence of anti-government ideologies on the Right.

The strength of the liberal movement has been one of the greatest political

* Used by permission of the author.

strengths of the American system. It has allowed the business forces to retain their power without direct dictatorship and without direct political responsibility even at times of greatest crisis, such as the Great Depression.

The result has been a strategic dilemma which has haunted American radicalism throughout its course. If it attacked liberal movements as mere supports for the capitalist system, it cut itself off from the real mass movements against the status quo; if it supported the liberal movements, it strengthened one of the system's greatest props. The first horn of the dilemma was classically illustrated by the policy of the Communist Party U.S.A. in the 1928–34 period, attacking the New Deal fanatically and labeling efforts at reform "social fascism"; while the second horn is illustrated by the all-out Communist support for the New Deal and Roosevelt after 1935 as part of the United Front policy. Any study of the strategic debates in the Left of the 1960's reveals the same dilemma.

In approaching this problem, we must recognize that there is no simple "correct line" which will make it go away. Rather, what is necessary is a historical process in which, through their experience with its failures, people come to see the weaknesses of liberalism. It is the function of radicals to play midwife to that process.

The essence of liberal movements is that their motivation is an attack on the functioning of the system, but that they do not attack the system which spawns the evils they attack. What must be done then is to liberate the "content" of opposition to the system from the "form" of support for the system it takes within liberal movements.

The first essential for this is that the radical movement retain its separate identity, and avoid merely becoming a more radical wing of the liberal movement. Only thus can the *possibility* of something beyond liberalism be made real to people.

Second, the radical movement must continuously articulate its critique of liberalism, not only in terms of its moral failings (commitment to imperialism, collusion with the C.I.A., etc.) but equally important in terms of its fundamental inability to achieve the real objectives of its adherents.

Third, it must especially show how liberalism fails to achieve its followers' aims precisely when it is in power. In the long run, it is only the visible and repeated failures of liberalism which can shake the popular faith in it. Thus the liberal sponsorship of the Vietnam war and their inability to end it, and their inability to deal with the racial crisis and end black oppression, have been the two great factors in the 1960's which have weakened support for liberalism and strengthed support for radicalism. Only if this process is repeated many times can the hold of liberalism finally be shaken.

Fourth, it is essential that radicals recognize the radical content of truly popular liberal movements. As such movements develop, their orientation toward liberalism is by no means inevitable. Within every popular movement, there should be a radical leadership, proposing an alternative course for the movement as a whole, pointing out how the liberal orientation makes it impossible to achieve the movement's objectives, and drawing out the lessons implicit in each of liberalism's failures.

Fifth, it is essential that radicals be both the voice of reason and of decisive action. We must not be afraid to engage liberalism in reasoned debate; if we are correct we have nothing to fear; in mud-slinging and appeals to unreasoned emotion, on the other hand, radicals will almost always lose out in the end to the forces of red-baiting, superpatriotism, and the like. Since liberals usually have little sense of how to achieve their objectives, the willingness of radicals to lead decisive action based on a reasoned position gives them a great advantage within liberal movements, despite the general hold liberalism has on people's minds.

PART 5

ALTERNATIVES AND STRATEGY

It seems obvious to us that the basic purpose of an economy should be to use all resources at its disposal to meet the most pressing needs of the people and to lay the basis for future development. This means (1) identifying needs and priorities, (2) employing resources toward meeting basic needs and toward creating the capacity to meet those and other needs in the future, and (3) eliminating both the use of resources for low priority, wasteful or destructive ends as well as the failure to employ productive resources at all.

Just look at America today. Ten to twenty million people suffer from hunger. Many more live in abject poverty. Food, clothing, decent housing, schools, clear air and water, space and recreational facilities, fast mass transportation, child care facilities, decent medical care—these are basic needs that go unmet for significant minorities and in some cases majorities of the American people.

Socialist development would meet these basic needs first. This would be true not only on a national but also on an international scale. In other words, a rich socialist country like the United States would be expected to make a great contribution to the development of poorer socialist countries around the world.

Socialism would liberate a large quantity of social resources. To begin with, large amounts of potential labor goes unused in our society. This is true of those who are unemployed, those who can find only part-time jobs and those who have given up looking for work only because they have not been able to find jobs. In addition, it includes large numbers of people (especially women) who are not in the labor force but who would jump at the opportunity to do productive work, especially with the institution of collective child-rearing arrangements and shared housework that would free women from traditional roles in the home. It is likely that the amount of labor our society is capable of could be increased by a factor of one half to three quarters. This does not include the added productivity of labor that could result from greater morale among workers who felt a sense of meaning and purpose in the work. (On the other hand, efficiency might be *decreased* through changed work techniques, slower work pace and shorter hours—so this should not be overemphasized.)

Second, large quantities of labor are wasted in unproductive work. For example, probably greater than $50 billion a year is wasted in the effort of the giant corporations to increase their sales. There is the $25 billion a year spent in advertising alone. It costs very little to spread the word on what there is to buy. Billions more are spent in the actual process of discovering, developing and producing new products which differ from the old only in superficial ways but which are pawned off as "new and improved." The cost of changing styles of automobiles, for example, is tremendous. Billions more are wasted in the production of goods that fall apart before they have to and must be replaced by new products. When one adds to all of this the production of materiel for the military and of luxuries for the rich (yachts, mansions, travel expenses, private planes), it is possible that from a third to a half of all the work in America might be considered unproductive.

In other words, a rationally conceived socialist economy might be capable of producing *more than twice* what our economy is capable of producing today—by utilizing *all* the labor of the society for *productive* work.

ALIENATION

Socialism holds out the vision of people identifying the problems that face them and their society and seeking to solve them by creating a new society. The revolutionary process involves from the beginning the mobilization of peoples' energies toward understanding their own oppression and needs and acting on them. Making the revolution itself, rather than being an alienating act, is something that is done out of a sense of acute desire—the desire to see the end of an inhumane system and the creation of a decent one.

Life in a revolutionary society is much more intense and demanding than life for most people in American society today. Constant demands are being made on people to participate in the effort to formulate the shape of the new society and to help build it. Work in such a context is no longer something external to one's life, a way of getting money so you can live. It is an activity that encompasses one's contribution to the collective effort to build new institutions, new values, new social relationships. The lines of division between work and leisure begin to break down as one begins to get satisfaction from one's work and seeks to make leisure more than simple escape. Similarly, education in a revolutionary society means learning skills that are needed to build a new society and learning to think in a critical manner. Both skills and a critical approach are necessary to establish decent social relationships and to evolve people who perceive the needs and priorities of their society in a creative manner.

In other words, life in a revolutionary society is given a social meaning, a purpose. People are encouraged to work out for themselves a way of making a contribution to a collective effort, to forge an identity for themselves. Those who have witnessed the lives of the people in revolutionary societies like Cuba and China know the fantastic commitment, energy and sense of purpose that has been unleashed by the revolutionary process. Revolution has transformed the lives of even the most destitute and degraded. According to Oscar Lewis, for example, who visited Cuba after the Revolution there, the "culture of poverty" that he had found in the slums of Havana before the Revolution had disappeared. It had given way to revolutionary enthusiasm and a sense of having a place on the face of the earth.

VALUES

The revolutionary process and the construction of a socialist society also transforms values related both to the life and personality of the individual and to his social relationships. The main values of capitalist society revolve around materialist pursuits—that is, making money and acquiring possessions. This means, in the first place, that life consists of an individual effort to advance oneself—if necessary, at the expense of others, and also at the expense of one's own sanity. One's value to society, and therefore to oneself, is measured by one's success in the materialist endeavor.

Socialism holds out a whole new set of values, based on cooperation. Whereas capitalism sees the duty of each person as the striving for greater and greater personal benefit, socialism ties personal benefit to the benefit of the community. Whereas capitalism pits people against one another in competing for scarce benefits, socialism involves people in a collective effort to build a society that can aid everyone.

This transformation of values comes in the first instance from the common bonds that are forged through revolutionary struggle and through the conscious assertion of values of solidarity. Further, socialism sets up a whole set of institutions that help to develop and deepen these new values. For example, a simple institution like a child care center can work to put children into more prolonged close contact with other children and to give parents experience in taking care of children other than their own together with other parents. In the school, in the work place, in the community, collective projects are formulated, planned and carried out. For example, frequent meetings would be organized in the community and in the work place to identify things that have to be done and to work out ways of doing them. The state would provide the resources to permit this kind of independent initiative. In addition, all sorts of collective entertainment would be instituted—group dancing, free camps, collective eating arrangements, etc.

The consequences of all of this for social relationships, for the individual personality and for the overall development of society are immense. The sense of social purpose in such a society and an educational system that helps people find ways of making a unique contribution to that purpose will develop individuals with a sense of identity and direction. The importance of this can be seen when we compare it to the lack of self-confidence and aimlessness that characterizes the lives of most people in American society today. The failure to achieve a positive identity has many serious consequences. People are unable to relate to other people in an honest manner from fear of exposing themselves; they are prey to manipulation at the hands of a culture that attempts to mold people into set roles through appeals to "masculinity," "femininity" or "success"; they have difficulty in moving beyond themselves to relate to the problems of other people; they look for chauvinist self-definition in terms of the superiority of one's race, sex or nation.

The dedication and commitment achieved by revolutionary youth in a socialist society together with the cooperative modes of living and working that have been encouraged throughout one's life lead to totally new kinds of social relationships. Honesty becomes possible once again—there is much less reason to play games. Real sympathy for other people is possible. The necessity to prove one's masculinity, or to look and act feminine, or to protect one's ego by being right all of the time—all this diminishes without anxiety-producing conditioning, competition and materialism.

The development of cooperative values and self-confident individuals is absolutely essential to the development of a truly humane socialist society. The quality of the people in a socialist society is crucial in determining the extent of its success. The ability to work hard, to act responsibly, to take criticism, to transmit information honestly, to exercise good leadership—all of these depend on the depth and maturity of the revolutionary commitment of the people. In other words, the transformation of socialist society also makes possible the transformation of human relationships and values, which in turn guarantees the success of the revolution.

In addition to the transformation of the values of the society and the development of a sense of social purpose, particular institutions can be constructed in such a way as to provide for a satisfying life and to contribute to the overall growth of the society. We will concentrate on the work place and the school.

Work can be and should be a sphere of activity where men feel they are making an important contribution to a collective undertaking. It should also be something that gives people a sense of satisfaction in doing and in accomplishment. Socialist society will give high priority to adapting the work place to these goals.

Here are some of the adaptations possible in work under socialism. There is the nature of the work process itself. No matter how important it is to turn out trucks on an assembly line, or to cut sugar cane, it is backbreaking and difficult work. Certain simple things can be done to reduce the burden on those who now must perform the most difficult and obnoxious tasks in the society. For example, large investments can be made to develop machinery to take the place of manual labor. This will never be done in capitalist society, as long as the product can be produced more cheaply with the use of labor. But since the humanity of the worker is valued in a socialist society, this is an important investment to make. Unlike capitalist society, where automation spells unemployment, a socialist society will take care to provide other work for someone whose place is taken by machinery.

Short of eliminating jobs entirely, the community can reduce hours substantially and make unpleasant jobs a collective burden. There is no reason why particular groups of people should always be saddled with the worst jobs. This could be part of a general scheme of rotating jobs—for the purpose of lowering the level of boredom as well as spreading the workload.

Conditions on the job can be improved by putting in safety machinery, slowing down the work pace, putting in good lighting, etc. One of the things about many jobs in factories today is that workers are being worked harder and harder so that they will turn out more in the same period of time, or the same amount with fewer people. At the same time, safety conditions are atrocious, both from the speed of the work and the reluctance of the company to spend money to maintain good safety conditions. (There are over two million disabling industrial accidents each year.) The only reason any of this happens today is because the capitalist is interested in his workers only for what they can produce, and he wants them to produce as much as possible as fast as possible.

Socialist society can spend a great deal of creative effort working out new techniques of work that increase the opportunity to exercise skills, that diminish the routine character of the job. In some cases, this may involve a certain reduction of efficiency.

Workers themselves can make all the decisions over the conditions, organization and uses of their labor. Such control by workers is important to establish the sense that the factory is one's own, to developing the spirit of collective effort and to making work satisfying. Workers will have the power to institute changes in the work place that will improve the quality of the product and the conditions of work.

Under capitalism, the worker works *for* a boss; he does not work to accomplish a job that he knows needs to get done. Whereas he does the hard labor, and the boss may do nothing at all, it is the boss who pockets a substantial amount of the product of his labor—in the form of exorbitant salaries, expense accounts, bonuses and dividends. Under socialism those in leadership would come from the workers, would be subject to the authority of the workers, would periodically work next to the workers and would live like the workers.

Further, as the productivity of labor increases and the ability of the economy as a whole to produce skyrockets, such a society can choose whether to take increases in productivity in the form of production or in the form of leisure. The requirement that everyone work full time could gradually be reduced to the point where work was optional. At the same time, new definitions of work and leisure would make it likely that most people would engage in what could be considered socially productive activity. In fact, it would be the responsibility of the society to expand the range of such activity. But the point is that the society would be free to make decisions about whether to produce more or to work less—a decision which capitalism is incapable of making.

None of these ideas, *in themselves,* nor any others that one could think of, could make work a satisfying experience in a socialist society. But these possibilities give an idea of the extent to which the rotten experience of work under American capitalism is not inherent in industrial society itself—it depends on who the work is for and how it is carried out. Machines and technology are not inevitably alienating. A serious attack on the problem of work, mobilizing the energies of the workers themselves, could accomplish a great deal in making work an activity that can satisfy human needs. The possibility of decent and creative work opens up the possibility of a satisfying life.

EDUCATION

Che Guevara wrote in his "Man and Socialism in Cuba": "Society must become a huge school." Education is a process that is not limited to the schools; people learn and shape their ideas and values from many different experiences in society. Work can teach people the possibility of using one's skills and creativity to contribute to the growth of the society. Child care centers can teach children the possibility of cooperating with other children. Movies, wall posters, newspapers and speeches can give people an awareness of what is happening in the country and in the world and how one's particular situation fits into an overall picture.

Schools under capitalism are subordinated to the need of the system for a disciplined work force. Most of education in America is extremely authoritarian, its form as well as its content communicating to its students the necessity of doing what one is told, what one is supposed to do.

Schools under socialism would be aimed at giving students an understanding of themselves and their potential, of their society and their history. Schools would attempt to teach the ability to look at society critically and get involved in the process of making the changes they saw had to be made. The desire to learn skills would come out of a recognition that those skills were necessary to make a contribution to the development of the society. The schools would try to teach by their form as well as their content the possibilities of human cooperation. They would recapture for each generation the years of revolutionary experience that produced the new society. They would identify difficulties honestly with the intent of developing the understanding and commitment among the younger generation capable of dealing with those difficulties. The schools in socialist society would support socialism, but not in the way schools in capitalist society support capitalism. Truth can never hurt when the society has nothing to hide.

Outside of schools, formal and informal educational processes would take place constantly. Open-air movies and speeches; classes and discussions each day at work; community meetings; these and many other forms would be developed to encourage the participation and understanding of the people in the development of the society.

OBJECTIONS TO SOCIALISM

Many people have specific and general criticisms of socialism as a system—reasons why *socialism* could never meet the standards laid out in the last few pages. What reason is there to expect that the masses of people would come to agreement on the policies needed to create a decent society? What guarantee is there that the leaders of the revolution will not simply exercise power in the revolutionary society for their own purposes? What reason is there to expect that the selfishness that has characterized mankind since time immemorial will not pop up its ugly head to screw up any and all idealistic plans that one might conceive? Who could be so naive as to think that a classless society—in which everyone essentially gets the same pay and rewards—can work? There's no reason to go to school, or to work hard, in such a society, and any economic plan that depends on people going to school and working hard will fail. More generally, isn't it true that socialism invariably means the institution of totalitarian controls and the destruction of individuality?

Let's now take up some of the arguments raised by critics of socialism: What reason is there to expect that the people would be able to come to some kind of agreement as to the shape of the new society they were trying to build?

In the first place, socialism will be created through a revolutionary process. In this process, people will be grappling to achieve an understanding of their own oppression and to formulate institutions and goals that can deal with that oppression.

Furthermore, the revolutionary process will see the development of new values on which the development of socialism after the revolution will depend.

In other words, socialism does not simply mean giving power to the people at their present level of understanding and organization, expecting people to immediately know how to proceed and where to go. Rather, it means the implementation of a program that is fairly well understood in the course of the revolutionary process—in fact, it will be the power of this program to mobilize the energy of the people that will make such a revolution possible in the first place.

To see this at a more concrete level, let's consider what socialist development might look like in one community. The community would be responsible for carrying out certain commitments as part of a national economic plan. At the same time, however, it would have a great deal of autonomy over how its resources would be used. Before the revolution, the largest businesses of the community used community resources to pay the top managers and directors high salaries, bonuses and expense accounts; to pay profits to the stockholders; to spend large amounts of money on advertising; and to invent and develop wasteful new products and styles.

After the revolution the people of the community would probably not have complete agreement about how the resources of the community should be used. But they would have concluded without much difficulty that those executive salaries, those dividends, those wasteful expenditures on advertising, those taxes for missiles and those puny wages would have to go. They would know that there were certain things that had to be done—develop new or better productive capacity, build schools and hospitals, reduce the work week, develop machinery to get rid of some of the most obnoxious jobs and improve working conditions.

Cynics will say that all of this is nice in theory, but that man is naturally selfish. What they forget is that the selfishness, anonymity and coldness that we see in today's society is in many ways a rational response to a society in which "the good guy always finishes last." The whole thrust of capitalist society is to encourage people to think mainly about themselves—from the media and educational process that systematically deprive them of any kind of deep understanding of the problems that other people are confronting, to the educational system that asks people to compete with one another for scarce grades and degrees to qualify for scarce jobs. The preoccupation with the accumulation of material possessions is, furthermore, not so unreasonable when the possibility of realizing other kinds of values (like satisfying work or making a contribution to society) are so difficult to achieve.

At the same time, despite the whole thrust of our society, we can see the seeds of a new man within the old. Most people recognize that they would not cheat their buddy. Many people have worked on projects, played on teams or planned events with other people in which they experienced a real common bond. *Despite* the limited opportunities for decent work open to people in this society, more and more youths have made a serious effort to find jobs that could make a contribution to the society. Rightly or wrongly, this was the source of the popularity of the Peace Corps. Further, many have simply dropped out—rejecting the materialist road without having worked out any alternative.

Further, this country has a history of political struggle which together with the resurgence of activism in the last decade reasserts the possibility of collective action. The heroism of the labor struggles of the 1930's, despite their limitations, cannot help reminding people of the possibility for collective action and cooperative values in this society.

But won't socialism merely mean the takeover by one group of leaders from another? Power always corrupts, it is often argued; one can expect these leaders or any leaders to exercise power in their own name rather than in the interests of the people. Furthermore, the historical experience has always shown that Communist takeovers have ended up suppressing the people beneath the heavy hand of the party bureaucracy.

Perhaps the basic fear of revolution comes from a mistrust of revolutionaries, and a sense that they are ignoring the practical problems with their vision, making promises that they cannot keep and using peoples' grievances for their own ends.

These fears come from many things. They in part come out of the cynicism that pervades American society. People in America have had so many disappointments, so many experiences of being sold down the river, that it is hard to believe that it will ever be different.

They also come out of an incessant propaganda against communism that predates World War II. Anti-Communist propaganda has pictured Communist revolutionaries as conspirators, manipulating events behind the scenes. Every social movement that America has seen, from the labor movement through the civil rights movement through the antiwar movement, has been attributed to a "small minority of troublemakers and instigators." Communist revolution as in Vietnam is pictured, in the first place, as a "takeover," and in the second place, as an outside force.

But revolutions are not made by small numbers of troublemakers and instigators. There are always some who make the first sparks, but it is the masses of people who make a revolution. There is no other way to defeat the awesome power of the state. During every revolution, thousands of people become members of the leading revolutionary organization; after the revolution, thousands more again join to help construct the new society. There is nothing mysterious about it.

What has been the actual experience of revolutions? Is it true that they have often resulted in disappointments?

How about the history of *socialist* revolutions? The experience has been varied (not the same everywhere as one might think), but it is possible to make some general statements. Since Japan began to industrialize at the end of the nineteenth century, there has been *no* underdeveloped country which has been able to succeed in conquering backwardness under *capitalist* auspices. The only poor countries that have been able to develop have been socialist countries. Fewer people die in the socialist countries of hunger than in the United States. Health benefits, education, improvements in housing, food, clothing—socialism has been able to provide for the basic needs of its people and to do so on a relatively egalitarian basis in a manner that even advanced capitalism has never been able to accomplish.

This is of course most true of the Soviet Union, a country that in fifty years has become the world's second industrial power, despite the destruction of much of Russian industry and thirty million people at the hands of the Germans in World War II. The Soviet Union proved once and for all that socialism as an *economic* system was capable of living up to its promise of rational utilization of social resources for the good of the society.

At the same time, the promise of socialism goes further than this—to the elimination of classes and creation of an egalitarian society, to the creation of a society in which the leaders are responsive to the people and can be said to represent the people, to the guarantee of fulfilling lives. It is here that the Soviet Union has not lived up to its promise. A group of leaders developed in the Soviet Union that stood above the people, using their position in part for power and privilege, exercising their rule in an authoritarian manner, increasingly separating themselves from the concerns and lives of the people and neglecting their responsibilities to the revolutionary peoples of the poor countries of the world.

But we must remember that while Russia was a backward country in a sea of hostile and powerful enemies, the United States is a relatively rich country in a relatively secure world position. And further, the practice of socialism has gone well beyond that of the Soviet Union *already*—in some of the newer socialist countries of the third world.

Countries like Cuba and China, which had revolutions well after that of the Soviet Union, have had opportunities to learn from the Russian experience. They have worked out means of dealing with some of the mistakes and failures of the Russian experience which they have been able to place in the context of a total critique of the Russian model of development.

To begin with, it is instructive to compare the Russian and Chinese experience with regard to the peasantry. In both countries the majority of the country was composed of peasants, though this was somewhat more true of China than of Russia. But Russia based its revolution on the proletariat, while China based it on the peasantry. The Bolsheviks in Russia never believed it was possible to organize the peasantry in depth in a way that could support a socialist revolution—they felt the commitment of the peasant to private ownership of small plots of land was too great. When the Russian proletariat was decimated in the Russian Civil War, the Bolsheviks had lost their entire conscious socialist base. Collectivization of agriculture—absolutely essential for the industrialization of the Soviet Union—was carried out from the top and was perceived in a hostile manner by the peasantry, even those who were helped by the measures in certain ways. The results showed up for years in the low productivity of Russian agriculture, and even in recent years, as Russian agriculture has thrived, the enthusiasm for the Russian regime is not great.

The Chinese, led by Mao Tse-tung, based their revolution on the peasantry. The Communist party was largely recruited from the peasantry, and party organizations were set up in every village composed of members of the village. The party mobilized the peasantry and laid the basis for a slow socialist transformation of the countryside. Though the movement toward communes has traveled in fits and starts, they are pretty well established throughout the country. Serious attempts have been made to move slowly and flexibly, retreats were made when the peasants resisted certain measures, and gradually the peasantry has been recruited to accept the Communist agricultural policies as desirable and necessary.

These differences have of course had a tremendous impact on the nature of the Chinese regime, which has been very close to the people, and the Russian regime, which has been much more remote.

In general, both Cuba and China have developed means of maintaining close contact between the leadership of the Revolution and the masses of people and have struggled successfully thus far against the formation of an elite. This has been done through requiring leaders to share a common experience with the people and through involving the people in the selection and criticism of the leaders.

In both countries, leaders (party cadre, managers, technicians, scientists, teachers) are remunerated in the same basic range as the people as a whole. In addition to this renunciation of privilege for those in authority, the managers of Chinese factories customarily work one or two days in the factory itself alongside the regular workers.

Party cadre are selected especially for their willingness to do hard work and to serve the Revolution. The Soviet Union recruited party people through an educational system that rewarded people mainly for performing well on exams, and then conferred certain privileges on these people. The effect was to encourage those who were in for prestige or privilege to join the party or to take on other positions of authority. In addition, the emphasis on pure academic qualifications in the selection of leaders biased the system toward those who had come from old middle-class or even upper-class backgrounds (they had more verbal skills) or those whose parents were in a position to prepare them for school. The result was that a class system started in which people from the lower classes were systematically excluded from higher education and resulting positions of authority.

Cuba and China both renounce material rewards as a means of attracting leaders, knowing that this only encourages the opportunists. They both make an effort to overcome the natural bias in the educational system toward the children of the higher classes. They both use political commitment and the willingness to work for the Revolution as criteria for selection. And they both make exacting demands on the party cadre. In Cuba, for example, it is the party people who work the hardest, who do the most volunteer work, who provide the example to the other people. In fact, the way party membership is chosen in Cuba is that the workers at a given work place will nominate for party membership fellow workers whom they think could do a good job. One of the main criteria they use is how much effort a particular worker puts into his job.

Further, both societies are moving toward setting up various institutions of popular control over the leaders. Cuba has set up various local institutions which are run through mass organizations that are run completely democratically. In addition, both countries give the workers in factories certain control over the selection of managers and the operation of their factories. Probably most important, the people are being told that they have the right to criticize the party and public officials.

Skeptics often say very simply that a classless society is not practicable, that there is no way to get people to work without providing monetary incentives. This position comes from a very correct perception about American society itself. Namely, people in our own society work and study mainly for the money. We know that if people could get ahead and make money in other ways, they wouldn't be breaking their backs in schools and jobs.

What this position does not recognize is that people are not responsive only to material incentives. It is not human nature to want to work only for the money. It is only a rational response in a society in which work has no real purpose and in which people are told that their main enterprise in life should be to succeed. But even in our own society people have had experiences of meaningful work. The Peace Corps, teaching, social work and other professions attract people who think that they will be able to make a real contribution to society. Many people may hate their jobs, but they may return home to work hard on a project or hobby. People are willing enough to work hard without reward, but the work that they do must be satisfying and important.

In a socialist society, born of a revolutionary transformation in which millions of people have worked together for common goals, there is an overriding sense of purpose and a common recognition of what has to be done. People recognize that it is their duty to their society to make some kind of contribution. Further, this is not a selfless contribution, since they know that others will be making their own contributions.

A classless society, in other words, is practical if the society gives its members reasons to make their contributions without the prodding of foremen and bosses or the attraction of extra money. The new values of the society encourage collective effort to build up the new society, and they also recognize a new definition of accomplishment and success that does away with old notions of a big house and lots of money and reestablishes standards more capable of making possible satisfying lives. It is the promise of such a society which gives socialism its hope and its power.

31 SOCIALISM AND COMMUNISM AS IDEALS*

by PAUL SWEEZY

We have offered as a major theme of this anthology the idea that capitalism as a social system cannot solve the major social problems facing it and thus create a Good Society. It will be burdened irreparably with problems like wastage on an immense scale, unemployment, imperialism, oppression of women and blacks, bad education, work alienation and inequality. The implication is, of course, that we can imagine a social system that can solve these problems. That system would be socialism.

Why would it be that socialism could solve these problems where capitalism couldn't? The answer is very complicated; we could compose another anthology on the subject; but here are elements of an answer.

Naturally, socialism would eliminate some of the dynamics fundamental to capitalism that produce these problems. For example, it would eliminate the structural antagonism between the worker and his employer based around the pursuit of maximum production for minimum cost.

Second, socialism would wipe out the vested interests that presently stand as obstacles to the implementation of solutions to social problems. Thus socialism by nationalizing industry would undermine the basis for the present opposition by private builders to the construction of housing and other public works by the government.

But on the positive side of the ledger, socialism would make available to society the resources and mechanisms needed to put solutions into practice. Thus planning and the rational allocation of investment could all but obliterate unemployment. More important on the employment scene, the fruits of automation would be liberated from the chains of profit and monopoly competition considerations, to be used to humanize work and to develop products and facilities that ministered to individual and social needs.

Finally, decision-making power in all areas would be democratized, made ultimately responsible to the will of the people. Ferocious debates can be generated over how much of this decision-making power should be decentralized into the hands of small groups—workers, neighbors and consumers—and how much centralized to insure efficiency or maintain equality. But what is clear is that once such authority is removed from the hands of socially irresponsible groups like corporations, decisions are sure to bear much greater correspondence to the real needs of the people. Production for the sake of collectively determined purposes—and high among these the solution of our remaining social problems—will have come into being.

Sweezy, in the article immediately following, lays out the basic elements of such a theory of socialism.

The conception of a communist society in which all property is owned in common is, of course, an old one, dating back at least as far as Thomas More's *Utopia,* written early in the 16th century.[1] But what the world understands by communism today is almost entirely a product of Marxian thought and practice. For this reason, attention will be confined here to what may be called Marxian communism. To begin with, a terminological clarification seems called for.

The word socialism was first used around the beginning of the 19th century in France, and first in its present-day sense by the socialist sects in France and England during the 1820's and 1830's. The Owenites, for example, meant by socialism a society in which collective ownership of the means of production is substituted for private ownership, and that is what most people regard as the *differentia specifica* of socialism today. But during the later 1830's and the early 1840's, writers calling themselves socialists of one sort or another came forth with a great variety of schemes, all intended to improve or perfect the human condition but differing so widely about the means to be employed that anyone seeking to define socialism in that period would have been hard put to find any common core of meaning to the numerous "socialisms" of the day. It was at just this time that Marx and Engels came on the scene. Feeling a need to differentiate themselves from the various existing schools of socialism, they adopted the label communist. The famous document issued on the eve of the revolutions of 1848 was thus the Communist Manifesto, not the Socialist Manifesto.

Subsequently, however, as Marxism rose to dominance among the radical tendencies of the day, the word socialism returned to favor and came to be more and more identified with the Marxian conception of the society of the future. So it came to pass that by the time national parties came into being in the 1870's and 1880's, most of them called themselves socialist or social democratic and proclaimed their goal to be socialism—a state of society in which private property in the means of production has been replaced by public ownership, and the guidance of production by prices and profits has been replaced by planning. Marx and his followers, however, did not hold the view that history would stop with the establishment of socialism. Socialist society would undergo development and evolution and would eventually be transformed into a higher form of society which was now given the old name of communism.

Thus before the end of the 19th century, the two words had acquired fairly

This is the text of a lecture delivered at the School of Advanced International Studies of Johns Hopkins University. The school is located in Washington and trains future U.S. diplomats and others preparing for a career in international affairs.

[1] Most historians of the subject would trace the origins of communist doctrine to the world of classical antiquity, citing Plato and the Essenes as outstanding protagonists. Plato's "communism," however, rested on a basis of slavery; and the Essenes were a religious sect preaching withdrawal from the world rather than its reform. Doctrines and movements like these, while recurring from time to time prior to the 16th century, can hardly be considered true forerunners of modern socialism and communism.

generally accepted meanings: socialism was the first or lower stage of the collectivist society which would take the place of capitalism; communism was the second or higher stage. From the Marxian point of view, therefore, communism must be thought of as growing out of socialism just as socialism grows out of capitalism; and to understand the sense in which communism is the goal of the whole movement, one must view it not as an abstract utopia but as the end product of an historical process which has to be treated as a continuous whole. What this end product will be like and why it is regarded as an ideal worth striving for are therefore questions that can best be answered in a step-by-step fashion. First, let us inquire in what respects socialism represents an advance over capitalism, and then proceed to a consideration of the further transformations which socialism is expected to undergo on the road to full communism.

As already noted, the *differentia specifica* of socialism as compared to capitalism is public ownership of the means of production. This does not mean *all* the means of production: what it does mean is that those branches of the economy which are *decisive* for its functioning must be in what is nowadays often called the "public sector." There is no general rule for determining exactly what must be included, the branches which are to be considered decisive varying in different economies at different stages of development. To take an example, one might hazard the guess that in the United States today the socialization of all corporations with assets of a million dollars or more would amply suffice to bring the economic levers of command into the hands of public authority. It is worth noting that this would leave several million private enterprises and wide opportunity for anyone to set up a business of his own. The only requirement would be that it must remain a small business; if it grew beyond a certain point it would automatically "graduate" into the public sector. And of course all the big corporations, which dominate U.S. economic life and which are already collectives in all but name (though still run by and for private individuals and groups), would have to be transferred to the public sector from the outset.

Socialists believe that this transfer of the levers of command from private to public authority will make it possible to eliminate the major economic evils of capitalist society. Evidently, the guiding principle of the managers of firms and industries can no longer be to maximize the profits of the enterprises for which they are responsible. The public sector—and, since it is assumed to be dominant, this means the whole economy as well—must be governed by an economic plan, and each enterprise must be given a specific role in the plan. The goal of managements must then be to fulfill, and if possible overfulfill, the targets set for them in the plan. Success (or failure) with all its consequences is judged accordingly, just as under the present system success (or failure) is judged by the yardstick of profits (or losses).

Nota bene that while this arrangement does away with production for profit (in the public sector), it does *not* by any means eliminate what is often called the profit *motive,* which economic theory since long before the time of Adam Smith has rightly regarded as the mainspring of economic activity. When we speak of the profit motive, we mean simply that those who engage in economic activity are moved primarily by the desire to reap as large a material reward as possible, and this of course applies not only to the owners or managers of capital but also to workers and farmers and lawyers and professional baseball players. Each has his job to do, and each expects that the better he does it the more he will be paid. It is this expectation that motivates him to work efficiently and hard. There is nothing in the nature of socialism that conflicts in any way with the continued operation of the profit motive in this sense. What changes is only the definition of the jobs of the managers, not the motives which lead them to strive for optimum performance. In General Motors, the president is selected and paid well if he contributes to the profitability of the company; under socialism, the head of the automobile industry will be selected and paid well if he contributes to the fulfillment of the industry's part of the plan. As we shall see, in the Marxian view it is the retention of this material-gain incentive system that more than anything else marks socialism as the first or lower stage of collectivism and differentiates it from communism, the higher stage.

What, then, are the weaknesses and evils of capitalism which it is expected will be removed or cured under socialism? A full list would be long, much too long to be included in the brief space available here. But we can note those which socialists regard as of the greatest importance.

1. *Exploitation of man by man.* Socialists believe that the wealth and income of society are produced by the collective labor of society, and that the existence of a class of owners which reaps far more than a proportionate share by virtue of its ownership and without the necessity to work is *ipso facto* proof of exploitation of workers by owners. The results of this are very far-reaching, going way beyond the extreme inequality of incomes to which it gives rise. All of history shows that exploitation inevitably divides society into hostile classes and degrades not only the exploited but also the exploiters. In such a society, human brotherhood and solidarity are mere empty slogans impossible of realization. Seeing each other as means rather than ends, human beings become alienated, hostile, and embittered. Socialists consider that overcoming this tragic human condition, which has persisted in various forms for so many millennia, is the first and greatest achievement of socialism.

The abolition of exploitation does not imply the end of all income inequality. The material-gain incentive system, which still characterizes socialism, presupposes and requires differentiated incomes for different kinds and intensity of work. But the extreme and demoralizing forms of income inequality which are such prominent features of capitalism will definitely be done away with. These owe their existence on the one hand to private ownership of the means of production and on the other hand to the destitution which comes from chronic unemployment. As we have already noted, abolition of private ownership of the means of production is of the very essence of socialism, and it will be argued presently that in a comprehensively planned economy there can never be any reason for unemployment as a massive and persistent phenomenon. It follows that a much greater degree of material equality will exist under socialism than under capitalism.

2. *Economic instability and unemployment.* Even when it is performing at its best, capitalism is subject to booms and busts which take a frightful human toll in terms of insecurity and enforced idleness. At other times, as during the 1930's and to an increasing extent in the last few years, a condition of chronic stagnation and continuing mass unemployment is superimposed upon the normal ups and downs of the system. All of this is due to the anarchy of the capitalist market in which millions of individual units make decisions without

knowledge or thought of the effect on the whole, to the concentration of wealth in the hands of a few while the great majority are poor, to the planlessness of saving and investment when all decisions are made with a view to private gain rather than public welfare. These are, of course, precisely the conditions and aspects of capitalism which not only can but must disappear with the adoption of a system based on public ownership and planning. Full employment of human and material resources can be planned for and maintained at all times, and the savings-and-investment process can be so geared as to yield a high or low rate of growth according to society's needs. In the world of today, in which most countries are underdeveloped and most peoples hungry, it is usually taken for granted that something close to the maximum attainable rate of growth is an obvious desideratum. To the extent that this is so, socialism can provide it. What is required is simply a pricing policy which will yield large "profits" to the publicly owned enterprises, and an investment plan which will channel these funds back into expanding society's powers of production. But it should not be overlooked that the planning mechanism is equally adapted to the implementation of entirely different economic policies. Suppose, for example, that a socialist society has built up its productive apparatus to a point where all reasonable needs can be satisfied and it is desired to shift production away from further investment and into rapidly increasing consumption. There are two chief methods which the planners can follow: first, they can lower prices, which will have the effect of reducing "profits" and raising the real incomes of consumers; and second, they can spend a smaller proportion of public revenues on investment and a larger proportion to satisfy society's collective consumption needs (education, recreation, conservation, etc.). Nor is there any reason why automation and other methods for increasing the productivity of human labor should carry with them a threat of unemployment. If, for example, productivity were rising at a rate of x percent a year and further increases of per capita income were not desired, it would only be necessary to reduce hours of work by x percent. The problem for a socialist society in this situation would be to educate its citizens to put their increasing free time to socially and morally worthy purposes. Some socialist thinkers—for example, the eminent British scientist J. D. Bernal—envisage a time when education will be a lifelong process, with more and more of society's human energies being withdrawn from productive pursuits and devoted to teaching on the one hand and studying and learning on the other. But these are more likely to be problems of the higher (communist) stage than of the lower (socialist) stage.

3. *Neglect of public needs.* It has always been true that capitalism has neglected the needs of society which can only be satisfied collectively, but this situation becomes particularly obvious and painful in a society like that of the United States today where education is neglected, resources are wantonly wasted, cities are allowed to turn into slums, and the people's health is left to the whims of private enterprise—while at the very same time a flood of trivial or even harmful goods and services is thrown upon the market, industries operate at 70 to 80 percent of capacity, and unemployment (by the admittedly inadequate official count) averages 6 or more percent of the civilian labor force. This is the ironically named "Affluent Society" in which the private wealth of the privileged stands starkly opposed to the indigence of the many and the neglect of all. Under socialism, by contrast, the pressures to concen-

trate on private trivia and to neglect public essentials are removed: at long last society can satisfy its collective needs directly from the publicly owned and appropriated surplus of its collective labor.

4. *Finally, the debasement of values and tastes.* As a capitalist society develops and enters the stage of "affluence," it becomes increasingly difficult to dispose of a growing surplus which is appropriated and owned by a relatively few individuals and groups caring only for their own narrow private and class interests. As a result, more and more resources are poured into a burgeoning sales effort. This sales effort, in turn, becomes the dominant factor in shaping the popular culture. The senses and sensitivities of human beings, their intellect and passions, are twisted and manipulated to the service of profitable sales—sales of ever-changing automobile models, of soap powders, of dog foods, of patent medicines and hair creams, of a thousand and one things that people may or may not need but which in any case should serve them as human beings, not dominate their lives and shape their minds. Under socialism, mercifully, this sales effort, multiplying and spreading like an uncontrolled cancer, dies a natural death. There can *never* be a problem of shortage of demand under socialism. Planners can *always* cut prices to clear a market if too much has been produced, and they can *always* divert resources to other uses or withdraw them from production altogether if a smaller volume of production in the future is indicated. And under socialism, leadership in educating and shaping popular values and tastes—in literature, in the arts, in science, in entertainment—can be assigned to those to whom it naturally belongs—the writers, the artists, the scientists, the entertainers, in a word to the people who are equipped by training and experience and interest to exercise leadership for the good of the whole society and not for the sake of selling this or that gadget or nostrum.

Is it a mere unsupported conjecture that socialism can eliminate these grave weaknesses and evils of capitalism, or is the theory set forth above supported by relevant historical evidence? Evidently, this is much too large a subject to be explored within the confines of a brief lecture. I will, however, indicate my own view which is, I think, that of the great majority of socialists all over the world. We believe that on each of the issues selected for particular mention, the actual experience of the USSR and the other socialist countries of Eastern Europe and Asia lends strong confirmation to the theory. In the socialist third of the world, exploiting classes of capitalists and landlords no longer exist, and the extremes of inequality have been eliminated. There have been no cyclical depressions, no stagnation of production, no mass unemployment. Collective consumption—especially in the fields of education and health—has been enormously increased relative to private consumption. And public morals and standards have been steadily if slowly raised, not lowered and debased by mass media of communication geared to the needs of the cash register. There is of course no implication that everything is perfect in the socialist countries, or that weaknesses and evils of other kinds do not exist. Quite to the contrary. Nothing is ever perfect in human affairs, and one has only to read critically what the socialist countries have to say about themselves to understand that weaknesses and evils still abound. What is maintained is that the specific weaknesses and evils which have been discussed above, and which have been associated with capitalism wherever it has appeared, have either disappeared from the socialist world or are clearly of declining importance.

In these respects, much has been achieved in a relatively short time and starting from a very low base. It would be legitimate to conclude from this experience, I think, that socialism in an already developed country like the United States could achieve much more in an even shorter time.

Let us now turn to the question of the advance from socialism to communism, remembering that communism presupposes socialism and is unthinkable except as a further development of forces and tendencies which are released and set into full motion under socialism.

The basic condition for the advance to communism is a tremendous increase in the productivity of human labor. Scarcity as it has existed in the world up to now—and as it has been taken for granted by the science of economics—must be perhaps not altogether abolished but at any rate greatly reduced. And of course this can be accomplished only as a result of a considerable period of rapid technological advance, improvement of living standards, rebuilding of physical environments, etc. These are, from an historical point of view, the specific tasks of the socialist stage. The transition to the communist stage will be gradual and may occupy a period measured in decades rather than years. It will be marked by fundamental changes, of which we may single out for mention the following:

(1) The attitude toward labor will change. This is not only desirable; it is also absolutely necessary for the functioning of an economy which has largely solved the problem of scarcity. If everyone enjoys an income high enough to satisfy all his reasonable needs—perhaps mostly distributed in the form of free goods and services[2]—very few will be motivated to work simply for the sake of earning money. They must work because they want to or because they feel it to be their social duty. In the communist stage, as Marx put it, "labor has become not merely a means to live but has become itself the primary necessity of life." [3] But this implies very far-reaching changes in the character of the labor performed by most workers. Many categories of jobs must be eliminated altogether (e.g. coal mining and domestic service), and insofar as possible all jobs must become interesting and creative as only a few are today. The ideal situation, of course, is that everyone should find satisfaction and enjoyment in work. To the extent that this is an unattainable goal, everyone must perform a certain amount of labor as a social duty, just as at the present time in most nations the whole population, or some specified part of it, is subject to military service as a social obligation.

(2) Social divisions such as those connected with the different modes of life in city and country will be eliminated. This does not mean that everyone will live exactly like everyone else, only that living conditions, cultural opportunities, etc., will be equally favorable for all. Similarly, the great present-day social division between mental and manual labor will have to be overcome. In part, this can be achieved by the progressive elimination of many categories of manual labor and the proliferation of categories of mental labor—a trend

[2] Free distribution involves very substantial economies and can therefore make a not unimportant contribution to solving the problem of scarcity. Only think, for example, how large a part of the cost of telephone service at the present time is incurred because of the need to keep track of all calls, bill customers, and so on. If telephone service were free, all of this footless paperwork could be dispensed with.

[3] Karl Marx, *The Critique of the Gotha Program,* Sect. I.

which is already in operation—and in part it will require that at some time in his life everyone should participate in both kinds of labor.

(3) Distribution of income will not be according to productivity but according to need. Whereas in the socialist stage, the principle of distribution will be "from each according to his ability, to each according to his work"; in the communist stage, it will be "from each according to his ability, to each according to his needs." This is already touched upon in what was said above in connection with the necessity for a changed attitude toward labor, but it has to be emphasized and what it implies has to be spelled out. Above all, "needs" in this context must not and cannot be interpreted in what may be called the Madison Avenue sense of the term. In capitalist society, the consumer is supposed to "need" not only the necessities and comforts of life but also an infinite accumulation of luxuries—several motor cars, a town house and two or more country estates, a yacht, etc., etc. What prevents consumers from satisfying these "needs" is only a shortage of the necessary purchasing power. As productivity increases and incomes rise, presumably everyone will be able to satisfy more and more of his "needs": the capitalist's utopia would then be a society in which everyone lived like one of today's Texas oil millionaires. Actually, this whole conception is an absurd contradiction in terms. The lavish scale on which the wealthy live under capitalism is possible only because they are able to command, directly and indirectly, the services of a far more numerous class of relatively poor people. In addition, much of their consumption is what Veblen called conspicuous waste, designed only to advertise their wealth and to arouse the envy of their countrymen. In a society of equals—one in which everyone stands in the same relation to the means of production and has the same obligation to work and to serve the common welfare—all "needs" that emphasize the superiority of the few and involve the subservience of the many will simply disappear and will be replaced by the needs of liberated human beings living together in mutual respect and cooperation.

Perhaps it will occur to some of you that what I am describing is not so much a new society as a new human being—one who expresses himself through his work, recognizes his responsibilities to society, respects and supports his fellows, and wants only what he needs to live a cultured life in a civilized environment. Am I not saying that communism will come into being and will prove viable to the extent that it is a society made up of human beings of this description? Yes, I am saying that. But I am saying more than that too: I am saying that the evolution of socialism will in due course *create* such human beings and precisely in that way will transform itself into communism. The society and the human beings who compose it constitute a dialectical whole: neither can change without changing the other. And communism as an ideal comprises both a new society and a new man.

In closing, allow me to quote a famous passage from Marx's celebrated *Critique of the Gotha Program*:

> In a higher phase of communist society, after the enslaving subordination of individuals under division of labor, and therewith also the antithesis between mental and physical labor, has vanished, after labor has become not merely a means to live but has become itself the primary necessity of life, after the productive forces have also increased with the all-round development of the individual, and all the springs of cooperative wealth flow more abundantly—only then

> can the narrow horizon of bourgeois rights be fully left behind and society inscribe on its banners: from each according to his ability, to each according to his needs.

That was written nearly a century ago, but the intervening years have done nothing to dim its brilliance. Karl Marx's conception of the communist society of the future is still the most humane and generous perspective that has been given to a suffering world, and today there are many more millions than ever before striving to make it a reality.

32 THE NEW MAN AND THE NEW ORDER IN CUBA*

by MIKE GOLDFIELD

Of course, it is difficult to decide what socialism would be like in America by looking at socialism in any other country. Up until now it has only come into being in underdeveloped countries like Cuba. The road to a humane socialism there is obstructed by the twin problems of (1) gnawing poverty and underdevelopment and (2) the implacable hostility of the most powerful country in the world.

This is all the more reason to be impressed with what Cuba has been able to achieve in ten short years. Mike Goldfield describes briefly some of the economic accomplishments of Cuba—the schools, the health care, the public services and the rational planning. Then he goes on to talk about how Cuba has attempted to deal with some of the contradictions that it has confronted. What kind of freedom has it given to intellectuals and artists? How has it treated groups that are obsolete from the perspective of the revolution—small, independent farmers, prostitutes, the old property-owning classes? And perhaps most important—through what incentives does Cuba encourage its people to perform the productive labor necessary to build up the country? Much more than the Soviet Union, Cuba has relied on moral incentives—the sense that hard work and extra work is necessary in order to realize the collective effort.

As Goldfield explains, central political problems still exist, especially those resulting from the fact that the Cuban Revolution did not grow out of a mass political movement. Thus the locus of decision-making remains to be shifted from Castro to the people as a whole. But in Cuba, politics has taken on a new, positive meaning, for the people have seen that things can change. *That in itself is a message that can transform any society.*

Through the Cuban experience we get some idea of what socialism might be like in a developed country. We get a glimpse of the new sense of optimism. Far from the old tone of suspicion and individualism, the dominant atmosphere now seems to be one of cooperation, enthusiasm and sense of collective purpose. Life and society are experimental; things change in response to needs, new ideas and people's reactions. A cultural revolution is taking place. Politics has taken on a new positive meaning: it is the process by which people decide where they are going, by which they come to understand the new developments in the society, by which leaders and led are united and work given a sense of purpose.

A visit to Cuba has an exhilarating, yet indescribable effect on many Americans. Upon returning, they find it difficult to communicate to their countrymen exactly what is going on there: it is not that they lack details, but that they fail to show how these details fit together. Even the *New York Times*' James Reston, normally a glib liberal apologist for the American corporate structure, grows contradictory as he tries to explain away and undercut some of his obviously positive reactions to Cuba (see Reston's series in the *Times* from his July 21–August 3, 1967, visit). Reston is impressed by everything from the new "status of the Cuban woman" to the incredible gains made in education, housing, health, and the economy. He is taken aback by the relaxed, yet politically charged atmosphere: the friendliness of the militiamen, the lack of hostility toward Americans; the sense of political purpose and the high-level political consciousness among ordinary people. New Leftists, when seeing these and other things, often wax into a dreamy inarticulateness upon returning, talking of a beautiful trip, happy peasants, delicious ice cream, and high revolutionary spirit, none of which does justice to Cuba, or to ourselves.

Perhaps the best way to begin to understand a society in its totality is to examine its ideology—the way the society comprehends itself. In its ideology one can see its view of the ideal man and the ideal society, and the projected pattern of development for reaching these goals. One must also examine the ways and the extent to which the economic structure and the socializing institutions embody this ideology.

By way of comparison, it is fruitful to look at the ideology of our own society—pluralism. The ideal man in a pluralist society is one who has particular (selfish) material and status interests, is competitive and inventive in advancing those interests, and is tolerant of people with interests other than his own, as long as their satisfaction does not threaten the assumptions of the system. Pluralist man is forever ready to bargain and compromise his interests, since by doing so he may obtain other possibilities to advance them. Pluralist interests are peculiar in that they are quantifiable (thus making them amenable to bargaining). The pluralist society is one in which interest groups (composed of pluralist men with similar interests, e.g., doctors or businessmen or auto workers) battle in numerous arenas for secondary and lesser levels of power and influence, while the key levels of power—which determine what types of goods the society produces, what the mass media will be saying and who shall have access to it, what occupations and roles shall be available to people —are guided by the needs of American capitalism, and the institutions and men that manage it. Pluralists tend to argue that pluralist man and pluralist society are natural—pluralism is, thus, the only realistic view. Other views of man's potential and the good society, while nice in theory, create, when implemented, inhumane perversions and gross deprivations of human freedom. It is this ideology which throws light on why James Reston has trouble explaining how a non-pluralist system can be as open and as politicized as is Cuba.

Cuba makes no bones about what she is trying to do: she is trying to create a socialist economy and communist men, and ultimately, a completely communist society.

CUBAN MARXISM

The generally accepted theory of the new man and the new order in Cuba is presented in Che Guevara's essay, "El Socialismo y El Hombre en Cuba" (Man and Socialism in Cuba), a piece which seems to have walked right out of the pages of Marx's 1844 *Manuscripts* (published when Marx was barely 26). Che puts forth several propositions dealing with the new man and the new order:

1. Under capitalism men are forced to compete for jobs, advancement, status, and goods. The men who reach the highest positions, like a Rockefeller, get there at the expense of many others. The consciousness of all men (especially the way they regard their fellow men) is formed by their participation in this "race of wolves." Also, economic development under capitalism is based on profit, not on what human beings need.
2. To create a communist society, economic priorities must be reversed. Income must be redistributed, and economic development must take place according to human needs, not as a result of the interplay of the profit-maximizing forces in the market.
3. In the Soviet Union and many other communist countries, it is felt that the establishment of a planned, socialist economy and the subsequent economic development will bring into being communist men. In Cuba, it is felt that communist men are not created merely by the economic structure; they must also be created internally (by their own will), and by a long-term and difficult educational process. "To build communism, a new man must be created simultaneously with the material base."
4. The communist man is one who does not think in terms of self-interested desires, but sees his self-realization closely linked to the welfare of his fellows. In spite of his communal orientation—or rather, because of it—Che claims that a communist man will have more opportunities for self-realization, and, thus, more freedom than man could ever have in a capitalist society.

This theory does sound nice, but much of what has happened already in some socialist countries has not only made rhetoric cheap, but suspect. In examining how the Cubans carry out their theory, three considerations will be studied: the economy, socialization of the new man, and how the society deals with obsolescent groups.

CUBA'S SOCIALIST ECONOMY

The prerequisite for socialist economic planning in Cuba was state control of the economy. State control of agricultural land was gained by the passage of two Agrarian Reform Laws, one in May, 1959, and the other in October, 1963. These laws limited the maximum size of large farms, gave ownership of some land to small farmers, and gave the state control of 70% of the land. Control of large industry was obtained in 1960: All U.S. investments were nationalized in August, in response to the refusal of U.S. oil companies to refine Russian crude oil; during October, the railroads, the department stores, and the remaining large industries were all nationalized.

Having control of the economy, the government pumped money into services, basic consumer goods, and economic development: hospitals, schools, housing, domestic food production (e.g., eggs, milk, vegetables, fruit, meat, chicken, and coffee), bus transportation, etc. Conscious decisions were made not to import cars or luxuries, and to eliminate the gambling and much of the night life around Havana. Some results are that Cuba has eliminated commercials, billboard ads, and gaudy gas station signs; Havana has little traffic (but a highly efficient bus system), the city is clean and has little smoke and smog.

From the very beginning, an attempt was made to redistribute income. One of the first things the *fidelistas* did upon their entry into Havana was to cut all rents in half and lower costs for utilities (particularly, phone calls). The basic policy now towards necessities is that they should be free or very low-priced. Among things free in Cuba are medical care (as one government official explained to me "everything from a scratch to a heart transplant"), nurseries for small children, books for students, water, funerals, beaches, local phone calls, and most sports. Good meals, eaten at one's school or work-place likewise are free. Scholarship students (of which there are now 400,000 out of a non-adult school population of 1,700,000) obtain free room, board, and clothing, in addition to their schooling. Further, there is a 10% of income ceiling on rents, and over a hundred thousand families pay no rent; in 1970, rent will be abolished for everyone. There is an elaborate social security system which provides a minimum of half one's salary at retirement or upon receiving any incapacitating injury or sickness whether or not it is related to one's work. Among the things eliminated last year in the attempt to cut down on bureaucracy were the tolls for the tunnel going under the bay in Havana and income tax.

Some necessities, of course, must still be paid for, but the way pricing works is strange to our capitalist-trained eyes. Rather than being regulated by the market, the prices for necessities are kept low; if the good is scarce, it is rationed, rather than allowed to rise in price and become a privilege for the rich (one of James Reston's complaints about Cuba was that coffee—a necessity—runs out as easily at the best hotels as anyplace else). It is also significant that Cuba, unlike some other socialist countries, has not allowed scarce goods to become privileges of high-ranking party members or government officials. The only prices that are exorbitantly high in Cuba are those of luxury items, making it quite expensive for those who still have large amounts of money, to flaunt even a shadow of their old style. The Cubans claim that as their economy grows, more and more things will become free and eventually money will be abolished, since under communism, "from each according to his ability, to each according to his needs."

Not the least important advantage to a planned economy like Cuba's is that there is virtually full employment, and complete job security for those who work. (Before the Revolution, unemployment ranged from 16% to 25% depending upon whether it was the sugar harvest season or not.)

SOCIALIZATION OF THE NEW MAN: VOLUNTARY WORK

Economic development for an underdeveloped country in the twentieth century is a very painful process. In both Russia and China, economic development has required the mobilization of the population for long hours of extra work. Though called voluntary, the method of mobilization was often highly coercive. The Cubans claim, however, that the development of communism and the elimination of money require more than a developed society. *How* the economy is developed is extremely important. The economy must be developed by—and while simultaneously developing—people who are willing to work hard for the social good, rather than for their own material gains, or because they are coerced. Voluntary work provides both the means to develop the economy and the new man:

> Through work we will create human wealth; through your work we will create human awareness . . . we will bring up human beings devoid of selfishness, devoid of the defects of the past, human beings with a collective sense of effort, a collective sense of strength (Castro, 7/26/67).

Cuban Marxism is characterized by what would traditionally be called its idealist tendencies, since almost as much emphasis is placed upon how people are socialized as on the level of economic development.[1]

Voluntary work is largely connected with agriculture. It consists, for many people, of leaving their normal jobs during the harvest times and working long hours in stints of anywhere from 30 days to several months. For other people, particularly those who cannot leave for such long periods (store workers, employees of periodicals, certain types of factory workers, students during the school year, and some administrators) doing voluntary work entails spending regular several-day periods (often weekends, or Sundays) in the fields. The most intensive periods of voluntary work come during the height of the sugar *zafra* (harvest), and with somewhat less intensity when work is needed in coffee and in tobacco. Something similar to voluntary work is done by large numbers of factory and agricultural workers. Many of them throughout the country have voluntarily renounced all overtime pay, in addition to the voluntary work they may do in agriculture.

Since one of the key premises about the new man is that he must create himself (one cannot coerce someone into feeling communal), an attempt is made to persuade people (through speeches and the educational work of the party) that self-fulfillment comes by voluntarily working for the social good rather than merely for one's own material benefits. The whole structure of social recognition in the schools and the society at large emphasizes these values; the close relation between the material conditions for communism and the use of voluntary work to change one's consciousness is continually stressed.

"What most characterizes the Revolution at the moment is work," said Castro at the 26th of July celebration in 1967, and his assessment is most likely correct. One can already see a large change in the way people look at work. Manual labor and hard work are now held in great esteem, whereas ten years ago they were not. Cutting cane, once thought to be the lowliest of jobs, seems to be done with an intense eagerness and desire for improving one's skill. Formerly, it was a mark of high status to live a comfortable life in Havana. Now young teachers, technicians, doctors, and lawyers have more desire to work in the rural areas because that is where the country needs them. The desire to do work where one is needed, to work hard, and to undertake the most difficult work is instilled in good part by example.

[1] Socialization is a complex phenomenon and must minimally include the school system, the military, the family, local meetings and groups, mass organizations, and the cultural apparatus. I am examining voluntary work because it is probably most indicative of what is unique about Cuba's attempt to form communist men.

A similar pride attaches to election to party membership. While in Cuba, I talked to few people (not counting counter-revolutionaries) who did not think it would be a great honor to be chosen to be a member of the Communist Party, and who did not hold in high esteem those who were already in the party. Selection for the party is based upon a person's workplace (or school). He must be a hard worker, a member of the militia, and active in one or more of the mass-based civic or political organizations. One who fulfills these qualifications may then be selected by his co-workers to be a member of the party. The person must finally be approved by the sectional branch of the party. To stay in the party one must retain the enthusiastic support of his co-workers. Though being in the party was a great honor, members seemed mainly distinguished by their willingness to set an example in work, to take on the most difficult jobs, to work the longest hours, to work the hardest; members of the party were those willing to go where they were needed, and there appear to be very few privileges, if any, associated with membership (no extra money, no car, no nicer house, etc.). In fact, the contrary is often the case; party members often voluntarily take lower salaries and live in more arduous circumstances than other people. A compelling example (one which even people neutral to the revolution seem to admire) is set by the leaders of the country; Fidel was in a lead tank and almost got killed at Playa Giron (the Bay of Pigs); he also supposedly narrowly missed being killed while manning a rescue boat during Hurricane Flora. Che was purported to have taken his Sunday rest by spending twelve hours cutting cane in a swampy place that was particularly bad for his asthma. Such examples go a long way toward making voluntary work different from self-sacrifice.

In many of the people with whom I talked, one could see the "communist mentality" developing. I asked one worker why he did voluntary work. He told me that before the Revolution profits from his work went to rich men—now they went to ordinary people like him. He asked me whether I had seen the schools to which all children could go for free, the new hospitals and housing. He told me that people are all equal, and did I not think it was better that a society should try to fulfill everyone's needs, not just some people's. He and other people emphasized that voluntary work was not for someone else because the whole society, the factories, and the profits belonged to everyone, including themselves. Though we skeptical Americans know better than to accept such rhetoric at face-value (men and society are just not like that!), when one stops to think and sees how much the lives of most ordinary people have changed, the logic of what these workers say is compelling. At the other end of the spectrum, I talked with a young economist from Juceplan (Central Planning Agency) who certainly could have been living a comfortable life in most any other country. He said, "I may be crazy for not wanting a car, a TV, and a nice house, and in fifty years I may end up changing my mind. But now we believe that a society that develops for everyone is the best way."

But, for Americans especially, the question of how *voluntary* is voluntary work, continues to linger. And not without reason. Other countries had their voluntary work, and the problems for those who did not volunteer are not particularly heart-warming. Cuba, however, seems to be different. Approximately 40% of the people are said to engage regularly in voluntary work, a figure much lower than that given in Russia. Given the high revolutionary fervor in Cuba, it would appear that coercion could raise that figure quite a lot. But the concern in Cuba *does* seem to be that people should want to do it; there is a confidence that the percentage will rise eventually and that there is no need to resort to the type of figure falsification that the Russians always proved so good at.

I suspect that the social pressure in adolescent groups is often coercive (it is hard to imagine an adolescent group in which it would not be), particularly since many Cuban adolescents tend to be superrevolutionary. Also, in most cases where 95% of the people in a group or factory do voluntary work, it is hard to imagine things not being a little tight for the other 5%.

In one factory I visited I spoke to people who did not do voluntary work. One man who forcefully described himself to me as a non-socialist, looked perplexed when I asked him whether there were any problems for those who did not do voluntary work. "Why should there be?" he answered. When I went into great detail to explain, he interrupted me and said simply "That's silly." In effect, the heaviest social pressure appears to be felt by those people in high and intermediate-range government positions.

ARTISTIC FREEDOM

Another significant sphere where coercion is low and the ideology of voluntarism runs rampant is art and literature. Though I had heard of the intellectual openness in Cuba before I went there, one's skepticism is only finally buried by facts. Perusing through used bookstores, I found old copies of the *New Leader,* Samuelson's *Economics* in abundance, and even in one bookstore a large selection of books glorifying America, including such titles as *The Story of American Freedom, Building America,* and *Trading With Latin America* by the Irving National Bank. Since 1963, Cuba has published a wide range of literature including titles by such authors as Tolstoy, Dostoievski, Gogol, Chekhov, Proust, Joyce, Hemingway, Faulkner, Scott Fitzgerald, Sinclair Lewis, John Steinbeck, Mark Twain, and a host of others, including the Cuban best-seller *In Cold Blood* by Truman Capote. Works by Trotsky, Deutscher's *Stalin,* and Deutscher's biography of Trotsky are all about to be published. A wide range of foreign films are available in Havana (American ones are unavailable because of the U.S. embargo), and among the most popular have been Antonioni's *Red Desert,* and *Morgan* which just won a film award. By the time I saw Talcott Parsons and Amitai Etzioni in the University of Havana bookstore, I found myself arguing to Cuban intellectuals that such a large degree of bourgeois literature was not conducive to developing communist men—and, with a paper shortage in Cuba, couldn't they be more selective. In such arguments the most decadent examples of bourgeois culture that I could find were two things I had seen at Expo '67: a Cuban fashion show with the latest style mini-skirts, et al., and a grotesque Broadway-type musical to celebrate the 26th of July, the biggest national holiday, commemorating the first act of the Revolution.

Here is the argument I got in return: many of the older intellectuals in Cuba are not particularly revolutionary. A large number exiled themselves before the Revolution (for reasons of cultural preference, rather than political reasons) to New York and other Western cities; some even abandoned the Spanish language. These people returned in force after the triumph of the Revolution; they not only produce bourgeois art now (like the musical), but poor imitations. Such art is not what we would like produced in Cuba. But there is another problem, potentially more dangerous, that of socialist realism. Revolutionary art cannot be mandated from above, it must be produced by revolutionaries who are free to create. Any state control would take away freedom, and stifle artistic creativity. We must encourage people to be exposed to all forms of art and culture, and hope that the young artists who are more revolutionary than the older ones will produce revolutionary art for Cuba.

OBSOLETE GROUPS

The humaneness which runs deeply through Cuba's revolution is most clearly seen in the way that they treat those classes and groups which are not seen to have a functional role in the development of the new society. The Agrarian Reform Law of May, 1959, gave over 100,000 peasants land in the form of private farms. Though small farmers are not considered irrelevant to the growth of the economy, they are seen as the most inefficient part of the agricultural plan. Besides their inability to use equipment that is suitable for large state farms, they do not utilize the soil for what it is best suited, but grow a variety of crops to suit the needs of the individual farmer. So what does the Revolution do? It clearly wants this land to eventually be part of the state farms or cooperative farms, but it is in no hurry. Farmers can keep their lands, and even hand them down to their sons. Meanwhile, they are considered allies in the task of agricultural development and given fertilizer, equipment, technical aid and credit. If a farmer wants to sell his land to the state or receive a pension he can, but no one pesters him. Though he may make more money than a farm laborer, he still gets the free goods and services that other Cubans do. Eventually, children of farmers will want to go to school and be technicians, some farmers will not have children, and others may opt for the pension. Twenty years from now there will be less private farming, and in another 20 years still less, but no one seems particularly concerned.

The bourgeoisie who have remained in Cuba have also been treated in a benevolent fashion. They still have their houses (though they are forbidden to hire servants), their cars, and what they have not spent of their bank accounts. One can bump into former large landholders in any of the big hotels, where they can be seen living in style off of more than adequate pensions. Those who had jobs in big companies or were private doctors or lawyers often still have the same jobs and salaries they had before the Revolution. Eventually, they will disappear as a class, since there are no up-and-coming bourgeoisie to replace them. Cuba is not exactly the type of place that a wealthy, or even a moderately wealthy man would want to recommend to his friends these days, but for a country that is still in the midst of a socialist revolution, one cannot help feeling that they could not have been treated more royally.

For another example of this humaneness, one might turn to the elimination of organized prostitution. With the large number of tourists in Havana, many of them American businessmen, prostitution flourished. In 1961, a decision was made to end it. Squads of people from the Ministry of Interior (somewhat in the fashion of community organizers) went into the red light districts. They spoke to prostitutes and gave them this line: the Revolution was made to free people from oppression, and it was made for everyone. Before the Revolution it may have been economically necessary for one to be a prostitute, but now one need not be so degraded. If you want to give up being a prostitute, we will send you to school to be trained for a job; we will find you a job and a decent place to live. After a year's time many had accepted this offer; some even found husbands while retraining. The government set up day nurseries to take care of their children, while the former prostitutes were in school. Then, in 1962, the government closed all the brothels, though there is still no law against prostitution and free-lance prostitutes can occasionally be seen.

DEALING WITH PROBLEMS

Examining the ideology of a society, and the way that society implements its ideology by necessity gives one a rather simplified view of how that society operates; many of its complexities, both positive and negative, are omitted. To gain a little perspective on the overview I have presented so far, it is helpful to look at some of the problems besetting Cuba and to check how she deals with them. One set of problems arose during the 1962 period and is self-described by many highly-placed Cubans as their Stalinist era; the second set of problems to be discussed must be faced in the next several years.

In the fall of 1961, Cuba began to take what appeared to be an authoritarian turn. At that time open-slate elections in the unions were abolished in favor of single-slate elections; rather than being nominated from the floor, union officials were now nominated on a single-slate chosen by the party, then given rubber stamp approval by the workers. Union meetings became smaller and less important; the unions and the industries became dominated by a section of the party bureaucracy. As a result of Playa Giron and the high-level of counter-revolutionary activity, many political prisoners were taken in late 1961 and in 1962—a good number of them for seemingly minor crimes. Homosexuals were also treated harshly during this period; they were rounded up and taken to camps to be rehabilitated. Some well-placed persons were advancing the notion that homosexuality was a "bourgeois hang-up" that need only exist under capitalism. And finally, the publishing policy tightened up in 1962; most of the books published were Soviet and those that were not echoed the Soviet line.

The general causes of these policies are easy to find. This was the period when Cuba had just moved close to the Soviet Union, was dependent on her economically, and had still not developed an independent course. There were also many Stalinists of pre-revolutionary vintage left in the newly consolidated Communist Party. Finally, Playa Giron and the continued threat from the United States created a (not particularly unjustified) paranoia against counter-revolutionaries. Each of these problems was met in different ways. The publishing policy changed the next year, largely from criticism by intellectuals and as a result of a critique of Soviet Marxism developed at the University of Havana. The policy toward homosexuals was also changed by the next year; the experiment had failed and people with better sense asserted themselves. The arrest of the large number of political prisoners has only been half-solved. Many have been released and even given education, job retraining, and aid in resettlement with their families, but many more still remain in prisons or rehabilitation camps (not too much is known about these prisoners; one of the few sources of information is Lee Lockwood's *Castro's Cuba, Cuba's Fidel*).

The situation in the unions was finally changed in 1965. The change seems to be due to the labor unrest during 1962 and 1963, and pressures exerted by local unions; an additional factor was the removal of a number of old communists from places where they could influence the unions. Since the return of the unions to the open-slate system, a number of other changes have taken place that give people more control of local decision-making. The CDR's (Committees for the Defense of the Revolution), originally set up in 1961 as local surveillance units to spot counter-revolutionary activities, have gradually changed their functions. Now they are similar to local block clubs, expressing the concerns of their members and performing neighborhood services (e.g., administering vaccination campaigns, running education and literacy classes, cleaning the neighborhood). Representatives chosen by the CDR's also make up the majority of members for the councils of the local community governments which have been set up all over the island in the last year.

Cuba seems to have developed a set of institutions on the local level (both in the workplace and in the community) which are responsive to and at least partially controlled by the persons they effect. It appears that procedures for expressing grievances are well-functioning. But, with respect to larger issues (particularly those connected with economic planning and international relations), there are no structured relations between the leaders of the people. There is a kind of Rousseauian democracy. Even as early as 1964, Che expressed concern about the need for more formal relations between the leaders and the people. Currently, the ultimate power for making broad policy decisions rests with the Central Committee of the Communist Party, a body of around 100 men and women. Possibly, as few as six or seven people hold the real power. Much of the influence that ordinary people have over the direction of the government in these areas is based on the responsiveness, the style and the openness to criticism shown by Cuba's leaders. The problems inherent in such a situation seem to be of concern to the leaders of the country. Fidel has mentioned them a number of times in his recent speeches; he even says that the problem of institutionalizing the Revolution, giving more structure to the relation between the leaders and the masses, will be partially solved at the First Party Congress. Whether this change will take the form of local workers councils, a new variety of representative democracy, or some uniquely Cuban institution which has little historical precedent remains to be seen.

33 DEMOCRACY UNDER SOCIALISM: THE CASE OF THE CULTURAL REVOLUTION*

by LEO HUBERMAN
AND PAUL SWEEZY

The Russian Revolution brought Russia a long way—from a poor, backward country to a leading industrial power. The Russian people have seen significant improvements in their lives. At the same time, many enthusiasts of socialism have been disappointed by the development of Russian socialism—the emergence of class distinctions; the separation of the leaders from the masses of people; the failure to develop significantly new values of cooperation and participation; the politically repressive nature of Russian society; the counterrevolutionary nature of Russian foreign policy. The Russian Revolution proved that socialism could bring a backward country into the modern world and provide clear material benefits for the people. But it did not prove that it could make possible a truly liberating society.

The Chinese experience has gone a long way toward showing that problems with Russian development were not inherent in socialism; rather they were the product of the particular conditions that faced Russia as the world's first Socialist country. The Chinese have long been aware of some of the drawbacks of Russian development and have sought to deal with them in a resolute fashion.

Huberman and Sweezy attempt in this selection to give some feel for the way in which the Chinese have approached these problems, and also an understanding of some of the specific policies that have characterized Chinese development.

They discuss some of the ways the leaders of the Chinese Revolution maintained their responsiveness to the needs of the people; they also describe the functioning of the Chinese workplace. In each case, one can see where China has advanced beyond the experience of the Soviet Union—at the same time, the contrast with the elitist nature of the political system of our own country is rather striking.

It is pretty generally agreed by now that the Cultural Revolution in China is an event of world-shaking import. And yet much of what is being said and written about it, at least in the sources to which we have access, is uninspired and uninspiring. Endless accumulation of details yield little useful or usable knowledge; steady proliferation of hypotheses contributes more to confusion than to understanding. Why?

There are doubtless many reasons, but perhaps the most important is that most commentators on the Cultural Revolution interpret it in terms of some experience which is familiar to them. Not that this procedure is necessarily bad: if the kind of upheaval which is now taking place in China had already occurred elsewhere, the method could certainly be fruitful. But if, as we believe, the Cultural Revolution is something genuinely new in history, interpreting it according to criteria borrowed from some past experience can only lead to muddle and confusion.

Most prone to fall into this trap, for obvious reasons, are those whose attentions and emotions have long been fixated on the Soviet Union. For them, Soviet experience provides ready-made models and norms for interpreting all subsequent revolutionary developments, including what is now happening in China.

Thus partisans of those now in power in the Soviet Union, for whom the ruling Communist Party is by definition the repository of all revolutionary wisdom and virtue, are bound to see in the Cultural Revolution a nihilistic and ultimately disastrous attack on the very essence of the socialist revolution itself. In their eyes no progress is possible save through what they regard as the tried and true methods developed during a half century of Soviet experience.

A similar obsession with Soviet experience is shown by the Trotskyists who see in present Chinese developments a re-enactment in a different setting of the Stalinist conflicts and purges of the 1920's and 1930's. Mao Tse-tung, in this view, heads one segment of the "bureaucracy" which is struggling for predominance against other segments. Whoever wins, the result can only be the continuation of "bureaucratic rule"—unless by some miracle there is a return to a golden age of "proletarian democracy" such as is supposed to have prevailed in the Soviet Union under Lenin and Trotsky.

Unfortunately for all these "explanations," China is not Russia; Mao is not Stalin; no Communist Party is or ever was infallible; and the years 1917–1924 in the Soviet Union were characterized by civil war and chaos and revolutionary dictatorship. No clear thinking about the Cultural Revolution is possible unless we are prepared at the outset to try to see the situation in China today as it really is and as it has developed out of centuries of Chinese history and decades of Chinese revolutionary experience. This is of course not easy, far from it; and with essential facts as hard to come by as they are under present circumstances, even the best informed and most perceptive analyst is certain to overlook significant happenings, make mistakes, see some things in wrong perspective. But difficulties provide no excuse for not trying.

What one needs above all in seeking to understand such a huge and complicated event as the Cultural Revolution is what may perhaps be called historical imagination. No one, not even the most favorably situated individual, can have personal knowledge of more than a very small fraction of what goes on in a country the size of China, and even knowledge acquired at second hand is limited. If nevertheless it is possible to have a conception, and a vivid conception at that, of the whole rapidly changing scene, the reason is obviously the enormous creative power of the imagination, that faculty which, according to Karl Marx, differentiates human beings from the rest of the animal world. Whether the imagination does its work well or badly depends partly on its natural power (for it seems that people are very differently endowed), partly on the training to which it has been subjected, and partly on the appropriateness of the materials with which it works. And it is with respect to this last that an eager receptivity to the new, the unexpected, the significant, the illuminating, must be zealously maintained and cultivated.

It is in this connection that we would like to direct the reader's attention to certain pieces of "evidence," partly speculative and partly factual, which seem to us to be most helpful in clarifying the true nature of the Cultural Revolution.

The first involves a comparison of China with the Soviet Union—not, however, of what is now happening in China with what actually happened in the Soviet Union but with what might have happened if Lenin had lived as long as Mao Tse-tung has lived. For it is surely obvious that in any comparative study of the two revolutions, Mao's role must be likened to that of Lenin, certainly not to that of Stalin. Mao was born in 1893 and will therefore be 74 years old this year. Lenin died in 1924 at the age of 54. If he had lived as long as Mao, he would have survived at least into the middle 1940's, and most likely there would never have been a Stalin era. Nor, probably, would there ever have been such a thing as Trotskyism: the most natural assumption is that Lenin would have remained the unchallenged leader of the Soviet state and that the relationship between him and Trotsky would have continued to be what it was from 1917 to 1923. How would Lenin have handled the great problems which faced the Soviet Union in the later 1920's and the 1930's?

Obviously no one knows for sure, and on many subjects there are not enough clues to justify even a highly speculative answer. But this is not so with respect to the problem which is our chief present concern. For we know that during the last two or three years of his life, Lenin became increasingly worried about the kind of regime which was emerging in the Soviet Union. To quote E. H. Carr, a leading historian of the Bolshevik Revolution:

> On November 20, 1922, he had made the last public speech of his life to the Moscow Soviet. Shortly afterwards he had his last conversation with Trotsky—a conversation to which Trotsky in retrospect attached much importance. . . . Lenin expressed his horror and fear of the growth of bureaucracy in the Soviet apparatus. Trotsky retorted that bureaucracy was to be found not only in state, but in party institutions; and Lenin half-jestingly proposed "a bloc against bureaucracy in general and against the Orgbureau in particular." [1]

The problem was neither new nor one which no previous attempts had been made to solve. In 1919 a Commissariat of the Workers' and Peasants' Inspectorate (Rabkrin) was created to combat bureaucracy and corruption in the state apparatus; and in 1921 a Central Control Commission was set up within the Communist Party to perform a similar function with respect to the party apparatus. The methods adopted by the Control Commission were specially characteristic of Lenin's approach. Local control commissions held public meetings open to Communists and non-Communists alike, at which the conduct of all members of the Party, from highest to lowest, was submitted to searching examination. Those found guilty of misdeeds could be rebuked or, in extreme cases, expelled

[1] *A History of Soviet Russia: The Interregnum, 1923–1924,* p. 257. See also Isaac Deutscher, *The Prophet Unarmed: Trotsky, 1921–1929,* Chapter 1 ("The Power and the Dream").

from the Party. The idea was that the people should have the power not to accept or reject the dictatorship of the Party as such but to control the behavior of the particular people who ruled in the name of the Party.

In the circumstances of civil war and chaos which existed at the time, neither Rabkrin nor the Control Commission was effective. In the last article he ever wrote, Lenin felt obliged to denounce Rabkrin in the strongest terms; and in later years the Control Commission was turned into the opposite of an organ of popular control and became instead an instrument of the Stalinist purges. Summing up Lenin's final position, Carr writes:

> If Lenin was driven by practical necessities to recognize a constantly growing concentration of authority, there is no evidence that he wavered in his belief in the antidote of "direct democracy." But he began to understand that progress would be slower than he had at first hoped and the bogey of bureaucracy more difficult to conjure.[2]

In the light of this record, are we not entitled to assume that if Lenin had lived, he would have been continuously, and indeed increasingly, concerned with the struggle against bureaucracy, corruption, and privilege, especially inside the Party? And when the problem proved to be as persistent and intractable as we now know it to be, is there any reason to doubt that he would have been drawn to increasingly radical experiments in "direct democracy" to find a viable solution?

Precisely what form these experiments might have taken we cannot know. But there is nothing in the least far-fetched or implausible in assuming that they would have climaxed in something very like the Cultural Revolution. For according to all available evidence, the overriding purpose of the Cultural Revolution is to free the Communist Party of China from the influence of those who "are taking the capitalist road," which we take to be a Chinese way of saying those who use their positions of authority to accumulate special privileges and to lord it over rather than serve the people. It is certainly no part of the purpose of the Cultural Revolution to undermine, let alone abolish, the Party's monopoly of power, any more than that was the purpose of Rabkrin and the Central Control Commission in Lenin's day. In present-day China, as in early revolutionary Russia, the aim is to purify the Party, to rid it of evil inheritances from the feudal and capitalist past, to enable it to perform more effectively its role as leader and guide along the road to socialism and communism. And the means chosen—especially the mobilization of the younger generation which has received its education since the Revolution, and the formation of Paris Commune-type "cultural revolutionary groups, committees and congresses" in localities and places of work—seem to be eminently appropriate and in full accord with Lenin's ideas of "direct democracy." The truth would seem to be that Mao's Cultural Revolution is the purest kind of Leninism. For if Lenin had remained in power twenty years longer, is it not likely that he would have seen the problem in much the same way Mao has seen it? After all, real revolutionaries—and Lenin and Mao are unquestionably two of the greatest revolutionaries of all time—do tend to think alike.

The second bit of "evidence" we want to call attention to comes from that segment of China's revolutionary history which is so brilliantly analyzed by William Hinton in *Fanshen*. The village of Long Bow which is the locus of

[2] *A History of Soviet Russia: The Bolshevik Revolution, 1917–1923,* Volume 1, p. 224.

Hinton's story was liberated in August, 1945, and immediately came under a new village government of revolutionary cadres and militiamen. Less than two years later, the new regime had disastrously deteriorated. It was no longer possible to ignore

> what had become increasingly obvious for a long time—that the revolutionary cadres and militiamen of Long Bow were gradually alienating themselves from the people by arbitrary orders, indiscriminate beatings, the assumption of special privileges, and "rascal behavior." Nor was Long Bow the only community in the district where a relatively small number of active young men had "mounted the horse," as the peasants so aptly put it, and were riding around to suit their own fancy. By the same token the Fifth District was not the only district where such things were occurring in Lucheng County, nor was Lucheng County itself an exception among the counties of the Taihang Region. In the spring of 1947, the government and the Party organization of the Taihang Region took note of the critical situation and launched a "Wash Your Face" campaign designed to put a stop to all such tendencies, and to overcome the opportunist and hedonist attitudes that fostered them.
>
> The method adopted in this campaign was to set up a *gate* or council of delegates, elected by the peasants at large, before which all the cadres had to answer for their motives and their actions. The phrase "Wash Your Face" came from Chairman Mao himself who had many times explained that the thoughts of revolutionary leaders inevitably became spotted and stained by the corrupt habits of the past and the rotten social environment that surrounded them on every side, just as their faces became spotted and stained by the dust and dirt of the natural environment. These spots and stains had to be washed off frequently just as people daily washed their faces to make them clean again. And just as one could not see the dirt on one's own face without consulting a mirror, so one could not clearly see one's own bad thinking and bad behavior without consulting the people who suffered as a consequence of both and could therefore reflect a truer image. (*Fanshen,* pp. 238–239.)

Here we have in embryo the whole idea of the Cultural Revolution—a gigantic, nation-wide "Wash Your Face" campaign.

To launch such a campaign, however, is one thing, and to carry it through successfully is quite another. Hinton's account of what happened in Long Bow, both in 1947 and later, throws valuable light on both aspects of the problem.

In the first place, the 1947 campaign was a failure. When the cadres were subjected to public examination, all sorts of grievances and criticisms were advanced, some constructive and some designed to secure the downfall and dismissal of the guilty ones—and all were guilty in one degree or another. A little reflection will show, however, that getting rid of those who had misbehaved could not provide any solution. For one thing, it left open the question as to who would replace them; and for another, even if satisfactory replacements could be found, there was no guarantee that they would not succumb to the temptations of power as their predecessors had done. What was needed was to *reform* the cadres, not to liquidate them. And this those responsible for the 1947 campaign in Long Bow were unable to accomplish. As Hinton explains it:

> Instead of allowing this storm of criticism to rage and using it to educate the peasants to distinguish honest from dishonest opinions so that the cadres could reform and all the people profit from a living political lesson, the district leaders lost their nerve and retreated. They intervened on behalf of the cadres and in effect suppressed criticism, both honest and dishonest. As a result, although

> some cadres, getting a scent of things to come, changed their outlook to a certain extent and corrected some of their faults, others . . . only became more arrogant than before and retaliated against those who had dared to criticize them. Clearly something more drastic was needed if the tendencies which were already alienating the leaders from the people and undermining not only the village administration and the Peasants' Association, but the Communist Party branch as well were not seriously to undermine and compromise the Revolution. (*Fanshen,* p. 239.)

This paragraph occurs less than a page before the end of Part II of Hinton's book, and it is no exaggeration to say that a large proportion of the remaining five parts, constituting nearly two thirds of the whole, is devoted to describing and analyzing the fascinatingly intricate process, reaching its climax in the spring and early summer of 1948, by which the situation in Long Bow was radically transformed for the better—for the people, for the leaders, and for their mutual relations. There can be no question of providing even the barest summary here: the process simply does not lend itself to summarization. Suffice it to say that the experience of Long Bow shows how, in the Chinese style of work, practice enriches thought and thought guides action; how there can be purification without purges and progress without victims. It is a very reassuring and encouraging story Hinton tells about Long Bow. And if, as one can hardly help assuming, similar things are now happening on a large scale all over China, then one can feel reassured and encouraged about the outcome of the Cultural Revolution too.

Our final bit of "evidence" comes from an unexpected source—a professor at a leading United States business school. Barry M. Richman is Chairman of the International Business Program and of the Management Theory and Industrial Relations Divisions at the Graduate School of Business Administration, University of California, Los Angeles. He is also the author of well-regarded works on the industrial management systems of the Soviet Union and India. With this background it was quite natural that he should want to study the Chinese system, and since he has the good fortune to be a Canadian it was possible for him to make the necessary arrangements. In his own words:

> With my Canadian citizenship and letters of introduction from a number of leading Canadian educators and businessmen, the Chinese were quite willing to issue me a visa, and this enabled me to undertake my first-hand study of industry and management. I visited [in April-June, 1966] 11 major cities and surveyed 38 enterprises (factories) in a wide range of industries as well as 3 of the country's largest retail department stores. In addition to interviewing and observing managers, workers, Communist Party cadres, and trade union officials at work, I also met many key personnel at various central, provincial, and municipal-level planning, industrial, and commercial organizations.[3]

Precisely because of his capitalist-business background and point of view, Richman's report throws an extraordinarily revealing light on the kind of society which is being constructed in China. And his frequent contrasts between Chinese and Soviet practices keep reminding us that there is a very different road the

[3] Barry M. Richman, "Capitalists and Managers in Communist China," *Harvard Business Review,* January–February, 1967, p. 58. A fuller account of the author's findings appears in *Industrial Society in Communist China,* New York, Random House, 1969.

Chinese might be traveling. His topic is not the Cultural Revolution—it was still in its earliest stage when he left China—but as one reads his report the thought continually recurs that he is, whether he knows it or not, dealing with the most fundamental issue at stake in the Cultural Revolution: Will China stick it out on the revolutionary road Mao has charted for her, or will she succumb to what must be enormous pressures, both internal and external, to return to an essentially bourgeois conception of economy and society? As Richman himself recognizes, the future of mankind will be profoundly influenced by the answer.

Let us summarize some of Richman's major findings.

(1) First and perhaps foremost, the Chinese have abandoned the bourgeois conception of the factory as a highly rationalized production unit. Richman's remarks on this crucially important subject are very striking:

> The Chinese do not seem nearly as concerned as the Soviets about economic inefficiency at the factory level resulting from state planning and resource allocation problems. For the Chinese enterprise is not viewed as a purely economic unit where economic performance clearly takes priority. In fact, Chinese factories seem to pursue objectives pertaining to politics, education, and welfare as well as economic results. Moreover, in their overpopulated country, with very low wages, the regime is not very concerned about underemployment or disguised unemployment which lowers per capita productivity at various factories.
>
> The Chinese factory is a place where much political indoctrination occurs both at the individual and at the group level, with the aim of developing the pure Communist man as conceived by Mao. It is a place where illiterate workers learn how to read and write, and where employees can and do improve their work skills and develop new ones through education and training. It is a place where housing, schools, recreational facilities, roads, shops, and offices are often constructed or remodeled by factory employees. It is also a place from which employees go out into the fields and help the peasants with their harvesting.
>
> Hence, if supplies do not arrive according to the plan, Chinese factory workers generally do not remain idle or unproductive—at least, by the regime's standards. In factories I visited where this type of situation arose, workers undertook some education or training during the period of delay in order to improve their skills; or they studied and discussed Chairman Mao's work; or, as was the case at the Tientsin Shoe and Wuhan Diesel Engine factories, they undertook various construction and modernization activities; or they worked on developing new or improved processes and products.
>
> This type of activity makes more sense than meets the eye in a country where illiteracy has been widespread, the level of industrial skill generally low, and factory housing and other welfare facilities sparse and inadequate. The benefits of political indoctrination seem more questionable, but even this activity seems to have a favorable motivating impact which is difficult for the capitalistic Western mind to grasp fully. (pp. 61–62)

Richman does not realize it but what he is describing here is the replacement of narrow bourgeois, balance-sheet rationality by a comprehensive socialist rationality. If he did realize it, he would not be able to assume so glibly that the Chinese conception of the role of the factory makes sense only for an underdeveloped country. On the contrary, it is only through developing and extending this kind of socialist rationality that the advanced industrial countries can hope to overcome the dreadful social diseases—poverty in the midst of plenty, confusion of wants and needs, proliferation of high IQ idiots, urban blight, alienation, mass neuroses, and all the rest—which capitalism has visited upon them.

All praise to the Chinese revolutionaries who are pioneering the road we must all travel if we are to survive as human beings!

In the meantime, it should be noted that the further the Chinese depart from bourgeois conceptions of rationality, the more impossible and meaningless will become quantitative comparisons between their and other countries' levels of income, productivity, etc. The Chinese are on the way to demonstrating in practice how all these seemingly hard statistical facts are in reality nothing but elaborate bourgeois rationalizations.

(2) In economic matters the Chinese practice flexibility and a relatively high degree of decentralization, and their method of getting good results puts major emphasis on having people with the appropriate understanding and motivation in decision-making positions.

> The reason that flexibility in planning does not get completely out of hand in China is that this country has a higher degree of decentralization of authority than does Russia. This means that administrators closer to the operating level have the authority to take more timely action in light of changing conditions. . . .
>
> The Red Chinese leaders have always been anti-bureaucracy in attitude, since they feel that bureaucracy impedes the right interpretation of national and party policy because of vested interests, localism, and routinization. . . .
>
> Since local party cadres have been viewed as generally dependable, the regime has not established a cumbersome system of checks, controls, and super-controls similar to that in the Soviet Union. . . .
>
> A prominent official of the Chinese State Planning Commission whom I interviewed declared that in the 1950's Peking went too far in imitating the Soviet system of bureaucracy and control. He said that this proved highly ineffective. . . . He also pointed out that in China more stress is placed on education and on controlling individuals in key positions than on controlling the performance of the organization. (pp. 62, 63)

In the light of this, certain other aspects of Chinese policy become easier to understand. For a decentralized socialist system—i.e. one which is not controlled by the impersonal forces of the market—to work smoothly, it is essential that those who make the important decisions should think alike on fundamental problems of economy, society, and morality. This consideration alone is enough to explain why the dissemination, study, and acceptance of "Chairman Mao's thoughts" plays an important role in the Chinese system: it is not a matter of glorifying an individual but of securing general agreement on what is right and important. Further, the policy of placing primary reliance on people rather than on organizations goes far to explain the particular form and function of the rectification campaigns which have been a recurring feature of Chinese revolutionary development and of which the Cultural Revolution is the biggest and most ambitious to date.

(3) The building of socialism requires the increasing separation of work from material rewards. And this is indeed Chinese policy and practice.

> While the Soviet regime has accepted monetary incentives and self-interest as key motivating forces for both managers and workers, the Chinese regime takes a less sanguine view toward such rewards. . . .
>
> I found during my visits to 38 Chinese factories that piece-rate incentives for workers had been completely abolished. However, at about 80 percent of

the factories workers could still earn monthly or quarterly bonuses. And, interestingly enough, such bonuses were not based solely upon productivity; politics and helping co-workers were also key criteria. . . .

During the past few years, directors, vice directors, and party secretaries have not been eligible to receive bonuses at any enterprises. . . . (pp. 64–65)

Richman's reaction to this strange state of affairs is what we might expect from a business school professor:

Can top-level enterprise managers (or middle managers, too, for that matter) be adequately motivated over time to perform efficiently without bonuses? I doubt it. At present there seems to be considerable dedication, zeal, patriotism, and other non-material stimuli motivating many of them to do the best job they can. But these stimuli cannot do the job alone for long. Complicating the difficulty is the fact that salaries, powers, and living conditions of top managers are relatively low in relation to those of their subordinates. (p. 65)

The "difficulty," it seems, is not so much with the Chinese system as with the bourgeois conception of "human nature." But Richman believes that this is a purely temporary state of affairs: in the long run "human nature" will triumph. All the same, he finds the problem worrisome and he keeps coming back to it.

(4) As indicated in the last paragraph quoted, there is a high degree of equality in Chinese salary scales: "At most factories the ratio between directors' incomes and the average factory pay was less than 2 to 1; the highest ratio I found was about 3 to 1." (p. 65) But this equalitarianism goes beyond money income and reaches into all aspects of life.

In a Soviet or an American industrial enterprise there are generally clues which enable an outsider to distinguish the top managers from the workers, and perhaps even the top managers from the lower-level managers. During my visits to Russian enterprises a few years ago, observable differences in the salary and wage scales, working and living conditions, dress, appearance, education, work patterns, and even interpersonal contacts gave me adequate clues to guess who was who. But in Chinese enterprises there are fewer clues than in probably any other country in the world.

In order for a Western [read: bourgeois] mind to make sense out of some of the more surprising and strange things going on in Chinese factories, one must be aware of two pure Communistic ideological tenets which the regime takes seriously and has gone a long way in implementing; (1) the abolition of classes, class distinctions, and elites; and (2) the abolition of distinctions between mental and physical labor. . . .

At Chinese enterprises there . . . seem to be no really very substantial differences in the housing conditions of managers, technicians, Reds, or workers. At the Nanking Chemical Fertilizer, Wuhan Iron and Steel Corporation, and Peking Cotton Textile No. 3 enterprises I spent quite a bit of time inspecting the factory housing. Top managers, lower-level managers, engineers, technicians, party cadres, and workers are all integrated in the apartment houses, for which a nominal monthly rent—typically 1 to 4 yuan [40¢ to $1.60] per room—is paid. . . .

All personnel eat together in the same canteen during working hours. Even though the larger factories have cars (some of them old U.S. models), top managers, key experts, and party officials claim that they walk, ride bikes, or take the bus to work. I was told that cars are only for official use or emergencies, and are used by all personnel. One can tell usually very little from dress

> or personal appearances in Chinese enterprises. Most personnel at all levels generally wear the conventional blue suits with caps—even the women. (pp. 65, 67)

All of which prompts the author to ask again: "In the absence of income and living standard differences, what does motivate the directors, party officials, and experts to perform well and to improve their performance at Chinese enterprises?" And he answers: "Dedication, loyalty, identification with the country's goals and progress, a deep sense of commitment and purpose—all these must play significant roles, particularly for the Reds and possibly for many of the experts." (p. 67) Again he assures us, however, that it can't last:

> It seems to me that in the long run material gain and self-interest will have to play significant roles in motivating the Chinese experts, and perhaps even the Reds, unless the regime can actually mold a nation of pure Communist men. The Russians have tried that, failed, and seem to have given up the attempt. The Chinese are much more persistent, but centuries of world history and experience are clearly against them. (p. 68)

It is true that the Russians tried a policy of equalitarianism—but only for a very short time under Lenin and in extremely unfavorable conditions. After Stalin had consolidated his power, he deliberately reversed this policy and it has never been tried since. Russian experience therefore has little to teach in this respect. And as for the lessons of "centuries of world history and experience," only a bourgeois professor can be so certain that they prove the universal validity of the laws of the capitalist jungle.

(5) Workers play a considerable and increasing role in choosing and controlling their own managers, and the effects are generally positive. Elections and worker participation, says Richman, "give the workers a sense of identification, loyalty, belonging, and commitment to their enterprises. They also keep managers on their toes, since they must at least listen to the workers. . . . Perhaps more important to the regime is that worker participation results in a form of bottom-up control not only over economic performance, but also over the proper interpretation of state policy and ideologically correct behavior." (p. 68) Here again we see that tendency, commented upon earlier, for a strictly economic rationality to give way to a more comprehensive socialist rationality.

(6) The same tendency is observable in the policy of requiring managers to engage in manual labor. At first Richman could hardly believe what he saw:

> During my first visit to a Chinese factory, Peking Wool, I thought it was a joke or strange aberration when, during lunch in the cafeteria, I was introduced to the director who was cooking dumplings in the kitchen. He was doing one of his two days a week of physical labor. I soon learned that all enterprise directors, vice directors, party secretaries, and trade union leaders spend from one to two days each week in physical labor. . . . (p. 69)

And the effects? They seem to be favorable in creating "a type of cohesive team spirit" and in enabling "managers to observe and keep in close touch with concrete operating conditions and problems in their enterprises." But again the doubts: "But where experts—in a country that has a critical shortage of experts—are forced to spend as much as two days each week in physical labor, may not the disadvantages outweigh the advantages, especially in terms of economic performance?" (p. 69).

The answer probably is that it is hard to tell, but that in any case building socialism is more important than economic performance—at least for real socialists.

(7) The Chinese system works pretty well. In general, and not surprisingly, Richman finds that the performance of Chinese factories is inferior to that of Soviet factories, much inferior to that of American factories, but well above that of Indian factories. What is particularly significant from our point of view is that China's achievements have been due more to human and social than to scientific or technological factors:

> Thus far Red China has achieved substantial industrial progress, more because of managerial motivation and attitudes than because of managerial or technical know-how. . . .
>
> Chinese industry has also made significant progress because of the motivation, dedication, resourcefulness, hard work, and other attitudes of its labor force. Here greater credit must be given to the Reds than to the experts or managers. The Communist Party has organized and motivated workers on a national scale to identify with and strive for national economic progress and power. Hence enterprise management has much of its job of motivating personnel done at the outset. (p. 70)

Economic policy has been both to build up heavy industry and to increase the quantity and variety of consumer goods. On the latter point, Richman observes:

> There is a surprisingly wide variety of consumer goods of relatively good quality in the stores, even in areas which are seldom frequented by foreigners, such as Wusih and Loyang. The largest Soviet department store—GUM in Moscow—does not come close to the large department stores in Peking, Shanghai, or Tientsin in terms of variety or quality of consumer goods available. For example, Shanghai's General Department Store No. 1 carries more than 50,000 different types of products. (p. 72)

As a final evaluation of China's industrial development, Richman states: "In spite of numerous managerial and technical problems at many of the Chinese enterprises, I am impressed by the wide range of goods that Chinese industry is capable of producing. China seems to be able to produce nearly anything it wants, but often it must produce very inefficiently and at a tremendous cost." (pp. 77–78)

In his concluding remarks, Richman returns to the question whether what seems to him to be a through-the-looking glass economy can go on developing and advancing; and once again he evokes those "centuries of world history and experience" to support a negative answer. He then adds:

> If by some miracle, the Reds do succeed, this would have a very great philosophical and cultural impact on the functioning of the world. But I am betting against such a miracle. I am also betting against the workability of a classless society with no noticeable distinctions between managers and workers, leaders and followers, experts and nonexperts, and mental and physical work. (p. 78)

We'll take those bets. As we see it, the Cultural Revolution is designed to make sure that China will accomplish just what Barry Richman and all the other bourgeois professors in the world regard as impossible. Marx and Engels believed it was possible. So did Lenin. So does Mao. We are happy to be in that company.

34

THE PROSPECTS FOR REVOLUTION IN AMERICA*

by JEREMY BRECHER

In January 1969, Barrington Moore, Jr., writing in the New York Review of Books, *asked whether there are "grounds for taking seriously the prospects of revolution in American society?" His own answer was No! Moore argued that conditions which have historically produced revolution do not exist in the United States today.*

Jeremy Brecher wrote a reply (which was never printed) that appears as the following selection. Brecher parries Moore's objections and argues that revolution is indeed possible, offering concrete reasons why we may be optimistic about revolutionary change in the United States.

January 30, 1969

The New York Review
250 West 57th Street
New York, N.Y. 10019

To the Editors:

Barrington Moore has done a real service by treating the possibility of revolution in America not as a slogan but as a subject for historical analysis. He has failed, however, to deal with the basic argument of those who see revolution as a real historical possibility.

1) No sensible observer argues that revolution in America is at hand, for precisely the reasons Moore spells out: essentially, the rulers are still able to run society and the ruled have not become desperate enough simply to ignore their authority. Those who believe revolution possible do argue that America's rulers are faced with a series of objective problems with which they seem unable to cope—problems which, if they persist, will lead to both a weakening of their power and an increase of mass discontent.

a) The United States has built its economy on world dominance through alliances and interventions which now appear to be beyond its resources to maintain. If it continues to defend this empire, it is faced with all the economic and other problems that have become evident during the Vietnam war. If it allows the empire to dissolve, it is faced with a domino effect that would have

* Used by permission of the author.

major repercussions on the domestic economy. At present, the ruling groups appear unwilling to extricate themselves from this dilemma by following either course vigorously.

b) America's post-war prosperity has depended on its domination of the capitalist economies of Europe, and the consequent suppression of inter-capitalist economic rivalry. The international monetary crises of the past two years are essentially a manifestation of the underlying fact that this imposed unity is now breaking up. Each monetary crisis has been accompanied by dire warnings from the authorities that disunity will lead to economic disaster. There is reason to expect that international competition will increasingly undermine the controlled economy which has circumvented depression in the U.S. for the past 25 years.

c) With the concentration of black people in the inner city, the system has put an impoverished and rebellious group in a strategic location. Its efforts to ameliorate the conditions of this group have been blocked by veto power over social legislation held by small-property and Dixiecrat representatives in the Congress, and by the fact that social investment in the not-for-profit sector reduces the effective demand available to private industry—refrigerators and helicopters are profitable for industry, but the poverty program isn't. The demand for the former is the keystone to our general economic prosperity.

d) Finally there is the less definable but equally important crisis of legitimate authority. The official management of the large institutions of the society are increasingly viewed not as the necessary organizers of society, but as a superfluous and irrational "they." This has been especially evident with regard to the Presidency and the university administrations under student attack.

Whether revolution is possible depends on whether the present rulers are able to resolve these problems. The reason revolution has begun to seem a real possibility to some people is the evidence that they cannot. First, the rulers seem to be hopelessly out of touch with reality; it was their star genius, Robert McNamara, who was the key architect of the Vietnam disaster and it was their great political mediator, Lyndon Johnson, who undermined the 20-year-old cold-war unity of the country. Second, the ruling class seems to be unable to pull itself together and follow a coherent class policy to meet the problems it confronts. Business failed to develop a program for solving the American problem in Vietnam long after it was clear to business leaders themselves that the war was both a military disaster and a threat to the international monetary system. Nor has business developed effective support for such class-conscious efforts to deal with the race crisis as the Urban Coalition. Of course, the ineffectiveness of ruling class response to these objective problems has not forced a revolutionary crisis on the system yet, but if the problems grow worse and worse, eventually it will.

2) Moore notes the absence in the United States of the traditional revolutionary lower-class base. But he appears to assume without arguing that any deviation from the class configuration which obtained in previous revolutions makes revolution less likely. Those who believe in the possibility of revolution in the United States point out a number of unique aspects of the American class situation which, they argue, make revolution more, not less, likely.

a) The traditional middle class of businessmen and farmers which has always been the basic mass constituency for the rulers of capitalist society has now become a tiny minority within American society. The overwhelming majority of the society has become proletarianized in the sense that it does not own the means of production but works for others who do.

b) The centralization of poor and impoverished blacks in the central city leads to an extreme vulnerability of the country to direct disruption, through strikes which hit the public services, sabotage to power, water, gas, transport, etc., and through other forms of mass action.

c) The rise of a militant movement of educated youth adds a new historical factor which in a number of situations has already played a catalytic role.

d) The industrial working class in the United States has reached a uniquely high standard of consumption, while at the same time retaining much of the insecurity and job oppression to which this class has been traditionally subject. In the event of economic dislocation and mass unemployment, this class would be subject to extreme drops in living standards due to foreclosures on mortgages, car loans, etc. Its political behavior in such circumstances is unpredictable to say the least.

It is the significance of these unique factors which will determine whether revolution is possible in the American future.

3) Moore's comments on the dangers of radical revolution presumably are directed toward the New Left, since they are virtually the only people around advocating revolution these days, and must be dealt with in that light.

a) Moore suggests that "a revolutionary takeover in quasi-Leninist fashion by some tiny but resolute minority" is what "a segment of young American radicals apparently seeks. . . ." But he fails to point out what anyone familiar with the American New Left knows—that it started out with a specific critique and rejection of this concept of revolution. There are many political sects today exhibiting the approach Moore describes, but not one of them has been able to win substantial mass support within the radical movement itself, precisely because such a view goes against the fundamental politics of the New Left.

b) Moore argues that "a revolution that tries to remold society against the mores and folkways of the mass of the population must turn to terror and propaganda on a gigantic scale in order to stay in control." It is true that if the revolutionary forces outlawed ham sandwiches and popcorn in movie theaters they would lose favor with the population and might have to resort to terror. But it is difficult to see why a revolution which ended conscription and war taxes, let the workers run their own factories, built decent housing for everyone to live in, and reduced the work week would need to oppress the population.

c) As always, the final argument against revolution is to point to the horrors of the Russian experience. Moore himself recognizes that Russia was a primitive country with no tradition of popular self-rule whose masses were unable to organize the economy—but he does not draw the obvious conclusion that entirely different conditions would obtain in an advanced country with a tradition of self-rule like the United States.

d) It is true that revolutionary movements tend toward a centralized authoritarianism when they have no alternative program for organizing society. This is as true for the liberal revolutions Moore defends as the radical revolutions he criticizes—the English revolution ended with the dictatorship of Cromwell and the French revolution with that of Napoleon. The New Left has put forward participatory democracy as its program precisely because it recognizes that both the revolutionary party and the revolutionary state tend toward authoritarianism. The critics are right in maintaining that the New Left has failed to spell out its concept of how a society based on participation instead of authority would work. But which of them has contributed more to a solution to this problem?

e) Within all recent revolutionary crises, organs for the direct self-government of the masses have developed. The Soviets in Russia, the Workers Councils in Germany, are classic examples. Whether a revolution results in authoritarian or democratic development, I would suggest, depends primarily on whether these organs and the masses they represent are strong enough to organize society under their own direction. If we don't want authoritarian development of revolutions, the way to combat such tendencies is not—as Moore suggests—by somehow incorporating elements of liberal revolution within radical revolution (whatever that means), but rather by seeking to strengthen the organs of self-government which revolutions engender.

If this is in fact the case, then one of Moore's own views would contribute greatly to authoritarian development. A revolutionary mass, he asserts, "cannot take power on its own. For a revolution to take place there must exist some group, such as the Russian Bolsheviks in 1917, that knows what it wants to accomplish and is willing to seize power in the midst of chaos and exercise it ruthlessly to restore order." It is precisely this argument which was used in an effort to justify the destruction of rule by the Soviets in Russia, and which the French Communists used against the workers councils that sprang up in the spring of 1968. While it may well have been true in the Russian context that direct self-government of the masses was impossible, to assert, as Moore seems to do, that this is true at all times and all places is simply to give the color of historical inevitability to authoritarian usurpation.

4) In discussing the possibility and desirability of revolution, Professor Moore neglects the most important question: is revolution necessary, not in the sense of *inevitable* but in the sense of *needed?* After all, those who advocate revolution do not do so out of an affection for violence, but rather out of a belief that human needs can be met in no other way. Essentially they argue revolution is necessary for these reasons:

a) It is the only way to overcome the overwhelming poverty of the underdeveloped world majority and of the poor within the United States—a poverty perpetuated by the power of America's rulers.

b) It is the only way to end the domination of the everyday lives of ordinary people in all advanced societies by bureaucratic authoritarian structures.

c) It is the only way to prevent the eventual outbreak of nuclear war in defense of established interest of one or another great power—or by accident.

Of course, if these are not the real needs faced by civilization, or if they can be fulfilled without revolutionary change, then revolution is unnecessary. Some of us who believe that it is necessary also believe that others can be as sensitive to their own and civilizations' needs as we are. "If we appear to seek the unattainable," as the Port Huron statement declared, ". . . then let it be known that we do so to avoid the unimaginable."

5) If read against the grain, Professor Moore's article suggests a number of points that those who support the idea of revolution must note.

a) The current radical forces—essentially militant youth and blacks—

constitute far too narrow a social base for any successful revolution. Only at the point when large sections of the now-conservative population swing over to social opposition can revolution possibly succeed. This is particularly true since only at that point will it be possible to politically neutralize the instruments of violence. The statement of the French police that they would not fire on the workers in the upsurge last spring is an example of the kind of situation in which the overwhelming capacity for violence of the state begins to lose its effectiveness; this can only happen when the classes from which the army and police are drawn have swung against the status quo. Thus, it is essential in the long run that black and youth movements break out of their isolation and seek a broader constituency for change. Premature attempts at disruption lead to disaster.

b) The most devastating social splits tend to be over which social groups are to bear the costs of new social arrangements. Therefore, the key issue on which to split the ruling groups in our society and win the support of subordinate groups for opposition to the powers that be is the attempt to put the burden of paying for the social crisis on the backs of the lower strata of the population. This is also the only program which can reunite the poor and the working class. So far, the left has been very weak in developing an economic program which draws on this basic social conflict.

c) Radicals must recognize the great differences Moore points out between urban and peasant revolutions, and not assume that they can apply the concept of "liberated territories" with their independent economic, military, and geographical base to the "counter-communities" of an urban culture. Instead, they must look toward some equivalent of Rosa Luxemburg's idea of antagonistic engagement with the society—a movement which builds on the friction generated at every point at which the needs of the people are attacked by the interests of the rich and powerful.

d) Much has been made of the overwhelming power of modern societies, but Moore's article makes clear the real point of their vulnerability—a popular movement which gains control over essential community services. Moore may consider such action "the anarchosyndicalist dream of the general strike and revolution" drawn from "the museum of social history," but such mass strikes have been the core of every Western revolutionary movement from 1905 to May, 1968. As Moore's argument indicates, the success of such a movement depends on whether the workers in essential services join it, and whether they participate in the democratic reorganization of the society.

Yours sincerely,
JEREMY BRECHER

35 THINKING ABOUT THE UNTHINKABLE: SOCIALIST REVOLUTION *versus* PESSIMISM*

by TOM CHRISTOFFEL

Many people agree with the argument of this book—that fundamental social improvement requires the destruction of capitalism as the economic system of ownership and control—but they feel that such a goal is idealistic, naive—in short, impossible. They argue that the power of the capitalist ruling class is too great, that no strong force for change exists in the society, or that human nature makes equalitarian progress impossible.

In the following selection Tom Christoffel argues that socialist revolution can take place in the United States, and he provides some guidelines for thinking about strategies for revolutionary change.

> *Men are products of circumstances and upbringing and . . . therefore changed men are products of other circumstances and changed upbringing.* [*But*] *circumstances are changed precisely by men.*
>
> —KARL MARX

The essays in this volume have focused thus far on three major arguments: first, that the "promise" of American capitalism is illusory because it is based on an economic class structure that is inherently exploitative, inequitable and unjust; second, that liberal attempts to reform this system cannot have any significant effect on the conditions of life for the vast majority of people; third—and most important—that the inherently inequitable state of capitalist affairs is maintained and controlled by a small class of individuals who profit from its continuance.

Many people, while agreeing with these arguments, react to them with hopelessness and cynicism. The power of the powerful is so great, it seems, and their vested interest so immense, that it appears naively idealistic to consider the possibility of fundamental social change. This essay will attempt to counter this pessimism by offering some suggestions on how such change could come about and by examining why it is so difficult for people in the United States to think realistically about radical change. (It is intended only as a *framework* for thinking about radical strategy, rather than as a strategy itself.)

The alternative to a capitalist form of economic organization is, of course,

* Used by permission of the author.

socialism. While capitalism consists of production for the profit of private owners, true socialism requires production according to collective need and with collective ownership. Without the replacement of the profit motive, all other attempts at social betterment will prove unsuccessful.

To achieve the desired society—to distribute wealth and control rationally according to participation in the work of society—the power of the capitalist ruling class must be fought and destroyed. Such a change runs counter not only to the structure of the capitalist economy and the interests of the capitalists, but also to the very value system attached to capitalism (and implanted most firmly on the college campus). For socialism is defined by more than the base of production relations—it is also a political organization, a culture, an ideology. Improvement is sought in the advance of all, not through private gain.

The idea that society's needs and work should be organized for society's good is hardly new. Socialism has been instituted, successfully and unsuccessfully, in many parts of the world. In the United States, working-class socialist movements have at times been fairly widespread, especially during the first two decades of this century. But since such movements have always been successfully co-opted or repressed, the feeling among much of the political Left is that American capitalism is invincible and radical change is therefore impossible. This sense of hopelessness has become so pervasive that it is difficult even to think about what social change means. In the back of quite a few heads there remains the notion: Radical Change = *The Revolution* = Guns in the Streets—a vision whose fantasy quality makes pessimism quite natural. There are a number of variations to this stereotype. For many people, both hopeful and fearful, the scenario for the New American Revolution involves some version of the following:

—American capitalism staggers into a crisis situation reminiscent of the 1930's. Unemployment skyrockets; tens of millions are without food or shelter; hopelessness affects everyone.

—Because their misery is so intense, the most oppressed class is driven to riot and revolt. Although some necessities of life are "liberated" by mob action, the rioting is generally spontaneous, without direction or goals, and destructive.

—As a political leadership slowly emerges from among the oppressed class, last-ditch repressive measures are taken by the ruling class. The activity escalates to the point of gunfire and barricades in the street.

—The government of the United States is overthrown by force and violence; a New People's Government is established.

Few, if any, would argue the actual likelihood of such developments in the United States within the foreseeable future (say, forty years). Nevertheless, the conscious or unconscious assumption that such a scenario must be the basis of radical or revolutionary change underlies many of the arguments against the possibility of such change.

The fact is, however, that revolutionary change can occur in ways dramatically different from the progression outlined above. The process of change is no mechanical structure built by rule. Perhaps most important, the sense of desperation and the blatant oppression that have just been posited are not necessarily prerequisites for social change. It is quite possible to conceive of broad movements for change that can develop despite the fact that the majority of Americans are not starving and despite the fact that capitalism has the government's enforcement power of several million men under arms, and the mass media, the local politicos and obedient labor "leadership" at its disposal.

In trying to figure out what radical change might look like, it is important to note that strategy for change is not so much a plan as it is an articulation of a process already going on—an attempt to grasp the dynamic of change and help it in the right direction. Thus strategy must be discussed not in an abstract, mechanical way but, rather, in light of, and growing out of, the unfolding events of the times. A good way to begin is to ask ourselves: Are we in a revolutionary era?

Not too long ago, the answer to this question would have been a sharp "No." But something has happened to the seemingly monolithic stability of the United States of the early sixties. The one fourth of the population which is poor (and only recently "discovered") has become increasingly militant—particularly the black and ghettoized. And a growing number of both blue- and white-collar workers have also shown a marked increase in rank-and-file militancy. This does not mean that workers are taking up arms to smash the state; but it does mean that they are doing what they are not supposed to be doing. The same is true of students. Just as working people did not respond to George Wallace's racism the way the pundits had predicted, so today's younger generation has largely rejected the electric facism of Marshal McLuhan. "The anti-political," writes E. P. Thompson, "find themselves once again in the arena of political choice." In such a situation, the superstate begins to lose some of its psychological punch. As Norman Birnbaum has noted:

> The vulnerabilities of a system of this kind are at this historical moment somewhat closer to the surface of events. In the first place, the system's chief claim to legitimacy is its sheer weight and factuality: it must be right, because it is there and it works. Insofar as it does not work, legitimacy can erode rapidly.[1]

Events in France in May and June 1968 provide a striking example of the vulnerability of the modern industrial capitalist state, even though the process of radical change was eventually aborted. Although the French universities and the French working-class tradition differ significantly from their American counterparts, it is instructive and encouraging to examine what happened in France in the spring of 1968. Most important, perhaps, was the new mentality generated throughout the society by the action of the students. The example of the student revolt cut away much of the apathy and hopelessness of the workers and demonstrated that workers and students need not be antagonistic to one another—that the struggles of the two groups are separate yet joined. Moreover, the fact that the workers' strikes were aimed not simply at bread-and-butter improvements, not only at better working conditions, but at creating a new government, underlines the fact that deprivation and economic

[1] "Staggering Colossus: The Surprising Vulnerability of Industrial Societies," *Nation*, September 2, 1968.

depression are not the sole fuses that ignite militant movements for radical change.

What are the likely elements for revolutionary change in the United States? Most important is an ever-growing, ever-more-militant working-class movement that isolates the capitalist ruling class from more and more of its bases of support. For although many different blueprints for socialist revolution exist, all involve such a progressive isolation of the capitalist ruling class until only a small hard core is faced with the alternative of fighting to the death or surrendering, on assurances of amnesty. Isolated instances during recent years—specifically in France 1968 and Italy in 1969—have shown that when the going gets rough the ruling class cannot fully depend on the police and the military which are drawn, after all, from the working class. (Such a defeat of capitalism does not eliminate the possibility that someday, with the help of bureaucratic elitism, capitalism may be restored—à la European revisionist "communism." Because such a danger will long exist, a revolution must effectively go on indefinitely.)

As has been pointed out earlier, extreme misery and oppression are not necessary preconditions for this development. If only those with nothing to lose but their chains were willing to struggle, change would be virtually impossible, since even the most oppressed members of society have something to risk. In fact, the incentive for change can come from an awareness of the exploitative and dehumanizing aspects of the existing system and from a recognition of the wide and unchanging disparities of wealth and power. "Proletarianization," according to William Appleman Williams, "concerns the general condition of the wage laborer in terms of his humanity and his sensitivity, and in terms of his lack of participation in the formulation of alternatives and in choosing between them."

Thus a crucial element of revolutionary incentive is the realization of the working class that its real power is not reflected in the distribution of power and that its relative power position—that of being exploited by a capitalist ruling class—will always remain the same under capitalism. Economic crisis in all likelihood highlights this relative position, since increased pressures expose the fact that it is working people who bear the burden and the brunt of capitalism's inequity. (Thus the enormous importance of capitalism's unemployment-inflation dilemma.) But this growing awareness is not dependent on a severe, depression-level crisis. It can, in fact, develop even during a period of generally advancing conditions and expectations. While Keynesian tools may—or may not—help capitalism avoid another Great Depression, and while U.S. imperialism may—or may not—manage to withstand the severe economic consequences of wars of national liberation around the world, American capitalism will continue to generate the incentive and argument for its own destruction. For disparities in wealth, high levels of unemployment, inhuman working conditions (continually intensified by speedup and stretchout), the growing discrepancy between the condition of the working class at work and in leisure time, the alienation of working people from what they produce—all these are part of the very nature of capitalism. And the contradictions of capitalism are most strongly felt where people are most strongly affected—in their major activity, their jobs.

It was the system of capitalist production that first brought men together into dense collections of humanity, while at the same time failing to take care of their communal needs. These two factors—the bringing of people together (making it possible for them to act together), and the failure to provide collective, nonexploitative relationships—provide the seeds for capitalism's destruction.

This is why labor insurgency is so important. American capitalism's greatest accomplishment in this century has been to divert and contain such insurgency, as the history of the American labor movement makes clear. (The activities of the National Civic Federation, the NLRB, the Gompers, Meanys, Reuthers, etc., worked to this end. See, for example, the Wiley selection, Part II.) But the workers' struggle to combat the ever-increasing pressures of capitalism, while often misled, has never been halted. Most of the time, however, this fight has been limited to the "here and now," with unions serving as defense mechanisms at the point of production rather than fighting for state power.

Labor insurgency is not, in itself, revolutionary. Without a revolutionary ideology, workers' struggles are simply holding actions—and in fact, the last thirty years have been, for the American working class, a gigantic holding action, not, as is often claimed, because of the affluence of American life, but because of the disorganization and diversion of the working class. It is the task of radicals in working-class struggles to point out that short-term militant drives must be part of a larger campaign for change if workers' gains are to be maintained and broadened. That awareness is essential to a radical working-class movement.

The most important aspect of labor insurgency is its potential. If, as many signs seem to indicate, labor insurgency is growing, the prospect of radical change becomes bright and clear. The aim of this essay is not to "prove" that revolutionary change *will* take place in America, but to point out that such change *is* a realistic possibility. The argument can be summarized along the lines of the following scenario:

—American capitalism continues to produce great disparities in wealth and power, with few trends toward greater equality. Problems relating to employment, income, race, and so on, continue to fester.

—Periodic capitalist crises expose the fact that capitalism cannot meet the needs and demands of the great majority of people living under it. Economic crisis fosters increased working-class demands, and vice versa.

—Escalated economic demands spur on escalation in working-class militancy among both private and public employees, to which the capitalists can offer only partial concessions.

—Heightened militancy and counterattacks on such militancy create greater and greater polarization of society, with fewer and fewer people willing to serve the interests of the capitalist ruling class.

—A point is reached where physical repression by an isolated ruling class is unlikely to succeed and may even be irrational. Attempts at a pre-emptive civil war are defeated. The capitalists are faced with a losing—although hard fought—battle. But the possibility continues that the dynamics of bureaucracy, elitism and bourgeois values may yet herald a return to the "capitalist road."

Viewed in this way, the American superstate at least ceases to be the unchallengeable controller of our destiny and, though formidable, becomes vulnerable. The key to that vulnerability lies in a radical consciousness—an awareness of the possibility of change. People will not become involved in a long-term struggle for change unless they have both a vision of a better future and a conviction that they are able to bring it about. Ironically, the very realization that there is a ruling class is cause for optimism. For that realization, and the recognition of a counterpart working class with opposing interests, makes it possible to organize a specific struggle for change. It is the liberal vision of bad things happening at random, without systematic cause, that is so depressing and pessimistic, for since it presents no enemy to fight, and no logical explanation for the oppressive status quo conditions, it can only condemn a "state of affairs." Such a liberal outlook leads to a logic of no cause, no solution.

The task for political radicals is to join in ongoing struggles against the ruling class—in antiwar/anti-imperialism movements, in black rebellions, in labor insurgency, in community campaigns against government—and to inject into all of these a coherent radical analysis. It is in the fire of such struggles that radical consciousness is developed, splits in the working class are overcome, and divisions between white and black, women and men, white-collar and blue-collar, are exposed as contrary to the interest of all working people.

Of course, it is to be expected that intensified struggle will produce a counterreaction of token concessions and repression from the capitalist ruling class. Once class consciousness begins to grow, however, the carrot becomes less and less effective, and the stick becomes dangerous. For repression is a two-edged sword: the more often it is used the more it polarizes society. "Repression," Daniel Webster wrote, "is the seed of revolution." And because of the very nature of capitalism, a thorough polarization leaves the ruling class very much isolated at one pole. This is the goal of radicalism.

The chief roadblock to revolution is not the immutable nature of man or the monolithic nature of the American superstate, but inertia and apathy. And as recent events in the United States, France and elsewhere have demonstrated, apathy is an alterable state.

Changing the circumstances of our lives requires both time and hard work. But the harshness of reality, measured against the potential of man and of society, can provide the incentive and optimism needed to fire the struggle. And if there are any who would argue that man's human nature is too base to sustain such struggles, we refer them to E. P. Thompson (himself quoting from Marx's *Theses on Feuerbach*):

> Human nature is neither originally evil nor originally good; it is, in origin, *potential.* If human nature is what men make history *with,* then at the same time it is human nature which they make. And human nature is potentially *revolutionary;* man's will is not a passive reflection of events, but contains the power to rebel against "circumstances" (or the hitherto prevailing limitations of "human nature") and on that spark to leap the gap to a new field of possibility. It is the aim of socialism, not to abolish "evil" (which would be a fatuous aim), nor to sublimate the contest between "evil" and "good" into an all-perfect paternal state (whether "Marxist" or Fabian in design), but to end the condition of all previous history whereby the contest has always been rigged *against* the "good" in the context of an authoritarian or acquisitive society. Socialism is not only one way of organizing production; it is also a way of pro-

ducing "human nature." Nor is there only *one,* prescribed and determined, way of making socialist human nature; in building socialism we must discover the way, and discriminate between many alternatives, deriving the authority for our choices not from absolute historicist laws nor from reference to biblical texts but from real human needs and possibilities, disclosed in open, never-ceasing intellectual and moral debate. The aim is not to create a socialist state, towering above man and upon which his socialist nature *depends,* but to create an "*human* society or socialised humanity" where (to adapt the words of More) man, and not money, "bearethe all the stroke." [2]

Why, then, is there such widespread pessimism within the student New Left? Why is revolutionary change in the United States viewed cynically as a nice dream and nothing more? One reason would seem to lie in the fact that the student Left, coming basically from a rather powerless middle-class background, is conceptually ill-equipped to think in terms of struggles for power. This weakness can be seen in the evolution of the New Left itself.

The pre-New Left student generation of the 1950's reacted to the Cold War, the Korean War and McCarthy with feelings of complete impotence. As a result the fifties were characterized by apathy and inertia. As Christopher Jencks has pointed out, those reaching maturity in the fifties "mostly assumed that our discontents were the result of personal maladjustments rather than societal ones. Even when we suspected that established institutions were unnecessarily hierarchic, authoritarian, and repressive, it seldom occurred to us that they could be changed."

By the 1960's, however, a variety of discontents brought people together and broad movements were organized—first against nuclear testing, then around civil rights, and finally in opposition to the war in Vietnam. E. P. Thompson described this move from political passivity to political involvement:

> The anti-political find themselves once again in the arena of political choice. Because, in retreating to the personal, they found themselves in the atomized, impersonal jungle of *Room at the Top,* they find that they must reach out once again towards the values of community. Because "love" must be thrust into the context of power, the moralist finds that he must become a revolutionary.[3]

The college activists who began to reach maturity in the sixties—the first of the Cold War generation—grew up with pessimism. The security of their middle-to-upper-middle-class economic affluence was more than balanced by the constant threat of total destruction. The illusion of instant communication merely emphasized their inability to communicate beyond the pressures of mass media culture. The exhilaration of witnessing the (almost romantic) struggles for national liberation in other parts of the world was dampened by realization of ever-increasing power and pervasiveness of the American ruling class. Even as they watched the process of fundamental change reach a high

[2] Thompson, "Outside the Whale," in Thompson, ed., *Out of Apathy,* London, New Left Books, 1960, pp. 184–185. For a powerful example of how people can change circumstances, habits, and beliefs, the reader is strongly urged to read William Hinton's *Fanshen: A Documentary of Revolution in a Chinese Village,* New York, Vintage, 1966, 613 pp. Hinton's account cannot help but fortify one's faith in man's ability to bring about positive *change.*

[3] In Thompson, *op. cit.,* p. 190.

point in other countries around the globe, they sensed that the possibilities for such change in their own country were constantly fading. Agonized by these paradoxes, they have become, intellectually and emotionally, the first full citizens of the superstate.

Despite their inherent pessimism, however, this generation, as it reached maturity, began to analyze, condemn and oppose the superstate. Predictably, this response was conditioned by the class background—or more precisely, by the class outlook—of the politically most active students. The young people who gathered at Port Huron in 1962 to found SDS, who traveled South in 1964 for Mississippi Summer and who marched in the first large anti-Vietnam War demonstration in Washington in 1965 were a rather homogeneous group. They came, for the most part, from the narrow upper strata of the middle class and from the more prestigious and more expensive colleges and universities. They were generally not pressed to find employment immediately upon graduation. Their parents made up the petty bourgeoisie: professionals, businessmen, college teachers, administrators, and so on. And even those for whom this was not so behaved as though it were, for the training they had received in secondary school and in college had given them the attitudes of this class.

As a result of their common background, these students tended to look at the country around them in a particular way, with an outlook best characterized as liberal. In this view, society is a classless collection of competing interests, history is an inevitably progressive process of morality overcoming technological problems and backward ideas, and politics has more to do with heroes than with movements. The petty bourgeoisie, whose contribution to the functioning economy was important but not crucial and who were and felt essentially powerless, did not view politics in terms of power or of powerful interests and neither did their sons and daughters. (Without the petty bourgeoisie the nation could still produce wheat and autos, missiles and profits. This powerlessness contrasts sharply with the potential power of the American working class—the great majority of the people, from lathe operator to secretary—by virtue of its crucial productive role. The organized exercises of that power, as in the 1930's, has from time to time won important concessions from capitalism.)

The early civil rights movement and marches, for example, represented an appeal to the Federal government to "do its job" by passing and enforcing various equal rights statutes. And the early antiwar movement viewed the American involvement in Vietnam as an ugly and irrational venture, rather than as a natural and logical aspect of U.S. imperialism. It was very difficult for those involved in civil rights and peace activities to accept the fact that the evils and injustices they fought were anything other than anachronisms. The concepts of a ruling class, of imperialism, of systematic exploitation, were dismissed as conspiratorial and paranoid. Unaccustomed to thinking in class terms, these young people found it difficult to conceive of events in terms of struggles between different class interests.

Yet these early militant liberal movements had a distinctly radicalizing effect. A great deal of middle-class innocence and liberal illusion were washed away by the sheer force of reality and experience. The growing New Left began to ask deeper questions about American society. Monopoly capitalism was consciously identified as the crux of an exploitative, alienating society—and as the enemy that must be destroyed and replaced. And it was recognized more and more clearly that the governmental structure functions not as a neutral arbiter of competing interests, but as the administrator and protector of interests of the capitalist ruling class.

Thus the goals and rhetoric of the New Left moved from reform to revolution. But in many ways, it seems, the analysis has gotten ahead of the strategy. For it has been difficult for the participant to react to these realizations. Liberal illusions give their holders the false comfort of believing—or hoping—that the Good Society can be attained in a slow but steady, peaceful and easy way. When such illusions disappear, so does the comfort they provide.

There are then a limited number of ways in which a person of middle-class background can react. Working-class individuals have more circumscribed options: to give in or to fight back. The middle class, however, can say "The hell with it!" and try to get as much out of this wicked world as possible. One can become totally pessimistic and accept the suggestion of Gabriel Kolko that "rational hopes for the twentieth century now rest outside America and in spite of it" and that, therefore, "at best a new left may only be able to define a new intellectual creed at home which permits honest men to save their consciences and integrity even when they cannot save or transform politics." Applying this "save-your-soul" psychology in a more militant way, one can permit this sense of pessimism and frustration to lead to unreal romantic and cataclysmic visions in which the chaos of wars abroad and ghetto and student explosions at home disintegrate the superstate, while the working class as a whole sits morosely by. Or, finally, one may reason that fundamental social change in this country can only come about with the organized power of those who make the country run—the working class—and that this organization is a long, hard process which, while neither certain nor immediate, is possible.

Certainly it is clear that working people in this country, steel worker and secretary alike, would benefit from radical change in direct relation to their current exploitation and oppression under capitalism. The working class stands to gain most from a decent reconstruction of society and, unlike other classes, cannot be permanently bought off. It is also clear that the working class possesses the potential of great power, for without its participation the business of capitalism cannot go on. Without such power of its own, the student Left can only hope to work along with the working class in struggling for change. Yet, especially during the period of the Cold War, American workers have been disorganized, divided and misled to the point of appearing to be practically their own worst enemy. Why then a continued faith in the working class as the force for fundamental change?

The simple answer is that there is no other alternative. But beyond this explanation lies a whole complex of national and world events of recent years; events which point to an increasingly rebellious working class. While the decade from 1956 to 1965 was one of relative labor calm, the last several years have been marked by a dramatic increase in labor militancy. In 1967, for example, close to three million workers were involved in 4475 recorded strikes, a fourteen-year high.[4] What is even more important, a considerable number of these were wildcat strikes—often over speedup and control over working conditions—challenging the existing leadership of unions as well as management. Most dramatically, the number of strikes in the public sector grew

[4] Manpower Report of the President, 1968, p. 323.

from 15 in 1958 to 254 in 1969. Within several unions radical and black caucuses have been formed and the "misleadership" of union bureaucrats is beginning to face organized opposition.[5] And when, for example, the superstate's largest super-city is repeatedly thrown into chaos by strike actions, the power relationship between capitalism and its workers can be seen in a different light.

Labor militancy, therefore, plays an important role in exposing the nature of capitalism and in countering an environment which is structured to teach the working-class individual his "proper" role. The several levels of a system of universal education concentrate on training rather than educating a working-class youth and provide him with limited pragmatic skills rather than with the ability to understand overall processes and concepts. An important part of his "education" is an ethical framework that encourages competition with other workers and sanctions collective efforts only with respect to "national interests"—oriented according to a Cold War ideology. The mass media tell him over and over again that his primary goal in life is a middle-class consumption pattern. Labor struggle is depicted as antisocial, and his present labor "leadership" asks him to accept a stipulated set of working conditions in return for a bit more bread and butter. In a hundred different ways it is made clear to him that he is lucky to get what he does and that he—a lone individual—can't hope to change the system. Despite all this, American workers are doing what they are not supposed to do: actively fighting the status quo.

More and more people are beginning to organize around their jobs. Perhaps the most dramatic politicization has occurred at the white-collar level, among teachers and social workers who, in the past, were often misled by the myth of "professionalism," but who are increasingly coming to see that they share a common interest with blue-collar workers. Other government workers have also begun to organize around their jobs, though—as with teachers—often in misdirected ways. Increased education and technology, instead of making the working class more heterogeneous and individualistic, apparently have made it more homogeneous. Not only factory workers, but secretarial and other clerical workers as well, find themselves in an assembly line system of production. And all workers are becoming more and more aware of exactly what capitalism is all about, as are students. This, then, is the hope for a revolutionary future—an awareness of the class nature of capitalism and of the need to fight to change it. As Jeremy Brecher has written:

> Despite the false consciousness, the continuous official propaganda, and the narcotizing pacifiers of the media, consumption, national glory and the rest, as long as people are human and therefore able to respond to their own needs, they pose a potential threat to the functioning of the system—the threat of revolution.

[5] See Stanley Weir, *A New Era of Labor Revolt,* Boston, New England Free Press, 1967.

ABOUT THE CONTRIBUTORS

PAUL BARAN was, until his death in 1964, Professor of Economics at Stanford University. His book *The Political Economy of Growth* is widely recognized as one of the most important contributions to economic thought in recent years.

HAROLD BENENSON is a graduate student in sociology at New York University.

ROBIN BLACKBURN is on the editorial committee of the English radical magazine *New Left Review* and—before being dismissed for his radical political activity—taught at the London School of Economics. He has coedited the books *Student Power, The Incompatibles,* and *Toward Socialism.*

EDWARD BOORSTEIN is a radical economist who worked for several years —until 1963—in the Cuban Ministry of Foreign Commerce.

JEREMY BRECHER was recently a visiting fellow of the Institute for Policy Studies in Washington, D.C., and is currently engaged in writing a United States history text for high school use.

TERRY CANNON was a member of the Oakland Seven.

TOM CHRISTOFFEL is a lawyer who teaches political science in the Boston area.

G. WILLIAM DOMHOFF is Professor of Psychology at the University of California, Santa Cruz. In addition to *Who Rules America?,* he has coedited *C. Wright Mills and The Power Elite.*

DAVID FINKELHOR is a graduate student at Harvard University and is active in the Boston radical movement.

DANIEL GILBARG, who graduated from Harvard College in 1968, is currently teaching American Civilization and Sociology at Bristol Community College and doing political organizing in Fall River, Massachusetts.

BRIAN GLICK is a Law Instructor at the Columbia School of Social Work and former Associate Director of the Center on Social Welfare Policy and Law, Columbia University.

MIKE GOLDFIELD is a graduate student in history at the University of Chicago and a former member of the Radical Education Project national staff.

ANDRE GORZ is on the editorial board of the French magazine *Les Temps Modernes* and has written, in addition to *Strategy for Labor, La Morale de L'Histoire, Le Socialisme Difficile* and *The Traitor.*

RICHARD GREEMAN was involved in the 1968 student rebellion at Columbia University.

EDWARD GREER, formerly assistant to Mayor Richard Hatcher of Gary, Indiana, now teaches at Wheaton College.

JOHN GURLEY is Professor of Economics and past Chairman of the Department of Economics at Stanford University. He was formerly managing editor of the *American Economic Review.*

LEO HUBERMAN was, until his death in 1968, coeditor of *The Monthly Review.* His works include *The Labor Spy Racket, We, the People, Man's Worldly Goods,* and *The ABC of Socialism.*

BEVERLY JONES, active in antiwar and student movements at the University of Florida, now resides in Pennsylvania and writes on women for movement and professional journals.

KATHERINE KAUFER is a student at Tufts Medical School.

GABRIEL KOLKO is Professor of History at the State University of New York, Buffalo. His books include *The Triumph of Conservatism* and *The Roots of American Foreign Policy.*

ERIC LESSINGER is a student at NYU Medical School.

ERIC MANN was active in the Newark Community Union Project and taught in the Newark public schools.

RALPH MILIBAND, Senior Lecturer in Political Science at the London School of Economics, is author of *Parliamentary Socialism* and editor of the annual *Socialist Register.*

BERNARD NOSSITER is a reporter for the Washington *Post.*

MILES RAPOPORT is a former Harvard student currently involved in political work in the Boston area.

MICHAEL REICH is a graduate student in economics at Harvard University.

PAUL ROMANO is the pseudonym of a Detroit factory worker.

PAUL SWEEZY is presently coeditor of *The Monthly Review.* He is the author of *The Theory of Capitalist Development* and has taught economics at Harvard, Stanford, Cornell and the New School for Social Research.

BRAD WILEY is on the West Coast staff of *Leviathan.*

JOHN WILHELM is involved in trade union activity in the New Haven area.

BIBLIOGRAPHY

PART I: ECONOMIC CONSEQUENCES OF CORPORATE CAPITALISM

PAUL BARAN, *The Political Economy of Growth,* 2nd ed., New York, Modern Reader Paperbacks, 1968

ROBERT ENGLER, *The Politics of Oil,* Chicago, Phoenix Books, 1967

DAVID HOROWITZ, *Corporations and the Cold War,* New York, Monthly Review Press, 1969

DAVID HOROWITZ and REESE ERLICH, "Big Brother as a Holding Company," *Ramparts,* November 30 and December 14–28, 1968; reprinted by New England Free Press*

ESTES KEFAUVER, *In a Few Hands: Monopoly Power in America,* Baltimore, Pelican, 1965

PAUL MATTICK, *Marx and Keynes,* Boston, Porter Sargent, 1969

SEYMOUR MELMAN, *Our Depleted Society,* New York, Delta/Dell, 1966

RALPH NADER, *Unsafe at Any Speed,* New York, Essandess, 1965

HAROLD NIEBURG, *In the Name of Science,* Chicago, Quadrangle, 1966

PAUL SWEEZY, *Theory of Capitalist Development,* New York, Modern Reader Paperback, 1968

WILLIAM APPLEMAN WILLIAMS, *The Great Evasion,* Chicago, Quadrangle, 1964

PART II: CORPORATIONS AND GOVERNMENT

T. B. BOTTOMORE, *Classes in Modern Society,* New York, Pantheon, 1966

PAUL CONKIN, *FDR and the Origins of the Welfare State,* New York, T. Y. Crowell, 1967

ELLIS HAWLEY, *The New Deal and the Problem of Monopoly,* Princeton, N.J., Princeton University Press, 1968

GABRIEL KOLKO, *The Triumph of Conservatism: A Reinterpretation of American History, 1900–1916,* Chicago, Quadrangle, 1967

JOHN McDERMOTT, "Technology: Opiate of the Intellectuals," *New York Review of Books,* July 31, 1969
C. WRIGHT MILLS, *The Power Elite,* New York, Galaxy, 1959
SHINYA ONO, "The Limits of Bourgeois Pluralism," *Studies on the Left,* Vol. 5, No. 3, Summer 1965
JAMES WEINSTEIN, *The Corporate Ideal in the Liberal State 1900–1918,* Boston, Beacon, 1968
ROBERT PAUL WOLFF, "Beyond Tolerance," in Wolff, *et al., A Critique of Pure Tolerance,* Boston, Beacon, 1969

PART III: PROBLEMS OF U.S. CAPITALISM

Work

ROBERT BLAUNER, *Alienation and Freedom,* Chicago, Phoenix, 1964
ELY CHINOY, *Automobile Workers and The American Dream,* Boston, Beacon, 1965
JOHN GOLDTHORPE and DAVID LOCKWOOD, "Affluence and the British Class Structure," *The Sociological Review,* July 1963
JIM JACOBS, "UAW Settles with Ford: Sellout and Insurgency in the Auto Industry," New England Free Press*
WALTER LINDER, "The Great Flint Sit-Down Strike Against G.M. 1936–37," *PL* magazine, February/March 1967; reprinted by New England Free Press*
PROGRESSIVE LABOR PARTY TRADE UNION PROGRAM, *PL* magazine, August 1969
HARVEY SWADOS, *On the Line,* Boston, Little, Brown, 1957
HARVEY SWADOS, *A Radical's America,* Boston, Little, Brown, 1962
STANLEY WEIR, "USA: The Labor Revolt," New England Free Press*

Race

ROBERT ALLEN, "The Dialectics of Black Power," New England Free Press*
TOM CHRISTOFFEL, "Black Power and Corporate Capitalism," *Monthly Review,* October 1968
ELDRIDGE CLEAVER, *Soul on Ice,* New York, Delta, 1968
LEO HUBERMAN and PAUL SWEEZY, "Reform and Revolution," *Monthly Review,* June 1968
JULIUS LESTER, *Watch Out, Whitey, Black Power's Gon' Get Your Mamma,* New York, Dial, 1968
ELLIOT LIEBOW, *Tally's Corner,* Boston, Little, Brown, 1967
The Autobiography of Malcolm X, New York, Grove, 1966
CHARLES SILBERMAN, *Crisis in Black and White,* New York, Vintage, 1964
HOWARD ZINN, *SNCC: The New Abolitionists,* Boston, Beacon, 1964, Chap. 10

Women

SIMONE DE BEAUVOIR, *The Second Sex,* New York, Bantam, 1968
MARILYN GOLDBERG, "New Light on the Exploitation of Women," *Liberation,* October 1969
JULIET MITCHELL, "Women: The Longest Revolution," *New Left Review,* December 1966; reprinted by New England Free Press*

Imperialism

PAUL BARAN, *The Political Economy of Growth,* 2nd ed. New York, Modern Reader Paperback, 1968

DAVID HOROWITZ, *Containment and Revolution,* Boston, Beacon, 1968

DAVID HOROWITZ, *Free World Colossus,* New York, Hill and Wang, 1965

NEIL HOUGHTON, *Struggle Against History,* New York, Simon and Schuster, 1968

GEORGE M. KAHIN and JOHN W. LEWIS, *The United States in Vietnam,* New York, Delta/Dell, 1969

HARRY MAGDOFF, *The Age of Imperialism,* New York, Modern Reader Paperbacks, 1969

CARL OGLESBY and RICHARD SHAULL, *Containment and Change,* New York, Macmillan, 1967

JAMES PETRAS and MAURICE ZEITLIN, *Latin America: Reform or Revolution?* New York, Fawcett, 1968

Viet-Report, "Pre-War Latin America" issue, April/May 1968

WILLIAM APPLEMAN WILLIAMS, *The Roots of the Modern American Empire,* New York, Random House, 1969

WILLIAM APPLEMAN WILLIAMS, *The Tragedy of American Diplomacy,* rev. ed., New York, Delta/Dell, 1962

Education

HOWARD ADELMAN and DENNIS LEE, *The University Game,* Toronto, Anansi, 1968

HAL DRAPER, "The Mind of Clark Kerr," New England Free Press*

EDGAR Z. FRIEDENBERG, *Coming of Age in America,* New York, Vintage, 1965

EDGAR Z. FRIEDENBERG, "What the Schools Do," *This Magazine Is About Schools,* September 1969

PAUL GOODMAN, *Compulsory Mis-Education,* New York, Vintage, 1966

PAUL GOODMAN, *Growing Up Absurd,* New York, Vintage, 1960

JAMES HEARNDON, *The Way It's Spozed to Be,* New York, 1965

JULES HENRY, *Culture Against Man.* New York, Random House, 1963

JOHN HOLT, "Notes on American Education: The Destruction of Children," New England Free Press*

"How Harvard Rules," New England Free Press*

Viet-Report, "University at War" issue, January 1968

PART IV: LIBERAL SOLUTIONS

MARVIN GETTLEMAN and DAVID MERMELSTEIN, *The Great Society Reader: The Failure of American Liberalism,* New York, Vintage, 1967

SIDNEY LENS, *Left, Right and Center: Conflicting Forces in American Labor,* Hinsdale, Ill., H. Regnery, 1949, especially Chap. 35

MAO TSE-TUNG, *Combat Liberalism,* Peking, Foreign Languages Press, 1960

RUTH PRYWES, "The Poverty of Retraining," *Studies on the Left,* spring 1965

DAVID WELLMAN "Putting on the Poverty Program" New England Free Press*

PART V: ALTERNATIVES AND STRATEGY

PERRY ANDERSON and ROBIN BLACKBURN, *Toward Socialism,* Ithaca, N.Y., Cornell University Press, 1966

JOHN CAMMETT, *Antonio Gramsci and the Origins of Italian Communism,* Stanford, Calif., Stanford University Press, 1967

G. D. H. COLE, *Guild Socialism,* New York, Fredrick H. Stokes, 1921

FREDERICK ENGELS, *Socialism: Utopian and Scientific* (numerous editions)

WILLIAM HINTON, *Fanshen: A Documentary of Revolution in a Chinese Village,* New York, Vintage, 1966

PRISCILLA LONG, *The New Left: A Collection of Essays,* Boston, Porter Sargent, 1969

VICTOR NEE, *The Cultural Revolution at Peking University,* New York, Monthly Review Press, 1969

COLIN TRUMBELL, *The Forest People,* New York, Simon and Schuster, 1961

RAYMOND WILLIAMS, *Culture and Society, 1780–1950,* New York, Harper Torchbooks, 1966

RAYMOND WILLIAMS, *The Long Revolution,* New York, Columbia University Press, 1961

* New England Free Press
791 Tremont Street
Boston, Massachusetts 02118